A Time for War

A Time for WAR

The United States and Vietnam, 1941–1975

ROBERT D. SCHULZINGER

OXFORD UNIVERSITY PRESS

New York   Oxford

Oxford University Press

Oxford   New York
Athens   Auckland   Bangkok   Bogotá   Buenos Aires   Calcutta
Cape Town   Chennai   Dar es Salaam   Delhi   Florence   Hong Kong
Istanbul   Karachi   Kuala Lampur   Madrid   Melbourne   Mexico City
Mumbai   Nairobi   Paris   São Paolo   Singapore   Taipei   Tokyo
Toronto   Warsaw

and associated companies in

Berlin   Ibadan

Copyright © 1997 by Oxford University Press

First published by Oxford University Press, Inc., 1997

First issued as an Oxford University Press paperback, 1998

Oxford is a registered trademark of Oxford University Press

Library of Congress Cataloging-in-Publication Data
Schulzinger, Robert D., 1945–
A time for war: the United States and Vietnam, 1941–1975 /
Robert D. Schulzinger.
p. cm.
Includes bibliographical references and index.
ISBN 0–19–507189–1
ISBN 0–19–512501–0 (Pbk.)
1. United States—Foreign relations—Vietnam. 2. Vietnam—Foreign
relations—United States. 3. Indochinese War, 1946–1954
4. Vietnamese Conflict, 1961–1975. I. Title.
E183.8V5S37   1997
327.730597—dc20   96–24690

10 9 8 7 6 5 4 3 2 1

Printed in the United States of America
on acid-free paper

For my daughter, Elizabeth Anne, with love

Contents

Preface

The war in Vietnam is always with us. From the 1988 and 1992 controversies swirling around Dan Quayle's and Bill Clinton's draft status, to the emotions stirred by the movie *Forrest Gump* in 1994, to the sulphurous reception in 1995 of Robert McNamara's Vietnam apology, *In Retrospect: The Tragedy and Lessons of Vietnam,* memories of the Vietnam war continue to divide and sadden Americans. So deep were the feelings that it took twenty years, until 1995, for the United States and Vietnam to resume full diplomatic relations, an action that subdued but did not put to rest the arguments over Vietnam. Indeed, the lingering animosities, regrets, second thoughts, and bitterness of the Vietnam era may die only when the last public official involved in setting Vietnam policy and every Vietnam veteran and antiwar protester have left the scene. The Vietnam War stands as the sort of watershed event for American politics, foreign policy, culture, values, and economy in the 1960s that the Civil War was in the 1860s and the Great Depression was in the 1930s.

U.S. participation in the war originated from ignorance and excessive optimism and escalated even though officials became dubious of eventual success. The war's aftermath created self doubt and social fragmentation. The war became the dominant issue of foreign affairs by 1965 and acted as the catalyst for vast domestic social upheavals. In the aftermath of Vietnam, Americans changed the way in which they conducted their politics, foreign and military affairs, economic life, and culture.

The war had similarly wide ranging effects in Southeast Asia. For a while—until the collapse of the Soviet Union—it altered the geopolitical balance of power in the region. The triumph of North Vietnam and the NLF in the spring of 1975 appeared at the time to have represented the culmination of decades of Vietnamese nationalism against outside powers. Yet the ensuing poverty of Vietnam, the murderous regime of the Khmer Rouge in Cambodia, and the exodus of hundreds of thousands of boat people made postwar Southeast Asia a tragic place.

The war devastated Vietnam, exposed the limits of U.S. military power, altered the role of the United States in Asia, and destroyed the consensus over post–World War II U.S. foreign policy. By 1968 military stalemate made it nearly impossible for the U.S. government to conduct an effective foreign policy. Differences over Vietnam opened fissures within the major political parties (especially the Democrats), fractured overseas alliances, changed the shape of the American military, wrecked the credibility of public officials, and spawned the twentieth century's most massive protests against government policies. Suspicion of officials generated by Vietnam reinforced a pervasive distrust of authority and the sense that many of American society's major complex institutions (the military, the presidency, universities, business, labor unions, some religious groups, the mass media) were corrupt, arrogant, and unresponsive. The occasional revulsion, cynicism and despair felt by large segments of the American population as they contemplated an interminable and unsuccessful war undermined public confidence and personal self-assurance.

Enough time has passed and a mountain of archival material has appeared in the twenty years since the war in Vietnam ended to warrant a fresh historical investigation. This book, *A Time for War,* is the first of two volumes in which I examine the war in Vietnam and its legacy, and covers events from the nineteenth century until the end of the war in 1975. The second volume, *A Time for Peace,* will explain the legacy of the war on the contemporary politics and economy and the cultural and social lives of America and Vietnam.

A Time for War represents an effort I began over fifteen years ago to place the Vietnam War in the context of contemporary history and international politics. My earlier work has been in the history of twentieth-century U.S. foreign relations. While I pursue that interest with a detailed discussion of the diplomacy of the war and the decision making at the highest levels, I go beyond it to examine the impact of the war on the lives of ordinary Americans and Vietnamese. The book discusses at length domestic American politics, the role of Congress, the pro- and antiwar movements, and the way in which the war was fought. I have tried to incorporate the most recently available unpublished material from archives in the United States, Europe, and Canada. The unpublished records of many prominent members of Congress have greatly enriched my understanding of the domestic politics of the Vietnam era. The book is also based on as complete a reading as possible of the vast secondary literature on Vietnam. In that sense, I intend this book as a compendium of the current state of scholarship on the Vietnam War.

As this project developed, the Cold War ended. This dramatic and largely unpredicted upheaval in the political landscape called for a further re-evaluation of the Vietnam War. Participants in and historians of the war have long considered it the high point of the policy of containment, for it was always about something other than events there or even in the rest of Southeast Asia. As John Kenneth Galbraith told President Lyndon B. Johnson in

July 1965, "Vietnam is of no great importance. Had it gone Communist after World War II we could be just as strong now and we would never waste a thought on it."[1]

From the perspective of the end of the Cold War, I have tried to answer some related questions: Why did policy-makers think Vietnam mattered? Why did they persist in these beliefs even after they correctly absorbed the lesson that Vietnam meant little for its own sake? What impact did the growing U.S. involvement in Vietnam have on the development of the Cold War? Did it prolong it, hasten its end, make little difference? Inside the United States the war changed many people's ideas about the worth and the duration of the Cold War, which, like the Vietnam conflict, seemed to most people to have lasted too long. Just as the war in Vietnam emerged out of containment and the Cold War, so it hastened their end. Time is a major theme of this book. How decision makers and ordinary people measured time, how patient or impatient they were to see the results of their efforts, helped determine the way in which Americans and Vietnamese conducted themselves during the war.

This book would not have been possible without the generous support of many institutions and individuals. The National Endowment for the Humanities supported a summer seminar I directed, The War in Vietnam and Its Legacy, in 1981. It also directly supported the research for this book with a Travel to Collections Grant and a Summer Stipend in 1991. The Lyndon B. Johnson Foundation and the Gerald R. Ford Library Trust generously provided travel grants to use the materials in the Johnson and Ford libraries from 1988 to 1995. I also gratefully acknowledge the travel grants I received from the Carl Albert Center for Congressional Research at the University of Oklahoma in 1991 and the Ball Brothers Foundation for research at the Lilly Library of Indiana University in 1992. The Council on Research and Creative Work at the University of Colorado provided a faculty fellowship enabling me to devote my full time to research for this book during the academic year 1991–1992. The history department and Dean Charles R. Middleton of the College of Arts and Sciences at the University of Colorado supported two research assistants, Andrew DeRoche and Gerald Ronning, who tracked down sources and transcribed my tape recordings. Patricia Murphy, the manuscript assistant in the department of history, helped shape the final version for publication.

Historians cannot do their work without archives and achivists. I deeply appreciate the help extended to me by keepers of records at every stop along my research journeys. Archivists are rightly proud of the material they have preserved and are eager to share it. The presidential libraries are the jewels of the National Archives and Records Administration, and their archives boast highly skilled professional archivists, eager to share the riches of their collections with researchers. I am especially grateful for the help of Regina Greenwell, Linda Hansen, and David Humphrey at the Lyndon B. Johnson Library, and Karen Holzhausen at the Gerald R. Ford Library. My work at various archives has also been made easier by tips provided by friends and colleagues. T. Christopher Jespersen and Kent Sieg have been exceedingly generous in sharing their superb knowledge of the availability of archival material on the Vietnam War.

I have explored the ideas that form the basis for this book in various courses, seminars, and public lectures over the years. The participants in my NEH Summer Seminar have helped over the years to sharpen my ideas. Among them John Hellmann, Frank Burdick, Milton Katz and Marianna Sullivan have been most generous in sharing their ideas with me. The hundreds of students in my undergraduate course at the University of Colorado on the war in Vietnam and its legacy have been a source of inspiration with their questions and comments. Many veterans and Vietnamese refugees who have addressed my class have also provided numerous insights. I am very appreciative of the contributions of Tommy Le Van, Russell McGodwin, and Peter Steinhauer. I have delivered portions of this book in public lectures at Alfred University, Broward Community College, Colorado State University, the Gerald R. Ford Library, the Harvard University East Asia Institute, Tel Aviv University, the University of California, Santa Barbara, the University of Colorado, and the University of Denver. I also appreciate the comments by critics, notably William Becker and Maarten Pereboom, of papers on the Vietnam War I have delivered at meetings of professional societies.

The manuscript has also benefited from the encouragement provided by many people. My friend Leonard Dinnerstein urged me to undertake this work, the contours of which have been shaped by his wise advice. Nancy Lane, my editor at Oxford University Press, has been unflagging in her enthusiasm for this project. Everyone who has worked with her appreciates her vast knowledge of history and her excellent judgment about books. Fredrik Logevall, Kent Seig, and Thomas Zeiler, experts on recent U.S. foreign relations and the historiography and sources of the Vietnam War, each read draft chapters and offered numerous excellent suggestions for revisions. My friends Diane Kunz and Michael Schaller read every word and spoke with me regularly about how to improve it. They helped me think out loud about what kind of a book *A Time for War* should be. This is a much better work because of their superb suggestions about what to cut, what to add, what to clarify, and how to organize a coherent account of a sprawling subject.

My family is my strength. My wife Marie understands the joy I derive from research and writing. My seven-year-old daughter, Elizabeth, is a source of pleasure in her own right. This is the first book I have completed while she has been old enough to express her thoughts regarding what I do. When she reads it, I hope she finds an answer to the question she asked since she was four: "Why's Daddy always talking about that 'Nam place?"

Boulder, Colorado   R. D. S.
May 1996

A Time for War

Chapter **1**

* * * * * * * * * * *

Long Time Passing:
The Vietnamese, the French,
and the Americans to 1946

*W*HAT CONSTITUTES a long time? That is a central question of the Vietnam War. For the Vietnamese the fight represented the latest phase of a centuries-long, even millennial, effort to define themselves and cast out invaders. Vietnamese nationalists and revolutionaries who fought the French and Americans seemed infinitely patient, serenely confident that eventually outsiders would have to go. But for first the French, and then the Americans and their Vietnamese allies, war seemed to go on forever. The French and the Americans grew increasingly frustrated and impatient when the war did not end on their terms. The French, before the climactic battle of Dienbienphu in 1954 and the Americans in the 1960s and 1970s, heard a clock ticking ever more loudly with every battle, every report of a death in combat, every change in the government of Vietnam, and every anguished cry of opposition at home. No wonder two of the most popular American accounts of events in Vietnam after 1945 are called *America's Longest War* and *The Endless War*.[1]

The war in Vietnam helped shape the contours of world politics after the era of European domination. For four hundred years, from the sixteenth to the middle of the twentieth century, the history of international relations was the story of what European states did—with one another and with other peoples and with states in the Americas, Africa, and Asia. But the European epoch ended in the twentieth century. The First World War eroded European power and the Second nearly destroyed it. World War II set the future course of world politics. The end of European pre-eminence foretold the demise of European empires in Asia and Africa. Before 1940 challenges to colonialism in Asia and Africa were mostly theoretical; after the war they became real. Although another fifteen turbulent years of anticolonial agitation were to pass, direct European rule was doomed.

THE VIETNAMESE AND THE FRENCH

Some of the most profound changes in the relationship between European nations and colonial peoples occurred in South and Southeast Asia. There, local nationalism soared across a region encompassing the Philippines (under U.S. rule), Indochina (controlled by France), Burma and Malaya (controlled by Great Britain), Indonesia (under Dutch rule), and Thailand, after Japan's early successes in the war shattered the apparent invincibility of the Europeans. Nowhere was nationalism stronger than in French Indochina. Antiforeign sentiment in the three French provinces of Tonkin, Annam and Cochinchina, which together comprise contemporary Vietnam, often surpassed similar expressions in other Asian lands. Several local and international developments fostered this intense nationalism: strong antiforeign sentiment among the Vietnamese had persisted for centuries. France consolidated control over Indochina in the nineteenth century, and its rule was often incompetent, usually inconsistent, and regularly harsh. Finally, the collapse of French authority in Asia during the Second World War gave heart to Vietnamese nationalists hoping to evict foreign rulers.

The Vietnamese today trace their origin to a group of about fifteen tribes, called the Lac Viet, who lived in the northern part of what is now Vietnam from the bronze age. They created a kingdom called Van-lang that established an independent agrarian-based political system in the Red River Valley.[2] Thereafter Vietnamese commenced a complicated two-thousand-year relationship with first their neighbors and later Europeans. Vietnamese often borrowed from the culture of others, but they nearly always retained a sense of separate political, cultural, and ethnic identity.

The Chinese Han dynasty expanded into southern China and Vietnam in 208 B.C. The Chinese brought with them Confucian philosophy and the Mandarin administrative system, language, and writing. The religion of the Vietnamese married Indian Buddhism with Chinese Confucianism and Taoism. While Vietnamese borrowed these cultural attributes, they insisted on remaining a people separate and distinct from the Chinese.[3] Indeed, over the centuries Vietnamese often revolted against Chinese rule. In 938 Vietnam won independence from China, but the Vietnamese continued to live in the shadow of the large empire to the north. The Chinese and Mongol empires tried continually to expand into Vietnam, which fought wars against northern invaders in 1257, the decade of the 1280s, 1406–1428, and 1788. These engagements left a legacy of Vietnamese resentment of outsiders and glorification of military heroes. For cxample, the general in charge of the victory in the thirteenth century had his soldiers tatoo "kill the Mongols" on their right arms.4 Outnumbered by the invaders, the Vietnamese developed a distinctive military style that combined infinite patience with guerrilla warfare. Their persistent opposition to Chinese domination also helped forge a national identity that the historian William Turley characterized as "a myth of national indomitability."5

During the centuries of conflict with China, Vietnam developed a distinct political identity. The first independent Vietnamese dynasty established a Great Viet kingdom with a capital, Thang-long, located on the current site of Hanoi. Successive Vietnamese dynasties created mandarin civil service systems based on Confucian principles. Although the structure was imported from China, the Vietnamese did not believe they were ethnically or politically Chinese. The Vietnamese imperial civil service was not as successful as its northern model in creating social and political harmony. Political divisions often wracked Vietnamese society, with regional lords, notably the Nguyen and Trinh in central Vietnam, creating their own parallel civil services that exercised real control on a local level. By the eighteenth century, the Nguyen rulers themselves started to dominate other peoples, expanding their control southward into the six provinces of the Mekong Delta that the French later called Cochinchina. In 1802 the Nguyen established their own dynasty with a capital at Hué, controlling an area stretching from China in the north to the Gulf of Siam in the south. But their rule was never secure. Living standards were poor and peasants groaned under the weight of taxes and conscription into labor battalions to build roads, bridges, irrigation canals, and the new imperial palace at Hué.6

But during the nineteenth century the Vietnamese had less success resisting outsiders other than the Chinese. The turbulent political and social terrain left Vietnam vulnerable to European expansion. France, a latecomer to the European scramble for economic and political pre-eminence in Asia, fought a series of naval and land battles with the Vietnamese. French Catholic missionaries created the diocese of Vinh on the central coast in 1846. One year later there were sixty-eight thousand Christians in Vietnam. When Vietnamese officials resisted, often imprisoning missionaries and killing local Catholics, France responded, between 1859 and 1862, with a naval assault and a seizure of the southern city of Saigon and the three provinces surrounding it. In 1867 the French conquered three more southern provinces and established direct rule over a colony they called Cochinchina. At about the same time France placed the kingdom of Cambodia under its protection.[7]

By skillful manipulation of divisions between the Vietnamese imperial court and other members of the local elite, France consolidated its hold in the 1880s on the central and northern sections of the country, labeling them the provinces of Annam and Tonkin. While the Nguyen emperor continued to occupy the palace in Hué, France sharply limited his power. France controlled all taxation. Inspectors of Native Affairs had the final say on all laws and administrative matters. At the same time, France permitted the election of local councils in each of the twenty local divisions within Cochinchina. While the actual powers of these councils were minuscule, their existence allowed the development of a local elite whose fortunes were tied to the French rulers. France also overturned traditional Vietnamese laws, outlawing polygamy and limiting divorce. Most of all, the French administration of justice seemed harsh and inhumane. French magistrates rarely displayed the sort of mercy or the personal touch characteristic of earlier mandarins.[8]

To make matters worse for the Vietnamese (and eventually the French themselves), France did not develop a coherent policy of colonial administration directed from Paris until the beginning of the twentieth century. For the first thirty years of French control, naval and military officers, with no training in administration and little affection for the Vietnamese, were the true rulers of Indochina. While outlawing polygamy, they took Vietnamese concubines, and Vietnamese deeply resented their arrogance. One early nationalist complained, "In your eyes we are savages, dumb brutes, incapable of distinguishing between good and evil. You not only refuse to treat us as equals but even fear to approach us as filthy creatures."[9]

In addition, French rule battered the self-confidence of prominent, educated Vietnamese, who lamented that their Confucian philosophy and the mandarin administrative traditions were no match for the technology of the Europeans. Emperors ashamed of having lost the mandate of heaven (the Vietnamese metaphor for legitimate rule), retreated to the pleasures of their palace in Hué. The travail of Vietnamese intellectuals paralleled those of Chinese bureaucrats appalled by the inability of their empire to resist the penetration of Europeans. One provincial governor-general wrote at about the time of the formal establishment of a French protectorate, "When I open my mouth, I speak strongly and with a bookish authority. Yet my soft flaccid lips can also drink me into drunken stupors. When I think of myself I am disgusted with myself, yet even with all this . . . my name has appeared on the gold examination list."[10]

This sense of regret, self-loathing, and inferiority persisted among educated Vietnamese into the twentieth century, when the nature of French rule helped fan Vietnamese nationalism. French missionaries converted approximately 8 percent of the Vietnamese population to Catholicism. Those most likely to adopt European religion came from the traditional elite: families that held some land and whose sons had entered the government bureaucracy. Many of the Vietnamese Catholics joined the local French civil service. Their willingness to cooperate with the French provoked a backlash. A nationalist writer berated educated Vietnamese who adopted French ways: "You continue to bow your heads and work like dogs for the bandits." Another complained that "the life of 10,000 'Annamese' is worth less than one French dog; the prestige of blue-eyed 100 mandarins is less than that of one French female. How is it that those blue-eyed, yellow bearded people, who are not our fathers or elder brothers, can squat on our heads, defecate on us?" After Japan's surprising victory over Russia in 1905, Vietnamese nationalists rejoiced that "Japan is kin, France is foe." Nationalists composed a song aimed at Vietnamese serving in the French army:

> So you're in the Army! . . .
> You end your hitch, homeward bound,
> And you'll die of taxes and corvée. . . .
> Where's thanks from the French?
> Where's love from them to you?
> The woman's bra is being used to strangle her! [that is,
> Vietnamese are oppressing their countrymen][11]

HO CHI MINH AND THE RISE OF
VIETNAMESE NATIONALISM

While the economic, social and political circumstances of the French and Vietnamese changed in the twentieth century, the rage, often expressed in sexual and scatological fashion, persisted. In 1907, Phan Boi Chau, one early participant in the Scholars Revolt, a movement of mandarins opposed to French rule, organized a plot to poison French officials in Hanoi. The French authorities uncovered the plan, and Chau was forced to flee to Japan. While still living in Vietnam, Chau influenced Nguyen Sinh Sac, a fiercely anti-French nationalist who had begun adulthood by following a traditional mandarin course of study. Soon, however, Sac came to share the nationalists' disdain for the bureaucratic mandarin style of life. He refused to speak French and often commented that "being a mandarin is the ultimate form of slavery." Sac passed along his hatred of European rule, contempt for the traditional intellectual elite, and a longing for the renewal of the Vietnamese nation to his three children. One of them, born in 1890 as Nguyen Sinh Cung, later changed his name to Ho Chi Minh and became the leader of Vietnamese resistance to the French and later the Americans. His mother died when he was ten years old, and he and his brother and sister were raised by their intensely nationalist father. From him and other nationalists, Ho drew his love of action. Throughout his life he would quote the derisive remarks of a late-nineteenth-century poet: "Nothing is more contemptible than to seek honors through literature."[12]

The young Ho Chi Minh became fascinated with the opinions of a variety of nationalists. He alternated between supporting the anti-French views of Phan Boi Chau and the antimandarin sentiments of Phan Chu Trinh, who opposed the use of violence to oust the French. Trinh argued instead that true Vietnamese nationalists should make use of the French presence to destroy the traditional imperial court and the mandarin system. Vietnam then could create a modern educational system, democratic political institutions, and an economy based on industrial production rather than peasant agriculture. "The mandarins," he wrote, "hate this, considering it an open threat to position. . . . They . . . regard the people as morsels to be eaten and to declare those who are concerned with the people insane and development efforts traitorous."[13]

Ho Chi Minh left his home in Nghe An Province in Central Annam in 1910. For the next two years he taught school and enrolled for a year in a vocational course in Saigon. He never completed the trade school, since by 1912 he believed that he could not live freely in a Vietnam controlled by France. In early 1912 he left Vietnam for the next thirty years. He went to sea as a cabin steward on a French ocean liner, traveling to New York, South Africa, North Africa, and Europe. Along the way he sharpened his hatred of European rule over non-white peoples. His sojourn in the United States piqued his curiosity about democratic forms of government. On the eve of World War I he was working as a cook in London.[14]

Late in the war Ho moved to Paris, where there was a large, thriving colony of about one hundred thousand Vietnamese. He joined other Vietnamese nationalists, who, like him and his father, still wavered between calls for the immediate end to French rule or the immediate destruction of the mandarin system and its replacement with modern education and democracy. He wrote nationalist article for Socialist Party journals, signing himself Nguyen Ai Quoc (Nguyen the Patriot) or Nguyen O Phap (Nguyen Who Hates the French).

When the leaders of the victorious powers assembled in Paris for the peace conference after the war, Ho became the most prominent Vietnamese nationalist. He unsuccessfully sought an appointment with President Woodrow Wilson, forlornly hoping that the U.S. president's endorsement of the rights of nations to self-determination extended beyond Europe to Asia. Wilson probably never knew of Ho's desire for a face-to-face interview; low-level officials declined to schedule a meeting between Ho and the president. What Wilson considered the far more pressing issues of German reparations, French desires for a security guarantee, and the future of the League of Nations absorbed all of his diminished energy in the late winter of 1919. Even had such an unlikely meeting occurred, it is doubtful that Wilson, who believed that national self-determination applied almost exclusively to Europeans, would have done much for the slightly-built twenty-nine-year-old Vietnamese. Keeping the French happy would have been far more important to the U.S. president than opening a dialogue with an unknown Vietnamese nationalist.[15]

Even had Ho paid a courtesy call on Wilson, it is unlikely that the future course of relations between the U.S. and the Vietnamese nationalists would have been different. The meeting that never took place between Woodrow Wilson and Ho Chi Minh set a precedent that was to last for the next forty-five years in U.S. relations with Vietnam: until the war in Vietnam became an exclusively American operation in 1965, Washington consistently considered relations with Europe more important than anything that happened within Vietnam. U.S. officials knew little of the realities of Vietnamese history, culture, or nationalism. The preoccupation of most U.S. officials with European affairs or relations with the major powers had terrible consequences. The United States gradually became deeply involved in Vietnamese affairs, but at each key turning point issues other than what actually took place inside Indochina were more important to the Americans. As a result, American officials consistently underestimated the difficulties they would encounter in Vietnam. In addition, Americans on the ground in Vietnam usually realized that their superiors in Washington were preoccupied with events elsewhere. This understanding on the part of consuls, diplomats, and field-level military officers often colored their own reporting from Vietnam. They tried to find the formula to entice Washington's interest in Vietnam and support for one or another faction. As a result, even the Americans closest to events in Vietnam often distorted what actually occurred in that turbulent land.

Ho made a far greater impact on French than on American officials. He submitted an eight point program demanding Vietnamese elections for representation in the French parliament; freedom of speech, press, and association; release of political prisoners in Indochina; and equality of law for Vietnamese with the French in Indochina. According to Ho, these demands represented the last chance for the French to maintain their position; if they were not granted, French control over the empire would quickly vanish. The audacity of Ho's awkward petition made him the toast of Vietnamese expatriate society in Paris. French political authorities considered him a spokesman for the Vietnamese point of view, but the police increased their surveillance of him.

In 1920 Ho took another fateful step when he joined with the most militant faction of the French Socialist party in founding the Communist Party of France. He had grown discouraged by the French Socialists' tepid support for Vietnamese desires for legal equality or independence in Indochina, and expressed increasing disdain for the Socialists' legalism, regard for parliamentary form, and fear of taking direct, even illegal, action. The success in Russia of the most militant faction of the Social Democrats (Bolsheviks) in seizing power provided a model for a successful revolutionary group. The writings of the Bolsheviks' leader, Vladimir Illyich Lenin, also offered what Ho characterized as deep insights into the dynamics of French rule in his homeland. In *Imperialism, the Highest Stage of Capitalism* and *Theses on the National and Colonial Questions,* Lenin claimed that the European nations had sought colonial dependencies because of the demands of industrial monopolies for raw materials and new markets. European nations enriched themselves by impoverishing their colonies. The logic of imperialism was inexorable; the French could not leave Vietnam even voluntarily. The Europeans, and a small group of privileged Asians who staffed the local bureaucracy for them, become rich by depriving ordinary peasants and laborers of the fruits of their efforts. Only concerted action by the Vietnamese peasants—a revolution—could liberate colonies from their European masters.

Here was an analysis that appeared to offer most of the answers to questions that Ho and other Vietnamese nationalists had been looking for: Vietnam's plight resulted from Europe's greed. Both the eviction of the French and a new society were necessary. The local elite who had joined with the French had to be destroyed in order for most Vietnamese to achieve prosperity and cultural fulfillment. Most of all, responsibility for Vietnam's renewal rested with the Vietnamese themselves. Action in Indochina, not argument in Europe, represented the only effective means of successful revolution. Ho remembered feeling struck by lightning when he first read Lenin: "What emotion, enthusiasm, clear-sightedness and confidence it instilled in me! I was overjoyed. Though sitting alone in my room, I shouted aloud as if addressing large crowds: 'Dear martyrs, compatriots! This is what we need, this is our path to liberation.'"[16]

For the next twenty years Ho Chi Minh and a group of other committed Vietnamese radical expatriates constructed a communist movement for and in their homeland. Ho lived in Moscow in 1923 and 1924 studying how to organize a revolution. In late 1924 he left the Soviet Union for Canton, China, where he advised the Soviet representative. While in China the French asked Chinese authorities to monitor his activities, but he retained enough freedom of movement to encourage Vietnamese expatriates to return home and organize communist cells. He expected the Communist Party to lead a revolution in Vietnam, yet he believed that success against the French could come only if his party enlisted the support of most peasants. He wrote in 1924 that in "all the French colonies . . . conditions have combined to further an uprising of the peasants. Here and there they have rebelled, but their rebellions have been drowned in blood. If the peasants remain pacific today it is because they lack organization and a leader."[17]

For the remainder of the 1920s, Ho moved through Asia and Europe recruiting Vietnamese nationalists to the cause. In June 1929 Ho joined with such other anti-French nationalists as Le Duc Tho, Pham Van Dong, and Nguyen Luong Bang to create the Indochinese Communist Party. About the same time other Vietnamese nationalists formed the Viet Nam Quoc Dan Nang (Vietnamese National Party or VNQDD), made up of middle-class and upper-class Vietnamese opposed to French rule. Soon another Vietnamese nationalist, the eighteen-year-old Vo Nguyen Giap, joined the Indochinese Communist Party. Together these men formed the nucleus of the movement that fought first the French, then the Japanese, then the French again, and finally the Americans until 1975.

In 1930 the Great Depression extended beyond North America and Europe to afflict the colonial dependencies of the European powers. The collapse in international trade depressed rice prices, causing hardship to peasants who had to pay rents to Vietnamese landlords and taxes to the French government in cash, not rice. Tax revolts broke out spontaneously in central and southern Vietnam. In Nghe An Province, where Ho Chi Minh had been born and where the most intensive organization for the Indochinese Communist Party had taken place, party workers created local Red soviets to demand land reform, tax cuts, and the end to rents to landlords. The soviets' agitation culminated on September 12, 1930, when some six thousand Nghe An peasants marched peacefully on Vinh, the local capital, to present their grievances. The French authorities panicked and ordered an air attack on the marchers that killed 117 people. Later in the day the French called in another air strike to attack people coming to claim the bodies of their relatives, resulting in the deaths of another fifteen Vietnamese. The suppression of the Nghe An revolt hardened attitudes on both sides. The fierceness of the French response demonstrated that the colonial power would go to great lengths to retain control. For the French, the sight of six thousand peasants on the march revealed how much latent anger lay beneath the placid surface of rural Vietnam.[18]

French authorities followed up their victory at Vinh with an intensive search for revolutionary leaders. They arrested Pham Van Dong and jailed him for the next eight years. Le Duc Tho spent the 1930s in hiding and prison. Giap evaded capture, but the French imprisoned his wife and baby, who died in prison in 1940. Giap never forgave the French.[19] As for Ho, the French tried him in absentia and sentenced him to death. France prevailed on the British authorities in Hong Kong to arrest him. Rumors spread that he had died in jail, but sympathetic British officials, who detested the French, smuggled him from prison to Shanghai in late 1932. There Soviet representatives arranged for him to flee to Moscow where he remained until 1938. He then returned to China, and in 1939 he and Giap met for the first time. The same year, Pham Van Dong left prison in Vietnam and joined Ho and Giap in China on the eve of the Second World War in Europe.[20]

WORLD WAR II

The defeat of France by Germany in June 1940 presented an unexpected opportunity for Vietnamese wanting to rid their country of European rule. But quickly a new outside empire moved into Indochina. Japanese forces based in southern China occupied the northern province of Tonkin. The Japanese promised the representatives of the government of Vichy France that French control of the two southern provinces of Annam and Cochinchina would remain secure. In July 1941, however, Japanese troops occupied the remainder of Vietnam, although they permitted the French and Bao Dai, the emperor of Annam, to continue to exercise formal authority on paper. As the Japanese consolidated their hold on Vietnam, Ho Chi Minh returned for the first time to the homeland he had left in 1910. He and his followers set up camp in a cave in the mountainous Cao Bang Province.

There they planned a war against both the Japanese and the French. In May 1941 Ho sought to expand the Communist Party by including the remnants of the old VNQDD to form a common front uniting communists and nationalists. He created a political organization called the Viet Nam Doc Lap Dong Minh, usually shortened to Vietminh—the League for the Independence of Vietnam. He also stopped calling himself Nguyen Ai Quoc and adopted the name by which he later became known worldwide, Ho Chi Minh, or He Who Enlightens.

As Ho Chi Minh and his small band of nationalists organized to fight the French and the Japanese, the leaders of the principal wartime Allies—the United States, Great Britain and the Soviet Union—considered events in Southeast Asia a minor element in their overall strategy to defeat the Axis powers. Nevertheless, as the war went on the United States, Britain, China, and France developed plans for the future of Southeast Asia, the roles of the former colonial powers, and the political status of Asian peoples. U.S. policy proved inconsistent, sometimes supporting the Asians and sometimes the colonial powers. The confusion resulted from ignorance of Southeast Asia, a belief that other areas of the world were more important to the United States, and the crushing weight of other business. The false starts and contradictions of American attitudes and the rivalries among various branches of the government often confused and frustrated allied officials. The governments of Britain, France, and China each pursued their own interests, different from those of one another and the United States. Since American power far surpassed that of its partners, however, the future development of Southeast Asia depended largely on decisions made in Washington.

The attitude of President Franklin D. Roosevelt toward colonialism in general and European states in particular largely set the pattern for later U.S. policies. Suspicious of European motives, Roosevelt seemed sympathetic to the nationalist position in Southeast Asia. ''Don't think for a moment,

Elliott,'' he told his son early in the war, "that Americans would be dying in the Pacific tonight, if it hadn't been for the shortsighted greed of the French and British and the Dutch."[21] Roosevelt distrusted the French more than other Europeans. Although contemptuous of France's speedy surrender to Germany and Japan, he also despised General Charles de Gaulle, the leader of the Free French, the movement that had continued to fight Germany after the surrender. Roosevelt's detestation of de Gaulle made him resist the restoration of French control over Indochina after the war. In 1942 Roosevelt often told representatives to the Pacific War Council (China, the Philippines, Australia, New Zealand, and Canada) that he did not want to see French rule restored in Indochina, asserting that "Indochina is not anxious to see the return of the French regime. . . . [T]he French have been in Indo-China since about 1832 and little has been done toward improving conditions among the natives." He proposed that at the end of the war France's Asian territories be turned over to the United Nations, which would create a trusteeship over the former colonies.[22]

A trusteeship, in which one or more of the allies would temporarily rule Indochina before its eventual independence, raised questions and provoked opposition. Predictably, Britain considered American efforts to strip a European nation from its colonies a direct a threat to its own position as a power in Asia. More surprising was the resistance to trusteeship within the U.S. government. Undersecretary of State Sumner Welles reminded the president that the United States had promised a restoration of French colonial possessions, but Roosevelt replied that he had meant this promise to apply only to French colonies in Africa. In 1943 the State Department developed plans for the future of Indochina that differed from Roosevelt's. Planners at the State Department did not wish to single out the French for special treatment. Moreover, they came to realize that Japan, while occupying all of Indochina in 1941, had permitted the continuation of formal French rule. Yet the President seemed to ignore these plans as he and his personal advisers prepared for the conferences at Cairo with Winston Churchill and Jiang Jieshi (Chiang Kai-shek) and at Tehran with Churchill and Joseph Stalin. At Cairo Roosevelt sought Chinese support for a trusteeship for Indochina. Jiang declined the President's offer to become the sole trustee, but Roosevelt later recalled at Yalta in 1945 that China had agreed to participate in a multilateral trusteeship along with the United States, the Soviet Union, France, Indochina, and the Philippines.[23]

The week after the Cairo meeting Roosevelt repeated his anticolonial position at Tehran. Much to Churchill's dismay, Roosevelt and Stalin aligned themselves against the interests of the colonial powers. The Soviet leader told Roosevelt that he did not want the "Allies to shed blood to restore Indochina . . . to the old French colonial rule."[24] Roosevelt agreed that "after 100 years of French rule in Indochina, the inhabitants were worse off than they had been before. . . . He added that he had discussed with Chiang Kai-shek the possibility of a system of trusteeship for Indochina which would have the task of preparing the people for independence within a definite period of time, perhaps 20 to 30 years.'' Stalin assented.[25]

Roosevelt returned many times to the question of Indochina, which he believed symbolized everything wrong with European imperialism in Asia. Churchill became alarmed that Roosevelt's interest in Asian colonialism spelled trouble for British interests in India. The Prime Minister tried to make light of his transatlantic friend's obsessions. He once told Foreign Secretary Anthony Eden that Roosevelt's observations were only ''chance remarks,'' which Britain need not take seriously.[26] Yet Roosevelt spoke often of Indochina, even if his comments did not reflect deep analysis of the situation there. He considered trusteeship ''an ideal situation'' and he refused to take Jiang Jieshi's no as the final word on the subject of trusteeship, regretting that the Chinese leader would not take over Indochina because ''its people and the country as a whole were completely different from their [China's] own.''[27]

Despite Britain's unhappiness with Roosevelt's plans for Asia, Roosevelt instructed his subordinates to ''discuss with them at every opportunity'' the need to end European colonial rule in Asia.[28] For Roosevelt the future of Indochina should be decided by the Anglo-Americans, without the participation of the French. Roosevelt could not stand the imperious Charles de Gaulle, whom he often likened to Mussolini.[29] American hostility toward the Free French leader offered Britain an unexpected opportunity to frustrate U.S. policy goals. In 1943 the U.S. and Britain divided military responsibility for the war against Japan into several theaters of operation, with command for each given to different British and American generals and admirals. British Admiral Lord Louis Mountbatten led the Southeast Asia Command (SEAC), which included Indochina. The British used their primacy in SEAC to help French agents return to Indochina in the summer of 1944. In October the British included French representatives at SEAC over American objections.

Later that year the British helped France inject more soldiers into Indochina. French foreign minister René Pleven told his ambassador in Washington to present the United States with ''a fait accompli, meaning we shall be present in Indochina at the end of the war and see to it that this presence is not contested.''[30] Churchill also tried to portray the presence of French soldiers in their old colony as an irreversible fact. The British had recently evicted French troops from Syria, and the British prime minister wanted somehow to make amends. Roosevelt considered the implications of restoration of French authority but decided to defer decisions until after the war with Japan. He told Secretary of State Edward Stettinius on January 1, 1945 that ''I still do not want to get mixed up in any military effort toward the liberation of Indochina from the Japanese. . . . From both the military and civilian points of view, action at this time is premature.''[31]

Yet just four days later Roosevelt approved a plan by Admiral Mountbatten to use French commandos in Indochina to destroy Japanese communications. The President neglected to inform subordinates that he had seemed to reverse course, but he probably reasoned that this was only a small operation that might hasten the end of the war against Japan. In his own mind he remained committed to trusteeship and eventual independence for Indochina, but he did not clearly communicate his views to the rest of the U.S. government.[32]

THE END OF JAPANESE RULE

U.S. intentions about Indochina remained unfocused in the tumultuous first eight months of 1945. Roosevelt met with Churchill and Stalin for the last time in February at Yalta, where he rejected the advice of his military staff and raised the question of trusteeships for colonial areas. Churchill exploded, charging that the United States sought the dismantling of the British empire. The President partially mollified him by excluding British territory from the trusteeship scheme. Moreover, trusteeships for the colonies of other Allied states, such as France and the Netherlands, would require their assent before going into effect. While this concession seemed to offer the European nations a potential veto over the creation of trusteeships, the United States would have enormous persuasive powers after the war.

The President deliberately did not discuss Indochina with Churchill, but he did raise it with Stalin. He reiterated his plan for a trusteeship and told the Soviet leader that ''the British did not approve of this idea as they wished to give it back to the French since they feared the implications of a trusteeship as it might affect Burma.'' Stalin agreed that ''Indochina was a very important area,'' and he did not think that Britain would be a good country to protect the region.[33] On the way back from Yalta, Roosevelt told reporters about a trusteeship plan involving France, China, the United States, the Soviet Union, and possibly the Philippines. ''Stalin liked the idea. China liked the idea. The British don't like it. It might bust up their empire.''[34]

After Yalta, however, opposition from Britain and France, the declining position of China, disagreements within the U.S. government and the changing circumstances inside Indochina scuttled the trusteeship program. On March 9, 1945, the Japanese authorities in Indochina mounted a coup d'etat against the puppet French regime. Ho Chi Minh, who had established contacts in northern Indochina and Kunming, China with representatives of the U.S. Office of Strategic Services (oss) and Office of War Information, briefed his American counterparts on the Japanese seizure of power: ''The

French wolf was finally devoured by the Japanese fascist hyena. Compared with the gigantic World War this is only a minute event. . . . [But] it has a serious bearing on the World War in general, and on Indo-China, France, Japan and China in particular.''[35]

The connection between the Vietminh and the oss bestowed benefits on both, but it also led to misunderstandings later. After the Japanese took over from the French, the oss lost its contacts with French intelligence agents. Captain Charles Fenn, who directed oss operations in Indochina from headquarters in Kunming China, met with Ho in March to create a working relationship. On March 17 and 20 Fenn and Ho arranged for the United States to supply radio equipment and limited amounts of arms and ammunition. In return the Vietminh agreed to provide intelligence about the Japanese, coordinate sabotage against Japanese targets, and help rescue downed U.S. pilots.[36]

Japan enlisted the help of Bao Dai (the emperor of Annam), the king of Cambodia, and some conservative nationalists to create formally independent governments for the region. This seizure of power by Japan abruptly transformed the French army stationed in Vietnam from collaborators with the Japanese to potential partners with the Allies in the war against Japan. The outnumbered French forces asked the U.S. Air Force in China for assistance. Reluctantly, Roosevelt agreed, although the air force had few planes to spare.[37]

Once more, Roosevelt thought this limited support for the French forces represented a purely military move, but it had great political repercussions. On March 15 Roosevelt seemed to modify his plan to allow France to become the sole trustee of Indochina. He told a State Department official that "if we could get the proper pledge from France to assume for herself the obligations of a trustee, then I would agree to France retaining these colonies with the proviso that independence was the ultimate goal." Roosevelt reiterated that independence, not some intermediate status like self-determination or dominion status within the French empire, had to be the goal.[38]

The State Department had difficulty translating the president's wishes into a concrete policy for Indochina. On April 5 the Department called for an international trusteeship, even after the President signaled willingness to allow France to act as sole trustee. Yet the department also pressed policymakers to leave options open. It recommended avoiding "any action which would operate progressively to define the position of the United States with regard to the future disposition of Indochina." At the same time the Department's Division of Far Eastern Affairs raised an issue that the British had stressed for at least a year, the need to maintain France's position as a strong European power. "If France is to be denied her position in Indochina she will be to that extent weakened as a world power," warned State Department official George Blakeslee. He urged policy makers to consider carefully "whether it is of more interest to us and to the world as a whole to have a strong, friendly cooperative France, or have a resentful France."[39]

U.S. policy toward Indochina, France, and the role of the United States in Asia lacked definition on the eve of Roosevelt's death on April 12. The new administration of Harry S. Truman struggled to master an enormously complicated foreign affairs agenda. Indochina, always a secondary issue for the United States, was pushed into the background. When Truman took office, he led a government that sympathized with the idea of independence of European colonies but also wanted to defer action until the war was won. Moreover, tension persisted between policy-makers who favored more assertive U.S. action in Asia and those who believed U.S. interests remained in Europe. Roosevelt had stressed different issues at different times, and it remained for his successor to try to craft a coherent policy. Truman worked under the terrible handicaps of inexperience in foreign policy, ignorance of Roosevelt's intentions and commitments, and the crushing weight of dealing with the end of the war. Even had Roosevelt lived, Vietnam would have been a distinctly secondary—albeit familiar—issue. The inexperienced Truman knew nothing and cared little about Southeast Asia and Indochina.

THE VIETNAMESE REVOLUTION OF 1945

The Japanese takeover of all of Indochina on March 9 and the death of Franklin D. Roosevelt on April 12 radically altered the political landscape in Asia. The former encouraged a revolution in Vietnam, while the latter disrupted U.S. policy at a crucial time.

Immediately after Japan took over French positions, a scramble for pre-eminence emerged among various factions of Vietnamese. Emperor Bao Dai, who complied with most Japanese directives during the war, re-established imperial power in the former imperial capital of Hué. Tran Trong Kim, a nationalist historian, became prime minister and the new government adopted the name Vietnam, a yellow flag, and a national anthem. A weak leader who vacillated between accommodating the Japanese and creating a truly independent government, Kim has been characterized as "Vietnam's Kerensky" (a reference to Alexander Kerensky, whose ineffectual provisional government preceded the Bolsheviks in Russia in 1917). Emperor Bao Dai actually had wanted to select Ngo Dinh Diem, a man who had resisted collaboration with the Japanese and therefore possessed more authentic nationalist credentials, to form his new government. The Japanese authorities vetoed the choice, fearing that Diem might prove to be too independent.[40] The subsequent history of Vietnam might have been very different had Diem formed a government in 1945.

The Kim government expressed mild interest in including the Vietminh in a broad coalition, but the Vietminh did not take the offer seriously. Leaders of the Vietminh denounced Kim as "a clown on stage," "a traitor who would steal the people's rice" or an inveterate plotter who would "spare no means to sabotage our movement for national salvation."[41]

A famine throughout the countryside of Vietnam combined with the political crisis provided the opportunity for the Vietminh to mount their own revolution in August. The famine began in 1944 and intensified in 1945. It originated with poor harvests in 1944, but the disruption of transportation caused by the war made it much worse. Allied bombing had closed ports and the Japanese used the roads to move soldiers. Estimates vary on the severity of the famine. Ho Chi Minh claimed that two million Vietnamese had died. This number was repeated often during the Vietnam war, but it is probably too high. The historian David Marr estimates that about one million Vietnamese, about 5 percent of the population, died in 1944 and 1945 from starvation and malnutrition. Other estimates are between 360,000 and 1,000,000. In any event, the famine of 1944 and 1945 represented an unprecedented catastrophe for Vietnam.[42]

The devastation in the countryside coincided with the collapse of Japanese power. By this time Operation Deer Mission, as the collaboration between the United States and Vietminh was called, had grown into a small but significant political collaboration. The Vietminh considered the oss officials as a ticket for ending their political isolation and as a counter to the French. In July the American Major Allison Thomas, supervisor of Deer Mission, parachuted into Ho's headquarters where the Vietminh greeted him almost as if he were a savior. Thomas provided medicine to an ailing Ho, and the two men had long conversations regarding the future of Vietnam. Ho's vision of an independent Vietnam, friendlier to the United States than to France, struck a responsive chord with Thomas. He communicated his enthusiasm to Washington: "Forget the Communist body," he told Washington, "the Vietminh is not Communist. Stands for freedom and reforms from French harshness."[43]

The Vietminh used the collapse of Japanese authority, the suffering of the peasantry, and the potential of support from the United States to move against the Kim government. News that Japan planned to surrender quickly reached Vietminh headquarters. On August 12 Vo Nguyen Giap ordered his troops to "attack and cut off the withdrawing troops" of the Japanese. He issued Military Order No. 1, calling for a general insurrection throughout Vietnam. A congress of the Vietminh met from August 13 to 15, creating a National Insurrection Committee chaired by Truong Chin, approving Military Order No. 1, and adopting a resolution calling for an insurrection in areas of the countryside and cities where they believed they could win easily.

On the same day the congress transmitted a message asking the "United States, as a champion of democracy," to assist Indochina in achieving independence. Specifically, the Vietminh requested that the United States prohibit, or least not help, the French from returning to Indochina; keep the Chinese under control, to minimize looting and pillage; send technical advisers to assist the Indochinese to exploit the resources of the land; and develop those industries that Indochina was capable of supporting. Finally, the Vietminh wanted their country "placed on the same status as the Philippines for an undetermined period."[44] Washington did not reply, but the oss continued to support their cause.

Over the next ten days the Vietminh took power in the major cities. They captured Hanoi on August 19, Hué on August 24–25. On August 24, Emperor Bo Dai abdicated, and Ho Chi Minh granted him the title "Supreme Adviser" to the new republican government. The Vietminh then moved quickly to proclaim a new, independent Democratic Republic of Vietnam (DRV). Their aim was to preempt efforts to reestablish French control and to warn off the Chinese whose forces had entered the northern part of the country to disarm the Japanese. On September 2, 1945, Ho stood before a crowd of five-hundred-thousand in the center of Hanoi to read a declaration of independence for the new Democratic Republic of Vietnam. He began with a reference to the American Declaration of Independence and then went on to denounce French rule: "They have built more prisons than schools. . . . They have drowned our revolution in blood. . . . [T]hey have forced upon us alcohol and opium in order to weaken our race." He praised the fighters who had "smashed the yoke which has pressed so hard upon us for nearly one hundred years and finally made our Viet Nam an independent country." He also asked for recognition from the "Allied nations which at Tehran and San Francisco have acknowledged the principles of self-determination and equality of nations."[45]

U.S. POLICY AND THE EMERGING COLD WAR

Recognition did not come, however. China sent about 150,000 soldiers to the northern part of the country to disarm the Japanese, and the Chinese provided many arms taken from the Japanese to the Vietminh. Official Chinese policy was changing at the end of the war, and China soon began negotiating with France over a restoration of French rule. The British undermined the Vietminh's position in the southern part of the country when they sent a small force to Saigon on September 12. Admiral Lord Louis Mountbatten, the commander of SEAC, and Major General Douglas Gracey, who directed the local operation in the Saigon area, clashed over British policy. Concerned about the geopolitical future of the region, Mountbatten did not want SEAC to appear to back French claims to sovereignty. He relied on the French forces remaining in the southern part of the country to assist the British, while leaving the future of sovereignty open.

Gracey, however, faced the immediate problem of restoring order in a chaotic situation. On September 23 the British commander encouraged the local French authorities to reassert their control in the country south of the 16th parallel. Gracey ordered his troops and the French to "shoot armed Annamese on sight." Street demonstrations and guerrilla attacks erupted immediately as the Vietminh saw their hold slipping away. oss officials on the scene concluded that the British decision to assist the French turned the Vietnamese from passive resistance to armed assaults. William Donovan, head of the oss, wrote President Truman that "the situation quickly grew beyond the control of the nationalist Vietminh party, and the Annamese, professing their willingness to die in the cause of liberty took as their slogan—'Death to all Europeans.'"[46] One of the first casualties was Colonel Peter Dewey, head of the oss mission in the southern part of Indochina, who was shot dead in an ambush. Dewey had clashed with both the French and the British, and he had helped the Vietminh. His killing remained controversial for decades, but the official inquiry concluded that he had been killed by Vietnamese who had attacked randomly any passing white man.

The French extended their positions in the southern part of the country during the remainder of 1945, while the Vietminh's DRV continued to hold sway in the northern region surrounding Hanoi. Ho Chi Minh's government repeatedly requested official recognition from Washington to match the local support it was receiving from the oss. The State Department filed Ho's increasingly desperate appeals for help but did not acknowledge or reply to them, nor did a very busy President Truman take note of the reports from oss officers characterizing Ho as "a brilliant and capable man." Washington also ignored oss reports that "to Annamites our coming was the symbol of liberation not from Japanese occupation but from decades of colonial rule. For the Annamite government considered the United States as the principle champion of rights of small peoples."[47] The highest officials, preoccupied with the fast changing postwar world, did not have time for Vietnamese affairs.

Competition between advocates of an Asian and a European strategy continued to determine Washington's policy toward Indochina and France. The office of Far Eastern Affairs presented proposals from Abbott Low Moffat of the Division of Southeast Asia Affairs that the United States and Great Britain jointly sponsor an investigation of the present conditions in Indochina and make recommendations about the future of the territory. The French resentment provoked by this proposal would be far superior than the prospect of a colonial war. The Office of European Affairs, however, considered the danger of a colonial war small and the damage to French prestige too great for the United States to bear. Eventually, the State Department issued a vague statement hoping for a peaceful settlement and offering U.S. help in brokering an arrangement between France and the Vietminh.[48]

Truman and Acting Secretary of State Dean Acheson went beyond the State Department's bland formula to give active encouragement to France. The two men wanted first and foremost to help France; what happened in Southeast Asia was distinctly secondary. French President Charles de Gaulle met Truman and Acheson in Washington in late August. The Americans expressed support for France's right to reassert authority over Indochina, although they pressed him to allow the early independence of Indochina. The American ambassador to France reported on French plans for economic development in Indochina over the coming years. De Gaulle's government hoped to make post–World War II Indochina resemble prewar Shanghai. The ambassador also explained the high stakes for the western allies in the future of French rule in its colonies: "in the coming difficult period in the Far East, Indochina will be the only real foothold on the Asiatic mainland for the occidental democracies [France, Great Britain and the United States]."[49]

By the beginning of 1946 a complicated political puzzle existed in Indochina. The new DRV exercised power in the region of Hanoi and the northern part of the country, but French officials were committed to reasserting their country's control over all of Indochina. Otherwise, they feared the collapse of French prestige elsewhere in Asia, North Africa, and Europe. For their part, U.S. officials preferred to see the eventual independence of Indochina, but wanted any new government to arise with the consent of France. In December 1945 Archimedes Patti, an OSS operative in Indochina, met the State Department's Abbott Low Moffat to explain Ho Chi Minh's leadership capacity and the popularity of the Vietminh through the country. Patti and Jane Foster, an OSS agent who had returned from Saigon, predicted that the Vietminh could wage an effective political and military campaign against France, yet Major General Phillip Gallagher, the chief of the OSS mission to South China and Indochina, presented a more complicated picture when he briefed Moffat at the end of January 1946. Gallagher too noted the popularity of the Vietminh regime, but he doubted whether it could wage an effective guerrilla campaign against the French. A collision appeared inevitable, as the French were committed to exerting their power over all of Indochina while Ho Chi Minh was just as stubborn in his desire to resist the return of colonial rule. Ho might accept a compromise with France if that country promised concrete moves toward speedy independence and the arrangement were guaranteed by the United States and other outside powers.[50]

Thus, four months after the end of the Second World War in Asia, the future of Indochina presented the United States with a complicated and unappealing set of alternatives. The grand design of U.S. policy set down by Franklin Roosevelt predisposed the United States to favor national independence. Yet what sort of nationalism and what sort of independence did that entail? What effect would this independence have on the European powers, who lay prostrate in the wake of the war's destruction in Europe? Their political, economic, and even spiritual lives had been broken by the war, and the highest-level American officials believed that the restoration of their health represented the first priority of the United States in the postwar world. The difficulty in creating an effective policy toward Indochina also reflected deep divisions within the U.S. government that persisted for decades. Officials who had spent the most time in Indochina came to sympathize most with the desires of the Vietnamese. These on-the-scene representatives occasionally romanticized Ho's achievements—from both genuine admiration and their desire to influence Washington. Yet the knowledge and opinions of local experts often counted for the least in forging U.S. policy. In the 1940s, Indochina barely registered as an important arena of U.S. foreign policy. For senior officials, who knew very little about the political realities of Southeast Asia, relations with allies and the emerging competition with the Soviet Union counted for far more in their estimates of what was important for the United States. They were content to let France resume a major role in the affairs of Indochina if that would make France a better and more compliant ally of the United States.

Chapter

* * * * * * * * * * *

The Vietminh, the French,

and the Americans:

1946–1950

*R*ELATIONS between France and the Vietminh deteriorated in 1946, and full-scale war broke out between them in December of that year. In the beginning the United States looked on as a spectator. Washington followed its practice of considering Indochina a distinctly secondary region. Europe took first place in the estimate of U.S. planners; in Asia, Americans looked first to China and then Japan to fulfill their national ambitions. Officially the United States argued that the issue of the future of Indochina concerned France, but later, high-level American officials began to take a more active interest in the future of Southeast Asia. The growing American concern for France's success in its war against the Vietminh coincided with, and represented a part of, the development of the Cold War.

The Cold War emerged in the six months after World War II as a combination of conscious planning and day-to-day interactions between the United States and the Soviet Union. Both powers had expressed suspicions of the other's motives during the Second World War, but the events of the period after August 1945 hardened these concerns into fear and mistrust. By 1947 little room for accommodation existed.[1] While representatives from each side continued to meet at conferences ostensibly designed to resolve their differences, they presented their antagonistic positions more to score points in future disagreements than to restore the alliance of 1941–1945. Europe represented the original arena of the Cold War, but events in Asia played an important role in widening the gap between the United States and the Soviet Union. When the administration of President Harry S. Truman decided in 1946 that the Soviet Union threatened the safety and well being of the United States and its partners, Americans also concluded that issues in one region of the world were intimately linked to problems and crises elsewhere. As American planners came to see the problems of the world as interconnected, they gradually developed a global strategy to contain Soviet aggression. Although Southeast Asia did not become a primary area of concern for the United States in the five years after 1945, planners and policy-makers in Washington came to see the problems of the region as one component of the conflict between East and West.[2]

FRENCH-VIETMINH DIPLOMACY, 1945–1946

In late 1945 French military and civilian authorities pursued seemingly incompatible ends in Vietnam. The military expected a conclusive defeat of the Vietminh forces; simultaneously, civilian representatives negotiated a political settlement to the differences between the Europeans and the Vietnamese. The French government appointed Admiral Thierry d'Argenlieu high commissioner—significantly, not governor general—of Indochina in August 1945. (The distinction in title meant that the French government had not yet formally reasserted its sovereignty over Indochina.) At the same time, General Henri Leclerc, a hero of the Free French in Europe, became the military commander.

In October d'Argenlieu and Leclerc returned to Saigon to wage war on the Vietminh. Leclerc stepped off the cruiser *Gloire* to an arrival ceremony during which the bright sun was obscured by black smoke from a rubber depot ignited by retreating Vietminh guerrillas.[3] For the rest of 1945 Leclerc moved an army made up mostly of Foreign Legionnaires and local Vietnamese, with a smaller contingent of French soldiers, throughout the southern sections of Vietnam. In October his forces controlled the region surrounding Saigon. The arrival of armored units from France later that month allowed him to move columns into the Mekong River Delta. In December 1945 and January 1946 Leclerc's forces secured the central mountains and the coastal plains of southern Vietnam. By early February 1946, Admiral d'Argenlieu believed that French forces had pacified the southern parts of Vietnam. Relying on the precedent of the French conquest of Indochina in the nineteenth century, the high commissioner believed that France could now extend its control northward into Annam and Tonkin. France withdrew its garrison at Fort Bayard on the Luichow Peninsula in exchange for Chinese evacuation of their forces from Tonkin.[4]

Meanwhile, Ho Chi Minh reorganized his forces in the northern section of the country. Ho's policy, then and for the next twenty years, combined fervor, hatred of colonialism, rigid political control, and tactical flexibility. Both his nationalism and his communism made him so sure of himself that he could afford to be patient. Some of his Vietminh colleagues occasionally considered him too willing to accommodate France, the United States, or other Vietnamese factions, but Ho's absolute certainty that his cause would prevail allowed him the luxury of adaptability. In 1946 he formally dissolved the Indochina Communist Party, although it continued its clandestine operations. The Vietminh granted the VNQDD and the Dong Minh Hoi (two nationalist parties) a guaranteed share of seats in the National Assembly. Elections were held in the Vietminh controlled sections of Tonkin, Annam, and Cochinchina. The Vietminh won 97 percent of the vote, but gave up the places in the Assembly it had agreed to offer to the two smaller parties.

In early 1946 Ho also continued efforts at gaining recognition from the United States. In January he once more wrote Truman telling the United States that France had forfeited rights to control Indochina and called for American intervention. The United States did not reply directly, but it did send Kenneth Landon, Assistant Chief of the Division of Southeast Asia Affairs, to the region. Landon spent most of his time with French officials in Saigon, but he did travel to Hanoi and met Ho several times in February. Landon reported on the genuine popularity of Ho and the Vietminh.[5]

French civilian authorities did not share the military's optimism. Jean Sainteny had represented the French government in conversations with Ho Chi Minh, Vo Nguyen Giap, and other Vietnamese officials since arriving in Hanoi in August. Sainteny and the Vietminh continued their discussions throughout the fall, since both sides doubted whether a strictly military solution was within reach. The French blanched at the prospect of diverting precious resources from the task of reconstruction in Europe. For their part the Vietminh preferred to take power peacefully and receive international recognition for the government of the new Republic of Vietnam than to risk full-scale war against France. The failure of any outside power to recognize the independent Republic of Vietnam proclaimed in September had left the Vietminh isolated. Sainteny informed Landon, the American representative, that he would offer Ho self-government within the French Community (a commonwealth of French-speaking dependencies). France would control foreign affairs and the Vietminh army would be integrated into the French army. Ho Chi Minh and the Democratic Republic of Vietnam would have control over local affairs.[6]

On March 6, 1946 Sainteny, General Raoul Salan and General Giap signed a Preliminary Convention in Hanoi. The French promised to recognize the government of the Democratic Republic of Vietnam as a free state within the French Union. Vietnam would have its own parliament, army, and finances and be a part of an Indochinese Federation including Cambodia and Laos. The preliminary convention provided for a referendum in three parts of Vietnam (Tonkin, Annam, and Cochinchina—north, central, and south) to determine the final political status of Vietnam. An annex to the convention allowed France to station a limited number of troops in Vietnam until 1952.

This compromise solution roughly followed the designs of the Americans and British at the end of the war for the end to direct colonial rule in Indochina. At the same time it preserved a French presence in Indochina and left unclear the question of whether Vietnam was to be a single country (the Vietminh claim) or three separate provinces or possible republics (the French position). But the Vietminh liked the agreement more than the French military. For Ho Chi Minh and his top political associates, Sainteny had yielded on the core issue of Vietnamese independence. Ordinary Vietminh fighters and ardent nationalists thought Ho and Giap had given up too much by allowing a continued French presence. Nationalists in the Vietminh and VNQDD denounced the agreement as a betrayal, but Ho told Sainteny, "you know I wanted more than has been granted. . . . Nevertheless, I realize that one cannot achieve everything in a single day."[7] Ho may also have counted on a more sympathetic government coming to power in upcoming French elections.

The French military in Indochina felt an even stronger sense of betrayal than did the foot soldiers of the Vietminh. Admiral d'Argenlieu expressed disgust that civilians would rather negotiate than fight. Opponents of the agreement in Saigon argued that the arrangement represented only a "regional arrangement" covering Tonkin and the northern part of Annam. Officials in Paris echoed these views. Marius Moutet, Minister of Overseas Territories and a member of the Socialist Party, stated that the southern province of Cochinchina would remain a "free state" not covered by the Sainteny-Giap agreement.[8]

In the face of such opposition, the French and Vietnamese agreed to resume negotiations at Dalat in central Vietnam on April 17. The French delegation, consisting of Max André (former director of the Franco-Chinese bank), Pierre Mesmer (a representative of the colonial office), and two scholars of Vietnam (Pierre Gourou and Marcel Ner) demanded assurances from the Vietnamese that they would remain a part of the French Union. They also did not agree to a single, unified Vietnam. For their part the Vietnamese delegates, headed by the Republic's Foreign Minister, Nguyen Tuong Tam (head of the VNQDD party), and including General Giap, insisted on guarantees that France would quit Vietnam and commit to recognizing the Vietminh government in Hanoi as exercising control over the entire territory of Vietnam. After two days of conversations, during which the gap between the two sides did not narrow, Giap doubted whether the French would agree peaceably to yielding all of Vietnam to the Vietminh. He expected war to break out between France and the Vietminh. Ho Chi Minh, however, instructed Vietminh delegates to continue discussions.

In the late spring and summer of 1946 a complex, interrelated mixture of diplomatic discussions in Europe and political and military movements in Vietnam set the future course of events in Indochina. On June 1 the French military in Vietnam proceeded with plan to divide the country when d'Argenlieu proclaimed the "autonomous Republic of Cochinchina" to a large crowd in the center of Saigon. Jean Sainteny informed Ho Chi Minh of this unilateral declaration in Paris, where the latter had gone to attend the talks on implementing the Dalat Preliminary Convention. The news alarmed Ho, who declared that Cochinchina "is Vietnamese soil. It is the flesh of our flesh, the blood of our blood."

News that the weak French government wanted a delay of a month or two before opening formal discussions also irritated the Vietnamese. The French government shunted the Vietnamese representatives to Biarritz in the southeast of the country, ostensibly because France was in the midst of an election campaign. In fact, the French government wanted to isolate Ho's potential supporters in Paris. Georges Bidault, the leader of the victorious Christian Democrats who became prime minister, favored a union of French overseas states "closely linked by common institutions." Ho wanted a much looser confederation patterned on the British commonwealth.[9] Worse news for the Vietminh followed: On June 21 d'Argenlieu concretely demonstrated his contempt for the Dalat agreement by ordering French troops to began an offensive to bring the central highlands under control.

The delayed conference on the political future of Vietnam opened outside Paris at Fontainebleu on July 6. Max André, who had headed the French delegation at Dalat, resumed that position at Fontainebleu. Pham Van Dong of the Vietminh's politburo led the Vietnamese contingent. Little progress toward an agreement occurred for the remainder of July. Then, in the beginning of August, d'Argenlieu convened a parallel conference at Dalat. The ostensible purpose of this meeting was to map the future of the Indochinese Federation, but in fact d'Argenlieu wanted to weaken the Vietnamese position at Fontainebleu. The French commander in Vietnam claimed that the future of Indochina could not be decided solely by representatives based in Hanoi, the most ardently nationalist and anti-French people in the region. D'Argenlieu included representatives from the French-controlled governments of Laos, Cambodia, the newly proclaimed Republic of Cochinchina, and delegations from two entities he created specially for this conference— the Montagnards (mountain people) of southern Indochina and South Annam.

Word of the second Dalat conference infuriated the Vietnamese delegation at Fontainebleu, so Ho tried once more to gain American backing.

T. Jefferson Caffery, the U.S. ambassador to France, reported after meeting Ho that "he would be very pleased to use in some way or other in his future negotiations with French authorities." Abbott Low Moffat, head of the State Department's Division of Southeast Asia Affairs, agreed that d'Argenlieu had tried to sabotage the Fontainebleu conversations, and he predicted war between France and the Vietminh. Moffat urged the United States to tell the French that "in view of our interest in peace and orderly development of dependent people, our hope [is] that they will abide by the spirit of the March 6 convention."[10] The United States did not, however, formally intervene. Indochina remained a subordinate issue, and the French government had a firm position on maintaining Indochina within the French Union.

While the Fontainebleu meeting nearly broke up, the French representatives persuaded the Vietminh that d'Argenlieu had exceeded his authority by convening the Dalat conference. Ho and Pham Van Dong stayed at Fontainebleu to continue discussions. The French suggested settling easier questions first, leaving the political status of Indochina to a latter stage of discussion. Talks continued into September without reaching agreement on the basic issues of independence for all of Indochina (including Vietnam and the kingdoms of Laos and Cambodia, which existed as French protectorates), the political status of Cochinchina, and the political and diplomatic organization of Vietnam. Ho Chi Minh and French colonial minister Marius Moutet did sign agreements on economic and cultural issues. This modus vivendi represented a temporary truce between the parties. Yet the Vietminh believed they had made more concessions than had the French, since the agreement formally ratified a French role in the future of the country. Ho Chi Minh whispered, "I've just signed my death warrant" after the ceremony.[11] He then sailed for Vietnam, never to return to France.

When Ho returned to Hanoi in October, he faced disappointed militants who accused him of selling out to the French, yet most representatives to the National Assembly that opened in late October hailed Ho and elected him president of the republic under a new constitution adopted in November. Even as Ho received the cheers of the National Assembly, skirmishes around Haiphong between the Vietminh and French naval forces allowed d'Argenlieu to begin a new offensive.

WAR

War broke out between France and the Vietminh at the end of 1946, although both French and Vietnamese civilians tried to head off a final breach. Ho appealed to the French Parliament to honor the accord signed in September, and told a French journalist that neither France nor Vietnam "can afford the luxury of a bloody war." But he warned ominously that the Vietnamese would endure an "atrocious struggle" before they would "renounce their liberty." A new French government headed by socialist Leon Blum promised reconciliation with Vietnam "based on independence," but Blum's weak regime lasted barely a month.

Meanwhile, both Vietminh fighters and the French army wanted a fight. D'Argenlieu, in Paris to stiffen the spine of the government, radioed subordinates in Vietnam "we will never retreat or surrender." Outraged by the killing of three French soldiers by Vietminh fighters in Hanoi, the French commander in Haiphong said, "If those gooks want a fight, they'll get it."[12] A cease-fire lasted two days, but the French government, under advice from d'Argenlieu, demanded that the Vietminh withdraw. The Vietminh ignored the ultimatum and the French navy responded with a ferocious bombardment of Haiphong in which about six thousand Vietnamese were killed.[13]

The Vietminh responded on December 19 by sabotaging the Hanoi municipal power plant and breaking into the homes of French officials in Hanoi to kill or kidnap the residents. Spies warned the French, who counterattacked by shelling Hanoi and conducting a house-to-house search for Ho. Hundreds died in the battle, their corpses left to rot in the street. Ho, ill once more with fever, escaped to a town six miles south of Hanoi. Giap ordered "all soldiers . . . to stand together, go into battle, destroy the invaders, and save the nation." Ho issued his own battle cry to the Vietnamese: "Those who have rifles will use their rifles; those who have swords will use their swords; those who have no swords will use spades, hoes or sticks."[14]

The United States became sufficiently alarmed after the shelling of Haiphong to pursue the sort of intervention Moffat had recommended in August. Ambassador Caffery told the Foreign Ministry of American concern over French inflexibility. Moffat embarked on a special mission to Saigon and Hanoi in early December. Over French objection, he met with Ho, who told him that the Vietminh wanted an independent, not necessarily a communist, state. Such assurances made little impression on Washington officials, primarily concerned with French sensibilities. Undersecretary of State Dean Acheson told Moffat to explore with Ho whether the Vietminh would accept a referendum to determine the future of Cochinchina. By December, however, Vietminh sentiment firmly opposed another compromise on the question of including southern Vietnam in the republic. Moreover, Acheson informed Moffat that the United States did not formally want to mediate between France and the Vietminh. Perhaps most importantly, the State Department reminded its representative in Hanoi of "Ho's clear record as agent of international communism." Whatever happened, the "least desirable eventuality would be [the] establishment [of a] Communist-dominated, Moscow-oriented state in Indochina." Thereafter, Washington's plans to accommodate Ho diminished.[15]

Back in Vietnam, a battle for Hanoi raged throughout December; eventually all Vietminh fighters fled the city. The French government now stiffened its conditions for negotiations, demanding that the Vietminh lay down their arms and that "order must be restored" before talks could resume. D'Argenlieu said that further discussions with Ho would be "henceforth impossible," and he called for a return to Vietnam's "traditional monarchy"—the restoration of Emperor Bao Dai.

A new French government replaced d'Argenlieu with Emile Bollaert, who appointed as his personal representative Paul Mus, an Asian scholar sympathetic to the Vietnamese. Ho interpreted the dismissal of d'Argenlieu as a positive sign and asked for a cease-fire to avoid a war that would "only end in hatred and bitterness between our two peoples." He appealed to the French government and public to recognize Vietnamese "unity and independence within the French Union." He pledged "to respect French economic and cultural interests."[16]

Before progress could be made on this latest Vietnamese offer, the French government shifted policies again and the Americans became more deeply involved in the search for a political solution. The Christian Democrats within the coalition, who favored using force against the Vietminh, gained the upper hand. General Charles de Gaulle, who had left politics the previous year, added his voice to demands for force with his support of a new political party promising the restoration of French prestige. The U.S. government made another ineffectual gesture toward mediation in the beginning of 1947. Acheson told the French ambassador of his concern that the "unhappy situation" in Indochina might wind up in the United Nations. He offered American help in resolving the dispute before it came before the international organization.

French officials rejected American help. They promised to resume negotiations with the Vietminh only after they had restored order. Some State Department officials worried that France's actions threatened the position of the United States in the eyes of other Asians, but the communist domination of the Vietminh prevented the United States government from treating the future of Indochina solely as a colonial question. In February the new Secretary of State, George Marshall, summarized the elements both limiting and encouraging American action: (1) The United States recognized French sovereignty over Indochina. (2) Reports from the scene confirmed the "continued existence of [a] dangerously outmoded colonial outlook and method" on the part of the French in the region. (3) Finally, "Ho Chi Minh has direct Communist connections and it should be obvious that we are not interested in seeing colonial empire administrations supplanted by [the] philosophy and political organization directed from and controlled by [the] Kremlin." In the end Marshall threw up his hands: "Frankly, we have no solution of [the] problem to suggest."[17]

In May the French government instructed Bollaert and Mus to agree to a cease-fire only after the Vietminh lay down some of their arms, permit French soldiers free access to all of the territory they controlled, and return some Foreign Legion deserters. Mus would not have accepted this offer had he been in Ho's position, and the Vietminh leader turned it down as a demand for surrender. The first Indochina war had begun in earnest.

THE GROWTH OF U.S. COMMITMENT TO INDOCHINA

In 1947 the United States reviewed its policy toward Indochina. Policy-makers became convinced that the French could not defeat the Vietminh as long as France appeared to wage a war solely to restore their colonial mastery of Indochina. Yet even as the United States grew increasingly critical of France, it expressed no greater warmth toward Ho Chi Minh or the Vietminh. Washington began an elusive search, one which continued for the next decade, to find a third force—authentic nationalists, neither communist nor puppets of France—in Vietnamese politics. Americans hoped this middle way would include personalities with authentic nationalist credentials, untainted by either connections to the colonial past or to the international communist movement.

U.S. officials recognized the cost of the war and the political misjudgments and military shortcomings of all the parties to the dispute. Secretary of State Marshall consistently told the U.S. embassy in Paris that the United States wanted a solution to the "disturbed situation in Indochina." The United States sought a "pacific basis . . . for the adjustment of the situation."[18] Charles Reed, the U.S. consul in Saigon, neatly summarized the ongoing dilemma when he cabled the State Department that "something must be done to bring home to the French that times have changed and that the natives have a right to more than a semblance of independence." At the same time Reed expressed skepticism about the willingness of Ho Chi Minh's "totalitarian government" to yield power over the central and southern parts of Vietnam. Both sides had shown "bad faith," and Reed thought that the gap between the French and Vietnamese so wide as to make outside mediation necessary.[19] At a conference among U.S. diplomats held to discuss Southeast Asia in June 1948, most participants agreed with the assessment of William Hunter that "the French are no longer capable of carrying on the war in Indochina. All independence movement leaders can take courage from the fact that it has been demonstrated that no matter how large and well equipped an Army is, it can be worn down by stubborn resistance."[20]

James O'Sullivan, the consul at Hanoi, agreed that it was in France's interest to look for local Vietnamese nationalist leadership, other than the Vietminh, to end the war. But finding such leaders presented a daunting,

possibly insurmountable task. He believed that Emile Bollaert, the new
French commissioner, had "no intention of negotiating with Ho Chi Minh."
O'Sullivan also determined that "French troops here are insufficient to pacify
the country unless their strength [is] greatly increased . . . or unless political action parallels military and police operations." The consul therefore
concluded that "Bollaert must then seek [a] solution with some figures or
groups other than Ho Chi Minh and [the] Viet Minh (assuming of course that
[the] French wish to stop [the] destruction in Tonkin as soon as possible)."
O'Sullivan doubted that France could make enough concessions to any potential negotiating partner among the Vietnamese to validate their nationalist
credentials in the eyes of their compatriots. "In [the] event [the] French fail to
satisfy by concessions to [a] govt they establish," he informed the State
Department, "such [a] govt could only remain [a] puppet as Nationalists
would continue [to] support [the] Viet Minh and Moderates will inevitably be
driven to extremes and into [the] Communist Party seeking support from the
only place it is available, Russia." Unfortunately, O'Sullivan noted, there
was no evidence that the French were "willing to make concessions of [the]
size required to satisfy Vietnamese nationalism."[21]

U.S. representatives on the scene in Vietnam also doubted whether Ho
would accept the conditions offered by the French for a cease fire. O'Sullivan
told Washington that talks between Ho and Paul Mus had gone poorly. Mus
met with Ho in June and informed him that France wanted hostilities to stop
with a promise by the Vietminh not to retaliate against Vietnamese who had
helped the French. France also demanded that the Vietminh surrender their
arms and order their fighters to assemble in spots designated by the French
army. At the same time the Vietminh were supposed to allow French soldiers
to circulate freely throughout Vietnam.

Ho rejected these conditions. He likened the call for amnesty for Vietnamese collaborators with the French to a requirement that France ignore the
misdeeds of French people who had helped the Germans in 1940 and during
the occupation. "We ought to punish Vietnamese who have decided to deliver our country to a foreign nation," he told Mus. Ho berated Bollaert for
demanding that the Vietnamese troops assemble in predetermined positions
while the French army had the run of the country. Such a scheme reminded
Ho of the way in which "the Pétain government delivered arms and munitions
to the German Army, permitted German troops freedom of action in French
territory and obligated French troops to assemble in determined positions. Is
this an armistice?" he asked. Mus, who sympathized with Ho's position but
who lacked authority to negotiate a deal favorable to the Vietnamese, could
reply only that "in these circumstances, we have nothing more to say to
you." As Mus left the meeting, Ho reminded him of Vietnamese patience.
"We can resist five years, ten years or more," he said.[22]

U.S. representatives in Vietnam also understood that Ho's popularity with the Vietnamese and other Asians made him a formidable force. Reed expected France to "stall [in the negotiations,] hoping something [would] turn up enabling them to bypass Ho." Reed reported, however, that a "government without Ho, even given independence, will have little chance [to] succeed unless backed by force which France can ill afford and most observers feel pitting Nationalists against Vietminh can only lead [to a] continuance of trouble." More troublesome to American observers was "much more talk than in the past few months [regarding] communism." The French gleefully reported to the Americans of the increased Soviet interest in Southeast Asia as a way of diminishing whatever support the Americans might have considered giving Ho. Americans also worried that Ho had begun appealing to the "fine Asiatic family" by characterizing the Vietnamese struggle against France as a fight "for the liberty and independence" of other Asians against Europeans.[23]

Partly despite and partly because of the broad appeal Ho Chi Minh presented to nationalists across Asia, the United States continued to fear Ho's communist connections. Americans joined Britons in concluding that Ho represented a dangerous mixture of communism and nationalism. Americans endorsed a Foreign Office analysis: "Clearly Communists always disguise themselves as Nationalists when they can, but this does not make it any easier to decide whether a Nationalist is also a Communist at heart—nor, in the last resort, does it really matter." Ho's early communist affiliations disqualified him as a legitimate nationalist leader. His time in Moscow in the 1930s gave him an instinctive feeling for the current Communist Party line. Americans thought that Ho did not need to consult Moscow regularly because he knew what the Kremlin wanted. His actions helped Soviet policy by weakening France, thereby undermining the Western position in Europe. By 1948 the State Department characterized "the basic assumption of this government vis-a-vis Ho" to be "that we cannot afford to assume that Ho is anything but Moscow-directed."[24]

THE FRENCH SEARCH FOR AN ALTERNATIVE TO THE VIETMINH

France too looked for a way out. Facing a prolonged war and trying to undermine the popularity of Ho, the French explored the possibility of returning the deposed Emperor Bao Dai, now living in Hong Kong, to head a nationalist but non-communist government. Before his recall in early 1947 d'Argenlieu advocated "the return of the emperor." The French military commissioner believed that Bao Dai offered "the political prestige of legitimacy," and a government directed by him "would probably reassure all those who, having opposed the Vietminh, fear that they will be accused of treason.'' By March 1947 contacts between Paul Mus, Bollaert's special representative, and Bao Dai in Hong Kong became common knowledge. At first, the former emperor adopted a nationalist stance, telling Mus that he would demand as much of the French as had Ho. He insisted upon a unified Vietnamese state within the French Union.[25] As talks continued, however, Bao Dai realized that France seriously considered returning him to power, a hope he had abandoned since 1945, and thus became more amenable to serving French interests. French officials considered the restoration of Bao Dai as the magical solution to their related problems in Indochina: how to retain real control there; how to end the war with the Vietminh; and how to reduce the influence of the Vietminh.[26]

In late summer 1947 France seemed formally to end all chance of a rapprochement with the Vietminh. The government in Paris forced Bollaert to abandon efforts to forge a compromise with the Vietminh and Bao Dai. In July he had raised hopes of a settlement with a promise to ''work out a lasting peace . . . with all parties and groups.'' These remarks encouraged Vietminh radio to reply that ''if this clear view of the situation guides French policy, a peaceful solution can certainly be found.'' Bollaert prepared to deliver a detailed plan of reconciliation on August 15, the date on which Britain had promised to relinquish its two-hundred-year-long rule over India. Before he spoke, however, the most anti-Vietminh faction of the French cabinet prevailed on the government to disavow Bollaert's latest olive branch. When he finally addressed a rally at Ha Dong in northern Vietnam on September 10, Bollaert offered neither a truce in the war nor a unified and independent Vietnam. He promised only liberty within the French Union. France would no longer exercise control over internal affairs, but it would direct the Vietnamese army and the country's international relations. The Vietnamese would decide the future of Cochinchina, but he, as high commissioner, would be the final arbiter of disputes among various Vietnamese regions. He also would control the federal budget of Vietnam. He said that this final offer ''must be rejected or accepted as a whole.''[27]

Bollaert's ultimatum polarized opinion in Vietnam. The Vietminh naturally fulminated against what foreign minister Hoang Minh Giam called a ''narrow minded'' proposal. The newspaper of the Vietminh in Cochinchina suggested that Ho Chi Minh's organization try once more to ''establish friendly economic and cultural relations . . . with the United States'' in order to secure Vietnam's ''internal and external sovereignty.'' Pham Ngoc Thach, the Undersecretary of State of the Vietminh, wrote Trygve Lie, the Secretary General of the United Nations, requesting that the Security Council ''put an end to the war of aggression that France has undertaken these last two years against Vietnam.'' The United Nations did not reply. Supporters of Bao Dai did not like the parts of Bollaert's speech that indicated a continuing division of Vietnam, but they were heartened by his address to ''all political,

Red River

China

Tonkin

Burma

Dienbienphu

Hanoi

Haiphong

Gulf of Tonkin

Laos

20°

Luang Prabang

Hainan

Vientiane

Mekong River

Vinh

0   150 Miles

0   150 Kilometers

Quang Tri

17°

Hue

Siam (Thailand)

Da Nang

N

Cambodia

14°

Tonle Sap

Annam

Bangkok

Phnompenh

11°

Saigon

Gulf of Siam (Thailand)

Mekong Delta

Cochinchina

102°   105°   108°

French Indochina

35

intellectual and social factions of Vietnam," not just Ho Chi Minh. As the French had hoped, Bao Dai's circle of advisers broke with the Vietminh, despite the latter's call for a unified front against France. They appealed to the former emperor to assume leadership of Vietnam. He replied: "You have revealed to me the whole picture of your misery. . . . I accept the mission which you entrust to me and am ready to contact the French authorities." He said he wanted independence and unity for Vietnam, but he left it unclear whether he would act as a mediator between the French and the Vietminh or wanted to assume sole power. Many Vietnamese shared the suspicion of Ngo Dinh Diem that "Bao Dai may weaken and be directly under French influence, as he naturally desires to revive his dynasty and lead his people into better days."[28]

Amidst intermittent battles with the Vietminh in 1948, France worked with supporters of the former emperor to create a stable government led by Bao Dai. After months of negotiations General Nguyen Van Xuan formed a new central government in May 1948. The regime lacked prestige and few prominent people joined the cabinet. The U.S. consul at Hanoi complained that the installation of Xuan was "more that of a funeral than a christening. . . . The appearance of Xuan, his stocky figure clothed in mandarinal robes which he obviously did not know how to handle, almost succeeded in introducing a note of low comedy. Gilbert and Sullivan came to mind."[29]

The new government's complete subservience to France, however, did lead Paris to reverse its earlier opposition to considering the three provinces of Vietnam a single country. On June 5, 1948, Bao Dai briefly left Hong Kong to meet Xuan and Bollaert on a French warship in Ha Long Bay. The three recognized the independence of Vietnam as an independent state within the French Union. Only nominal independence came from this agreement, since the government of Vietnam protected French nationals and gave priority to the hiring of French advisers and technicians. After he signed, Bao Dai left for the Riviera, leaving Xuan in charge of forging a popular government. For the remainder of 1948 Bao Dai remained in exile, dangling before the French the possibility of his eventual return to take over formal power. Before doing so, however, he wanted more than the semblance of independence.[30]

Bollaert believed that the agreement represented a "psychological shock" that would undercut popular support for the Vietminh. It did not. Naturally, the Vietminh denounced the accord as a sham concluded between the colonial government and what Ho characterized as "a puppet central government ready to commit every kind of treason in the service of its foreign masters." Of even greater significance in undermining the Ha Long Bay accord was the chronic disarray within the French cabinet. U.S. Ambassador Caffery reported that "no two ministers are in accord" regarding "what should be done about Indochina."[31] Some members of the governing coalition interpreted the Ha Long Bay accord to change nothing. Others believed it meant that France had indeed agreed to Vietnamese unity and no longer insisted on control over Cochinchina. Prime Minister André Marie, a Radical Socialist colleague of Bollaert, would not specify whether the agreement's promise to consult all political and intellectual factions meant that Paris still would talk with the Vietminh.[32]

VIETMINH SUCCESSES

Meanwhile, the Vietminh consolidated control over the countryside of northern and central Vietnam. The Vietminh pursued a moderate economic policy, avoiding land redistribution or collectivization of agriculture. It did order a 25 percent reduction in rents, a move highly popular among the peasants. It also tried to make the economy self-sufficient by moving factories to the countryside and diversifying agriculture. Drawing on lessons learned during the famine of 1945, the Vietminh also encouraged the peasants to plant sweet potatoes, corn, and manioc as well as rice. The new authorities organized the peasants into teams to protect the dikes and to compete with one another to fight illiteracy, famine and the French. The economic program was popular but drafting peasants into the army to fight the French was not. A traveler in rural Vietnam found that "the people are very tired of the war. They don't care whether Ho Chi Minh or Bao Dai governs the country if peace can be restored. They are very much afraid of the French troops and particularly bombing planes. Every time they have to leave the village, they lose at least part of their pigs and chickens which are taken by the French army."[33]

As 1948 went on, however, the Vietminh gathered strength while the Xuan government languished. Even some members of the imperial family joined Ho Chi Minh's forces. As one royalist who had taken part in the Fontainebleu conference put it: "the former Imperial Family of Viet Nam regards with profound sadness the spilling of blood which is taking part in Vietnam because of the refusal of the French authorities to negotiate with the national government of president Ho Chi Minh. There will be no end to this fratricidal war while the French authorities continue the policy of creating and supporting artificial 'governments' without any roots in the Vietnamese people."[34]

France's international position weakened further in early 1949. The Chinese communist forces gained the upper hand in the Chinese civil war. In January Mao Zedong's People's Liberation Army captured the former capital of Beijing, dooming the Nationalists. In the event of the likely takeover of all of China by the communist forces, the Vietminh would have for the first time an ally on their border. Previously, the Vietminh had fought alone, smuggling arms from China and by boat from Hong Kong and the Philippines. As the People's Liberation Army approached the border of China and Vietnam its potential as a real, military ally of the Vietminh grew. Foreign recognition of the Republic of Vietnam could kill France's hopes to retain power. Ironically, the chance of Chinese support for the Vietminh also strengthened France's bargaining power with Bao Dai. "You cannot survive without our presence," a French representative told Xuan.[35] France redoubled its efforts to persuade Bao Dai to return to Vietnam and pry nationalist support from the Vietminh. In January Xuan traveled from Vietnam to France to urge Bao Dai to return.

THE STATE OF VIETNAM

On March 8, 1949 Bao Dai and French President Vincent Auriol exchanged letters outlining the future political status of Vietnam. In these Elysée Agreements (named for the presidential palace on the Champs Elysée where the two leaders exchanged letters) France formally agreed to Vietnamese unity and independence within the French Union. There, as at each previous stage of negotiation since 1946, France insisted that independence not jeopardize its future position in Indochina. French citizens had special legal rights; cases against them would be tried by French, not Vietnamese, courts. Vietnam was to join the French Union as an Associated State and France agreed to support the new nation's application for membership in the United Nations.

Yet Vietnam was hardly a truly independent state under this arrangement. It had far less freedom of action than did members of the British Commonwealth. France permitted it to open diplomatic relations with China (later changed to India after the communist victory in China), Thailand, and the Vatican, but France could exercise overall control of Vietnam's external affairs. Vietnam could send representatives to France's National Assembly, but so could the French protectorates of Africa, which everyone agreed were not independent. Vietnam also had the right to send delegates to a new body, the High Council of the French Union. This organization did not meet until 1951. The president of the French Union was also the president of the French Republic, confirming metropolitan France's domination of the Union. The Elysée Agreements promised Vietnam an armed force to maintain order and internal security. The Vietnamese pledged their military to the defense of the Union, and promised to use French equipment and advisers. A French Union armed force would remain in Vietnam with the right to circulate among their bases and garrisons. France did acknowledge that the southern province of Cochinchina would be absorbed into the new state. Two autonomous regions, made up of the Montagnards of the south-central highlands and the Thai people in the north, remained outside of the control of Vietnam. In summary, the Elysée Agreements put into practice the negotiating positions France had pressed since 1946.

Bao Dai had retreated from the nationalist positions he had occasionally adopted since 1946. The time for his return to Vietnam was now or never. He expected that the desperate need for U.S. support would force the French government to make additional concessions. After he signed the Elysée understanding, Bao Dai predicted that "an era of reconstruction and renovation would open in Vietnam." He did not, however, expect the gates of paradise to open automatically, and delayed returning to Vietnam until the French Assembly ratified the Elysée provisions for the incorporation of Cochinchina into the new state. On March 12 the French Assembly authorized the creation of a Cochinchinese Assembly. This body was hardly a representative legislature—sixteen of the sixty-four members were French and all were chosen indirectly by local councils and French professional, syndical, and corporative bodies. Only five thousand Vietnamese in Cochinchina were eligible to vote in the elections scheduled for April 10; a minuscule seven hundred actually did so. Once the Assembly met some new members readily sold their votes to General Xuan for about 20 million francs, but bribery was not enough to convince a majority of the assembly to attach Cochinchina to Vietnam. Only after Xuan and his subordinates exerted other pressures, including death threats, did the Assembly vote to join Vietnam on April 23. Bao Dai then returned on April 25, but he did not resume authority until the French assembly ratified the unification of Cochinchina and Vietnam. A French law acknowledging unification went into effect on June 4, and Bao Dai, under heavy protection from French guards, entered Saigon on June 13.[36]

U.S. CONTAINMENT POLICY

The United States came slowly and fitfully to support Bao Dai's restoration. The United States believed that no good solution to the problem of Indochina existed. The complex and conflicted U.S. policy toward the Bao Dai solution reflected significant differences of opinion among government officials over where to focus American efforts in the Cold War with the Soviet Union. The Truman administration committed itself to a policy of containment of the Soviet Union in 1947. In March of that year the President announced the Truman Doctrine under which the United States pledged to "assist free peoples" everywhere "in maintaining their freedoms."[37] In June Secretary of State George Marshall promised billions of dollars in reconstruction aid to Europe. In July the journal *Foreign Affairs,* an organ of the Council on Foreign Relations, a private organization made up of many of the most prominent foreign-policy practitioners and experts in the country, published "The Sources of Soviet Conduct." *Foreign Affairs* listed the author only as X. Walter Lippmann, an influential columnist for the New York *Herald Tribune,* soon identified the real X as George F. Kennan, the head of the

Policy Planning Staff of the State Department and one of the nation's premier experts on the Soviet Union. The X article, as it came to be called, offered the public justification for the policy of containment of Soviet expansion and communism that the Truman administration had adopted in 1946 and 1947.[38]

Containment provided the intellectual justification for the East-West conflict, and the Truman Doctrine authorized American assistance to government fighting local revolutionaries which might be considered to be inspired by communism. Neither the Truman Doctrine nor containment, however, specified precisely where or how the United States would act. Officials divided between those who believed the principal arena of the Cold War would be Europe and those who thought that Asia represented a separate area of concern. Europeanists tended to consider issues everywhere in the world related to events in Europe. Specialists on Asia, on the other hand, believed that events in that region followed specific, even unique, historical patterns. For Asia experts the development of a proper U.S. policy required detailed knowledge of local culture, history and current events. Asia experts saw events in that region as far more independent of Moscow than did Europe-oriented officials.

The top officials of the Truman administration—the President, Secretaries of State George Marshall (1947–1948) and Dean Acheson (1949–1953), and Secretary of Defense James Forrestal (1947–1949)—leaned toward a European strategy. Nevertheless, from 1947 onward they tried to weave together a comprehensive global policy. In 1947 they changed the direction of U.S. policy toward Japan. Previously they had allowed General Douglas Mac-Arthur a free hand in reorganizing Japan's political and economic structures. In early 1947, however, the State Department sent George Kennan to Japan, with orders to find ways of integrating the defeated power into new security arrangements for Asia. The head of the policy planning staff recommended much tighter control from Washington over MacArthur and a reversal of the occupation's hostilities to large business monopolies. Henceforth the American occupation strove to increase Japanese exports to Southeast Asia, thereby lending stability to a key anchor of what U.S. planners called a "great crescent" running from the Kurile Islands north of Japan through Southeast Asia through the Indian subcontinent to the borders of Iran and Afghanistan. Kennan later characterized the reverse course along with the Marshall plan as "the most significant contribution I was ever to make in government."[39]

U.S. RECOGNITION OF BAO DAI

Differences of opinion among government officials affected the development of U.S. policy toward Indochina and Bao Dai, and these disagreements soon became known to the larger public. A North Carolina member of Congress complained to Truman that an already desperate security situation in the Pacific and Asia had been made worse by "the tendency of various executive departments to act as isolated units, rather than integrated elements."[40] U.S. representatives in Vietnam favored an Asia-based policy. They believed that Bao Dai lacked popular support and Ho Chi Minh's hold on the country's nationalist aspirations could not be undermined. George M. Abbott, who succeeded Charles Reed as the consul in Saigon, wired the State Department in June 1948 that the United States should withhold support from the restoration of Bao Dai until France did more to satisfy nationalist aspirations: "If the Bao Dai solution fails," he wrote, "the United States would be on record as advocating a liberal solution crucial to the political problem but in no wise committed to monarchist, as distinct from non-communist, solutions."[41] Abbott believed that the "greatest obstacle" to the success of any French plan to restore Bao Dai was "the lack of comprehension by the French public of the depth and strength of nationalism in colonial areas which has emerged in the postwar era."[42]

Doubts about the ability of France to satisfy genuine nationalist aspirations represented the core of the Asia strategy. These concerns dominated U.S. policy toward Indochina until the conclusion of the Elysée Agreements of March 1949. In July 1948, for example, Secretary of State Marshall lamented that "the objective of United States policy can only be obtained by such French action as will satisfy the aspirations of the people of Indochina." He glumly acknowledged that the United States lacked "any practicable solution" to resolving the dilemma of preserving France's position in Asia while fostering the development of authentic nationalism.[43]

Yet this skepticism about the value of an unlimited U.S. commitment to France melted in 1949. The U.S. embassy in Paris and the Office of Western European Affairs of the State Department persuaded superiors to support France's policy toward Vietnam unconditionally. Ambassador T. Jefferson Caffery argued that Bao Dai was the only alternative available to Ho Chi Minh. He further claimed that the political balance in France was so delicate that France could make no further concessions to nationalist sentiment without destroying the governing coalition. Advocates of the European-centered strategy gained their final triumph after Bao Dai returned to Vietnam in April and established his government in June. On June 21, 1949 the United States endorsed the Elysée Agreements as a way of uniting the "truly progressive elements within Vietnam."

The United States moved closer to extending formal diplomatic relations to Bao Dai's regime after the communists achieved total victory in the Chinese civil war. The communists' defeat of Jiang Jieshi's Nationalists sent shock waves throughout Southeast Asia. The National Security Council considered Mao Zedong's success to be "a grievous defeat for us." The extension of communism to the rest of Southeast Asia would be "a major political

rout, the repercussions of which will be felt throughout the rest of the world."
In late 1949 the United States urged the governments of Burma, India, Indonesia, the Philippines, and Thailand to recognize Bao Dai. Each refused,
doubting the extent of Vietnam's independence from France. Their reluctance
infuriated Secretary of State Acheson who predicted that "this general indifference or lack of understanding may prove to be disastrous for those nations
as Communism relentlessly advances. It is impossible for the United States to
help them resist Communism if they are not prepared to help themselves."[44]

Washington took the final step of opening diplomatic relations with Bao
Dai in early 1950. China and the Soviet Union formally recognized Ho Chi
Minh's Democratic Republic of Vietnam in January. David Bruce, the U.S.
ambassador in Paris, told Acheson that the Soviet move attacked the integrity
of the French Union and would "induce [a] violent reaction in France."[45] In
early February Acheson formally reviewed the last five years of the conflict
between France and the Vietminh as he recommended extending recognition
to Bao Dai. Ho Chi Minh, "who, under various aliases, has been a communist agent in various parts of the world since 1925," had taken over the anti-
French nationalist movement in 1945. Recognition of Ho's government by
the Soviet Union and China threatened the position of France and the United
States. Acheson recommended the United States follow with its own formal
recognition, which would bolster the "national aspirations" of "non-
communist leadership for peoples of colonial areas in Southeast Asia," help
establish "stable non-Communist governments" in the areas adjacent to
China, "demonstrate support to a friendly country [France] which is also a
signatory to the North Atlantic Treaty," and finally, demonstrate U.S. "dis-
pleasure with Communist tactics which are obviously aimed at eventual
domination of Asia, working under the guise of indigenous nationalism."
Truman approved extending the diplomatic hand to Bao Dai on February 2,
and on February 7 the United States formally recognized the independent
state of Vietnam.[46]

The United States moved immediately after extending recognition to provide military and economic assistance to Vietnam through France. In March
Deputy Undersecretary of State Dean Rusk, whose long diplomatic career
pivoted on the issue of Vietnam, observed that "Southeast Asia is in grave
danger of Communist domination as a consequence of aggression from Communist China and of internal subversive activities."[47] A few weeks later the
Joint Chiefs of Staff reported to the National Security Council on the "critical
strategic importance" of the mainland states of Southeast Asia. They worried
that "the situation in Southeast Asia [had] deteriorated and, without United
States assistance, this deterioration [would] be accelerated." They concluded
that the security of Japan, India and Australia depended on "the denial of
Southeast Asia to the communists." The military perceived a direct threat to
U.S. interests too. They predicted that "the fall of Southeast Asia would

result in the virtually complete denial to the United States of the Pacific littoral of Asia.''[48]

By the spring of 1950 the United States had begun its commitment of direct political, economic, and military support to the anticommunist forces fighting a war in Vietnam. The commitment arose despite the skepticism of some of the highest officials about the chances for success. Support for the government of Bao Dai and the continuation of a French position in Southeast Asia came in the face of even more profound misgivings of U.S. officials present in Indochina. Yet the government took fateful steps toward involvement because officials considered alternative courses of action even more perilous. During the five years after the Second World War, as U.S. policymakers came to see the problems of the world as increasingly intertwined geographically, strategically, politically, and economically, they acted in Indochina to advance what they thought were U.S. interests beyond Vietnam.

Chapter

* * * * * * * * * * *

"The Fatal Weakness":
May 1950–April 1954

*I*N JULY 1951 Deputy Assistant Secretary of State for Far Eastern Affairs Livingston T. Merchant reflected gloomily that "our side cannot win in Indochina given the fatal weakness of the native regimes, the incurability of the French attitudes and the . . . continuation of an aggressive Communist China on its northern frontier."[1] Merchant held an influential though secondary position in the government hierarchy, but it was remarkable how similar his views were to those of the people who directed American policy toward Indochina, France, and the Cold War in Asia. Equally noteworthy was the gap, growing into a chasm, between this privately expressed skepticism about the prospects for victory in the war and the publicly stated optimistic support for France. U.S. officials backed France's war effort because French youth were dying in Indochina at a time when young Americans faced the ultimate sacrifice in Korea.

Many of the earlier differences of opinion over U.S. policy toward Southeast Asia—between Asia-firsters and Europe-firsters, between people on the scene and those in Washington—diminished after the outbreak of the Korean War in June 1950. From then until the battle of Dienbienphu in the spring of 1954, high U.S. government officials agreed on the importance of Indochina, although they differed over the best way to oppose the Vietminh. As John Foster Dulles, the principal Republican spokesman on foreign affairs, told the French National Political Science Institute in May 1952, "Indochina is the

44

key to Southeast Asia, upon the resources of which Japan is largely dependent. Its loss to Communism would gravely endanger other areas."

At the same time, American policy-makers believed that France had not done and probably could not do enough to preserve an independent, noncommunist Vietnam. Joseph Jones, the Truman administration's coordinator of foreign aid, explained that "the building up of a strong native army in Indochina is especially important. . . . The financing of an Indochinese army by the U.S., though it might be costly, might be one of the cheapest and most effective ways of bringing greater security and greater political stability not only to Indochina but all of Indochina."[2]

Officials in both the administrations of Harry S. Truman and Dwight D. Eisenhower believed that Indochina was an important arena in the conflict between East and West, so the United States needed to support the French in their war against the Vietminh. At the same time, however, prospects for a French victory were always uncertain and often bleak. As they sought to improve the chances to defeat the Vietminh, U.S. officials tried to strengthen the local, non-communist Vietnamese authorities and make the French more sensitive to Vietnamese nationalist aspirations.

Toward the end of the period, as the French military position collapsed, the Eisenhower administration faced a new situation. The President and Secretary of State John Foster Dulles crafted a new approach. They retained a U.S. commitment to the non-communists in Vietnam but came to see France as a liability rather than an ally in fostering an independent, non-communist Vietnam. After the forces of General Vo Nguyen Giap defeated the French at Dienbienphu in the spring of 1954, the United States tried to salvage a noncommunist Vietnam. The Eisenhower administration looked to replace France as the sponsor of what officials hoped would be more a more authentically nationalist but non-communist regime in Vietnam.

THE IMPACT OF THE KOREAN WAR

The Korean War has been overshadowed in popular and historical memory by the longer, more divisive and more costly war in Vietnam. Often called the "the forgotten war," the Korean conflict hardened the battle lines in Asia between the United States, the Soviet Union, and communist China.[3] Without the fighting in Korea, the United States may have followed a course other than the twenty-one-year freeze in relations with mainland China. The anxiety produced in the United States by the North Korean invasion of the South led public opinion and Congress to endorse an extraordinary increase in U.S. military expenditures from $13 billion to $48 billion per year. Without U.S. involvement in Korea there would have been little reason for the United States to become involved militarily in Vietnam.[4]

While the Korean War helped define East-West relations for the next thirty years, officials developed the plans that the war transformed into realities months before June 1950. In February a special working group of the State Department, consisting of representatives of the Office of Western European Affairs, the Office of Philippine and Southeast Asian Affairs, and the Mutual Defense Assistance Program, drafted recommendations on military aid for Indochina. In one of the most thorough reviews of events in Asia and public opinion in the United States, planners confronted the new situation posed by the communist victory in China. They noted that "Congress has shown considerable dissatisfaction with policies which are alleged to have contributed to Communist success in China." They observed that "Communism has made important advances in the Far East in the past year." Reviewing the history of French efforts to assert control in Indochina after the second World War, they found that the French had backed Bao Dai as an alternative to Ho Chi Minh, "a Moscow trained Communist." Had France continued its 1946 program of recognition of Ho's government "it would obviously [have made] their position in Indochina untenable [and it] would also open the door to complete Communist domination of Southeast Asia." Planners concluded that war against the Vietminh was in the interests of the United States, but that "the countries and areas of Southeast Asia are not at present . . . capable of defending themselves against Ho Chi Minh's forces." They recommended that the United States should "furnish military aid in support of the anti-Communist nationalist governments of Indochina."[5]

Later that month another group drafted NSC 64, the official position of the United States regarding Indochina. Formally adopted in April 1950, NSC 64 considered the communist war in Indochina "one phase of anticipated communist plans to seize all of Southeast Asia." The paper reviewed U.S. efforts to foster the creation of governments and leaders capable of attracting the support of "non-communist nationalist followers who had drifted to the Ho Chi Minh communist movement in the absence of any non-communist nationalist movement around which to plan their aspirations." NSC 64 explained that the United States and the United Kingdom had recognized the independent governments of Vietnam, Laos, and Cambodia on February 7 and hoped that other Asian countries would soon extend their own diplomatic recognition. Nevertheless, these newly formed states did not "as yet have sufficient political stability nor military power" to withstand the Vietminh. The French had an army of approximately 140,000 troops stationed in Indochina. They could maintain the status quo, but NSC 64 expressed doubt that they could "successfully contain Ho's forces should they be strengthened by either Chinese Communist troops crossing the border, or Communist-supplied arms and material in quantity from outside Indochina." The paper concluded by recommending the U.S. to take "all practicable measures to prevent further communist expansion in Southeast Asia."[6]

During the remainder of 1950, the United States pressed forward with the military aid to the French in Indochina promised by NSC 64. The aid program went forward in the context of the Korean War, the changing political balance in Europe, and the deteriorating French military position in Vietnam. Truman administration officials believed it necessary to support France's effort on the southern flank of China while American forces engaged communists on the Korean peninsula. U.S. policy-makers also believed that forthright support for the French war effort in Indochina would encourage a skeptical government in Paris to acquiesce in a U.S. effort to integrate the West German economy and, later, a reconstructed West German military, into the Western alliance. Much of the discussion over the future of Indochina involved sending signals to other parties designed to affect their perceptions of the future of U.S. actions.

In the spring Edward Gullion, the new American chargé d'affaires at Saigon, thought the well publicized arrival of American military aid would bolster the confidence of the Vietnamese.[7] But not everyone shared his optimism. Charlton Ogburn Jr. of the Bureau of Far Eastern Affairs commented that Gullion's proposal might "shoot so much adrenalin into the Bao Dai government as to bring about a fundamental change in prospects." Unfortunately, "maybe it wouldn't. The trouble is that none of us knows enough about Indochina . . . to hazard a really intelligent guess." Ogburn worried about Gullion's tendency to voice "breezy statements" without the support of facts. Ogburn, himself no expert of Southeast Asia, was more prescient. He observed that Ho Chi Minh's forces had already withstood 140,000 French troops for four years. They had a "blazing hatred" for France and France's friends. He predicted that

> they are not going to wilt under the *psychological* impact of American military assistance. They might on the other hand give way under the *physical* impact of American weapons—if we send enough. Should things get too hot for them, they will, I suppose, do what the Indonesian Republicans tell us they would do—i.e., go underground until a more propitious occasion presented itself. So unless the French are prepared to police Vietnam indefinitely or are enabled by the magnitude of our assistance actually to kill off a hundred thousand of the more ardent Vietnamese rebels, it may well be that a military decision now—even if it can be achieved—will be followed a couple of years hence by a take-over by Ho's party.[8]

Ogburn's dissent found few echoes. In April and May Gullion continued to urge U.S. support for France and Bao Dai. He thought the French had "come [a] long distance down [the] liberal road in Indochina." The United States should not ask them to do more than that, because he believed that a foreign army would be required in Indochina indefinitely, "not so much for suppression of the Vietminh as to check [the] threat from the north."

In May Gullion warned that the situation was precarious, with the Vietminh likely to announce receipt of outside military aid. Anti-communist morale in Vietnam could be devastated if the United States did not preempt it with its own public declaration of the amount of military assistance it was sending to Vietnam.[9]

Any public commitment of aid by the United States opened the central dilemma of the following twenty-five years of U.S. involvement in Vietnam: How to foster an independent Vietnamese government while providing the sort of aid likely to make it more dependent on American charity? Time and time again Vietnam seemed to need immediate infusions of aid to bolster morale and to prevent the imminent victory of communist forces. Yet every time the United States increased its support to meet an immediate emergency, the local Vietnamese government became weaker and more dependent on its overseas patron—first France, then the United States.

In May 1950, a government crisis in Vietnam further clouded the prospect for the war. Bao Dai, at the end of April, replaced Nguyen Phan Long, the prime minister of Vietnam, with Tran Van Huu, governor of Southern Vietnam. Long had irritated the French with his demands for greater independence. The United States had indirectly contributed to Long's fall, because the Vietnamese had become "hyper confiden[t]" after the rumors circulated regarding U.S. aid. Huu's appointment and the greater French involvement in Vietnamese affairs discouraged Bao Dai. The Emperor complained to the U.S. consul that "this government independence, what is it? Where is it? Is a government independent without a budget?"[10]

Bao Dai then left Vietnam for France. Most State Department officials thought this abrupt departure represented proof of his feckless laziness. Gullion, however, pleaded for understanding. "It would be a mistake to underestimate Bao Dai," he wrote on June 23, two days before the Korean war began. Gullion believed the Emperor was "still the only person capable [of] holding together or fronting for any non-Commie government in Vietnam" because he possessed a keen strategic sense of how to obtain Vietnamese independence. He pleaded for understanding because "this is a hard job for a man brought up as [a] puppet viceroy and not as Thomas Jefferson."[11] Yet Bao Dai remained highly unpopular. Ngo Dinh Thuc, the Catholic bishop of Hué and the brother of Ngo Dinh Diem, dismissed the Emperor: "Bao Dai relies on French bayonets," he grumbled. "There [is] no public opinion behind this government."[12]

On May 1 the United States formally announced plans to send $10 million to the military effort in Indochina. In August, after the outbreak of the Korean War, this amount rose to $107 million for fiscal year 1951.[13] According to Gullion, the North Korean invasion of the South had an "electric" and devastating effect on Vietnamese morale, because both the French and Vietnamese had discounted the possibility of a North Korean move.[14] Within a month, President Truman told Congress that the United States intended to speed up military aid to the Associated States of Indochina and the French forces fighting there. From July 20 to 24 representatives from the United States and Great Britain met in Washington to discuss the Korean War. They agreed that they would assist France "to the extent of their abilities in case of a Chinese communist attack, but the probability would be great that neither could provide forces for this purposes."[15]

Meanwhile, John F. Melby, an expert on Chinese affairs, traveled throughout South and Southeast Asia to report on the status of the region in the wake of the Korean War. He found the entire region "'ripe' for communism," and believed that Indian leader Jawaharlal Nehru "unwittingly or not is playing the Kremlin line." In Vietnam he thought that "the problem cannot be solved by military means alone." The French could apply sufficient force to "break the back of Vietminh military force," but the problem would crop up again later. He found the "hatred of [the] French so deep-seated and traditional that [the] French [are] incapable of selling [the] political, economic and propaganda follow-up required to make military successes stick." Bao Dai, he thought, lacked the "determination and training" required to provide the strong local Vietnamese leadership to overcome the Vietminh. He found a grudging admiration for the Vietminh among many Vietnamese who were "secretly pleased with [their] success in bogging down the French." He thought that "distaste for [the] white man [was] greater" than any fear the general population might have of their future under the Vietminh.[16]

French government officials considered the outbreak of the Korean War both a frightening prospect and an opportunity to consolidate support from the United States. If the threat of Chinese intervention materialized, then France's situation could be desperate. France was even willing to open relations with the new communist government in Beijing in order to prevent Chinese intervention. On the other hand, the possibility that China would enter the war seemed to French officials a way to make certain that the United States would do more for France. In August the U.S. government surveyed the likelihood of Chinese intervention in Indochina after the Korean War. Intelligence experts believed that Korean invasion had made immediate Chinese intervention less likely; Chinese troops had moved northward toward the Korean fighting rather than southward toward Indochina. The State Department encouraged David K. E. Bruce, the U.S. ambassador to France, to impress on the French the dangers of negotiating with China. The Chinese could not be expected to keep any agreements, and France would have to do more than just exchange diplomatic officials with Beijing. They would have to support China's claim to a seat on the United Nations Security Council. In the U.S. view this "yielded to [the] very blackmail on seating [the] Chi Commie member which we have resisted with such resolution and which is one of the strongest arguments in [the] present Security Council debate'' over Korea.[17]

The State Department's Policy Planning Staff concurred that the French government's ''inclination to appease Beijing'' was both futile and ''a disturbing commentary on the general state of mind in Paris.'' The planners repeated the now-familiar theme that the only way to assure success in Vietnam was for the French to adopt ''drastic political measures'' guaranteeing the complete independence of Vietnam. There should be a definite date for independence, no more than two years from the present. ''Such developments,'' the strategists wrote, ''would make our own military and aid role in Indochina more popular in the country.'' The situation had reached a point where France had to make the reforms suggested by the United States or ''the French and we may well be heading into a debacle which neither of us can afford.''[18]

The old division between European and Asian experts dissolved in the face of such apocalyptic warnings. David Bruce thought that an ultimatum to the French was ''impossible of realization in the immediate future.'' There simply was no alternative to Bao Dai.[19] During the rest of 1950 the military situation in Indochina deteriorated. Americans believed that any pressure applied on France toward relaxing its control over Vietnamese political affairs would backfire. Moreover, the United States had its hands full with the Korean War, leaving little opportunity for top political leaders to pursue a dramatically new course toward events in Indochina. In mid-September, General Douglas MacArthur led U.N. forces on a surprise invasion of Inchon, Korea. Within two weeks the U.N. forces had swept the North Koreans out of the South and had marched northward. The aims of the war shifted from repelling an invasion to evicting communists from Korea. In October Truman met MacArthur on Wake Island in the Pacific to discuss future U.N. moves in the war. The general persuaded the President that the war probably would be over by the end of the year.

Over the next months MacArthur and Washington ignored intelligence reports and diplomatic warnings from India that China considered the movement of U.N. troops near its own frontier to be a threat. The first Chinese troops entered the fighting at the end of October, but these skirmishes did not cause MacArthur to reverse course. Finally, on November 25, five months after the war began in Korea, the Chinese army entered the war in force. More than four hundred thousand Chinese troops attacked the Americans and their U.N. allies. The U.N. forces retreated in a near rout. Panicked officials in Washington considered the possibility of using atomic weapons to stop the calamity. Little time remained to craft a new policy toward Indochina that might have adjusted to the new reality of growing Vietminh strength.[20]

VIETMINH GAINS

While events in Korea preoccupied the Americans, the war in Vietnam intensified. The Vietminh followed a modified version of Mao Zedong's primer on
guerrilla war. In 1947 Truong Chinh, the chief theoretician of the Vietnamese
Communist Party, published *The Resistance Will Win,* a guide to the course of
revolutionary warfare. He predicted that the war would go through three
stages. In the first, the French would be strong, the Vietminh weak. In this
stage the Vietminh would concentrate on preserving its territory and training
soldiers. It would engage the French sporadically with raids on its bases and
convoys. He called the second phase "the equilibrium of forces and of active
resistance." During this period the French could make no further progress
clearing Vietnam of the Vietminh, but the resistance could not retake the
major cities. During this phase the Vietminh would engage the French in
larger battles, tie them down, and destroy some of their forces. Truong predicted that this second phase would be the most prolonged. It would end
when the Vietminh were strong enough to engage in a final victorious coun-
teroffensive in which the Vietminh would bring ever larger forces to bear
against the French.[21]

In 1950 the war entered the second of Truong's three phases as the Vietminh used ever larger forces against France. In February General Giap sent
units of his regular army against the French in the Red River Valley of northern Vietnam. He defeated the French with Chinese supplied mortars at the
city of Laokay near the Chinese border. In May Giap overran the French post
at Dong Khe on Route 4 in Tonkin. The French retook the area two days later,
and the rainy season stopped further fighting. In mid-September, however,
the Vietminh attacked once more and captured the eight-hundred-man French
garrison. The fall of Dong Khe cut off the northernmost French outpost at
Caobaong. The French needed to fight their way south to the town of Langson before being completely encircled by the Vietminh. They made it there in
early October with thousands of Vietminh attacking nearly at will. On the
night of October 17–18 the French abandoned Langson, leaving behind a
huge cache of weapons, ammunition and vehicles. In the month between the
Vietminh capture of Dong Khe and the French abandonment of Langson,
France lost six thousand men.[22] Bernard Fall, a prominent French expert on
the French-Indochinese war, later called the French loss "their greatest colonial defeat since Montcalm had died at Quebec."[23]

The debacle in Tonkin forced U.S. national security planners to fashion a
policy toward Indochina which integrated it into the broader needs of the
United States in Asia. The Joint Chiefs of Staff glumly reported in November
that a "critical situation" existed in Indochina. The military recognized that
however grave the military position in Indochina, it could be solved only by

political means. The Chiefs believed that "the fundamental causes of the deterioration in the Indochinese security situation lie in the lack of will and determination on the part of the indigenous people of Indochina to join wholeheartedly with the French in resisting communism."

The U.S. military tried to craft a program of assistance to the French that stopped "short of the actual employment of United States military forces," a move that could lead to Chinese military intervention. Most of the plan tried to generate popular support among Vietnamese for France. The Chiefs wanted to create local armies to help in the war. A national Vietnamese army might have minimal impact on the fighting against the Vietminh, but "the direct political and psychological benefits to be derived from this course would be great." The Chiefs also demanded that French officials change their rhetoric in Indochina to eliminate references to colonials. Fearful of a Chinese invasion, the Chiefs recommended that "the United States should not permit itself to become engaged in a general war with Communist China, but should, in concert with the United Kingdom support France and the Associated States by all means short of the actual employment of United States military forces."[24] Assistant Secretary of State for Far Eastern Affairs Dean Rusk explained that U.S. military aid to the Associated States meant that the United States actually supported independent nations in Indochina, not just France. A Canadian diplomat dismissed Rusk's words as a "nonsensical approach."[25]

FRENCH OPTIMISM: 1951

The pervasive sense of doom brought on by the Chinese intervention in the Korean War began to lift in early 1951, as American aid helped French forces fight more vigorously. About $50 million in U.S. military aid had been delivered and another $165 million was on the way. The infusion of U.S. aid had allowed the French to carry the fight to the Vietminh, although the latter also had been encouraged by the increase in support from China, which had supplied light artilleries, mortars, and automatic weapons. The Chinese had also set up training centers for Vietminh troops, about fifty thousand of which had completed training by March 1950. The Defense Department also estimated that there were fifteen to twenty Chinese technicians working with each Vietminh battalion. The Chinese-trained troops were considered the equals of the French forces. China also had stationed 200,000 to 300,000 regular soldiers near the Vietnamese border. France could hold its own only so long as these soldiers did not enter the war.[26]

The arrival of the new American aid coincided with the appointment of a new French high commissioner and commander, General of the Army Jean de Lattre de Tassigny, who vowed to win the war in 1952. He carried the fight more aggressively and spoke openly about granting full independence to the Vietnamese. Vietnamese nationalists liked what they heard from the blunt-speaking French general.[27] In February, U.S. minister to Saigon Donald Heath told the Southeast Asia Aid Policy Committee that "the situation was much brighter now" due to the arrival of U.S. aid and the appointment of de Lattre, "a first class commander," who had picked up the tempo of the fighting from "a previous pedestrian rate."[28] By May, de Lattre reported enthusiastically that the Vietminh "had been stopped and they knew it" in their offensive in the northern province of Tonkin.[29] Heath thought that de Lattre's military qualities "border on genius," but he also noted a darker side to the general's character. He brooded, he bullied subordinates and the Vietnamese, and he badgered the Americans for more aid. At the same time he rejected further American efforts to force the pace of independence.[30]

The death of de Lattre's son Bernard, a lieutenant in the French army, by Vietminh fire while defending the French garrison at Binh Dinh in late May temporarily unnerved the general. De Lattre looked "old and worn out," and he spoke in a low, bitter voice about how the Vietnamese refused to believe his professions of support for their interests. "What [is] the price of all this sacrifice if those on our side refuse to believe in our sincerity? If this constant sacrificing of our youths' flower does not prove us sincere in [our professed] desire to give Vietnam independence, what further is necessary to drive the idea home? Yet we are doubted on all sides. What is the use?"[31]

Yet de Lattre pulled himself together later in the summer, as he planned a visit to the United States to discuss the future of U.S. aid. His trip coincided with the efforts by some members of congress to exert pressure on France to yield formal independence to Vietnam. New York Democratic Congresswoman Edna F. Kelly's effort to block all aid to Indochina as long as Bao Dai remained in power brought a visit by Deputy Secretary of State Livingston Merchant to dissuade her. Kelly expressed the views of Ngo Dinh Diem, who by now bitterly opposed Bao Dai. Although privately Merchant thought the war in Indochina all but lost due to the weakness of the local authorities, he valiantly told Kelly that Bao Dai "was probably not pure as driven snow but . . . there was no other anti-communist native leader who combined his courage, political sense and strain of imperial legitimacy."[32]

In mid-September, de Lattre arrived in Washington. He met Truman, Acheson, and Secretary of Defense George Marshall and toured military bases. Washington praised his revitalization of the French armed forces yet did not pledge more aid than already authorized. The United States could not divert ground forces from Korea and from Europe (General Dwight D. Eisenhower had gone to Europe at the head of a U.S. expeditionary force in December 1950) to help France in Indochina. Despite de Lattre's military successes in the spring and summer, U.S. officials still doubted the extent of his and his government's commitment to offer genuine independence to Indochina. The State Department urged Truman to be wary of his "strong sense of mission and dignity" which had made "for occasional incidents of explosive friction with his associates and superiors."[33]

De Lattre came to the American capital with a chip on his shoulder. He complained that the "young men" in charge of dispensing aid to Indochina had shown "missionary zeal" in expanding the role of the United States in Vietnam. He lectured his hosts against what he viewed as efforts to " 'put rocks' into the machinery of the Franco-Vietnamese relationships and into the machinery of Franco-American friendship."[34] American diplomats and military officers had recent experience with difficult generals. Charles de Gaulle had shown similar haughtiness toward the United States during the Second World War, and Truman had his own bad memories of dealing with an irascible general that had culminated the previous April in his firing of Douglas MacArthur. Policy differences also divided Washington from de Lattre, because the Americans frankly believed that France could not prevail in Indochina without a bona fide effort to provide complete independence in the near future to Indochina.

BEYOND KOREA: 1952–1953

Nevertheless, when de Lattre left Washington, both the French and the Americans felt more satisfied with the situation in Indochina than they had during the past two years: the Americans believed that France had found a fighting general and de Lattre considered American aid secure. Unbeknownst to his hosts, however, de Lattre was a sick man. He returned to Paris for a checkup, where doctors discovered a fatal liver cancer. He never resumed his command in Indochina and died in January 1952. With him went much of the French enthusiasm for the war, and French corporations began pulling out of Vietnam.[35]

In 1952 a shift in perspective occurred in the major Western capitals as they dealt with Indochina and Korea. The Korean front stabilized, giving leaders the luxury of greater planning. The Americans, British, and French all continued to see Indochina as important in the global competition with the Soviet Union, but each power attempted to persuade the others to increase their commitment while minimizing its own. Truman met British Prime Minister Winston Churchill in early 1952, and they agreed on the strategic and economic importance of Indochina to the remainder of Southeast Asia. The Americans believed that communist control of Indochina threatened "70% of the world's natural rubber and 50% of the world's tin." Truman did not think the United States could do more to help France than already planned. "We do not want to assume a further responsibility," he told Churchill. Only if China sent troops might the United States "consider taking military action, short of the actual employment of ground forces, in Indochina, if it became apparent that such action was necessary to prevent the fall of the country to communism.''

The Americans saw no need for tripartite military talks, a course favored by the British.[36] The British agreed that France bore the primary responsibility for the defense of Indochina, but British officials worried more than did the Americans about the French commitment. According to the British, by 1952 the French believed that they were in Indochina to advance general Western interests in the struggle against communism. The British ambassador to France reported that "the French interests, narrowly interpreted, would dictate withdrawal. It is questionable how long the French, not a notably disinterested people, will continue to ruin themselves in a cause which they do not now regard as primarily their own."[37]

After de Lattre's death the French continued to fight in Indochina while they looked for ways to shift the burden of the war to their allies. A replacement for de Lattre, General Raoul Salan, a veteran of the restoration of French rule in 1945, spent fifteen months in Saigon. Then in May 1953, General Henri Navarre became the French commander. France found the war costly. Defense Minister Antoine Pinay informed the British foreign secretary and the American secretary of state that "the public in France were weary after six years of fighting in Indochina." Foreign Minister René Pleven told Secretary of State Acheson in May that the French burden in Indochina was a major obstacle to French participation in a newly proposed European Defense Community, or EDC.[38] American and European military planners conceived of the EDC as a way of including German troops, toward whom the victims of Nazi aggression naturally were extremely suspicious, in the Western armed forces arrayed against the Soviets. The EDC was designed to overcome the resistance of the French, Dutch, and Belgians to rearming Germany by placing German soldiers in a unified European, rather than national, army.[39] Acheson tried to mollify the French with promises to aid the creation of legitimate national armies in Vietnam. The British deplored the "thoroughly defeatist attitude" of the French foreign and defense ministers and their transparent efforts to "blackmail the Americans."[40]

Americans too noted the growing reluctance of the French to continue the war. The influential foreign-affairs newspaper columnist Walter Lippmann told the British ambassador in Paris that he expected the French to tell the United States that they could not carry the burden of the war beyond 1952. France now required one hundred thousand replacement soldiers. Sending conscripts to Vietnam was out of the question, and the Algerian and Moroccan troops who made up the bulk of the French expeditionary force in Indochina were proving restless. Lippmann warned of "some quite sudden diplomatic move by the French." He expected France would either seek a cease-fire or withdraw on their own from the northern province of Tonkin where the major part of the fighting took place. He also expected that the United States might furnish a token military force to monitor a potential cease-fire. In no circumstances, however, would the United States commit several divisions to land fighting. The Korean War had soured public opinion on fighting land wars is Asia. "Nobody understood what" the Korean War was about "or why it had to be continued."[41]

While the French wanted to shift the burden to the Americans, the United States was equally insistent that the war not involve U.S. ground troops. The appointment of General Navarre allowed the two countries to work out new ways of dividing responsibility for fighting the Vietminh. The CIA estimated in late summer 1952 that the war would continue to stalemate over the next year. The National Intelligence Estimate predicted that "France will continue its war effort in Indochina, but will attempt to transfer to the U.S. a progressively larger part of the economic and military burden of the war, and to reduce its manpower commitments by developing the national forces of the Associated States."[42]

Dwight D. Eisenhower won the presidential election in November 1952. He promised to visit Korea and end the fighting. The French asked him to include Vietnam on his trip, but he demurred, not wishing to dilute the impact of his Korean trip with another important but distinctly secondary issue. Two weeks after the election Eisenhower received a briefing on world developments from Truman and Acheson. The latter explained the Truman administration's concern over the course of the war. A significant portion of the French public considered the war a lost cause "that was bleeding France." Acheson expressed dismay at the "noticeable lack of French aggressive attitude from a military point of view in Indochina." He thought that the "central problem" was the refusal of the bulk of the Vietnamese population to "come down on one side or another until they had a reasonable assurance of who would be the victor and that their interests would be served by the victor."[43]

THE NAVARRE PLAN

In the first year of the new Eisenhower administration, the United States showed greater interest in Indochina. In June it sent Lieutenent-General John W. O'Daniel, the commander of the U.S. army in the Pacific, to Indochina to consult with Navarre over French intentions and the sort of aid wanted from the United States. O'Daniel found Navarre brimming with enthusiasm "to retake the initiative immediately." Navarre expected to use commando and guerrilla attacks in the summer of 1953. Beginning in mid-September he wanted to take the offensive in the north. He contemplated a climactic battle with the Vietminh in the winter of 1953–1954.[44]

Navarre acted as French public opinion grew ever more sick of the war.

Alert to the general war-weariness, the new government of Premier Joseph Laniel decided to end the war through ''military superiority in war operations which will make negotiations more fruitful.'' Laniel's elevation of military over political efforts to end the war dissatisfied British and Canadian diplomats. The British Foreign Office predicted that France's ''military position in Indochina is likely to go from bad to worse as soon the Viet Minh launches a new attack.''[45]

For years French commanders had believed that the way to defeat the Vietminh was to force them into a conventional battle. The technological superiority of Western armaments would negate the advantages the Vietminh had in guerrilla warfare. The success of the plan would require an additional 331,000 soldiers over the next three years, but the United States would not supply them and French public opinion would not tolerate any additional French troops. Yet the French had seen the American willingness to fund the war, and the Navarre plan therefore envisioned the creation of nine new battalions of the Associated States' army, to be paid for by the United States. Navarre called this the ''yellowing'' of the forces arrayed against the Vietminh.[46] Over the summer of 1953 representatives of the Departments of State, Defense, and the Treasury, the Central Intelligence Agency, and the Bureau of the Budget worked out the funding. In August they recommended an additional $400 million to fund the Navarre plan.[47]

On September 9 the National Security Council conducted a full review of American support for the Navarre plan. Vice President Richard M. Nixon and Secretary of State John Foster Dulles both spoke enthusiastically about Navarre and the government of Premier Laniel. ''For the first time,'' said Dulles, ''we have a French government which sees the necessity of building strength in Indochina.'' While Laniel and Navarre wanted to press forward with the creation of an authentic Vietnamese fighting force. Dulles lamented that ''the prevailing mood in France, especially in the Chamber of Deputies, was to get out of Indochina.'' Time was of the essence, and Dulles believed that speedy American approval of additional aid to the French war effort in Indochina might stiffen the French will. Nixon agreed that ''American stakes in Indochina were obviously very great,'' and he worried that the $385 million promised under the Navarre plan might not be enough. Dulles assured him that the amount represented the full French request. Officially, the NSC held that the United States would make it clear to the French government that the $385 million was everything the French government could expect from the United States in calendar year 1954. Dulles made it clear, however, how vital he considered Indochina. The United States was ready to do more, provided the French made progress.[48] By the end of 1953 the annual amount of aid had reached $500 million and the United States was providing ten thousand tons of equipment each month.

Vice President Nixon visited Vietnam in December 1953 as part of a twenty-nation tour of Asia and the Middle East. The Vice President admired Navarre's élan, which he thought had instilled a new fighting spirit among the Vietnamese, and believed the French officials who told him that public opinion had recently shifted against the Vietminh. "People [are] beginning to realize," he reported, "that the Vietnam side is [the] side of those who fight for national independence; the Vietminh side is [the] side which fights for foreign control."[49] He told a national television and radio audience that Indochina held the key to all East Asia. "If Indochina falls, Thailand is put in an almost impossible position. The same is true of Malaya with its rubber and tin. The same is true of Indonesia. If Indochina goes under Communist domination the whole of Southeast Asia will be threatened and that means that the economic and military security of Japan will inevitably be endangered also."[50]

Nixon displayed the same sense of urgency when he briefed the National Security Council. He asserted that "what happens in Indochina is more important, from the standpoint of the strategic interests of Europe, than what happens in Korea." Yet he was also far more skeptical about optimistic French claims of progress than he let the public see. He found the preparations of the new Vietnamese armed force wanting. Americans observing the training of Vietnamese believed that "at the present level and at the present rate [it] will not succeed." He considered some of the Navarre plan's expectations about relying on local Vietnamese troops wishful thinking. "The French generals simply have no confidence in independent units of natives, and the natives don't want to fight under French leaders."

Nixon also reported that the local French commanders distrusted the political leadership in Paris and believed that the future of the war would be settled in Paris. He predicted that "the effect on morale will be serious when the negotiation talks take place." Nevertheless, he thought that "the Navarre plan is a tremendous improvement." Whatever shortcomings existed among the Vietnamese troops, "the French troop morale is excellent." The French had made genuine strides toward granting independence to the Cambodians, Laotians, and Vietnamese.[51] Two weeks later Nixon was even more pessimistic about the ability of the French to make good on their commitment to build up a national Vietnamese army. "The French talk one way but feel another," he said. He had the "gravest doubts" about the current French leadership building up a local armed force to the level envisaged by General Navarre.[52]

DIENBIENPHU

Armed with American weapons and hopeful that the Vietnamese army could at least deny territory to Vietminh guerrillas, Navarre proceeded to draw the main force of the Vietminh into a major battle. He found what he thought was the perfect place for a "mooring point," a base from which French soldiers could employ aggressive tactics to search out the Vietminh from the surrounding mountains. The area he selected was Dienbienphu, a hamlet in western Tonkin, near the border of Laos. Though not a natural fortress, Dienbienphu possessed several tactical advantages. General Vo Nguyen Giap had sent his forces into Laos, alarming the French and the Americans. Brigadier-General Thomas J. H. Trapnell, the chief of the U.S. Military Advisory and Assistance Group (MAAG) for Vietnam, believed that the Vietminh invasion of Laos gave the communist forces the initiative.[53] Navarre believed that establishing a base at Dienbienphu would threaten the reserve forces of the Vietminh. He hoped to catch them in a pincer movement between his forces in the north and other French troops operating in the Red River Delta of the south. He also hoped to use the base at Dienbienphu to squash the opium trade centered in the region, thereby denying the Vietminh a major source of revenue for the purchase of armaments.[54]

Navarre believed that the creation of a base at Dienbienphu would present an unacceptable challenge to Ho Chi Minh's and Giap's position in Tonkin. He wanted to create a target "sufficiently tempting [for the Vietminh] to pounce at, but sufficiently strong to resist the onslaught." He expected that they would mass their forces for gigantic human-wave assaults, involving hundreds of thousands of troops, similar to the tactics employed by the Chinese in the Korean War. Navarre therefore established an airstrip to anchor the base at Dienbienphu in the center of a wide valley. Since France could expect to enjoy air supremacy over the valley and would install artillery at the base, Navarre anticipated that his forces would annihilate attacking Vietminh units.[55]

Giap saw the approaching showdown at Dienbienphu differently than did both Navarre and the hundreds of Chinese advisers who had joined his forces. Both the French and Chinese anticipated human-wave assaults, with different outcomes, of course. Giap, on the other hand, wanted slowly to encircle Dienbienphu but not engage in massive assaults until the last stage. In this way, he would deny the French the tactical advantages they had sought by building their fortress in the middle of a plain. Of ever greater importance for the Vietminh was the opportunity to tie down a large number of French troops and confine the remainder to their base in the cities. The Vietminh would then have a fuller run of the countryside in which to conduct brief raids, so deadly to the morale of uncommitted local peasants. Giap said that if the French "reduced their occupation forces in order to regroup them, our guerrillas would . . . increase their activity" in the countryside.

Navarre turned the day-to-day command of Dienbienphu over to Colonel Christian de Castries, a former cavalry officer who had suffered three wounds as an artillery commander during the Second World War. De Castries roamed through the valley surrounding Dienbienphu, wearing a red scarf with a riding crop in hand, selecting locations for fire bases at which to station large artillery pieces. He named three of them Isabelle, Beatrice, and Gabrielle, after mistresses he was keeping simultaneously, and named six other French outposts after earlier mistresses. He dropped in 13,200 French paratroopers and on January 1, 1954 announced that he expected "total victory after six months more of hard fighting."

Giap was just as confident. De Castries's placement of fire bases surrounding the main outpost at Dienbienphu made sense only if the Vietminh used human-wave assaults. If they somehow could move artillery into the mountains surrounding the valley, a feat the French believed to be beyond their capacity, and attack the firebases one by one, they could encircle and eventually strangle the paratroopers at Dienbienphu. The Vietnamese had promises of hundreds of howitzers and mortars captured by the Chinese from the American forces in Korea. The tight organization of the areas of Vietnam under Vietminh control over the past seven years also provided Giap with the labor of approximately one hundred thousand peasants, many of whom were women, boys under fifteen, and men over fifty, to carry supplies, and dig trenches and tunnels. Throughout the winter of 1953–1954 Giap did what the French considered impossible: he moved fifty thousand combat troops and fifty thousand support soldiers into the mountains surrounding Dienbienphu. They traveled by bicycle or on foot, wearing sandals made of strips of rubber tires, each carrying rifle, a shovel, clothes, a bag of rice, and a bottle of water. Heavy cloud cover rendered French aircraft bombing virtually useless in stopping the troop movements. The Vietminh disassembled artillery pieces and had the components carried by porters. French artillery strikes could temporarily disrupt major roads, but the tens of thousands of peasant laborers could quickly repair them under the cover of darkness.[56]

Movements toward an international conference to work out a political solution for Indochina made both the French and the Vietminh intensify their preparations for a climactic decision on the battlefield. French Premier Joseph Laniel, irritated by Bao Dai's persistent demands for complete independence, complained that France "has no reason to prolong its sacrifices if the very people for whom they are being made disdain these sacrifices and betray them." The Chinese communists worried that French weariness with the war might cause them to abandon Indochina to the Americans, whom the Chinese feared far more than the French. The Chinese told the Vietminh in late 1953 that they should respond to French peace feelers or risk losing some of the aid China provided.[57]

Moscow also wanted a political resolution of the Indochina problem as a way of reducing Western hostility. An end to the war in Indochina might also wean the French away from participation in the U.S.-sponsored European Defense Community. In late November Ho Chi Minh told a Swedish newspaper that he was willing to discuss the political future of Vietnam at an international conference. At the January 8 meeting of the National Security Council, at which Nixon expressed misgivings about the capacity of General Navarre to create an effective Vietnamese armed force, Eisenhower and Dulles made it clearer than ever before that U.S. and French interests diverged over the future of Indochina. They feared an abrupt abandonment of the region. "In this contingency," Dulles remarked, he did not believe that "this country would simply say 'Too bad; we're licked and that's the end of it.'"[58]

Despite objections from the United States, the French government agreed to discuss Indochina at an international conference. A five-power Conference on Far Eastern Problems, co-chaired by Britain and the Soviet Union, and including representatives of France, the People's Republic of China, and the United States, would have the French-Indochinese war on its agenda when it opened in Geneva on April 26.[59]

On March 12 Giap's forces began the battle for Dienbienphu. Vietminh artillery rained fire on the French artillery bases, and within twenty-four hours the Vietminh had captured firebases Beatrice and Gabrielle. The Vietminh suffered thousands of casualties, but the French had lost most of their precious artillery. The Vietminh then turned their guns on the French airfield, leaving it so pockmarked that supply planes could not land. Dienbienphu was under siege. On March 17 U.S. and French pilots started dropping food, weapons, and ammunition by air into the French encampment.[60]

Three days later, on March 20, General Paul Ely, chief of staff of the French army, arrived in Washington to consult with American leaders about the immediate problem in Dienbienphu and the larger context of the political future of Indochina. Ely carried apparently inconsistent instructions from the fractious French government. On the one hand, Premier Laniel wanted American blessing for reaching a political settlement with the Vietminh at the upcoming Geneva conference. On the other hand, France needed to negotiate from a position of strength by saving the besieged garrison at Dienbienphu. To this end, the French government wanted continued U.S. military backing and threats of airstrikes if the Chinese communists joined the fighting. The French government resisted, however, opening the possibility of actual U.S. troop participation. This last step would undermine French independence and make a political settlement at Geneva more remote. The historian Melanie Billings-Yun characterizes the French cabinet before the Vietminh assault on Dienbienphu as "balanced on the precariously thin line between its desire for a wholly believable threat of U.S. intervention that would strengthen its bargaining position at the Geneva conference and its fear that the United States might carry out that threat."[61]

News of the assault on the stronghold shocked the French government and turned Ely's trip to Washington from a routine briefing into a plea for more

American aid to France. While Ely represented the conflicting views of the French cabinet, one of his hosts, Admiral Arthur Radford, Chairman of the Joint Chiefs of Staff, used his visit to further his own efforts to have the United States more deeply involved in Indochina. Radford, a persistent advocate of a forceful role of the United States in Asia, actually seemed more alarmed by the French position at Dienbienphu than did Ely at their first meeting on the evening of March 20. He told a dinner attended by Ely, Vice President Nixon, Army Chief of Staff Matthew Ridgeway and CIA Director Allen Dulles that the Vietminh could overwhelm French forces at Dienbienphu "within the next few days if not the next few hours."[62]

Part of Radford's alarm was genuine, but part represented an attempt to implement the emerging military strategy of the Eisenhower administration. Concerned that the public could no longer abide costly and protracted ground wars, Radford and Secretary of Defense Charles Wilson had designed a "new look" for the U.S. military, one which diminished reliance on ground soldiers and enhanced the role of air power and nuclear weapons. Radford contemplated using tactical nuclear weapons in Indochina as a way of signaling the credibility of the American New Look.[63] Over the next two weeks Radford campaigned to have the U.S. air force attack the Vietminh, possibly using nuclear weapons.

THE INTERNATIONAL RESPONSE TO DIENBIENPHU

This plan to intervene militarily at Dienbienphu, which came to be known as Operation Vulture, set off a debate within the U.S. government and across the Atlantic. Operation Vulture drew support from Vice President Nixon but opposition from Army Chief of Staff Ridgeway, who resisted recapitulating the unpopular experience of the Korean War. Secretary of State Dulles advocated a much more complicated mixture of threat and diplomacy. Publicly he threatened military intervention by the United States against the communists. Yet Dulles thought France had become a liability in the war against the Vietminh. France had reneged on numerous promises to grant independence to the Vietnamese, thereby undermining their capacity to carry the war against the Vietminh. Privately Dulles assailed the French government for its willingness to negotiate with the Vietminh. Eventually he decided that the American position would be better served by the United States dealing directly with Indochina rather than through France. "We could lose Europe, Asia and Africa all at once if we don't watch out," he worried.[64]

Public airing of the possibility of U.S. military actions set off debate among congressional leaders and in the press. It also involved top officials of the British government who had their own interests to project. Eisenhower made the final decision on Dienbienphu, trying to balance his competing desires to prevent a communist victory while retaining domestic and international support for his foreign policies.[65]

On March 29 Dulles addressed the Overseas Press Club of America on "The Threat of a Red Asia." He repeated his oft-stated concerns for the importance of Southeast Asia: "Southeast Asia is astride the most direct and best developed sea and air route between the Pacific and South Asia. It has major naval and air bases. Communist control of Southeast Asia would carry a grave threat to the Philippines, Australia and New Zealand. . . . The entire Western Pacific area, including the so-called 'offshore island chain,' would be strategically threatened." He considered the imposition of a communist political system on Southeast Asia "a grave threat to the whole free community." He asserted that American policy was to meet such a threat with "united action."[66]

Dulles did not state precisely what he meant by united action. His ambiguity may have been a purposeful example of what was called brinkmanship at the time or what was characterized later as a studied use of threats to deter adversaries.[67] Whatever impact Dulles intended his remarks to have on opinion in Moscow and Beijing, or among the Vietminh leadership, it confused rather than clarified American and European attitudes regarding Indochina. Journalists thought that Dulles's speech was either simply a morale booster for the French and their Vietnamese allies or a threat of full scale war against the communists in Southeast Asia. The *New York Times* characterized Dulles's words as "carefully chosen if still somewhat ambiguous." The newspaper's editorial writers thought that "the administration sees no alternative except to continue the war under the plan of General Navarre until Indochina is in better position to defend itself, as a precondition to negotiating from a position of strength."[68]

Initial British reaction also was cool. The Foreign Office cabled the embassy in Washington their conclusion that the battle for Dienbienphu already was lost. "The conditions for a favorable situation in Indochina may no longer exist. Failure to consider this possibility now is likely to increase the difficulty of reaching . . . agreement should we be forced at Geneva to accept the policy of compromise with the communists on Indochina."[69] For its part, the French government feared that united action would prove an empty declaration. "Unless backed by intervention," the government told the French ambassador in Washington, "a warning would not produce any immediate effect." It might even "have a bad effect on French public opinion."[70]

Congress seemed equally confused. Senator John Stennis (D., Miss.) received no answer to his question: "Exactly what is meant by 'united action' and what is the necessity or the case for it?" The British and French too asked for clarification from Washington, but they did not receive a satisfactory definition of united action.[71] Only Eisenhower could have provided sharp definition of the meaning of united action, yet the President perceived dangers in specifying future U.S. behavior. He had long considered the French military position in Indochina nearly hopeless. "I'm convinced that no military victory is possible in that kind of theater," he wrote in his diary in 1951.[72] The President objected at a cabinet meeting when Ambassador to the United Nations Henry Cabot Lodge likened the situation in Indochina to the civil war in Greece where the United States had armed and trained the anti-communist government forces. Eisenhower called the Indochinese situation different because the "Greeks were sturdy people with [a] will to win." The Vietnamese, on the other hand, were "'backward people' who don't think France sincere in granting them freedom." Almost despairingly, Eisenhower said that "France presents difficult questions everywhere you look."[73]

But the president shared Dulles's and most other American policymakers' belief that Indochina held the key to the fate of Southeast Asia, a region crucial to American interests. Any public statement on his part explicitly ruling out military action would have a devastating affect on French and Vietnamese morale. He tried to preserve as wide a range of options for as long as possible. Eisenhower fielded a barrage of questions about united action at a press conference two days after Dulles spoke. He asserted that the Dulles speech "must stand by itself," but he then went on to qualify his statement. United action had a military aspect but it also had political and moral dimensions. It required the "united action of *all* nations and peoples and countries affected in" Southeast Asia. Here Eisenhower suggested that nations reluctant to use force to save the French position, notably Britain, might exercise a veto over deployment of additional troops. He also repeated his profound distaste for the involvement of American "ground forces, or any other kind of forces, in great numbers around the world, meeting each little situation as it arises."[74]

Dulles's and Eisenhower's remarks had not brought the U.S. government any closer to a decision regarding Radford's plans to relieve Dienbienphu. The chairman of the Joint Chiefs of Staff tried to force the issue. At a meeting of the National Security Council on April 1 Radford said that the French position had grown desperate in the previous forty-eight hours. "Many airdrops had fallen into the hands of the Vietminh," he said. "Unless the garrison were reinforced" he saw "no way to save the situation."

For his part, Eisenhower blew off steam at the folly of Navarre's and de Castries's tactics. "Why had the French ever committed forces to a remote area where these forces could not be reinforced?" Despite his irritation, Eisenhower recognized the gravity of the issue, and he said he believed that "the plight of the French certainly raised the question whether the United States ought now to consider any kind of intervention to help save Dienbienphu." He observed that all the members of the Joint Chiefs of Staff with the exception of Radford opposed airstrikes using U.S. planes and pilots.[75]

Ridgeway presented the most forceful opposition. He offered "an emphatic and immediate 'no' " to the question of whether the United States should use its planes at Dienbienphu. The outcome of the battle for Dienbienphu "would not in itself decisively affect the military situation there." Yet U.S. intervention "would greatly increase the risk of general war."[76] Highly cautious about committing forces unless success was guaranteed, Eisenhower leaned strongly against intervention. Yet he put off a final decision pending meetings with the British and the congressional leadership.

After the morning NSC meeting, Eisenhower had lunch with publisher Roy Howard, an ardent Republican, and went over the dilemma of relieving the French. He reported that the situation in Indochina was "getting really bad." The "French want more help from us, but want it at their terms." They were "very difficult to handle—almost impossible." He told Howard that he might soon "have to make [a] decision to send in squadrons from 2 aircraft carriers off [the] coast to bomb [the] Reds at Dienbienphu. Of course if we did, we'd have to deny it forever."[77] Eisenhower did not reveal whether he had decided on a course to follow, but what he did over the next two days indicated that he had made up his mind against direct military involvement by the United States at Dienbienphu.

The President left it to Dulles to conduct conversations with the British ambassador and congressional leaders. The opposition to military intervention Eisenhower expected surfaced at both meetings. British ambassador Roger Makins heard Dulles explain that his speech on March 29 was designed to prevent the French "from reaching a settlement at Geneva or elsewhere which would be disastrous to the French and the free world." Makins replied that the British government too acknowledged how bad the situation was in Indochina. London "even regarded it in more pessimistic terms than the U.S. government." The solution, however, from the British point of view was to end the war as quickly as possible "and yet keep Indochina out of Communist hands." Among several distasteful solutions—a cease-fire, a coalition government, free elections, and partition—Makins believed that partition of Vietnam into communist and anti-communist countries was the least undesirable.[78] Military intervention by Great Britain was out of the question. It could jeopardize Britain's sponsorship of the Geneva conference. The government of Prime Minister Winston Churchill also worried that direct military intervention in Indochina could raise the specter of nuclear war at a time when Britain hoped to foster detente and eventual arms control between Washington and Moscow.[79]

A meeting among Dulles and Radford and eight Democratic and Republican congressional leaders at the State Department on Saturday morning April 3 confirmed Eisenhower's judgement that opinion leaned against greater U.S. military involvement at Dienbienphu. Dulles and Radford reviewed the desperate situation. Dienbienphu could fall at any time, and a French defeat there could lead quickly to a rout. After the Vietminh conquest of Indochina, Dulles predicted that "it was only a question of time until all of Southeast Asia falls along with Indonesia." He asked for congressional authority for the President to "use air and sea power in the area if he felt it necessary in the interests of national security." Only Republican majority leader William Knowland supported introduction of this resolution (and he drew back after the other seven objected.) All of the others agreed that "we want no more Koreas with the United States furnishing 90% of the manpower." All eight told Dulles that they would not go forward with a congressional resolution supporting the use of military force until he could guarantee that U.S. forces would be part of a multilateral force including the major European allies. They presented three preconditions for their support of a congressional resolution authorizing the use of U.S. forces at Dienbienphu: Dulles needed to receive "definite commitments" from Britain and other allies to join a coalition; the French government had to promise to keep its forces in the fight until the war was won; France had to promise to accelerate the independence of the Associated States.[80] Since Dulles believed that he needed congressional support before he could convince the Europeans to join any plan of united action, the possibility that France's allies would join the fighting immediately passed.

Yet all policy-makers—whether the President, the Joint Chiefs of Staff, or members of the congressional leadership—agreed that Indochina remained important to the United States in the Cold War. All wanted assurances from other nations and other players within the U.S. government that they would share responsibility for the future course of the war. On the evening of April 4 Eisenhower met with Dulles and Radford. The President spoke more clearly than he had before about his own preconditions for miliary actions. He said that the United States would agree to use force in Dienbienphu only if Britain, Australia, and New Zealand agreed to include their own soldiers in a coalition. He wanted a "full political understanding with France and other countries" about the future of Indochina. The President hoped this would provide maximum pressure on France to accede to U.S. plans for the political independence of Vietnam. Finally Eisenhower wanted Congress as a whole, not just the leadership, to vote formally on the use of force at Dienbienphu before he would commit the U.S. military.[81]

Eisenhower helped foster an atmosphere in which the public recognized the importance of Indochina. He also wanted to create the maximum freedom of action for the United States. Years of competition with France had made policy-makers highly skeptical of the chances of success as long as the initiative for Indochina remained with French officials. Three days after he outlined his conditions for the use of American air power at Dienbienphu, Eisenhower explained at a television news conference what was at stake: "You have a row of dominoes set up and you knock over the first one, and what will happen to the last one is the certainty that it will go over very quickly. . . .

The loss of Indochina will cause the fall of Southeast Asia like a set of dominoes."[82]

Just as the April 4 meeting at the White House seemed to forestall immediate U.S. military intervention at Dienbienphu, the French formally requested implementation of Operation Vulture. General Navarre concluded that the outpost would fall within a few days unless airstrikes stopped the Vietminh advance. The French government told Washington that "immediate armed intervention of U.S. carrier aircraft at Dienbienphu is now necessary to save the situation."[83] Over the next three weeks Dulles traveled several times to European capitals to generate support for an American-led coalition to help France. He never could resolve the competing desires of the British to go forward with the Geneva conference and the French to retain control of the pace of the war. The British considered Dienbienphu lost anyway, although they also thought that a French defeat there did not mean a complete communist victory. For their part, the French continued to resist American demands that they promise to stay in the war for the long run. They also balked at Dulles's insistence that united action meant that the future of non-communist Indochina be decided by the entire coalition. France regarded united action as a fig leaf providing cover for what they considered the immediate need for U.S. airstrikes. The Americans, on the other hand, did not want to go in alone. French foreign minister Georges Bidault dismissed Dulles's requirement that the British participate, because France thought that the British contribution would not "amount to much of anything."[84]

Dulles made one final pitch to the British, but Churchill and Foreign Secretary Anthony Eden had already made up their minds not to go forward with a British contribution to united action. Britain was committed to the Geneva conference. Only if that gathering failed to reach a settlement would the British consider participating in united action. Eden repeated the long-held British position that "none of us in London believe that intervention in Indochina can do anything." Prime Minister Churchill scuttled any possibility of using British forces immediately. He told Admiral Radford that since Britain had given up India, the British people would not supply soldiers to keep Indochina French. More ominously, Churchill thought that only the use of "that horrible thing"—the atomic bomb—could save Indochina. Britain was much more vulnerable to nuclear attack than the United States, and in the new nuclear age policy-makers had to be more cautious than before.[85]

The rebuffs from France and Britain irritated Eisenhower. Privately, he berated France for its unwillingness to grant full independence to Indochina and for its continued suspicion of the United States. They insisted that the United States "come in as junior partners and provide materials etc., while they themselves retain authority in that region." These were unacceptable conditions for Eisenhower, and they guaranteed failure of the French cause. As for the British, the President complained that they demonstrated a "woeful unawareness'' of the dangers posed by a potential communist victory in Indochina.[86] Nevertheless, the French and British refusal to support united action on terms laid down by the United States ended the plan.

Yet the end of consideration of united action signaled not the end of U.S. involvement in Vietnam but exactly the opposite. The growing American frustration with France and, to a lesser extent, Britain, led the Eisenhower administration to look for ways to act on its own in Indochina without committing U.S. military forces. As the battle of Dienbienphu approached a climax, the U.S. government moved to take control of the future of Indochina into its own hands.

Chapter

* * * * * * * * * * *

"Good Intentions, a Clear Conscience, and to Hell with Everybody":
May 1954–December 1960

*I*N LATE 1955 Graham Greene, an English novelist, published *The Quiet American,* a bitter story of a love triangle involving a youthful and apparently naive American embassy official, a world-weary British journalist, and a beautiful young Vietnamese woman attempting to survive the chaos of the final days of French rule in Indochina. The names of Greene's characters seemed to leap from the pages of the works of Charles Dickens. The endlessly soliloquizing American named Alden Pyle was indeed an unrelenting pain to many of the people he encountered in Saigon. Thomas Fowler, the cynical, disengaged British reporter, was Pyle's rival for Phuong, the Vietnamese woman. Phuong pronounced Fowler's name Fowl-aire, representing the stale and fetid attitudes of old European powers. For her part, Phuong's name called to mind a phoenix, rising from the ashes of colonial rule.

Greene drew a devastating portrait of an American innocent marching down the road to hell. Pyle had studied Asian history at Harvard University, and he had come to Vietnam, "determined," Fowler recalled, "to do good, not to any individual person but to a country, a continent, a world." The earnest Pyle displayed no irony, expressed limited self-doubt, and spoke at tedious length about the desirability of finding what he called a "third force" of authentic Vietnamese nationalists, tied to neither the French nor the communists. Fowler mocked Pyle for his worship of abstract expertise—"He never saw anything he hadn't heard in a lecture-hall, and his writers and his lecturers made a fool of him. When he saw a dead body he couldn't even see the wounds. A Red menace, a soldier of democracy."[1] Yet despite his impeccable politeness and apparently insignificant job at the U.S. embassy, Pyle actually directed covert military operations in Saigon for the Central Intelligence Agency. Greene patterned his character roughly on the experience of Edward G. Lansdale, a prominent CIA operative in Vietnam in 1954 and 1955.[2]

At the climax of *The Quiet American,* Pyle, a far more sinister personality than his naive exterior suggests, organizes a terrorist attack on a café in the heart of Saigon, one which he hopes will discredit the communists and enhance the standing of a militia he favors. The death toll of civilians far exceeds Pyle's expectations. Finally roused to action by his fury with Pyle's insouciant disregard for the lives of innocent Vietnamese and his jealousy at Pyle for having stolen the affections of Phuong, who previously had been Fowler's mistress, the British journalist exposes Pyle's whereabouts to leaders of a Vietnamese faction, who track him down and kill him. Only at that point does the profoundly talkative Pyle become a truly "quiet American." Fowler's summary judgment of Pyle is that "I never knew a man who had better motives for all the trouble he caused." He expanded his indictment of Pyle to include much of American culture. Musing about the passing of world leadership from Britain to the United States, Fowler complained that "we used to speak of sterling qualities. Have we got to talk about dollar love? . . . A dollar love has good intentions, a clear conscience and to Hell with everybody."[3]

Not surprisingly, Greene's novel received a hostile reception upon its publication in the United States. A. J. Liebling, a stalwart liberal, dismissed Greene as a "minor novelist," and expressed outrage that an anti-American British author could defame U.S. representatives in Saigon for having promoted an explosion in the heart of Saigon in late 1954. (One did occur, but no one ever proved U.S. involvement.[4]) Greene's book sold poorly at first, but ten years later sales took off as many Americans, heavily engaged in their own war in Vietnam, reduced their earlier optimistic assumptions what the United States could accomplish in Vietnam.

From the time of the Geneva conference of May–July 1954 until the establishment of the National Front for the Liberation of Vietnam on December 20, 1960, the United States became ever more deeply engaged in Vietnamese politics. At every stage U.S. officials sought to thwart the efforts of

Ho Chi Minh and his colleagues to unify Vietnam under the leadership of the government of the Democratic Republic of (North) Vietnam. To that end, the United States backed the creation of an alternative regime south of the seventeenth parallel led by Ngo Dinh Diem called the Republic of Vietnam. American officials carefully distinguished their efforts from those of France or Great Britain. Diem enjoyed numerous successes in establishing his rule, although doubts arose about his political skills from the very beginning. Nevertheless, the United States chose to foster what experts characterized as nation-building in South Vietnam. The refusal of the Diem regime to reach an accommodation with Ho Chi Minh in the north and Vietminh fighters who remained in the south led to a revival of civil war by the end of the decade. The United States became the primary support of Diem's government in this civil war. Some representatives of the Eisenhower administration expressed occasional misgivings about the popularity and capacity of Diem's government, but by 1960 U.S. officials in Washington and Saigon chose to ignore the political shortcomings of the Republic of Vietnam. Instead, as the historian David L. Anderson writes, the Eisenhower administration became "trapped by success" in South Vietnam. The President and his advisers believed that Diem expressed a genuine nationalism that could deny Ho Chi Minh the fruits of the victory won by his fighters in the war against the French.[5]

THE GENEVA CONFERENCE

Vietminh forces surrounding the beleaguered French garrison at Dienbienphu conquered the outpost on the night of May 6–7, 1954. The attackers, aware that the Indochinese phase of the Geneva conference was due to open on May 8, wanted success on the battlefield to dictate the terms of a diplomatic settlement. While ordering the final assault on the French garrison, the Vietminh commander said "negotiations with the imperialists should be effected by means of bayonets, explosives and cannon. Tonight we shall `negotiate' with them."[6]

A few hours later Secretary of State John Foster Dulles addressed the nation by radio and television. After "paying tribute to the gallant defenders of Dienbienphu," the Secretary of State went on to outline the stakes for the United States in the future of Indochina. "What is going on in Indochina," he observed, "is a perfect example of the Soviet Communist strategy for colonial and dependent areas which was laid down by Lenin and Stalin and which the Communists have practiced to take over much of Asia." Nevertheless, Dulles observed that "in Indochina the situation is far more complex" than it had been four years earlier in Korea when the United States had sent its military forces. Accordingly, the United States now was willing to let negotiators at Geneva try to reach an agreement, but the settlement acceptable to the United States would somehow preserve a part of Indochina as non-communist territory.[7]

Dulles spoke from Washington, where he had returned following his attendance at the ceremonial opening of the discussions at Geneva. International politics and personalities made life difficult for Dulles for the short time he attended the conference. The approaching climax at Dienbienphu put France on the defensive militarily. The presence of Chinese Foreign Minister Zhou Enlai proved a profound embarrassment because of Republican hostility to the communist victory in China in 1949. Dulles coldly refused to shake Chou's proffered hand, a snub which loomed large in popular imagery of U.S.-Chinese relations (its actual effects on relations between the two powers has been highly exaggerated). Dulles fidgeted while at Geneva. A British diplomat described him seated at the conference table "not knowing where to look, his mouth drawn down at the corners, his eyes on the ceiling, sucking on his teeth."[8] Moreover, Dulles reflected on "how galling it was to the U.S. to be the center of the Red attack at Geneva, without any of our western friends speaking up . . . in our defense."[9]

Yet Dulles's discomfort was partly a pose to induce concessions from the communist side. He met privately with Soviet Foreign Minister Vyacheslav Molotov at the beginning of the conference and hinted that the United States and the Soviets should each speak for their respective clients. The result might be a tidy bilateral agreement, but the secretary reported his disappointment that Molotov declined to leap to "any of the flies I had cast."[10] Dulles returned home before the conference discussed Indochina, leaving his deputy Walter Bedell Smith in charge. Dulles ordered the American delegation to participate only as representatives of an "interested nation" rather than as a "belligerent or principal in the negotiations."[11]

When the conference formally took up the subject of Indochina on May 8, the United States still wanted to explore the possibilities of a military solution. At minimum, Dulles hoped to deny all of Vietnam to the Vietminh. He informed the U.S. delegation that his speech's reference to the way in which the United States had participated in the Korean war offered hope that the French would "have gotten the point and realize that we are ready to talk with them about internationalizing the war if they come to the conclusion that this is preferable to the harsh terms which no doubt Communists will seek to extract."[12]

U.S. officials hoped against hope for military success against the Vietminh. From May 8 until the middle of June, Washington's policy followed the winding path taken during the previous six months. The President and his principal advisers stressed three often inconsistent themes: a desire to defeat the communists militarily, or at least not negotiate with them while they held the advantage on the battlefield; frustration with, bordering on contempt for, the French government; and a simultaneous reluctance to commit U.S. forces without the presence of other nations' troops. Allen Dulles, the director of the Central Intelligence Agency, told the National Security Council that the French defeat at Dienbienphu had not resulted in widespread panic among the remaining French and Vietnamese soldiers fighting in the Mekong Delta of the southernmost part of the country. He acknowledged, however, the fluidity of the situation, and the future of the anti-communist forces "depended very largely on psychological factors." Secretary Dulles worried about the "growing sentiment in France to accept the current Vietminh proposal as the basis for a discussion at the Geneva conference. If this actually occurs," he went on "it would be nothing but a thinly disguised French surrender."[13]

Eisenhower continued to weigh the possibility of military action as long as the United States went to Indochina in concert with allies. He told Dulles that "he would not necessarily exclude sending some Marines. . . . He was, however, very emphatic," Dulles recalled, "that we must adhere to the position of not going in alone."[14] Dulles spoke with British, Australian, New Zealand, and French leaders over the next several weeks, attempting to revive the idea of united military action. Sometimes he seemed to hope that France would invite the United States into Indochina, as Britain had encouraged American participation in Greece in 1947. At other times the Secretary of State gave the impression that he considered discussions with the allies primarily an "academic exercise" to be used to influence the diplomats at Geneva into thinking that the United States was seriously contemplating military action in Indochina.[15] In any event, no potential partner chose to join the United States in forcing the issue on the battlefield while the international conference went forward.

The participants at Geneva—Great Britain and the Soviet Union (the two co-sponsors), France, China, the Vietnamese communists, delegates from Cambodia and Laos, and observers from the State of Vietnam—and the United States (which attended only as an "interested party" or observer) each advanced profoundly different interests.[16] The Vietnamese pressed the least complicated position, since they came to Geneva expecting the other nations to recognize that their military victory over France justified their control over all of Vietnam. For their part, the two co-sponsors, Britain and the Soviet Union, sought to balance their backing for France and the Vietminh, their respective allies, with hopes for a successful conference. Walter Bedell Smith characterized the British as "anxious to play a major role at Geneva as a peace maker," provided, of course, the British did not have to commit troops to the conflict.[17] An amicable resolution of the problems of Korea and Indochina would enhance the standing of each of the co-sponsors. This was an enticing prospect for the British, suffering the pangs of international decline, and for the Soviets, yearning for international acceptance. Chinese representatives had an even greater desire for international, and especially U.S., acknowledgment of their nation's legitimacy. In May little progress in the talks occurred toward arranging a cease-fire, the possible partition of the country, withdrawal of Vietminh troops from Laos and Cambodia, and the makeup of an international-control commission to supervise the future.[18] Surprisingly, U.S. efforts to organize an international military force to fight in Indochina may even have hastened progress toward a solution in Geneva, the outcome the United States wanted least. Propects of American military intervention encouraged Eden to redouble his efforts to bridge the wide gap among the participants.

The French came to the table with ambivalent aims, reflecting the persistent divisions within France over Indochina. The cabinet sought the incompatible goals of ending the war quickly and preserving French predominance in Indochina. The fall of Dienbienphu eroded parliamentary support for the government of Premier Joseph Laniel and Georges Bidault, his uncompromising foreign minister. They barely survived a series of parliamentary inquiries into the conduct of the war but resigned on June 12.

Pierre Mendes-France, a Radical-Socialist deputy and long an advocate of direct negotiations between Paris and the DRV, became the new prime minister on June 18 with the promise "to resign if by July 20 I have not obtained a cease-fire in Indochina."[19] Undersecretary of State Walter Bedell Smith met Mendes-France on June 20. The new premier told him that he expected that negotiations with the Vietnamese would prove difficult. He encouraged the United States to "help France by discreetly letting the Vietnamese representatives know that they would be wise to accept the French agreement with the Vietminh as the best agreement obtainable."[20]

The ascendancy of Mendes-France removed the last possibility that the United States might organize an international military expedition to Indochina. When British Prime Minister Winston Churchill learned that Mendes-France had become premier, he finally threw in the towel. He wrote Eisenhower of his longstanding belief that

> if the French meant to fight for their empire in Indochina instead of clearing out as we did of our far greater inheritance in India, they should have at least introduced two years' service which would have made it possible for them to use the military power of their nation. They did not do this, but fought on for eight years with untrustworthy local troops. . . . The result has thus been inevitable and personally I think Mendes-France . . . has made up his mind to clear out on the best terms available. If that is so, I think he is right.

He saw no foreseeable circumstances in which British troops might be used in Indochina. Instead, he recommended that the United States and it allies proceed with the formation of a Southeast Asia Treaty, similar to NATO, to "establish a firm front against Communism in the Pacific area."[21]

In the wake of this final British refusal to contemplate military action in Indochina, the Geneva conference got down to arranging a political settlement between France and the Vietminh. The departure of Walter Bedell Smith from the conference, and Dulles's suggestion that the conference suspend operations while the new French government was organized, may have encouraged greater flexibility on the part of the Soviet and Chinese delegations. The United States remained ambivalent about seeing the negotiations succeed. In early July Eisenhower considered keeping both Dulles and Smith away from the conference. He told James Hagerty, his press secretary, "The trouble, Jim, with this whole situation is that the French will try to get us, if we are physically there with Dulles or Bedell, to approve the terms of the settlement. We don't think it is going to be a good one and it certainly isn't one we can support." Eventually, however, Eisenhower decided that there was more for the United States to lose by not having a high level representative at the end of the conference.[22]

In Geneva, Soviet Foreign Minister Molotov assented to the creation of an international-control commission in which the communist states would be in a minority. Smith reported further that Chou Enlai "had taken an apparently reasonable position on Laos and Cambodia." China agreed to their future presence within the French Union and would consider them separately from Vietnam. As for the latter, the Soviets and Chinese favored partition between France and the Vietminh. China's willingness to have the negotiations concluded quickly derived partly from a desire to act independently of Moscow and partly out of fear of the United States. Dulles received an unconfirmed intelligence estimate from Republican Senate Majority Leader William Knowland, an ardent opponent of the Chinese communists, that Beijing feared a U.S. attack over Indochina and worried that the Soviets would not provide more than token military support.[23] Molotov's "friendly and mild tone" in his private conversations with Smith contrasted sharply with his "harsh and even insulting language" in the public sessions. Smith attributed both aspects of the Soviet foreign minister's demeanor to his conviction that the Vietminh held the upper hand militarily and their belief "that our intervention is improbable."[24]

In the beginning of July, Dulles continued to advocate a minimal U.S. role in the proceedings at Geneva. He wanted Smith to stay away from the conference entirely, leaving U. Alexis Johnson as the State Department's representative. Eisenhower overruled the Secretary of State, since the President believed that the alliance between the United States, France, and Great Britain eliminated the possibility of complete U.S. non-participation at Geneva.[25] Nevertheless, Dulles retained a significant measure of personal control by going to Paris to hammer out a coordinated U.S.-French position with Mendes-France.

While the U.S. Secretary of State met with the French premier, the negotiators in Geneva marked time. Dulles and Mendes-France agreed that any demarcation line separating a Vietminh zone from that of the French zone of Vietnam would be only temporary. Dulles reported to the NSC that news of his trip to Paris had indeed stiffened the resolve of Mendes-France and forced the Vietminh to back down from their demand that Vietnam be divided at the fourteenth parallel. Instead, the French held fast to the eighteenth parallel as the dividing line between Vietminh and French territory. But other officials thought that France would cave in to the Vietminh. Chairman of the Joint Chiefs of Staff Arthur Radford feared "the likelihood of severe Vietnamese revulsion against the French when the terms were finally announced."[26]

The scene then shifted back to Geneva. For the first time France revealed to its Vietnamese allies that it had conducted secret and direct conversations with the Vietminh. Vietnamese authorities, led by Prime Minister Ngo Dinh Diem, appointed by Emperor Bao Dai in June, formally objected to partition. The Vietnamese allies of the French also demanded an enclave north of any demarcation line should the Vietminh win the right to hold territory in the Mekong Delta. Diem's objections foreshadowed later problems with the Geneva agreement.[27]

As Mendes-France's deadline of July 20 approached, the parties had not yet agreed who would sign the accords. The Chinese insisted that Walter Bedell Smith commit the United States to the agreement, thereby implicitly recognizing the People's Republic of China. Molotov prevailed on Chou Enlai to drop this demand.[28] Nor had the negotiators set the line dividing Vietminh territory from that held by France and her Vietnamese allies. Under intense pressure from the Chinese, the Vietminh agreed to the seventeenth parallel, a line favored by the Americans, and one which gave the State of Vietnam (Bao Dai's government) some of the most significant towns of central Vietnam. Pham Van Dong, the Vietminh representative, accepted the Chinese demand because he had little choice, yet the memory of Chinese haste to arrange a cease-fire remained among the leaders of the DRV. After the final success of the communist forces in Vietnam in 1975 and the opening of outright warfare between Hanoi and the People's Republic of China in 1979, Vietnamese communist leaders denounced the Chinese for having "betrayed the revolutionary struggle of the peoples of Vietnam, Laos and Cambodia" in the last days of the Geneva conference.[29]

The announcement of an agreement came a few hours after midnight on July 21. Vietnamese delegate Pham Van Dong resented a settlement which did not recognize the full extent of Vietminh military success, especially in the southern Mekong Delta. Nevertheless, the Soviet and Chinese delegates made it clear that they valued the potential for future accommodation with the

Western powers more than they wanted to continue unconditional sponsorship of Vietminh aspirations. Dulles characterized the communists demands as "relatively moderate in terms of their actual capabilities." He believed that they drew back from pressing for the full realization of their military strength because they feared an adverse reaction from Washington "would increase the danger of general war, which they do not want now."[30]

On July 21 the conference participants signed a series of separate agreements establishing a cease-fire, a temporary division of Vietnam between French and Vietminh forces at the seventeenth parallel, the promise of elections to determine the future of a unified Vietnam within twenty-four months, the return of refugees, and the creation of an International Supervisory Commission made up of representatives from Canada, India, and Poland to oversee the implementation of the agreements. The United States took note of the agreements and did not sign them, because the policy of strict non-recognition of the People's Republic of China barred any official interchange with Chinese diplomats. But the United States did pledge to respect the accords. British Foreign Secretary Anthony Eden considered this American attitude "unreasonable," especially since Dulles was "at least as much responsible as we for the calling of the conference and the present terms of reference." Nevertheless, no one cared to disrupt the final ceremony because of objections to the U.S. positions. Eden believed that differences of opinion in the Western camp over procedures could not be permitted to contribute to "the continuation of the war in Indochina with all that will bring with it."[31]

THE GOVERNMENT OF NGO DINH DIEM

Events in Vietnam, far more than the negotiations at Geneva, determined the future of Indochina. Washington maintained abiding interest in the political arrangements in Indochina, despite its coolness toward the diplomatic negotiations. In 1954 and 1955 the United States took two fateful steps to fortify the position of anti-communist forces throughout Southeast Asia: support for Ngo Dinh Diem and the creation of the Southeast Asia Treaty Organization (SEATO). The United States helped establish a new government of the State of Vietnam under the leadership of Prime Minister Ngo Dinh Diem. After the cease-fire arranged by the Geneva conference, U.S. officials in Washington and Saigon deepened their commitment to creating a viable, independent regime under the leadership of Diem and his brother Ngo Dinh Nhu. For a while, some American officials believed that the Ngos represented the sort of authentic but elusive third force the United States had sought since 1946. American support for the Ngos contributed to additional estrangement between the United States and France. U.S. support for the Diem government augmented American hopes to reverse what they considered the most unsatisfactory provisions of the Geneva agreements: the likely unification of Vietnam under the leadership of Ho Chi Minh. U.S. sponsorship of Diem led to a policy of division of Vietnam, and the false expectation that a separate, viable society could be created south of the seventeenth parallel. At the same time, officials in Washington sought to broaden international involvement in Indochina by joining partners in Asia and Europe to create a Southeast Asia Treaty Organization. Together, U.S. support for the political aspirations of the Ngo family in the part of Vietnam below the seventeenth parallel and the creation of SEATO represented two more fateful steps on the road to the second Indochina war.

Diem became prime minister of Vietnam on June 18, 1954, the same day Mendes-France became premier of France. His appointment followed a complex and even astonishing relationship with Bao Dai. The Emperor had approached Diem in May 1950 about becoming prime minister, but Diem had refused on the grounds that France had not offered real independence. He had then fled the country fearful that his life might be in danger. After traveling in Japan and Europe, he had spent two years in a Roman Catholic seminary in Lakewood, New Jersey. He occasionally interrupted his meditations to meet with low-level State Department officials and several Catholic clerics and prominent laymen, including the archbishop of New York, Cardinal Francis Spellman; Democratic Senators John F. Kennedy of Massachusetts and Mike Mansfield of Montana; and Supreme Court Justice William O. Douglas. These men formed the nucleus of the American Friends of Vietnam, a group of prominent people dedicated to advancing the standing of the Diem government inside the United States.[32] A psychological profile of Diem later described him as distrustful of the counsel of any people other than his family. He spent long hours alone, meditating. When he met visitors, he engaged in monologues often lasting hours. He was extremely uncomfortable around women, with the exception of his brother's wife, and intelligence analysts made much of the fact that he had never had sexual relations.[33]

Given the persistent divisions between Bao Dai and Diem and Diem's later difficulties in creating a viable government in Vietnam, his appointment to the premiership has provoked a controversy among historians. The most persuasive explanation for the Emperor's selection of Diem was his close connection to influential Americans. Bao Dai reported that he gave up on the French during the Geneva conference and ''the Americans remained our only allies.'' They ''had the ability to help us continue the fight against communism,'' and Diem's contacts among U.S. officials might make the United States more helpful. The French reciprocated Diem's hostility with their own objections to his appointment.

This hostility made Diem an all the more attractive to the Americans. A few weeks before he actually assumed office, he met Bao Dai and swore on a crucifix to defend Vietnam against the communists and against the French if necessary. The Emperor offered Diem greater control over the government than had been given to any of Diem's predecessors. Some observers saw a sinister motive at work, with the Emperor expecting the failure of Diem and thus his elimination as a rival. A more reasonable explanation of the freedom granted by Bao Dai to Diem was the perilous situation that existed in the southern part of Vietnam after the Geneva conference. Bao Dai remained in the south of France throughout the period. Moreover, the constitutional structure of the region south of the seventeenth parallel was ill-defined by the conference. The State of Vietnam existed, with Bao Dai as emperor, but its relationship to the government of Vietnam led by Diem was unclear because France still exercised ultimate authority through General Paul Ely, who served as both high commissioner (the civilian authority) and commander of the French armed forces.[34]

The situation on the ground in Vietnam presented grave problems to the anti-communist forces. Secretary of State Dulles believed that the Vietminh had agreed to the seventeenth parallel demarcation line and had not sought a communist enclave in the Mekong River Delta region out of a "conviction that they will secure what they really want gradually in the course of time." Allen Dulles, director of the CIA, pointed out that the Diem government faced an enormous problem in maintaining order in the South, "where, to put it mildly, the French were extremely unpopular as a result of the partition."[35] The Dulles brothers perceived a looming dilemma in southern Vietnam: any viable government had to be independent of the despised and ineffectual French, yet the French Expeditionary Corps was for the time being the guarantor of order until a strong Vietnamese government could be created. The United States therefore wanted to reduce French influence while relying on the French military for the time being. The British government considered U.S.-French disagreements over Diem camouflage for American uneasiness about the viability of Diem's regime. "The Americans are obviously preparing to make scapegoats of the French in case their own backing for Mr. Diem turns out to have been misguided," wrote a Foreign Office official in October 1954.[36]

General John W. "Iron Mike" O'Daniel, the commander of the U.S. Military Assistance Advisory Group (MAAG) in Vietnam, also recognized the difficult military and political situation in Vietnam in the aftermath of the Geneva conference. He noted the professionalism of the communist forces and the weakness of previous governments under Bao Dai. He considered the "present situation made to order for the communists" now that "they need fear no armed interference." On the other hand, O'Daniel detected a "great opportunity" for the United States to point "Vietnam in the right direction." Conditions seemed ripe for the United States to provide more money, war materiel, and personnel to train the Vietnamese armed forces now that the French had lost popular support and the Diem government seemed genuinely interested in consolidating its position.[37] O'Daniel overlooked the French desire to retain some influence in Vietnam after the cease-fire.

THE POSTWAR POLITICAL-RELIGIOUS LANDSCAPE IN VIETNAM

Adding further difficulties to the Diem government was the fractured political-religious landscape at the end of the war. The cease-fire had stalled Vietminh actions south of the seventeenth parallel, and much of the energy of Ho Chi Minh's supporters went into reconstituting an effective government in Hanoi. French troops represented only a thin layer of leadership of the Vietnamese army in the South, and these forces did not exercise control over much of the territory below the seventeenth parallel. Catholics made up approximately 10 percent of the Vietnamese population, although they represented a far larger portion of the educated and wealthy segments. Most Catholics had opposed the Vietminh during the civil war because of their religion's anti-communism, though many, like Diem, had come to despise the French. Vietnamese Catholics, however, lacked a political movement, and at the end of the war many resided in territory controlled by the Vietminh.[38]

Three powerful political-military sects exercised real authority over the territory of Vietnam controlled by neither the French nor the Vietminh. The Cao Dai religious sect, a mixture of Catholicism, Buddhism, and local animism, had approximately one million followers. It had a headquarters in the town of Tay Ninh, north of Saigon, from which it collected taxes from most of the population in the area immediately to the north and northwest of the southern capital. One Cao Dai leader, Pham Cong Tac, often called the Cao Dai Pope, led an armed force of approximately ten thousand to twenty thousand troops. During the war between France and the Vietminh, Tac had often shifted his allegiance among Ho Chi Minh, French authorities, and neutralists to augment the power of the Cao Dai. A smaller sect, the Hoa Hao, with an armed force of several thousand men, exercised power similar to that of the Cao Dai in the area southwest of Saigon. The Hoa Hao practiced a more consistent and simple Buddhism than the eclectic theology and elaborate rituals favored by the Cao Dai. Support for the Hoa Hao came from some of the poorest peasants in the south.

A third sect, the Binh Xuyen, operated in Saigon itself. The Binh Xuyen resembled the Cao Dai and Hoa Hao not through religious practices—it had none—but in the unshakable allegiance of its followers to its leader, Bay Vien. The commander of the Binh Xuyen led a militia of about 2,500 well-armed bullies. They used their weapons to protect a sprawling vice establishment in Cholon, a suburb of Saigon, where they operated the largest brothel in Asia, a casino, several opium dens, and an opium factory. These and more legitimate businesses commanded revenues of several million dollars per year. During the Franco-Vietminh war, Bay Vien had sided with the French military, which had made him a colonel and later a brigadier-general.[39]

When Diem installed his first cabinet in July 1954 he included no representatives of the sects, which he despised as either thugs or illiterate peasants. Instead, the first Diem cabinet was made up largely of political unknowns, most of whom were related to the Prime Minister. Many Catholics, who might have been expected to make up the bulk of Diem's supporters, remained north of the seventeenth parallel. Diem therefore began to persuade as many Catholics as possible to come south.

Diem had the assistance of teams of the Central Intelligence Agency operatives, organized by Edward Lansdale. American officials believed that a massive migration out of the Vietminh-controlled North would prove a major embarrassment to Ho Chi Minh. Accordingly, priests informed anxious parishioners that "Christ has gone to the South" or "the Virgin Mary has departed from the North."[40] Lansdale and his men offered the incentives of five acres and a water buffalo for northern Catholics to support their coreligionists in the South. Some Catholics may have fled because of fears generated by Lansdale's propaganda: agents circulated stories of Vietminh concentration camps and the possibility of a U.S. atomic bomb attack on the north. Fifteen years later, the *Pentagon Papers* identified as "conceivably an example of Colonel Lansdale's handiwork" a map of Hanoi distributed among the Catholics of the North with three concentric circles destroyed by a U.S. atom bomb attack.[41]

In the last six months of 1954, the French army and the U.S. Seventh Fleet transported over 310,000 people to the South. This "Passage to Freedom," as the navy labeled it, proved extremely popular in dramatizing the plight of the Vietnamese to Americans. Another seven hundred thousand northern Catholics walked to the South. At the end of the year, the United States provided an additional $282 million to pay for the resettlement of refugees. Many whole villages with their priests relocated to the areas of Vietnam that Diem regarded as especially important in resisting the communists. They established some of the 203 villages in a cordon around Saigon and others in areas of the central highlands inhabited by non-Vietnamese tribes.[42]

The movement of nearly one million Catholics to the South fortified Diem, but he still faced intrigues swirling among the sects and Bao Dai. The Emperor, living comfortably in Cannes, relied on money from the Binh Xuyen's vice activities to support his lavish lifestyle. Any movement by Diem to curtail the Binh Xuyen would provoke retaliation from the Emperor. Even if Diem survived the machinations of Vietnamese factions, he faced formidable social, political, and military obstacles in creating a viable government. U.S. officials faced grim choices in the latter months of 1954. Most agreed that Diem should have a chance to prove himself, if only because no alternative seemed to exist. Senator Mike Mansfield (D., Mont.), the senate's leading expert on Vietnam, reported to the Foreign Relations committee his doubts that "a satisfactory substitute for" Diem existed in Vietnam. At the same time officials in Saigon and Washington thought that Diem faced a bleak future, given his limited base of popular support and the constant French opposition.[43]

THE COLLINS MISSION

Accordingly, the Eisenhower administration decided to dispatch a high level delegate to Vietnam. Secretary Dulles and the President expressed dissatisfaction with the performance of Donald Heath, the U.S. ambassador in Saigon, and believed a special representative with the confidence of the President could ease out Heath. In early November, Eisenhower selected an old, trusted subordinate, General J. Lawton "Lightning Joe" Collins (he had been a corps commander in Europe in the Second World War and Eisenhower's deputy chief of staff in 1947). Collins had the personal rank of ambassador in charge of all "the agencies and resources of the United States government in Vietnam." Eisenhower instructed Collins to assist the Diem government to maintain internal order and "foster economic conditions which will strengthen and promote the survival of a Free Vietnam."

Collins soon discovered that his mission had too many contradictory aims. On the one hand, Washington told him to reverse "the deteriorating situation in Vietnam." On the other, the means of doing so required that he "assist in stabilizing and strengthening the legal government of Vietnam under the premiership of Ngo Diem."[44] Collins quickly learned how difficult a task it was to reconcile the end of creating an effective government south of the seventeenth parallel with the requirement that he advance the interests of Prime Minister Diem. On the day of his appointment, Collins met with Diem's ambassador to the United States, who brusquely warned him against paying much attention to the views of General Paul Ely, the French high commissioner. The French, warned ambassador Tran Van Chuong, "had been and still were opposed to the government of Premier Diem."[45]

Collins reached Saigon on November 8, 1954 and almost immediately plunged into a maelstrom of political intrigue. Although Eisenhower had given him formal plenary powers, he lacked authority over General O'Daniel, the head of the Military Assistance Advisory Group, and Lansdale, the principal CIA official. Both O'Daniel and Lansdale supported Diem, as did a growing contingent of U.S. trainers of the South Vietnamese armed forces and police led by Professor Wesley Fishel of Michigan State University.

Lansdale, a model for the loquacious Alden Pyle in *The Quiet American*, bombarded Collins with endless memoranda on the need to support a popular government headed by Diem: "We have no other choice but to win here or face an increasingly grim future, a heritage which none of us would like to pass along to our offspring." He requested authority to coordinate all efforts of the United States, the French, and the Vietnamese in "giving the people a truly representative government."[46] Lansdale reported the French remained a force to be reckoned with, and they continued to oppose Diem's regime. Ely commanded some 160,000 French troops remaining in the southern part of Vietnam. While U.S. representatives hoped to reduce the number of French soldiers to under 80,000 in the next year, their presence for the time being seemed necessary to stop the resurgence of the Vietminh. Despite the Emperor's refusal to abandon his villa in Cannes and return to Vietnam, he seemed still a force in Vietnamese politics.[47]

At his first meeting with the Vietnamese Prime Minister, Collins formed an unfavorable impression of Diem as a "small, shy, diffident man with almost no personal magnetism." His refusal to act decisively put him a severe disadvantage when dealing with fast-changing events. While willing to withhold final judgment on Diem's political skills, Collins doubted his "inherent capacity to manage [the] country during this critical period."[48]

Over the next two months, Collins softened his initial harsh judgment of Diem. While the Prime Minister resisted Collins's suggestion that he broaden his cabinet by appointing Dr. Phan Huy Quat, a prominent Buddhist leader, as his secretary of defense, Diem did seem to understand the dangers posed by the sects. In January 1955 Collins reported to the National Security Council that Diem's prestige among the Vietnamese had risen, but that he still "has much to learn about practical politics and public relations. While at times he conveys the impression of being well over his depth, recently he has evidenced greater flexibility in handling people and increased self-confidence in dealing with his ministers and public issues."[49]

At the beginning of 1955, Collins glimpsed the hope that Diem could create a viable government. The Prime Minister advocated a seven point program of reorganization of the armed forces, resettlement of refugees, creation of a responsible national assembly, and economic development. In late January Collins returned to Washington and told Eisenhower that he saw "at least a 50-50 chance of saving South Vietnam from the Communists." Collins believed that the Vietminh intended to lay low for the time being. The real threat to the viability of the Diem regime came from continued activities of the sects.[50] In February, Dulles met Diem in Saigon and assured him that the United States had a "great stake in him and in Vietnam." Collins told Dulles that Diem had "developed a sound and progressive program." The

U.S. had to maintain support for Diem through the elections scheduled for 1956.[51]

Yet Collins' optimism soon faded. In March, the war between Diem and the sects flared up. The Cao Dai, Hoa Hao, and the Binh Xuyen formed a united front against the government, and rumors flew in Saigon of a coup against Diem. For his part, Diem saw French intrigue behind the alliance, and he considered using the Vietnamese National Army against the sects. Collins and members of his own cabinet advised patience, but this counsel only persuaded Diem that he could not trust any lieutenants other than members of his family. Diem denied to Collins that he was governing with his brothers, and he told Collins that "he had to act before the situation got worse." Once more Collins urged him not to move militarily against the Binh Xuyen gangs. Collins warned ominously that the Prime Minister "was making it very difficult for me to continue supporting his government. . . . [I]f he continued his present course we would be under heavy pressure to support a change in the government. If it were not for refugees, for whom we have heavy responsibility, I feared I might have to recommend a change in the government." Diem did not reply.[52]

Some of the pressure against the Prime Minister came from the French, whose low opinion of Diem had fallen even further as he had refused to enlarge his government. On the night of March 29–30 fighting broke out between the Vietnamese National Army and the Binh Xuyen police in the Cholon district. Ely sent French armored units into the street to stop further fighting. On March 31 Ely told Collins that "Diem must be induced to be more conciliatory and agree to enter negotiations looking toward enlarging his government. Otherwise the country is headed for civil war."[53]

Over the next week, Collins and Ely followed separate paths to the same goal—a peaceful resolution of the impasse between Diem and the sects. Both generals wanted Diem to reverse course and pull back from military confrontation with the sects. Failing that, they would remove support from Diem—the French enthusiastically, Collins reluctantly. A stubborn and distrustful Diem refused to budge. Moreover, American and French generals were not the sole western advisers to the government of Vietnam; Lansdale and Fishel bolstered Diem's resolve to remain firm in his campaign against the sects. On April 7 Collins cabled Dulles that he had finally come to the conclusion that "Diem does not have the capacity to achieve the necessary unity of purpose and action from his people which is essential to prevent this country from falling under Communist control." Collins's summary judgment of Diem foreshadowed much of the later U.S. efforts to control the government of South Vietnam. The United States engaged in an elusive and ultimately futile quest for a leader in Vietnam strong enough to stand on his own but simultaneously willing to take advice from the United States. Diem, Collins noted, has valuable spiritual qualities, is incorruptible, is a devoted Nationalist, has great tenacity. However, these very qualities, linked with his lack of practical political sense, his inability to compromise, his inherent incapacity to get along with other able men, and his tendency to be suspicious of the motives of anyone who disagrees with him, make him incapable of holding the government together. . . . *He pays more attention to the advice of his brothers Luyen and Nhu than he does to General Ely or me.*[54]

Collins's new view that Diem no longer deserved U.S. support alarmed Washington. Secretary Dulles and his principal Southeast Asia advisers believed that the United States had too much invested in Diem to turn back. Eisenhower, who relied on both Collins and Dulles for advice, was torn. Accordingly, the State Department arranged for Collins to return to Washington to discuss the future of U.S. support for the Diem government. Waiting for Collins upon his arrival was a "Dear Joe" letter from Dulles reminding the ambassador that "Diem was picked not by us but by the French. We backed him and backed him 100% because (a) nobody better appeared on the horizon, and (b) because no one can survive without wholehearted backing."[55] Yet in a series of meetings from April 22 to April 26, Collins nearly prevailed in turning Washington against Diem. Shortly after 6:00 p.m. on April 27, the State Department cabled the embassies in Saigon and Paris to withdraw support from Diem and replace him and his brothers with Phan Huy Quat and Tran Van Do, two officials with wider popular appeal to the Buddhists.[56]

Six hours after the original messages left Washington for Saigon cutting off support for Diem, Secretary Dulles blocked the order with two additional telegrams telling the embassies in Paris and Saigon to wait for further instructions. The Secretary of State's reversal came amidst receipt of news that Diem had ordered his soldiers to attack the Binh Xuyen, and it appeared that government troops had gained the upper hand. Diem had moved after hearing rumors that Collins had gone to Washington to dump him. The role of Lansdale in persuading Diem that the hour to strike was at hand remains shrouded in secrecy. Someone in Washington probably used the back-channel line that Lansdale had established to communicate with Washington independently of Collins to alert the cia operation in Saigon that the State Department had decided to drop Diem. Alerted immediately by Lansdale, Diem poured much of his army into the battle against the Binh Xuyen in Cholon.[57]

By April 30 Diem had clearly won, and Dulles cabled the embassies in Saigon and Paris that "American opinion is increasingly opposed to removal of Diem at this juncture."[58] A good soldier, Collins obeyed, but his opinion of Diem had not changed. In his final report from Saigon he offered a chilling vision of the future of the South under Diem's leadership:

I still feel that even if Diem manages to suppress Binh Xuyen, this will not change his own basic incapacity to manage the affairs of government. His present success may make it harder for us to persuade Diem to take competent men into government, to decentralize authority to his ministers, and to establish sound procedures for the implementation of reform programs. I am still convinced Diem does not have the knack of handling men nor the executive capacity truly to unify the country and establish an effective government. If this should be evident, we should either withdraw from Vietnam because our money will be wasted, or we should take such steps as can legitimately be taken to secure an effective new Premier.

Finally, Collins reminded Washington of the main objective in Vietnam, "to assist in saving the country from Communism." He believed that only cooperation and coordination among the Americans, French, and Vietnamese would work. "If this tripartite approach is not secure, we should withdraw from Vietnam."[59]

Dulles and Eisenhower chose not to follow Collins's prescient advice. It is hard to see how they could have done so, given their perception of the importance of Southeast Asia in the struggle against communism. Seeing no clear-cut alternative to Diem and wishing to preserve what the United States had already invested in Vietnam, the Americans became more committed to Diem over the next five years. As Collins predicted, the deepening U.S. support coincided with greater rigidity on Diem's part. His government became more closed off from other Vietnamese, and he finally broke with the French and Bao Dai. Fortified with increasing amounts of U.S. financial and military assistance, Diem embarked on building a separate nation, the Republic of Vietnam, south of the seventeenth parallel.

NATION-BUILDING IN THE SOUTH

Diem's defeat of the sects allowed him to consolidate his power. The last French troops departed in 1955. Thereafter Diem eliminated Emperor Bao Dai, created a separate Republic of Vietnam south of the seventeenth parallel, and refused to participate in the elections scheduled in 1956 by the Geneva conference. U.S. military and economic assistance fortified national police and the reconstituted Vietnamese National Army (renamed the Army of the Republic of Vietnam.) Diem used his armed forces and police to destroy the vestiges of the Vietminh forces left in the South. This "Denounce the Communists" campaign caused Vietminh leaders both south and north of the seventeenth parallel to reevaluate their strategy for obtaining power peacefully. By 1959 the communists remaining in the South had commenced a guerrilla war against the Republic of Vietnam. In 1960 they formally created a political organization, the National Front for the Liberation of Vietnam, to coordinate the revolutionary war against Diem. After considerable hesitation the communist authorities in Hanoi supported the efforts of their fellow revolutionaries south of the seventeenth parallel to topple Diem by force.

The United States used the five years after Diem's victory over the sects to pursue plans for what officials characterized as "nation-building"—the creation of a viable state, with legitimate political authority, a functioning economy, and a growing sense of community among different social classes, ethnic groups and religions. U.S. officials reasoned that if nation-building succeeded in creating a sturdy Republic of Vietnam, Southeast Asia would avoid the dire consequences of the domino effect outlined by Eisenhower during the Dienbienphu crisis. Most American policy-makers and opinion-leaders believed that the United States faced a stark choice should nation-building fail: either see communist regimes throughout Southeast Asia or enter Vietnam with large numbers of U.S. soldiers. Both prospects seemed so unappealing for U.S. officials that they misled themselves into believing that Diem exercised more effective leadership than he actually did.

Almost immediately after Diem defeated the sects, European observers criticized him as a creature of the Americans. Graham Greene reported on Vietnamese affairs in the (London) *Sunday Times*. He admired Diem for his incorruptibility and his Catholic faith, but he thought that the Prime Minister's piety "has been exploited by his American advisers until the Church is in danger of sharing the unpopularity of the United States. . . . An impression is given that the Catholic Church is occidental and an ally of the United States in the cold war." He contrasted Ho Chi Minh of the North, who reminded him, astonishingly, of Mr. Chips—"wise, kind, just"—with Diem. Greene expressed some sympathy for Diem, "for in a Saigon where there is nothing else but politics he represents at least an idea of patriotism." Yet Diem had separated himself from ordinary Vietnamese "by cardinals and police cars with wailing sirens and foreign advisers droning of global strategy." Sorrowfully, Greene characterized Diem as "the Patriot Ruined by the West."[60]

The question of the possibility of the unification of the two parts of divided Vietnam arose immediately after Diem's victory over the sects. Senator Mike Mansfield, one of Diem's strongest supporters in Washington, stated publicly that he doubted whether elections would occur before July 20, 1956 as promised at Geneva. He predicted the revival of civil war between Diem and the Vietminh. He believed that Diem needed an armed force of approximately one hundred thousand men to resist the communists. He advocated all means short of the deployment of U.S. combat forces to assist Diem, going even so far as to contemplate supplying the Diem with atomic weapons "if Ho had them and used them." The British Foreign Office considered "outrageous" the senator's thinking out loud about handing over nuclear weapons "to a small power like South Vietnam for a civil war." London expressed particular concern that such speculations and the apparent advice to Diem not to hold elections in 1956 came from Mansfield ''who has a reputation for being fairly steady and well informed.''[61]

The domino theory remained the dominant interpretation of events in Indochina for Americans. Only rarely did people treat the possiblity of falling dominoes skeptically. Newspaper columnist Joseph Alsop became one of its most persistent advocates. (Indeed, as late as 1971 President Richard Nixon, hardly a dove, considered him ''crazy'' on the issue of Vietnam).[62] In 1955 Alsop extended the danger of falling dominoes beyond Asia to the stability of India, the Middle East, Western Europe, and the future of the Western Alliance. This was too much for CBS New reporter Eric Severeid, who told Alsop that his fears reminded him of the story about the man who

> asked his doctor to give him a dose of the clap. The doctor said, ''I'm often asked to cure it, but this is the first time I've ever been asked to give it to anybody.''
> ''Well,'' said the fellow, ''There's a guy I hate.''
> ''I don't get it,'' said the doctor.
> ''It's this way: You give it to me, see. I'll give it to the old lady; I know she'll give it to Jacobson, the butcher; he'll give it to Mrs. Jacobson; she's bound to give it to that Baptist preacher on the corner, and *that's* the son of a bitch I'm after.''

Alsop replied that he did not think the story was very funny for the Baptist preacher, and besides the ''mass of Communist literature'' led him to believe that the communists did indeed plan what he called a ''backdoor attack on the West.''[63]

The government of Ngo Dinh Diem had little time for such geopolitical speculations as the Prime Minister consolidated his power. On October 23, 1955 the government held a referendum on the question, ''Do the people wish to depose Bao Dai and recognize Ngo Dinh Diem as the Chief of State of Vietnam with the mission to install a democratic regime?'' The election was rigged; no opposition leaflets or rallies were permitted. The question carried 98 percent of the vote. In one jurisdiction with four hundred thousand registered voters, six hundred thousand votes were counted.[64] Nevertheless, on October 26 Diem proclaimed the establishment of the Republic of Vietnam with himself as president to replace the monarchy. The following March Diem held elections for an assembly and a new constitution. Approximately 90 of the 123 members of the constituent assembly supported Diem.[65]

The elections promised throughout Vietnam by the Geneva agreements slipped away. Diem never wanted to measure his popularity against Ho's. The United States too had little use for elections throughout Vietnam. A few days after Diem's successful coup against the sects, the State Department called on Diem's government to ''center its position'' on elections, ''on insistence that the Communists agree to conditions which will guarantee genuinely free elections. If the Communists will not agree to such conditions, the United States believes that Free Vietnam should not allow itself to be draw prematurely into discussion of other questions relating to elections."[66]

Diem had no intention of being drawn at any time into a discussion of elections. He opposed them because he believed that Ho Chi Minh might exercise even tighter control over voters north of the seventeenth parallel than Diem did over voters south of the line. The American Friends of Vietnam opposed elections on the grounds that they had been promised by France, not a Vietnamese authority. Senator John F. Kennedy (D., Mass.) told the American Friends of Vietnam at a dinner that the United States should oppose anything proposed by France, a country which had presided over "centuries of colonial exploitation" in which they had pursued "deliberate policies of illiteracy." Kennedy went on to characterize South Vietnam as the "finger in the dike" keeping "the red tide of Communism" from washing over all of Southeast Asia.[67]

The communist authorities in the North publicly called for discussions leading to implementation of the plans for elections, but privately they acknowledged that Diem, with American backing, had no intention of submitting the fate of his rule to voters throughout the country. Foreign Minister Pham Van Dong told a foreign visitor, "You know as well as I do that there won't be elections."[68] Nor did North Vietnam receive more than token support for elections from the Soviet Union, ostensibly its backer, and cochair with Britain of the Geneva conference. British Foreign Minister Harold Macmillan found it "very odd" that Soviet Foreign Minister Molotov offered only half-hearted support for elections and unification in Vietnam. Macmillan surmised that his counterpart did not want international scrutiny of his contradictory policy of urging "unification based on free elections in Vietnam and resisting the same proposal in relation to Germany."[69]

A visit by Vice President Richard Nixon to Saigon in July 1956 further demonstrated U.S. support for Diem's government. The British Foreign Office, still smarting from the collapse of the Geneva elections proposal, sourly noted that Nixon's visit fortified "the view of the neutralist countries and some others that Diem continues to exist solely by dint of sitting on the knees of the U.S.A. like a ventriloquist's dummy."[70]

No elections took place, and over the next several years the United States expanded its aid to the Republic of Vietnam through private and governmental agents. Wesley Fishel, a close adviser to Diem, had his university sponsor an extensive technical-assistance program for the new republic. In 1955 the government of Vietnam and the U.S. Foreign Operations Administration signed contracts with the Michigan State University Group (MSUG) to provide advice in public administration and police training. The MSUG operated in Vietnam from May 1955 to June 1962. During the peak of its operations the

MSUG employed approximately fifty to sixty advisers, five to eight of whom at any time were actually agents of the Central Intelligence Agency. These operatives provided paramilitary training to mountain tribes people and dropped agents into North Vietnam. The most controversial element of both the CIA and civilian activities of the MSUG involved the training of South Vietnamese police and civil guards. The rural police forces became one of Diem's favorite elements in suppressing political dissent. The Americans tried to create a professional police force of approximately thirty thousand men to provide security in the countryside, but Diem wanted a larger and better armed force of about fifty thousand men, similar to the U.S. National Guard, who would more aggressively pursue opponents of the Saigon government.[71]

The United States also encouraged economic development in South Vietnam, although the results were mixed at best. American agricultural expert Wolf Ladejinski, a friend of Diem's, encouraged him to limit rents in the countryside and distribute land to peasants. Such issues bored the President, who considered his political standing more important. Diem also resisted Ladejinski's efforts to delegate more responsibility "on the grounds that the Vietnamese had little administrative ability." Diem told the U.S. land reform representative that he "deplored the deterioration of the mandarin system."[72] Rent control and the "land to the tiller" program also failed to strike a responsive chord with landlords or peasants. The former had not been able to collect their rents during the years of civil war, and they therefore resented government efforts to curtail what they could receive now that peace had come to the countryside. The peasants, for their part, believed that the communists offered more.[73]

The United States sought to bolster the Saigon government by channeling millions of dollars into South Vietnam's economy through the Commercial Import Program (CIP). Under CIP, Vietnamese importers deposited local Vietnamese piasters into special "counterpart funds" in Saigon. The counterpart funds could then be used to purchase U.S. goods for use in Vietnam. The South Vietnamese government also collected import duties on these goods. The U.S. government directly subsidized American exporters who sent their products to South Vietnam. U.S. officials hoped that CIP would foster economic expansion in South Vietnam while avoiding inflation, since U.S. dollars would not freely circulate in the South. In the period 1955–1960 the United States provided about $1 billion in counterpart funds (through the subsidies) and tens of millions in direct aid. While inflation did not develop, neither did the economy of South Vietnam take off into self-sufficient development. Many of the purchases made by the emerging South Vietnamese middle class were of consumer products rather than machinery that could be used to develop local industry. Some counterpart funds were stolen. By far the bulk of CIP went to fund the growing needs of South Vietnam's military.[74]

THE GROWING U.S. MILITARY COMMITMENT TO DIEM

In 1957 Ngo Dinh Nhu and Ngo Dinh Diem made separate visits to the United States. Before Nhu's arrival, Acting Secretary of State Christian Herter told Eisenhower that "Vietnam is our newest and one of our staunchest friends in Asia and we have great reason to be satisfied with President Diem's performance."[75] In May Diem made a triumphant two week visit to the United States. Eisenhower met him at the airport, and the South Vietnamese President addressed a joint meeting of Congress. He went to New York for a parade and a private Mass celebrated by Cardinal Spellman. He then traveled to East Lansing, Michigan, for a dinner in his honor hosted by Michigan State University. He inspected the dams of the Tennessee Valley Authority before flying to Los Angeles for more speeches and dinners. He ended his American tour in Hawaii, where he was the guest of the commander of the Pacific Fleet.

Diem's visit had a serious as well as a ceremonial side. In a series of conversations with Eisenhower, Dulles and high State Department officials in charge of Vietnam policy, Diem was gloomy and demanded additional American support. He wanted assurances that the current U.S. aid level of $250 million per year, of which $170 million went for the military, would be maintained. He needed a land army of 170,000 men and a highway system to move them quickly about the countryside. He failed to see the humor in Eisenhower's half-joking reference to the old military adage "that roads sometimes were a 'golden bridge for your enemies.'" Diem thought that any resumption of military activity by the North Vietnamese required powerful ground forces. He told the Americans that "because of the poor visibility of low cloud cover prevailing though most of the year, it would be difficult if not impossible to give adequate air support to the ground forces." He also expressed regret that "it would not be possible to use tactical atomic weapons" against any attack from North Vietnam through Laos, "since there would be no concentrated targets suitable for A-bomb attacks."[76]

While Diem fortified his position with the Americans, he campaigned against domestic opponents, especially Vietminh operatives who remained south of the seventeenth parallel after the Geneva agreements. At the beginning of his premiership in 1954 Diem launched a "Denounce the Communists" campaign, resulting in the arrest of 25,000 supporters of the Vietminh. Diem's police and civil guard killed approximately 1,000 and injured 4,231 Vietminh operatives by 1956. Diem also entrusted his brother Ngo Dinh Nhu to organize a political movement to combat communism. Nhu developed an ideology called "personalism," combining aspects of Catholicism and Marxism. Claiming that personalism married Asian views of communal responsibility to Western ideas of individual liberty,[77] Nhu favored long, windy expositions of his doctrines, in which he stressed "the transcendent, spiritual vocation of man and the need to provide the material minimum indispensable for his economic well being." Nhu often derided "traditional Oriental philosophies" for ignoring material needs while "confining [people's] attention only to the spiritual side of man's nature."[78]

THE REVOLUTIONARIES' DILEMMA

Diem's assertiveness disrupted the political plans of Ho Chi Minh and his associates in Hanoi. On the one hand Hanoi wanted to concentrate on political competition with the regime in the South, avoid the costs of renewed warfare, and build support for the communist regime in the North. "We must not allow the winning of the South to detract from the requirements of consolidating the North."[79] The North set up several autonomous zones among mountain people in the country designed to strengthen their ties to the government in Hanoi. The U.S. embassy in Saigon perceived the creation of these zones as "a potentially important line of propaganda directed at minority groups in Free Vietnam." The French representative in Hanoi concluded that Ho Chi Minh seemed more interested in "correcting mistakes in the regime than in sustaining Vietminh hopes for any imminent or speedy reunification with the South." A popular uprising against the authorities in Nghe An province midway between Hanoi and the seventeenth parallel, a region which had long been a center of nationalist sentiment, also worried Ho Chi Minh. The North Vietnamese government admitted cruelties in its land reform program and an "insensitive attitude toward its Catholic population."[80]

On the other hand, Hanoi perceived a grave threat from Diem, whom northern officials described as "dangerously crafty and different from the previous puppets" who had served the French or the Japanese. The South's Denounce the Communists campaign proved an even greater danger to the political fortunes and physical well being of communists south of the seventeenth parallel. In September 1956 General O'Daniel, head of the MAAG, reported that "the Vietminh's strength in Free Vietnam was rapidly decreasing."[81] Beginning in the winter of 1955–1956 Le Duan, the highest ranking Vietminh leader in the South and also a member of the Politburo of the Vietnam Workers Party (Lao Dong) of the North, urged the leadership of the DRV to send more organizers south of the seventeenth parallel and contemplate responding to Diem's raids with military action and local terrorism. Communist party officials debated Duan's requests off and on for a year until deciding in late 1956 to retain the policy of peaceful struggle in the South.

Duan grudgingly accepted Hanoi's request that the communists in the South resist a premature uprising against the Diem government, yet his submission to the party line could barely conceal the concern he and other southern communists felt as they saw Diem's power grow. In December 1956 Duan released a pamphlet entitled *The Path of Revolution in the South,* in which he called for more assertive political confrontation with Diem. While not formally abandoning the North's stated policy of peaceful struggle with the Saigon government, Duan called for the development of a revolutionary movement based on organizing the peasantry against the government. The corruption and inefficiency of the government's Civic Action Program of reducing rents and distributing some land to farmers offered an opening for the Communist Party in the South. Yet the Vietminh moved slowly to encourage seizures of land from the gentry in the countryside. In 1956 the communists in the South still hoped to create a coalition of the poorest peasants with some of the lesser gentry. Moreover, in 1956 the North Vietnamese cabinet admitted "serious mistakes in agrarian reform" among peasants in the North. Communist cadres had offended many of the middle-level gentry by the brutality with which they had seized land.[82]

Fighting between the communists and the government flared during 1957. Diem sent units of the Army of the Republic of Vietnam (ARVN) into communist strongholds in the Plain of Reeds, the Ca Mau, and the area north of Saigon. The ARVN killed about 2,000 suspected communists and arrested another 65,000 people by the end of 1957. Party membership fell from about 5,000 to around 1,700 throughout the year. U.S. Socialist Party leader Norman Thomas, a member of the American Friends of Vietnam, complained to his longtime personal friend Secretary of State John Foster Dulles about the government of Vietnam's "high handed actions against individual liberty." The U.S. embassy noted "increasing stridency in recent drv propaganda." U.S. officials believed that the North resented the "Government of Vietnam's gains and psychological advantages accruing from Diem's trip."[83]

In desperation the communists of the South regrouped and ordered a wave of assassinations of local officials, killing several hundred. By the end of 1957 Saigon officials labeled the fighters the Vietcong.[84] At the end of the year General Samuel T. Williams, the new head of the MAAG, reported that "the present military posture of Vietnam is not too strong."[85] In 1958 the Vietcong continued to respond to arvn attacks with small arms fire. Occasionally the Vietcong launched attacks of their own.

Le Duan surveyed the military situation in the South in early 1959 for the North Vietnamese Workers Party. He concluded that "it was time to resort to armed struggle combined with political struggle to push the movement forward."[86] Yet differences of opinion remained between Le Duan and the North Vietnamese leaders. Duan wanted to protect his fighters in the South by commencing an aggressive military campaign against the Diem government and kidnapping, torturing, and killing local officials. Back in Hanoi the ever-patient Ho Chi Minh still counseled caution. Ho thought that the Diem government's unpopularity held out a small but real possibility that it might fall without too much of a push from armed adversaries. Le Monde, reflecting the view common among French officials that both Vietnamese regimes had botched their efforts to consolidate popular support since 1954, reported on the fifth anniversary of the Geneva agreements that the infiltration of communist organizers from the North to the South "constituted a real danger" to the Republic of Vietnam.[87]

Nevertheless, Workers Party leaders of the North gradually adopted the view in 1959 that the communists of the South had to protect themselves from the ARVN, expand their numbers, and enlarge the harrassment of the Diem government if they hoped to displace it. By the middle of 1959 communists in the North and the South spoke openly of a revolutionary war against Diem. They contemplated a protracted war, which included military and political means. At first the communists expected small engagements which would gradually expand into battles between large troop concentrations. The war would proceed from the countryside to the small towns until a climactic attack on the cities of the South would defeat the government of Vietnam.[88]

Throughout 1959 the North increased the pace of infiltration into the South of some ninety thousand Vietminh cadres who had gone North after Geneva. After they reached the South they organized numerous demonstrations and occasional terrorist attacks against ARVN installations. By the end of the year they had caused four thousand casualties among gvn officials and ARVN troops. Ambassador Elbridge Durbrow, usually an optimistic booster of Diem's prospects, reported that internal security had become the primary problem of South Vietnam in 1960. He blamed "intensification of Viet Cong guerrilla and terrorist activities, weakness apparent in the GVN security forces and the growth of apathy and considerable dissatisfaction among the rural populace" for the weakening position of the government.[89]

DIEM'S UNPOPULARITY

Diem's government responded by creating rural development centers or "agrovilles." These encampments of three hundred to five hundred families attempted to deprive Vietcong guerrillas of their most fruitful fields of recruitment while giving South Vietnam's peasants the benefits of improved educational, health, and sanitary services. The ever-hopeful Edward Lansdale thought that there was "a lot of imagination, good planning, and hard work going into" the agrovilles project.[90] Peasants did not share Lansdale's enthusiasm. Instead of binding rural residents to Saigon, the agrovilles became another point of tension between the capital and the countryside. Peasants disliked leaving their ancestral homes for sterile, concrete huts, which they had to build themselves. Peasants protested against the agroville program, which was suspended by late 1960.[91]

Diem's inability to generate popularity in the countryside and his adamant refusal to delegate responsibility to anyone other than his brothers caused frustrations within the ARVN. Junior officers resented the "failure of the GVN to handle the VC threat, politics in military matters and the failure to announce traditional promotions."[92] The unhappiness of some officers boiled over on November 11, 1960, when two colonels ordered paratroopers under their command to attack the presidential palace in Saigon at 3:30 A.M. The attackers quickly isolated Diem, Nhu, and Madame Nhu in the wine cellar, but instead of capturing or killing them, the colonels only demanded that they agree to reform their government and allow more press and personal freedoms. Diem readily acceded to their demands in order to restore communications with loyal ARVN commanders. By 9:40 A.M. Diem's voice could be heard over the radio calling for tank units to proceed to the center of Saigon. They did so and the coup fizzled. Most of the rebel paratroopers fled to Cambodia. Diem arrested the leaders and reneged on his promises to reform his government. Foreign diplomats in Saigon worried that "Diem might leave no stone unturned in an effort to erase all opposition to his regime."[93]

Lansdale concluded that the coup had taught Diem to distrust the way in which the MAAG had trained the ARVN, since some of its important officers were willing to take up arms against him. Lansdale believed that Diem might blame Durbrow for having "sided with the revolters emotionally." He suggested recalling Durbrow and replacing him with someone in whom Diem had confidence, Lansdale himself. The new administration of John F. Kennedy, elected in November to take office in January 1961, made good on part of this suggestion, recalled Durbrow, and listened attentively to Lansdale's suggestions for more aggressive U.S. support for Diem. For his part, Durbrow heard more of Diem's rambling monologues in which he denounced his local rivals and the international press. The U.S. ambassador seemed even more gloomy at the end of the year. "Just below the surface," he reported, "there is much talk about another coup unless Diem relaxes some controls, puts in effective reforms, takes more effective action to fight VC and gives protection to the population."[94]

THE NATIONAL LIBERATION FRONT

Before the change of administrations in Washington took place a more momentous change occurred in the political landscape of South Vietnam. The communist leadership of North Vietnam dropped more of its opposition to full-scale revolutionary warfare in the South. The Vietnam Workers Party held its third congress in September 1960 and chose Le Duan as general secretary. He delivered a general report on the Party's strategy in the South which he characterized as a "long and arduous struggle, not simple but complex, combining many forms of struggle." General Vo Nguyen Giap, the victor at Dienbienphu and now the Defense Minister of North Vietnam, still advised caution in face of "the plots of United States imperialism and their lackeys." Giap favored achieving peaceful reunification while preparing "to cope with any maneuver of the enemy." In the fall of 1960 the Workers Party resurrected the Central Office for South Vietnam (COSVN), the southern branch of the party's Central Committee. Communists created a unified military structure to supervise the new People's Liberation Armed Forces (PLAF). The PLAF combined local southern communists with remnants of the sects to engage the ARVN.[95]

In order to coordinate the non-military struggle in the South, the party organized a political group which it hoped would galvanize a broad spectrum of anti-Diem sentiment. On December 20, 1960 representatives of the religious sects, some Buddhist and Catholic organizations dissatisfied with Diem's high-handedness, women's groups, the South Vietnam Democratic Party, and the Radical Socialist Party (two parties created by the communists) created the National Front for the Liberation of Vietnam (NLF).[96]

The creation of the PLAF and the NLF set the stage for the second Indochina war. The communists of the North now appeared ready to reunify the country, a project that had been interrupted but not halted by the Geneva agreements. The Geneva conference represented a truce, not a settlement of the conflict. The United States had become ever more deeply involved in setting the political agenda in Vietnam. The government of Ngo Dinh Diem represented the culmination of the U.S. efforts to find a third force, nationalists but not communist or tied to the French. The Diem government's performance demonstrated the few strengths and many weaknesses of the effort to create a third force. Honest and incorruptible, Diem did express sincere nationalist sentiments, yet his personal characteristics also made him a singularly unlikely candidate to build a nation. He lacked political skills, treated non-Catholic Vietnamese with contempt, and refused to enlarge his government to include representatives from other factions. His nationalism and stubbornness made him far more independent of the Americans than the "lackey" of communist broadcasts, editorials, and cartoons. His very independence drove successive American emissaries nearly to despair. Collins wanted to drop him in 1955 and Durbrow doubted whether he was up to the job in 1960. Yet neither U.S. representative questioned the principal flaw in the U.S. strategy of nation-building: The United States had embarked on the impossible task of creating a separate state and society in the southern part of a single land.

Chapter

*   *   *   *   *   *   *   *   *   *   *

From Support to
Intervention: 1961–1963

*T*HE NEW administration of John F. Kennedy vastly expanded the U.S.
commitment to support the Republic of South Vietnam in its war against the
National Liberation Front. Kennedy, along with most foreign affairs experts
of the late 1950s and early 1960s, believed that the Cold War was a global
struggle: events were interconnected, and weakness in the face of communist
adversaries' moves encouraged aggression elsewhere. Furthermore, many of
the more assertive American Cold Warriors believed that a languorous President Eisenhower had underestimated the growing threat to U.S. interests
posed by revolutionaries supported by the Soviet Union and China. Soviet
Communist Party General Secretary Nikita Khrushchev's promise at the beginning of 1961 to offer material support for revolutionaries waging ''wars of
national liberation'''reinforced these foreign affairs experts' sense of peril to
the United States.[1]

President Kennedy and his principal foreign affairs advisers considered
the communist-nationalist insurrection in South Vietnam part of this global
competition. Himself an early member of the American Friends of Vietnam,
the young President considered Vietnam and all of Southeast Asia a key arena
in the contest between communism and the West. By themselves the National
Liberation Front and North Vietnam posed no threat to the United States. But
they challenged the legitimacy of the Republic of Vietnam, a friendly government created largely by American actions. Victory for the NLF and North

Vietnam would mean a major gain for the Soviet Union and for China and an equivalent setback for the United States.

From the perspective of the 1990s, the Kennedy administration's obsession with communism and local revolutions seems tragically overblown, but the Cold War was real in 1961. While they differed occasionally over tactics, all American officials and nearly all elements of elite opinion believed that the Soviet Union and, to a lesser extent, China militarily threatened the United States. Kennedy administration officials perceived the growing rift between China and the Soviet Union, but their understanding of that split only intensified their opposition to Southeast Asian revolutions. American officials believed that with Moscow and Beijing bidding for the support of local revolutionaries, these insurrections could only gather strength, and the success of one would embolden revolutionaries elsewhere.

In September 1959, while planning his run for the presidency, Kennedy became one of four senators who delivered to all the other members of the U.S. Senate copies of William Lederer's and Eugene Burdick's best selling 1957 novel, *The Ugly American.* As a literary achievement the book fell far short of Graham Greene's *The Quiet American,* the book whose title Lederer and Burdick modified for their own work, but as political propaganda setting the stage for a war, *The Ugly American* had an impact similar to that of Harriet Beecher Stowe's *Uncle Tom's Cabin* in the years before the American Civil War.

The authors, both former naval officers, had experience in Asia. Lederer had recently retired as special assistant to the commander-in-chief of the Pacific Fleet while Burdick taught the government and institutions of Southeast Asia in the department of political science at the University of California at Berkeley. The ugliness of the title referred to the smug self-satisfaction and cultural insularity of many American foreign-service officers and foreign-assistance workers. Lederer and Burdick set the story in the mythic Southeast Asian country of Sarkhan, but the authors often referred explicitly to the French war with the Vietminh. Among the few Americans in the story who do not strut, preen, and isolate themselves in a "golden ghetto" from the concerns of the locals was the air force colonel, Edwin B. Hillendale, whose character was patterned even more closely than Greene's Alden Pyle on the life of Edward Lansdale. Kennedy admired Hillendale's intensity and persistence in working directly with Sarkanese peasants to foil a communist-led insurrection. Maybe, Kennedy hoped, real-life Hillendales could thwart a real insurrection in South Vietnam.[2]

Lansdale, the model for Hillendale, continued his longstanding interest in Vietnam with a visit to the country from January 2 to 14, 1961. He urged the new administration to "recognize that Vietnam is in a critical condition and should treat it as a combat area of the cold war, . . . requiring emergency treatment."[3] Kennedy met Lansdale at the White House a few days after his inauguration on January 20. When Deputy National Security Adviser Walt Rostow gave Kennedy a copy of Lansdale's report, the President read it in horrified fascination. Rostow recalls that after Kennedy read the report, he looked up and said "You know, this is the worst one we've got, isn't it? You know Eisenhower never uttered the word Vietnam."[4] Kennedy was so taken by Lansdale that he urged National Security Adviser McGeorge Bundy to arrange for publication of a favorable story about his exploits in the Philippines in the *Saturday Evening Post*.[5] But not everyone was smitten by Lansdale. Shortly after the President read Lansdale's report, Graham Parsons, the State Department's expert on Vietnam, characterized him as a "flamboyant lone wolf and operator."[6]

However bad Lansdale considered the situation in Vietnam, it was Laos that became the first country in Southeast Asia to occupy the attention of the new administration. Under the terms of the Geneva agreements of 1954, Laos was supposed to be neutral, but the pro-Western, communist, and neutralist factions could not put aside their differences. Civil war broke out in mid-1959, with the United States playing a major role in installing a government in Vientiane. By late 1960 both the United States and the Soviet Union were delivering military supplies to opposing factions, and it appeared as if the landlocked kingdom of Laos would be the next battleground in the Cold War. Kennedy asked for a meeting with Eisenhower on January 19, 1961, the day before the inauguration, to strengthen his hand with the public. He wanted "to get some commitment from the outgoing administration as to how they would deal with Laos." Precisely what Eisenhower told his successor cannot be determined, because note takers present at the meeting disagreed about Eisenhower's advice. The initial accounts made public of the meeting record Eisenhower as recommending "as a last desperate hope, to intervene unilaterally" to prevent Laos from falling to the communists. Such a victory would "bring an unbelievable pressure to bear on Thailand, Cambodia and South Vietnam." But records declassified later offer a different picture of the outgoing president's advice. Secretary of Defense-designate Robert McNamara reported that "President Eisenhower advised *against* unilateral action by the United States in connection with Laos." In a sensitive analysis of the record, the political scientist Fred I. Greenstein and the historian Richard H. Immerman surmise that Eisenhower followed the pattern of thinking out loud about the potential benefits and costs of military intervention he set out during the period of the Dienbienphu crisis in 1954. He foresaw bad consequences from either a communist victory in Laos or unilateral military intervention by the United States. As was his practice when he did not have to make a decision, he deferred making a fateful choice. Now responsibility rested with his successor.[7]

DEFINING THE U.S. RELATIONSHIP WITH
PRESIDENT NGO DINH DIEM: 1961

Over the next eleven months the new Kennedy administration avoided intervention in Laos. The British supported a call by the Soviets for an international conference on Laos, although some of Kennedy's advisers counseled him to intervene militarily in the Laotian war. Deputy National Security Adviser Rostow recommended that the government "orchestrate diplomacy and force" in its approach to Laos.[8] Despite this recommendation, the United States agreed to participate in a Geneva conference on Laos. This meeting eventually proposed a neutralization of the country.[9] Despite its avoidance of a war in Laos, the new administration consistently increased its commitment to South Vietnam. By the end of the year the British Foreign Office warned that "there may come a time if this build-up goes on when it may be difficult to distinguish between support for Diem to win his own war and direct intervention."[10]

Paradoxically, the Kennedy administration provided greater support for Diem as the South Vietnamese public withdrew their backing for his regime. In early 1961 the Central Intelligence Agency observed "widening dissatisfaction" with Diem among the South Vietnamese. They believed that the same unhappiness with Diem's high-handedness, his refusal to share power, and his inability to suppress the rebellion made another coup by the noncommunist forces likely over the next year.[11] Even Diem's staunchest supporters thought his autocratic ways harmed him. Assistant Secretary of State Graham Parsons thought that Diem's incessant "monologue" in Vietnam had encouraged the rise of the opposition.[12] Lansdale, Diem's closest American friend, told him directly that the opposition sentiment in Saigon was "so ugly and bad that I am afraid that it will prompt some thoughtless persons to attempt another coup." Even more worrisome to Lansdale was Diem's efforts to arrest opponents and suppress their newspapers. Lansdale warned that these efforts "will only turn the talk into deep emotions of hatred and generate the formation of more clandestine organizations and plots to oppose you."[13] But Diem was unmoved after he won a presidential election on April 9 in which he received nearly 90 percent of the vote.[14]

The Kennedy administration responded to the increasingly desperate situation by creating a presidential task force on Vietnam, chaired by Deputy Secretary of Defense Roswell C. Gilpatric, and by sending Vice President Lyndon B. Johnson to Vietnam. Lansdale crafted a first draft of the Task Force Report which characterized the situation as "critical, but not hopeless."[15] He recommended a substantial increase in U.S. financial and military assistance. But not everyone was convinced that the United States should embark on a substantial program of military and financial assistance to South Vietnam. Theodore Sorensen, Kennedy's chief counsel, thought "we need a more *realistic* look." He believed that the planners unrealistically anticipated tying down the communist forces in Laos and Cambodia, and also doubted the task force's expectation that Diem would broaden the base of support of his government.

Sorensen observed that

> there is no clearer example of a country that cannot be saved unless it saves itself—through increased popular support; governmental, economic and military reforms and reorganizations; and the encouragement of new political leaders. We do not want Vietnam to fall—we do not want to add to Diem's burdens—and the chief purpose of insisting upon such conditions should not be saving of American dollars but the saving of Vietnam.

As the task force on Vietnam proceeded with its work, members believed that the United States needed to do more to prod Diem to enact reforms. Robert Komer of the National Security Council staff wondered, "if we are bailing Diem out, why aren't we entitled to *insist*" that he enact the economic reforms the Americans thought necessary to make his regime more popular.[16]

On May 1, the task force's recommendations went to the President. Its views reflected the consensus on a deteriorating situation in Vietnam. Vietcong attacks had increased over the past two years to the point "where South Vietnam is reaching the decisive phase in its battle for survival." Since the situation in Vietnam had approached a crisis, the task force recommended that "for the time being, primary emphasis must be placed on providing a solution to the internal security program." Nevertheless, the report thought that military means alone would not reverse the communist tide. The task force recommended that "an equally strong, equally positive political-economic program" supplement the military program.[17]

The task force also looked for ways to bolster Diem. It recommended that Vice President Johnson focus his impending trip to Vietnam on gaining Diem's confidence and obtaining "broad agreement on joint objectives in Southeast Asia." Like scores of officials who had earlier evaluated Diem, the members of the task force acknowledged the difficult position South Vietnam's president occupied because of the government's inability so far to stop guerrilla attacks. They also acknowledged that the NLF exploited Diem's own weaknesses. Yet Diem's shortcomings were real, and they consistently undermined his popularity. Having expressed sympathy for Diem's predicament, the task force sounded the same alarms that J. Lawton Collins expressed at the end of his tour of duty in Saigon in May 1955. Diem seemed incapable of bridging the communications void between the government and the people of South Vietnam. "For many months," the task force wrote, "United States efforts have been directed toward persuading Diem to adopt political, social and economic changes designed to correct this serious defect. . . . Our success has only been partial.'' Some of the experts on the task force believed that ''that Diem will not succeed in the battle to win men's minds in Vietnam.''[18]

On May 11, eleven days after the submission of this report, Kennedy approved National Security Action Memorandum 52, setting the contours of upcoming U.S. policy toward South Vietnam. NSAM-52 reaffirmed the general U.S. objective toward South Vietnam ''to prevent Communist domination . . . , and to initiate, on an accelerated basis, a series of mutually supporting actions of a military, political, economic, psychological and covert character designed to achieve this objective.''[19]

Vice President Johnson arrived in Vietnam the same day Kennedy approved NSAM-52 and remained until the morning of May 13. During the thirty-six hours he spent in Saigon, he delivered a letter to Diem from Kennedy and spoke at a public meeting. Kennedy's message reaffirmed the points made in NSAM-52 regarding a joint program of military, political, economic, psychological, and covert operations.[20] In his private conversations with Johnson, Diem launched into another interminable monologue about the history of the conflict, the difficulties he encountered with his own people, the interference of the Western press, and the slowness of the Americans to respond to his requests for military assistance. All the while, Johnson fidgeted and tried to get Diem to focus on the substance of Kennedy's offer. Eventually, Diem agreed about the high sense of urgency needed at the moment, but the overall impression he gave was of resistance to American interference. He suspected that the United States did not fully understand or appreciate the complexities of the political and social situation in his country. While he gave lip service to the idea that ''political and military action [was] of equal importance with military measures,'' he reminded Johnson that ''political and economic actions must be those appropriate to Vietnam.'' Beyond that, Diem pressed Johnson for a commitment of $200 million per year in military and economic aid, $30 million more than budgeted for 1961.[21]

In his public address, Johnson effusively praised Diem as ''the Winston Churchill of Southeast Asia.'' But even in these lavish remarks the Vice President noted the need for reform in the government of South Vietnam. The British ambassador to Saigon considered the Vice President's praise for Diem mere ''thickening paper over the cracks'' to hide some deep divisions between Washington and Saigon.[22] The *New Times* of Hanoi thought that Johnson's visit with Diem ''opens the way for the U.S. imperialists to introduce more weapons and military personnel into South Vietnam.'' Yet the Canadian ambassador in Saigon reported that American diplomats assured him in the wake of Johnson's visit that Washington had ''no intention of sending United States troops into Vietnam.''[23]

Johnson's report to Washington on his visit was more optimistic than the observations of the presidential task force. His impression of Vietnam reflected his sympathy for Diem and his distrust of journalists; both sentiments grew in later years, with significant consequences for U.S. policy. He found the "situation in Vietnam . . . more stable than is indicated by newspaper and other reports reaching Washington in recent weeks," and thought that the journalists were excessively nervous and obsessed with their own personal security, likenening their reporting from Saigon to the sometimes hysterical reports of murders in Washington's Rock Creek Park, events which may have been deplorable but which did not, by themselves, "mean that the United States is about to fall apart." Many of the journalists operating in Vietnam wanted the United States to offer more assistance than it presently provided, and the only way to generate more aid was to make the situation look as frightening as possible. The embassy in Saigon reinforced these fears by relying on reports from Saigon officials, many of whom also wanted to frighten Washington into supplying more aid. The Saigon government had forced the U.S. embassy into an unhealthy reliance on governmental sources because the South Vietnamese authorities had consciously discouraged travel outside Saigon by foreign embassy personnel.[24]

Unlike earlier delegates to Vietnam who focused on Diem's shortcomings, Johnson shared Secretary of State John Foster Dulles's view that the United States was too deeply committed to Diem to accept any alternative. Believing that Diem's regime was "the only realistic alternative to Vietminh control in South Vietnam," he thought the government of Vietnam possessed the will to pursue the war against the communists but lacked the most current methods and the organizational skills to overcome the Vietcong effectively. He detected differences between the commitment of the Ngo family, which he considered unwavering, and the more limited "self-dedication and self-sacrifice" of the rest of the South Vietnamese bureaucracy.[25]

But foreign observers disagreed with Johnson's optimistic assessment of Diem. Canadian representatives to the International Commission for Supervision and Control, established by the Geneva conference of 1954, noted shortly after Johnson left that "Diem's regime is rapidly losing whatever popular support it had in the past." The very skills which had served Diem well in the past—tenacity, willfulness and a messianic sense of a "divine mission of saving his country from Communism"—prevented him from broadening his appeal. His self-importance made him "virtually impervious to advice and criticism" from anyone outside his family or immediate entourage.[26]

While Johnson differed from the view prevailing among most diplomats and military officers that Diem lacked the political skills necessary to overcome the Vietcong, he also reinforced the conventional thinking that Vietnam needed a comprehensive program of military and diplomatic initiatives. He noted a disturbing trend on the part of the government to rely exclusively on military means to produce social stability. The authorities seemed to shy away from dramatic and potentially popular social and economic reforms. Evidence mounted that the government feared its own people as well as the Vietcong. The Vice President wondered whether the increased military aid might not encourage the ARVN to use its firepower even more indiscriminately against the Vietcong and anyone else who opposed the government. The predictable result would be to increase public dissatisfaction with the government and provide a great boost to claims that Diem's regime did not permit any sort of dissent. Johnson thought that Diem's current resistance to the idea of unification and neutralization of Vietnam made sense in the current situation. If the planned assistance to Vietnam worked, however, he believed that eventually Saigon might become less dependent on U.S. aid. Under such circumstances South Vietnam might "lay a valid claim to represent the entire Vietnamese people, north and south." That represented the best possible outcome. The alternative seemed very dark: "If these steps fail . . . we shall be able to hold even the present unsatisfactory situation only by larger and larger infusions of aid. Ultimately, perhaps, even our direct military involvement may be required to hold the situation."[27]

Johnson recommended what he characterized as a liberal but not extravagant three-year program of military and economic aid. He paid lip service to the need for respecting the sensitivities of the Vietnamese government, but he thought that the United States had to retain overall control of aid. The aim of the ambitious aid program had to be to persuade the Vietnamese government "from the President on down to get close to the people, to mingle with them, to listen for their grievances and to act on them." He believed the United States should insist on advanced agreement in writing with the South Vietnamese government on details involving specific, measurable goals. Johnson intended all these measures to convince the Vietnamese of the seriousness of the situation and their own responsibility to remedy it. The United States had to make it clear to the Vietnamese that "barring an unmistakable and massive invasion of South Vietnam from without we have no intention of employing combat U.S. forces in Vietnam." The lessons of the French experience seemed clear enough to Johnson in May 1961. The French had been unable to prevail with a force of several hundred thousand men, even though little appreciable Soviet or Chinese intervention had occurred.

Johnson anticipated some of the subsequent criticism of his own administration's later conduct of policy toward Vietnam after 1963. He urged that before the United States plunged into a war "we had better be sure we are prepared to become bogged down chasing irregulars and guerrillas over the rice fields and jungles of Southeast Asia while our principal enemies China and the Soviet Union stand outside the fray and husband their strength."[28]

Over the next four years Johnson and other policy-makers regularly repeated warnings like this one, yet these reservations merely slowed the growing U.S. commitment to the war. Most policy-makers believed the cost of a communist victory in Vietnam too high for the United States to bear. They also were serenely self-confident that they could discover a way to help the government of South Vietnam defend itself at a relatively low cost to the United States. In August 1961 foreign diplomats in Saigon heard American representatives predict that they would have the war "under control" within the next six to twelve months. British, French, and Canadian diplomats shook their heads in disbelief and pointed to the political weakness of Diem's government. The Americans told them not to worry, because "once military victory is assured the people [of South Vietnam], having gained confidence in the government, will offer a greater measure of support."[29]

STRATEGIC HAMLETS

While Johnson expressed concern but not panic over the extent of the communist insurrection in Vietnam, Deputy National Security Adviser Walt Rostow was alarmed. He told Kennedy that the "situation is extremely dangerous to the peace. . . . [W]e must push on all fronts to force a deflation of that crisis before it builds to a situation like that in Laos."[30] Rostow's assertive approach prevailed. Military aid rose form $220 million to $262 million for the rest of 1961.[31] The administration also pushed the deployment of Army Special Forces, called Green Berets because of their distinctive headgear, to South Vietnam. Their mission consisted of training the ARVN in the intricacies of fighting against guerrillas.

The CIA pressed forward with a program it had developed over the previous year for a program designed to help the villagers of South Vietnam defend themselves. William Colby, the CIA station chief in Saigon, originated the Citizens [or Civilians] Irregular Defense Groups (CIDGS). These were teams of local Vietnamese farmers who worked with Green Berets in a complicated scheme of irregular defensive operations. Colby also persuaded Diem to receive a six-member team of British counterinsurgency experts, led by Robert K. G. Thompson, who had wide experience in waging a counter insurgency in Malaya. They recommended the creation of strategic hamlets, concentrations of rural villagers behind sturdy barbed wire fences guarded by forces from the ARVN, the Green Berets, and the CIDGS. The hamlets reversed the government's previous strategy of going after the guerrillas by trying to isolate the rural population from the guerrillas.[32] As Douglas Blaufarb, an analyst of counter insurgency, put it, advocates of stategic hamlets self-consciously parodied Mao Zedong's advice to guerrillas to "swim in the sea of the peasantry": "As was repeated endlessly in public explanations of the plan, the purpose was to dry up the sea of friendly peasantry in which swam the VC 'fish.' "[33]

The Thompson mission immediately encountered difficulties. The Americans and South Vietnamese wanted speedy results, since officials in both Washington and Saigon considered the situation desperate. For their part, the British believed they had gone far beyond their position as skeptical observers of the growing U.S. involvement in Vietnam to sponsoring the visit of Thompson's mission. Thompson predicted that five painstaking years of effort "clearing one area after another on the Malay pattern" were necessary before the South Vietnamese government could triumph over the insurgents. He favored a strategy of "clear and hold" rather than the techniques of "search and destroy" previously advanced by the Americans, and offered a medical analogy in which "the remedy should be clinical rather than surgical." Thompson also believed that "the insurgency can only be overcome by the Vietnamese with, of course, extensive assistance from the U.S." Thompson agreed with the Americans that the stakes were extremely high. He offered the Canadian ambassador his own version of the domino theory: "The political effects of a successful campaign against the Viet Cong will spread far beyond Vietnam" to Malaya, Cambodia, Thailand, and the Philippines.[34]

U.S. ambassador Frederick Nolting in Saigon resented Thompson's interference in planning the war. Nolting believed that Thompson presented plans to Diem without prior coordination with the U.S. authorities. Given Diem's habitual delays in agreeing to concrete proposals, Thompson's end run around the Americans offered the Vietnamese President another opportunity to avoid making a firm commitment on aggressive deployment of ARVN forces. Elements of Thompson's proposals also seemed to delay the reforms most American advisers believed Diem desperately needed to make in his government. Thompson recommended direct control by Saigon over the counterinsurgency effort in the delta region south of the capital. Since the Americans continually urged Diem to delegate more authority to local military commanders, Nolting resisted any proposal which might diminish Diem's already tenuous desire to reform his government.[35]

Disagreements between Nolting and Thompson reflected differences among experts over the proper tactics to defeat the Vietcong. By the end of 1961, however, there was widespread agreement among officials that the United States needed to do more to help the government of South Vietnam wage the war more aggressively. Otherwise, many observers believed, "the Communists could march in at any time and take over."[36] Deputy National Security Adviser Walt Rostow favored an aggressive approach, including the dispatch of a force between five thousand and twenty-five thousand U.S. soldiers to Vietnam. Rostow considered the recent settlement of the war in Laos to have further weakened South Vietnamese morale.[37] Yet most of Kennedy's advisers and the President himself shied away from a direct commitment of ground forces.[38]

THE TAYLOR REPORT

Instead, Kennedy sent a special mission to Vietnam headed by the army's General Maxwell Taylor. A prominent critic of the Eisenhower administration's efforts to reduce the size of the army, Taylor found Kennedy much more receptive than Eisenhower to his belief that the United States should adopt a more assertive new military posture. Taylor's ideas of flexible response, employing a whole array of military options, seemed the perfect complement to Rostow's belief that the developing world represented the new arena of the Cold War.[39] Taylor headed a mission including Rostow and Lansdale that left for Vietnam on October 15. The President's instructions ordered Taylor to "evaluate what could be accomplished by the introduction of SEATO or United States forces into Vietnam."[40]

En route to Saigon, Taylor's delegation stopped in Hawaii for a briefing from Admiral Harry D. Felt, the commander-in-chief of the Pacific Fleet. Felt considered the situation in Vietnam critical; it could be saved only with substantially more U.S. assistance. While reluctant to deploy combat units, Felt favored the introduction of engineering and helicopter units to assist the ARVN.[41] He repeated the continuing impatience of U.S. military officers with the refusal of district ARVN commanders to fight aggressively rather than remain in static defense positions, and urged Taylor to encourage Diem to prevent his local commanders from interfering in the conduct of the war.[42]

Upon arriving in Vietnam, Taylor listened to one of President Diem's familiar monologues on the history of Vietnam and his achievements in opposing the communists. On the more practical matter of the level of U.S. aid Diem desired, the South Vietnamese leader stated that the Laos settlement had made his people more inclined to welcome U.S. forces. Specifically, he requested tactical aircraft, helicopter companies, coastal patrol forces, and ground transportation to move the ARVN forces around the country. Despite Rostow's leading question about whether the United States should mount a concerted effort to convince the world that South Vietnam now faced an international invasion, Diem did not consider this issue significant. He seemed far more concerned to receive reassurances of support from the United States, and claimed that the "Vietnamese people are worried about [the] absence [of a] formal commitment by [the] U.S. to Vietnam. They fear that if the situation deteriorates Vietnam might be abandoned by the United States."[43]

Taylor met with South Vietnam's generals, intelligence service leaders, and the major American representative during his stay in South Vietnam. Most of his informants confirmed the earlier pessimistic assessment of the course of the war. General Duong Van Minh, in charge of the ARVN field command, told Taylor that the situation was "extremely grave." The population had supported Diem in 1955 and 1956, but now they seemed to have lost heart.[44]

Back in Washington other government officials looked for ways to make the government of South Vietnam more amenable to U.S. interests. Some of Kennedy's advisers considered Vietnam so vital to U.S. interests that they would consider deploying U.S. troops to prevent a communist victory. Others wanted to avoid the introduction of combat forces. In either case, officials who thought about Vietnam expressed ever more serious reservations about Diem.

The Vietnam experts of the State Department readied a contingency plan to be used in the event of a new coup d'état against the Ngos. Under the new guidelines, the United States would initially support Diem. If and when the embassy in Saigon determined that the President no longer could effectively exercise control, U.S. officials should ''quickly support the non-Communist person or group who then appears most capable of establishing effective control over the Government of Vietnam.'' The contingency plan considered Vice President Nguyen Ngoc Tho or Defense Minister Nguyen Dinh Thuan possible candidates. In any event, the plan recognized the delicacy of U.S. attempts to dictate the shape of the government of Vietnam. The plan recommended that ''the nature of U.S. support'' for a new government of Vietnam ''should be strong enough to achieve rapid results but not so blatant as to make such a person or group appear as a U.S. puppet.''[45]

John Kenneth Galbraith, one of Kennedy's early supporters from Massachusetts who had become ambassador to India, watched the growing commitment to Vietnam with mounting concern. He sent the President a series of increasingly frustrated memoranda on the deteriorating situation in Vietnam. He asked, ''Who is it in your administration who decides what countries are strategic? I would like to have his name and address and ask him what is so important about this [Vietnamese] real estate in the space age.''[46] He thought that the United States was approaching a point of no return in Vietnam. He recommended the administration seek a neutral South Vietnam, clearly independent of the North. To achieve this ambitious end, he suggested replacing Ambassador Nolting with a high-level envoy such as Averell Harriman.[47] Senator Mike Mansfield, one of Kennedy's old colleagues in the American Friends of Vietnam, also tried to preempt any aggressive recommendations from Taylor's mission. He recalled that Diem had resisted the introduction of U.S. troops for the past several years, and he believed that the same argument against Americanizing the war applied in 1961. He continued to believe that Vietnam represented an important arena of the Cold War, but he predicted that ''we cannot hope to substitute armed power for the kind of political and economic social changes that offer the best resistance to communism.''[48]

These reservations paled before the force of Taylor's recommendations. The members of the Taylor mission met with Kennedy for over an hour on the afternoon of November 3. They presented a report drafted by Taylor and Rostow which, according to the authors of the *Pentagon Papers,* combined "urgency . . . with optimism." Their report repeated the conclusion that South Vietnam faced a crisis in its war with the communists. The United States had a vital interest in the future of South Vietnam, and if it acted promptly and energetically "a victory can be had without a U.S. takeover of the war."[49]

Taylor urged Kennedy to increase the size of the Military Assistance Advisory Group and favored introducing a U.S. military task force into Vietnam. This new group of soldiers would have both psychological and tactical functions. It would "provide a U.S. military presence capable of raising national morale and of showing to Southeast Asia the seriousness of U.S. intent to resist a Communist takeover." In practical terms, the new task force would conduct self-defense military operations and maintain the security of the area in which it was deployed. It would also provide a strategic backup for the ARVN "in case of a heightened military crisis."[50]

Taylor's views represented a consensus of the members of the delegation. Not all of them, however, expressed the same faith in the ability of the United States to reverse the downward course in Vietnam. Sterling Cottrell, the director of the interdepartmental task force on Vietnam, wrote Taylor about the nearly insoluble dilemma facing the United States in Vietnam. He believed that the United States had failed to force Ngo Dinh Diem to reform his government or change his ways of doing business. The United States now should recognize that Diem never would alter his high-handed ways. He considered Diem to be "an oriental despot" like Sukarno of Indonesia, Syngman Rhee of Korea, and Jiang Jieshi of Nationalist China. Threats coming from the United States would not alter Diem's behavior. Suggestions that he delegate authority also conflicted with Diem's personal experience of coups led by the military. Therefore, he believed that the United States "should now direct our major efforts from the bottom up, and supply all effective kinds of military and economic aid."[51]

In the next breath, however, Cottrell doubted whether such aid would enable the government of South Vietnam to overcome the communist insurrection. He therefore thought it might be a mistake for the United States to commit itself "irrevocably to the defeat of the Communists in South Vietnam." Yet Cottrell did not favor abandoning the fight in Vietnam at the present time. He thought that the current level of support for the insurrection from the drv should be stopped, and favored eventual adoption of Rostow's plan of "applying graduated punitive measures on the drv with weapons of our choosing."[52] This idea of providing a convenient exit for the United States should the situation continue to deteriorate stood at the center of Cottrell's observations.

Subsequent policy-makers also occasionally pondered graceful ways to leave Vietnam. Their efforts were sporadic, and the costs of an American departure always seemed too great to bear. Furthermore, most officials directing Vietnam policy had their hands full with daily operations. They had little time to plan for the long term, and they had less inclination to devise exits from Vietnam. A departure of the United States from Vietnam or even a diminution of the U.S. commitment there would lead to a communist victory. The sight of unification of Vietnam under Ho Chi Minh would be tangible. The costs of an enhanced U.S. presence in Vietnam could only be imagined.

Cottrell neatly summarized the dilemma facing the United States in deciding between supporting a stubborn Diem or providing more direct military aid. William J. Jorden, the chief political officer accompanying Taylor and Rostow, outlined the bleak political situation in the South. He saw the pressure for political and administrative changes in Vietnam approaching an "explosion point." Even Lansdale agreed that "Vietnam is dangerously far down the road to a Communist takeover, against the will of its people."[53]

In the twelve days between the time Taylor presented his report to Kennedy on November 3 and a meeting of the National Security Council on November 15 adopted a version of his recommendations, top officials in the State and Defense Departments and the White House mulled over options for Vietnam. In these discussions the personalities differed from those in the earlier Eisenhower administration, but the range of opinions remained remarkably unchanged from those discussed from 1955 to 1960.

Secretary of Defense Robert S. McNamara supported Taylor's view that the United States approached a crisis in Vietnam and repeated the theory of falling dominoes. He believed that a communist victory in South Vietnam put at risk the rest of mainland Southeast Asia "right down to Indonesia." While Southeast Asia had relatively little direct importance for the United States, McNamara believed that U.S. strategic interests worldwide would suffer after a communist victory in Southeast Asia. McNamara also believed that without the introduction of U.S. forces the chances were "sharply against" defeating the insurrection. Even the eight thousand to ten thousand man contingent proposed by Taylor for flood relief "will not convince the other side (whether the shots are being called from Moscow, Beijing or Hanoi) that we mean business. Moreover, it probably will not tip the scales decisively." Therefore, McNamara told the President to face the possibility that the United States might have to deploy as many as six to eight divisions, or about 220,000 men.[54] The next day, on November 5, McNamara noted that the Joint Chiefs of Staff believed that the eight thousand troops proposed by Taylor represented only the first installment of a larger increment to come later. They believed that the eight-thousand-man force would not be enough to preserve the independence of South Vietnam.[55] Civilians in the Defense Department favored waiting to see how well the force would do. If, however, Hanoi actually invaded the South, the United States should be ready to move fast.

In their recommendation to Kennedy to adopt the Taylor report, McNamara and the Joint Chiefs agreed that the government needed to commit itself clearly to preventing the fall of South Vietnam to communism. It had to support this commitment with immediate military actions and entertain the possibility of even greater military actions later. Without this formal promise to see the policy through to the end, Mcnamara and the Chiefs recommended against introducing major units of U.S. forces into Vietnam. If, however, as they expected, the President committed himself, they endorsed Taylor's proposals. Secretary of State Dean Rusk joined McNamara and the Chiefs in endorsing the Taylor report.[56] Yet Rusk and his closest advisers also worried about pressing forward with U.S. forces without a clear cut statement of objectives. Rusk spoke contemptuously of Diem's lackluster commitment to the war. The United States had recently drafted some college students during the Berlin crisis, he complained, while the Vietnamese "students stay in school." Paul Nitze, an old colleague of Rusk's from the Truman State Department, now the Assistant Secretary of Defense for International Security Affairs, thought that the introduction of U.S.troops might provoke Hanoi into stepping up infiltration into the South. Averell Harriman, the U.S. ambassador-at-large who had guided the U.S. position in the Laotian negotiations, argued that putting additional U.S. forces into Vietnam would "blow open the Laotian situation." Harriman thought the rest of the world did not believe that the North gave much support to the Vietcong in the South. Rather, world opinion blamed Diem's fecklessness for the poor showing of the ARVN in the war against the communist guerrillas.[57]

President Kennedy wrestled with the Taylor report over the next week. Like Eisenhower before him, he often talked out loud, weighed options, and perceived dangers in whatever course of action he took. Like many of his advisers, he considered South Vietnam's fate intimately linked to the fortunes of the United States in the Cold War, even while he shared many of their anxieties about the dangers of deeper military involvement. In many cases Kennedy believed that his advisers over-simplified the complex problem of Vietnam and offered overly optimistic solutions.

On November 7, he hosted Indian Prime Minister Jawaharlal Nehru at a meeting attended by Ambassador Galbraith, who opposed deeper U.S. involvement in Vietnam, and Rostow, who favored it. Kennedy explained to Nehru that the United States supported the concept of the inviolability of national sovereignty, even if that meant "unhappily, that we support governments not fully supported by their own people." In the case of South Vietnam, the President said that if the United States withdrew, "communism might take over by subversion."[58]

Kennedy met with his top advisers to discuss the future of U.S. actions in Vietnam for two hours on November 11. Among those present were Secretary of State Rusk, Secretary of Defense McNamara, General Taylor, Attorney

General Robert Kennedy, National Security Adviser McGeorge Bundy, and Walt Rostow, his deputy. Kennedy revealed his anxieties about making the war in South Vietnam an American affair. He considered troops to be "a last resort." If at all possible, he wanted any combat force in South Vietnam to represent SEATO rather than the United States. He also grumbled about the insistence of McNamara, the Joint Chiefs, and Rusk that a firm presidential commitment to South Vietnam precede adoption of the Taylor plan. Having raised public anxieties with his combative approach to the Berlin crisis, he wanted to avoid statements like the ones he had made over Berlin in the summer of 1961. He foresaw "a tough domestic problem" if he raised the stakes in Vietnam.

Already Senator Richard Russell (D., Ga.), the highly respected chairman of the Armed Services Committee, opposed involvement of the United States in a war that might turn out to be as costly as the engagement in Korea. Yet the President's brother Robert, his most trusted adviser, explained that the Taylor report could not be implemented without a public presidential endorsement of the objective of defeating the communists in Vietnam. Besides, Robert Kennedy said, "We are not sending combat troops" at this time, and we are "not committing ourselves to combat troops."[59]

When Kennedy met with the National Security Council on November 15, he still had serious reservations about a major commitment of U.S. forces to Vietnam. The United States presently confronted the Soviet Union in Berlin, and he feared "becoming involved simultaneously on two fronts on opposite sides of the world." In contrast to Korea, where there had been "a case of clear aggression" and which the United States had been joined by the members of the United Nations, the issues in Vietnam seemed far murkier. He pressed his advisers for assurances that some other nations would support the United States. Neither France or Britain would support the United States in military actions in Vietnam, and he doubted Secretary Rusk's assertion that Pakistan, Thailand, the Philippines, Australia, and New Zealand would provide assistance. Nevertheless, McNamara told Kennedy that he would recommend U.S. actions in Vietnam even if SEATO did not exist. At the end of the meeting, Kennedy still had not made up his mind about implementation of the Taylor report and he deferred consideration of the draft NSAM.[60]

One week later, on November 22, Kennedy approved NSAM-111.[61] NSAM-111 granted some but not all of the additional military forces recommended by Taylor. The United States promised South Vietnam that it would join it in "a sharply increased joint effort to avoid a further deterioration in the situation." The United States promised South Vietnam helicopters, light aircraft, and transport aircraft manned by U.S. uniformed servicemen. In addition, the United States would provide intelligence equipment and troops for aerial reconnaissance. The United States would enhance its training of ARVN and civil guard forces. It would also increase economic aid.

In return, the government of Vietnam would promise to go on a wartime footing.[62]

GROWING U.S. FRUSTRATIONS WITH DIEM: 1962

By 1962 Americans grew even more frustrated with Diem's unwillingness to delegate authority and broaden the base of his support. Despite the provision of the additional military assistance and U.S. advisers recommended in the Taylor report, Diem would not change. General Paul D. Harkins, a protege of Taylor's, replaced General Lionel C. McGarr as head of the MAAG in early February. Maxwell Taylor personally selected Harkins and convinced Kennedy to award him a fourth star in December 1961. A tall, handsome man who had served in the calvary and played polo, Harkins promised to add the dash the ARVN desperately needed.[63]

Yet Harkins's appointment failed to convince Diem to use his army more aggressively. The President continued to believe that the coup against him in November 1960 had originated with ARVN fear of casualties.[64] Holding back from the fighting also did not satisfy many officers. Two or three dissatisfied air force officers, still upset by their poor pay, food, and living conditions, bombed his presidential palace at 7:15 on the morning of February 27, 1962.[65]

Diem dismissed the attack as the work of pampered young men who had an "exaggerated interest in comfort and conveniences." He urged the Americans to "point out to his airmen that their role was not only one of glamour and grandeur, but also of service."[66] American and international reporters seized upon the bombing of the palace as evidence that Diem's support had collapsed. They berated U.S. policy for supporting the Diem government rather than the people of Vietnam.[67] For his part, Diem used one of his lengthy monologues with Ambassador Nolting to vent his rage at Western journalists. They had written that the bombing of the palace stood as a warning to the President. Ominously, he saw the bombing "as a warning to them" and to factions opposed to him. Joseph Mendenhall, the counselor for political affairs at the Saigon embassy, wrote in disgust that Diem "never learns."[68]

Diem's insularity affected the war effort, and the ARVN refused to take the initiative against the Vietcong. The poor battlefield situation exacted a toll among officials who planned the U.S. commitment. Theodore Heavner, deputy director of the State Department's working group on Vietnam, complained that American officials in comfortable offices in Washington or Saigon were brimming with ideas, but "it's easy to win a war on paper." He worried that the Vietnamese "don't change quickly," and the Vietcong's continued offensive did not provide much time.[69]

Despite Heavner's skepticism, he and other planners continued to draft action proposals. In the summer the Vietnam task force refined its directives, requiring a commitment by both the Americans and the Vietnamese to fight the war more vigorously. The Americans wanted Vietnamese agreement to go onto a war footing. The South Vietnamese authorities were supposed to strengthen popular support for the war effort. Convinced that something had to be done to open up the Diem regime, the Americans urged the development of democratic institutions at all levels of Vietnam. The planners were quick to note, however, that "this means developing a governmental system responsive to the needs and desires of the Vietnamese people and does not imply an obligation to adopt western political forms." The Americans wanted Diem to open relations with the Hoa Hao and Cao Dai sects and announce an amnesty for defectors from the Vietcong. For their part, they promised to "make clear our confidence and support." This promise included offers to continue supplying administrators and advisers to the government of South Vietnam. These civilian and military personnel would "plan and carry out [a] program of military civic action aimed at winning popular support and cooperation for the armed forces and the government of Vietnam."[70]

The administration adopted NSAM-178, a program of crop destruction by herbicides in nine areas of South Vietnam. The aim of the program was to deny food and jungle shelter to the Vietcong.[71] Edward R. Murrow, the director of the U.S. Information Agency, counseled caution in the use of defoliants. He referred to the series by Rachel Carson running in the *New Yorker* exploring "with devastating impact the consequences of insecticides on insect-plant life balance and human health." Only if the use of defoliants could guarantee victory and refraining from their use guarantee defeat would Morrow support their use. He thought that "we cannot persuade the world—particularly that large part of it which does not get enough to eat—that defoliation is good for you."[72]

These misgivings did not stop the program of chemical defoliation, which went forward over the next three months. General Harkins reported that defoliation improved visibility by 80 to 90 percent and significantly reduced the susceptibility of areas sprayed to ambush. U.S. advisers in the areas sprayed happily reported that there had been "no apparent reaction by the populace to the spray operations." McNamara also was encouraged that no news organizations in neutral or friendly countries had commented on Radio Hanoi's report that the defoliation campaign had injured hundreds of Vietnamese peasants.[73]

Vietnam experts believed that the six months following the end of the Vietnamese rainy season in November would be critical.[74] Some signs of hope existed.[75] Taylor visited Vietnam in September and had long discussions with Harkins who exuded optimism. Harkins invited Lieutenant-

Colonel John Paul Vann, one of the most aggressive advisers who had led ARVN forces on several missions in the Mekong Delta since May, to lunch with Taylor. Vann had read *The Ugly American,* and patterned his efforts in Vietnam on those of Lansdale, whose earlier exploits he hoped to match and surpass. Vann had prepared to tell the Chairman of the Joints Chiefs of Staff that whatever progress had occurred in the past several months was tenuous. The ARVN forces still lacked an aggressive fighting spirit, and they relied almost exclusively on the heavy fire provided by U.S. helicopters. The Vietcong had lost some of their earlier fear of helicopters and had learned how to dig underground to avoid some of the worst pounding from heavy artillery. Harkins did not let Vann speak up at the lunch, and Taylor did not seem especially keen on ferreting out negative information.[76]

Taylor later told the Vietnamese that "he was much encouraged by the progress which had been made" in the war since his visit in October 1961.[77] The Vietnamese now fought more than before, although their commanders still feared casualties. They had cleared several areas near Saigon of Vietcong. Ambassador Nolting believed that an invigorated bombing campaign has "done considerably more good than harm," and "the populace is not being driven into the communists' arms" by the additional bombing.[78] U.S. officials in Saigon estimated in September 1962 that the government controlled 49 percent of the population and the Vietcong 9 percent, with the rest remaining in dispute.[79] This intensification of the war meant, however, that casualties would likely mount and U.S. public opinion would pay greater attention to U.S. deaths. Support would continue "if on balance it seems that we are getting somewhere."[80] In Washington Averell Harriman warned the embassy in Vietnam against over-optimism. While acknowledging the progress made in the past year, Harriman told Nolting that "I think we are by far safer in carrying out the President's directive to save Vietnam if we lean in the direction of emphasizing our problems rather than our successes."[81]

Signs of optimism collided with other examples that the South Vietnamese government obstructed what the Americans thought needed to be done to succeed in the war. John Hebel, the U.S. consul in Hué and one of the few Foreign Service personnel to travel widely in the Vietnamese countryside, reported that the rate of deterioration had slowed, but the "deterioration itself has not stopped." Worse, he observed that "the strategic hamlet program is mostly pure facade."[82] Higher officials in the State Department, such as Harriman, and in the White House, such as Michael Forrestal, the National Security Council's official in charge of Vietnam affairs, also disputed the effectiveness of the strategic hamlet program.[83] Since Diem's brother Ngo Dinh Nhu was in charge of the strategic hamlets, American frustration with the pace of the program intensified their misgivings about the Ngos' rule.

Despite Washington's reservations, the few indicators of success in late

1962 emboldened Diem to crack down on critics. He expelled journalists from NBC, CBS, and *Newsweek,* and banned the distribution of *Newsweek* in Vietnam. The journalists had incurred Diem's wrath by reporting on flaws in the strategic hamlet program, criticizing the President's dictatorial methods, and revealing his exclusive reliance on his family. Most bothersome to Diem had been reports on his interminable monologues in which the President took "a great deal of time saying nothing." Nolting begged Diem to rescind the expulsions and restore *Newsweek* to the newsstands. He explained that American public opinion would turn sharply against Diem if Americans believed he suppressed their press. The best cure for negative reporting, Nolting observed, was demonstrable success in the war against the Vietcong. These admonitions could not move Diem, who repeated that he thought that the journalists lacked "elementary respect for the chief of state." Nolting, usually a strong supporter of Diem, warned him explicitly that the expulsion of journalists could do more than anything else to encourage "changes in U.S. policy, which I do not think desirable or justified." Nolting also expressed bewilderment that Washington did not seem too concerned about the problems of American journalists in Vietnam. He thought that the preoccupation with the Cuban missile crisis might have had something to do with the State Department's apparent lack of interest in the fate of U.S. reporters in Vietnam.[84]

More disturbing still for the conduct of the war, Diem decided that the ARVN could no longer tolerate the casualties American advisers thought were necessary if they were to develop into a mobile, aggressive fighting force. On October 5 a forty man platoon of ARVN Rangers disembarked from a helicopter in a guerrilla-dominated area near the Plain of Reeds west of the town of My Tho. The platoon advanced across rice paddies toward a hamlet where they believed a Vietcong force had concentrated. Attacks from the ground were to be coordinated with machine-gun fire from helicopters designed to flush the Vietcong fighters into open fields. In earlier operations the Vietcong had panicked and run at the sound of the helicopters. This time they dug into camouflaged foxholes in a dike, waited until the Rangers approached within thirty yards, and opened fire, killing or wounding a majority of the Rangers in the initial gun battle. When reinforcements arrived by helicopters, the Vietcong shot at them, forcing five of the helicopters to crash land. When fighter bombers dropped bombs, napalm, and rockets the Vietcong did not flee, but stayed in their foxholes until they could retreat in good order under cover of trees and darkness. This Vietcong success convinced Vann that the ARVN forces needed more experience in close in combat. Diem, however, drew a different lesson. In one of his familiar monologues, Diem told Colonel Huyen Van Cao, Vann's favorite Vietnamese officer, that he had decided not to risk additional casualties.[85]

THE BATTLE OF AP BAC

American officials grew increasingly apprehensive as conditions in South Vietnam deteriorated in 1963. Their anxiety led them to redouble efforts to persuade or force the government of South Vietnam to change. The war went badly, the NLF fought better than the ARVN, and Diem's support nearly collapsed in the face of an uprising by Buddhists who made up a majority of the population of the South.

On January 2, 1963 a Vietcong battalion, outnumbered four to one, scored a major victory over ARVN forces supported by armor, artillery, and U.S. army helicopters at the town of Ap Bac, approximately thirty-five miles southwest of Saigon. Ap Bac proved to be a defining moment in the war. The actual events of the battle were bad enough for the South Vietnamese. For months Vann and his superiors in Saigon had hoped that the Vietcong would be reckless enough to abandon guerrilla tactics and fight a battle in the open in which the superior firepower of the ARVN could cut the Vietcong fighters to shreds. Like the French before them at Dienbienphu, U.S. advisers got their wish at Ap Bac, but the results were far different from what they had anticipated. Despite the overwhelming advantages in weaponry the ARVN enjoyed, they refused to take the initiative in the fighting, and would not leave the protection of their armored personnel carriers. General Cao would not send mobile reinforcements after the Vietcong to capture them. The battle of Ap Bac did not rout the guerrillas as the American advisers expected; instead, it exposed the weaknesses of the ARVN and revealed that the Vietcong had learned how to shoot down helicopters.[86]

But Ap Bac represented more than a defeat for the ARVN. Armies often learn useful lessons from tactical setbacks, but several additional elements made Ap Bac emblematic of the growing difficulties of the Americans in forging an effective military regime in Saigon. Reports in the *Washington Post* and the *New York Times* of a "major defeat" at Ap Bac brought the issue before the public.[87] Most U.S. journalists in Vietnam in late 1962 supported the aims of U.S. policy in Vietnam, but they had grown skeptical of the optimistic claims of success emanating from Harkins's headquarters and from the South Vietnamese government.[88] The embassy in Saigon dismissed some of the griping by journalists as the work of young, inexperienced correspondents who relied on "equally young American advisers." Both "tend to be shocked, angry and indignant because they think [the] U.S. is being 'suckered'" by the South Vietnamese. Besides, the "American newsmen and this particular regime dislike each other to a degree that verges on the neurotic."[89]

Beyond the negative publicity generated by the Vietcong defeat of the ARVN at Ap Bac was the bitter after-action report of the battle prepared by John Paul Vann, the American adviser to the ARVN forces. Vann berated the

Vietnamese for their "damn miserable" performance and accused their officers of cowardice. Vann became even angrier when he discovered that
Harkins and his staff in Saigon seemed unconcerned that the ARVN commanders had falsified reports of the battle to turn an obvious defeat into a victory. General Cao had even gone so far as to stage a phony battle at Ap Bac
for the benefit of credulous American officers the day after the real engagement.[90]

The White House reacted to the catastrophe at Ap Bac and the bad publicity it generated by sending General Earle Wheeler, the army Chief of Staff,
and Major-General Victor Krulak of the marines to Vietnam to assess the
situation. Wheeler and Krulak prepared another optimistic report. The two
generals complimented the Diem government on having survived since 1955.
The bad relations between the government and the foreign press corps had
created a public relations nightmare, which might have serious repercussions
back in the United States. Wheeler and Krulak warned that "opinion in
the United States has been influenced toward thinking that the war effort in
Vietnam is misguided, lacking in drive, and flouts the counsel of United
States advisers."[91] Wheeler exuded "rosy euphoria" when he met Kennedy
on February 1. His upbeat assessment of the situation in Vietnam precluded a
tough discussion of whether U.S. officials have "been as firm as we should
with the GVN in putting our views across on our military, domestic and foreign policy."[92]

Staff members of the National Security Council, who were losing patience daily with Diem's refusal to take orders from the embassy, began
looking for a new ambassador to replace Frederick Nolting. Nolting's two-
year term in Vietnam was due to expire in April, and his loyal support for
Diem now seemed more of a liability than an asset. The stubborn South
Vietnamese President did not seem to take seriously Nolting's recommendations on how to organize his government and defeat the Vietcong. Roger
Hilsman, the director of the State Department's Bureau of Intelligence and
Research, and Michael Forrestal of the National Security Council Staff, both
of whom had grown disillusioned with Diem, wrote Kennedy that "we are
probably winning" in Vietnam, "but certainly more slowly than we had
hoped." They recommended that a "single strong executive" was needed to
"use all the leverage we have to persuade Diem to adopt policies which we
espouse."[93]

Finding a suitable replacement took several months. In the summer the
administration asked a prominent Republican, Henry Cabot Lodge, to become U.S. ambassador to Vietnam. Lodge and Kennedy had a long political
rivalry. Kennedy had displaced Lodge from the U.S. Senate in 1952, and
Lodge had lost again as the Republican vice presidential candidate in 1960.
Kennedy wanted a Republican ambassador to South Vietnam to minimize
domestic criticism of his policy in Vietnam before the presidential election of

1964.[94] The U.S. administration also believed that the perception of bipartisan support for Vietnam policy would "demonstrate to President Diem, to the Vietnamese people, and to the world the importance which the U.S. attaches to its support of Vietnam and to demonstrate that this policy has the support of both political parties."[95]

The Americans wanted a popular government in Saigon, one which could foster nationalist, anti-communist fervor on the part of the largely rural and Buddhist population. Only such a government had a chance to create an armed force that could move effectively against the NLF fighters. Currently, the leadership of the ARVN seemed more interested in preserving its own privileges than in fighting the war. For his part, Diem worried more about disloyal army officers threatening his regime than he did about fighting the Vietcong.

THE FALL OF DIEM: MAY–DECEMBER 1963

American anxiety regarding Diem's unpopularity and his army's reluctance to fight boiled over in the spring and summer of 1963. Religious leaders of the Buddhist majority had long resented the rule of the Ngo family, who barely concealed their contempt for Buddhism and rejected calls to relax restrictions on Buddhist religious and political activities. On May 8 the long-simmering dispute erupted into street demonstrations in Hué when the Buddhists demanded to fly their religious flags. The government responded with clubs, tear gas, and gunfire, that killed several demonstrators and bystanders, including children. Some of the deaths resulted from government fire; others from a bomb, a concussion grenade thrown into the crowd, and the general panic following the soldiers' firing into the crowd.[96]

The Buddhist leadership demanded that the government allow Buddhists the same privileges accorded Catholics, "stop arrests and terrorization" of Buddhist followers, and compensate those slain.[97] Further demonstrations took place for the next month. The Buddhists pressed for greater autonomy while President Diem asserted that no crisis existed. He told his senior ministers he was convinced that "the NLF and the Vietcong are exploiting the situation."[98] The climax occurred on June 11, when a seventy-three-year-old Buddhist monk, Thich Quang Duc, turned the local Buddhist rebellion into an international crisis by pouring gasoline over himself and burning himself to death in the midst of a busy Saigon intersection. He had alerted members of the international press before taking his life and gory pictures of his suicide were captured on film and broadcast around the world.[99]

The shocking images horrified many Americans who previously had given little thought to Vietnam. Senator Frank Church (D., Idaho), told the Foreign Relations Committee that "such grisly scenes have not been witnessed since the Christian martyrs walked hand-in-hand into the Roman arenas.''[100] President Kennedy told ambassador-designate Lodge that ''no news picture in history has generated as much emotion around the world as that one [has].''[101] Immediately after the immolation the State Department pressed Diem to reach an agreement with the Buddhists to defuse the crisis. William Truehart, the highest ranking official at the Saigon embassy while Ambassador Nolting was in Washington, informed Diem's secretary that the ''government of Vietnam's position abroad and probably in the country was very precarious. I doubted that position could be restored without many immediate, dramatic and conciliatory move by President Diem personally.''[102] Some members of Diem's circle wanted to press the President to extend an olive branch to the Buddhists. Whatever hopes these advisers had of reaching an accommodation faded when U.S. newspapers reported that the U.S. government had warned Diem it would condemn his actions unless he assuaged their grievances.[103]

Within the White House, however, staff members of the national security council finally abandoned what little hope remained of encouraging the Diem government to reform. Assistant Secretary of State for Far East Affairs Roger Hilsman told Kennedy that ''no matter what Diem [does] there will be coup attempts over the next four months.'' White House staff members decided to move up the date of Lodge's ambassadorship.[104] Presidential assistants informed South Vietnam's Vice President that the United States was ready to support him if President Diem were to lose power. Negotiations with the Buddhists did not end the demonstrations, and another monk burned himself in August. The outrageous comment of Tran LeXuah (Madame Ngo Dinh Nhu) to CBS News on August 1 that the Buddhists had only ''barbecued a *bonze* [monk] with imported gasoline'' provoked the White House to inform Diem that he had to get his sister-in-law out of the country.[105] Diem responded on August 21 by proclaiming martial law. His brother Nhu's special forces and police units raided Buddhist pagodas throughout the country, arresting monks and killing several who refused custody.

Lodge arrived in Saigon the next day. He immediately learned of a plot on the part of several of the ARVN's top generals to oust Nhu and possibly Diem. Diem had survived several earlier coup attempts, but now the generals believed they had, for the first time, the unqualified backing of the United States. The Ambassador supported their efforts, as did Forrestal and Hilsman. Forrestal, acting in the absence of the President, who was vacationing on Cape Cod, prepared a cable to Lodge promising the generals ''direct support'' should they oust Diem.[106] Despite assurance of U.S. backing, the generals aborted their coup on August 31, fearful that Diem had learned of their plans.

Their reluctance to go forward without certainty of success left American officials more perplexed than ever about what to do about Vietnam. Most

American officials were almost desperate for a government in Vietnam eager to press the war against the Vietcong. As plans for the coup unraveled in late August, Secretary of Defense McNamara, Chairman of the Joint Chiefs of Staff Maxwell Taylor, and CIA director John McCone expressed support for Diem, but by the end of August, Washington had lost all confidence in the Diem government. Moreover, future relations between the Kennedy administration and Diem were likely to get even worse, since Diem suspected that Lodge had joined with his rivals in the ARVN. The plotters' desire for more aggressive action against the Vietcong made Diem and Nhu wonder if fighting the communists was in their own personal best interests.

In September, the future of U.S. policy toward Vietnam riveted the public. Kennedy addressed Vietnam in several interviews. He said "we are for those things which help win the war there. What interferes with the war effort, we oppose." He identified Diem and Nhu as interfering with the war. "I don't think the war can be won," he told Walter Cronkite, "unless the people [of South Vietnam] support the effort, and in my opinion, in the last two months, the government has gotten out of touch with the people." He thought the Saigon government might regain some of that trust as he signaled the American desire for Diem to drop his brother: "with changes in policy and perhaps with personnel, I think it can."[107]

Some journalists in Vietnam and academic experts went much further and publicly called for an end to support of Diem. Stanley Karnow, reporting in the *Saturday Evening Post* on the battles between the government and the Buddhists, condemned the Ngo family as "the strongest communist allies in the country. . . . They have sown suspicion and chaos."[108] Cornell University political science professor George McT. Kahin, later an outspoken critic of U.S. escalation of the war, encouraged Senator Church to "press the administration to . . . take the calculated risk of opening the way for new leadership, rather than *half* encouraging this while at the same time continuing with the existing policy of backing Nhu and Diem."[109]

Behind the scenes, the White House moved fitfully toward a final break with Diem. Rumors flew that Nhu was looking to make a "deal with North Vietnam for a truce in the war, a complete removal of the U.S. presence, and a neutralist" South Vietnam.[110] Kennedy sent two fact-finding missions to Vietnam in September. The first, led by General Victor Krulak and Joseph A. Mendenhall, a Foreign Service officer who had served in Vietnam, returned with wildly divergent opinions. Krulak supported Diem and reported that despite the political divisions with the Buddhists the war was going well. Mendenhall, however, brought back a gloomy assessment of a religious civil war and a government on the verge of collapse. An exasperated President asked, "You two did visit the same country, didn't you?" After his advisers debated whether the war was being won or if the Diem government could be salvaged, Kennedy exploded. "This is impossible," he said, "we can't run a policy when there are such divergent views on the same set of facts.''[111]

Kennedy thereupon sent another fact-finding mission to Saigon led by Secretary of Defense McNamara and Chairman of the Joint Chiefs of Staff Taylor, both strong supporters of the war. Both men returned optimistic about the military effort. They proposed that the sixteen thousand members of the U.S. advisory contingent could be withdrawn in 1965 if things continued to go well. They also proposed that the President remove a one-thousand-man construction battalion once it finished its work at the end of 1963. Kennedy agreed to do so but stipulated that an additional thousand men were to be sent as replacements. McNamara and Taylor presented a much grimmer view of an unpopular and oppressive Diem government, suggesting that the announcement of proposed troop withdrawals would be another mode of pressuring Diem.

By the middle of October communications had broken down between Washington and Diem. Nhu publicly charged that the cuts in U.S. aid to his country had ''initiated a process of disintegration'' in Vietnam.[112] The generals who had plotted Diem's overthrow in August once more approached the United States to determine its attitude. The White House responded that it ''did not wish to stimulate'' a coup but would not ''thwart'' one either. Internally, White House officials wanted to make certain that the coup would succeed and that it could maintain a ''plausible denial'' of Lodge's involvement.[113] On October 29 Kennedy met with his Vietnam advisers to discuss the prospects for a coup, but once more they reached no consensus. On November 1 the Vietnamese generals moved anyway, convinced that once they succeeded support would flow from the United States. The army installed General Duong Van Minh as president. Lodge, deeply involved in plans for the coup, barely lifted a finger to protect Diem and Nhu from the wrath of the rebellious generals. When Diem, aware that soldiers loyal to the plotters were marching on Saigon, asked Lodge what the United States intended to do about the coup, the Ambassador blandly and dishonestly replied: ''I do not feel well enough informed to tell you. . . . It is 4:30 A.M. in Washington and the U.S. government cannot possibly have a view.'' He made an equally perfunctory offer to the President and his brother of safe conduct out of the country, but they refused, not trusting him to keep his word.[114] The next morning they were murdered in an armored car after having been captured by their military opponents. When Kennedy heard the news his face turned white and he fled the room. He had been one of Diem's earliest supporters; he had wanted him replaced as president, not slain.[115] Three weeks later he too was murdered.

Kennedy bequeathed a terrible legacy to his successor, Lyndon Johnson. The United States was committed to participation in a civil war in Vietnam without guarantees of success. Sixteen thousand U.S. army, navy, and marine corps troops led ARVN soldiers in daily operations against the NLF, who exercised control over large parts of the countryside.

In later years, when the war turned into a catastrophe for the United States, some of Kennedy's loyal supporters claimed that he had contemplated withdrawing U.S. forces from Vietnam. In 1992 the director Oliver Stone presented the movie *JFK,* a grotesquely fictionalized version of the assassination of the President, in which conspirators from the military and Central Intelligence Agency combined to killed him. According to this bizarre view, Kennedy had run afoul of government officials and military contractors who wanted the United States to become involved more deeply in Vietnam.

Stone equivocated when asked if he literally believed that Kennedy had been killed because of his plans to quit Vietnam. He claimed that his views on the transition from the Kennedy to the Johnson presidencies had been deeply influenced by the work of the historian John M. Newman, whose book, *JFK and Vietnam,* argued that a central feature, perhaps even the most significant aspect, of Kennedy's policy toward Vietnam had been his insistence that the United States not employ ground forces in the war. While Newman acknowledged that Kennedy consistently upheld the importance of preventing a communist victory in Vietnam, he argued that Kennedy placed an even higher value on avoiding a Korea-style engagement for the United States in Asia.[116] Newman argued that Kennedy masked his dovish instincts with hawkish rhetoric for political reasons. Like other observers of the final weeks of the Kennedy presidency, Newman noted that Kennedy had told Kenneth O'Donnell, his appointments secretary, and Senate Majority Leader Mike Mansfield that he wanted to wait until the election of 1964 and then withdraw. He may have made such remarks, although there is no contemporary evidence of them.[117]

But even if Kennedy did tell some people (although not his most intimate advisers) that he hoped to remove U.S. forces in eighteen months, these comments represented more the musings born of the frustrations of dealing with Diem than an acceptance of a communist triumph. Like Eisenhower before him and Johnson after, Kennedy often perceived the risks posed by a more forceful course in Vietnam. Throughout his presidency, however, he also perceived the stakes in Vietnam as high and growing for the United States, and wanted to retain as much freedom of maneuver for as long as possible. Hence, while he continually scaled back efforts on the part of some of his more militant advisers for the deployment of ground forces, he always retained the option of ordering just such a deployment at a later date. The day of reckoning came, however, after his death.

Chapter

* * * * * * * * * * *

To the Brink—And Beyond:
1963–1964

*W*HILE THE Kennedy administration had undertaken a reassessment of its tactics in Vietnam in September and October, the basic policy remained victory in the civil war over the NLF. Despite improvements in U.S.-Soviet relations in 1963, administration officials believed that the Cold War dominated international relations. The danger of direct nuclear confrontation with the Soviet Union had diminished with the signing in August of a treaty banning the testing of nuclear weapons in the atmosphere, outer space, and under the oceans, but competition between the superpowers for preeminence in the underdeveloped world might even have intensified. Limited improvement in relations with the Soviet Union did nothing to decrease U.S. rivalry in Asia with the People's Republic of China. As long as the United States and the communist powers remained adversaries, the original reasons for the United States to help the Republic of Vietnam put down the insurrection remained as valid as ever to the principal U.S. government decision-makers. They continued to fear that a communist victory in South Vietnam would have repercussions throughout Asia and possibly in other areas of the underdeveloped world.

For more than fifteen years, the American public heard officials across the political spectrum explain the danger of dominoes falling in Asia. While it may have been possible to reverse public fears of communist revolution, it would have come at a terrible political cost domestically. As long as Kennedy

124

lived, he expected a hotly contested presidential election in 1964. Reducing the U.S. commitment to the Republic of Vietnam might provide a Republican opponent with the opportunity to renew old charges that Democrats cared little for the fate of Asians fighting communist revolutionaries.

Once Lyndon B. Johnson became president, he too wanted nothing to interfere with election victory in 1964. Therefore, in both the last weeks of the Kennedy administration and the first year of the Johnson government, officials saw many reasons to continue what they thought was their established course in Vietnam and had few incentives to change direction. But their commitment to continuity was profoundly wrong. As Washington planners looked forward to the upcoming election and paid attention to changes in the international environment, they continually missed the vastly changed situation within South Vietnam. The United States could not maintain the status quo in the war without a far greater commitment. Although some officials sometimes recognized the costs of such a commitment, those who mattered the most decided at every step that additional escalation of U.S. resources to the war represented the best way to maintain continuity with the past, preserve the government of the Republic of Vietnam, and leave open options for the future.

Near the end of his life, President John F. Kennedy privately told South Vietnam's President Ngo Dinh Diem that he gave "absolute priority to the defeat of the Communists." He maintained the same position publicly. In remarks prepared for delivery in Dallas on the afternoon of November 22 he maintained that Americans "dare not weary of the task" of supporting South Vietnam no matter how "risky and costly" that support might be.[1] Yet by November 1963 the White House recognized a painful dilemma in U.S. policy toward Vietnam: doing more, doing less, or doing the same all entailed enormous risks. Perceiving no way completely to eliminate these risks, officials throughout late 1963 and all of 1964 supported a series of South Vietnamese governments which they hoped might prevail over revolutionaries.

Two days before Kennedy was shot, Secretary of Defense Robert S. McNamara, Secretary of State Dean Rusk, and National Security Adviser McGeorge Bundy met with Ambassador Henry Cabot Lodge in Honolulu to discuss the situation in Vietnam. Lodge thought that the immediate future of Vietnam looked "more hopeful" after the coup d'état of November 1. He believed the urban population of Vietnam was more enthusiastic about the government than they had been in a long time, but admitted that the war would be won or lost on the basis of the attitude of the rural population. The Defense Secretary, valuing quantifiable facts more than what he considered evanescent emotion, thought that Lodge and the other U.S. representatives in Vietnam had been overcome by euphoria since the coup. He believed that the generals who had staged the coup, although friendly to the United States for the time being, led a highly fragile government. The Vietcong had shown enormous resilience, tripling the rate of attacks in the week immediately after the coup. McNamara believed that the Vietcong were as strong in late 1963 as they had been a year or two years before. The Defense Secretary doubted that the United States had committed enough resources to stop further deterioration in the military and political standing of the South Vietnamese government.[2]

At the conclusion of the Honolulu meeting McGeorge Bundy flew back to Washington to preside over the daily staff meeting of the National Security Council. The meeting in Hawaii left Bundy with two indelible impressions that had long term repercussions. First, he thought traveling a twelve-thousand-mile round trip for a one day conference had been effortless and comfortable; he recommended holding more such intercontinental meetings in the future. Over the next years White House staff members, the Defense Secretary, and eventually the President himself became frequent visitors to Pacific islands and the Asian mainland in their search for a suitable strategy in Vietnam. Second, Bundy noticed the testy interaction between McNamara and officers serving in Vietnam. He reported that the briefings "tend to be sessions where people try to fool him [McNamara], and he tries to convince them that they cannot."[3] These scenes were to be repeated many times in the next several years. That afternoon, Kennedy was shot.

JOHNSON AND THE KENNEDY LEGACY

Johnson became president promising continuity with his predecessor's personnel and policies. Keeping the advisers proved easy: Johnson told each White House staff member how vital he was to the success of the new administration. Press Secretary Pierre Salinger announced on November 24 that the President had urged all staff members to stay at their jobs.[4] Many of the mid-level and junior staff members from the Kennedy White House walked though the first weeks of the new administration in a daze, unable to assuage their grief at the sudden death of their beloved president. Men at the top, such as National Security Adviser McGeorge Bundy and Secretary of Defense Robert McNamara, maintained iron control over their emotions. They quickly impressed Johnson with their intelligence, drive, and loyalty. Johnson often called McNamara "the brightest star in the cabinet."[5] Bundy served Johnson so loyally in the first months of the new administration that some of the junior staff members from the Kennedy White House said darkly that he had betrayed the memory of their fallen hero.[6]

But it proved far more difficult for Johnson to determine the precise policy that Kennedy would have followed in Vietnam than it was for him to assimilate the Kennedy staff into his own advisers. From November 1963 until July 1965 Johnson was alternately active and passive in setting Vietnam policy. He took a series of steps, some small, some large, which made the war a fully American affair.

Johnson took an interest in Vietnam from the very beginning of his presidency. He met with Ambassador Lodge, Secretaries Rusk and McNamara, CIA Director John McCone, and National Security Adviser Bundy on Sunday afternoon, November 24. Lodge repeated his upbeat assessment of the improvement in the morale of the South Vietnamese government since the coup. CIA director John McCone was far more pessimistic, reporting that the Vietcong had continued to raise the level of their attacks since the coup. The new military authorities had not consolidated their power with civilian representatives who sat on the sidelines and continued "their traditional role of critics." President Johnson expressed his frustrations with recent American efforts in Vietnam, citing misgivings about U.S. participation in the coup against Diem. The deed had been done, however, and Johnson was committed to "see that our objectives were accomplished" in Vietnam. He wanted action, not the constant bickering among the members of the U.S. team. General Paul D. Harkins, the commander of MACV, could not seem to get along with Ambassador Lodge. The Ambassador, in turn, had lost confidence in William Truehart, the counselor of the embassy, who did not seem able to run an effective operation. Johnson also lashed out at U.S. efforts at social reform in Vietnam. It was a mistake for the U.S. to try to "reform every Asian into our image." The need now was to "win the war" before the voices in Congress calling for a U.S. withdrawal from Vietnam grew louder.[7]

Over the next several weeks, Johnson became even more deeply involved in planning the U.S. engagement in Vietnam. On November 26 he approved NSAM-273 authorizing planning for increased military activity against North Vietnam. Johnson directed the State and Defense Departments to assess the "plausibility of denial" of U.S. involvement. Later, John M. Newman, a prominent critic of the Johnson administration's actions in Americanizing the war, claimed that the version of NSAM-273 approved by Johnson significantly changed the language of the draft proposed by Bundy before the Honolulu conference,[8] which had authorized "additional government of Vietnam resources" for sea-going activities against the North. The version approved by Johnson, however, dropped any reference to government of Vietnam resources and replaced it with a vague call for "increased activity" against North Vietnam. The revised proposal could include U.S as well as ARVN activities against the North. The difference was more imaginary than real, however. Roger Hilsman, the Assistant Secretary of State for Far Eastern Affairs, went forward with joint CIA-Defense Department plans to step up the pressure on North Vietnam.[9]

INCREASED U.S. MILITARY AID: WINTER 1963–1964

Within two weeks of his accession to the presidency, Johnson characterized the situation in Vietnam as "our most critical military area." He urged the Defense and State Departments and the CIA to move quickly to shakeup the personnel in Saigon.[10] Rusk told Ambassador Lodge that Johnson wanted "our effort in Vietnam stepped up to the highest pitch."[11] He perceived a loss of momentum since the coup and bewailed the fact that "we as a government were not doing everything we should" in South Vietnam. Johnson ordered McNamara to make an unscheduled stop in Vietnam on the way home from a NATO meeting. He wanted McNamara to be in Saigon for Johnson's announcement that three hundred members of the U.S. force in Vietnam would go home at the end of the year and another seven hundred in 1964. Without the presence of the Secretary of Defense in the Vietnamese capital, Johnson feared that morale would suffer when news of the departure of the U.S. contingent became public knowledge.[12]

In early December the CIA reported a serious ebbing of the initial enthusiasm for the new government generated by the coup d'état of November 1–2 despite the apparent advantages in numbers of soldiers and quality of weapons the ARVN enjoyed over the Vietcong. Since May 1963 the government had increased the size of its armed forces to about five hundred thousand. Two hundred fifteen thousand served in the regular army, eighty-three thousand were in the civil guard, and over two hundred thousand were in paramilitary groups such as the self-defense corps, the hamlet militias, and the Citizen's Irregular Defense Groups (CIDGS). Although the South Vietnamese forces had a monopoly of air power and significantly superior weapons, and had stepped up the tempo of their tactical operations, they had not weakened the Vietcong. The CIA estimated Vietcong strength at twenty-one- to twenty-three thousand regular forces, with an additional sixty- to eighty thousand irregulars. The Vietcong had been able to organize larger units of regimental size. Supplied North Vietnamese weapons and approximately three thousand cadres in the past year, the Vietcong had sufficient manpower to replace any losses suffered in the engagements initiated by the South Vietnamese.[13]

Concern that the situation in Vietnam had not significantly improved since the coup d'état permeated official Washington. On December 2 President Johnson complained that "Lodge has got it screwed up good out there."[14] Staff members who had backed the plan to remove Diem grumbled about his successors. No one had worked harder to replace Diem than had Michael V. Forrestal of the National Security Council Staff and Roger Hilsman of the State Department. By December 11, however, Forrestal told Johnson that inertia had overtaken the provincial leadership since the coup. The strategic hamlet program, the brainchild of Ngo Dinh Nhu, now seemed moribund. The Vietcong enjoyed freedom of movement in the Mekong Delta region.[15]

Hilsman concurred that the generals leading the November 1 coup had had difficulty organizing a new government, thereby slowing the war effort.[16] Long An Province, a showcase of the strategic hamlet program, had been particularly hard hit. The provincial representative of the U.S. mission in Long An reported that "the only progress made in Long An Province during the month of November 1963 has been by the Communist Vietcong."[17] An American official visiting the province agreed that the strategic hamlet program in Long An had fallen far short of expectations. Of the 219 hamlets reported as completed, *"no more than* 35 are now considered to be capable of achieving the purpose for which [they were] built—that is, of separating the people from the Vietcong while providing them both security and an opportunity for social and economic development." Even in the best of the hamlets, the security was appalling. Without radios, the hamlets depended on clearly visible and easily cut wires to communicate with the soldiers who were supposed to protect them. Many villagers believed that they remained in the hamlets only at the sufferance of the Vietcong.[18]

Other officials agreed that the situation in the delta approached a crisis. CIA Director John McCone believed that conditions in the whole delta, and particularly in Long An province, had deteriorated rapidly since the coup. John Mendenhall, another member of the Special Interagency Group for Counterinsurgency, believed that the government's inability to seize the initiative since the coup had let the strategic hamlet program falter. Forrestal agreed that the delta was in grave danger of falling to the communists but thought that perhaps the responsibility lay with the Diem government he had tried so assiduously to replace. In the past Saigon authorities had consistently been optimistic; the new government might have a more realistic grasp of the situation.[19] The Director of the Defense Intelligence Agency reported to McNamara that "the government has apparently been unable to materially reduce the strength of the Vietcong in spite of the increased number of ARVN offensive operations."[20] The CIA staff officer in the delta observed "a lack of forward motion on the part of the country's new rulers in getting on with the many sided struggle against the Vietcong."[21] Forrestal wanted McNamara to whip the generals in Saigon into line. They should stop their political bickering and make certain that the provincial officials pressed forward with the war.[22]

PESSIMISTIC ASSESSMENTS: DECEMBER 1963–JANUARY 1964

The only dissent from this view came from Senator Mike Mansfield, the majority leader and a longtime supporter of Diem. In 1963, Mansfield had grown increasingly disillusioned with Diem and had warned Kennedy in August against excessive U.S. involvement in Vietnam.[23] He thought that the current efforts to secure a victory over the Vietcong in South Vietnam might "in time, involve U.S. forces throughout Southeast Asia, and finally throughout China itself in search of victory. What national interest in Asia would steel the American people for the massive costs of an ever-deepening involvement of that kind?" Instead of heading for this kind of war, with inestimable costs in terms of morale, Mansfield favored a truce in Vietnam leading to a peace throughout Southeast Asia, with a neutralized Vietnam and a Southeast Asia less dependent on U.S. aid and support, dominated neither by the United States nor by China.[24] Yet no other of the President's advisers recommended such a substantial reversal of Kennedy's policies. Still new to the job, Johnson was not ready for a dramatic break with recent policy toward South Vietnam.

Meanwhile, McNamara came away dismayed from a two-day visit to Vietnam on December 19–20, 1963.[25] The new government seemed to drift and had many of the same shortcomings of the Diem regime. Sounding like Diem, General Minh even complained about the negative stories appearing in *Time* and *Newsweek*. There seemed to be no clear hierarchy in the new government. General Minh was the chief of state, but he would step aside if an abler individual could be found. There was no backstabbing among the generals of the sort characteristic of other military regimes, but this collegiality came at the expense of activity. McNamara pressed Minh to speak to the people personally in terms that "would give them hope and faith in the future." Minh replied lamely that he had given a couple of press conferences and there was no national television in Vietnam. Anyway, the Vietnamese public probably would not respond in the positive way Americans had to the speeches Johnson made in early December after he became president. The Vietnamese might believe that Minh and the other generals were behaving like dictators.[26]

Back home, McNamara told Johnson that a crisis was near. Unless current trends were reversed in the next sixty to ninety days, a communist-controlled or, at best, a neutralist Vietnam would emerge. The major problem lay with the indecisiveness and weakness of the new government. Officials had no idea how to reorganize the strategic hamlet program. The generals in Saigon had not provided clear guidance to the provincial chiefs, most of whom were new and inexperienced. The political future of the generals' government so preoccupied them that they gave little attention to directing the war. They had even abandoned aggressive pursuit of the Vietcong in III Corps, the region immediately surrounding Saigon.

The disarray of the new government was bad enough, and it was made even worse by the persistent ineffectiveness of the U.S. diplomatic and military missions. Communications between the diplomats and military advisers had broken down. Ambassador Lodge operated as a loner as he had through-out his career, and so he and General Harkins had virtually no official contact. McNamara, Rusk, and McCone had repeatedly told him to consult more with Harkins, but Lodge seemed incapable of changing. The Vietcong had taken advantage of the weakness in the new government and the lack of coordina-tion of the American authorities. They had stepped up attacks since Novem-ber 1, but McNamara believed that the situation had deteriorated since the middle of the summer. The Vietcong had control over the population in the key areas south and west of Saigon. They had destroyed most of the key roads, making it impossible for the government to communicate with the region, and they collected taxes at will. While the Secretary of Defense's overall assessment was gloomy, he lacked specific suggestions for improve-ment, and doubted that a significant addition of U.S. forces would affect the outcome. He did believe, however, that the U.S. military needed to send better, more aggressive people to Vietnam.[27]

Although CIA Director John McCone was slightly less pessimistic than McNamara, he concurred with the gist of the Defense Secretary's conclu-sions. McCone decided that "there are more reasons to be pessimistic than to be optimistic about our success in South Vietnam."[28] Both men agreed that no organized government existed in Saigon. The Military Revolutionary Committee exercised overall control, but it did not issue strong orders to provincial administrators. They agreed that the coup had occurred at a time when conditions in Vietnam were far worse than Americans had believed. The Diem government, having lost the support of the population, had vir-tually ceased to function, and the Vietcong had made vast inroads into the hearts and minds of the peasantry that had continued after the coup. The weakness of the new government had prevented the ARVN from waging an effective offensive, and the North continued to infiltrate soldiers and equip-ment into the South. The new government may have been an improvement over the previous regime, but that reflected more on the weaknesses of Diem than on the abilities of the current rulers. Its political future remained in doubt; McCone thought that even with some moderate expansion of harassing raids by the South against the North "there are more reasons to doubt the future of the effort . . . than there are reasons to be optimistic about the future of our cause in South Vietnam."[29]

One pessimistic assessment after another poured into the White House. William Jorden, Harriman's assistant on Vietnamese affairs, reported that the mood in South Vietnam among both Vietnamese and Americans was much grimmer than he had expected. Instead of solving problems, both Americans and Vietnamese dwelled on the sins of the Diem regime. As a result anyone who had held any position under the old regime spent more time defending themselves against charges of malfeasance than trying to wage the war against the Vietcong.[30] The reports moved Johnson to encourage Lodge and the generals to try to reverse the downward spiral. The President told Lodge that McNamara's gloomy assessment of the situation meant the future of the war depended on Minh's exercise of strong personal leadership. The Vietnamese public wanted to see and hear their president.[31]

The advisers whom Johnson retained from Kennedy had an interest in the success of the policy of American intervention to determine the government of South Vietnam. They agreed that abandoning the U.S. commitment to Vietnam would represent a setback in the Cold War. Reversing the course of additional involvement in Vietnam also held domestic political perils. According to National Security Adviser McGeorge Bundy, "if we should be the first to quit in Saigon" Johnson would face the same sort of damage that President Harry S. Truman and Secretary of State Dean Acheson encountered when the Korean War went badly.[32]

Johnson raised a different unpleasant political precedent—the communist victory over the Nationalists in China in 1949. Senator Mike Mansfield, worried that "we are close to the point of no return in Vietnam," believed that both the Korean and Chinese precedents should caution the Johnson administration against deeper involvement. In both China and Korea, Mansfield believed, U. S. officials had raised the stakes too high with "overstatements of our purpose and commitment only to discover in the end that there were not sufficient American interests to support with blood and treasure a desperate final plunge." Mansfield recommended a diplomatic offensive which would enlist France, Britain, India, and perhaps even the Soviet Union in an effort to end the conflict between North and South Vietnam. He believed that a neutral Vietnam was far better than the alternatives: endless U.S. involvement in Southeast Asia "at great cost in resources and, probably, lives," or, equally unpalatable, "an ignominious and dangerous abandonment of the Southeast Asian mainland to Chinese political domination."[33]

Johnson respected Mansfield, and he asked McGeorge Bundy, Rusk, and McNamara to comment on his plan for a neutral Vietnam. Bundy believed that the analogies between Korea, China, and the current situation in Vietnam all pointed to a more, not less, aggressive stance by the United States. Public opinion had grown frustrated with the Truman administration's handling of these earlier Asian conflicts because "most Americans came to believe that we could and should have done more than we did." Bundy predicted that should the U.S. government even *seem* to move in the direction of neutralization the anti-communist forces would collapse in South Vietnam. The dominoes would start to fall. The rest of Indochina would become communist or neutralist. There would be heavy pressure on Malaya and Indonesia. The governments of Japan and the Philippines would shift toward neutrality. The South Korean and Taiwanese governments also would believe that the United States had suffered a severe blow to its prestige. In order to recover, the United States would have to commit more resources than it otherwise might have chosen to deploy in both South Korea and Taiwan.[34] Rusk thought that any scheme to neutralize Southeast Asia simply would not work. He accused Hanoi and Communist China of repeated violations of the 1954 Geneva agreement. The Soviets did not seem interested in any scheme of neutralization of South Vietnam other than the creation of "a regime which would have no support from the West and be an easy prey to a communist takeover."[35]

McNamara urged the President to reassure Mansfield that the war was essentially a Vietnamese responsibility. The United States remained committed to the withdrawal of advisers in 1965. Everything else the Secretary of Defense recommended, however, demonstrated how high he considered the stakes to be. He wanted Johnson to tell Mansfield that any deal to divide South Vietnam or to neutralize the country "would inevitably mean a new government in Saigon that would in short order be communist dominated." While McNamara's visit to Saigon had left him discouraged about the strength of the current government of Vietnam, he thought that it still could win the war. To do so, however, required constant reassurance from the United States. From the Defense Secretary's point of view the best way to assure the defeat of the anti-communists in Vietnam would be for the United States to suggest a diminution of its support.

As for the nature of U.S. interests at risk in Vietnam, McNamara repeated the justifications for U.S. involvement in Southeast Asia made by previous officials going back to the late 1940s. Events in Indochina reverberated throughout the world in the Cold War competition with the Soviet Union and China. A communist-dominated Vietnam would weaken the U.S. position in the rest of Asia and "indeed other key areas of the world." He believed officials in other regions threatened by communist insurgencies considered the U.S. reaction to the war in South Vietnam "a test of U.S. firmness and specifically a test of U.S. capacity to deal with 'wars of national liberation.'" He concluded that the stakes for the United States in preserving an anti-communist South Vietnam were "so high that . . . we must go on bending every effort to win."[36] That clinched it for Johnson. Support of neutralization as a viable option declined for policy-makers in 1964.

Theodore Sorensen, President Kennedy's counselor who remained on Johnson's staff, concurred with Bundy, Rusk, and McNamara. He stressed the political implications of the U.S. commitment to South Vietnam, one which "was not made by Democrats—but we are not free to abandon it."[37]

Johnson had argued against U.S. complicity in the November coup because he had foreseen the irrevocable repercussions. Now he was stuck; Americans had definite opinions about who should take charge in Saigon and what policies should be pursued. Other Vietnamese factions, dissatisfied with the authorities, justifiably looked to Washington for support. Faced with what Ambassador Lodge characterized as the deep "dry rot and lassitude" within the government of South Vietnam, the new Johnson administration looked for ways to stiffen the nerve of the authorities in Saigon.[38]

GENERAL NGUYEN KHANH'S COUP

In January 1964 Johnson's militant advisers decided that the war had reached the point of a "definitive crisis" requiring more aggressive U.S. action. Walt Rostow warned of widespread defeatism in South Vietnam that could contribute to "the greatest setback to U.S. interests in the world scene in many years." To reverse the sense that the United States lacked a "viable concept for winning the war" he advocated "a direct political-military showdown with Hanoi" before the end of the year.[39] The Joint Chiefs of Staff also concurred in January 1964 that the United States had to go further than before in carrying the war to the North. Maxwell Taylor urged McNamara to "put aside many of the self-imposed restrictions which now limit our efforts and undertake bolder actions which may embody greater risks." Taylor and the other Chiefs believed that "if support of the insurgency from outside of Vietnam in terms of operational direction, personnel and material were stopped completely, the character of the war in South Vietnam would be substantially and favorably altered."[40] General Harkins agreed that if the United States could stop the flow of supplies to the South the South's armed forces would be in a better position to overcome the NLF.[41]

Yet Johnson hesitated before fully Americanizing the war in an election year. He hoped to downplay the Vietnam story before election day. Johnson did not directly discourage his subordinates from pursuing an assertive Vietnam policy, but he wanted a delay in any showdown with the North. He seemed to agree with McGeorge Bundy's caution that the worst political damage would come from appearing to "quit Saigon." With the situation so desperate, the time was not ripe to contemplate a peaceful settlement. *"When* we are stronger," Bundy wrote, *"then* we can face negotiations."[42]

Echoes of Bundy's fears of neutralization reverberated in Vietnam. General Nguyen Khanh, the commander of I Corps (the region nearest the border with North Vietnam), told an adviser from the MACV that he believed General Minh planned a French-sponsored coup leading to the neutralization of Vietnam. The CIA station chief in Saigon reported that Khanh identified the leaders of the Military Revolutionary Committee as pro-French and pro-neutralist. The CIA suspected that Khanh "feels this alleged tendency on their part is becoming so pronounced that he and his like-minded military associates must act to prevent a neutral solution." Lieutenant-Colonel Tran Dinh Lam, a close associate of General Minh, had recently returned from Paris. While there, he had spoken with French officials about achieving the neutralization of South Vietnam. The CIA chief in Saigon reported that the French had promised to provide two billion piasters to achieve the neutralization of Vietnam.[43]

Lodge too notified Washington that General Khanh expected "a strong move by the government of Vietnam" in the next couple of days. He advised the State Department to protest directly to President Charles de Gaulle that the United States knew French money and agents had subverted the South Vietnamese government. Although Lodge did not believe that de Gaulle would change his course, "it is well for him to know that we know what is going on, and that we suspect a secret agreement between him and the Chicoms. We should give him a sense of pressure."[44]

On January 29 General Khanh, believing that Minh planned to arrest him and the other corps commanders,[45] staged his coup against the Military Revolutionary Council with the support of the commanders and other top military leaders. The leaders of the insurrection had concluded that Minh had "moved too slowly in restoring the momentum of the counter insurgency effort." They believed he had been too closely associated with the former Diem regime and had promoted his cronies to positions of authority. Many of these people had ties to the French: they had served in the French-created Vietnamese National Army, had been aides to General de Lattre, spoke French, and met frequently with French officials in Saigon. Khanh believed that Colonel Lam actually was a French agent. Since President de Gaulle had publicly called for an end to the war and a neutral South Vietnam, Minh's association with France made him a suspect figure in the eyes of Khanh and the other generals close to the Americans. Khanh went on the radio to explain that he had organized the coup to halt the "inefficiency" of the Minh government. He charged that "a number of people" in the former government had been paving the way for a communist government by conspiring with "colonialists" (meaning the French) to create a neutral regime.[46]

Khanh's coup provoked a mixed reaction in Vietnam and Washington. Buddhists greeted the new regime warily, since Buddhist leaders had found the previous regime more sympathetic than Diem's government. More secular leaders supported the new government, since they had grown disillusioned with Minh's movement toward neutralism.[47] *New York Times* columnist James Reston explained that Washington officials "were obviously embarrassed that the regime they helped bring to power only last November had been overthrown."[48] American officials seemed more concerned about the effectiveness of the new government to wage the war. Yet Khanh promised to "rely heavily" on the American ambassador "for political assistance because of [Khanh's] relative unfamiliarity" with civilian politics and diplomacy.[49] Besides, Minh had proved to be a profound disappointment to the officials who had wanted a change from Diem's ineptitude. No one in Washington wanted to see a neutral South Vietnam. Johnson told a press conference on February 1 that Washington might look with sympathy on the neutralization of both North and South Vietnam, but that was not the scheme presently advocated by President de Gaulle.[50]

On the other hand, Washington experts distrusted Khanh's claim that he had acted to prevent the neutralization of South Vietnam. Personal ambition had been Khanh's main reason for seizing power. While Khanh had impeccable pro-U.S. credentials and might want to wage the war more energetically than had Minh, a new period of confusion was bound to follow the latest coup. Now that coups had become the norm in determining the government of South Vietnam, Khanh had to fear for his own safety. That meant diverting military resources away from the war to protecting the authorities in Saigon. That was the way Diem had reacted to threats to his position. Three months after Diem's ouster it appeared to American officials that the new government in Vietnam would have many of the same problems that had bedeviled Diem.

Lodge saw Khanh two days after the coup to warn him against "another 6 weeks inter-regnum . . . devoted to fumbling around and to so called 'reorganization.'" Khanh seemed to willing to act quickly and even offer "a few kicks in the rear end where necessary." But he also expressed a naive longing for guidance from the United States on how to organize his government. He wanted Lodge's nominations for prime minister. Lodge wisely pretended not to know enough about the personalities to offer suggestions. Khanh also asked for help in confronting France. He contemplated immediately expelling the 450 or so French schoolteachers and scores of physicians who provided assistance throughout the country. Lodge warned against a hasty move and said that the United States did not want English to supplant French as the major European language used by the Vietnamese. While Lodge behaved correctly on the surface, the very fact that Khanh wanted his advice on the make-up of his government showed how dependent the Vietnamese were on the Americans.[51]

BOOSTING THE MORALE OF THE
SOUTH VIETNAMESE GOVERNMENT

After Khanh's coup, Americans in Saigon and Washington spent the next six months looking for ways to demonstrate U.S. support for the government of South Vietnam. Lodge quickly reversed his initial impression that the coup had set back the progress the United States had made with Minh. He believed that Khanh probably was right in asserting that Minh had surrounded himself with generals with fond memories of their days on the staff of General de Lattre during the French war against the Vietminh. Lodge liked the way Khanh seemed to want to press the war effort. "I am getting all the generals out of town and with troops as fast as I can," Khanh told Lodge a few days after the coup.[52]

Lodge also decided that changing a government by bloodless coup was an appropriate way of arranging Vietnam's affairs. "In this country," he wrote, "it rarely occurs to anyone that an election is an efficient or appropriate way to get anything important accomplished. The traditional way of doing important things here is by well planned, well thought out use of force." As time went on more and more U.S. officials used similar excuses for the shortcomings of South Vietnam's government. Lodge believed that Khanh seemed able, had a lot of drive, and would not tolerate the sort of delays in the war that General Minh had allowed. Later, Lodge told Khanh that nothing would please the Americans more than "the sight of an Oriental chief of state who wanted to go fast and did not hesitate to kick people in the rear end."[53]

A few days after Lodge refused to offer an opinion to Khanh about the makeup of the new government, the State Department weighed in with its own advice. John Mendenhall, the department's senior official on Vietnam, suggested Khanh keep the post of premier himself. If Khanh or Lodge thought this a bad idea, the department recommended Tran Quo Buu, the president of the Confederation of Vietnamese Trade Conferences, as a prime minister who could unite disparate factions within the government.[54]

But two weeks after Khanh's coup, the new government had done little to press the NLF in the war. On February 14 the CIA reported that the war was "not progressing favorably in I Corps area [the northernmost area of South Vietnam] which was generally regarded before the 1 November coup as one of the areas of greatest counter insurgency progress." Neither the Minh nor the Khanh governments had found the right personnel to run the war in I Corps. The analysts believed that some of the difficulty experienced by the new regime came from the interruption of the Tet (new year) holiday. The Americans, however, thought that interrupting a war for a holiday demonstrated much of what was wrong with the commitment of the Vietnamese authorities.[55] Four days later the CIA presented an even bleaker picture: The "tide of insurgency in all four corps areas appears to be going against the government of Vietnam."[56]

The bleak picture prompted Secretary of Defense McNamara to prepare for another visit to South Vietnam in early March. Forrestal told him before he left that the next four or five months might be the crucial juncture in the war. "If a favorable political and military trend does not develop in that period, we will slowly lose our position in Vietnam and the rest of Southeast Asia."[57] General Taylor also analyzed the changes since the coup of January 30. Khanh had, at the urging of the U.S. military command in Saigon, created a National Pacification Plan. The plan set forth a "combined military, political and economic offensive against the Vietcong in two stages." In the first phase the ARVN forces and their American advisers would move gradually from the most secure and densely populated areas to insecure and less densely populated ones. Planners labeled this concept as "spreading the oil drop."

In the second phase the government forces would attack the Vietcong's secret bases and end the insurgency. The area to be cleared under phase one would be the region surrounding Saigon, extending south into the Mekong Delta. The planned completion date of this move was July 1, 1965, with the war expected to end by January 1, 1966.[58] Lodge believed that before this optimistic scenario could come to pass the United States needed to put great pressure on North Vietnam through covert operations.[59] Johnson agreed, at least insofar as speeding up the drafting of contingency plans for "pressures against North Vietnam . . . so as to produce the maximum credible deterrent effect on Hanoi."[60]

Upon receiving the president's directive to plan future moves against North Vietnam, McNamara instructed Taylor to examine alternatives. The Secretary of Defense wanted options ranging from relatively minor covert activities to open South Vietnamese or U.S. air or sea attacks on the North. He asked Taylor for an assessment of likely responses from both the North Vietnamese and the Chinese military to U.S. attacks. Could the Chinese, for example, broaden the geographical area of the conflict to include Korea or Taiwan? He also wanted to know the capabilities of the South Vietnamese armed forces to undertake action against the North. If the ARVN forces were too weak to mount a serious campaign against the North, could the United States do so "without public acknowledgment?"[61]

The Joint Chiefs replied that the Chinese and the North Vietnamese had approximately twenty-two divisions which they could support in actions against other Southeast Asian lands during the dry season. During the rainy season their capacity would be severely limited. The Chinese could conduct limited ground and air attacks simultaneously in widely separated areas such as Southeast Asia, South Korea, and Taiwan. Realistically, though, the Chinese could not sustain a major land, air and sea offensive in more than one area. As for the strengths of the South Vietnamese, the Joint Chiefs believed that they had "very limited capability to conduct air strikes, amphibious raids, and sabotage operations in North Vietnam." If the United States used its fighter bombers covertly, the attacks would have a far greater chance of successfully destroying North Vietnamese targets. If the United States were willing to announce openly that it was using air power against the North, there would be far greater chances of deterring the North.[62] The Chiefs preferred removing restrictions on "ground and air cross-border operations."[63] So did Walt Rostow of the State Department's Policy Planning staff.[64]

These views did not yet persuade the Secretary of Defense or the President. Johnson told Taylor shortly before the latter left for Vietnam that political realities intruded on the purely military decision to authorize attacks against the North. Johnson told the Chairman of the Joint Chiefs of Staff that he did not want to lose South Vietnam before the election, but he did not "want to get the country into war" before the vote either.[65]

The CIA provided the most balanced view of the rewards and risks of crossing the border into North Vietnam. John McCone, the Director of Central Intelligence, thought that if the government of General Khanh proved stable, it was worth attacking the North, even at the risk of provoking a response from China. McCone predicted that the "loss of the game in South Vietnam would have too serious consequences to be acceptable." On the other hand, McCone doubted the premise about the strength of Khanh's regime. He predicted:

> If the Khanh government remains fragile, if the people remain disinterested, and disaffected, and we are continually confronted with coup plotting and the consequent hazards, if the resentment of the American presence continues, then it appears to me that carrying the war to North Vietnam would not win the war in South Vietnam and would cause the United States such serious problems in every corner of the world that we should not sanction such an effort."[66]

McNamara and Taylor returned to Vietnam in March. Their mission: to survey the current strength of the South Vietnamese government; review the trends of the past several months; estimate the outlook for the future, assuming no changes in the present level of U.S. commitment to the South; and map out alternatives should it appear that "current policies will not lead to the attainment of our objectives.[67]

McNamara was brusque when he met top South Vietnamese officials, rudely dismissing Khanh's claim that the South Vietnamese armed forces numbered over 422,000. Khanh meekly backed down and agreed that at any given time his government might not have more than three hundred thousand men arrayed against the NLF fighters. McNamara urged Khanh to announce a national mobilization. Only if President Johnson could tell the American public that Vietnam was on a full war footing could Khanh expect the United States to increase its support for the war with more action. McNamara's bullying became too much for General Harkins, who interjected that South Vietnam already had a national mobilization law; it simply had not been well publicized. McNamara considered this point absurd.[68] The Defense Secretary craved verifiable data on which he could make rational decisions, and formal decrees left him cold.

Upon returning to Washington, McNamara reported on the present situation in Vietnam and the ways in which he believed the United States could improve it. He stressed the advisory role of the U.S. military. It was still sound policy for the United States to want to reduce the number of advisers where the ARVN was able to take control. Although he did not expect many U.S. trainers to come home before the end of 1965, he believed the United States could gain credit in the court of world opinion by portraying the conflict as one for the South Vietnamese to win on their own.[69]

Yet South Vietnam had foundered since the previous September. McNamara noted that the Vietcong controlled anywhere from 30 to 40 percent of the territory. In twenty-two of forty-three provinces the Vietcong controlled at least 50 percent of the land area. Even in those areas outside of Viet Cong control many Vietnamese displayed apathy and indifference to the fate of the government in Saigon. Desertion rates ran high among the ARVN and even higher among the paramilitary forces. Young men dodged the draft in the cities, while in the countryside the Vietcong had successfully recruited fighters.

The government's legitimacy had also nearly disintegrated since the November 1 coup d'état. The new government had not effectively established control over strategic hamlets. Many of the hamlet militias had turned in their weapons; others were suspected of siding with the Vietcong. Power vacuums existed on the local level because of the constant turnover among provincial chiefs since the coup. General Khanh still had not exerted control over the armed forces. While he appeared to McNamara to be "a very able man within his experience," he lacked a wide appeal. He and his senior advisers worried constantly about the threat of another coup, "which would drop morale and organization to zero." At the same time the North Vietnamese had increased their support for the Vietcong.[70]

Facing a potential military and political collapse in South Vietnam, McNamara recommended that the United States do more to boost the morale of the Khanh government. He wanted to scotch any talk of neutralization as proposed by French President Charles de Gaulle. On the positive side, McNamara recommended that U.S. officials reiterate that the United States was prepared to support the South Vietnamese authorities "for as long as it takes to bring the insurgency under control." He wanted Saigon to use additional conscripts to increase their armed forces by at least fifty thousand. The United States would help train this enlarged force to create an offensive guerilla force, and would provide additional attack aircraft and armored personnel carriers. He also wanted the United States to use its own planes to patrol the borders of Laos and Cambodia to prevent the infiltration of supplies into South Vietnam. Finally, he recommended that the U.S. government proceed with plans for direct military action against North Vietnam.[71]

The National Security Council discussed McNamara's report on March 17, 1964. Johnson believed that the United States had little choice but to endorse McNamara's prescriptions. All other actions entailed terrible diplomatic or political costs. Neutralization would certainly lead to a complete breakdown of morale among non-communist South Vietnamese, and pulling out U.S. forces hastily would also devastate their spirit. Increasing the size of the U.S. commitment would have nearly as bad an effect on public opinion in the United States during a presidential election year.

The best thing about McNamara's proposals, Johnson thought, was that they seemed to offer maximum freedom of maneuver and permitted delaying more fateful decisions regarding Vietnam until a later date. He commented that they did not "foreclose action later if the situation did not improve." The council then approved nsam-288 authorizing McNamara's recommendations.[72]

None of this seemed to produce the desired impact. Johnson delayed implementing a "political scenario" in which the government of South Vietnam would ask Washington to initiate attacks against the North. Forrestal believed it was very important that "political initiatives should surface in Saigon and not in Washington, so as to maintain the credibility of the sovereignty of the government of Vietnam."[73] The President did not want to go that far at the time. His resistance led Pentagon officials to scale back their own plans for attacks on the North. Instead, they advocated cross border, tit-for-tat raids on the North.[74]

Meanwhile, the South Vietnamese government continued to founder. General Khanh required continuous hand-holding from visiting American dignitaries and Ambassador Lodge. Khanh told Secretary of State Rusk that he favored the U.S. taking the war to the North before he went on a war footing in the South. Rusk replied that should the U.S. attack the North it risked expanding the war to the point where the United States "would have to consider using nuclear weapons." That did not bother Khanh, who said "that as far as he was concerned we could use anything we wanted against China."[75] Khanh asked Lodge for advice on whether to put the country on a war footing. "I always feel better after I talk with you," he told the Ambassador. Putting the country on a war footing would throw the politicians out of Saigon. Like Lincoln during the Civil War, Khanh would impose a curfew and suspend civil liberties. Lodge seemed to agree. He gave his personal view that winning the war came before democratizing South Vietnam. "After the war was won," Lodge said, "there would be plenty of time to go ahead with democratic reforms."[76]

Officials in Washington thought that both Khanh and Lodge were losing faith in the ability of the ARVN to stem the tide. McGeorge Bundy believed that Khanh had linked putting his country on a war footing with attacking the North. Bundy observed that Khanh would agree to the sort of mobilization the Americans wanted "only if there were to be action against the North; and in turn that action would make sense only if the United States would fully support it."[77]

Lodge contemplated the possibility of another Dienbienphu in the near future. He thought "a massive Communist success is possible which could end the war if the U.S. were not to react promptly. I think it may be possible for North Vietnam to seize the Northern provinces."[78] The Ambassador explained that Khanh was frustrated by the heavy losses the ARVN had recently experienced and the inability of the arvn to prevail over the Vietcong.

Lodge reported that Khanh "is not happy in contemplating a long drawn out guerrilla war offering no decisive victory. Hence, he looks to the North as a battlefield offering more attractive targets."[79]

McNamara and Taylor returned to Vietnam in May. They heard General Harkins and his deputy, General William Westmoreland, scheduled to take over as commander of the MACV in June, disagree over the progress in the war. The ever-optimistic Harkins believed that the ARVN and their U.S. advisers would establish acceptable control over all of Vietnam with the exception of the Delta by the beginning of 1964. The more cautious Westmoreland dissented. He thought it would take another year to establish effective control over the area north of Saigon and two to three years to exert control over the Delta.[80]

When McNamara met the country team on May 12, he heard that nothing seemed to have changed since the establishment of the Khanh government. Lodge and Harkins reported that the "greatest psychological weakness in South Vietnam is the attitude of 'every man for himself.'" Like Diem before him, Khanh had centralized authority exclusively in his own hands.[81] Khanh confirmed that he did not know how to handle political issues. He was proud that he was "a soldier and not a politician." He relied on the U.S. ambassador to help him open relations with the Buddhists. Unlike Diem, however, he thought that he had the full support of Ambassador Lodge. He urged McNamara to approve guerrilla raids against the North. "Whereas the North attacks us with guerrillas that squirm through the jungle, we would attack them with 'guerrillas' of our own, only ours would fly in at tree-top level and blow up key installations or mine the port of Haiphong." Khanh acknowledged that attacks on the North would present the United States with a new sort of war. The North might retaliate in force and China might enter the war. Nevertheless, he thought that the NLF and the Vietcong were "but the arms and legs of the enemy monster; its head was in Hanoi and maybe further North."[82]

U.S. AND SOUTH VIETNAMESE PLANS
TO ATTACK THE NORTH

McNamara came away from his meeting with Khanh gloomy about the future. The government was too slow in improving its effectiveness, and the strategy of expanding oil drops worked only in a few areas. Khanh himself had an effective idea of pacification, but he had trouble translating those ideas into action. The government had not concentrated its resources in the areas of greatest vulnerability to Vietcong attack. The fighting strength of the Vietcong had risen to the point where "they are now able occasionally to stand and fight rather than to retire and dissolve in the face of government pressure." All was not lost, however, since the Vietcong were not yet able to seize an area and hold it for an extended period of time in the face of a government attack. He reported Lodge's view that U.S. air strikes against the North represented the best chance to diminish the morale of the North and raise the spirits of the civilians and military in the South. But McNamara still had not yet made up his mind on air strikes.[83]

Lodge's enthusiasm for bombing the North went further than Johnson cared to go in the spring of 1964. The President did not want any escalation in the war to detract from his ambitious legislative agenda. Congress was set to debate the Civil Rights Act in the summer, and Johnson wanted no foreign policy crisis to weaken the tenuous support for this legislation. Johnson told Lodge that neither Secretary of State Rusk nor Assistant Secretary of State William P. Bundy had understood how far along Lodge was in planning attacks against the North when they had spoken with him in April. Johnson told Lodge that he considered it "vital that you and I at all times fully and clearly understand each other's minds."[84]

McNamara briefed Johnson, the National Security Council, and important congressional leaders at a special Sunday meeting of the NSC on May 15. He explained that things had gotten worse in Vietnam in the previous three months. The Khanh government had fragmented and a new crisis brewed with the Buddhists. Khanh seemed to McNamara to be less inclined to strike against the North at the present time than was Ambassador Lodge. For all of his faults, Khanh seemed to the Secretary of Defense to realize that his current difficulties were more political and religious than military. He wanted to improve the security situation in the South before striking against the North, possibly in the fall.

Johnson interjected his own dispirited gloss on McNamara's assessment. The President thought that the fortunes of the South Vietnamese government were deteriorating at a rate which caused his administration "to be extremely alarmed. The religious situation is explosive. A great effort will be necessary to turn the tide back to our side." Members of Congress seemed most concerned about whether the United States would receive help from others if it participated in a Vietnamese war. Senate Republican leader Everett Dirksen wanted assurances that the South Vietnamese were drafting more young men into their armed forces. McNamara said the results of the previous three months had been encouraging. Regarding foreign assistance to the cause, Rusk explained that the State Department had asked about twenty nations to help in South Vietnam. West Germany, France, the United Kingdom and Australia had given verbal support. That did not satisfy one Republican congressman, who accused the administration of "merely puttering around instead of launching a campaign against the Red Chinese." He grumbled that "our allies really do not give a damn about Communist aggression."

The views of McNamara, Rusk and members of Congress represented the unattractive options available to Johnson. The advisers he had retained from Kennedy wanted deeper involvement, but they could not promise success. Congress wanted victory over communism in Asia, but at low cost. At the end of the meeting Johnson expressed some of the same frustration that had bedeviled both Eisenhower and Kennedy as they had faced the vexatious problems of Vietnam. "Even with increased U.S. aid," he complained, "the prospect in South Vietnam is not bright."[85]

The same day, the CIA reported that the situation in South Vietnam remained "extremely fragile." The Vietcong still seemed able to operate where and when they chose throughout much of the South. Their freedom of action had depressed South Vietnamese morale and made it difficult for the U.S.-sponsored assistance programs to work. The next several months presented a period of maximum danger. During this time there could be "an assassination of Khanh, a successful coup, a grave military reverse, or a succession of serious military setbacks." These could have a devastating effect on the already tenuous state of South Vietnamese morale. "If the tide of deterioration has not been arrested by the end of the year," the CIA predicted, "the anti-Communist position in South Vietnam is likely to become untenable."[86]

Each way Johnson turned he faced unpleasant prospects. South Vietnam was likely to be lost to the communists, but he certainly did not want this to happen before the 1964 presidential election. The effort needed to prevent the worst outcome, a communist victory, also might provoke a backlash among Americans. Before he would authorize the dramatic attacks on the North pressed by Lodge and sometimes by Khanh, he wanted the South Vietnamese to do more.

The frustrations of U.S. officials boiled over into a contempt for the South Vietnamese, the very people they ostensibly wanted to help with their program of assistance and military activities in the war. Rusk angrily cabled Lodge that "in the face of the prospect of a deepening crisis and the possible necessity for asking the American people to accept larger sacrifices and grave risks, we want to be sure nothing is left undone which could be done to strengthen the position of South Vietnam itself." Specifically, he wanted General Khanh to work together with General Minh "as patriotic Vietnamese even though it may require General Khanh to take some chance on working with some of those he displaced when he assumed power." He wanted Vietnam to intensify its "puny diplomatic effort abroad," and demanded that the government approve a budget, stalled since Khanh took office in January. "I can't see why," he raged, "materials in warehouses and pipelines cannot be moved promptly to the countryside." He remembered his experience in the China-Burma-India theater during the Second World War. He knew "how deliberate all deliberate speed can be in that part of the world." Nevertheless, Rusk demanded that "somehow we must change the pace at which these people move, and I suspect that this can be done only with a pervasive intrusion of Americans into their affairs.''[87] As the United States became more deeply involved in Vietnam, views like these became more pronounced, and the United States came more and more to dominate the political life of the people whom it claimed it wanted to make independent.

Lodge thought Rusk overwrought. He reminded the Secretary of State that South Vietnam had only emerged from colonialism ten years before and that no one in Saigon wanted to recapitulate the colonial experience with the Americans in the role of the French. Lodge was not averse to the United States exercising full power in Vietnam through a commissioner general ''or a man who really gives the orders under the title of Ambassador,'' but he thought that at least the South Vietnamese should invite the Americans to take over before the United States actually moved in to call the shots.[88]

PLANNING A CONGRESSIONAL RESOLUTION

At the same time a group of Vietnam experts in Washington was drafting a congressional resolution authorizing Johnson to use as much force as he wanted. The draft resolution charged that North Vietnam, aided by China, had ''systematically flouted'' its obligations under the 1954 Geneva accords to respect the independence and territorial integrity of South Vietnam. It authorized the President to ''use all measures, including the use of armed forces,'' to assist the governments of South Vietnam or Laos ''against aggression or subversion supported, controlled or directed from any Communist country.''[89] Advocates of a resolution wanted Congress to make a public display of support for the government of South Vietnam, but they did not believe that the resolution had great political significance inside the United States. They realized, however, that the debate over Johnson's civil rights bill absorbed most of Congress's attention. They asked Johnson ''to persuade [Georgia Democratic Senator] Dick Russell to accept a three day truce in Civil Rights on straight patriotic grounds.''[90]

Still, Johnson believed that the time was not right for a resolution. He did not want to generate public attention on a festering war in Southeast Asia in the midst of the presidential election campaign. Arizona Republican Senator Barry Goldwater, the likely Republican presidential candidate, accused Johnson of lacking a decisive strategy to achieve victory in Vietnam. ''I think the first decision is that we are going to win,'' he said on network television on May 24. He thought that the United States was waging a defensive war and ''a defensive war is never won.'' He urged the bombing of bridges, roads, and other supply lines from the North to the South. He even explained that ''defoliation of the forests by low yield atomic weapons could well be done,'' although he said that he did not presently favor such a course.[91]

Johnson seemed tormented by the rising tide of public discussion over

Vietnam in the newspapers. Columnist Walter Lippmann had supported de Gaulle's call for neutralization of all of Southeast Asia.[92] On May 27 Lippmann met Johnson, McNamara, McGeorge Bundy, and Undersecretary of State George Ball. Lippmann reiterated his support of neutralization even though he thought that the United States could not stop the advance of communism in the region and that all of Southeast Asia was destined to become a zone of Chinese communist control. The best that could be hoped for was to seek political means by which to slow the expansionism and "make it less brutal."

Johnson argued with Lippmann. He seemed deeply impressed by Lippmann's assertion that the United States "was presenting itself in a bad light to the world by refusing to negotiate and entertaining the possibility of enlarged military action." Johnson wondered out loud about how he could maintain "his posture as a man of peace in the face of the Southeast Asian crisis." He asked Ball, Bundy, and McNamara "how could he carry a united country with him if we were to embark on a course of action that might escalate under conditions which the rest of the world would regard as wrong-headed." Johnson's caution reinforced Ball's skeptical view. Ball presented a series of questions about the likelihood of a move against the North having the desired effect. "Are we proposing action against the North because we are reasonably confident it will, in fact, work, or merely because we are becoming reasonably confident that the present course of action will not work and we are not able to think of anything else to do?"[93]

High officials in Washington and Saigon spent the next two months trying and failing to think of something other than an attack on the North. Michael Forrestal told Johnson that the political atmosphere in Saigon was rife with fatalism. He saw "doubt that the war will ever be ended the way it is being waged now," and believed that "some dramatic change in the atmosphere" was needed within the next six weeks. He recommended "action by the United States in some part of Southeast Asia which gets across forcefully to the Vietnamese a sense that we believe communist insurgency can be contained and that we will do whatever is required to insure this."[94]

Another meeting occurred among the top military and diplomatic officials from Washington and Saigon in Honolulu in June. Westmoreland called the situation "tenuous but not hopeless."[95] Rusk thought that things were actually a little better than they had been the year before. The Secretary of State thought that the United States should distance itself from the fortunes of General Khanh. If he fell, so be it; the United States would have to start all over again. The Secretary of Defense was more pessimistic about the prognosis for the next six month. He also thought that air strikes could work, at least in the short term, to raise the morale of the South Vietnamese. McNamara was certain that the United States could "plan an air attack on targets in North Vietnam which would avoid running into their defended areas."[96]

Everyone wanted something dramatic, but they differed over the value of introducing a congressional resolution. Walt Rostow, now the Counselor of the Department of State and Chairman of the Policy Planning Council, claimed that the public did not understand the international dimensions of the war. They were uninformed about Hanoi's responsibility for the fighting in the South. Rostow blamed the negative reporting by David Halberstam in the *New York Times* for confusing the public about the nature of the war. He recommended a concerted but low key campaign of public information to convince reporters, editors, publishers, congressional leaders, and key citizens that Hanoi had sponsored the war in the South.[97]

Assistant Secretary of State for Far Eastern Affairs William P. Bundy said something like the passage of a congressional resolution was needed to grip the public imagination and convince people that the war was going better for the United States and its South Vietnamese allies. He noted a continuing "press bias toward reporting the unfavorable." If current trends continued, Americans would think things were getting worse, even if the South Vietnamese made modest progress.[98]

From Saigon, however, Ambassador Lodge told Johnson that he was "not yet persuaded that such a resolution [was] in fact required." Lodge considered the commitment of one hundred thousand men envisioned by advocates of a congressional resolution far too high. "The climate and other conditions in this area are of incomparable difficulty for Americans." Moreover, Lodge thought that the U.S. contingent would make up the bulk of the force assisting the South Vietnamese. The South Vietnamese had committed as many young men as they were able. The resolution and the commitment of seven divisions, therefore, seemed to Lodge to foreshadow "a largely U.S. venture of unlimited possibilities which could put us onto a slope along which we slide into a bottomless pit."[99]

While Johnson temporized over the introduction of a congressional resolution, his staff thought a replacement for Lodge as ambassador might provide the necessary boost to the morale of the South Vietnamese. National Security Adviser McGeorge Bundy, arguing that Vietnam "is more important than poverty, and the right man harder to find," listed some important—and unusual—personalities as potential replacements for Lodge. Sargent Shriver, married to the sister of John and Robert Kennedy, whom Johnson had named to head the effort to eradicate poverty, was Bundy's first choice. He also suggested Roswell Gilpatric, the former Deputy Secretary of Defense who had drafted some of President Kennedy's earliest plans for Vietnam. Bundy praised Gilpatric's style and judgment but expressed a measure of doubt about "whether he has the energy and the political insight to take the call to the provinces and the case to the people." Bundy also proposed McNamara for the position, but his endorsement was surprisingly tepid. Bundy noted that the Secretary of Defense "has been trying to think of ways of dealing with the problem for so long that he has gone a little stale. . . . He has rather mechanized the problem so that he misses some of its real political flavor."

Bundy's last two suggestions were even more curious. He thought that Robert F. Kennedy, whom Johnson deeply distrusted, had "tremendous appeal to younger people and to non-Americans all around the world. He will give a picture of idealism and peace-seeking which our case will badly need, especially need, especially if we have to move to stronger measures." Johnson considered the appointment of Robert Kennedy as the ambassador in South Vietnam a wild idea. Finally, Bundy nominated himself, pointing to his understanding of the issues, his knowledge of French, and his "heavy dose of the ways of thinking of all branches of the U.S. team in South Vietnam."[100] Not included in Bundy's list was Maxwell Taylor, the man Johnson named to replace Lodge on June 23.[101] Johnson's selection of Taylor expressed his conviction that military considerations were paramount in the growing U.S. involvement in Vietnam.

Many of Johnson's principal advisers, including Rusk, McNamara, McGeorge Bundy, Secretary of the Treasury Douglas Dillon, Attorney General Robert Kennedy, Walt Rostow, and William Bundy, met at the White House on June 10 to discuss the benefits and drawbacks of introducing a congressional resolution on Southeast Asia. The group rehearsed the familiar arguments. In favor of a resolution was the boost to the morale of the government of South Vietnam. McNamara said that most Vietnamese did not think the United States would "take actions necessary to save the situation." A resolution might help change their minds. William Sullivan, the State Department's chief planner for Vietnam, expressed exasperation that the United States had "to reassure the Vietnamese every day." Rusk shared Sullivan's irritation, and he complained that "we cannot build our policy on the constant need to reassure nervous friendly countries."

But a resolution also had dangers. A congressional declaration that did not have nearly unanimous support would be worse than nothing at all. Senator Wayne Morse (D., Ore.) had gone on record opposing further U.S. involvement in Vietnam, so he could be counted on to oppose any resolution. The group hoped that his would be the only negative vote. To assure such unanimity Rusk argued that "we should ask for a resolution only when the circumstances are such as to require action, and, thereby, force congressional action." The Secretary of State believed that "there will be a rallying around the president the moment it is clear to reasonable people that U.S. action is necessary." Robert Kennedy agreed that "heavy ground work with Congress will be necessary." He recommended delaying the introduction of a resolution until the administration had dramatic evidence of North Vietnamese action against the South. The group also agreed that nothing could be done while the civil rights bill was under consideration, and the debate on that legislation was expected to continue until July. Furthermore, McNamara thought that although the situation appeared bad in South Vietnam, he did not think that the United States had to take major action in the next two or three months.[102]

Summarizing, McGeorge Bundy told the President that his principal advisers believed the advantages for the resolution were in the international arena. It would raise the profile of Vietnam and demonstrate a greater U.S. commitment to the South. The effect on South Vietnamese morale might be impressive, yet the very increase in attention given to Vietnam was the major drawback in asking for a resolution in the midst of debate over the Civil Rights Act and the upcoming Republican presidential nominating convention. Bundy noted that Johnson could do things other than request a formal resolution to achieve bipartisan support for his Vietnam policy. He could consult Eisenhower and Barry Goldwater, appeal directly to the people in a televised address, and discuss the issue with the congressional leadership. On balance Bundy concluded that the costs of an immediate resolution outweighed the benefits. Introduction of a resolution in June or July would create "a substantial increase of national attention" toward Vietnam and generate greater "international tension."[103]

His brother, William Bundy, disagreed. He believed that the best time to introduce a resolution was the third week in June, after the Civil Rights debate. July was out, he said, because of the Republican convention. The Democrats met in August, so there would be little time that month either. This timetable was upset when Congress did not complete the civil rights debate until early July. Johnson refused to introduce the resolution while Congress was preoccupied.[104] Bundy believed that the impending presidential election made it all the more important for Johnson to have the strong backing of Congress. He thought that the administration should prod Congress to act even "without the type of dramatic event that would, inevitably call for convening the Congress." Previously, advocates of the congressional resolution had stressed the importance of stiffening the spine of the South Vietnamese government. William Bundy added the element of using the resolution to convince the communist side that "America means business." Without an official congressional resolution, he feared the communist side would assume that the United States was "unlikely to act firmly during an election year."[105]

As he had done before, Johnson undertook measures less dramatic than the introduction of the congressional resolution. He authorized a major public relations push to explain the reasons for the U.S. commitment in Vietnam.[106] He also publicly announced that Maxwell Taylor would be going to Vietnam accompanied by U. Alexis Johnson, who had help create the State Department's policy on Vietnam since the Eisenhower administration, as his deputy ambassador.[107] Johnson gave Taylor full control over all U.S. operations in Vietnam. Previously the military had not been willing to grant the ambassador such plenary powers, but Taylor, coming straight from the chairmanship of the Joint Chiefs of Staff, could not be denied. When Johnson met with Taylor before his departure, the President stressed that he wanted the "strongest possible effort to move ahead *within* South Vietnam. Large scale moves 'to the North' are not the present answer."[108]

THE GULF OF TONKIN RESOLUTION

While the White House advisers foresaw dangers in Khanh's desire to move to the North, the South Vietnamese government seemed more ready than ever to take the war to the North. Ambassador Taylor reported that Khanh considered the ARVN rife with intrigue. His own position was not secure at the top of the armed forces, many generals distrusted him, and the disaffection at the highest levels might seep into the lower ranks. This unrest within the armed forces was intolerable, because Khanh believed the armed forces to be the "only real solid instrument in South Vietnam capable of exercising power and exercising the affairs of state." Taylor thought that Khanh might be tempted to send the ARVN north of the seventeenth parallel to close the rifts among his top officers. Events outside Vietnam also led Khanh to think the time was ripe to attack the North. Goldwater's nomination for president led South Vietnamese generals to believe they could apply pressure on the United States to expand the area of conflict. The Sino-Soviet split and President de Gaulle's repeated calls to neutralize Vietnam made the South Vietnamese authorities think American officials might relax their restrictions on an attack on the North. These new international developments reduced the risk of Soviet or Chinese intervention in case of such an attack.[109]

Taylor thought that Khanh's talk of marching north had a calculated air about it, intended to whip up public enthusiasm for the war effort among South Vietnamese. This might be exactly what the Americans had proposed in their demands that Khanh put the country on a war footing. The discussion of a march to the North might be a ploy to encourage the United States to begin a campaign of reprisal bombing against the North, but Khanh might seriously want to use the military to reunify Vietnam "as soon as he felt he had us inextricably involved beyond the point of possible detachment." Whatever Khanh's specific intention, he knew he could manipulate the United States into more aggressive involvement in the war.[110]

Then, in early August, everything changed with two controversial incidents off the coast of North Vietnam. Two U.S. destroyers, the *Maddox* and the *C. Turner Joy,* had conducted so-called De Soto patrols in connection with a covert operation, OPLAN 34-A. In De Soto patrols the American vessels supported the activities of the South Vietnamese navy by conducting surveillance, sometimes within the twelve-mile coastal limits claimed by North Vietnam, along the North Vietnamese coast bordering the Gulf of Tonkin. The destroyers approached the coast in order to provoke the operators of coastal radar installations to activate their machines. The radars would then emit radio signals which would reveal their location to the sophisticated electronic equipment on the American ships. In response, the *Maddox* and the *C. Turner Joy* would notify the accompanying South Vietnamese patrol boats of the position of the North's radar, allowing the South Vietnamese to attack.[111]

These De Soto patrols provoked the North Vietnamese navy to attack the *Maddox* at 3:40 A.M. on August 2.[112] Immediately after this attack, General Earle Wheeler, Chairman of the Joint Chiefs of Staff, authorized the De Soto patrols to approach to within eleven miles of the North Vietnamese coastline. The North Vietnamese claimed a twelve-mile territorial zone, but the United States recognized only a three-mile limit. Authorizing ships to approach within eleven miles was a way of defying the twelve-mile claim. Michael Forrestal urged that the naval vessels do more and engage in hot pursuit of North Vietnamese vessels to within three miles of the coast.[113]

Two nights later the commander of the *C. Turner Joy* believed that his destroyer also was under attack and ordered his gunners to return fire. They did so but hit nothing, probably because no attack had occurred. North Vietnamese PT boats did track the movements of the *Turner Joy*, whose crew members were aware of what had already happened to the *Maddox*. Nervous, they fired into the murky night. After evidence mounted in later years that these attacks had not taken place, Johnson said, "For all I know, our navy was shooting at whales out there."[114]

Nevertheless, Johnson ordered air strikes against four North Vietnamese bases. He met his principal advisers and told them that nothing should be made public about the attacks and possible retaliation for the time being. Secretary of the Treasury Douglas Dillon said that there was "a limit on the number of times we can be attacked by the North Vietnamese without hitting their naval bases." Later at lunch, Johnson agreed with McNamara and Rusk that "a firm swift retaliatory strike must be carried out." Johnson authorized air attacks against five PT boat bases and an oil depot on the coast of North Vietnam. Johnson rejected a suggestion that the United States attack ships in Haiphong harbor and mine the port in that city.[115]

The incident in the Gulf of Tonkin provided precisely the sort of provocation advocates of a congressional resolution had sought for months. Johnson submitted to Congress the resolution prepared earlier in the spring. McNamara testified before Congress that both the *Maddox* and the *C. Turner Joy* had been attacked, although at the time he knew that only scanty evidence existed of the second attack. He also clearly did not tell the truth when he assured lawmakers that "the *Maddox* was operating in international waters and was carrying out a routine patrol of the type we carry out all over the world at all times."[116]

McNamara's testimony and the conviction expressed by Secretary of State Rusk that "an immediate and direct reaction by us is necessary," carried the day in Congress.[117] Rusk told the congressional leadership meeting secretly at the White House that the attack had been a deliberate effort on the part of the North Vietnamese to intimidate the United States. "We must make it quite clear," he told the leaders, "that we are resolved not to overlook any threat that is posed our forces." All the leaders present agreed that a resolution was necessary, but their complaisance won them little respect at the White House. National Security Adviser Bundy told the National Security Council that "leadership" was a "funny word" to use in reference to the Democrats and Republicans who had called on the President on August 4. "There was nothing Congress could do in the way of leading," he said, "in a situation in which the president's role was so primary."[118]

On August 7 both houses passed the Gulf of Tonkin Resolution, which granted congressional support for the President to "respond instantly with the use of appropriate force to repel any unprovoked attack against the armed forces of the United States." Congress also authorized, upon request from any nation in Southeast Asia, "all measures including the use of armed force to assist that nation in the defense of its political independence and territorial integrity against aggression or subversion."[119] The vote in the House of Representatives was unanimous, while in the Senate only two Democrats, Ernest Greuning of Alaska and Wayne Morse of Oregon, voted no.[120] Greuning considered U.S. involvement in Vietnam a "putrid mess" and felt that "all Vietnam is not worth the life of a single American boy."[121] Morse spoke at great length and with great passion against the resolution.[122] He asserted that the United States had provoked the attacks by the North Vietnamese by escorting the South Vietnamese boats close to the shore, and complained that the Pentagon and the State Department had performed a "snowjob" on Congress with their dishonest denials of the South's attacks on Northern coastal installations.[123] He thought the United States ignored its obligations under the United Nations Charter to resolve disputes peacefully by bombing the North in retaliation for the attacks on the U.S. destroyers. Morse also foresaw a catastrophic outcome for the United States, similar to the defeat suffered by France in 1954, predicting the deployment of hundreds of thousands of U.S. troops and tens of thousands of casualties. He believed that "the administration responsible" for such a prolonged war "will be rejected and repudiated" by a disgusted public.[124] Off the Senate floor he complained that the Johnson administration had "joined the vicious lying Communist leaders of North Vietnam and Red China . . . in treating as scraps of paper our international law obligations."[125] He predicted that Americans would

later vindicate him and Greuning for voting against the Gulf of Tonkin Resolution. "The day of the White Westerner is over in Asia," he explained.
"Like the European countries before us we must find a way to withdraw
gracefully from Vietnam."[126]

But withdrawal was the last thing on Johnson's mind. The resolution's
extraordinarily broad grant of authority had no time limit. Later Johnson
would use it to justify the greatly expanded American role in the war. Members of Congress in 1964 hardly anticipated the later uses to which the resolution would be put; they supported it as an appropriate response to what
seemed to be a reckless North Vietnamese attack. Some hoped that the
display of congressional fortitude would make it easier for the North to back
away from a major escalation in the fighting.[127]

The Gulf of Tonkin Resolution and the limited air strikes against the
North did little to fulfill the planners' hopes of bolstering the morale of
General Khanh's government. Khanh was moody and impatient and wanted
the United States to mount a continuing bombing campaign. Assistant Secretary of State Bundy thought that Khanh's chances of remaining in power were
only 50-50. He told Johnson that "even if the situation in our own view does
go a bit better, we have problems in maintaining morale."[128]

Yet the resolution and the air raids of August removed Vietnam from the
political debate during the 1964 election in the United States. Johnson followed the advice of his assistant Bill Moyers to "keep the public debate on
Vietnam to as low a level as possible."[129] Goldwater dropped his earlier
condemnations of Johnson's timidity. The President broadcast an air of mod-
eration toward the war, refusing to recommend either withdrawal or intensification. Most of his listeners believed that he wanted to keep the United
States out of a full-scale shooting war while at the same time preventing a
communist victory. Most supported that course. He made one major campaign speech on Vietnam in which he sounded moderate while leaving himself considerable room for a deeper U.S. commitment at a later date. He said
that only "as a last resort" would he "start dropping bombs around that are
likely to involve American boys in a war in Asia with 700 million Chinese."
He could not predict the future, he said, but "we are not going north and drop
bombs at this stage of the game, and we are not going south and run out and
leave it for the Communists to take over."[130]

Johnson's soothing rhetoric helped him sail serenely to a landslide victory
over Barry Goldwater in November, but nothing his administration did in its
first year resolved the dilemmas of U.S. intervention in the war in Vietnam left
by President Kennedy. The North Vietnamese and National Liberation Front
remained confident and patient; the South Vietnamese government and military divided and hesitant. The United States became more deeply involved in
South Vietnamese politics, and stood on the threshold of fighting the war itself
without having helped the Republic of Vietnam fortify its legitimacy.

Chapter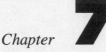

* * * * * * * * * * *

Days of Reckoning:
August 1964–July 1965

*B*ETWEEN LATE 1964 and the middle of 1965 the U.S. passed the point of no return in Vietnam. The number of U.S. troops in Vietnam rose from fifty thousand to ninety thousand with a promise of another hundred thousand by the end of 1965. Their role changed from advisers to combatants. In the fall of 1964 President Johnson and his principal advisers on Vietnam policy watched in horror as a succession of unstable governments in Saigon failed to develop popular support and wage the war effectively. The United States took a series of steps designed to bolster the flagging morale of the South Vietnamese authorities, but nothing seemed to work. For both political and military reasons, in early 1965 the United States escalated the air war over North Vietnam. By June, Johnson had taken a series of decisions that irrevocably transformed the Vietnam conflict into an American war. In July the President presided over a celebrated discussion with his key advisers about whether to increase the number of U.S. ground forces. By the time these discussions took place, Johnson had so deeply committed the United States to the fighting that it seemed far easier to go forward than to diminish American involvement.

Throughout this period of gradually increasing American participation in the fighting, the Johnson administration struggled to limit the U.S. role. Planners hoped to break the will of the North Vietnamese and force them to stop the NLF fighters without at the same time provoking retaliation from the

154

Soviet Union or China. Most officials thought that limiting the geographical scope of the war would lessen the impact on the American public, sustaining support for the war. At the same time, Johnson and his advisers did not want the war to get out of hand—to "get the American people too angry," as Dean Rusk put it.[1] But it proved nearly impossible both to limit the war and wage it effectively. Each step up the ladder of escalation alarmed the Soviets and Chinese and also provoked reactions from a growing anti-war movement at home.

THE ELECTION OF 1964

Congressional passage of the Gulf of Tonkin Resolution on August 7, 1964 gave Johnson political breathing room during the election of 1964. The nearly unanimous congressional endorsement of air strikes against the North and future military action deflected criticism. Barry Goldwater, the Republican nominee, had earlier called on the United States to step up the pace of bombing and attacks with ground troops. Now that the Gulf of Tonkin Resolution was law, with Goldwater's approval, further statements by Goldwater about the advisability of using nuclear weapons or increasing the level of bombing of the North made the Republican candidate appear reckless. Johnson cleverly played on public fears that Goldwater was a dangerous man. "Sometimes our folks get a little impatient," he told a campaign rally. "Sometimes they rattle their rockets some, and they bluff about their bombs. But we are not about to send American boys 9 or 10,000 miles away from home to do what Asian boys ought to be doing for themselves."[2]

Ironically, Johnson's calls for restraint in Vietnam won him the support of a wide spectrum of Americans, even as he laid plans to expand the war. Johnson hoped for a landslide, demonstrating a broad consensus in support of his domestic and international policies. Moderate Republicans, most Democrats with the exception of Southern segregationists, and political radicals and pacifists all supported Johnson's candidacy. Deputy Secretary of the Treasury Henry Fowler helped set up a presumably "independent" committee of mostly Republican business leaders to support Johnson.[3]

Senator J. William Fulbright (D., Ark.), chairman of the Foreign Relations Committee strongly supported his friend Lyndon Johnson's candidacy as he had the Gulf of Tonkin Resolution because, he recalled, "I had no wish to make any difficulties for the president in his race against a Republican candidate whose election I thought would be a disaster for the country." Fulbright spoke out for Johnson as a president who could better manage relations with the Soviets. "The Goldwater Republicans propose a radical new policy of relentless ideological conflict aimed at the elimination of Communism and the imposition of American concepts of freedom on the entire world. The Democrats under President Johnson propose a conservative policy of opposing and preventing Communist expansion while working for limited agreements that will reduce the danger of nuclear war."[4] Even radicals such as David McReynolds of the War Resisters League and pacifists such as David Dellinger also supported Johnson's candidacy because they believed he wanted to limit U.S. involvement in Vietnam.[5]

As Johnson went forward with the presidential campaign promising to limit the U.S. fighting role in Vietnam, political turmoil continued in South Vietnam. In August General Nguyen Khanh resigned as president and dissolved the Military Revolutionary Council, but retained the post of prime minister. He left Saigon for a long stay in the more relaxed atmosphere of Dalat, citing high blood pressure and hemorrhoids. Ambassador Taylor believed his worst ailment was an "obsession over the preponderant strength" of his domestic opponents. He continued to worry about the possibility of a coup led by younger military leaders. Like a series of U.S. ambassadors before him, Taylor assumed the role of a big brother to a timid South Vietnamese president. Taylor and U. Alexis Johnson, his deputy, demanded that Khanh pull himself together. He sounded, they told him, like "practically a mental case" in interviews he gave to local reporters. He had to get hold of himself and return to Saigon. Taylor and Johnson managed to convince Khanh that, since he retained the support of nearly all Catholic clergy, most Buddhist leaders, and nearly all the upper echelons of the armed forces, he need not fear his domestic opponents. He promised to return to work soon.[6] Within days, he created a provisional government, including himself and Generals Duong Van Minh (the man he had ousted in January) and Tran Thien, that was intended to last two months.

Khanh's near mental collapse sent shock waves to Washington. McGeorge Bundy told the President that "we do not know whether Khanh still has it in him to resume full control." Bundy thought that the United States should continue to show solid support for Khanh, "so that if he falls it will in no sense be our doing." Such assurances represented more political posturing than an effective strategy for dealing with the war. Bundy stressed pressing forward with contingency plans to escalate U.S. involvement in the war, including naval harassments along the coast of North Vietnam, air strikes over the Laotian panhandle, and sending the U.S. fleet into the Gulf of Tonkin. The goal of these moves, like those of so many before, "would be more to heighten morale and to show our strength of purpose than to accomplish anything very specific in a military sense." Bundy thought that the United States might even have to contemplate using its own ground troops in the war against the Vietcong. Until then the Pentagon had not drafted contingency plans for such a major escalation. For his part, though, Bundy believed that before the United States let South Vietnam go "we should have a hard look at this grim alternative." Alert to Johnson's fears of a repetition of the stalemate during the Korean War, Bundy doubted that the analogy would hold in the Vietnamese case. He thought that the introduction of a couple of brigade-size units in mid-October, just three weeks before the U.S. presidential election, "might be good medicine."[7] Johnson, gifted with greater political insights, thought nothing could be worse than raising the profile of U.S. involvement in Vietnam right before the election.

Ambassador Taylor returned to Washington in September to confer with Johnson and Rusk on the deteriorating situation in South Vietnam. He reported that Khanh did not seem to have the stuff of leadership. His government was "exhausted and frustrated" following recent demonstrations against it in the northern part of the country. The turmoil had eliminated the government's earlier enthusiasm for a march north to raise the stakes for Hanoi. Any successor would not do any better. "Only the emergence of an exceptional leader could improve the situation and no George Washington is in sight," Taylor lamented.[8] General William C. Westmoreland, the commander of the MACV, was even blunter. He believed that Khanh had nearly destroyed the effectiveness of the ARVN by negotiating with Buddhist leaders on their demands to fire some of the top commanders of the ARVN and the national police. He believed that such moves were "calculated to destroy the morale, the unity, the pride and confidence of the Armed Forces."[9]

Like Bundy, Taylor saw no alternative to an augmented U.S. military presence in Vietnam. The ambassador faced the daunting challenge of running a military campaign against the Vietcong, at the same time carrying out "a remodeling job of the government [of South Vietnam] under hostile fire."[10] Walt Rostow, the chairman of the policy planning staff of the State Department, believed that the task went beyond reforming the government of South Vietnam to a complete reformation of its political culture. A literate, professional urban middle class demanded a say in a modern government.[11] Rostow and Taylor recognized a political fork in the road of Vietnam policy. One path would lead to the development of a popular front movement that would eventually force the United States to abandon Vietnam; the alternative course required the United States to assume increased responsibility for its fate.

Taylor differed from Bundy, however, on the timing of a steep increase in United States military participation in the war. The ambassador believed that the U.S. needed two or three months, until the beginning of December and well after the U.S. presidential election, to foster a strong and effective government in Saigon. After December 1, Taylor believed that the United States would be in a position to "begin escalating pressures on the DRV for the purpose of holding the government of Vietnam together, of raising morale and of creating conditions required for a negotiated termination of hostilities on favorable terms." He wanted the United States to position ground forces in South Vietnam to prevent the North or the Chinese communists from attacking the South. Once assured of sufficient protection of the civilian areas of South Vietnam, the United States would conduct air strikes against infiltration routes in Laos and against North Vietnam. These would be primarily U.S. operations. The South Vietnamese air force would operate only out of the range of the North Vietnamese MiGs.[12]

The CIA also warned Johnson about the continued instability of the South Vietnamese government. The aftermath of the overthrow of the Diem government had unleashed previously suppressed political forces. Buddhists, students, labor leaders, and intellectuals and politicians at home and abroad pressed their own demands. Many of their interests conflicted. A few civilian politicians wanted to play a constructive role and resolve differences, but "most remain[ed] more concerned with personal power and prestige than national unity." The top leadership of the armed forces also seemed incapable of maintaining a steady course among the competing demands of groups within South Vietnamese society. The CIA considered the situation in Saigon "far more serious than that of November 1963." Then, at least, there had been the initial burst of enthusiasm following Diem's ouster. Now, few people in Saigon believed that Khanh's new provisional regime was up to the task. Moreover, the Vietcong were now stronger than they had ever been before. The CIA did not believe that the NLF had been responsible for the recent outbreak of anti-government demonstrations in the northern part of the country, but the civil disturbances in Hué had fortified the Vietcong's propaganda that a communist victory would "come primarily from South Vietnam's political failures and instability."[13]

The President met with Taylor on September 9. They discussed a modest plan of increased military actions against the North that Taylor had previously worked out with McNamara and Chairman of the Joint Chiefs of Staff Earle Wheeler. The military men agreed that the United States would resume De Soto patrols (the effort to locate North Vietnam's shore batteries and radar installations) in the Gulf of Tonkin outside the twelve-mile limit around September 12. The South Vietnamese would continue 34-A operations designed to harass the North. The military leadership also wanted the South Vietnamese armed forces to commence air and ground operations near the Laotian border in order the slow the flow of supplies through the Ho Chi Minh Trail into South Vietnam.

Taylor, McNamara, and Wheeler thought that these operations would be more important in keeping the South Vietnamese armed forces busy than in actually affecting the military situation in the South. The three men deferred offensive actions by the United States against the North. Instead they recommended that the United States be "*prepared* to respond on a tit-for-tat basis" to the North should the DRV attack U.S. units or should the forces of the DRV engage in any extraordinary actions against South Vietnam. They recommended that whenever the United States employed air strikes against the

North, the targets should be specifically chosen to relate to the attacks on the U.S. forces or the South Vietnamese installations.[14]

Johnson found the limited scale of the recommendations puzzling, given the recent reports by American military officers in South Vietnam detailing the desperate state of the Khanh government. McNamara told him that Taylor did not believe the time was ripe for a major escalation, but that the commandant of the Marine Corps and the commander of the Air Force now wanted the United States to embark on a sustained bombing campaign of the North. Taylor explained that the current fragility of the Khanh government made any greater escalation of the war politically difficult. John McCone, the Director of Central Intelligence, observed that sustained air attacks against the North would expose the Saigon government to greater internal dissent. Moreover, the CIA foresaw the danger of intervention in the war by the Chinese should the United States move immediately to a sustained bombing campaign against the North.

Ever the alert politician, Johnson wondered what could be done to strengthen the government of South Vietnam. He thought that the United States should not go forward with a bombing campaign of the North until the government in Saigon could defend itself in the streets. "With a weak and wobbly situation," the President remarked, "it would be unwise to attack until we could stabilize our base." He also grumbled that the United States had had its best personnel in place in Vietnam for the previous sixty days, and yet the situation seemed worse than before. Taylor, who heretofore had proven a far less optimistic ambassador than his predecessor, reassured the President that things might not be as bad as they appeared. Even though the Vietnamese public did not seem to like President Khanh any more than they had Diem, the military was making headway in pacifying the countryside— nearly half the provinces, which seemed to please Westmoreland. Seeing no other real choice, Johnson approved the military courses of action McNamara, Taylor, and Wheeler had drawn up.[15] NSAM-314, issued on September 10, authorized their proposed actions against the North, which based U.S. policy on the need to strengthen the government of South Vietnam.

Johnson then reflected on his own need to have the support of the congressional leadership in the midst of the U.S. presidential election campaign. He said he wanted to brief the congressional leaders regularly so they would understand that the administration did not presently plan a major escalation of the war. But National Security Adviser Bundy thought the less Congress was seen the better. He criticized the steady stream of congressional visits to Vietnam which, he claimed, made it all the harder for the embassy and the MACV to do their jobs. Even worse, congressional visitors often met with figures opposed to the government of South Vietnam. They encouraged opposition leaders to believe that Ambassador Taylor's was not the only voice speaking for the United States. President Khanh, a chronically insecure man, did not easily comprehend the role of Congress in the U.S. government. The President and Taylor agreed that to press on the congressional leadership the "hope that Congress would let the government get stabilized, and that at this delicate moment when the government is fragile we should have only one spokesman on the scene—the ambassador."[16]

In the seven weeks before the presidential election, American officials tried to keep the government of South Vietnam intact despite mounting evidence that it had lost the support of important factions within the military. Two generals attempted a coup on September 13.[17] It failed, but left Khanh in a black mood, complaining about the disloyalty of his army colleagues with whom he had been friendly for years.[18] The attempted coup also infuriated officials in Washington who reminded the Vietnamese generals that they "need not look among themselves for enemies; they all have a common enemy in the Vietcong."[19] The coup had failed because the plotters had been disorganized and had little popular support. Even so, the confidence in President Khanh expressed by the U.S. embassy had been the crucial factor in keeping the South Vietnamese government in place.[20] Taylor thought that Khanh's position had actually been strengthened by the commonly held recognition that there was no one else around who could do a better job. This was hardly a ringing endorsement of Khanh's strong leadership. He had lost his zest for the job, and seemed to survive by "making virtually unending concessions to every pressure group" in Vietnam.[21] Moreover, his unhealthy dependence on the United States made it all the more difficult for any government of South Vietnam to wage a successful war.

The turmoil among the South Vietnamese generals was bad enough, but incidents in the Gulf of Tonkin threatened once more to deepen the military involvement of the United States. Two destroyers on De Soto patrols in the Gulf of Tonkin reported that North Vietnamese patrol boats had followed them in the gulf. President Johnson doubted the incident had occurred, and denounced the Pentagon for leaking news of the episode to the press. He did not want "rapid escalation on so frail evidence and with a very fragile government in Saigon." Johnson seemed more skeptical than Secretary of State Rusk, who "pressed on the President the importance of not seeming to doubt our naval officers on the spot." Rusk believed the stakes in maintaining the De Soto patrols in the Gulf of Tonkin were very high. He called the North Vietnamese "bandits" who needed to know that "we were in the area and had no intention of being driven out." Johnson remained torn between the need to do something and the need to keep the American public calm. He wanted to maintain a tough stand, but he feared terrible domestic political consequences should the North Vietnamese attack U.S. vessels with officials in Washington looking unprepared. He predicted the future appearance of "a brutal prosecutor'' investigating how the United States had become involved in a messy war.[22]

Johnson instructed McNamara and Rusk, two of the more militant of his advisers, to survey the state of the U.S. military and diplomatic options. At the same time he asked Undersecretary of State George Ball to analyze the situation in Vietnam from the point of view of the possibility of reducing the U.S. role.[23] Johnson wanted specific proposals to stop the further deterioration of the government of South Vietnam. They concluded that there was little the United States could do inside South Vietnam beyond what Taylor had done to fortify Khanh's resolve. They proposed extending the life of his provisional government for another sixty days beyond the end of October when it was due to expire. They thought that U.S. military actions might bring effective pressure on North Vietnam. Rusk and McNamara established a modest war aim: they wanted North Vietnam ''to be satisfied with a lesser degree of direction and assistance to the VC in South Vietnam.'' They believed that additional U.S. raids against the North could encourage Hanoi to be more amenable to reducing its support for the revolutionaries in the South.[24] Rusk encouraged Vietnam experts in Washington to ''scratch their heads and think of more ways of pulling the body politic [of South Vietnam] together.''[25] Rusk had said things like this many times before, and he had few effective suggestions. He hoped that a declaration of unity among all the prominent civil and military leaders of South Vietnam might focus their attention on the war against the revolutionaries, but offered little hope that such a paper agreement would solidify the faltering government in Saigon.

Taylor was blunter in his dismissal of Khanh's chances to create a sound government. Twice recently the United States embassy had helped him survive domestic challenges to his authority. In August the embassy had helped Khanh when the generals wanted to oust him because he seemed to accept Buddhist demands. In September embassy officials had resolutely refused to utter any words of encouragement to the leaders of the coup against Khanh. Now Taylor was fed up with Khanh's ''lack of fundamental qualities of leadership.'' He submitted to the most outrageous demands of pressure groups, then stayed away from Saigon for weeks at a time. Everyone in the country knew that Khanh was afraid for his physical safety in Saigon, and these fears had turned into morbid suspicions of his oldest and closest associates. He now distrusted the Americans too, believing that they had been behind the coup of September 13, and had authorized leaks to the press accusing the United States of sponsoring the coup and stirring up opposition to Khanh among the Montagnards. Still, Taylor thought that the United States should stick with Khanh until he seemed ''clearly to be going down.'' Surprisingly, given the hostile U.S. attitude at the beginning of 1964, Taylor now thought that General Duong Van Minh, whom he thought had behaved well recently, might be a man who could organize an effective government. Surely, Taylor acknowledged, Minh was "no world beater as we all know," but he now seemed committed to waging the war. Back in the winter of 1963–1964, the United States had grown disenchanted with Minh because of fears that he planned to open negotiations with the North leading toward the neutralization of Vietnam. However bleak the situation appeared, Taylor thought "we must hang on, keep up the war and play for breaks."[26] Taylor had stripped the Johnson administration's Vietnam policy to the bare essentials: Every alternative seemed unpalatable; preventing the victory of the NLF and the North for the foreseeable future was essential. Otherwise, all of the catastrophic consequences officials had predicted for years would come to pass should the communists win. In the fall of 1964, most important decision makers firmly believed that the costs to the U.S. position in the Cold War competition with the Soviets and China of a communist victory in South Vietnam far exceeded the costs of greater U.S. involvement in the war.

Taylor's pessimism alarmed McGeorge Bundy, who had pressed for more assertive military action since the Gulf of Tonkin incident of August. Bundy thought that the Ambassador's gloom had made the intelligence analysts in Washington lose hope. He urged the President not to say anything in public that might undermine Khanh; the man's sense of himself seemed so fragile that another discouraging word might make him drop out of public life. Bundy, who had no qualms about ordering additional U.S. air raids on the North before the U.S. presidential election, did not want a governmental crisis in Saigon before Americans went to the polls.[27]

The CIA estimate which worried Bundy was as downbeat as he had feared. The CIA analysts foresaw "increasing defeatism, paralysis of leadership, friction with Americans, exploration of possible lines of political accommodation with the other side, and a general petering out of the war effort." The CIA doubted whether the civilian government scheduled to take office at the end of October could improve the spirits of the government of South Vietnam. The rot had seeped into the officer corps. Men in the field seemed to have given up on pressing pacification. Even worse, anti-American demonstrations had occurred in Hué, Da Nang, Qui Nhon, and Nha Trang.[28]

In Saigon General Westmoreland agreed that "time is running out." Although he believed that the current governmental turmoil in Saigon made it unlikely that an expanded military effort on the part of the United States would be enough to reverse the unfavorable trend in Vietnam, he was not willing to abandon hope. He believed that the South Vietnamese might be able by the end of the year to craft a successful government.[29]

At the same time the CIA presented its gloomy assessment of the political turmoil in Vietnam, Undersecretary of State Ball, one of the few high-level skeptics of the value of increasing U.S. involvement, offered a choice of four options the United States might take to limit a deeper commitment: continuation of the present course, a full U.S. takeover of the war, escalation of the air offensive against North Vietnam, or a move towards a political solution. He favored the last course—"covert probing of a deal with the Viet Cong elements." Each of the earlier choices either had no chance of changing the political situation on the ground or would involve the United States in a war in which it could not choose its way of departure.[30] In retrospect, of course, Ball was right. Why did his warnings, like Cassandra's, go unheeded? Assistant Secretary of State William P. Bundy gave the answer. He did not dispute Ball's contention that the United States faced unpalatable choices in Vietnam. For Bundy, however, the prospect of a communist victory was intolerable.[31]

The Joint Chiefs also believed that the United States approached the "collapse" of its position in Southeast Asia. The generals seemed especially concerned that the CIA, which had consistently proven to be accurate in its assessments of the facts, would present such a gloomy prognosis that the highest political officials in Washington would lose heart. Like every other official or office studying Vietnam, the Joint Chiefs recognized that the chronic instability of the South Vietnamese government greatly reduced the chances of success for additional U.S. actions. They believed that Washington had to order a plan combining political and military actions, and hoped that each phase would reinforce the other. Then, maybe, the deterioration would stop. They wanted authority to conduct U.S. air strikes within South Vietnam as a way of deterring "a major communist aggression" in Southeast Asia. In any event the Joint Chiefs wanted to demonstrate to the people who mattered in South and North Vietnam American resolve and the ability to escalate military action in Southeast Asia. This demonstration, they hoped, would stiffen the spine of the Southerners and frighten Ho Chi Minh and his advisers.[32]

Back in Saigon Taylor pursued his nearly endless discussions with Khanh and the other generals about creating a new government. A group of generals led by Duong Van Minh, called the High National Council, moved to form a new regime with a strong central executive. Khanh referred to the potential of creating a Gaullist style government in Saigon, yet he continued to insist that he had no political ambitions, a pose which nearly drove Taylor mad. He expressed too much enthusiasm for French President Charles de Gaulle, a man whose grand imperial style contrasted sharply with Khanh's shyness and dithering. For someone who seemed clinically depressed in August and who could not summon interest in anything, his excitement over a government with a strong executive represented a remarkable change.[33]

By now Taylor had given up on Khanh's political instincts. The Ambassador believed that the new charter proposed by the High National Council (HNC) established a dictatorship. Vietnam was not France, nor Khanh de Gaulle. Taylor did not believe the future looked bright, and he tried to arrange a power-sharing triumvirate to rescue the situation. Minh would remain the nominal chief of state, Khanh would continue as commander in chief of the armed forces, and a civilian would take over as the prime minister. Khanh agreed, but Minh, doubting whether Khanh would accept a triumvirate, seemed "plunged in gloom" when Taylor presented the same proposition to him.[34]

Taylor tried walking the delicate line between helping the Vietnamese form a government and telling them what to do. As he grew more frustrated, however, he and Westmoreland demanded more and more tokens of compliance from the South Vietnamese. Taylor used some "deliberate anger" when he told the HNC that the United States could not allow it to take important decisions regarding the makeup of the government of Vietnam without first consulting the United States. At the same time he told them that the United States did not want to impose any personalities on the South Vietnamese.[35] No wonder Vietnamese of all political factions did not believe American officials when they denied any desire to dictate the personalities or policies of the government of South Vietnam.

Despite Taylor's show of irritation, the High National Council went ahead with its choices to form a new government. On October 27 Khanh made good on his promise to resign. He turned authority over to Pham Khac Suu, a civilian who would head a government established along a pattern designed by the HNC. The HNC slipped Suu in over General Minh at the last minute. A coalition of Buddhist, Catholic, Hoa Hao, and Cao Dai leaders prevailed on the HNC to appoint Suu. Taylor dismissed Suu as weak and worn out, but the Ambassador did not think it would matter much in the long run. Suu probably would not last long and even if he did, he would probably be more a figurehead than an effective leader. Nevertheless, Taylor lectured Suu about how the United States insisted on having a veto over a final slate of candidates for high government office. Suu seemed to get the message and called Taylor to discuss a list of potential members of his government.[36] By this time American officials had grown so accustomed to giving orders in Saigon they did not notice the irony of selecting the members of the cabinet of an ostensibly independent country.

Khanh returned to his position as head of the military in the new government. The return to full-time military duty did not appear to have the tonic affect on Khanh that his earlier statements about his desire to be only a general indicated. He still seemed listless. He could not do any more than he had before to stop the bickering among the officer corps, the most senior of whom were the most lukewarm to the new government. On the other hand, the young Turks, a coterie of officers led by air force Colonel Nguyen Cao Ky bent on waging the war more aggressively, seemed far more enthusiastic. Taylor remained the major power in Saigon. He told Khanh that since he no longer had governmental affairs to worry about, he could meet weekly with Westmoreland to discuss the state of the war.[37]

Westmoreland too believed that the United States had to require more from the South Vietnamese armed forces. The commander of the MACV finally understood the monster that the United States had created by providing such massive aid to the South Vietnamese. The government now had come to take U.S. aid for granted. Instead of behaving like the compliant clients U.S. officials wanted, the South Vietnamese continued their own personal intrigues. Westmoreland could have tolerated this show of independence on the part of the Vietnamese if they had operated effectively or even given evidence of a "real desire to do what was required to win the war." That was not the Vietnamese way, however. Westmoreland evaluated the government's conduct as characterized by "inefficiency, corruption, and lack of motivation." The result was that South Vietnam was not winning the war and the only realistic choice for the United States was to "lay things on the line" to the Vietnamese.[38]

Westmoreland wanted no more blank checks issued to the South Vietnamese. Like many other Americans in Saigon and Washington, the commander of the MACV had unbounded faith in what the U.S. could accomplish if not restrained by incompetent allies or self-imposed limits. Rarely did Westmoreland consider that the strengths of the North and the NLF were major causes of the government's difficulties. Those strengths would hamper the Americans too.[39]

The stakes for the United States in Vietnam rose when a Vietcong mortar attack on Bien Hoa airfield on the night of October 31 killed four U.S. servicemen and damaged twenty-seven aircraft. Officials in Saigon and Washington differed over the proper response. The diplomatic and military leadership in Vietnam wanted to demonstrate U.S. support for the South Vietnamese, while official Washington expressed more concern about the international implications of the escalation of the war. In Saigon Taylor wanted an immediate retaliatory air raid against a similar North Vietnamese base. He believed that the time had come for the United States to announce that in the future it would always retaliate against North Vietnamese targets on a tit-for-tat basis.[40] Coming just two days before the U.S. election, however, the White House chose not to strike at the North.[41]

PLANNING ESCALATION: NOVEMBER–DECEMBER 1964

The election of President Johnson removed one brake on a more assertive U.S. policy in Vietnam, but planners still could produce no attractive option to stiffen the spine of the South Vietnamese government. By the end of November an NSC committee chaired by William P. Bundy developed a plan of military escalation for the United States. They laid out three options: A continuation of current policy, with the addition of reprisals for attacks on

U.S. targets; heavy military pressure against the North, with negotiations not ruled out entirely; and a ''slow controlled squeeze on North Vietnam in order to bring about negotiations.'' As he had done so many times before, Johnson expressed misgivings about any of these courses of action. None of the proposals promised success in the near future. He complained that he ''could not face the Congressional leadership'' unless the military commanders offered assurances of their support.[42]

For the first time planners in Washington contemplated the consequences of a communist victory. The government of South Vietnam had become so weak that the Bundy committee believed the communists could win in the foreseeable future. The committee believed that ''the loss of South Vietnam to Communist control, in any form, would be a major blow to our basic policies.'' It did not foresee the immediate victory of communist forces in the remainder of Southeast Asia; ''the so called 'domino' theory,'' it concluded, ''is over-simplified.'' But if the United States were forced out of Vietnam in a military defeat, communist movements in other Southeast Asian nations would receive a major boost in morale. A communist victory in South Vietnam might or might not have terrible consequences for the United States in other areas of vital concern. Should the United States draw down its forces from Europe to fight in Vietnam and then lose, or should the end of the war in Vietnam be followed by a ''wave of 'isolationism''' in the United States, then U.S. allies would doubt the ability of the United States to come to their aid in the future. The loss of South Vietnam probably would not have the ''totally crippling effect in Southeast Asia and Asia generally that the loss of Berlin would have in Europe, but it may be that bad.'' In the final analysis, the Bundy committee could not estimate the precise impact of a communist victory but preferred not to risk the outcome.[43]

The committee therefore recommended continuing the current course in Vietnam until the end of 1964. (Taylor reported that the South Vietnamese government functioned but made little progress in the war or with its own people.)[44] At the beginning of 1965 the committee suggested that U.S. government planners revisit Vietnam to see whether dramatic escalation was necessary. In the meantime the problem of the low morale of the government of South Vietnam remained a pressing problem. The committee suggested that another strong presidential statement on Vietnam would help feelings in Saigon. They also advocated reprisal raids against targets in the North in response to any spectacular attacks on U.S. forces in Vietnam.[45]

Other officials considered the consequences of a communist victory in Vietnam far worse for the position of the United States. The Joint Chiefs of Staff thought that communist success in Vietnam would inevitably lead to the early loss of Southeast Asia and the ''progressive unraveling of the wider defense structures'' the United States had created over the past decade.[46] Deputy Ambassador to Vietnam Alexis Johnson said that the proper response to the question whether the war in Vietnam could be won was, "It *must* be won." He likened the situation in Vietnam to what had happened in Cuba at the time of the missile crisis, and believed that the "risks of doing nothing are much greater" than the dangers involved in an additional commitment of U.S. resources to Vietnam.[47]

Over the next several weeks the NSC working group, Taylor, and the President worked out plans for a significant increase in U.S. military operations in Vietnam. The Ambassador concluded that "war weariness and hopelessness" pervaded the urban areas of Vietnam. The government and the United States played a losing game. For Taylor it obviously was "high time we change and find a better way" to prevail. He recommended greater U.S. involvement to raise the cost to the North. Whatever the United States decided to do, Taylor stressed the importance of avoiding negotiations with the North until Hanoi felt substantial pain. Even if the DRV were to win in Vietnam, he wanted them to pay such a high price that victory would not be worth it. But the United States had to walk a very fine line to make certain that the war did not become a strictly American affair. Taylor wanted Washington to keep the government of Vietnam "in the forefront of the combat and the negotiations."[48]

On December 1 Johnson met with his principal advisers to discuss plans drafted by the Bundy committee. The President expressed boundless frustration with the dithering of the South Vietnamese government. He thought that there was "no point in hitting the North if the South [was] not together." Right now the Saigon regime was so weak that giving them a sign to strike the North would be like sending a "widow woman to slap Jack Dempsey." He wanted Taylor to tell the South Vietnamese that if the factions continued to squabble he could "not send Johnson City [his home town] boys out to die." Having blown off steam Johnson repeated what every official in Washington thought: The "day of reckoning is coming." He agreed with the NSC's recommendations to prepare the way for stronger reprisals against the North over the next several months. In the end Johnson asked his principal advisers to try to round up support from allies in Asia and Europe for increased aid to South Vietnam.[49]

On December 2 Johnson accepted the NSC's proposals for a two-phase program of escalation. In the first thirty days the U.S. officials would stress the importance of the stakes in Vietnam. Behind the scenes Ambassador Taylor would tell the South Vietnamese authorities to shape up. Beyond the thirty day initial phase, the NSC recommended that the United States deploy more aircraft to Vietnam and keep open the option of increased military pressure on the North. The United States would start by bombing infiltration routes south of the nineteenth parallel and then work up to targets north of that line. Eventually the United States might attack military targets, mine the ports of the North, and institute a naval blockade of the North. The committee believed that "the whole sequence of military actions would be designed to give the impression of a steady, deliberate approach, and to give the United States the option at any time . . . to proceed or not, to escalate or not, and to quicken the pace or not."[50]

But political instability persisted. The South Vietnamese government seemed impervious to Taylor's outline of the minimum criteria of performance it needed to meet before the United States would go forward with escalation. "At a minimum," Johnson instructed Taylor to insist that the South Vietnamese be "capable of maintaining law and order in its principal centers of population, make plans for the conduct of operations and assure their effective execution by military and police." The South Vietnamese must "have the means to cope with the enemy reactions which must be expected" once the United States escalated the fighting.[51] The Saigon government still did not comprehend the Americans' frustration. Prime Minister Huong seemed disappointed that the Americans thought that "he had not been carrying out government in a capable manner."[52]

The Huong government's weakness seemed obvious to overseas observers less inclined than Washington policy-makers to continue failing policies. The British thought the Huong government was making a valiant effort but seemed incapable of mounting an effective response to the NLF guerrillas and the North Vietnamese. Britain had had long experience with weak dependencies trying to dictate London's policy, and British officials feared that the Americans might also be succumbing to the tyranny of the weak. In preparation for a visit by British Prime Minister Harold Wilson, National Security Adviser Bundy informed the President that "the British will find it very, very difficult indeed to increase their commitment to Vietnam right now." No British politician of any party wanted to do more in Vietnam. For the past ten years the British had provided only polite support to U.S. efforts, refusing to do more because of their position as co-chair of the Geneva conference on Indochina.[53]

When Johnson met Wilson and British Foreign Secretary Patrick Gordon Walker, the British officials warned the Americans against any "disproportionate retaliation" against the North. Should that happen, the participants in the Geneva conference on Asia might demand that Britain reconvene it. Moreover, Wilson told Johnson that he expected fierce questioning from members of his own Labor party in the House of Commons over the British government providing even minimal support for the American effort in Vietnam.[54]

Similar qualms arose within Congress. On December 9 Senate Majority Leader Mike Mansfield warned Johnson that "we remain on a course in Vietnam which takes us further and further out onto the sagging limb." Mansfield urged Johnson to promise not to expand the war beyond the borders of South Vietnam.[55] National Security Adviser McGeorge Bundy replied that it would be a mistake for the United States forthrightly to declare its intentions. The President had often said that "we seek no wider war and intend no reckless action." Bundy believed that Johnson's current course of continuing in Vietnam for a long struggle represented the beliefs of most thoughtful Americans who had considered the Vietnam issue. "We do not want a big war out there," Bundy and Johnson agreed, "and neither do we intend to back out on a ten-year-long commitment."[56]

South Vietnam was gripped in what Ambassador Taylor characterized as "another first class governmental crisis" from late December 1964 to February 1965.[57] The Young Turk generals, led by Nguyen Cao Ky and Nguyen Van Thieu, once more demanded that General Khanh break up the High National Council and again take charge as prime minister. Ky seemed particularly concerned that the HNC had interfered with pensions for retired officers.[58] This was too much for Taylor. Everything he had said over the past several months regarding the need for subsuming personal needs in order to achieve progress in the war seemed to have been so much wasted breath. Taylor told the generals that the entire world interpreted their actions as a military coup, and "we Americans were tired of coups."[59]

Still, the generals would not back down. Ky tried to have Taylor thrown out of South Vietnam as persona non grata. Furious, Taylor wanted to let the generals know that the United States might stop further military support and end air operations designed to stop infiltration. Back in Washington, however, Rusk took a calmer view. He thought that any direct threat of reduced military assistance would only make matters worse. Publicly, Rusk stated that "what is important is unity, the setting aside of personal rivalries or lesser issues in the interests of maintaining the strength and the unity of the country. Unity would be worth many, many divisions."[60]

Yet the South Vietnamese remained divided in the midst of continuing Vietcong activity. Another attack by the NLF against a U.S. officers' billet in Saigon on Christmas Eve killed two U.S. servicemen and wounded thirty-eight Americans and thirteen Vietnamese. Taylor asked for a reprisal air raid to be launched against a North Vietnamese barracks. After long discussions with his principal aides, President Johnson decided against another tit-for-tat air raid against Northern positions. While acknowledging that a reprisal would "do wonders for the morale of U.S. personnel in South Vietnam," Johnson decided that Taylor was too close to the situation. McGeorge Bundy warned Johnson against following the militant advice of the officials closest to the situation in Saigon. "It is easy for advisers to be brave," Bundy told the President, "but it is the President who must live with the decision." Moreover, the lessons of the events of the past several months confirmed that the "central problem is and remains the establishment of political stability in South Vietnam." The situation seemed to Bundy "more unstable than ever," and he and Johnson doubted that a reprisal air strike would do much to make the South Vietnamese get their own affairs in order. It might produce exactly the opposite effect of further convincing the South Vietnamese that they did not need to take seriously the American demands for internal reforms because Washington would eventually be willing to ratchet upward the level of force to be used against North Vietnamese.[61]

THE DEVELOPMENT OF CONTINUOUS BOMBING: JANUARY–APRIL 1965

In 1965 the United States no longer attempted to encourage the South Vietnamese to reform their government by withholding additional military support. At the beginning of the year, American journalists in Vietnam became fatalistic. A *New York Times* reporter told one of Johnson's speech writers that "the next six months may mark the end of the road." He wanted the United States to look for ways to "withdraw with honor."[62] But most officials in Washington believed that withdrawal and honor could not coexist. The succession of military regimes drove Johnson nearly apoplectic. "I don't want to hear any more of this coup shit," he exploded to aides.[63] Believing withdrawal and a communist victory unacceptable, officials in Washington eventually sided with Taylor's argument that the South Vietnamese would pull themselves together only when they believed that the American commitment was unshakable. The war became an increasingly American affair, something U.S. government planners wanted to avoid. All the while they hoped to strengthen the independence and spirit of the government of the Republic of Vietnam, but everything they did made it behave more like a vassal of the United States.

After General Khanh returned to power in a coup in late January 1965, McNamara and Bundy concluded that "our current policy can lead only to a disastrous defeat." They voided the directives of December 1964 that the United States would not engage in wider action against the North until a stable government existed in Vietnam. They now believed that there was little hope for an effective government in South Vietnam without greater U.S. support. The South Vietnamese avoided taking responsibility for firm anticommunism as long as they saw that the United States was "unwilling to take serious risks." No matter how "outrageous" the South Vietnamese attitude seemed to Bundy and McNamara in "light of all that we have done and all that we are ready to do if only they will pull up their socks," it was a fact of life.[64] Johnson finally agreed that the United States had to do more for the South. "Stable government or no stable government," the President said, "we'll do what we ought to do. I'm prepared to do that."[65]

A continuous series of high level visits went from Washington to Saigon and returned with the conclusion that the war was nearly lost. The morale of the ARVN had continued to sink as the initiative in the battle passed to the NLF fighters. ARVN field commanders and the government in Saigon seemed paralyzed with fear that the United States would not support them. In this atmosphere, U.S. military advisers continued their search for morale boosters for the Saigon regime. Taylor told Johnson early in 1965 that a program of air raids, lasting longer than the retaliatory strike of the previous August, would "inject some life into the dejected spirits" in Saigon. Johnson was willing to try, but recognized that the air raids had more to do with encouraging the flagging spirits in Saigon than changing the military fortunes of the war. He predicted to Taylor that "this guerrilla war cannot be won from the air." Taylor thought it would buy time and "bring pressure on the will of the chiefs of the Democratic Republic of Vietnam. As practical men, they cannot wish to see the fruits of ten years of labor destroyed by slowly escalating air attacks."[66]

How revealing the contrast between Taylor's time frame—a decade—and the patience of the Vietnamese communists. They considered their current fight the latest episode in a thousand-year-long effort to expel foreigners. The North Vietnamese continually adjusted the intensity of their attacks in the South to conserve their forces and raise the price, first for the French and then for the Americans. Their goal of ridding the country of foreigners and unifying it under their control remained constant. They could wait; a clock ticked ever louder for the Americans.

The program of sustained bombing of the North, code named Operation Rolling Thunder, began in mid-February. At the beginning of the month the United States still tried to limit its role. McGeorge Bundy visited Saigon from February 4 to 7. As usual, General Khanh pressed him for help "liberating the North." Once more Bundy observed that the United States was in Vietnam to win the war in the South, not liberate the North. He agreed that the United States would put pressure on the North, but Washington wanted to act "only if it involved frank and loyal partnership with a stable and reasonably popular government of South Vietnam." He told Khanh that "the main burden inevitably falls on Vietnamese, who must learn to work together more cohesively and effectively."[67]

The American approach toward North Vietnam stiffened on February 7 as Bundy prepared to leave Saigon. NLF fighters fired artillery at the barracks of American Marine base at Pleiku in the central highlands of Vietnam, destroying ten planes and killing 8 Americans and wounding 126. American officials considered the attack another episode in a series, but they believed that the cumulative impact of assaults on Americans would panic the already demoralized South Vietnamese. The South Vietnamese officials seeing Bundy off at the airport told him that the bombing of the Pleiku barracks "was a test of whether Washington meant what it said." They asked the National Security Adviser, "Do they mean to stay with us and back us up, or are they going to let this sort of thing happen with no answer?"[68]

Upon returning to Washington, Bundy told the President that the bombing of the barracks "produced a practical point of departure" for a new, more assertive U.S. military policy in Vietnam.[69] Others agreed, and only George Ball expressed serious reservations about the wisdom of sustained bombing of the North. He thought that nothing "short of a crushing military defeat" would convince Hanoi to "abandon the aggressive course it has pursued at great cost for ten years and give up all the progress it has made in the communization of South Vietnam."[70]

After first ordering a single retaliatory strike against the North, Johnson authorized Rolling Thunder on February 13. Public reaction was largely supportive. A Gallup Poll reported that 67 percent of the public approved of the President's actions. Telegrams to the White House, however, ran fourteen to one against the bombing.[71] Most Democrats, with the exception of the two senators who had voted against the Gulf of Tonkin Resolution, believed the bombing of the North strengthened the U.S. position.

Yet a significant number of Democrats appeared worried that the United States had started a course in Vietnam from which it could not exit easily. Senate Majority Leader Mike Mansfield repeated his concern that the United States had staked too much on a weak government in South Vietnam. Senator Frank Church (D., Idaho) called for a negotiated settlement, quoting approvingly columnist Walter Lippmann's argument for the neutralization of South Vietnam. But the administration easily stifled these doubts—at least for the time being. Lippmann told Bundy that he thought the situation in South Vietnam was "hopeless." After Bundy informed him that the bombing was designed to turn the tide in South Vietnam, Lippmann said he would "do his best" to support Johnson.[72] Johnson boasted to a reporter that he told Church, "the next time you want a dam in Idaho, Frank, go see Walter."[73]

Other members of congress also expressed misgivings. Senator Joseph Clark (D., Pa.) privately expressed his qualms to McGeorge Bundy. Clark told the National Security Adviser that the United States seemed to be "fighting unnecessary wars when we should be making a basic settlement with Moscow against Peking."[74] Republicans expressed more unqualified support for the bombing. Senate Minority Leader Everett Dirksen became one of the most outspoken defenders of the policy of bombing the North. Yet columnist Drew Pearson, a friend of Johnson's, warned that the Republicans hoped the President might fall into a trap in Vietnam.[75]

The Rolling Thunder bombing was extensive. In April, U.S. and South Vietnamese air force and navy planes flew 3,600 sorties against fuel depots, bridges, munitions factories, and power plants in the North. They bombed factories and power plants in the North. They inflicted much damage, but nothing that the Vietnamese could not restore with will power and assistance from the Soviet Union and China. North Vietnam quickly adapted to round-the-clock bombing. There were few industrial targets in the North, and the North Vietnamese used darkness and cloud cover to rebuild destroyed highways and railroad bridges. Far from breaking North Vietnam's will, the bombing intensified anti-American feeling.[76] The morale of the South Vietnamese government did not rebound sharply, because the infiltration of supplies and troops continued virtually unabated from the North to the South.

And the results of the offensive did not meet the expectation of the planners who had advocated bombing. Bundy believed that the air actions had had only a marginal impact on the morale of the Khanh government. He lamented that "there is no evidence that the new government has the necessary will, skill and human resources which a turn around will require."[77] In Washington officials worried that Rolling Thunder would not accomplish its goal. James Thomson, an NSC staff member, worried about the appearance of desperation in the bombing campaign. He feared that observers would consider the bombing "a *substitute* for political stability in Saigon."[78] In early March, Bundy presented Johnson his gloomy assessment that "the chances of a turn around in South Vietnam remain less than even." Aware that Rolling Thunder offered little more than a temporary respite from the Vietcong's ability to strike at will against the ARVN, General Westmoreland called for the American troops to conduct ground operations on their own throughout the South. The time had come, he told the President in March, "to put our own finger in the dike."[79]

Despite this advice, Johnson still resisted a complete Americanization of the war. Speaking at Johns Hopkins University on April 7, he offered "unconditional negotiations" with North Vietnam to end the war. He promised a one-billion-dollar development agency modeled on the Tennessee Valley Authority to serve nations along the Mekong River. Bill Moyers, then a personal assistant to the President, later concluded that the proposal of a TVA for the Mekong Basin reflected the limitations of Johnson's political outlook and his lack of experience in dealing with people of different culture. Johnson, who had grown up in the deal-making world of Texas politics, believed all conflicts could be settled at the right price. The President told Moyers before the speech, "Old Ho, he can't turn that down." Moyers noted, "Had Ho Chi Minh been [AFL-CIO President] George Meany," a man used to cutting deals with his rivals, "he would have agreed."[80] For Ho Chi Minh and the other revolutionaries of North Vietnam, however, there was nothing Johnson could offer short of an American departure from Vietnam that would satisfy.

The Johns Hopkins address promised continuing U.S. involvement in South Vietnam. Johnson asserted that "we will not be defeated. . . . We will not withdraw."[81] Hanoi responded by demanding that the United States quit Vietnam and the South accept the program of the NLF to end the war.[82] A few low-ranking officials in Washington, fretful about the direction the war was taking, thought Hanoi had not flatly turned Johnson down but had only provided "a statement of final objectives."[83] Yet Johnson and his top advisers chose to regard the North Vietnamese statement as a rejection of calls to negotiate, setting the stage for the final decisive escalation of U.S. participation in the war.

On April 20, McNamara, Taylor, and Westmoreland met in Honolulu. They reluctantly agreed that bombing alone would not force the North and the NLF to stop their war against Saigon. All agreed that the North and the Vietcong would not capitulate "or come to a position acceptable to us in less than six months." They believed that the only strategy to improve the chances of the South Vietnamese was to convince the North that the communist forces could not win. Such a strategy depended on avoiding, "for psychological and morale reasons," a spectacular defeat of South Vietnamese and U.S. forces.[84] They decided that American forces had to fight the war on the ground in the South, if the Saigon government were to have a chance to stabilize. Still, concerned about the implications of Americans fighting throughout the South, they called for forty thousand additional U.S. soldiers to fight within fifty miles of American enclaves on the coast of Vietnam.[85]

THE FINAL DECISION FOR AN AMERICAN GROUND WAR: MAY–JULY 1965

The enclave strategy lasted barely a month. The NLF operated at will in the remainder of the South, and the Saigon government, now led by Air Marshall Nguyen Cao Ky, lost more authority daily. Chairman of the Joint Chiefs of Staff Earle Wheeler believed that "the communists may be on the threshold of moving the conflict in Southeast Asia to a new and higher level of intensity." The Joint Chiefs believed that the situation on the ground had deteriorated to the point where the United States had to provide a "substantial further buildup of U.S. and allied forces" in South Vietnam.[86] Westmoreland requested an additional 150,000 troops to carry the war throughout the South. McNamara returned to Vietnam and decided that Westmoreland was right. He recommended that Johnson approve sending an additional 100,000 men to Vietnam and ask Congress to authorize the potential call-up of an additional 236,000 reservists. He told the President that "the situation in South Vietnam is worse than a year ago (when it was worse than a year before that). After a few months of stalemate, the tempo of the war has quickened."

McNamara, returning home after travelling to Saigon in late June, weighed the last starkly unappealing choices: to cut U.S. losses and leave under the best conditions possible—"almost certainly conditions humiliating the United States and damaging to our future effectiveness on the world scene''; to continue with present level of U.S. forces, approximately seventy-five thousand, which would make the U.S. position progressively weaker and ''would confront us later with a choice between withdrawal and an emergency expansion of forces, perhaps too late to do any good.'' Rejecting both, McNamara concluded that Johnson could do nothing but follow his third option: ''Expand promptly and substantially the U.S. military pressure against the Vietcong in the South and maintain military pressure against the North Vietnamese in the North.'' While no guarantee of eventual success, ''this alternative would stave off defeat in the short run and offer a good chance of producing a favorable settlement in the longer run.''[87]

In late July, Johnson consulted with his principal advisers on the future of American involvement in the ground war. In a series of meetings Johnson appeared frustrated with the inability of the South Vietnamese to make progress, bewildered at the unresponsiveness of the North to his proposals for negotiations, and skeptical about the usefulness of the dispatch of additional United States troops. Despite his misgivings about deeper involvement, Johnson agreed with nearly all of the advisers that the costs of an NLF victory were unacceptably high. The lives and money the United States had spent so far in Vietnam would have been wasted. The price would be paid in places far removed from Asia as the world's confidence in American credibility deteriorated. Secretary of the Navy Paul Nitze, primarily interested in maintaining good relations with Europe and appearing strong to the Soviet Union, remarked that ''the shape of the world will change'' were the United States to acknowledge that ''we couldn't beat the VC.'' Secretary of the Army Stanley Resor concurred that ''we can't go back on our commitment. Our allies are watching carefully.''[88]

The only course tolerable to Johnson was continuation of a gradual buildup of U.S. forces—the very policy that had failed to defeat the NLF or bolster the morale of the South Vietnamese government for the previous year. He hoped to keep the buildup quiet and present it as a continuation of policy, not a dramatically increased American commitment. He wanted to avoid provoking the Soviets or ''stir talk about controls over the economy and inflation.''[89] Johnson expected that by downplaying the significance of the new commitment, he would avoid a divisive public debate and prevent the sort of public war weariness that had wrecked the Truman administration during the Korean War. At the height of his authority with Congress, he feared that congressional discussion of Vietnam would interfere with passage of his ambitious program of domestic reform legislation, the Great Society. Some of the President's aides believed a forthright statement that the United States had raised the stakes in Vietnam ''would create the false impression that we have to have guns, not butter—and would help the enemies of the president's domestic legislative agenda.''[90]

The July reappraisals held elements of tragedy—and folly. Jack Valenti, a political adviser, told the President he wanted to ''weep because the options are so narrow and the choices are so barren.''[91] A sentimental man, Johnson liked this sort of histrionics from subordinates eager to show their empathy for the burdens borne by the chief executive. For his part, the President often expressed greater awareness of the risks than did some of his more militant advisers. He wanted assurances that the efforts to encourage other nations to support the U.S. effort in Vietnam had ''wrung every single soldier out of every country we can.''[92] Johnson voiced doubts about the usefulness of additional U.S. troops. He once turned to General Earle Wheeler, Chairman of the Joint Chiefs of Staff, and asked: ''Tell me this. What will happen if we put in 100,000 more men and then two, three years later, you tell me we need 500,000 more? How would you expect me to respond to that? And what makes you think that Ho Chi Minh won't put in another 100,000 and match us every bit of the way?'' To which Wheeler replied: ''That makes greater bodies of men from North Vietnam, which will allow us to cream them.''[93] Johnson's fears proved prophetic, and Wheeler's reply foretold some of the military's foolish and wasteful tactics of attrition they waged in the war.

Johnson also recognized the fragility of public support for the war. A June public opinion poll by Louis Harris gave the president an overall approval rating of 69 percent. Sixty-five percent of the public approved and 35 percent disapproved of his handling of Vietnam issues. Forty-seven percent favored sending more U.S. ground troops, while 19 percent thought the present number appropriate. Eleven percent wanted the troops removed, and 23 percent were not sure.[94] Yet when the Secretary of the Army pointed to public opinion polls showing strong support for a continuation of the American commitment, Johnson, an old political professional, rebuked him: ''But if you make a commitment to jump off a building, and you find out how high it is, you may withdraw that commitment.''[95]

Only one of Johnson's principal advisers, Undersecretary of State George Ball, openly voiced dissent from the prevailing willingness to go forward with one hundred thousand more soldiers. A staunch Europeanist, with limited knowledge of or concern for Asia, Ball asserted that U.S. security interests lay in the preservation of a strong Atlantic alliance. Rather than believing that a U.S. defeat in Southeast Asia would shrink America's standing with important European allies, Ball thought that an excessive U.S. commitment in Vietnam would cause NATO partners to wonder about the depth of American concern for them. Ball had delivered a series of strongly worded memoranda opposing greater involvement in Vietnam for the previous year. He quoted Ralph Waldo Emerson's admonition to avoid conditions where ''things are in the saddle and ride mankind.'' He believed that Johnson's most difficult continuing problem in Vietnam was ''to keep control of policy and prevent the momentum of events from taking command.''[96]

Ball argued that the United States should cut its losses in Vietnam. Bombing had failed and "there is no assurance that we can achieve our objectives by substantially expanding American forces in South Vietnam and committing them to direct combat." He believed that "this is our last clear chance" to avoid escalation into a war in which thousands of Americans would lose their lives. Once casualties mounted it would become ever more difficult and more costly for the United States to reduce its commitment and nearly impossible to extricate itself.[97]

Ball thought that the United States could not win in Vietnam without risk of drawing China, and possibly even the Soviet Union, into the fighting. He predicted that public opinion would not tolerate a long war. During a prolonged war with high U.S. casualties an impatient public would demand that the government "strike at the very jugular of North Vietnam." This greater escalation risked provoking retaliation by the Soviet Union or China. Ball thought that even greater dangers to U.S. credibility existed should the war go on for more than a year. "If the war is long and protracted, as I believe it will be," he said "then we will suffer because the world's greatest power cannot defeat guerrillas." Ball referred to the long history of the Vietnamese fighting outsiders and doubted that "an army of westerners can successfully fight orientals in an Asian jungle." Johnson seemed struck by the image. "This is important," the President told McNamara and Wheeler. "Can Westerners, in the absence of accurate intelligence, successfully fight Asians in jungle rice paddies?"[98]

Why did Johnson reject Ball's pessimistic although ultimately accurate recommendations? The President believed that cutting U.S. losses in the middle of 1965 represented a new course in Vietnam. He wanted to make it seem as if he had not changed policy, even though a new course was precisely what the United States undertook in 1965. Moreover, Ball did not offer sharp, consistent, and easily followed practical advice. The Undersecretary of State acknowledged that it would not be easy to cut losses in the middle of 1965, but every delay raised the costs higher. Ball provided no immediate mode of deescalation, but he thought that the pressure to move toward a larger war would be "almost irresistible" after July. He acknowledged a substantial risk that Southeast Asia would become dominated by communists, but he believed that the losses to the United States would be of a short-term nature.[99] Ball also thought that a continuation of the bombing of the North without "massive troop deployments" would be enough to raise the morale of South Vietnamese forces.[100] For Johnson to have followed Ball's advice he would have had to part company with nearly all his other lieutenants, most of whom refused to acknowledge the limits of American power and let nature take its course. They concurred with Chester Cooper of the NSC staff that Ball simply wanted to "wash our hands of the problem." For most of Johnson's advisers that was an unacceptable solution. Cooper asserted that "good men and true should concentrate on how a peaceful South Vietnam can also be a non-communist one."[101]

No other advisers joined with Ball in expressing such pessimism in the public meetings. Sensing that Johnson believed the risk of a communist victory greater than the challenges of greater commitment, they recommended sending the troops McNamara thought were needed. Longtime presidential adviser Clark Clifford did telephone a dissent; he too doubted that the United States could win because China and the Soviet Union would see to it that the nlf continued to fight. China was likely to send in troops, as they had done in the Korean War. He accurately predicted an unacceptably high number of U.S. fatalities. "If we lose 50,000 men there," he forecast, "it will be a catastrophe for the country. Five years, billions of dollars, hundreds of thousands of men—this is not for us."[102] In the end, however, Clifford supported Johnson's decision to increase the American troop commitment.

Johnson also received some advice from people outside official circles to downplay the significance of Vietnam. The economist John Kenneth Galbraith encouraged Johnson to instruct his official spokesmen to "stop saying the future of mankind, the United States and human liberty is being decided in Vietnam"; it was not. Galbraith believed that "no question of high principle is involved." Vietnam was "of no great intrinsic significance." He also reminded the President that he alone would have to "take the political heat" should the decision to Americanize the war go wrong.[103]

Galbraith's politically prophetic note raised caution flags in the White House, but it could not overcome the weight of the advice coming from other influential outsiders. Galbraith's suggestions, like Ball's, required the President and his principal advisers to think anew about the stakes involved in Vietnam. But mid-1965 was not a time when the senior leaders could effectively examine a fresh approach. Whatever their anxieties about mounting costs, they did not believe the United States would fail in Vietnam. And if it did so without making more of an effort, they projected a severe international backlash. Johnson, McNamara, Rusk, and Wheeler agreed that the perception of failure in Vietnam would shake the foundations of U.S. foreign policy. A panel of so-called Wise Men, including General Omar Bradley, former Deputy Secretary of Defense Roswell Gilpatric, and the prominent banker and former diplomat John McCloy, told Rusk and McNamara that "the stakes in Vietnam were very high indeed." They considered South Vietnam "a crucial test of the ability of the free world and the U.S. to counter the Communist tactic of `wars of national liberation.'" They were certain that a communist or neutralist government of South Vietnam would be perceived as a defeat for the United States. Such a setback "would necessarily lead to worldwide questioning whether U.S. commitments could be relied on."[104]

Another Wise Man, former U.S. ambassador to Vietnam Henry Cabot Lodge, also considered the issues in Vietnam to be nothing less than the future of U.S. foreign policy. He supported the decision to escalate in the expectation that "our grandchildren will not live to see the day that a united China does not probe in Southeast Asia."[105] Lodge even dismissed the efforts of the past year to bolster the government of South Vietnam. He did not think that the United States should take the government of Air Marshall Ky seriously. "We have to do what we think we ought to do regardless of what the Saigon government does." He fully backed the Americanization of the war as a way of providing greater freedom of action to "do certain things with or without the government's approval."[106]

Eventually the President and all of his advisers with the exception of Ball and possibly Clifford, concurred that adding one hundred thousand Americans to the ninety thousand troops already in Vietnam would stave off defeat without provoking a backlash against the war in Congress or with the public. The President told his advisers that "he regretted that we were embroiled in Vietnam. But we *are* there."[107] Johnson and most advisers hoped to characterize the doubling of troops as only a continuation of current policy. To that end they rejected McNamara's request to call up reserves. Even so, Johnson's advisers worried about the implications of the Americanization of the war. Horace Busby, one of Johnson's most politically astute advisers, told the President that it was "self-deceptive" to claim that the troop buildup represented only an extension of what the U.S. had done in the past several years.[108] Yet Johnson encouraged such deception, hoping to maintain a wide consensus in support of his policies.

Johnson informed congressional leaders on July 27 of the decision to send another one hundred thousand soldiers but not to call up reserves. Most Democratic and Republican leaders expressed support. Speaker of the House John McCormack thought there was no alternative. He reflected that the "lesson of Hitler and Mussolini is clear."[109] Republican leader Gerald Ford agreed. But the mood among members of congress not called to the White House was apprehensive. Mike Mansfield told the President that many senators supported the president because they sensed "that your objective [is] not to get in deeply." Yet lawmakers worried about the administration's inability to define success in Vietnam. "Even if you win, totally," Mansfield reported, "you still do not come out well. What have you achieved? It is by no means a 'vital' area of U.S. concern." Senators sensed deep currents of public anxiety. They noted that the French had never used conscripts in their war in Indochina. News of casualties among American draftees could ignite angry revulsion at the war. Mansfield told Johnson that "the country is backing the president on Vietnam primarily because he is president, not necessarily out of any understanding or sympathy with policies on Vietnam; beneath the support there is deep concern . . . which could explode at any time; in addition racial factors at home could become involved."[110]

Despite the prophetic content of these reservations, they did not sway

Johnson. Quite simply, he believed that the cost of seeing the NLF win quickly appeared too great. He announced the dispatch of additional troops at a low-key midday press conference on July 28, 1965. For the rest of 1965 the White House continued to insist that the additional troops did not change American policy in Vietnam, and Johnson stressed the Great Society as the centerpiece of his administration's accomplishments. When Secretary of the Treasury Henry Fowler complained that the fighting strained the economy and had caused prices to rise, the White House warned him to keep his views quiet. "What the President doesn't want to do," Bill Moyers told Fowler, "is, in essence, say to the business community that we have declared war in Vietnam."[111] Keeping the buildup quiet, however, backfired dramatically. The stealth with which Johnson announced the additional commitment of American troops contributed later to a widely held belief that administration officials did not tell the truth, and a wide "credibility gap" thus opened.

The United States was fully at war, whether declared or not, after July 1965. The decision to send an additional one hundred thousand troops by the end of 1965 did not stop the buildup. During 1966 and 1967 the number of U.S. soldiers in Vietnam rose from 190,000 to 535,000. Many were conscripts, and perhaps as many as half of those who ostensibly volunteered did so because they faced induction through selective service. Yet this huge expeditionary force could not prevail against the NLF and several hundred thousand regulars from the North Vietnamese People's Liberation Army.

After public opinion turned against U.S. participation in the war in Vietnam in the years following 1967, Americans reflected on the decisions taken in 1965. In 1971, when the *New York Times* published excerpts from the Pentagon's history of U.S. decision-making in Vietnam, popularly known as the *Pentagon Papers* many observers deeply regretted that Johnson chose not to follow the advice of George Ball to cut U.S. losses in Vietnam before the price mounted even more steeply. In later years commentators and historians questioned whether Johnson made the proper use of his advisers if the results of the advisory process turned so catastrophically wrong. Supporters of President Kennedy's style of decisionmaking contrasted his successful handling of the 1962 Cuban missile crisis with the bad results of Johnson's decision to Americanize the war in Vietnam in 1965.

In retrospect, it was obvious that Ball and outsiders like John Kenneth Galbraith were correct when they argued that most of Johnson's advisers had overstated the importance of Vietnam to the United States. Whatever costs to U.S. credibility would follow a defeat of the pro-American government of Vietnam were far less than the eventual price paid in American blood, treasure, and domestic harmony caused by Americanizing the war.

This picture, so clear after 1968, was but a potential nightmare in 1965. Johnson and some of his advisers dimly recognized some of the dangers, but they did not believe that the worst possible outcome would occur. Later

Johnson often dismissed critics of his war policies as "nervous nellies" paralyzed with fear that a disaster awaited the United States in Vietnam. They were right; he was wrong. But nothing as catastrophic as the Vietnam experience had happened before in U.S. foreign policy, so why should the doomsayers be right now? The United States had succeeded in most of its overseas undertakings since 1941, so why should not the good results continue? While the experience of the previous ten years in Vietnam made policy-makers pause, their successes in other places in the world in World War II and the early Cold War gave them a sense of near invincibility.

Nearly all of Johnson's senior advisers in 1965 believed it was better to do something—almost anything—to solve a problem than to admit that American action would not make things better. There lay the key to explaining why Ball did not carry the day. In the face of the unanimous opinion of such forceful individuals as McNamara, Taylor, Rusk, Bundy, and Wheeler, all of whom preferred action to what they considered torpor, Lyndon Johnson was bound to put aside his real misgivings and proceed with an American war in Vietnam.[112]

Chapter

* * * * * * * * * * *

Fighting the War:
1965–1967

*F*ROM THE END of 1965 until the end of 1967 the war in Vietnam became more and more of an American affair. At the beginning of 1965 the United States stationed 23,000 troops in Vietnam. A year later the number was 184,000, rising to 385,000 at the end of the year and 535,000 by the beginning of 1968.[1] Although the United States preferred conventional "big unit" confrontations with the NLF and the North Vietnamese, the enemy decided when to engage the Americans and ARVN forces, thereby limiting their own casualties until the time they expected the Americans would weary of the war.

General William C. Westmoreland, the U.S. commander, tried unsuccessfully to counter these tactics with an attrition strategy of his own.[2] He sent giant B-52 bombers and smaller fighter bombers over South Vietnam to terrorize the Vietcong. After the bombers had prepared the battlefield, helicopter-borne American units descended on the countryside on search-and-destroy missions to root out and kill enemy soldiers. Americans would fly out from their bases in the morning, pursue the Vietcong or North Vietnamese in fire fights, and return to bases in the evening. The tokens of progress in the war became the "body count" of soldiers killed, rather than territory captured or decapitation of the enemy's command and control structure. Westmoreland adopted the procedure because it seemed to provide the quantifiable data that McNamara insisted upon. Washington and MACV headquarters in

Saigon hoped to reach an elusive crossover point at which they destroyed troops faster than North Vietnam could replace them. The lightning helicopter raids also reduced American casualties by limiting their exposure to hostile fire.

These tactics encouraged serious abuses. Body counts rarely reflected the accurate number of enemy soldiers killed, as officers were rewarded for producing high numbers. Sometimes officers had the number of dead killed in a battle ready at the next dawn. Cynical reporters complained that "American soldiers had apparently stayed up all night counting enemy bodies with flashlights" in range of NLF snipers.[3] Official reliance on the body count induced soldiers to shoot first without asking questions. A marine recalled that "any Vietnamese out at night was the enemy." Others said, "If it's dead, it's VC."[4]

By the end of 1966 the U.S. commitment had stopped the deterioration of the government of South Vietnam, but the end of the war was not yet in sight. American military tactics proved ineffective in forcing the North Vietnamese to either stop infiltration into the South or negotiate a settlement with the United States. The United States fought the war it did because it possessed abundant air power, mobility, technology, and firepower. Technology—as much as logic—drove the plan. Since technology seemed to save American lives, planners assumed it would be effective. As the historian Larry Cable observed, "American policy makers did not attempt so much to understand the goal definitions and theories of victory which arose organically within the conflict as to impose upon the belligerent those of an American manufacture."[5] When finally the commanders concluded that using more ground troops and small arms might prove more effective, it was nearly too late. Public patience had already worn thin. All along, North Vietnamese leaders predicted that the U.S. public would tire of the war more quickly than would the Vietnamese. This view proved prophetic. American soldiers fought for twelve months in the faraway jungles of Vietnam before returning home. When their North Vietnamese counterparts went South they were told, "The trip has no deadline for return. When your mission is accomplished you'll come back." Ho Chi Minh declared "Your mission is to fight for five years or even ten or twenty years."[6] They did, and their perseverance carried the day.

THE BATTLE FOR THE IA DRANG VALLEY

When President Johnson announced the decision to send an additional one hundred thousand soldiers to South Vietnam in July 1965, he specifically mentioned that the airmobile division was among the first to go.[7] It left on a troop ship from Charleston, South Carolina on August 16 and arrived in

Vietnam a month later. (Later U.S. soldiers flew directly to Vietnam from the West Coast.)[8]

As the airmobile division embarked on its six-week sail to South Vietnam, Henry Cabot Lodge arrived in Saigon as ambassador to South Vietnam as a replacement for Maxwell Taylor. The choice of Lodge seemed perplexing at first glance, since the Johnson administration had brought him back home the previous summer. At that time, Lodge supported the presidential campaign of Pennsylvania's Republican governor William Scranton. However unlikely the prospect that Scranton would receive the Republican nomination or be elected president, Johnson knew that Lodge had not supported him for re-election. Moreover, the White House and State and Defense Department advisers on Vietnam had considered Lodge's lackadaisical performance as ambassador as a minor but significant factor in the turmoil of the South Vietnamese government. In the summer of 1964, therefore, General Taylor, former Chairman of the Joint Chiefs of Staff, seemed a perfect choice to bend the South Vietnamese authorities to the Americans' will. But now that the war in Vietnam was more of an American operation, Washington no longer wanted a tough ambassador in charge. General William Westmoreland, the commander of MACV, became the principal U.S. official in Saigon. The complacent Lodge was less likely to cause Westmoreland difficulties than the strong-willed Taylor.[9]

In the fall of 1965 the 1st Airmobile Cavalry Division of the U.S. army conducted a major search-and-destroy operation in the central highlands of South Vietnam near Pleiku. For years the Vietcong had controlled the Ia Drang River Valley south of Da Nang, and General Westmoreland decided to use helicopters to transport the 1st Cavalry into battle to root out the communist fighters.

In mid-November the 1st Cavalry encountered the 66th Regiment of the North Vietnamese People's Liberation Army commanded by Brigadier General Chu Huy Man in the Ia Drang Valley. General Man's troops had left North Vietnam in mid-August, about the time the 1st Calvary departed from Charleston. The North Vietnamese walked down the Ho Chi Minh Trail, thousands of miles of roads, paths, and trails winding through the thick brush of North Vietnam, Laos, and Cambodia. The North Vietnamese often claimed that only volunteers went to the South. Technically many North Vietnamese soldiers did ask to go. Many were recruited to make the long march after giant rallies denouncing the Americans and the South Vietnamese authorities. Some were asked to go by Communist Party cadres. Most complied the way soldiers in all wars at all times act. One reported to an American interrogator, "I felt it was my duty to go and comply with national policy." Another reported, "To tell the truth, I was very worried about the trip south. But I had no choice since it was my duty to go. . . . If the other men could go, why couldn't I, who was in no way different from them?"[10]

Each soldier wore a uniform of a khaki shirt and pants and carried one spare outfit in his pack. Each had a pair of sandals cut from old truck tires as well as ankle-high green canvas Chinese communist boots.[11] The uniforms and sandals were expected to last the recruit for five years. Each soldier carried twenty-two pounds of food expected to last for the entire two-month walk from North Vietnam to the Ia Drang Valley. They also carried weapons manufactured in the Soviet Union, China, Czechoslovakia, and Albania. The Kalashnikov AK-47 assault rifle was the most effective infantry weapon. Units also lugged heavy machine guns, mortars, and anti-aircraft weapons down the Ho Chi Minh Trail. As had been the case during the Vietminh war against the French thousands of young, mostly female Vietnamese peasants maintained the network of trails with campsites every nine miles extending from the North through Laos and Cambodia to the border with South Vietnam. Each soldier was expected to take a malaria pill each day, but most contracted the disease anyway. About three or four men out of each 160-man company died on the trip from the North to the South from disease, accidents, snake bites, and U.S. air raids.[12]

Initially the North Vietnamese felt "very nervous, very worried by what they were hearing" about the arrival of the Airmobile Cavalry, a "strong, mobile unit so well equipped with helicopters." The North Vietnamese fretted that they "moved mainly by foot [and] were poorly equipped. Our hospital and food services were not so good."[13] Soon, however, the North Vietnamese recovered their spirit. They developed a strategy of confrontation with the South Vietnamese and the Americans which was a virtual mirror image of the American effort to root out the Vietcong and the North Vietnamese. Both the North Vietnamese and the Americans sought a confrontation in which they could kill as many of the opposing forces as possible. General Man decided to attack the less-well-equipped ARVN forces. Man expected the ARVN forces to be no match for the North Vietnamese. The Americans would therefore be forced to assist their allies under conditions favoring the North Vietnamese.

On November 14 the Airmobile Cavalry and the North Vietnamese 66th Regiment engaged in a fierce battle in the Ia Drang Valley. The American forces attacked with air strikes and artillery in preparation for the landing of troops on helicopters. The North Vietnamese shot at helicopters and tried to seize the helicopter landing ground and encircle the Americans. A helicopter pilot recalled that "we landed too close to some trenches the gooks had dug. . . . The guys inside [the helicopter] didn't know Charlie was that close. . . . They got us on our approach."[14] Despite sustaining significant losses, the American forces were able to land at the Ia Drang and begin a search-and-destroy operation. On November 16 B-52s rained bombs on the North Vietnamese. Over the next three days the Americans lost 79 killed and 121 wounded. After the fighting the American forces combed the battlefield in a grisly body count of the enemy soldiers, counting 634 dead and adding another 1,215 estimated killed or wounded by artillery, air attacks, and aerial rocket bombardment. General Harold Moore, the U.S. commander, told reporters that "Brave American soldiers and the M-16 rifle won a victory here." *New York Times* reporter Neil Sheehan, who had helped break the news of catastrophic defeat of the ARVN forces at Ap Bac in January 1963, told Moore "This could be the most significant battle of the Vietnam war since Ap Bac."[15]

The fighting on November 14–16 represented the fiercest engagement of a month-long engagement between the North Vietnamese and the Americans over the Ia Drang. In thirty-four days the North Vietnamese lost 3,561 killed versus 305 American dead. The battle marked a significant turn for both the Americans and North Vietnamese. Both sides believed that they had crossed a threshold favorable to their own position. Each adopted methods of fighting the war which mirrored their adversary. Each sought to achieve their own version of the crossover point. For the Americans, that point had a quantifiable although ever changing value, namely the pace at which the North Vietnamese forces were being killed at a faster rate than they could be replaced.

The North Vietnamese, for their part, had a less quantifiable but still real crossover point in mind as they pursued the Americans. They believed that eventually they could raise the price of waging the war high enough for the Americans to quit Vietnam. Having made life impossible for the South Vietnamese armed forces, the North Vietnamese now saw the Americans as the principal foe. During the battle for the Ia Drang the North Vietnamese for the first time engaged the Americans with division-sized regular forces. Not since defeating the French at Dienbienphu had the communists used such large concentrations of troops against invading forces. General Vo Nguyen Giap believed that having fought the Americans without having been annihilated meant that "we could fight and win against cavalry troops."

Like the French before them, the Americans believed that the communists made a serious mistake by challenging the superior fire power and mobility of the U.S. forces. General Westmoreland welcomed the ratio of twelve enemy soldiers killed for every American death as a way of eventually grinding down the North Vietnamese. Giap thought the United States made a fatal mistake relying solely on the tactic of attrition. He reflected later to an American general, "You had tactics and it takes very decisive tactics to win a strategic victory. If we could defeat your tactics—your helicopters—then we could defeat your strategy."[16]

Giap adopted a plan of "strategic mobility" in which he deployed strong multi-division forces in dispersed, well supplied areas. These highly maneuverable forces would tie down the Americans in defensive positions. In frustration, the Americans would attack these well-supplied positions. Giap

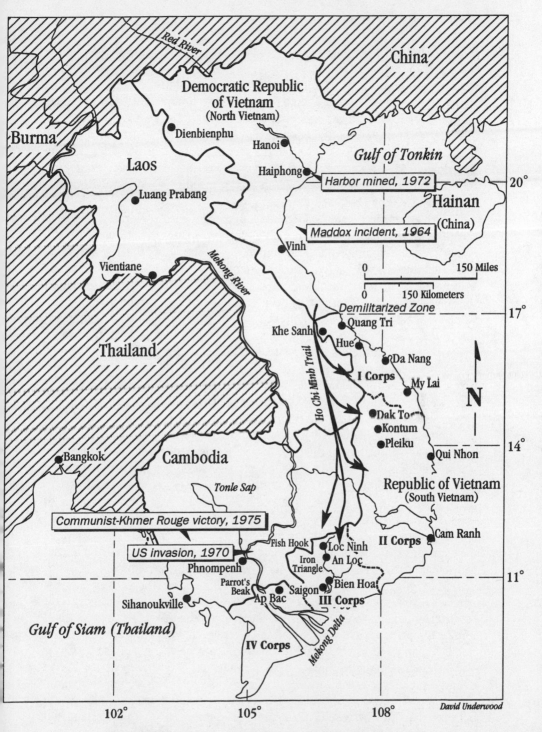

Vietnam During the War, 1960-1975

187

hoped to inflict sufficiently heavy casualties on the Americans to make them rethink their participation in the war. The North Vietnamese hoped to turn the highland regions in which the Ia Drang campaign had been conducted into a killing field that would force the Americans to lose heart. A North Vietnamese broadcast after the Ia Drang battle boasted that "we were able . . . to force the U.S. Marine division to leave its base on the coast and rush into the jungle so that we could exterminate them." As the United States became tied down and suffered ever-heavier causalities, the North Vietnamese and the Vietcong could turn their attention toward capturing the population centers of the Mekong Delta and the coastal plains.[17]

Shortly after the battle, Americans recognized what the North Vietnamese hoped to accomplish. The 1966 MACV command history determined that the North's strategy attempted to demoralize the Republic of Vietnam and force the withdrawal of the United States. General Giap drew the lessons from the Vietminh's struggle against the French, when the communists had "relied on the unwillingness of the French people to support a long and costly `dirty war.'" The North Vietnamese believed that the Americans, too, would eventually withdraw their forces in the face of "the high financial cost, the loss of American lives, international pressure and domestic dissension."[18]

Westmoreland and Secretary of Defense Robert McNamara also recognized that the North Vietnamese hoped to build up their forces faster than the Americans could add to theirs and faster than the Americans could kill the North Vietnamese. In the aftermath of the battle for the Ia Drang Valley, Westmoreland wrote to the Pentagon that the buildup rate for the North Vietnamese was double that of the U.S. forces. He desperately wanted at least an additional 25,000 U.S. and 23,000 Korean soldiers. He hoped Washington would send 41,500 more U.S. troops. These new soldiers would free a division of U.S. troops (approximately 20,000 men) for mobile operations of the sort the 1st Air Cavalry had recently undertaken in the Ia Drang.[19]

McNamara visited Saigon once more in late November in the wake of the campaign in the Ia Drang. Some things had not changed much, and McNamara provided another downbeat assessment of the situation for Johnson. The "government of generals" led by Prime Minister Nguyen Cao Ky had lasted since June 1965. Yet except for having survived the revolving door of governmental authority in Saigon for five months, it seemed only a slight improvement over its predecessors. Ky's regime had not attracted much public support and its efforts at pacification had been completely stalled.

McNamara lamented the lack of permanent security anywhere in the country, which made it nearly impossible that "able and willing leadership will emerge" to wage the war effectively in South Vietnam. McNamara believed that "the increased willingness of the communist forces to stand and fight, even in large scale engagements" represented a dramatic change in the character of the war. The communists believed as they had for years that the war would be prolonged and that "time is their ally, and their staying power is superior" to that of the Americans.

This willingness on the part of the communists to challenge the Americans once more forced McNamara to ask for more U.S. troops. Unless the Americans and their allies had a superiority of at least two to one over the communist forces, the war could not be won. He believed that a level of approximately six hundred thousand U.S. troops could ultimately sap the resources of the North Vietnamese and the Vietcong. Nevertheless, even raising the U.S. commitment to nearly six hundred thousand "[would] not guarantee success." He predicted that in early 1967 the United States might be faced with another decision "at significantly higher levels of casualties," perhaps one thousand U.S. deaths per week.[20]

TURMOIL IN THE SOUTH

Continuing disarray within the government and military command in South Vietnam validated McNamara's growing pessimism. ARVN commanders demonstrated more interest in squabbling among themselves than in fighting the NLF. Three South Vietnamese generals, Nguyen Van Thieu, Nguyen Cao Ky and Cao Van Vien, shared power. Thieu chaired the Committee for the Direction of the State, commonly known as the Directory, the committee of younger generals and senior colonels who acted as the supreme governing power in Vietnam. Ky was the prime minister and Vien chaired the Joint General Staff of the Armed Forces. The commanders of the four tactical zones within the South also shared power. Few of these men trusted one another, each had supporters, and their rivalries continued to detract from the conduct of the war. On January 15, 1966 Ky announced that he and the Directory intended to return South Vietnam to civilian rule over the next year.[21]

Plans for a constitution drafted by the military provoked protests from Buddhists throughout the country. Buddhist religious leaders complained about the generals' subservience to the Americans. Monks and students took to the streets in what they characterized as the "Struggle Movement" in the major cities of South Vietnam. The largest demonstrations occurred in the northern cities of Hué and Da Nang. General Nguyen Chanh Thi, the commander of I Corps, had his headquarters in Da Nang. Thi, a decorated airborne brigade commander who was popular with both the people of the Northern region and the Americans, refused requests from Ky to put down the demonstrations forcefully. As a member of the Directory, Thi believed he was Ky's equal, and he resented being asked to do the dirty work of the generals in Saigon.

Ky and Thieu accused Thi of aligning himself with the Struggle Movement and harboring political ambitions of his own. On March 11 Ky fired Thi. Lodge and Westmoreland both felt a sickening sense that the Saigon authorities had reverted to their old ways of personal intrigues. Nevertheless, they stifled their objections. Lodge had long believed that the corps system had given the local commanders too much independence, to a point where their activities resembled those of the Chinese warlords during the 1920s. Lodge thought that firing Thi might signal the "subordination of corps commanders to central authority" and foster "Vietnam's march toward nationhood."[22]

The firing of Thi touched off a full-blown political crisis that lasted until June. Supporters of the Struggle Movement mounted huge demonstrations in Hué and Da Nang demanding an immediate resignation of Ky and Thieu, a return to civilian rule, and, most ominously for the U.S. war effort, less dependence on the Americans. The Struggle Movement's animosity toward the Americans led to some of the deepest American involvement in South Vietnamese politics in the war. Lodge assailed the Struggle Movement's demands as a pastiche of "hypocrisy and cant" that amounted solely to a "naked grab for power."[23] Some South Vietnamese army commanders, including General Thi, joined the Struggle Movement. On April 9 a large task force of dissident troops advanced on the U.S. air base at Da Nang. A contingent of U.S. marines, supported by marine corps fighter bombers, blocked the advancing rebel forces. After some tense negotiations, the rebels withdrew.[24]

Evidence of support for the Struggle Movement among the military startled the generals in Saigon, who ordered the withdrawal of their forces from Da Nang. The demonstrations cooled, but beneath the surface agitation against the government continued. American officials became alarmed at reports that Buddhist chaplains in the armed forces told troops that the war aims were Washington's, the enemy was China, not North Vietnam, and the ARVN troops should lay down their arms. The claims of a subversive network of Buddhists were probably manufactured by Saigon in order to gather American support for a swift strike against the rebels.

On May 15 Ky ordered South Vietnamese marines, army units, and air force planes to take over Da Nang. There was some fighting, but most of the rebel forces withdrew into Buddhist pagodas. On May 19 Thieu and Ky ordered 3,300 troops to attack the pagodas. As they had done so many times before, the top American leadership temporized. Most of all, they wanted the crisis to end quickly. Chairman of the Joint Chiefs of Staff Earle Wheeler told Westmoreland to use whatever influence he had to get the South Vietnamese generals to stop their suicidal squabbling and concentrate on the war. Wheeler wondered, however, if the South Vietnamese government thought that the United States was so "firmly hooked in Vietnam" that the authorities could ignore the wishes of the Americans.[25] Westmoreland tried to calm Washington, saying that overzealous "reporters on the scene attempting to make a name for themselves and play a role'' in the future of South Vietnam had blown the affair out of proportion.[26]

The Buddhists did soon surrender their pagodas in Da Nang, but opposition to the government spread. Priests set up altars blockading the main roads in Hué, Da Nang, Quang Tri, and Qui Nhon. The Directory sent loyal troops to these cities. Beginning on June 10, the government troops fought intermittent battles for two weeks with the Buddhists. On the twenty-third the government seized control of the Buddhist Institute in Saigon, effectively ending all resistance. The end of the revolt strengthened the authority of the Directory, but at a terrible political cost. No middle ground now remained between the government and the Vietcong. Thieu and Ky felt domestically fortified, but their strength gave them less reason to accept advice from the Americans.

All the while, ordinary South Vietnamese soldiers grew more estranged from their leaders' intrigues. A wide gulf separated the top ARVN officers from the troops they led. In a country where about 80 percent of the population were Buddhists, only about 5 percent of the senior colonels or generals said they were Buddhists. Unlike the NLF fighters, who endured hours of political indoctrination each week, ARVN soldiers often were left in the dark about the reasons they fought and their nation's politics. After the fall of Ngo Dinh Diem, ARVN fighters often did not know the names of the government's leading figures. One told a reporter ''he figured he would still be a soldier regardless of who was leading the country.''[27] ARVN pay was low by American standards. An enlisted man of the lower ranks earned the equivalent of $600–$1200 in 1965. By 1966 inflation had effectively cut that wage in half. Men had to pay for their food out of their wages, and by the beginning of 1966 rising prices meant that most ARVN field soldiers depended on American surplus rice for their sustenance.[28]

Americans regularly belittled the ARVN as poor fighters without considering the hardships endured by the ordinary Vietnamese soldier, and complained of the ''politics, corruption and nepotism'' at the highest levels of the South Vietnamese armed forces. Millions of dollars worth of goods provided as aid by the United States were stolen from warehouses and PXs, fueling wild inflation throughout the Republic of Vietnam. American cigarettes, whiskey, and razor blades as well as rifles, ammunition, uniforms, boots, and helmets were available on the black markets of the teeming cities of South Vietnam. One American senior adviser reflected that too many officers lacked ''aggressiveness, leadership ability, and a full professional outlook.'' Commanders spent more time fighting one another than engaging the enemy. Officers pocketed the pay of thousands of ghost subordinates—deserters, men on leave or in hospitals or even dead. As many as 25 percent of the 261,000 men supposedly in the regular armed forces and 30 to 40 percent of the territorial guard were missing at any time. To make the ARVN fight better Westmoreland tried to unify the American and South Vietnamese command under his leadership, but he eventually drew back in recognition that South Vietnam's proud generals would resist "something approaching de facto U.S. control of the RVNAF [Republic of Vietnam Armed Forces]"[29]

For the most part ARVN soldiers guarded secure areas and their own bases. When they did take the field, American observers thought the ARVN fighting man's small physique disqualified him as a modern soldier. Draftees from the rural areas had little in common with the better educated, urban, and often Catholic officers. Fearful of ambushes by the Vietcong, ARVN truck and jeep drivers often roared through villages at high speeds oblivious to the safety of peasants they supposedly were protecting.[30] But the ARVN, poorly armed and unable to call on air support or helicopters to evacuate the wounded as could their American counterparts, displayed remarkable tenacity. One Australian reporter recalled "how tough they were. They kept on, with no sign of tiredness, weighted with their spare ammunition and crazy collection of guns, most of which were too big for them: M-1 carbines from World War II, Thompson submachine guns; Browning automatic rifles, and the new American M-16s." They waded stoically into streams where the water surged over their heads, carrying their rifles and packs safely in the air.[31] But with the war an American affair by 1966, the ARVN's activities went largely unnoticed by the outside world.

LARGE UNIT OPERATIONS: 1966–1967

The U.S. conducted search-and-destroy operations designed to sap the ability of the Vietcong and North Vietnamese to fight. The turmoil within the ARVN relegated the South Vietnamese to an even more subordinate role in the fighting. In 1966 and 1967 ARVN units sometimes helped in American-led search-and-destroy operations, but they more often helped defend villages already under government control.

U.S. commanders mistakenly believed that the vast technological advantages of the American forces changed the ground rules of guerrilla warfare. Traditional military theorists had concluded that a government needed an advantage of about ten to one over guerrilla forces, yet Wheeler claimed that the helicopter and fighter bombers provided to "South Vietnamese and to U.S. forces an advantage in mobility and firepower—the fundamentals of combat—greatly exceeding that available to counter-insurgency forces in any other guerrilla war."[32]

Experts in guerrilla warfare expressed skepticism at the time that air mobility had upset the traditional balance between the belligerents. Sir Robert Thompson, a British expert on fighting guerrillas who had advised the Kennedy administration on counterinsurgency, believed that the U.S. army relied too heavily on the helicopter. The Americans, he recalled, were never mobile on their feet. "You got landed from helicopters and the battle took place, but when the battle was over and you had won the battle you even went out by helicopter." An American reporter who grew increasingly frustrated with the army's reliance on the helicopter rattled General Robert Williams, an advocate of air mobility, when he told Williams, "You are doing more in your helicopters to prevent our side from winning this war than anyone else." He asked, "How do you expect our forces to win the hearts and minds of the people when all they do is take off from one army base and fly overhead at 1500 feet while Charlie [a GI-given nickname for the Vietcong] is sitting down there and he's got 'em by the testicles jerking, and every time he jerks their hearts and minds follow."[33]

The United States tried to make vast areas of South Vietnam unlivable to the Vietcong. Air force and navy planes rained bombs on suspected Vietcong strongholds in Operation Arc Light. The American army sent villagers scurrying away from their homes into larger hamlets that could be defended by the ARVN. The United States also sprayed a variety of different herbicides on the forests of Vietnam from 1962 to 1971 in order to deprive NLF and Vietcong fighters of leaf cover. The different types of herbicides were identified by color-coded bands around the drums containing the chemicals. The defoliants were thus named Agents Orange, White, Blue, Purple, Pink, and Green. Agent Orange was the mostly widely used defoliant during the period of the most intensive defoliation, called Operation Ranch Hand, from 1965 until 1971. During Ranch Hand 17.6 million gallons of Agent Orange were sprayed over approximately 3.6 million acres of Vietnam.[34]

The goal was to deprive the Vietcong guerillas the sanctuary of a friendly or at least neutral population,[35] but the result often was to make peasants fear the Americans. After B-52s dropped their bombs a villager said, "The earth quaked. My ears were sore. . . . All the trees in the bombed area were uprooted or cut down."[36] One woman likened an American attack to rid her village of Vietcong fighters to "a raging elephant stomping on red ants too far down in their holes to feel the blows." She saw U.S. troops go from house to house "tearing everything apart to find the Vietcong hideouts. Whenever anything suspicious was found, the house was burned and its occupants tied up and taken away for interrogation."[37] More and more ordinary Vietnamese peasants felt estranged from all sides and only wanted the fighting to stop. A Vietnamese nun told an American relief worker that her country "was beautiful once . . . until *you* arrived."[38]

The war turned life in Vietnam upside down. A country that once fed itself now imported rice. The bombing forced millions of people to flee their rural homes. At any given time about four million people, roughly one quarter of the republic's population, were refugees crowded into squalid suburbs of South Vietnam's cities or large towns. Many suffered from tuberculosis, dysentery, or other diseases, or had limbs blown off during the fighting. They lived off the Americans. Tens of thousands of people, including youngsters under ten years of age, offered goods on the black market. Many people begged. Many women tended bar, and some sold their bodies to the Americans. Thousands of children were born of relations between the GIS and Vietnamese women. This disintegration of their traditional way of life made many Vietnamese yearn for an end to the bloodshed. The refugees' desperation touched the hearts of many Americans who offered friendship and relief. U.S. aid for refugees ran at a rate of about $30 million per year, most of which was spent on food, medicines, farm equipment, and temporary buildings. But the misery of ordinary Vietnamese also contributed to a deepening sense that the very people whom the Americans had come to help had seen their lives disrupted or even ruined by the Americans' arrival.[39]

Critics of the Americans' reliance on search-and-destroy missions believed that the Americans left the field to the guerrillas, who then could decide whether and when to engage the Americans. Advocates of traditional methods of counterinsurgency wanted the Americans to keep their soldiers on the ground, protect the population centers, and use long range patrols to drive the guerrillas into ever more remote areas. Eventually, guerrillas would find that they had been denied their supplies from the rural population. They would then have to come out in the open. At that point the Americans could use their technological superiority to annihilate the main force of the Vietcong.

Yet Westmoreland and his principal lieutenants rejected suggestions that the army spend more time in the field, rely more on small arms, and express less confidence in helicopters, fighter bombers, and heavy fire power. "That's not the American way," one said, "and you are not going to get the American soldier to fight that way."[40] He may have been right. Ordinary soldiers wanted to be in the field for as short a time as possible. During the entire Vietnam War era, from 1961 to 1975, about 2.25 million American men served in Vietnam.[41] Soldiers' slang suggested how strange they found Vietnam. They fought "Charlie" in " 'Nam" and counted the days until they could return home to "the world." The experience of entering Vietnam was profoundly disorienting. One day a man would board a commercial plane in the United States, and after a twenty-hour flight he would land at Cam Ranh Bay, Da Nang, or Saigon, to be hit with a blast of hot, humid air. Newcomers to Vietnam could often see artillery or smoke from bombs as they approached the airport. A nurse remembered a deadly quiet settling over the passenger cabin of her plane as soon as the coast of Vietnam came into view. The captain announced that the Vietcong "were mortaring the airfield. He said he was going to drop us off and get right back into the air. The plane made a steep landing into the airfield. They opened the door. We ran out and the troops going home ran onto the plane."[42] A frightened young conscript felt moments before landing that "they're gonna just be standing there and they're gonna blow our ass away."[43]

Men changed emotionally and physically soon after reaching Vietnam. Many of those who volunteered for combat duty in Vietnam out of a sense of duty, obligation to a father or brother who had fought in an earlier war, or a conviction that the cause was just changed their minds. Little progress against the enemy seemed to take place. Vietnamese civilians often appeared ungrateful for the Americans' aid. The brutalization of the body count offended some men. More were disgusted and angered by the deaths of their comrades-in-arms. A lieutenant lashed out at a minister who offered words of comfort and hope, "Hey, Chaplain! Do you have any idea how tough it is to live in Vietnam after the kids you love and led die? Do you have any idea how hard it is to wash their blood out of your brain?"[44] In the field they stopped shaving, grew their hair long, and threw away their extra pair of socks—refusing to remove their boots because of fear of a deadly booby trap, poison-tipped "punji sticks." A foot soldier recalled that "I didn't brush my teeth for two months in Vietnam" because the troops needed their tooth brushes to clean their rifles.[45]

Foot soldiers (``grunts'' or "dinks") did not like being on patrol where no one could tell who was the enemy or when he would strike. Twenty percent of the men wounded in South Vietnam fell victim to booby traps rather than direct enemy fire. The enemy wired bodies with mines, and dug holes on trails covered them with leaves and twigs so the Americans would fall into them to be impaled on sharpened bamboo stakes. Reporters wrote derisively that troops would "search and avoid" the enemy.[46] One combat soldier bitterly recalled "they booby-trapped the trails they knew we'd take, because we always took the same trails, the ones that looked easy and kept us dry."[47] No wonder combat soldiers far preferred the relative comfort of base camps. They made them seem as American as possible with rock 'n roll blaring from Armed Forces Radio, steaks grilling on makeshift barbecues, and beer flowing freely. The familiarity of base camps also diminished some of the resentment that combat soldiers, who made up no more than 20 percent of the American force at any time, felt toward the other 80 percent who had relatively safe jobs as support personnel—supply officers, mechanics, medical personal, cooks, or laundry workers.[48]

The heat during the dry season, the cold during the rainy months, the dampness year-round, and the dirt took their toll. Men could never stay dry or clean on search-and-destroy missions. Out in the field they worked eighteen-hour days, and would rather sleep than eat. Some forgot to take their malaria pills or keep their feet dry. Others patrolled without helmets or flak jackets to avoid the oppressive heat. Their carelessness made them prime targets for disease or snipers. Better leadership at the platoon level would have helped, but the army decided to rotate officers every six months to broaden their experience. This personnel policy made officers less likely to bond with their men.[49]

The twelve-month tour of duty of the ordinary soldier (spread over thirteen months, with one thirty-day break for rest and recreation or "R and R") also contributed to the alienation GIs felt in Vietnam. Commanders originally praised the twelve-month tour of duty as a means of reducing stress on combat soldiers by giving them a fixed date on which they would return home. Besides, there was such a large pool of men available for the draft it did not seem fair to make men stay any longer than necessary. But soldiers did not develop strong ties with their units in their twelve months. Worse, after their break for "R and R" many men could think only of their return home and had less desire than ever to expose themselves to the NLF. Frightened, unfamiliar with guerrilla warfare, not well led, many American soldiers soon saw all Vietnamese as the enemy. "I'd just as soon shoot a South Vietnamese as a VC," was a common refrain.[50]

Between 7,500 and 11,000 American women also served in the military in Vietnam. All of these women were volunteers, over twenty years of age, and most of them were officers. Eighty percent of them served as nurses, all of whom held officer rank. About half of the 1,300 women who did non-medical work were enlisted personnel, serving as clerks, air traffic controllers, photographers, and cartographers. Like the men in Vietnam, women served a twelve month tour of duty spread over thirteen months. They came and left Vietnam individually, not as members of units.[51] But the women saw a different sort of war. A tiny minority, women saw their special needs ignored by commanders. When women got sick, they shared wards and bathrooms with men. Helmets did not accommodate women's smaller heads or larger hair styles. Most women adapted to this overwhelmingly male environment as they played out what the sociologist Elizabeth Norman characterized as an unwritten rule of traditional gender relations in Vietnam: "Men protected women; women, in turn, comforted the men."[52]

The nurses who made up vast majority of women in Vietnam saw first-hand the destruction wrought by the war. They served twelve hour shifts, six days a week, in trauma units in evacuation hospitals. The ready availability of helicopters profoundly changed the nature of wartime casualties in Vietnam. Wounded men who would have died in World War II or Korea were quickly evacuated by air to forward field hospitals. One nurse recalled looking at a wounded man's wristwatch as she prepared him for surgery; it had stopped seventeen minutes earlier. If a man reached the forward hospital, mortality rate was low, about 3 percent. The wounded spent an average of four days in the hospital before being flown to more fully equipped facilities in Japan, Hawaii, or the mainland United States. Many of the women found their initial exposure to the badly wounded men shocking. "I quickly learned," one recalled, "that I was not in a John Wayne movie. The devastating injuries just came in and came in." Many of the wounded were very young men, averaging nineteen years of age, while the nurses were in their mid-twenties. The nurses thought the soldiers looked like their high school classmates, and they sometimes wept over the tragedy of youths crippled before they could enjoy the fullness of life.

But the hard work, companionship of the trauma units, and the sense of helping very needy people strengthened the nurses. Unlike many combat soldiers who grew ever more disillusioned as their tours of duty went on, the nurses developed a strong sense of accomplishment in Vietnam. Military commanders recognized how vital were their services. While few special facilities existed for women, commanders valued their professional skills. The macv ordered that in the event of an attack on a field hospital nurses were to be saved before patients. One nurse recalled that "it seemed that everyone was expendable but us." Many nurses served multiple tours of duties, and they often married men whom they met in Vietnam, sharing unique memories of stress under fire. "I cannot imagine life without him," one nurse remarked about her husband fifteen years after the war. "We understand each other the way few people could."[53]

Meanwhile, the Vietcong continued to recruit among the South Vietnamese peasants. In the middle of 1966 there were approximately forty-six thousand Vietcong soldiers in the South. Recruiters stressed patriotism, opposition to the government of South Vietnam, and hatred of the Americans. A man would join the NLF and go back for nephews and friends. Villagers who had family members serving in the Vietcong would ask men who remained behind why they had not joined. A recent member of the Vietcong would tell a young man: "You can't sit on the fence forever. You are a young man living in a country in danger. You must defend it! I myself have left my own family to serve the Front! But here you are, hiding your face in your mother's skirts! You don't even deserve to live!"[54] Once in the Vietcong tightly organized three-man cells and the strict control of information kept fighters in line. One political commissar recalled that he did everything possible "to ensure that not a single soldier should have a single doubt as to why and for whom he was fighting."[55]

To counter the appeals of the Vietcong the United States conducted psychological operations designed to convince North Vietnamese and Vietcong fighters to rally to the government side. Plane dropped millions of leaflets over South Vietnam to induce fear and encourage surrenders. One showed a B-52 dropping bombs with the caption "This is the Mighty B-52. Now you have experienced the terrible rain of death and destruction its bombs have caused. Your area will be struck again and again, but you will not know where or when. The planes fly too high to be heard or seen. . . . Leave this place to save your lives." A famous leaflet superimposed an ace of spades on a skull and read "Viet Cong! This is a sign of death! Continue your struggle against the national cause and you will surely die a mournful death like this!" Later the psychological operations branch learned that the Vietnamese did not use an ace of spades in their playing cards and so it had no death symbolism.[56] Another more effective set of leaflets appealed directly to the appalling loneliness and separation from loved ones felt by Vietcong and North Vietnamese fighters. One showed a weeping woman saying "Darling! My eyes are flooded with tears, when will you leave the Communists and return home!"[57] Others read "Compatriots: Come Home! Your family needs you."[58] Some stressed sex appeal, showing attractive young Vietnamese women asking "Why do you deny yourself the satisfaction of life?"[59]

In 1967 the CIA also developed a harsher program to "neutralize" (a euphemism to kill, capture, or cause to defect) members of the Vietcong. Under this program, code-named Phoenix, small teams of CIA operatives, often clad in black pajamas to make them appear to be Vietcong fighters, would enter the dwellings of suspected Vietcong in the middle of the night. They would grab a suspect and demand that he or she confess. If the terrified Vietnamese agreed to work for the Americans, he or she would sometimes have the words "Kill the Communists" tattooed on the chest to prevent the suspect from ever returning to the Vietcong. Others were turned into double agents. Those who refused to change sides sometimes had their throats slit or were thrown to their deaths from helicopters. Others were turned over to the South Vietnamese who ran their own parallel program called Phung Hoang. The South Vietnamese killed more Vietcong suspects than did the Americans, and imprisoned others for more than two years in horrible conditions. In 1970 an American prison reformer broke the news that the South Vietnamese held hard-core Vietcong operatives in "tiger cages" at Con Son prison. Three to five men were shackled to the floor in stone compartments five feet wide, nine feet long, and six feet high. They were beaten, and many were mutilated.[60]

Thousands of Vietcong and North Vietnamese fighters did defect to the South. Over 11,000 rallied in 1965, 20,242 in 1966, and 27,178 in 1967. Nevertheless, the Americans' loudspeakers, leaflets, and radio broadcasts had far less effect on the Vietnamese than did personal appeals from the Vietcong recruiters.[61] Many North Vietnamese and Vietcong fighters believed the appeals insulted their intelligence. One told his captor that "We all knew there were always hardships while fighting a war. We disregarded them because we were fighting for the country." Another reported a common feeling that the appeals for a comfortable existence with the South Vietnamese could not overcome hatred for the Americans who "came to Vietnam and brought death and destruction."[62]

Still, the American military resisted prolonged engagement on a personal level with the Vietnamese rural population. High commanders believed that waging a classic counter-guerrilla war would take longer and produce higher levels of U.S. casualties. Were these men blind? Maybe not. The American generals in Vietnam knew as well as their critics that the Vietnamese seemed to possess almost infinite patience. Unless the United States could make demonstrable progress within a limited period of time (under Westmoreland's 1965 schedule the war would be won by late 1967), the American public would lose heart.[63] Moreover, generals believed that the use of quick search-and-destroy operations limited U.S. casualties. With an army of conscripts, it was essential to keep casualties low and predict the end of the war in a reasonable period of time.

While McNamara, Westmoreland, and their principal advisers were not ignorant of the strengths of the Vietcong and the traditions of the Vietnamese in 1965, they often exaggerated insignificant military engagements into major successes. They did so because the alternative would have required them to fight a war for which they believed that the other side had the advantage.

Westmoreland tested the effectiveness of the attrition tactics in a series of major search-and-destroy operations in the fall of 1966 and the first half of 1967. The MACV hoped to force the enemy into the open where the superior firepower of the allies could annihilate them. Despite killing thousands of the Vietcong and North Vietnamese fighters and seizing hundreds of weapons and thousands of rounds of ammunition, the operations did not significantly affect the Vietcong's ability to wage the war. Experienced guerrillas, they simply waited for the Americans to leave. They often retreated into elaborate underground tunnel systems or returned home to their villages. From September to November 1966, twenty-two thousand troops from the U.S. army and the ARVN engaged in Operation Attleboro in the area northwest of Saigon. B-52s rained bombs and artillery fire made the battlefield unbearable for the fighters of the Vietcong. The MACV thought the operation a success because one thousand Vietcong soldiers were killed, while the Americans and South Vietnamese lost fewer than two hundred men.

Pleased with the results of Attleboro, the MACV launched operation Cedar Falls in the same area, the so-called Iron Triangle, northwest of Saigon, in January 1967. This time the Americans and their Vietnamese allies used forty thousand soldiers for nineteen days. Once more the initial results proved appealing to the Americans and South Vietnamese. Westmoreland reported seven hundred enemy deaths and the capture of 613 weapons.[64] At the beginning of Cedar Falls a five-hundred-man battalion led by Lieutenant-Colonel Alexander Haig helicoptered into the village of Ben Suc. They set up loudspeakers telling the population, "You are surrounded by Republic of South Vietnam and Allied Forces. Do not run away or you will be shot as v.c."[65] The Americans then rounded up six thousand people from Ben Suc and the surrounding hamlets. They moved the women to an area controlled by the ARVN and interrogated the men of fighting age, looking for Vietcong guerrillas. Those not arrested as Vietcong were drafted into the ARVN.[66]

After Ben Suc was depopulated, American troops fanned out looking for Vietcong fighters buried in a maze of tunnels in an area called Cu Chi. The army used tanks with bulldozer blades and slightly-built soldiers, called "tunnel rats," to uncover an underground city. They found stoves, furniture, men's and women's clothes, and thousands of pages of documents. The American command brought Westmoreland to inspect what they thought was a major headquarters of the Vietcong in the Saigon region. While the commander was there, however, the senior non-commissioned officer in charge of exploring the tunnel system was killed by a booby trap. The U.S. army decided it was too dangerous to explore further, so they pumped in tear gas and set off explosives. Despite their glee at having unearthed a major Vietcong stronghold, the Americans missed the underground headquarters of the NLF, which was located several miles north. The bulk of the tunnel system, where thousands of NLF fighters rode out the American offensive, remained undisturbed.

An even larger operation, Junction City, followed Cedar Falls. This time the United States used two divisions, approximately forty thousand soldiers, to return to War Zone C, the area northwest of Saigon. This time the American forces used paratroopers, tanks, and heavy artillery to root out the Vietcong. The operation lasted from February 22 to April 15. The Americans reported killing 1,776 and capturing eight hundred tons of rice and a huge cache of weapons and ammunition. For Westmoreland, the results of Attleboro, Cedar Falls, and Junction City taught the Vietcong that it was "foolhardy" for them to keep their units near the major population centers, but other U.S. commanders later realized that whatever gains were achieved were temporary. Major-General William DuPuy recalled that when Vietcong casualties got "too high . . . they just backed off and waited." Another general observed that "it was a sheer physical impossibility to keep the enemy from slipping away whenever he wished." The United States used several tons of artillery and bombs for every Vietcong fighter killed. As a Vietcong manual put it, "the enemy may be several times superior to us in strength and modern weapons, but he will not chase us from the battlefield, because we will launch surprise attacks from within the underground tunnels."[67]

Westmoreland believed that the Vietcong and North Vietnamese had decided to abandon guerrilla warfare and concentrate their forces in divisional strength in eight to ten different areas.[68] Westmoreland's command understood from captured documents that Giap's strategy was to keep his forces in the more remote frontier areas of South Vietnam. He expected that the United States would engage in more fruitless operations to seek them out and annihilate them. Meanwhile, the United States would not concentrate its efforts in securing the population centers, from which the revolutionaries drew their strength. The North Vietnamese generals hoped "for a spectacular victory in the highlands employing main forces already located there and possibly reinforced by continued infiltration from North Vietnam." Giap did not expect "to hold ground permanently, but rather to create a psychological shock designed to affect U.S. public opinion against continuation of the war." Westmoreland acknowledged that Giap's strategy was "a practical and clever one to continue a protracted war and inflict unacceptable casualties on our forces."[69]

Time, then, became the crucial factor in planning the future of the war for both the North Vietnamese and the Americans. For the communists in North and South Vietnam, the longer the war, the better their chances. Their patience was nearly inexhaustible and their forces were not going anywhere. Giap boasted that the Americans had wanted to fight a blitzkrieg, but he had forced them "to fight a protracted war" which he characterized as "a big defeat for them."[70] For the United States, on the other hand, the end had to be in sight, otherwise public opinion would not tolerate the continuation of the effort. Professional pollsters told the White House that "the people are in a foul mood over Vietnam." The overwhelming public sentiment was not for withdrawal but they wondered, "Why can't we get it over with?" George Gallup, Louis Harris, and Oliver Quayle, the major independent public opinion pollsters, told Johnson that "you will continue to go down [in public opinion] until there is some movement—either toward a military victory or toward a negotiated settlement."[71]

In this environment, Americans longed for evidence of success. Robert Komer, the President's special assistant for the civilian pacification effort in Vietnam, became Johnson's principal eyes and ears on what happened at the local level in the country. Known as the "blowtorch," he traveled to the country often in 1966 and 1967, creating both the Civilian Operations and Revolutionary Development Support (CORDS) and Phoenix programs.[72] In June 1966 Komer returned with a glowing report on Westmoreland's "spoiling operations."[73] In 1967 he told the President that he was "more optimistic than ever before." He believed that by the end of 1967 the war would be all but won. How similar these words sounded to the expectations of the French generals in 1952 and 1953. Komer and the other Americans remembered the French experience, but they believed that the United States's vast superiority in wealth and modern equipment would make the outcome different. Komer believed that "wastefully, expensively, but nonetheless indisputably we are winning the war in the South. . . . We are grinding the enemy down by sheer weight and mass."[74]

The desire to show progress and the emphasis on winning the war within a predictable period of time, however, made it difficult for American military commanders to assimilate the information that the war remained a guerrilla engagement. Despite Attleboro, Cedar Falls, and Junction City, over 96 percent of all engagements with the Vietcong and North Vietnamese occurred at company-size strength (under two hundred men) or smaller.[75] The proper way for the United States to have responded to these tiny confrontations with the enemy would have been to employ small-unit guerrilla-like tactics of their own. To have done so, however, would have meant reversing the military's reliance on technology and mobility in favor of infantry and foot patrols, and such a reversal seemed to the military planners likely to prolong the war, raise the number of U.S. casualties, and reduce public support for the effort. Even worse, it seemed to detract from the main advantages the Americans had in the war—wealth, technology, destructive power, and mobility. Try as they might, critical dissenters never could convince most senior American officials that the way to defeat a primarily guerrilla force was through adopting tactics that the guerrillas had perfected. The Americans always believed that the guerrillas would be better at guerrilla warfare than would the Americans. The only way to prevail over them would be to play to the Americans' strength. Much to their dismay, the Americans learned as time went on that the guerrillas refused to accommodate them.

THE AIR WAR

Even as the U.S. army tried to engage the Vietcong and North Vietnamese in large scale ground operations, the air war over the North went forward. When the Johnson administration embarked on the Rolling Thunder bombing of North Vietnam in February 1965, planners expected that the bombing campaign would buy time for the government of the South.[76] Planners hoped that a revitalized South Vietnamese government might take more initiative.

By June 1965, Johnson's principal military advisers concluded that Rolling Thunder alone would not stabilize the military situation in the South. By the end of July Johnson decided on an additional forty-four battalions of troops for South Vietnam, and the role of the bombing of the North changed. Now bombing was to combine political initiatives designed to bring North Vietnam to the bargaining table with the physical destruction of the North's ability to fight the war.

For the remainder of 1965 Rolling Thunder attacks averaged about 750 sorties per week. For the entire year U.S. bombers and fighters flew about 55,000 sorties over the North. About half of these were attacks, and the rest reconnaissance or rescue missions. These missions over the North represented about 30 percent of the total amount of U.S. air actions in Southeast Asia.[77] In late July 1965 McNamara argued that air raids would put ''a ceiling on the size of the war that the enemy can wage.''

But McNamara seemed more interested in the political aspects of the bombing of the North. He outlined the principles behind the bombing designed to encourage the North to negotiate while avoiding the risks of a larger war. He wanted the United States to emphasize the threat to the North of the potential for *future* attacks against it, and encouraged Johnson to allow the North Vietnamese to save face. The best way to encourage the North Vietnamese to negotiate on American terms was to design the bombing program in a way which allowed for pauses, since the North could more easily open discussions when bombing of their territory was not taking place. McNamara believed that the most effective military impact of the bombing campaign would be to prevent the flow of supplies and men (known as "interdiction" in military parlance) from the North to the South. In terms of starting negotiations to end the war, he thought it essential to "avoid bombing which runs a high risk escalation into war with the Soviets or China and which is likely to appall allies and friends."[78]

As the bombing of the North continued in the years after the decision to Americanize the war, the campaign followed rubrics McNamara had laid down. McNamara and Johnson kept off limits major targets such as bridges, port facilities, power plants, and munitions factories in the Hanoi-Haiphong area. They wanted to make the North Vietnamese constantly worry that the United States might in the future attack the most industrially advanced areas of the North. Initially Johnson fully supported McNamara's program of gradual escalation and political incentives. Later, however, McNamara's commitment to this political program of bombing brought him into conflict with the Joint Chiefs of Staff, Congress, and Johnson.

The Joint Chiefs and their supporters in Congress disputed McNamara's belief that the best use of air power was to stop the flow of supplies to the South. Hawkish critics of McNamara's policy believed that the United States should follow a more punitive policy to force the North Vietnamese to yield. Critics pointed to a CIA report which stated that "almost 80 percent of North Vietnam's limited modern industrial economy, 75 percent of the nation's population, and the most lucrative military supply and lines of communications targets have been effectively insulated from air attack." The House and Senate Armed Services Committees repeatedly questioned McNamara about the decision to avoid the Hanoi-Haiphong industrial areas.[79] Defending his decision, he explained that the bombing was "directed primarily against the military targets that are associated with the infiltration of men and equipment into the South. . . . [W]e have not struck in the Hanoi area because the targets are not as directly related to the infiltration of men and equipment as those outside the area."[80]

The United States paused in its bombing of the North and reduced the amount of Arc Light bombing of the South for thirty-seven days from December 24, 1965 to January 31, 1966. Some of Johnson's advisers believed that a pause might encourage the North to explore negotiations on terms acceptable to the Americans. They realized that no movement toward peace talks would take place while the bombing went forward. One group reviewing the bombing policy concluded in the fall of 1965 that "it would be difficult for any government, but especially an oriental one, to agree to negotiate while under sustained bombing attack."[81] National Security Adviser McGeorge Bundy endorsed the idea of a pause as a potential prelude to a cease-fire. He thought that if the North rejected a proposal for a cease-fire "the international political rewards [would be] very great indeed."[82]

Yet as had happened many times before, officials of the Johnson administration divided over the proper course to follow during the bombing halt. Initially Johnson believed that the suspension would "last only hours or a day or so at the most." But soon the President decided to follow McNamara's efforts to allow the North a face-saving method of opening negotiations. Not that Johnson fully believed that the North wanted to negotiate; even before the pause, Hanoi had condemned the idea as a trick. Lodge, Westmoreland, and Admiral U. S. Grant Sharp, commander of U.S. forces in the Pacific, all opposed the bombing halt as providing the North and the Vietcong an opportunity to resupply their forces.[83] Rusk also doubted whether the bombing halt would work, on the grounds that "a pause should be undertaken only when and if the chances were significantly greater than they now appear that Hanoi would respond by reciprocal actions."[84]

Nevertheless, the skeptics went along in order to put the onus on the North. Rusk undertook an international effort to bolster the American case. The Secretary of State dispatched ambassadors Averell Harriman, Llewelyn Thompson, Arthur Goldberg, and Foy Kohler, National Security Adviser McGeorge Bundy, Assistant Secretary of State G. Mennen Williams, and Vice President Hubert Humphrey to open channels with the North Vietnamese. They emphasized to the North Vietnamese the need for a reciprocal reduction in the level of infiltration from the North to the South and told the North that "if your government will now reciprocate by making a positive contribution toward peace, it would obviously have a favorable effect on the possibility of further extending the suspension."[85]

The Johnson administration considered generating public support a central factor in deciding how long to extend the bombing pause. During the pause, the Harris poll found that 73 percent of the public favored a new effort for a cease-fire, 59 percent supported the bombing pause, and a similar proportion, 61 percent, favored increasing the bombing if negotiations did not take place soon. As they had done when starting the bombing campaign, Johnson and McNamara calibrated the political and military advantages of the bombing pause. John McNaughton, McNamara's principal aide in charge of crafting a program of escalation for Vietnam, believed that the political situation inside South Vietnam was as bad as ever. He lamented that "the ARVN is tired, passive and accommodation prone." The military situation also had not improved and the United States and the North Vietnamese now faced "an escalating military statement." The United States had raised its stakes in Vietnam over the past several years in order to avoid the damage to its reputation that would come had it defaulted on its commitments to the government of South Vietnam. He now saw that "the ante (and the commitment) is now very high. . . . [S]ince it is our reputation that is at stake, it is important that we not construe our obligation to be more than do the countries whose opinions of us are our reputation." Accordingly, McNaughton perceived a stark dilemma in mid-January 1966. The United States needed to find a compromise solution to the war, but the only way to do so, he believed, was to try to win. "While going for victory," he predicted, "we have the strength for compromise, but if we go for compromise we have the strength only for defeat."[86]

Johnson went through a smaller version of the debate he conducted among his principal Vietnam advisers the previous July before deciding on resuming the bombing at a higher level. This time, however, the general public paid closer attention. A significant peace faction emerged. The *New York Times* and Senator J. William Fulbright (D., Ark.), Chairman of the Senate Committee on Foreign Relations, called for extending the bombing pause "as long as it is militarily feasible." Critics accused the Johnson administration of having issued what amounted to an ultimatum to the North Vietnamese to halt attacks in the South before the United States would agree to a permanent bombing halt. The *New York Times* urged the President to accept Hanoi's ambiguity regarding its conditions for negotiations.[87]

Once more some of Johnson's advisers urged caution. U.N. ambassador Goldberg urged the President to extend the pause for an additional three weeks at the end of January. He believed it "would have a very good reaction among those who have supported the pause but who have not given up hope."[88] Undersecretary of State George Ball warned of the dangers of a widening war should the United States resume bombing of the North. He believed that it was only a matter of time before the United States increased the size of the area bombed and included more targets. He noticed how it had become a "widely accepted" rationale among government planners "that for bombing to have [the] desired effect" of pressuring Hanoi to stop the war "we must gradually extend our attack to increasingly vital targets." He feared that *"sustained bombing of North Vietnam will more than likely lead us into war with Red China—probably in six to nine months."*

Despite Ball's warning that escalation of the bombing held greater dangers of a wider war (something Johnson was determined to avoid) than it offered the promise of convincing Hanoi to open negotiations, the President decided to resume bombing the North at the end of January 1966. He received advice from former officials who had served in high positions during the Korean War who recommended a resumption of bombing. Many of them agreed with former Secretary of the Air Force Robert Lovett, who claimed charter membership in the "Never Again Club" (officials with bad memories of public impatience during the later phases of the Korean War). "Now that we are in," Lovett told McGeorge Bundy, "he would go a long way." The banker John J. McCloy, another of the so-called foreign-policy Wise Men on whom Johnson relied for advice on Vietnam, agreed that "the pause has been good and useful on political and military rounds, but it has had no response." Clark Clifford, who had expressed some quiet reservations to the buildup of ground troops the previous summer, also recommended a resumption of the bombing. He said that the pause "has now clearly failed with Hanoi," and adopted a position similar to McNaughton's that the best way to achieve a compromise settlement was to try for a military victory. Clifford told Bundy that "he wants to get out of Vietnam more than any other man he knows but the only way to do it is to use enough force and show enough determination to persuade Hanoi that a political contest is better than a military one."[89]

Why did Johnson agree to resume bombing? Skepticism within the military in Washington and Saigon about the bombing halt played a role. So did the negative responses from Hanoi to the diplomatic initiative undertaken by prominent ambassadors and political figures. The President characterized Ho Chi Minh's response as "nothing but repeated denunciation . . . and of feverish effort to repair and retrain and resupply."[90] At each step Hanoi replied through intermediaries that North Vietnam would be willing only to negotiate the modes by which the United States withdrew its troops from Vietnam. The political future of Vietnam should be decided by the Vietnamese. Hanoi refused publicly to acknowledge the pause as a concession from the United States which required a response. Hanoi's diplomats told the Americans through intermediaries that the United States "has no right to bomb or strafe North Vietnam and the DRV regards such actions as an act of war against its sovereign government." The United States realized that this formulation was a recipe for the collapse of the South Vietnamese government. The United States's conditions were just as unacceptable to the North. Washington made it clear through its various intermediaries that it demanded "reciprocal reductions of hostilities" by the North in order to continue the bombing pause.[91]

Moreover, public opinion wanted an immediate and positive response from the North to unconditional negotiations. Failing that, a majority of the public favored increasing the bombing. McNaughton's advice to use additional military action to hope for a compromise solution resonated with the public. Johnson stressed to the congressional leadership that "if we give up the bombing we get nothing but a brutal 'No' from Hanoi, [and] we will give them a wholly wrong signal and strengthen the hard liners among them." Finally, the skeptics did not seem to offer an alternative to the resumption of the bombing that would satisfy the White House's keen need to preserve face. The columnist Walter Lippmann told National Security Adviser Bundy that "the best answer is to let the place go communist as gracefully as possible."[92] Lippmann, a committed Europeanist, believed that the U.S. preoccupation with Vietnam had badly damaged relations with its far more important European allies. But Johnson and all of his close advisers considered such a notion heresy, striking at the heart of their belief that the United States could and should act globally in the Cold War. Johnson found persuasive McNaughton's formulation that the United States might achieve a compromise but only if it appeared to try for a victory. Eventually Johnson decided to resume Rolling Thunder on January 31, 1966. Once more he tried to split the differences among his advisers and held back from a decision to extend the scope of the bombing of the North.[93]

Lost in the January discussions over the future of the bombing of the North was the important question of what the bombing of the past nine months had accomplished. In fact, the bombing produced very limited effects on what was a primarily rural economy. A joint CIA-Defense Department evaluation of the bombing estimated that only about 12 percent of North Vietnam's economy fell into the modern industrial sector. The analysts estimated that the "economic deterioration so far has not affected the capabilities of North Vietnam's armed forces, which place little direct reliance on the domestic economy for material." Six months later Ambassador Ellsworth Bunker believed that bombing had helped slow the rate of infiltration of troops and supplies from the North to the South. He acknowledged, however, that bombing had "neither stopped infiltration nor broken the will of the North Vietnamese and it is doubtful that it can accomplish either." The compilers of the Pentagon Papers, writing in 1968 after Secretary of Defense McNamara had decided that bombing had not worked, concluded that "the idea that destroying or threatening to destroy North Vietnam's industry would pressure Hanoi into calling it quits seems, in retrospect, a colossal misjudgment."[94]

Yet throughout 1966 the Johnson administration tried to refine the bombing to apply more pressure on the North. It did so because the alternatives seemed unpalatable. Without bombing, officials believed the war would last longer and U.S. casualties would be higher. Without bombing they thought that the South Vietnamese authorities would lose heart. Convinced that the end of bombing would make matters worse, officials took the next erroneous step to believing that more bombing would help end the war on U.S. terms. During the first six months of 1966 Johnson mulled proposals to increase the air war to include attacks on the petroleum supplies of the North. The CIA and Joint Chiefs of Staff recommended heavier attacks against targets designed to break "the will of the regime."[95] By April McNamara agreed that attacks on the petroleum storage facilities would "create a substantial added burden" on North Vietnam which might lead eventually to negotiations. Not that officials favored immediate negotiations in the late spring of 1966. The fighting among South Vietnam's generals made it difficult for Saigon to contemplate participation in talks with the NLF. Maxwell Taylor, now the special military adviser to the President, warned against stopping bombing as a precondition to talks. Taylor advised using bombing as a "blue chip" once negotiations began.[96] Lodge agreed that "the bombing must not be stopped without a *quid pro quo*." Lodge did not even believe that negotiations would hasten the end of the war. He insisted that there be "an incentive for the enemy to come to a *prompt* settlement. Without such an incentive the talks could drag on indefinitely."[97]

In February 1966 Johnson appointed Walt Rostow National Security Adviser. He replaced McGeorge Bundy, who was tired after five years in a grueling job and was growing increasingly concerned about the costs of the U.S. commitment to Vietnam on American standing with its allies. Rostow, a fervent advocate of deep U.S. involvement in the war, was far less torn over the ambiguities of the war than Bundy. Rostow's appointment signaled a hardening of Johnson's position and a reduced willingness of the President to consider advice to reduce the American commitment in the war. Rostow advocated air attacks against the North as "the only course open to us to raise the cost to Hanoi and hasten the decision to desist in their aggression." He believed that bombing the oil storage facilities would make it difficult for the North to fuel the trucks carrying goods to the South since approximately 60 percent of the oil used in North Vietnam went to the military.[98] He recalled what he considered to have been the positive military experience of the World War II allied bombing of German petroleum supplies as support for a program of "systematic and sustained bombing of POL [petroleum, oil, and lubricants] in North Vietnam."[99]

In June 1966 Johnson decided to strike the petroleum depots in North Vietnam. Approval of action against the POL facilities was ready at the beginning of June, but the President deferred because Chester Ronning, the Canadian ambassador to the United States, visited Hanoi to explore the North's willingness to open talks with the United States. Dean Rusk encouraged a delay until Ronning returned because the Secretary of State believed that "general international revulsion" would take place "if it becomes known that we took an action which sabotaged the Ronning mission to which we had given our agreement." When Ronning returned, Assistant Secretary of State William P. Bundy found him "markedly more subdued and sober" than he had been before he left. The Canadian discovered no change in North Vietnam's position that the United States must take its troops out of South Vietnam, drop support for the government of President Thieu, and recognize the NLF before opening negotiations. After one more delay caused by the publication of the plan to attack the POL storage facilities in the *Wall Street Journal*, U.S. planes struck simultaneously at oil storage facilities in Hanoi and Haiphong.[100] The oil tank farm in Hanoi was completely destroyed, and the depot at Haiphong was 80 percent destroyed. In July McNamara, following Johnson's instructions to complete the "strangulation" of North Vietnam's POL facilities, authorized attacks against POL depots throughout the North.[101]

The results of the raids on the POL facilities briefly buoyed the spirits of U.S. officials, but the euphoria was short-lived. Eventually the attacks on POL failed to curtail the infiltration into the South. An air force commander in Saigon characterized the first attack as "the most important strike of the War." By the end of the summer, however, the air force planes had destroyed most of the large POL facilities. Faced with diminishing returns from bombing the petroleum facilities, commanders of Rolling Thunder ordered a return to "attrition of men supplies and equipment."[102]

U.S. planes stepped up psychological warfare against the North by dropping millions of leaflets containing crude cartoons, drawings, and photographs designed to diminish popular support for Ho Chi Minh and the Lao Dong (Peoples' Workers) Party. Some contained pictures of destroyed POL facilities with the warning "STAY AWAY FROM TARGETS LIKE THIS. Bombing is not directed against you. Don't risk your life. Stay away from all military targets such as oil tanks and other petroleum storage areas."[103] Others showed bombed bridges and cautioned "Compatriots who are forced to repair bridges and roads, BEWARE! Roads and bridges will continue to be bombed to prevent the Lao Dong Party from sending troops and weapons to attack the South. The quicker they are repaired, the sooner they will be bombed again. Compatriots, try to avoid working on roads and bridges. You will save yourself from a needless death."[104] Leaflets played upon the traditional Vietnamese hatred of the Chinese. A cartoon showed a North Vietnamese official trading Vietnamese rice to the Chinese for weapons. The caption read in part: "Ask the Communist government to keep the food and increase the rations so that the people of both the North and South can earn their living in peace."[105] Another leaflet asked: "Who is the aggressor? Are there any South Vietnamese troops in North Vietnam? No! Are there more than 100,000 North Vietnamese troops in the South. Yes!"[106]

The campaign of psychological warfare against the North backfired. The North Vietnamese responded with a morale boosting campaign of their own. Ho Chi Minh told the National Assembly in April 1965 that "to oppose the United States and save the country is the most sacred task of every Vietnamese patriot." The Lao Dong Party used face-to-face encounters with soldiers and common citizens, its monopoly of radio and the press, and wall posters to counteract the puny U.S. leaflet campaign. Every bombed-out bridge, air field or petroleum depot made it easier for the government to rally popular support. One captured North Vietnamese soldier told his U.S. captors that after air raids "the people got very mad and cursed the Americans. . . . To them the Americans were the cruel enemy who had bombed the civilian population." Another captive told the Americans that "if we don't fight the Americans would conquer our country."[107]

Yet neither the bombing of the POL nor the leaflets had a significant impact on the infiltration of troops and supplies into the South. Deep flaws marred both the attacks on the POL and the psychological warfare operations. The North prepared for the attacks on the POL facilities in the first six months of 1966 by importing more oil and dispersing its storage facilities. The planners of the attacks on the POL greatly overestimated the North's reliance on the docks at Haiphong or storage facilities throughout the country. When the bombers blasted the Haiphong docks or storage depots, tankers simply stayed offshore and loaded their oil at night into barges. Shallow draft boats then took the oil along a series of internal waterways to small, concealed storage facilities. Some of the oil already was in drums which could be hidden easily. Ho Chi Minh also used the attacks on the POL facilities to bolster his requests to China and the Soviet Union to provide additional financial and military aid. Forty-seven non-governmental scientists employed by the Institute for Defense Analysis estimated that approximately $86 million worth of damage had been done to North Vietnam since the beginning of Rolling Thunder in February 1965. The Soviet Union and China supplied approximately $250–$400 million in economic and military aid in 1965, and they provided more in 1966. From 1965 until 1969 about 320,000 Chinese troops were sent to North Vietnam. In 1967, the peak year, 170,000 Chinese troops were present. They operated antiaircraft facilities, maintained roads, bridges, and rail lines, and built factories. The Chinese forces freed Vietnamese men to go south to the fighting, and their presence also deterred the United States from additional air attacks near the Chinese border.[108]

MCNAMARA'S DISILLUSIONMENT

Disappointed with the results of the raids on the POL facilities, Secretary of Defense McNamara changed his mind about the value of bombing the North. He told the Senate Armed Forces Committee in early 1967 that "the bombing of the POL system was carried out with as much skill, effort, and attention as we could devote to it, starting on June 29, and we haven't been able to dry up those supplies."[109]

In the second half of 1966 McNamara became profoundly disillusioned with the fundamental tenets of the bombing campaign. The effects of bombing on the will of the North Vietnamese government to continue the war until the United States left had not been noticeable. By mid-1966 McNamara received disturbing evaluations from civilian experts that while it was reasonable conceptually "to assume that some limit may be imposed on the scale of military activity that Hanoi can maintain by continuing . . . Rolling Thunder . . . there appears to be no basis for defining that limit in concrete terms." The report asserted that there had been no "tangible" evidence that the bombing had weakened the Northern population's "will . . . to con-

U.S. marines slog through a rice paddy on a search-and-destroy mission.
NATIONAL ARCHIVES.

Ho Chi Minh. UPI/CORBIS-BETTMANN

ARVN troops climb out of the mud after a patrol in the Mekong Delta to board U.S. navy boats.
NATIONAL ARCHIVES

North Vietnam's General Vo Nguyen Giap, the victor
over the French and Americans.

The U.S. military used the body count as
a grisly measure of progress in a brutal war.

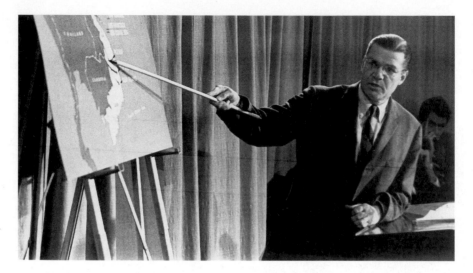

Above. Secretary of Defense Robert S. McNamara explains the stakes in Vietnam. NATIONAL ARCHIVES

Below. President Dwight D. Eisenhower welcomes President Ngo Dinh Diem to Washington (1957). NATIONAL ARCHIVES

Facing page. U.S. troops interrogate a terrified Vietcong suspect. NATIONAL ARCHIVES

Left. During Operation Ranch Hand U.S. planes sprayed millions of tons of defoliants on the forests of Vietnam. NATIONAL ARCHIVES

Below, left. Fast helicopter evacuation of the wounded substantially reduced the number of U.S. soldiers killed in battle. NATIONAL ARCHIVES

Below, right. A U.S. marine gunner peers out of a helicopter flying low over South Vietnam. NATIONAL ARCHIVES

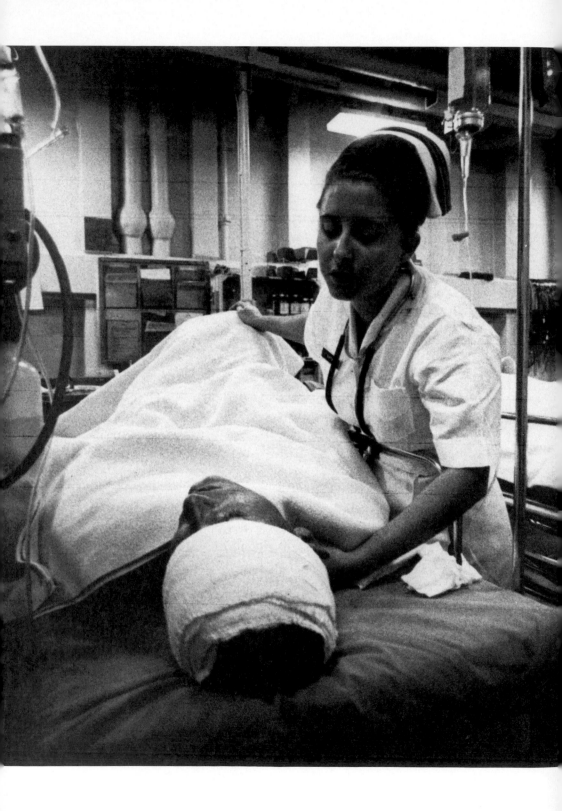

Above. President Nguyen Van Thieu of the Republic of Vietnam inspects U.S. troops. NATIONAL ARCHIVES

Below. Secretary of Defense Robert S. McNamara and General William Westmoreland meet ARVN commanders. NATIONAL ARCHIVES

Facing page. A U.S. navy nurse cares for a wounded soldier. NATIONAL ARCHIVES

Some American soldiers were touched by the plight of
millions of refugees made homeless by the war.
NATIONAL ARCHIVES

The devastation in Saigon during the Tet Offensive
(February 1968). NATIONAL ARCHIVES

Above. President Lyndon B. Johnson visits the U.S. mission to Vietnam at Camranh Bay. NATIONAL ARCHIVES

Below. An American pilot shot down over North Vietnam is held captive by villagers. NATIONAL ARCHIVES

Facing page. Thousands of desperate South Vietnamese crowd the gates of the U.S. embassy in Saigon hoping to leave the capital before NLF and North Vietnamese troops capture it (April 1975). NATIONAL ARCHIVES

Anguished and exhausted, a South Vietnamese family runs to board
a U.S. evacuation helicopter at the end of the war (April 1975).
NATIONAL ARCHIVES

tinue fighting and . . . their leaders' appraisal of the prospective gain and costs of maintaining" their antagonism to the United States.[110]

This was a devastating assessment for McNamara, who valued concrete, quantifiable information far beyond intuitions, guesses, or sentiments. Still, he drew back from reversing course and advocating an end to the U.S. military role in Vietnam. His faith in technology remained strong. He sought concrete suggestions to diminish infiltration from the North to the South. For a few months he believed that the creation of an electronic barrier would turn the war in favor of the United States and its South Vietnamese allies. The same scientific experts who doubted the effectiveness of the bombing advocated construction of a barrier along the Demilitarized Zone (the no-man's land separating North and South Vietnam) and the northern Laotian panhandle. Making use of the recently developed electronic sensors to spot the movement of trucks and people, the barrier would block the transportation of equipment and men down the Ho Chi Minh trail. U.S. airplanes would fly overhead and drop bombs when alerted by the sensors. Planes would also drop thousands of small "button bomblets" which would not injure people walking on the trail but would give off a loud noise, making it easier for the acoustic detectors to sense movements. The electronic barrier would also distribute acoustic detectors every mile or so to detect the movement of trucks. McNamara believed that diverting approximately ten thousand to twenty thousand soldiers to the construction of the electronic fence would be well worth the effort. While he acknowledged that it might take some time for the barrier to work, he predicted that eventually it "would be persuasive evidence both that our sole aim is to protect the South from the North and that we intend to see the job through."[111]

The idea of an electronic barrier opened fissures between McNamara and the military commanders in Saigon and Honolulu. The military commanders believed that more bombing and search-and-destroy operations in the South were the keys to winning the war. These divisions soon widened into an unbridgeable chasm. By the end of 1966, McNamara believed the war had stalemated. He thought that no amount of military pressure the United States could conceivably apply could break the will of the North Vietnamese. The only way out of the war was a negotiated solution. He no longer advocated the position taken by John McNaughton at the time of the December 1965–January 1966 bombing halt that the way to a compromise ran through applying maximum pressure on the North.

McNamara considered the creation of an electronic barrier as an alternative to bombing most of North Vietnam. In October he advised Johnson either to stop bombing all of the North or to restrict bombing to the area immediately above the Demilitarized Zone. Such a pause or bombing restriction would test North Vietnam's position that it could not negotiate with the United States while bombing went on. He recommended stopping the bombing "without fanfare, conditions or avowal whether the stand-down was permanent or temporary." The United States would then see what the North did, and if their reply did not satisfy the President, the U.S. could resume bombing.[112]

It is hard to see how McNamara believed that changing the bombing policy would not generate a fierce debate inside the United States and among foreign leaders. Any bombing pause would result in calls to make it permanent from people who wanted the United States to reduce its activities in Vietnam. Reducing the bombing would also provoke outrage among advocates of bombing. McNamara acknowledged that "any limitation on the bombing of the North will cause serious psychological problems among the men who are risking their lives to help achieve our political objectives." Nonetheless, McNamara could perceive no other way out in late 1966.

The uniformed military commanders opposed both the creation of the barrier and any restrictions on the bombing of the North. Admiral U. S. Grant Sharp, commander of U.S. forces in the Pacific, opposed the creation of the barrier. He believed construction and monitoring of the barrier would divert far too many badly needed combat troops from operations in the South and the bombing campaign of the North. The Joint Chiefs also dissented from McNamara's recommendation for a bombing halt. General Wheeler observed that the chances of a negotiated settlement were remote and that "far from inducing negotiations, another bombing pause will be regarded by the North Vietnamese leaders and out allies as renewed evidence of lack of U.S. determination to press the war to a successful conclusion."[113] Westmoreland believed that the search and destroy missions and the bombing of the North were "of transcendent importance" in the war. When Westmoreland met Johnson in Manila in late October, he told the President that he shuddered at the thought of stopping the Rolling Thunder campaign against the North. He characterized the bombing of the North as "our only trump card," and recommended lifting the restrictions presently in force against bombing airfields, the port of Haiphong and power plants. No more than McNamara could Westmoreland guarantee that bombing additional targets would have the desired political effect. Rather, he thought that bombing more highly visible targets would work wonders for the morale of the flyers and the American public. The loss of aircraft and capture of flyers in raids against easily repaired roads and bridges had alarmed the flyers and their families. Westmoreland suggested that the United States at least attack something that was hard to replace.[114]

McNamara's and Westmoreland's position represented astonishing reversals in a little more than eighteen months. When the Johnson administration began the bombing of North Vietnam in February 1965, McNamara hoped to bolster the morale of the South Vietnamese armed forces. By the fall of 1966 raising the morale of the U.S. armed forces in Southeast Asia became Westmoreland's reason to continue bombing the North. The political objectives of bombing had been lost. Once more Johnson perceived no good solutions to the problem of the United States in Vietnam. Westmoreland's earlier prediction that 1966 would be the year of the major battles in the war, leaving 1967 for the mopping up of remaining pockets of Vietcong and North Vietnamese strength, had not come to pass. The will of the North to resist the United States remained as strong as ever. Neither publicly nor privately had the North indicated that it wanted to negotiate on the terms set by the United States. Indeed, the North had gained considerable sympathy internationally by having withstood U.S. air attacks. The North continued to maintain that the United States had interjected nearly one half million troops improperly into Vietnam. Should negotiations occur the subject the North wanted to discuss was the timetable under which the United States would quit Vietnam.

The United States greatly increased the bombing of North Vietnam in 1966 over 1965, dropping 33,000 tons over North Vietnam in 1965 and 128,000 tons the next year. Planes attacked 185 targets on a list of 242 compiled by the Pentagon. The United States lost 318 aircraft in 1966 compared with 171 in 1965, at a cost of $1.247 billion. The cia estimated that the bombing caused $94 million in economic damage and $36 million in military damage to North Vietnam. It cost the United States $9.6. for every dollar in damage in 1966 compared to $6.6 for every dollar in damage in 1965. Civilian and military casualties in North Vietnam nearly doubled from 13,000 in 1965 to 23–24,000 in 1966.[115]

Johnson faced 1967 with less progress in the war than his more optimistic advisers had predicted in early 1965. Yet the situation did not seem desperate at the end of 1966. While McNamara had lost heart in bombing as a means of bringing the North to the table, nearly all of the top advisers believed that the massive Americanization of the war in 1965 and 1966 had gained the minimal objective of depriving the revolutionary forces of a victory. The usually overly optimistic Lodge cabled Washington that "we are not losing . . . indeed never have things gone so well."[116] A government functioned in South Vietnam and the ARVN troops still went on patrols with the Americans. That in itself was far superior to the situation that existed in early 1965 when McGeorge Bundy predicted that the government of South Vietnam would collapse within six months if the United States did not step in with bombs and troops.

The war in Vietnam could not go on indefinitely without decisive military resolution, but at the end of 1966 Johnson temporized once more. He deferred any decision on changing the role of bombing until after the midterm congressional election. Then he waited some more. By year's end, he decided that neither McNamara's advocacy of a bombing halt nor the Joint Chiefs' demand for adding more targets would help. Each course would provoke domestic and international opposition without a guarantee of changing the conditions of the war. Instead of changing the bombing, Johnson decided to increase the troop levels to approximately 450,000 in the middle of 1967. He also resolved to pay more attention to the "other war" in Vietnam, the effort to pacify the countryside and wed the South Vietnamese to the side of the government. Whether 1967 saw the culmination of Westmoreland's plan to mop up operations against the North and the NLF or not, the Johnson administration was committed to seeing tangible progress before the election year of 1968. Without strong evidence that the United States could leave South Vietnam to a strong, stable government, the rumblings of domestic and international dissent against the U.S. presence in Vietnam could overwhelm Johnson's presidency.

Chapter

* * * * * * * * * * *

Bringing the War Home:
1964–1967

CONTROVERSY over the war in Vietnam brought vast changes to the United States in the 1960s. The war profoundly affected every institution in American life: universities, Congress, the presidency, the Democratic Party, the armed forces, labor unions, religious organizations, and the mass media. At the beginning of U.S.involvement in the war most Americans trusted their leaders to make appropriate choices, and the public held most large organizations in high regard. The prosperous white middle class created by the post–World War II economic expansion maintained an abiding faith in the future. A wide consensus, crossing party and social and economic lines, agreed that the United States had properly confronted the Soviet Union and other communist movements around the world since 1945. Nearly all public officials and most citizens believed that the United States was properly waging the Cold War. Most thought that the cost of the confrontation with the Soviet Union and its allies was equally borne by the United States. The minority of dissenters seemed marginal, nearly outlandish, figures who lacked understanding of the nature of the threat posed by communism and the ability of the United States to resist.

By 1968 this landscape had changed beyond recognition. A sizeable portion of the public no longer believed that government officials waged the Cold War properly. Many thought that the war in Vietnam had become a burden which the country no longer could afford. Quickly labeled "doves" by the mass media, these people wanted the United States to reduce its role in Vietnam and reach a negotiated settlement with the North Vietnamese and the NLF. Many others, often a larger proportion of the public, believed that the U.S. involvement in the war had initially been a proper course of action, but they now thought that leaders had badly mismanaged the conduct of a war which seemed to drag on endlessly without the traditional indicators of success. These so-called hawks wanted the United States to fight the war more vigorously and end it soon.

The desire for a speedy end to the fighting crossed all lines as the public grew disgusted with the war. The largest political demonstrations since the 1930s took place as opponents of the war demanded the end of U.S. participation. Some of the most dramatic demonstrations against the war took place on college and university campuses. Many protesters challenged the basic assumptions of U.S. foreign policy in the Cold War. By 1968 opposition to the war forced Lyndon Johnson to withdraw from the presidential race, while the Democratic Party nearly tore itself apart over the Johnson administration policy in Vietnam. For a generation most Democratic members of Congress had advocated the containment of communism as the proper foreign policy for the United States, but a group of Democratic senators and representatives opposed the Johnson administration's policy in Vietnam. As this group grew from about eleven in 1965 to more than thirty in 1968, many of the members also questioned the basic assumptions of American foreign policy. They concluded that Vietnam represented an overextension of U.S. resources. The majority of Democratic office-holders continued to support Johnson and his Vietnam policy, but many did so out of a sense of duty rather than conviction.

A huge generation of 53 million men and women were between the ages of eighteen and twenty-six sometime during the era of U.S. involvement in Vietnam from 1961 to 1973. The war affected this so-called Vietnam generation most directly. Some men eligible for conscription into the armed forces during these years faced painful choices about whether to serve. Unlike in the Second World War, when nearly every man eligible for military service was inducted, the armed forces needed fewer soldiers during the Vietnam era. Of the 26.8 million men in the Vietnam generation, 10.93 million served in the military. Of these 8.7 million enlisted and 2.215 million were drafted.1 Many of those who enlisted did so because they believed that their options in the military would be better than if they waited until they were drafted. Many of the nearly sixteen million men of the Vietnam generation who did not enter military service during the Vietnam era also made major life choices because of their attitudes toward the possibility of their service in the military. Women of the Vietnam generation selected careers, political affiliation, and spouses in part because of their attitudes toward the war in Vietnam.

Reaction to the war among men and women of older generations not eligible for military service also profoundly affected the way they thought about their families, their communities, the nation's politics, and the role of the United States in world affairs. The main impact of the war was divisive and fragmenting. Most people thought about the war some of the time, and many opinions were passionate. Americans came to question the veracity of their government's leaders. A "credibility gap" opened between what government officials said and what the public believed about the war in Vietnam. At first, reporters in Vietnam perceived the gap between the optimistic statements of high officials in Saigon and what the reporters saw with their own eyes in the field.[2] As the war continued, more Americans back home saw a gap between what Johnson, Secretary of Defense McNamara, and Secretary of State Dean Rusk said about American war aims and intentions and progress in the war and the reality of the stalemate in the fighting. Some people concluded that they had been deliberately misled into supporting a war where the basic interests of the United States were not at stake.

Yet there never was a single dominant opinion regarding the purpose of U.S. involvement in the war, the morality of American activities, or what to do next in the fighting. By the end of 1967 a consensus did emerge that the war had lasted long enough. A weary public wanted the war to end, but even then, no consensus emerged about how that should come about. Until 1971 opinion polls consistently indicated a plurality of the public favored more intensive military action by the United States to end the war on terms favored by Washington. From 1964 until 1968 more and more Americans agreed that it had been a mistake for the United States to have entered the war in Vietnam in the first place. Over the same period of time a greater proportion of the public wanted the United States to withdraw from Vietnam immediately. Before late 1967 fewer than 10 percent of the public favored immediate withdrawal of U.S. forces from Vietnam. From 1968 onward a larger proportion of the public favored an immediate withdrawal of U.S. forces, but no more than 25 percent ever backed that course.[3]

CONGRESSIONAL OPINION AND THE WAR

From 1945 to 1965 Congress customarily accorded presidents wide latitude in conducting policy toward Southeast Asia. The presidents and their principal advisers decided what should and could be done. Often the people directing policy acknowledged limits set by public opinion expressed through Congress. President Dwight Eisenhower consulted congressional leaders at the time of the crisis over the assault on Dienbienphu in April 1954. The reservations expressed by Democratic Minority Leader Lyndon B. Johnson and Democratic Senator Richard Russell of Georgia helped persuade Eisenhower not to send U.S. planes to relieve the French garrison.[4] In September 1963 public outrage over Ngo Dinh Diem's government's repression of the Buddhists led to some members of Congress questioning U.S. support for Diem. Senator Frank Church (D., Idaho) introduced a resolution calling on the United States to cease military and economic aid to the government of South Vietnam unless it "abandons policies of repression against its own people and makes a determined and effective effort to regain their support." Church claimed that to continue to aid Diem without his government's agreement to stop the assaults on the Buddhists would "identify the United States with the cause of religious persecution, undermining our moral position throughout the world."[5] Twenty-two other senators joined Church in sponsoring this resolution. They included a mixture of liberals, moderates, and conservatives, each with his own reasons for advocating an end to aid to the South Vietnamese government. The extent of senatorial concern led the Kennedy administration to intensify its efforts to change the conduct of the Diem government.[6]

Congress approved the Gulf of Tonkin Resolution in August 1964. In later years the resolution became a highly controversial element in the debate over the validity of U.S. policy in Vietnam. The Johnson administration and its supporters referred to the Tonkin Gulf resolution as the congressional authorization for U.S. participation in the war. Later critics of the Johnson administration's war policy disagreed that the resolution offered the president a blank check in escalating the war. Illinois Republican Senator Charles Percy said that he doubted that congress would have approved the resolution if lawmakers had known that "it would have involved the commitment of 540,000 Americans." Oregon Democratic Senator Wayne Morse, one of two members to vote against the Tonkin Gulf Resolution, asked Secretary of State Dean Rusk in February 1966 if he thought "that the vote would have been the same if my colleagues in the Senate had contemplated that it would lead to 200,000 or 400,000 or 600,000 American troops in Vietnam?" Rusk replied that he believed Congress would have voted as it did.

Others claimed that the administration had misled Congress into approving the resolution, because at least one of the two purported attacks on U.S. naval vessels in the Gulf of Tonkin had not occurred. The U.S. navy had not been engaged in "routine patrols," as Secretary of Defense Robert McNamara claimed, but had provoked the attacks by escorting South Vietnamese boats inside the twelve-mile North Vietnamese territorial limit. Arkansas Democratic Senator J. William Fulbright (D., Ark.), Chairman of the Foreign Relations Committee and the floor manager for the bill, later lamented that "I was hoodwinked and taken in by the President of the United States, the Secretary of State, and the Chief of Staff and the Secretary of Defense who told us about certain alleged events that I do not believe occurred."[7]

At the time Congress passed the resolution, however, few members expressed misgivings. The House considered the resolution for a brief forty minutes before approving it unanimously on August 6. The Senate debated the resolution for eight hours over two days and passed it by a vote of 88 to 2 on August 7.[8] Nearly all of the supporters of Frank Church's earlier resolution opposing the religious repression of the Diem government supported the Gulf of Tonkin Resolution. Church explained that "we must unite behind the president" even though he still thought U.S. policy toward Southeast Asia was "more a product of our own addiction to an ideological view of world affairs . . . rather than a policy based on a detached and pragmatic view of our real national interests."[9] He said "the attacks upon our ships cannot be justified." Nevertheless, even during the debate on the Gulf of Tonkin Resolution, Church explained that he supported the resolution because he believed a show of toughness in the summer of 1964 might encourage the North Vietnamese to slow infiltration into the South. At any rate, Church expressed his support for the resolution as preventing a full scale war in Southeast Asia.[10]

While managing the bill, Fulbright decried the "fact that the North Vietnamese have for years been sending in trained personnel, materiel, guns, and ammunition to attack their neighbor." He doubted that Johnson would attack the cities of North Vietnam should Congress adopt the resolution but acknowledged that the resolution authorized him to do so. He also acknowledged that in modern conditions of warfare a president probably would not ask for a declaration of war but the resolution would serve as one. Fulbright later renounced all of these points.[11]

Wayne Morse (D., Ore.), one of two senators who voted against the resolution, accurately predicted that the public would eventually repudiate the Johnson administration's Vietnam policy. They did, but the doves also felt the voters' wrath. Alaska's Ernest Greuning, the other senator to vote no on the Gulf of Tonkin Resolution, lost in the 1968 Democratic primary to Mike Gravel. Republican Robert Packwood defeated Morse in 1968. Moreover, passage of the Gulf of Tonkin Resolution slowed the pace of congressional efforts to share foreign policy-making with the President. So many senators who earlier had moved toward limiting the President's freedom of action in foreign policy supported the resolution that it took until late 1965 before members of Congress began once more to offer institutional opposition to Johnson's handling of the war.

Fulbright gradually reversed his support for the war in the spring and summer of 1965. Like George Ball within the administration, Fulbright believed that the U.S.-Soviet relationship was paramount. Instead of bolstering U.S. credibility with allies and potential foes, deeper American involvement in Vietnam could dissipate valuable resources. He broke with Johnson over the U.S.-led invasion and occupation of the Dominican Republic in April. By June he opposed further escalation of the war. He also opposed "unconditional American withdrawal from South Vietnam," and he praised Johnson for withstanding pressures to expand the war. He believed that Johnson's goal was "ending the war at the earliest possible time by negotiations."[12] People who wrote his office divided over whether he supported or opposed Johnson's policies.[13]

After Johnson escalated the war in July, Fulbright became more forceful in his condemnation of U.S. policy in Vietnam. In September, he spoke out against what he characterized as the "arrogance of power" by which the United States had sought to impose its vision on world politics since 1945.[14] With members of the staff of the Committee on Foreign Relations he lamented the apparent rise in tensions between the United States and the Soviet Union in the previous two years. Instead of fostering detente with the Soviet Union, U.S. policies had increased the danger of nuclear war. Public opinion throughout the world now feared the United States "as the nation most likely to precipitate a nuclear war." In the last two years Fulbright and his staff on the committee believed that the United States had "tried to force upon the rest of the world a righteous American point of view." He also decried the tendency to demand immediate results from U.S. foreign policy. The Johnson administration justified its opposition to communist power in Vietnam as a way of blocking Chinese influence throughout Asia. Fulbright believed that the Chinese threat had been overblown. "Who is to say what China will be like tomorrow? She is as capable of change as any nation."[15]

Over the next several months Fulbright undertook a crash course in the history of American policy toward Vietnam.[16] Fulbright's chief of staff informed him in early 1966 that "the powerful force of nationalism, which was instrumental in freeing Vietnam from the French, has been captured by the Viet Cong." Fulbright was particularly downcast by reports that

> U.S.-Vietnamese polices are found to be highly objectionable in Northern Europe: the Labor government in Britain would fall if it were to offer troops for use in Vietnam; the position of France [a persistent critic] is clear; the Japanese government would fall if it were to support the U.S. in Vietnam; Germany provides only medical support—just enough to encourage the United States not to withdraw its troops from Germany and Berlin.[17]

In late January and early February 1966, Fulbright chaired televised hearings on the U.S. role in Vietnam. Privately he confessed he was "at a loss as to how we can stick an olive branch in Uncle Sam's fist."[18] The hearing began two days before Johnson ended the suspension of the bombing of North Vietnam begun in December. Committee members displayed some initial optimism that the bombing pause might lead to negotiations. Once bombing resumed on January 31 the mood became somber and even angry. Secretary of State Dean Rusk, aware that Fulbright intended to use the hearings to discredit the way in which the United States conducted the war, resisted testifying in an open session in support of the administration's policies, but eventually he agreed to appear.[19] Fulbright asked tough questions: How long would the United States be in Vietnam—five, ten, twenty years? What were U.S. objectives? Did the United States want to impose a Pax Americana around the world? Rusk replied that he was not a prophet and could not say how long the United States would be in Vietnam. He explained U.S. objectives in Vietnam as enabling the South Vietnamese to choose their own future policies "without having them imposed on them by force from North Vietnam or elsewhere from outside."[20] Fulbright seemed unpersuaded.

A high point of the hearing for the public watching was the testimony of numerous academic, military, and diplomatic experts, many of whom had been architects of American policy in the Cold War. Many told the committee that the United States risked jeopardizing its most cherished relations with Japan and European allies. George F. Kennan, the man who had coined the term "containment" as a description of U.S. policy toward the Soviet Union during the early Cold War, observed that Vietnam was under normal circumstances one of the most marginal regions of the world. Even should the communists come to power in Vietnam, he expected that they would follow a course independent from that of China or the Soviet Union. Were the United States not already involved militarily in Vietnam, Kennan "would know of no reason why we would wish to become involved." He thought that Japanese public opinion had grown unhappy with the United States because of the American use of strategic bombing over Vietnam, and also dismissed Rusk's concern that the European allies would lose faith in the United States should it end its involvement in Vietnam. The Western Europeans had themselves withdrawn from territories in Asia and Africa, so Kennan believed they might sympathize with the United States should it limit its exposure in Vietnam. He believed that "there is more respect to be won in the opinion of this world by a resolute and courageous liquidation of unsound positions than by the most stubborn pursuit of extravagant or unpromising objectives."[21]

Retired General James M. Gavin, the former commander of the 101st Airborne Division who had served as Assistant Chief of Staff of the Army at the time of the fall of Dienbienphu, also testified that the United States had committed too many resources to Vietnam. He repeated before the committee the gist of an article he published in *Harper's* in February 1966.[22] In both the article and his testimony, he validated the misgivings of other critics of the war that the United States had committed too many resources in return for too little gain in Vietnam. Gavin's views stood out, however, because of his credibility as a military leader. In the late summer of 1965, after Johnson announced the additional deployment of one hundred thousand U.S. troops to Vietnam, Gavin decided that the commitment of the United States to Vietnam had become "alarmingly out of balance." The United States had let the initiative drop and "we were being escalated at the will of our opponents rather than at our own judgment.'' He thought the $10.5 billion the administration planned to spend on the war over the next year too much to bear. He asked, ''Is Vietnam at this point worth this investment of our national resources with all the other commitments we have world wide?''[23]

Since leaving government service Gavin had headed the Massachusetts-based industrial consulting firm of Arthur D. Little, and he believed that economic, scientific, and cultural factors had taken precedence over the military in waging the Cold War. Gavin opposed deeper U.S. involvement in Vietnam because it weakened the United States in the Cold War. He warned that commitment to Vietnam had come at the cost of resources for an economic and cultural struggle with the Soviets, and thought that the United States had unwittingly fallen into a ''very dangerous position'' by turning its back on international economic endeavors ''to support a tactical confrontation that appears to be escalating at the will of an enemy.''[24] Gavin recommended maintaining the current level of U.S. troops in Vietnam but sending no more. The United States could use the forces it had to hold onto the coastal areas of Vietnam. He advised the United States to commence a permanent halt to the bombing of the North in order to open negotiations. The enclaves the United States held along the coast would become bargaining chips.

Millions of Americans watched these hearing on television. The Foreign Relations Committee received over twenty thousand letters and telegrams from citizens.[25] Most people who wrote to the committee supported critics of the administration's policies. Some writers were thoughtful, others nearly apoplectic with rage. A woman pleaded with committee members to be ''crusaders'' against ''this impossible foreign policy.'' ''Do all of you have to say yes . . . to Lyndon Johnson? Do everything he stupidly asks, like children afraid, or too unhealthily apathetic?''[26] Fulbright commented that the hearings ''filled a deeply felt need on the part of the American people for an exploration of the reasons why the United States was once again involved in a war thousands of miles from home.''[27] Random House quickly published the complete transcripts of the hearings.[28]

The response to the hearings revealed the extent of public anxieties about the course the country followed in Vietnam, yet the depth of public concern did not lead to concrete alternatives to the Johnson administration's policies. One reason was that critics felt uncomfortable about going too far in challenging Johnson's autonomy in foreign policy. Arthur M. Schlesinger Jr., a former aide to Kennedy and later one of the Democratic liberals' most outspoken critics of Johnson's Vietnam policy, explained to Fulbright the dilemma facing many liberal critics of the war. Such people wanted to place a ceiling on the war without at the same time ''placing the Senate in the vulnerable position of interfering in the details of military operations and superseding the constitutional authority of the commander in chief.''[29] In 1966 these liberal dissenters still believed that the Soviet Union represented a deadly threat to the United States.

In the fall of 1966, Fulbright planned more hearings in 1967 on the declining role of the United States in the world. He aimed to shortcut the normal process of exchanging ideas within the intellectual community because the results of such discussions generally took "several years to enter the governmental bloodstream." His staff arranged for prominent witnesses "with strong personalities" to testify to "gain and retain both television and broad press coverage." They wanted hearings with "enough sex appeal to attract the attention of the press and the Committee, and with the potentiality of changing (reversing) policy within the next year or two." Fulbright and the committee staff thought that the two years before the 1968 presidential election crucial for the future of U.S. foreign policy and even, in a more apocalyptic vision, the fate of the earth. Arguing for the most concrete sort of hearings, Carl Marcy, Fulbright's chief-of-staff, feared that "we may not need to worry about what makes us tick if LBJ becomes so convinced of the need for a 'victory' before 1968 that he inadvertently brings on the holocaust."[30]

Congressional supporters of the administration's policy complained that the critics offered no concrete alternatives. Senator Stuart Symington (D., Mo.), who had served as Secretary of the Air Force in the Truman administration and was a firm believer in the policy of containment, characterized General Gavin's prescriptions as "fuzzy."[31]

Even many supporters of the administration's policy wanted to assert congressional oversight and the prerogative to declare war. Jacob Javits (R., N.Y.) and Jennings Randolph (D., W. Va.), both of whom backed the commitment of U.S. forces to Vietnam, introduced a resolution supporting the U.S. presence in South Vietnam but asking for an accelerated program of social and economic development there. Javits said that the President had only himself to blame for the erosion of public support for the war, since he and his aides seemed to have ducked appropriate debate. The New York Senator complained that "for more than a year the administration has not come to Congress for a support resolution on our Vietnam policy."[32]

More militant members of Congress also questioned Johnson's handling of the war. Some conservative Republicans complained that "the inconsistency of the administration is that they severely criticized Senator Goldwater for what the administration is doing now."[33] As the war went on without conclusive victories by the United States or the South Vietnamese, members of Congress who supported the premise of U.S. involvement in the fighting objected to the administration's performance. "The biggest mistake," wrote Oklahoman Page Belcher, a conservative Republican representative, is that "President Johnson apparently runs this entire war from the White House or the LBJ ranch." Like many frustrated hawks, Belcher believed that Johnson and McNamara had interfered excessively with the military's conduct of the war. "There is no need to have Annapolis, West Point and the Air Force Academy to train officers if we are going to let a man who made Fords tell them how to run a war."[34]

Other supporters of the military voiced similar complaints about McNamara's apparent condescension and high-handedness. In many cases the congressional critics acted on information provided by senior military officers. As early as July 1965, when Johnson decided against the Joint Chiefs of Staff's recommendation to call up reserves, the upper echelons of the military chafed under what they considered McNamara's and Johnson's micro-management of the war. They objected to the civilian leadership's performance on subjects as varied as the selection of targets for the bombing of the North to the choice of rifles carried by U.S. troops. Most members of the Senate Armed Services Committee strongly backed the U.S. commitment in Vietnam. Their support, however, did not always provide much comfort to the Johnson administration. Senator Sam Ervin (D., N.C.) was one of the most ardent backers of the President's position on Vietnam, but even he acknowledged that the original commitments of the United States to Vietnam had been a mistake. Nevertheless, Ervin wrote, "we are now in South Vietnam as a result of such commitments. I wish I could find some honorable way to extricate ourselves from that area. I am compelled to confess, however, that I do not see any way in which we can bring this about short of a retreat which would be more likely to endanger than secure our future."[35] At the time of the Foreign Relations Committee's hearing on the war, Ervin chided opponents of the war for ignoring the "stern realities." Like most Senate hawks, Ervin endorsed both the domino theory and the assertion that U.S. credibility was at stake in Vietnam. "Communism has not yet forsaken its purpose of world domination," he said. For the United States to follow the advice of George Kennan or James Gavin implied a withdrawal from Vietnam. Such a withdrawal meant that "all the Asiatic countries, including India, will fall under Red Chinese domination, and all the free world will lose whatever confidence its people may have in us."[36]

Senator Richard Russell (D., Ga.), Chairman of the Armed Services Committee, expressed grave doubts about involvement in a ground war in Asia. In 1954, he counseled Eisenhower against U.S. engagement in the relief of Dienbienphu. But once Johnson, one of Russell's oldest friends in the Senate, decided to Americanize the war, Russell believed that Congress had to suppress doubts and offer comfort to the soldiers fighting it. Accordingly, Russell called McNamara before the committee to explain why the President restricted the bombing of the North to avoid cities and the Chinese border. The committee also grilled McNamara regularly about the slow pace of supplying the M-16 rifle to the soldiers in the field.[37]

With friends like these, Johnson grumbled. Representative Belcher's complaints about McNamara's overruling the military bore an unlikely similarity to the President's own complaints that "if we start making the military decisions, I wonder why we paid to send them to West Point." What would the dissenters from his policy have him do? he constantly asked. Visitors to his office and people who listened to his speeches received massive doses of the Johnson treatment. The President would lean forward, grab a visitor with advice on Vietnam on the knee and arm and then put his massive face inches from that of the by-now terrified politician, professor, journalist, or business leader. *"What would you do?"* he would nearly shout.[38]

The President reacted peevishly to the advice of the Foreign Relations Committee. He complained that Senate critics wanted power without responsibility. They objected to the way he conducted the war, but he believed that they proposed futile alternatives. His senior advisers, especially National Security Adviser Walt Rostow and Secretary of State Dean Rusk, derided the critics' suggestions for negotiations because they believed that Fulbright and the other doves never stated concretely what to do if negotiations failed.[39] Johnson alternately flattered Fulbright and sought to discredit him. One day he invited Fulbright to the White House and the next he ordered aides to investigate him for subversive activities. "It's easier to satisfy Ho Chi Minh than it is Fulbright," he would explode.[40] The President loved derogatory reports on the Senator. He was cheered by the news that an Israeli diplomat thought that Fulbright "reminded him of a 'modestly endowed don' at Oxford. He was full of historic parallels which did not bear serious examination."[41] The President encouraged the FBI to circulate comparisons of the positions taken by Fulbright at the 1966 hearings and those of the U.S. Communist Party.[42]

Fulbright's dissent from the war particularly rankled Johnson because the two men had previously been so close. They came from the same region and had shared many of the same commitments to social reform legislation (although Fulbright had done next to nothing in promoting civil rights for African-Americans). Fulbright supported Johnson for president over John Kennedy in 1960 and he had offered unstinting praise for his old friend during the 1964 presidential campaign. His ardent championship of the Gulf of Tonkin Resolution derived from his expectation that Johnson's experience and sure political touch would never lead him into a major war unless the most significant U.S. interests were at stake.[43]

Fulbright was only one of the most prominent congressional doves. By 1967 about a dozen senators of both parties opposed the war. Several senators, who had supported the Gulf of Tonkin Resolution despite earlier misgivings about deepening American involvement in Vietnam, joined Morse and Greuning, who had opposed the Gulf of Tonkin Resolution, in their criticism of some aspects of the war. For example, Frank Church, always looking for a middle way out of a painful dilemma in Indochina, agreed that the Foreign

Relations Committee's hearings on Vietnam had not produced "any miracle cures in Vietnam. I think it is generally recognized that what has been done there cannot be suddenly undone." He pointed out that "there are some omelettes that are not digestible, but I don't know of any that can be unscrambled. And the President's options are narrowing." While Church often drew back from unqualified condemnation of the Johnson administration's conduct of the war, he was a constant scold. He peppered administration officials with requests for information abut what other countries besides the United States did in Vietnam.[44]

Congressional critics of the administration's war policy persistently called on the President to end the bombing of the north in order to encourage negotiations with Hanoi. Opposition to the President's conduct of the war from Robert F. Kennedy, elected to the Senate in 1964, represented the most serious blow to Johnson from within the Democratic Party. Ambassador-at-Large Averell Harriman warned Kennedy that his dissent would be considered "support for Hanoi against your government," a charge Kennedy resented.[45] Kennedy berated Johnson for not permanently "halting the bombing in exchange for a beginning of negotiations."[46] The White House complained that such dissent only made it more difficult to begin meaningful negotiations with the North. "We must avoid 'negotiating with ourselves,'" Rostow told Johnson. In any event the White House remained as skeptical about the North's intentions in proclaiming its willingness to begin negotiations as it had been at the beginning of the buildup. "The North Vietnamese might merely be seeking alternative methods of achieving the domination of South Vietnam," Rostow warned.[47]

THE WAR IN THE STREETS

While important members of Congress, both Democratic and Republican, gradually drew away from Johnson's policy on the war, even more far-reaching changes in popular attitudes toward the war in particular and government institutions in general took place outside Washington. Unhappiness with the war began slowly on university campuses in 1965; by 1968 major universities were in constant turmoil over the war. At the start professors took the lead in voicing discontent with the war. Students joined later as part of a larger movement for social change.

Opposition to the war in Vietnam became bound up with the movement for civil rights and economic advancement for African-Americans and other people of color. Advocates of civil rights and opponents of the Vietnam War disagreed nearly as often as they aligned their efforts. The civil rights movement began before opposition to the war in Vietnam became a significant element in American political or social life. Efforts to end racial discrimination absorbed most political energies of socially aware college students in the early 1960s. Later, however, students became more concerned about Vietnam. The personal blended with the political. College students eligible for conscription worried about their own participation in the war, but concern over the war extended far beyond anxiety about whether individuals would go to Vietnam. Some college anti-war protesters came to see the war in Vietnam as interfering with efforts to create a fairer society at home.

As the war in Vietnam intensified, advocates of civil rights wrestled with the question of whether to link opposition to the war in Vietnam with their commitment to domestic justice. On the one hand, the Johnson administration had done more to advance the civil rights of black Americans than had any administration since 1865. Proponents of civil rights hoped to maintain momentum for further gains, and were loath to alienate Johnson by criticizing his conduct of the war. On the other hand, proponents of civil rights gradually came to believe that progress stalled because of involvement in Vietnam, and unless the administration reversed course all momentum would be lost.

No one felt the dilemma of reconciling support for civil rights and speaking out over Vietnam more keenly than did Martin Luther King Jr. Reluctant to break openly with Johnson for fear of undermining the President's commitment to civil rights, King initially kept his doubts about Vietnam to himself. By late 1966, however, King believed that silence gained nothing in terms of further progress on civil rights while it undermined his authority to speak on issues of political morality. He therefore became a prominent opponent of the war in Vietnam. King joined hundreds of other religious leaders in condemning the U.S. position in the war. By 1968 a significant portion of the public discussion of Vietnam involved concepts of morality. This made the discussions intense, positions hard, and compromise of the sort customary in public life nearly impossible.

The first teach-in took place on the campus of the University of Michigan during the night of March 24–25, 1965. About three thousand students and faculty members spent part of the night attending lectures, discussions, and debates on the war. Economics professor Kenneth Boulding said, "The poorest peasant in Vietnam should have as much right as the richest American. The world has become much too small and crowded for what we are doing."[48] The next morning six hundred remained to demonstrate against escalation and for a negotiated settlement. Teach-ins spread quickly to other campuses: 35 in the next week and 120 by the end of the academic year. The teach-in movement culminated on May 21–22 when over twenty thousand students took part in a thirty-six-hour marathon on the campus of the University of California at Berkeley.

The Berkeley teach-in was a distinctly more radical affair than the earlier ones had been. Many of the organizers, working from the apartment of Jerry Rubin, had helped form the Free Speech Movement that had galvanized the

Berkeley campus the previous fall. These veterans of protest against what they considered a large, impersonal bureaucratic university created an ad hoc Vietnam Day Committee. Radicals at the Berkeley teach-in argued that the war had originated with post–World War II liberalism. They urged opponents of the war to leave the "liberal-labor-Negro coalition" and advocated a "new 'do-it-yourself' revolution." Such talk irritated and bewildered some participants who opposed the war but did not believe that the United States needed or was likely to have a revolution. One traditional liberal characterized the call to revolution "so much crap." Norman Thomas, leader of the Socialist Party who had abandoned his earlier support of the U.S. presence in Vietnam, said, "I am interested in peace" in Vietnam and peace "does not require us to hate America."[49]

The militant language foreshadowed deep divisions within American society, but opponents of the war were a distinct minority in 1965. At the beginning of U.S. escalation of the war student opinion roughly paralleled that of the public at large. At many colleges where teach-ins occurred, students who supported the war organized demonstrations of their own. Six thousand students at the University of Wisconsin signed a petition supporting Johnson's policies. One quarter of the undergraduates at Yale University did the same thing.[50] In April 1965 Chester Cooper of the National Security Council staff explained the need for an organized effort on behalf of the war. He concluded that "the noisy protests against U.S. policy in Vietnam emanating from the universities by no means constitute a majority view."[51]

Despite the fact that more students supported the administration's position in Vietnam than opposed it, the teach-ins and protest rallies on college campuses in 1965 had a profound effect on the Johnson administration. Johnson had won election in 1964 as a candidate of consensus. Now, just a few months into his term, that unity seemed to have frayed. The sense of foreboding over greater involvement in Vietnam lay behind the President's decision to outline the chances for negotiations during his speech at Johns Hopkins University in April. Fear of alarming the public about the potential for involvement in a major war also caused the President to downplay the significance of his authorization of additional troops to Vietnam in late July 1965.[52]

Rumblings of dissent over Vietnam among intellectuals threatened the unity of the Democratic Party. Johnson and his supporters began to harass opponents of the war. The teach-ins helped the publication of several books highly critical of the Johnson administration's policy.[53] Robert Scheer, a Berkeley activist, published *How the United States Got Involved in Vietnam* and distributed copies to sympathetic members of Congress. California Democrat George Brown, a liberal, passed it on to colleagues with an endorsement as "the best short treatment of this subject I have ever seen." Richard Ichord, a Missouri Democrat who strongly backed Johnson's handling of the war, reacted furiously to a publication he characterized as "filled with half-truths, distortions, implications, innuendoes, and inferences which lead one to believe that Ho Chi Minh is the George Washington of Vietnam and any American who has any part in our involvement is guilty of stopping a legitimate revolution." An angry Representative Ichord circulated files on Scheer compiled by the House Committee on Un-American Activities showing his support for Fidel Castro and his previous travel to North Vietnam.[54]

The President and National Security Adviser McGeorge Bundy became alarmed that many prominent intellectuals addressed the teach-ins. Intellectuals had formed an important segment of the coalition backing Johnson in 1964. They had identified with the Democratic Party since the 1930s, and their opinions carried enormous weight with the editorial boards of major newspapers. Bundy helped organize visits by top administration officials to campuses across the country to present the case for the war. Initially, Bundy refused to meet with a group of his former academic colleagues from Cambridge, Massachusetts, to discuss the war. He dismissed their invitation as poor propaganda filled with errors and distortions, and said he would have given it a poor grade had it come to him "for grading as a professor of government."[55]

As criticism from the academic community intensified, Bundy reversed himself. In May Bundy was scheduled to debate Vietnam policy with Professor George Kahin of Cornell University, a major critic of the war, at a national teach-in in Washington, broadcast live to one hundred thousand students across the country. At the last minute Johnson sent Bundy to the Caribbean to avoid confronting Kahin. A few weeks later Bundy did appear on another televised teach-in debating the wisdom of U.S. policy with Professor Hans Morgenthau, a leading realist thinker on international relations at the University of Chicago. Morgenthau's dissent from the administration's handling of the war deeply wounded Bundy, who also considered himself a consummate realist.[56]

In 1966 and 1967 the anti-war movement became a major element in American political and social life. Demonstrations involving first tens of thousands and later hundreds of thousands of protesters erupted across the country. Yet because of deep internal divisions, the opposition to the war was less successful in ending it than it might have been. Opponents of the war disagreed among themselves over reasons for opposing the war and the best tactics to stop it.

The smallest identifiable group of opponents of the war were political conservatives, some of whom called themselves libertarians. These people maintained the pre–World War II skepticism of non-interventionists or isolationists who believed that involvement in a world war would vastly augment the power of the federal government. Senator George Aikin (R., Vt.) and libertarian scholar Murray Rothbard maintained this point of view.[57] Political liberals, often aligned with realist scholars of international relations, represented a larger group of critics of the war. For Hans Morgenthau, the war greatly dissipated American resources best deployed in Europe. From the start of U.S. involvement in the war, political liberals dubious of U.S. policy augmented realist themes about the limitations of U.S. resources with complaints about the nature of the government of South Vietnam. In 1963 Senator Frank Church complained about the oppressive nature of the government of Ngo Dinh Diem.[58] In 1967 Allard Lowenstein, the former executive director of the National Student Association and a stalwart supporter of liberal causes, complained that the government of Prime Minister Nguyen Cao Ky was undemocratic and unpopular. He organized a committee to supervise the elections, complaining that "the prospects for meaningful elections . . . are very dim. . . . An unfair election could well give the semblance of a popular mandate for an unrepresentative regime and more firmly tie American policy to a very narrow Vietnamese base."[59]

From the very start, liberal and realist voices were not alone in calling for changes in policy toward Vietnam. Pacifism revived in the 1960s to challenge both the assumptions of the Cold War and participation in Vietnam. Pacifist critics of the war in Vietnam themselves divided sharply into liberal and radical alignments. Liberal pacifists, such as Norman Cousins of the Committee for a Sane Nuclear Policy or Alfred Hassler of the Fellowship of Reconciliation, believed that U.S. involvement in the war was a mistake to be corrected. They valued persuasion of elected officials and proposals they thought would be palatable to the Johnson administration. Hence in 1965 and early 1966 they favored negotiations and the sort of de-escalation proposed by the witnesses before the Senate Committee on Foreign Relations in February 1966. Liberal pacifists, committed to the redemptive power of nonviolence, sought alliance with like-minded groups inside the United States and Vietnam. They refused to endorse the Vietcong for tactical reasons—it would alienate most Americans—and because the Vietcong used violence. Instead, when liberal pacifists commented on events inside Vietnam, they tended to support the claims of Buddhists trying to create a third force between the government and the NLF.

Radical pacifists like David Dellinger, editor of *Liberation,* expressed a much more sweeping condemnation of the nature of contemporary U.S. society.[60] Radical pacifists condemned post–World War II American society for fostering racial and economic inequality at home and injustice and violence abroad. Radicals believed that the country needed a revolution, a nonviolent resistance movement made up of opponents of the war, African-Americans, and disaffected young people and students. Radical pacifists believed that, just as the United States needed a revolution to save the country from violent and unresponsive authorities, salvation for Vietnam lay with the NLF. Their support for the Vietcong often isolated radicals from liberals within the peace movement. Waving the flag of the nlf and calling for a Vietcong victory often alienated members of the broader public who, although anxious about the war and opposed to deeper U.S. involvement, felt revulsion at the idea of an American defeat. After some raucous anti-war demonstrations in October 1965, *Time* lambasted "Vietniks" whose behavior validated a report of the Senate Committee on Internal Security that "The control of the anti-Vietnam movement has clearly passed from the hands of the moderate elements who may have controlled it at one time, into the hands of Communists and extremist elements who are openly sympathetic to the Viet Cong and openly hostile to the United States."[61]

This was a clearly erroneous evaluation. The movement to oppose U.S. involvement in Vietnam was far too amorphous to be controlled by anyone. Hundreds of thousands of people participated at some level in anti-war activities—attending demonstrations, voting, wearing armbands, passing out leaflets, organizing. They moved in and out of anti-war events depending on what happened in the war, their own levels of concern, frustration, and burnout, the weather, and the calendar of the academic year. Opposition to the war never was an organized movement, and the vast majority of participants never shared the radicals' analysis of the irredeemable flaws in American society.[62]

Nevertheless, radical rhetoric and ostentatious display of the symbols of the Vietcong helped the opponents of the anti-war movement. Nothing discredited it more in the eyes of President Johnson and his principal aides than the display of the banner of the NLF and the photograph of Ho Chi Minh. He was unlikely to compromise with his critics in any event, but his perception that sympathizers with the adversary directed the anti-war movement made accommodation between Johnson and his critics all but impossible.[63]

In their opposition to the war and their demands for vast changes within the United States, radical pacifists often made common cause with the Students for a Democratic Society and other groups that made up the burgeoning New Left in the years after 1964. Originally members of the New Left concentrated on changing society inside the United States. The movement to end legal discrimination, eradicate poverty, and augment the standing of students at large, impersonal universities first absorbed the energies of the SDS in the period 1962–1964. When New Leftists thought about foreign policy before 1965, they concentrated on Cuba. Fidel Castro held the imagination of many young people in the early days of the revolution. Opposition to U.S. sponsorship of the Bay of Pigs invasion spawned the creation of the Fair Play for Cuba Committee, with branches in major cities and nearby universities. The small group of sympathizers with the Castro government were among the few people inside the United States who opposed the Kennedy administration's policies during the October 1962 Cuban missile crisis. This dissent from a widely popular foreign policy helped set the stage for members of the New Left later to express wholesale disagreement with U.S. policy in Vietnam and the Cold War.[64]

Many of the organizers of the May 1965 Berkeley teach-in identified with the New Left. Activists from the sds and a variety of groups from the Old Left such as the Communist Party, the Socialist Workers Party, and the Young Socialist Alliance formed a bewildering array of groups to coordinate anti-war activity. In the months following the teach-in they created a loosely organized National Coordinating Committee to End the War in Vietnam (NCCEWVN). Initially Jerry Rubin, the moving spirit behind the NCCEWVN, tried to interest the SDS in housing the organization in its Chicago headquarters, but the SDS declined, citing the importance of student issues and civil rights. The NCCEWVN occupied offices in Madison, Wisconsin, and set about planning demonstrations to stop the war in Vietnam. From the beginning, the NCCEWVN struck a militant but non-violent tone.[65]

The NCCEWVN enjoyed some early successes, but it fell victim within a year to factional divisions within the peace and New Left movements. The NCCEWVN organized international days of protest on October 15–16, during which over one hundred thousand people attended rallies across the United States. Speakers were militant and demanded the immediate withdrawal of U.S. forces. Signs read SUPPORT THE TROOPS, BRING THEM HOME, and END THE WAR IN VIETNAM NOW. From the beginning, however, factionalism bedeviled efforts of the NCCEWVN to create a unified opposition position to the war. When the SDS raised the possibility of a nationwide student strike to take place in conjunction with the October 15–16 demonstrations, the NCCEWVN opposed. Most members of the NCCEWVN steering committee believed that the "SDS was proposing this without real consideration as to whether or not strikes were ever a realistic consideration."[66]

The NCCEWVN also refused to participate in what turned out to be a highly successful March on Washington sponsored by SANE (the Committee for a Sane Nuclear Policy) on November 28, 1965. This march was the largest antiwar gathering in the nation's capital since the Second World War. Speakers such as Senators Ernest Greuning and Wayne Morse and the prominent pediatrician Benjamin Spock called for a negotiated settlement to end the war in Vietnam. SANE discouraged signs calling for the victory of the NLF and refused to allow speeches by radical pacifists such as David Dellinger.[67] The NCCEWVN refused to endorse the march, however, on the grounds that sane had traditionally excluded groups affiliated with the American Communist Party and the Trotskyist Young Socialist Alliance.[68]

Leftist factional fighting engulfed the NCCEWVN in 1966. Members of the American Communist party aligned with some liberal members of the NCCEWVN to organize support for anti-war candidates during 1966. Trotskyist participants in the NCCEWVN believed that this represented wasted effort, since a majority of the public did not yet oppose the war in Vietnam. More radical members of the NCCEWVN believed that the best way to channel public opinion away from the war was to make it impossible for the government to conduct business as usual. They advised following Johnson around, shouting him down, taunting him with the chant "Hey, hey, LBJ, how many kids did you kill today?" and making him a prisoner in the White House. Some of the original organizers of the NCCEWVN became disenchanted with endless meetings and the successful efforts by the Trotskyist faction to take over. One complained about a "gruesome" meeting in Cleveland. "All the decisions were made in a smoke-filled back room. They didn't even make a pretense of democracy."[69] Afterwards the NCCEWVN, dominated by a small Trotskyist faction, lost influence. The Fifth Avenue Peace Parade Committee, also dominated by Old Leftists, soon became a more visible organizer of protest marches.[70]

From the early days of anti-war protest in 1965, opponents of the war in Vietnam confronted the dilemma faced by anyone who considers a public issue one of right or wrong. Political activists wanted to convince a majority of the public or elected representatives to adopt their course of action. That required patience, subtlety, and the willingness to allow people with different points of view a graceful way to change their minds. But if the issue truly involved morality it was hard for the activists to accept that more Americans supported the war than opposed it. In the fall of 1965 a Gallup Poll revealed a huge majority of 70 percent supported the war and that people between the ages of twenty-one and thirty backed the war more strongly than did any other group. That fall, college students expressed pro-war feelings at least as strongly as they did anti-war sentiments. Sixteen thousand students at Michigan State University signed a petition backing Johnson, 2,000 at the University of Michigan and 175 at the Harvard Law School sent telegrams to the White House supporting Johnson's position.[71]

Being outnumbered only frustrated anti-war activists. The bitterness led to dramatic acts, most of which hardened public attitudes against the anti-war movement. The violence and self-defeating activities of a few anti-war activists also deepened the divisions among opponents of the war. As time went on the differences over tactics—non-violence versus direct action, political involvement designed to change the minds of politicians versus demonstrations designed to raise the costs of continuing the war for both the public and government officials—tended to overshadow the agreement among opponents of the war that the fighting should end.

Two political suicides in late 1965 raised the stakes. On November 2, 1965 Norman Morrison, a Quaker active in the peace and civil rights movements, held his eighteen-month-old daughter in his arms near the entrance to the Pentagon, poured kerosene over himself and the child, and set themselves afire. Bystanders rescued the child, but Morrison died. He had previously expressed despair at the "terrible predicament" of speaking out against the

killing without reversing government policy. The day he killed himself he
read the anguished cry of a French priest in Vietnam who had "seen my
faithful burned up in napalm." Morrison thought his previous efforts to
organize letter writing campaigns to members of Congress futile. "What else
can we do?" he wondered. He wrote a suicide note to his wife in which he
said, "Know that I love thee but must act for the children of the priest's
village." A week later Roger LaPorte, a twenty-two-year-old participant in
the Catholic Worker Movement's opposition to the war in Vietnam, also took
his life in a gasoline immolation in front of the United Nations headquarters in
New York. Before he died LaPorte said, "I'm a Catholic Worker. I'm against
all wars. I did this as a religious action." Morrison's death had inspired
LaPorte, as did the hatred directed at anti-war demonstrators in New York a
few days after Morrison's suicide, where a mob shouted at a group of pacifists
gathered to burn draft cards, "Burn yourselves, not your cards."[72]

The two suicides did not inspire others to follow. Religious pacifists
encouraged people to live their lives for peace. Practically, that meant continuing the sorts of political organizing, rallies, and opposition to the draft
that had so frustrated Morrison and LaPorte. In 1966 liberals and moderate
pacifists overshadowed radicals in their opposition to the war. For the sds the
war itself came to represent a world revolutionary movement of which New
Leftists believed themselves a part. Frustrated delegates to the sds convention
in December 1965 said "no one knows what to do really" to end the war.
Some sdsers, recognizing how anti-war rallies seemed to galvanize *supporters* of Johnson's policies, said public demonstrations against the war had
become "an essential ingredient of the war effort; our protest activities, in the
context of contemporary American life, convert more people into the war
consensus than into the antiwar movement."[73]

While New Leftists dismissed the usefulness of traditional public protests,
liberals and moderate pacifists became more important in expressing dissent
from the administration's positions in 1966. The spontaneous public response
to the Senate Foreign Relations Committee's hearings in February dominated
discussion of the war in the early months of the year. Later the midterm
congressional elections became an important barometer of public sentiment
about the Johnson administration's handling of the war and public affairs in
general. In June Senate Majority Leader Mike Mansfield warned that his
survey of Democratic senators revealed terrible foreboding about the impact
of the war in the November elections. He found "deep confusion and concern
that we have not yet found the way to end" the fighting, "either by extension
or contraction of the military effort." The senators predicted that "candidates
of the Democratic Party will be hurt by the war."[74]

The Democrats' uneasiness proved prophetic. The Republican Party,
given up for nearly dead after the debacle of the Goldwater election campaign
of 1964, roared back in 1966, gaining over forty seats in the House of

Representatives and capturing seven from the Democrats in the Senate. But Vietnam was rarely an explicit issue in the campaign of 1966. When it was, more people favored escalation of the American effort than sympathized with the anti-war movement's call to negotiate or withdraw. Only in the city of Dearborn, Michigan, did voters pass a resolution explicitly calling for an end to U.S. participation in the war. Candidates seldom referred directly to Vietnam; when they did they usually divided between supporters of the President and candidates who thought the United States should do more, not less, in the war.

The Democrats' defeat had more to do with a white backlash against the urban riots by African Americans in the summer of 1965 and 1966. In California Ronald Reagan defeated two-term Democratic governor Edmund G. Brown by over one million votes. Reagan had supported Goldwater's call for an intensification in the war in 1964, but as a gubernatorial candidate he avoided direct references to Vietnam. He did base part of his campaign, however, on opposition to the anti-war demonstrators on the Berkeley campus of the University of California. Two Republicans won election to the Senate on platforms calling for a reduction of U.S. activity in Vietnam. In Oregon Republican Mark Hatfield had the support of Democrat Wayne Morse, one of the most vocal critics of Johnson's escalation of the war in Vietnam. In Illinois Republican Charles Percy defeated Democrat Paul Douglas, one of Johnson's most ardent backers of the war in Vietnam. Percy implied, but did not say explicitly, that he favored ending the war by negotiations, and won by tying Douglas directly to Johnson on domestic and foreign policy.

Douglas's advocacy of legislation barring discrimination in housing on racial grounds cost him the support of many white ethnic voters who cast their ballots for Percy. These voters generally favored the war and certainly had little sympathy for anti-war protesters. Their desertion of the Democratic Party foretold the break-up two years later of the New Deal coalition. The election of 1966 also revealed that the 1964 consensus behind Johnson had completely dissipated. Some Democrats wondered whether Johnson might not become a liability in 1968 if the war continued and racial divisions mounted. Allard Lowenstein began to explore the possibility of encouraging one of the Democratic senators opposed to the war in Vietnam to challenge Johnson for the nomination in 1968.[75]

Anti-war protest activities exploded during 1967 with the largest demonstrations yet demanding a negotiated settlement, reduction of the U.S. role, and even withdrawal. White House aides who spoke with students in early 1967 noted that they had "deeply troubled attitudes about Vietnam."[76] In 1967 more ordinary citizens without ties to traditional peace groups, religious pacifist organizations, or the New Left attended marches and vigils, wrote members of Congress, and told friends, neighbors, co-workers, or fellow students that in one way or another they wanted the war to end. A myriad of organizations opposed to the war either sprang up or were rejuvenated: Another Mother for Peace, Clergy and Laity Concerned about Vietnam, the Student Mobilization Committee to end the War, Women Strike for Peace. More popular support for opposition to the war, however, did not translate into tangible measures to end it. Anti-war activity produced more demonstrations of support for the President. The Johnson administration, always suspicious of its critics, increased its program of infiltrating and provoking the anti-war movement.[77]

Tensions among liberals, radical pacifists, and New Leftists continued within the anti-war movement in 1967. Liberals wanted their opposition to the war to be perceived as support for traditional American values. Most hoped to persuade Johnson to alter course; a growing minority sought to replace him as the Democratic party's nominee for President in 1968. Radical pacifists believed that the liberals' emphasis on "responsible" protest would not work. They believed that the United States had become morally compromised in Vietnam. Radicals argued that "U.S. involvement in the `bloody mess' is not the result of error upon error, mistake upon mistake, committed by *stupid* men. Every decision to escalate the war has been carefully programmed."[78] They believed any non-violent tactic appropriate to end the war, and rejected the liberals' argument about the need for responsible protest on the grounds that the liberals had not succeeded in ending the war. For New Leftists the war remained one important part of a larger picture showing the need for revolution in the United States and the rest of the industrial world.

In February 1967, Martin Luther King Jr. spoke out forcefully against the war. For the previous year he had privately voiced misgivings about the course of U.S. policy in Vietnam, but said that his civil rights work took up all of his time. He changed as the war seemed to absorb more energies of the administration and the momentum for civil rights drained after the elections of 1966. In February King called for an alliance of the civil rights and peace movements "until the very foundations of our country are shaken." Later he became the co-chairman of the Clergy and Laity Concerned About Vietnam, a prominent liberal religious coalition opposed to the war. He called the government "the greatest purveyor of violence in the world today." He characterized American involvement in Vietnam as a "symptom of a far deeper malady," the reflexive fear of revolution that had led the United States to oppose people throughout the underdeveloped world who wanted to assert their rights. "Somehow this madness must cease," he said. "The great initiative in this war is ours. The initiative to stop it must be ours."[79] As he anticipated earlier, King's outspoken opposition to the war caused a breach with other civil rights leaders, the national media, and the Johnson administration. Roy Wilkins, Executive Director of the NAACP, denied that Vietnam had hindered the advancement of African Americans. The national board of the NAACP rejected King's call to merge the civil rights and anti-war movements. Vice President Hubert Humphrey criticized King publicly. Behind the scenes John Roche, Johnson's aide in charge of liaison with intellectuals, told the President that King had "thrown in with the commies." Roche recommended that "the Communist origins of the operations must be exposed, the leaders discredited."[80]

Most of the various anti-war organizations had no ties to the Communist Party, Hanoi, or Moscow. Many groups worked uneasily together to sponsor a variety of protests against administration policy in the spring, summer, and fall of 1967. The Spring Mobilization to End the War in Vietnam began as an effort to unite liberals, pacifists, and radicals. Organizers hoped to undermine the Johnson administration's "claim to legitimacy through the electoral process."[81] Eventually some liberal groups such as Women Strike for Peace, sane, and the Fellowship of Reconciliation, uneasy with the radicalism they anticipated at some rallies, declined to be official sponsors. They wanted the massive protests to be "anti-administration, but not anti-American." But the refusal of national liberal organizations officially to endorse the protests did not dampen attendance at huge rallies in San Francisco and New York on April 15. The rally in San Francisco drew fifty thousand people; the one in New York two hundred thousand. Among the signs carried by the marchers were "STOP THE BOMBING," "NO VIETNAMESE EVER CALLED ME NIGGER," and "CHILDREN ARE NOT BORN TO BURN." Some young demonstrators shouted "Hey, hey, LBJ, how many kids did you kill today?" and "Hell no, we won't go." In New York Martin Luther King Jr. called on the United States to "honor its word" and "stop the bombing of North Vietnam." His wife, Coretta Scott King, addressed the rally in San Francisco, also urging an end to the bombing of the North.[82]

For the organizers of the rallies the tactical differences among various factions of the anti-war movement took on huge importance. For the people who attended the rallies, however, these doctrinal disputes hardly mattered. Both the leaders and the followers were right. The disagreements among organizers were sectarian and tedious and highly important. The massive rallies were important for showing how many people opposed the war and giving many people a sense that they had done something to try and end it. Specific tactics mattered too, however, if the anti-war movement was to have an effect. People went to these rallies for a variety of reasons: to hear speakers, to show support for the few hundred young men who burned their draft cards, to join a festival of music and art, or just to show that they did not like what the war did to the United States. For the most part, people who attended anti-war protests were middle class and better educated than the public at large. College students and other young people made up a substantial portion of the audience. Crowds were mostly white, although there was substantial representation among African Americans who drew the same connection between the push for civil rights and the war in Vietnam that had encouraged Martin Luther King Jr. to speak out against the war.[83]

Organizers of the protests considered the demonstrations huge successes because they showed that a significant number of people did not like the war, and believed that the demonstrations gave "visibility to the ever-widening base of the antiwar movement" and produced cover for "many new groups and persons to enter the political struggle against this war."[84] Protest rallies alone, however, did not seem to brake the momentum of the war. The public remained in flux, confused and disheartened by the war but unwilling to advocate withdrawal. Polls taken in the summer of 1967 revealed that a majority could not specify the war aims, but a plurality did not believe it had been a mistake to enter the war. Majorities opposed increasing troop levels and withdrawal. Approval of Johnson's handling of the presidency dropped to 38 percent in October 1967.[85] While most leaders of the anti-war movement understood that their views did not represent the thinking of a majority of the public, they gradually came to believe it did not take a majority to change policy. If somehow the Johnson administration could appreciate that the cost of the war at home had risen too high, the government might change course.[86]

In 1967, a coalition of liberals, radicals, and New Leftists created a Vietnam Summer, patterned on the highly successful Mississippi Summer of 1964 organized by the civil rights movement. At the April 15 rally in New York Martin Luther King Jr. urged students to "use this summer and coming summers educating and organizing communities across the nation against the war."[87] Vietnam Summer participants went to mid-sized and large cities to raise sentiment against the war. Volunteers canvassed door to door, hoping to "bring the war home" and make ordinary people feel the same anguish experienced by ordinary Vietnamese as the bombs fell on their homes and fields.[88]

Organizers of the Vietnam Summer hoped to expand the scope of opposition to the war in Vietnam from middle-class college students to working-class young people, who were more likely to be drafted into military service. The Vietnam Summer proved a pale imitation of the Mississippi Summer of three years earlier. People slammed doors in the faces of organizers or simply did not want to talk about the war. Volunteers drifted away from the project. Some volunteers did not like the persistent wrangling over leftist doctrine and tactics that organizers seemed to delight in. Others became discouraged by support for the war prevalent among working-class people and lack of interest among the poor. By the summer of 1967 ordinary people wanted to hear less, not more, about Vietnam, and the Vietnam Summer never overcame this sort of resistance.[89]

The issue raised by volunteers during the Vietnam Summer that resonated most with young people was the draft. Conscription into the armed forces was fraught with inequities. Because the potential pool of men eligible for the draft—26.8 million between 1961 and 1973—so vastly exceeded the number drafted or enlisted—2.15 million and 8.72 million respectively—the burden of military service fell unevenly across the population. Men from higher income families and those with greater education were less likely to serve in the war than were men from low-income families who had only a high school education. Aware that the military needed fewer men than the pool available, the Selective Service System developed a system of "channeling" men into desired occupations. General Lewis B. Hershey, who directed Selective Service from 1941 to 1969, described Selective Service as "exerting 'pressurized guidance' to encourage young people to enter and remain in study, in critical occupations, and in other activities in the national health, safety and interest." Hershey wanted someone eligible for the draft to feel as if "he is standing in a room which has been made uncomfortably warm. Several doors are open, but they all lead to various forms of recognized patriotic service to the Nation."[90]

The anti-war movement developed an internal network of draft counselors developed to help the young men facing Hershey's "uncomfortably warm" room. As William Strauss and Lawrence Baskir, the two staff directors of a clemency board set up by President Gerald R. Ford to handle cases of men who had committed various offenses against Selective Service or the military, observed, "The draft became a sieve for men who got the right advice at the right time, or who were clever enough to wage an independent fight against the system."[91] Until 1968 attendance in college or graduate school deferred men from the draft. After the Supreme Court decided *U.S. v. Seeger* in 1965, conscientious objector status became available to people who opposed participation in war based on a well-thought-out moral code; a prospective conscientious objector no longer had to be a member of an organized religion to be granted CO status.[92] Draft counselors explained how men could keep college deferments, obtain certificates from medical practitioners about conditions that disqualified them from military service, or fashion a claim for CO status that would withstand scrutiny. Some draft counselors also advised resistance to selective service. Thousands of young men refused to register for the draft or ignored induction notices. Hundreds burned draft cards in 1967; thousands fled the country. Selective Service struck back by trying to remove the student deferments for young men who engaged in anti-war protests.[93]

Liberals tried to influence the President more directly than the organizers of the Vietnam Summer in July 1967. Allard Lowenstein organized a delegation of seven college student-body presidents and newspaper editors to go to the White House to urge that Johnson seek a negotiated settlement. The President responded by having Assistant Secretary of State William Bundy explain somewhat condescendingly that government officials had already considered all of the "questions and doubts" about Vietnam policy that the student leaders wanted aired. The President also sought information from the

FBI about whether Lowenstein had connections to the American Communist Party and whether communists had organized the meeting of the editors and student body presidents. The FBI reported no communist connections. Douglas Cater, the President's aide who followed up on Lowenstein, reported him to be "aggressively ambitions and appears to be trying to establish his own communications system with the leaders of Hanoi." Cater also thought that the college leaders came from too many different backgrounds and were too numerous to have been manipulated by the anti-war movement. He did believe, however, that the White House might be capable of some manipulation of its own, since an invitation to meet with top aides of the President probably carried more weight than an appeal to sign a letter opposing the war. He suggested "inviting a selected group of next year's college student presidents to Washington early in the fall. . . . [I]t could be helpful at heading off more militant protests on their part."[94]

Militancy certainly was in the air in the middle of 1967. Hundreds of delegates to a National Conference for a New Politics met in Chicago over the Labor Day weekend. Convinced that both the Democratic and Republican Parties were conservative organizations resistant to social change, the NCNP considered organizing an effective alternative radical political group. Leftist factionalism doomed this prospect before the three-day meeting ended. Delegates gave only polite applause to Martin Luther King Jr., whose speech they believed was far too moderate. Vietnam was not high on the agenda of the gathering. Instead, the growing importance of Black Power within the civil rights movement nearly broke up the meeting. After furious and sometimes heart-wrenching debate, white delegates agreed to a set of demands presented by the black caucus, including a stipulation that half of the representatives be African Americans and a condemnation of Israel following its victory in the Six Day War in June 1967. For the majority at the September meeting of the NCNP, Vietnam became only one of many issues.

The NCNP stayed alive briefly after the Chicago meeting, but it became the focal point for creating a new political organization.[95] The agreement to the demands of the black caucus shocked liberal delegates, many of whom had been drawn to the NCNP as a way of ending the war in Vietnam. Liberals viewed the Chicago convention with dismay or fury. One reporter called the debate over the demands of the black caucus "a scene worthy of Genet or Pirendello."[96] Their frustration mounted in the fall, since they desperately wanted some alternative to Johnson but they were fed up with radical politics.

Widespread demonstrations occurred from California to Washington in October, culminating in a giant march on Washington on October 20–21. The activities ranged from hundreds of vigils, to picketing outside the White House, to acts of civil disobedience. A group called Resistance organized turn-ins of draft cards. Over 1,100 young men across the country turned in their draft cards on October 16 as thousands more female supporters and adults of both genders applauded and endorsed their actions. In the days before the march on the Pentagon 3,500 radical demonstrators tried to shut down the army induction center in Oakland, California. Police officers waded into the crowd waving clubs, sending twenty people to the hospital. Three days later ten thousand angry people showed up in front of the induction center to fight with two thousand police officers. In Madison, Wisconsin, sixty people were injured when police attacked students demonstrating to stop representatives of the Dow Chemical Company, the maker of napalm, from recruiting on campus.[97]

This activity was but prelude to the march on Washington on Friday, October 20 and Saturday, October 21. The President became frantic as he learned of plans for a gathering of more than one hundred thousand people to demand a bombing halt, the withdrawal of U.S. troops, and immediate negotiations to end the war. At a cabinet meeting, he asked his Attorney General, Ramsey Clark, who had usually been solicitous of the civil liberties of anti-war demonstrators, "Who are the sponsoring groups? Pacifists? Communists?" Clark replied that "there [was] a heavy representation of extreme left wing groups with long lines of Communist affiliations." When Secretary of State Rusk interjected, "Wouldn't it help to leak that?", Clark responded that "the fact of Communist involvement and encouragement [had] been given to some columnists." "Let's see more," was Johnson's comment.[98]

Deputy Attorney General Warren Christopher pursued a more cautious policy of coordinating the ground rules of the demonstration with organizers. For the first time since the bonus marchers went to Washington in 1932, authorities called out troops to protect the capital from citizens petitioning the government.[99]

About one hundred thousand people began gathering in Washington on Friday, October 20. That afternoon a group organized by the Resistance went to the Justice Department to deliver a collection of draft cards turned in by protesters. Officials refused to accept them, claiming that they did not want to be a party to a criminal activity. That evening hundreds attended a fundraising event at a theater. An obviously drunk Norman Mailer delivered a rambling speech that later became a focal point of a celebrated memoir of the demonstration.[100] The next morning over one hundred thousand people gathered at the Lincoln Memorial to begin the largest anti-war demonstration held up to that point at the Capital. After a few hours of denunciations of Johnson and speeches demanding immediate negotiations, a bombing halt, and withdrawal of troops, about fifty thousand of the demonstrators slowly walked across the Arlington Memorial Bridge to a Pentagon parking lot. Nearly all of the marchers milled around, gave flowers to the soldiers, sat down in the parking lot, and sang protest songs. A small group joined beat poet Allen Ginsberg in attempting to levitate the building with Tibetan chants. A group called the sds Revolutionary Contingent rushed the entrance to the Pentagon

and were thrown back by military police. Police then sprayed tear gas on
other demonstrators. Some ran in panic or went limp for arrest; a few threw
bottles or taunted the police. About six hundred people entered an area declared off-limits before the march and were arrested. Forty-seven demonstrators and police officers went to the hospital.[101]

Press accounts of the rally at the Lincoln Memorial and the Pentagon
pointed out the diversity of the crowd and how the vast majority had been
non-violent. Commentary focused, however, on the behavior of a few. David
Brinkley of NBC News characterized the march as ''a coarse, vulgar episode
by people who seemed more interested in exhibitionistic displays than
any redress of grievances.'' Barry Goldwater called it a ''hate-filled, anti-
American, pro-communist violent mob uprising.'' Opinion polls revealed
that the public believed by a 3 to 1 margin that people thought anti-war
demonstrators endangered the safety of Americans fighting in Vietnam. Seventy percent agreed that the anti-war demonstrations encouraged the NLF and
North Vietnamese to fight harder. Johnson took comfort in these numbers,
and demanded heightened government efforts to link the anti-war movement
to Moscow or Hanoi.[102]

A group of Vietnamese students in France sympathetic to the NLF and Ho
Chi Minh wrote the organizers of the march expressing gratitude. The Vietnamese students believed that the large gathering in Washington refuted
the administration's claim that the anti-war protesters ''do not represent the
United States and are only giving illusions to our people, supposedly on the
verge of being crushed under the deluge of U.S. bombs, and thus you are
betraying the U.S. by needlessly prolonging the war.''[103]

Johnson and supporters of the administration continued to make exactly
that sort of argument in the last two months of 1967. The election of 1968 was
only a year away, however. The administration needed concrete signs of
progress in the war to dampen the growing anti-war movement. Allard Lowenstein's efforts in the fall to persuade a liberal Democratic senator to challenge Johnson for the Democratic nomination bore fruit in late November
when Eugene McCarthy of Minnesota announced his entrance into the New
Hampshire Democratic primary. McCarthy's candidacy represented more of
an irritation than a threat to Johnson, but only if something could be done to
remove Vietnam as a potential issue in the 1968 campaign.[104]

ECONOMIC EFFECTS OF THE WAR

As the war continued, many people believed that it cost far more than it was
worth. As early as August 1965 an economist warned the House Committee
on Foreign Affairs that spending an additional $10–$14 billion a year in
Vietnam risked ''a serious breakdown of the world monetary system.'' By

December scientists worried that the money used to fight the war meant that less would be available to pay for important basic scientific research.[105] President Johnson himself acknowledged that the war drained resources from his Great Society programs. In his 1966 budget, he confidently predicted that the United States could afford both domestic reform and the war. A year later he admitted that funding for Great Society programs needed to be restrained by "the claims of our commitments in Southeast Asia upon the Nation's resources." By 1967 a White House economist complained that "Vietnam has taken our pin money." In his budget message of January 1968, Johnson said, "We can't do everything we would wish to do."[106]

The war's economic impact went beyond budget allocations. Most of the effects were negative, some positive. Prices rose, but so did wages. Spending for the war had a noticeable impact on the general rise in prices that took place after 1964. In both 1964 and 1965 the Consumer Price Index rose around 1.5 percent. The rate nearly doubled to 2.9 percent in both 1966 and 1967, and it hit 4.2 percent in 1968. While the rise in prices was not great in comparison with subsequent years, it far outpaced the experience of the previous decade, when prices had risen a little more than 1 percent per year. The most dramatic increase was the cost of labor. As the Vietnam War absorbed more and more young men, wages went up. In the three years before the massive American buildup, wage increases averaged 3 percent. In 1965 it was 3.7 percent. From 1966 to 1970 it was 6.6. percent.[107]

The economic impact of the war was also psychological. Opponents of the war continually derided it as a terrible misallocation of scarce resources. Sometimes the complaints were that the United States did not get its money's worth for its vast expenditure in Vietnam. A *Fortune* magazine study of the war's impact, based in part on research conducted by the economist Alan Greenspan, complained about the "profligate disparity between the huge quantities of U.S. bullets and bombs poured from the air upon targets in Vietnam and the military and economic damage the bombs do." It cost $1,300 per hour for the ten-hour trip a B-52 bomber made from Guam to Vietnam and back.[108] The popular economics writer Eliot Janeway turned against the war in Vietnam because it seemed to enrich America's economic competitors. He was especially incensed that nearly half of the aid the United States provided to South Vietnam "goes right back to France as ammunition in her war against the dollar." Even the ardently anti-communist *Wall Street Journal* questioned whether "the U.S. is inflicting more injury on the Communists or on itself."[109]

Antiwar activists believed that excessive spending for the war in Vietnam helped recruit otherwise indifferent citizens to their cause. A Quaker group noted how many worthy projects could be paid for with the money spent in Vietnam. They urged citizens to write their representatives in Congress explaining that the $2.5 billion spent in Vietnam in one month in 1966 could provide 169,000 schoolteachers, 125,000 nurses, and 50,000 doctors. The $10 billion spent in Vietnam over the next four months could replace one million of the four million substandard housing units.[110] For Janeway the solution was a negotiated settlement; for the more militant *Journal* the preferred course was harder pressure on the North; for the Quakers the idea was to end the war immediately. Whatever conclusions critics drew from the economic consequences of the war, they intensified their opposition to Johnson's policies.

IMPACT OF OPPOSITION TO THE WAR

By the end of 1967 the war in Vietnam had come home in ways that neither supporters nor opponents of it expected or fully comprehended. The growth of opposition to the war had wrecked the consensus constructed by Johnson in 1964. Distrust of the government was at its highest point since the Second World War. But the anti-war movement had not convinced most people to support its views either.

At the time and for a generation after the events of the middle 1960s, participants in the movement and outside analysts argued over its tactics. Sometimes the discussions became so intense and the points at issue so arcane that observers concluded that the existence of the arguments themselves detracted from the success of the anti-war movement. Certainly it was diverse, noisy, divided, and angry. The rhetoric often was overblown, even apocalyptic. The fringe of the anti-war movement engaging in violence attracted more attention than the hundreds of thousands of ordinary people who occasionally marched, went to vigils, or wrote members of Congress. The tumult within the anti-war movement turned away as many people as it recruited. At its most basic level the discussion of the tactics of anti-war protesters addressed the question of whether the movement shortened or prolonged the war. Sympathizers with liberal protesters, such as Charles De Benedetti in his massive study, *An American Ordeal: The Antiwar Movement of the Vietnam Era,* argue that the responsible form of protest favored by the traditional peace groups stood a good chance of shortening the war. Unfortunately, De Benedetti and other liberals claim, radical elements in the anti-war movement adopted such extreme positions and engaged in such foolish acts of romantic revolutionary violence that more people came to revile anti-war activities than supported them. Tom Wells, another veteran of the antiwar movement, argues exactly the opposite position in *The War Within: America's Battle over Vietnam,* claiming that the very disruptions of the anti-war movement eventually made it impossible for the United States to continue the fight.

The anti-war movement did not end the war in Vietnam, but it did alter, almost irrevocably, the perceptions of ordinary citizens of their society and their government; it also altered the perceptions of leaders toward the public. Secretary of State Dean Rusk claimed that he overestimated the patience of the public to fight a long war.[111] By the end of 1967 that patience had worn out.

Chapter **10**

*   *   *   *   *   *   *   *   *   *   *

Crack-up: 1967–1968

*T*HE WAR in Vietnam overwhelmed the United States in 1967 and 1968. When President Johnson escalated American involvement of ground personnel in 1965, General Westmoreland optimistically promised that the United States and its South Vietnamese ally would turn the tide of the war in 1966. Mopping up would occur in 1967 and the war would effectively be won in 1968. These estimates proved wildly out of line. The number of U.S. troops in Vietnam surpassed four hundred thousand in 1967 and the resistance of the nlf and the North Vietnamese remained intact and powerful. Secretary of Defense Robert S. McNamara's doubts about the effectiveness of bombing the North caused him finally to conclude that "the war in Vietnam is acquiring a momentum of its own that must be stopped." Further escalation "could lead to a major national disaster."[1] The growth of anti-war sentiment had a vast impact on the thinking of top officials of the Johnson administration. The intellectual leadership of the country, supportive of presidential action in foreign affairs since the Second World War, turned against deeper U.S. involvement in Vietnam.[2]

Faced with growing popular opposition to the war, the United States sought a way out. In 1967 the United States hoped that elections would solidify the position of the government of the Republic of Vietnam and refute criticism that the United States supported an unpopular and corrupt clique in the South. U.S. officials wanted a popular government in the South to alter the face of South Vietnamese society, reduce chronic corruption, recruit soldiers from across a broad spectrum of society, and wage the war more

246

effectively. None of these hopes were realized. The United States also failed in an ambitious effort to open negotiations with the North to end the war. Private mediators working on their own behalf and special representatives of the U.S. government sought avenues of dialogue with Hanoi. These did not materialize because of the profound distrust between North Vietnam and the United States.

Nineteen-sixty-eight proved to be a climactic year in the war. At the beginning the Johnson administration concluded that peace efforts would not work but that the military momentum had shifted in favor of the United States and the ARVN. While Westmoreland's earlier predictions of victory by 1968 had proven premature, Washington still thought that 1968 would turn the tide. All of these hopes vanished in the fiery Tet Offensive begun on January 30. While fighting raged in the major cities of Vietnam for the next three weeks, the hopes of Lyndon Johnson for a second full term vanished. On March 31 he announced that he would not seek the Democratic presidential nomination. He rejected Westmoreland's request for an additional 206,000 troops for the war effort, and he dispatched Averell Harriman and Cyrus Vance on a quest for a negotiated settlement. While the diplomats began a slow dance across three continents looking for ways to bridge the gap between Hanoi and Washington, the bloodiest fighting of the war occurred in Vietnam.

Meanwhile, following the assassinations of Martin Luther King, Jr. and Robert F. Kennedy, the United States experienced the greatest domestic upheaval since the end of the Civil War. All of this occurred in the midst of a presidential election campaign. In the fall voters in the United States narrowly elected a Republican, former Vice President Richard M. Nixon. He defeated Democratic Vice President Hubert Humphrey, who had loyally supported Johnson's policies on the war from 1965 to 1968 but who suggested that he favored de-escalation of the U.S. role, and Alabama Governor George Wallace, who implied that he would wage the war more aggressively. Nixon did not make his own plans for Vietnam clear, but he rode the crest of public frustration with a seemingly endless war. Most of those who voted for Nixon did so in the hopes that he would cut loose the albatross of Vietnam from around the American neck.

NEGOTIATIONS

In the winter of 1966–1967, the Johnson administration stepped up efforts to seek negotiations. A committee headed by Averell Harriman met regularly to "find out specifically, if possible, what 'reciprocal action' the North Vietnamese leaders would take if bombing were stopped."[3] At the same time Congress noticed an upsurge in constituent demands for negotiations. Even Democratic legislators usually supportive of Johnson's war effort complained about reports of divisions within the administration over opening negotiations with the North.[4] U.N. ambassador Arthur Goldberg told Secretary of State Rusk that he wanted to leave the United Nations and return to the Supreme Court because he felt that "we have not done enough for peace."[5]

In the midst of these rumblings for peace, the administration paid attention to overtures from Polish diplomats to open communications with Hanoi. Januscz Lewandowski, Poland's representative to the International Control Commission, met secretly with Henry Cabot Lodge and North and South Vietnamese officials in a series of encounters the U.S. code-named Marigold. At first the United States was skeptical of Lewandowski and his superior, Foreign Minister Adam Rapacki. President Johnson contemptuously dismissed Rapacki's "Nobel prize fever."[6] As time went on, however, the administration took Lewandowski more seriously. A Soviet diplomat told U.S. officials that "there was definitely something" in Hanoi's approach.[7]

Lewandowski presented ten points for the United States and the North Vietnamese to agree upon. Essentially, his program called for negotiations to settle all outstanding military issues. The United States would be willing to accept the reunification and neutralization of Vietnam after the restoration of peace. The future of bombing represented the key element in starting negotiations. In Lewandowski's formula the United States would stop bombing the North "if this will facilitate . . . a peaceful solution." He wanted the United States to "avoid any appearance that North Vietnam is forced to negotiate by bombings or that North Vietnam has negotiated in exchange for cessation of the bombing. Stopping the bombing would not involve recognition or confirmation by North Vietnam that its armed forces are or were infiltrating into South Vietnam."[8]

Throughout the discussions with Lewandowski, American officials pressed to know what the communists would do if the U.S. stopped the bombing. He refused to accept this question as the point of departure for worthwhile negotiations, explaining that Hanoi was bound to reject it because "de-escalation would be viewed as strengthening the governmental status quo in South Vietnam, whereas it was precisely a change in the South Vietnamese government that the Communist side required."[9] Yet while Polish diplomats tried to convince the United States to halt the bombing in order to encourage Hanoi to enter negotiations, the United States increased the bombing of the Hanoi region. A few days after the United States escalated the bombing, Assistant Secretary of State William P. Bundy reported that "our bombing actions had left the Soviets—and by implication, Hanoi—in complete doubt as what our intentions and views really were."[10]

Any hopes that Marigold might bear fruit vanished in early 1967 when the secret negotiations became public with stories in the *Washington Post* and the *International Herald Tribune*.[11] In early February Johnson claimed that he had not found "any serious indications that the other side is ready to stop the war.''[12] Washington eventually concluded that the Polish diplomats spoke only for themselves and could not deliver representatives with the authority to make commitments on behalf of Hanoi.

Unhappy with the results of Marigold, the administration acted to forestall other private diplomatic initiatives. Early in 1967 the White House summarily rejected efforts by two newspaper editors, Harry Ashmore and William C. Baggs, to act as go-betweens with the North Vietnamese. In January Ashmore and Baggs traveled to Hanoi. They went to Vietnam hoping to break the impasse between American officials who wanted assurances that the North would begin fruitful negotiations once bombing stopped and the North Vietnamese who insisted on an unconditional halt to American bombing, the departure of U.S. troops from Vietnam, and the recognition of the National Liberation Front as the "sole genuine representative of the South Vietnamese people."[13] In Hanoi, Ashmore and Baggs noted that the bombing of the North had not disrupted the economy of the mostly agricultural country. Secretary of Defense Robert S. McNamara, by now thoroughly disenchanted with the effectiveness of bombing, agreed with Ashmore and Baggs. He told them that "the decision to bomb the North was political, and those of us who tried to halt it took a beating when the Vietnamese didn't make any political response to the bombing pauses [in the winters of 1965–1966 and 1966–1967]."[14]

After the two Americans met Ho Chi Minh, they gushed over his fluency in French and English, his "extraordinary mobility of expression which thoroughly gives the lie to the legend of the inscrutable Oriental," and his command of the issues dividing North Vietnam from the United States. Ho told the Americans that the North was not at war with the United States. "We are supporting our fellow Vietnamese in the South in their war of liberation, but this is a matter among Vietnamese." When the two visitors asked the standard American question about his willingness to specify the conditions under which he would talk if the bombing stopped, he refused. He told them "it is like being asked by a Chicago gangster who has you at gun-point what you are willing to pay him not to shoot you." Ashmore and Baggs asked the North's leader if he could do something to relax the Americans' suspicions. Ho angrily declined to guarantee that he would talk without conditions if the U.S. halted the bombing. "I am not willing to guarantee anything under these conditions. . . . I want to see the goods before the price is established."[15]

Over the next month Ashmore and Baggs tried to bridge a wide gap between Hanoi and Washington. While the North Vietnamese welcomed their efforts, the Johnson administration considered them kibbitzers. The journalists sought to soften the administration's demands for the North Vietnamese to reduce their infiltration into the South in return for a bombing halt. Their efforts proved unsuccessful. Johnson told Ho that the North's demand for an unconditional and permanent halt to the bombing and all other military actions against the North was unacceptable. Johnson agreed to stop bombing and shelling the North "as soon as I am assured that infiltration into South Vietnam by land and sea has stopped." Ho angrily rejected these demands. He repeated that "the Vietnamese people will never submit to force, they will never accept talks under the threat of bombs." Ashmore felt crushed. He accused the State Department and Johnson of double dealing. For his part, National Security Adviser Walt Rostow encouraged journalists to write columns arguing that the domestic clamor for peace negotiations "hurts the war effort in South Vietnam and tends to lengthen the war."[16]

Yet by the middle of 1967, the Johnson administration seemed ready for serious negotiations with Hanoi. In the summer and early fall, the administration felt such intense pressure to show progress that it sent its own private intermediary, Harvard professor Henry Kissinger, to Paris to seek North Vietnamese negotiating partners. Two Frenchmen, Herbert Marcovich and Raymond Aubrac, who had long personal connections with Ho Chi Minh and Pham Van Dong, came forward as intermediaries between the United States and North Vietnam.

In July the two French intermediaries met with Ho Chi Minh and Pham Van Dong in Hanoi, who assailed the United States but held out hope for a negotiated settlement. Unlike Ashmore and Baggs, who had been impressed with Ho's intelligence and grasp of the issues, the Frenchmen, who had met him twenty years before, found the revolutionary leader old, frail, and unconcerned with details.[17] In contrast, Pham Van Dong, the North Vietnamese premier, seemed fully in control. He informed them, "We have been fighting for our independence for four thousand years. We have defeated the Mongols three times. The United States army, strong as it is, is not as terrifying as Genghis Khan."[18] Pham Van Dong assured the French negotiators that "the Marines are in difficulty. The United States is forced to replace its well-trained troops by ever younger soldiers. We fight only when we choose; we economize on our resources, we fight only for political purposes."[19]

Despite such brave talk, the North's leaders wanted the United States to stop bombing. National Security Adviser Walt Rostow thought he heard "flexible noises" coming from Pham Van Dong.[20] The very success of the revolutionaries in the South made the Northern leaders worry that the United States might take the next step in escalation and bomb the elaborate system of dikes protecting the fields of North Vietnam. To prevent such a catastrophe, Pham Van Dong wanted the United States to stop bombing. Once Washington made it clear that the end of bombing was "permanent and unconditional," North Vietnam would talk with the United States.[21]

But the Johnson administration was not ready for either a private or public declaration of a complete and permanent end to the bombing. Johnson considered the air war over North Vietnam one of his best bargaining chips. Moreover, Johnson believed that continued bombing of the North or the resumption of the bombing, if talks with the North Vietnamese failed to produce progress toward negotiations, improved his standing with uniformed officers. Many of them urged increasing the tempo of bombing and targeting the dikes. Wanting a payoff on the investment of planes and captured airmen, air force commanders thought that additional bombing validated their original efforts. Johnson's principal foreign policy advisers concluded that the most productive quid pro quo from Hanoi would be a promise not to augment its forces in the South in return for a bombing halt.[22]

Reports from Aubrac and Marcovich were encouraging enough to send Henry Kissinger to Paris. In talks, code-named Pennsylvania, Kissinger relayed to the North Vietnamese an administration offer to cease bombing with the understanding that a pause would "lead promptly to productive discussions" with the North. The United States was willing to talk either openly or discreetly with the North Vietnamese. If Hanoi wanted secret talks, however, the United States argued that it would not be possible to order a complete stop to the bombing. To do so would let the world know that something was up.[23] Hanoi considered this argument nonsensical. The United States would not demand that North Vietnam remove its troops from the South, but would expect the North not to take advantage of a bombing pause to increase its supplies flowing to the South. The United States would remain committed to the government of South Vietnam headed by President Nguyen Van Thieu and Vice President Nguyen Cao Ky. The United States might permit NLF participation in a coalition government, but the NLF would have to drop its revolutionary program.

As the secret contacts went forward in Paris, Johnson outlined publicly Washington's requirements for peace. In a major speech he delivered at San Antonio, Johnson promised to stop air and naval bombing of North Vietnam "when this will lead promptly to productive discussions." He elaborated that the United States would assume that as the talks went forward "North Vietnam would not take advantage" of the halt to the bombing.[24] Both the North Vietnamese and the NLF representative in Paris publicly blasted this San Antonio formula as "sheer deception."[25]

In private discussions, North Vietnam expressed some interest in Kissinger's proposals once the United States stopped bombing within a ten-mile radius around Hanoi. But as time went on Hanoi concluded that the United States would not take the crucial step of halting the bombing completely. Throughout much of September and October Washington and Hanoi danced around the issue of how complete a halt to the bombing the United States would undertake, what reciprocal gestures the North would offer, and what negotiations might accomplish. Hanoi wanted a complete bombing halt before going forward. Officially it complained that "the essence of the American propositions is the stopping of the bombing under conditions. The American bombing of the Democratic Republic of Vietnam is illegal.

The United States should put an end to the bombing and cannot pose any conditions."[26] It rejected the "words of peace" coming from Washington as "only trickery."[27]

Johnson too suspected trickery—on Hanoi's part—and believed the North's leaders "are keeping this channel going just because we are not bombing Hanoi." He also did not trust Marcovich or Aubrac. "They aren't our people are they?" he asked. Dean Rusk answered, "No, Aubrac is a scientist, Marcovich is a Communist."[28] Finally the President accepted the judgment of two of his more militant advisers, Supreme Court Justice Abe Fortas and Maxwell Taylor, to keep bombing. Taylor believed that the North had made its first genuine response, but he cautioned that "by showing weakness we could prejudice any possible negotiations." Fortas, perhaps closest to Johnson's thinking, recommended that Kissinger tell the North Vietnamese, "Thanks, it's too bad. You know you could have gotten somewhere if you had really wanted to."[29] Kissinger did as he was told.

Marcovich and Aubrac told him that changes in language in a message from Hanoi (the DRV had called on the United States to halt escalation, not bombing, in return for receiving Kissinger in Hanoi) suggested movement. This was not good enough for Kissinger. He informed the French intermediaries that "the issue was really quite simple. If Hanoi wanted to negotiate it should be able to find some way of expressing this fact by means other than subtle changes in tense and elliptical references full of double meaning."[30]

Hanoi's public attitude stiffened just as the White House concluded that Pennsylvania was not likely to succeed. The Australian journalist Wilfred Burchett, a long-time supporter of positions adopted by the DRV, reported on October 20 that Prime Minister Pham Van Dong and Foreign Minister Nguyen Duy Trinh demanded a complete bombing halt before talks could begin. Burchett concluded that Hanoi "is in no mood for concessions or bargaining and there is an absolute refusal to offer anything—except talks—for a cessation of the bombing. The word stressed is 'talks,' not negotiations."[31] With neither the Americans nor the North Vietnamese willing to budge privately from their entrenched public positions, Pennsylvania collapsed.

THE SOUTH VIETNAMESE ELECTIONS

The effort to open negotiations between the United States and North Vietnam proceeded as presidential elections went forward in the South. Since 1964 U.S. government officials had been frustrated by the turnover in governments in South Vietnam. A succession of military regimes had failed to generate much public support. At one point a frustrated White House aide complained that the national symbol of South Vietnam should be the turnstile.[32] The changes at the top seemed to end in early 1966 when air force marshall Nguyen Cao Ky became prime minister and General Nguyen Van Thieu took over the largely ceremonial position of chief of state. A showman and a dandy, Ky designed his own uniform and loved to be photographed wearing dark aviator sunglasses at the controls of his fighter jet. The flamboyant, egotistical Ky was made of tougher stuff than his predecessors. He slapped down dissident military commanders, forcing a showdown with one rebellious local leader in the northern district (I Corps) in March.[33]

Ky seemed willing to carry the war more vigorously to the NLF fighters in the South, yet he also was far more brutal than some earlier South Vietnamese leaders. Under his regime the government imprisoned thousands of NLF suspects in tiny, filthy tiger cages along the banks of the Mekong river. For a while the Ky denied these atrocities, but pictures in the American news media provoked an outcry against him.[34] Ky inspired both intense support and deep loathing among wide elements of the military and the civilian population.[35]

Both Vietnamese leaders and American officials desperately hoped that the government in Saigon could achieve legitimate, broad, popular support. Ky believed that a constitutionally elected president would represent "a great source of pressure on Hanoi."[36] No presidential elections had occurred in South Vietnam since the Diem era. Vietnamese civilian opponents of military rule and American opponents of the war often pointed to the dependence of the military rulers of Vietnam on the United States as proof that South Vietnam did not control its own destiny. If the Republic of Vietnam was not a truly independent and viable state, then what was the United States doing in the war? American planners believed that the best way to diminish these criticisms would be to hold a fair election in the midst of war. That could create a government "strong and unified enough to continue to prosecute the war (or to negotiate a peaceful settlement) and at the same time broadly enough based to attract increasing local and national strength away from the V.C."[37]

From January to September 1967 American officials in Saigon and Washington carefully tracked the fortune of candidates in the presidential election. The Americans walked a fine line between guiding the electoral process to assure fairness and acquiescing in decisions made by the military government. Pursuing the first course gave weight to the communist charge that the Saigon authorities were "dirty lackies of the Americans . . . running dogs, traitors, and country sellers."[38] Yet if the Americans let the Saigon government do what it wanted, it could make a mockery of democratic processes. In the end the Americans interfered enough in the election to invalidate it as democratic, but not enough to force the victors to respect the rights of their opponents.

U.S. planners hoped against hope that military and civilian leaders inside Vietnam would come together. Officials in Washington were ready to lean on the military, whom they feared would "instinctively think in terms of their domination of the government with some democratic window dressing." Ambassador Lodge, on the other hand, reminded Washington that the military government represented the "most experienced, cohesive and reliable of the nation building forces of the country."[39]

The potential for a split in the military leadership during the presidential election produced even graver anxieties among U.S. officials. Both Ky and Thieu wanted to be "the military candidate for president," and Americans feared that their rivalry would "create once again a situation where senior officers devote their time to politicking rather than defeating the common enemy."[40] In May, many senior ARVN commanders deserted Thieu for Ky, and Thieu told Ellsworth Bunker, the U.S. ambassador since March, that he did not think he could win if he ran.[41] But Bunker encouraged him to try. At that point forty-eight ARVN generals met in an extraordinary two-day meeting in Saigon to decide between Thieu and Ky. Men shouted, denounced one another for corruption, tore their stars from their uniforms, wept, and threatened alternately to turn things over to civilian rule or to stop the elections and government through martial law. In the end, Thieu became the presidential candidate and Ky agreed to serve under him as vice president. Ky explained to the Americans that he had "laid down the condition that he would have the right to name the cabinet and control the armed forces."[42]

Almost immediately Thieu and Ky, with the assistance of the Americans, made it impossible for any other candidate to win the election. They turned their attention first to General Duong Van Minh ("Big Minh"), the leader of the coup which had overthrown Ngo Dinh Diem in 1963, who announced from exile in Thailand that he would seek the presidency. Minh had a substantial following among his fellow Buddhists and urban opponents of the military weary of the war. He also enjoyed support among some military officers resentful of Ky's irascibility and Thieu's Catholicism. Bunker feared that Minh's candidacy threatened "to open religious conflict such as that which erupted between Catholics and Buddhists in 1964."[43] Thieu and Ky sent a military envoy to Minh telling him he would be arrested if he returned to run for president. The National Assembly banned him from the ballot. The legislature also blocked the candidacy of a former minster of economics under Ky who ran as a peace candidate favoring a cease-fire in the war.[44]

A month-long election campaign began on August 3. Ten tickets challenged Thieu and Ky. Tran Van Huong, a onetime Vietminh fighter and former mayor of Saigon under Diem and General Nguyen Khanh, seemed the strongest civilian candidate. His impeccable nationalist credentials and his leadership of the Buddhist movement in 1963 combined with his international reputation to make him appear a strong challenger, yet Huong never articulated a forceful position about what he would do in the war, and his candidacy never caught on with the public. Truong Dinh Dzu, a wealthy lawyer and former head of the Saigon Rotary Club, who once had close ties to the Ngo family but who had also plotted against Diem, eventually emerged as the principal threat to an easy victory for Thieu and Ky. Dzu ran as a peace candidate, calling for a brief, twenty-four-hour halt to the bombing against the North to test Hanoi's willingness to negotiate. Even more disturbing to the government was Dzu's acknowledgment that the National Liberation Front "does represent some people in the country and they control some villages." He promised to "invite them to a private conference and . . . ask them to present to us their reasonable proposals." He also advocated the revival of the Geneva conference to work out peace between the two Vietnams.[45]

As the campaign went forward, opposition candidates charged that the government prevented them from traveling throughout the country, tore down their signs, ripped out wires from amplifiers, and arrested people en route to campaign rallies. Critics of the war in the United States also condemned the government's handling of the election. Fifty-seven liberal House Democrats demanded that Johnson assure a fair election, encouraging him to warn the Saigon authorities that the United States would "undertake a serious reappraisal of its policies in Vietnam" if Thieu's forces continued to interfere with a fair election.[46] Allard Lowenstein, the liberal activist thoroughly disillusioned with the prospects of Johnson ever ending the war, organized an independent team of electoral investigators to go to South Vietnam.[47]

Facing a rising tide of complaint about the elections, American officials in Saigon and Washington conducted a spirited counterattack. Johnson sent a delegation to Vietnam to report on the fairness of the election. Three senators, three governors, two mayors, and various veterans, business leaders, clergymen, and reporters spent five days in Vietnam. They came back praising the overall achievement of having any election at all in the midst of a war, but they also raised questions about its fairness. Johnson made it clear to the observers that he only cared to hear positive comments about the elections. One editor complained that their meeting with the President was "a performance, not a report." When he mentioned that the government had barred several prominent peace candidates, Johnson "glared at [him] with obvious anger."[48]

When the ballots were counted Thieu and Ky achieved only 35 percent of the vote, far less than the 45 percent the U.S. embassy anticipated just a week before the voting. Dzu came in second with 17 percent. Thieu and Ky received a plurality of the votes in each of the four tactical zones of Vietnam, but they lost six provinces and came in second in the major cities of Saigon, Hué, and Da Nang. They ran strongest among government workers, soldiers, Catholics, and moderate Buddhists. Dzu's support came from militant Buddhists and the Cao Dai and Hoa Hao sects. Eight of the defeated candidates filed charges of fraud after the election, but their complaints were ignored. The opposition fought among themselves; some of the charges were directed at opponents of Thieu and Ky. The victors, who could not stand each other, also could not maintain the slightest appearance of unity. The Sunday after the election Thieu refused to appear on NBC's *Meet the Press* alongside Ky, his new vice president.

But none of this confusion and bad blood within the South Vietnamese government publicly fazed the Americans. Johnson praised the election as "a milestone along the path toward . . . a free, secure, and peaceful Vietnam."[49] Vice President Hubert Humphrey attended the inauguration of Thieu and Ky on October 31 and sent back a glowing report: "We are winning, steady progress is everywhere evident."[50]

A REEVALUATION IN WASHINGTON: NOVEMBER 1967–JANUARY 1968

Privately the view from Washington was much more somber. The South Vietnamese election made no impact on the relentless complaints inside the United States about the endless war. Enough South Vietnamese thought the election flawed that Thieu had difficulty consolidating his power. Humphrey told a friend after returning home, "America is throwing lives and money down a corrupt rat hole." He threatened to tell Johnson directly that "We're murdering civilians by the thousands and our boys are dying in rotten jungles—for what? A corrupt, selfish government that has no feeling—no morality." This was just so much brave talk. Like most people, Humphrey wilted in Johnson's massive presence. When given the chance to report on the elections, Humphrey told a meeting of congressional leaders with the President that he had come back "encouraged" from his trip to Saigon.[51]

With the disintegration of the Pennsylvania channel in late October 1967, Johnson sank into gloom, skeptical of the value of escalation but unwilling to stop the bombing to move negotiations forward. Morbid fatalism gripped the President for the next year as one after another of his close advisers changed their minds about the war. In the fall of 1967, Robert McNamara completely abandoned hope that the war could be won through bombing and escalation. He proposed a policy of "stabilization" in which "we will gradually transfer the major burden of the fighting to the South Vietnamese forces." He opposed further bombing of the dikes, locks, or population centers of the North and hoped to hold down civilian casualties. McNamara also recommended a complete bombing halt, which he predicted would lead to talks with Hanoi. "At a minimum," he wrote, "we would have made clear that our bombing is not preventing a peaceful political settlement."[52]

National Security Adviser Walt Rostow, Dean Rusk, Maxwell Taylor, and Abe Fortas all rejected McNamara's advice for a complete bombing halt. They expressed more support for his suggestion to stabilize the war and turn more of the fighting over to the South Vietnamese.[53] Having lost the President's confidence, McNamara wanted to leave the administration. In November Johnson accepted McNamara's resignation as Secretary of Defense and announced that the following February longtime Democratic Party adviser Clark Clifford would replace him. After the announcement of McNamara's departure, the President's remaining advisers temporarily became more militant. Clifford himself changed his initial position resisting involvement in the war to advocating continued bombing. He expressed doubts about the North's commitment to negotiate through private intermediaries. "I do not think they will use *this type of channel* when they are serious about really doing something." He believed that a bombing halt would invariably fail to yield negotiations and that the United States would increase its troop levels in the aftermath.[54]

In early November Johnson convened a group of about sixteen senior foreign policy advisers, the so-called Wise Men who had met in July 1965 to offer support for his escalation of the war. He wanted their opinions regarding what changes the United States should make in waging the war and what could be done to shore up public and congressional support for it. McGeorge Bundy, William Bundy, Dean Rusk, Walt Rostow, and Maxwell Taylor agreed that Johnson could not satisfy his domestic critics with a bombing halt. McGeorge Bundy wrote Johnson that "I think your policy is as right as ever and that the weight of the evidence from the field is encouraging." He thought that "we are in for a long, slow business in which we cannot expect decisive results soon." He also opposed an unconditional bombing pause on the grounds that he expected the United States would have to resume bombing after the North refused to limit its infiltration into the South. Such a resumption would prove "very damaging" to a public desperate for peace.[55]

When the Wise Men convened on November 1–2, they all sympathized with the President's burdens. Frustrated by congressional oversight, Johnson complained he was "like the steering wheel of a car without any control." Dean Acheson, who remembered the way Congress had brutalized Harry Truman, commiserated with the President: "The cross you have to bear is a lousy Senate Foreign Relations Committee. You have a dilettante Fool [J. William Fulbright] at the head of the Committee."[56] The Wise Men unanimously opposed a withdrawal from South Vietnam "without a satisfactory settlement with the North." They divided more on a public relations strategy to bolster fading support for the war at home. Some participants suggested reaching out more to television anchors, educators, and Congress. They wanted to disseminate widely an optimistic assessment of the war that CIA analyst George Carver gave to the group of Wise Men on November 1. McGeorge Bundy thought these views hysterical and advised staying calm as the best policy. He believed that public support ebbed because of deaths on the battlefield "with no picture of a result in sight." He predicted that if the administration could persuade people that "we are seeing results and the end of the road," support would revive.[57] Johnson agreed about the need to lower public anxiety, but he seemed almost muscle-bound with ambivalence. "We'll do all we can to win the war," he told another group of senior advisers as they considered the merits of sending U.S. troops across the border into Cambodia.[58]

Johnson hoped than an optimistic assessment of the war from the battle-field commander might reduce public dissatisfaction. In late November General Westmoreland returned to Washington. Upon his arrival he told reporters that "I have never been more encouraged in my four years in Vietnam."[59] The President complained about the negative press stories on congressional disillusionment with the war when he met Westmoreland. No wonder the public mood had turned so sour, Johnson said; "we need to get them more information of a factual nature."[60] Westmoreland told Congress that the North Vietnamese and Vietcong could not resist much longer and he hoped the American part of the war effort could end within two years. Ambassador Bunker confirmed this optimistic assessment to the Senate Committee on Foreign Relations. He could not predict when the war would end but he assured the senators that "we are going to win." Like Henry Cabot Lodge, his predecessor, he believed that the war would end with the Communists simply fading away.[61]

At the end of 1967, the State Department, the military command in Vietnam, and the CIA weighed in with their individual assessments of the prospects for the next year. The State Department and the military believed things would look better in a year. They agreed however, that "there will not have been a decisive and undeniable breakthrough . . . the enemy will still be very much with us . . . and it will remain difficult to produce dramatic and convincing evidence of a victory in the near future." The military had a more elaborate plan for the next year. Westmoreland's staff wanted to keep the NLF and the North Vietnamese constantly on the move to deny them the opportunity to refit, rest, or resupply. They expected to bomb the North more heavily to diminish the North Vietnamese supplies and force them to concentrate more on events at home. The military thought that these operations would result in "increased casualties, desertions, sickness and lowered morale."[62] The CIA had a far less rosy outlook. They noted that the communists had been able to adapt their tactics to the increased U.S. pressure. The NLF and North Vietnamese armed forces remained effective enough to "tie down U.S. forces on widely scattered fronts and to deny the degree of provincial security essential to the pacification program." Even more ominously, the CIA analysts understood perfectly the North Vietnamese conception of pro-tracted war. The analysts noted that Hanoi harbored no illusions about winning a Western-style victory over the Americans. Instead, they were willing to accept the high costs of American air attacks in the belief that they could hold out longer than the Americans or the South Vietnamese.[63]

1968

All planning for the future changed abruptly on January 30, 1968. At 2:45 that morning, during Tet, the Vietnamese New Year, a squad of nineteen Vietcong commandos blasted their way through the wall surrounding the U.S. embassy in Saigon. A young U.S. Army Spec. 4 fired at the invaders and shouted into his radio, "They're coming in! They're coming in! Help me! Help me!" He then was shot dead.[64]

It was mid-afternoon in Washington when the attack occurred. Johnson was meeting with his senior foreign policy advisers to discuss another crisis in Asia—North Korea had seized the U.S.S. *Pueblo* and imprisoned the crew. Suddenly Rostow burst into the meeting to report that "we are being heavily mortared in Saigon. The presidential Palace, our BOQ's, the embassy and the city itself have been hit." Johnson immediately grasped how devastating the attack could be on public confidence. "This could be very bad," he said. Whatever progress had been made in the past three years could vanish. "This looks like where we came in," he said as he reflected on the attack on the Marine barracks at Pleiku that had led to the Rolling Thunder bombing of North Vietnam in early 1965.[65]

The attack on the embassy came as part of a coordinated Vietcong–North Vietnamese offensive of sixty-seven thousand veteran troops plus an additional seventeen thousand recently impressed men and boys against the population centers of South Vietnam during the Tet truce. NLF and North Vietnamese units fought the Americans and ARVN for control of forty-four provincial capitals, five of six major cities, and sixty-four district capitals. The most intense fighting lasted about two weeks, and in most areas the Americans and South Vietnamese repulsed the attackers. The fighting lasted longest at the old imperial capital of Hué. Vietcong troops captured Hué and held it for more than three weeks. For the first ten days the U.S. commanders gathered reinforcements to retake the city. During that time the pro-government citizens of Hué lived in terror. After raising the NLF banner over the ancient citadel in the center of town, the revolutionaries released all of the inmates of the city jail, many of whom had been held for secretly helping the Vietcong. The victors also went on a rampage of vengeance, gunning down more than two thousand civic leaders, policemen, and ordinary citizens whose neighbors turned them over to the revolutionaries. When the American marines and ARVN forces finally retook the city on February 23, they found a moonscape of charred remains of wooden buildings, rotting corpses, and starving abandoned animals.[66]

Casualties on the communist side were enormous, as many as forty thousand dead, while the ARVN and Americans lost about thirty-four hundred men. The U.S. forces and the ARVN captured about three thousand men and disabled another five thousand through wounds. All told, the communist side lost about one fifth of its total forces, and its effective strength was reduced by a third. The South Vietnamese armed forces were not badly hurt physically; the U.S. military estimated that it would take them approximately six months to recover fully.[67] "Their problems are more psychological than physical," Westmoreland estimated.[68] The Tet Offensive took an enormous toll on the civilian population, with as many as one million refugees swelling already-teeming camps.

General Vo Nguyen Giap planned the simultaneous attacks as a reprise of the defeat of the French at Dienbienphu in 1954, one which he hoped would lead to the collapse of the American will to continue in Vietnam. He also hoped that the South Vietnamese population would turn against its government and overthrow them, believing the claims of the North that the regime was nothing but a puppet of the Americans.[69] In late 1967 North Vietnamese leaders had grown concerned that the United States had made progress in its efforts to pacify densely populated areas of the South.[70] At the same time the Northern armed forces engaged in fewer battles with the Americans and their South Vietnamese allies "in order to mislead the Government of Vietnam and its allies" into a false sense that they were winning the war. In reality, the North moved a vast amount of men an equipment into the South. The North and the nlf expected that the United States would augment its forces throughout South Vietnam in 1968, in anticipation of a climactic battle before the presidential election. For their part, the cia concluded that the "Viet Cong also planned to put the greatest pressure on the U.S. during 1968, the year of the U.S. presidential elections."[71]

Ten days before Tet, Giap created a diversion with persistent shelling of Khe Sanh, a marine base in the northwestern corner of South Vietnam. Every night in the days before the Tet Offensive, reports on the evening news in the United States showed the faces of marines, battle-hardened far beyond their tender years, as they ran for cover beneath the hail of shells. Yet unlike the siege of Dienbienphu, planes could land supplies at Khe Sanh, except during periods of bad weather when they parachuted bundles into the camp. Back home viewers heard soldiers bravely promise never to give up the garrison and saw them run to help wounded buddies or unload supplies planes. The U.S. air force and navy pounded the thirty-five thousand North Vietnamese soldiers attacking Khe Sanh with round-the-clock air raids. Giant B-52 bombers flew over 2,500 miles from Guam, and hundreds of fighter bombers took off from bases in South Vietnam, Thailand, and aircraft carriers. The planes dropped tons of defoliants and the green jungle surrounding Khe Sanh soon became a desert.[72]

U.S. journalists, commanders in Saigon, the White House staff, and the President himself saw eerie parallels between Khe Sanh and Dienbienphu. Both were in the northwestern area of the war zone near the Laotian border. Like the French before them, the Americans had established their base partly to block the flow of supplies. But unlike the battle for Dienbienphu, Giap never intended to overrun Khe Sanh. He hoped to keep the Americans distracted from the buildup of forces for the Tet Offensive. He later explained that "Khe Sanh was not that important to us. Or it was only to the extent that it was to the Americans." The Americans completely misjudged Giap's intentions at Khe Sanh. They considered it a success that despite the North's assaults during Tet "they were not able to bring about the diversion of major U.S. forces from Khe Sanh."[73] In the aftermath of the Tet Offensive, Giap withdrew the bulk of his forces from the area surrounding Khe Sanh. On April 15 a relief column opened the road to Khe Sanh. The marines remained for three more months, but in early June they abandoned the bases. They called in bulldozers to obliterate any signs of the encampment so the North Vietnamese could not create a monument to victory at the spot.[74]

The U.S. military command in Vietnam called Tet "a very near thing." The initial attack nearly succeeded in a dozen places, and only the quick reinforcement by U.S. soldiers saved the day.[75] Nevertheless, General Westmoreland declared the results of Tet a major defeat for the North and the NLF. He told Johnson that "the enemy decided to abandon his attrition strategy and go for broke" and he "failed in his maximum objective."[76] Chairman of the Joint Chiefs Wheeler also returned from a quick inspection tour of Vietnam after Tet to report that the attackers had failed to achieve their three objectives of a general rising, forcing the collapse of the ARVN, and holding territory.[77] The Vietcong forces were especially hard hit and it would take them years to recover. One NLF colonel recalled that "the Tet objectives were beyond our strength. . . . Our losses were large, in material and manpower, and we were not able to retain the gains we had already made. Instead we had to overcome myriad difficulties in 1969 and 1970."[78]

A more important loss was suffered, however, at home, where televised scenes of the grisly fighting turned public opinion against continuing the war in the same direction. On February 3 General Nguyen Ngoc Loan, the Director of the National Police and a close friend and adviser to Vice President Nguyen Cao Ky, took custody of a high-ranking Vietcong fighter who had killed some Saigon civilians, many of them relatives of police in the capital. Loan grabbed the man by the arm, pulled out his revolver, and shot him in the head. An AP photographer snapped a still picture, which became one of the most famous photographs of the Vietnam War. A television camera operator also captured the horrific event, which was seem by twenty million American viewers of the NBC Evening News on February 3. Every night Americans recoiled from equally mad scenes on the evening newscast. At one point a marine colonel told an reporter surveying the damage of a town in the central highlands relieved by the Americans that "we had to destroy the village to save it." Another time, CBS news anchor Walter Cronkite, often regarded as the most trustworthy public figure in the country and a long time supporter of the U.S. war effort, dramatically changed his mind on television. "What the hell's going on here," he exploded in the early days of the Tet Offensive. "I thought we were winning this war." Congressman Henry Reuss (D., Wis.) expressed the shock many people felt watching the brutality in the streets of South Vietnam. None of the horrible acts committed by the Vietcong or the North Vietnamese army, Reuss said, could "justify or excuse actions by the United States or allied forces which sink to this level. Murder or torture of prisoners is horrible and un-American."[79]

An even worse massacre took place on March 16. At 8 o'clock that morning troops of Charlie Company of the Americal Division dropped from helicopters into the hamlet of My Lai in the village of Song My. The area was in Quang Ngai Province, near the coast north of Da Nang, and it had long been a center of Vietcong. The soldiers, led by twenty-four-year-old William Calley, were frightened and angry. One GI recalled that the company "had revenge on its mind" for losses suffered during Tet. They called the town Pinkville, certain that the villagers harbored Vietcong fighters. Most of them, however, melted into the countryside as soon as the Americans approached. Instead of finding guerrillas, Calley's troops discovered only old men, women, and children. Almost immediately the Americans rounded up the Vietnamese for interrogation. When they refused to talk, the Americans went on a rampage. Soldiers threw an old man down a well, bayoneted others, and shot children and women running down the road. Then Calley ordered them to push hundreds into a ditch and start firing. When it was over by 11:00 A.M., more than five hundred Vietnamese civilians lay dead. The next day the command in Saigon said that "sporadic contact" between U.S. forces and Vietcong fighters had occurred at My Lai on March 16. The army covered up what happened, and news of the extent of the atrocities committed by the Americans at My Lai remained hidden from public view for the next eighteen months.[80]

In 1968 the initial reports of the North Vietnamese successes were greatly exaggerated, yet journalists who had grown disgusted with the optimistic assessments from Westmoreland's staff refused to believe that Tet represented a defeat for the revolutionary forces. *Time, Newsweek,* and *U.S. News* all characterized the Tet offensive as a major psychological blow for the United States. Herblock, the *Washington Post*'s editorial cartoonist, portrayed the U.S. commanders happily cranking out reports of battlefield victories blissfully unaware of the Vietcong shells exploding in their offices. "Everything's okay," says one, "they never reached the mimeograph machine."[81] The *New York Times,* long critical of the Johnson administration's handling of the war, claimed that Tet revealed "the weakness of the political structure on which the American military effort is based."[82]

Later critics of the press's behavior during Tet claimed that excessively negative coverage of Tet colored the public's perception of the war. That view is hard to sustain, however. The public's reaction to Tet occurred in the context of the dashed hopes for victory before the end of 1968. Even Johnson acknowledged that his own representatives had raised hopes too high at the end of 1967. He railed against onetime congressional supporters of the war who changed their minds during Tet and charged that "we had the people believing we were doing very well in Vietnam when we actually were not." Rostow, Johnson's most hawkish adviser, acknowledged that public opinion followed the situation on the battlefield: "If the war goes well, the American people are with us. If the war goes badly they are against us." He found little solace in the U.S. press. Only the lead article on Tet in the London-based *Economist* cheered him up. Long a supporter of the American war effort, the *Economist* believed that the "big push" at Tet and Khe Sanh "is intended to hustle Mr. Johnson into accepting the sort of negotiations that will eventually leave South Vietnam to the communists; or, if Mr. Johnson won't, to frighten the Americans into electing someone who will."[83]

From North Vietnam to New Hampshire the Tet Offensive signaled a turning point in the war. General Giap recalled that while Tet did not trigger an immediate rising of the population against the Saigon government, it vindicated the strategy of protracted war. He claimed that "our biggest victory was to change the ideas of the United States." Before early 1968 the primary aim of the United States, he claimed, been "to find and kill: it was replaced by a new strategy of defense." He noticed that "until Tet they had thought they could win the war, but now they knew they could not."[84] After Tet 78 percent of the American public told opinion pollsters that they did not think the United States was making progress in the war. A small minority of 26 percent approved of Johnson's handling of the war. In New Hampshire pollsters detected signs of life in what had appeared to be a quixotic campaign by Minnesota Senator Eugene McCarthy to challenge Johnson in that state's presidential primary.[85]

THE DECISION TO DE-ESCALATE

Johnson asked Clark Clifford to take a hard look at Vietnam policies before officially taking over as Secretary of Defense in late February. Specifically, he wanted Clifford's advice on Westmoreland's request for an additional 206,000 troops. The discussions became more urgent in early March when Neil Sheehan, the Pentagon reporter for the *New York Times,* broke the story that Westmoreland had requested that many additional soldiers.[86] A debate ensued among Clifford's military and political advisers. Most of them agreed that things could not continue as before.

Unless there was assurance that the additional troops would bring victory soon, the public would not stand for more escalation. Former ambassadors to Vietnam Maxwell Taylor and Henry Cabot Lodge favored using U.S. troops already in Vietnam differently than the way in which Westmoreland had deployed them in the past. Lodge reckoned that public patience approached the breaking point in Vietnam. Concluding that search-and-destroy tactics had caused too many U.S. casualties, he argued that public opinion could stand a long drawn out war with few casualties or a short war with high casualties. "But American public opinion cannot stand a *long drawn out war* with *high* casualties." Unlike World War II, Lodge argued, "it is not possible to win the war by killing the enemy *by military means on the ground* in South Vietnam." Guerrilla warfare would continue. He recommended a shift away from search-and-destroy to "split up the enemy and keep him off balance." The U.S. military would then act as a shield behind which Vietnamese nation-building and pacification operations took place.[87] For his part, Maxwell Taylor thought that the United States might use bombing more effectively to signal the North that the United States was ready to talk.[88]

Most of Clifford's civilian advisers within the Defense Department, veterans of McNamara's re-evaluation of the bombing campaign in 1966 and 1967, counseled against sending additional soldiers to Vietnam. Air Force Secretary Harold Brown advocated intensifying the air war over the North to include the mining of the harbor of Haiphong, and suggested substituting bombing of the South for more ground forces.[89] Assistant Secretary of Defense Paul Warnke, a close personal friend of Clifford, advocated pressuring the South Vietnamese government to accept speedy negotiations with the North. He doubted that a quick military victory in Vietnam would occur. Like Lodge, he believed the public could tolerate the continuing presence of a significant American force in Vietnam only if casualties declined. He advised continuing the long process of nation-building. To do so, he told Clifford, "we have to scale down military activities to the point where our costs, particularly their human costs, are at a level that the American people will be willing to sustain for the long haul." Instead of sending 206,000 more troops to Vietnam, he advocated announcing soon "our intention to withdraw some 50,000 troops as early as September." Undersecretary of the Air Force Townsend Hoopes was blunter, deriding the idea of a military victory in Vietnam as a "dangerous illusion."[90]

Only the Joint Chiefs of Staff supported Westmoreland's call for more troops. Chairman Earle Wheeler argued that maintaining the current force levels would leave the initiative to the NLF and the North. Wheeler believed that withdrawing U.S. forces to protected enclaves near the population centers would make matters worse in the countryside and eventually leave the cities exposed. He predicted that "the enemy could mass large forces anywhere in the mountain and jungle hinterland and strike deeply, with force and surprise, into the population areas." Westmoreland needed the additional troops because the U.S. commander "has been stripped of his reserves." Wheeler also misread completely Giap's ideas regarding the siege of Khe Sanh. He thought it "better to have the two divisions which surround Khe Sanh back in the mountains than in the city of Hué."[91] Giap would have been delighted to have read this assessment in March 1968, for that was precisely his aim in creating the diversion at Khe Sanh.

In the end, Clifford sided with his civilian advisers' recommendations to de-escalate the U.S. role in Vietnam. He had trusted these men for years. Their advice to de-escalate was similar to the ideas McNamara had developed with his principal civilian aides in 1967.[92] Clifford himself had expressed a few doubts about the effectiveness of escalation since 1965. He had voiced quiet misgivings in July 1965 on the grounds that the initial deployment of ground forces could not assure victory, and had then shelved public criticism of Johnson's actions in Vietnam.[93] When Johnson appointed him Secretary of Defense in late 1967, the President believed he had selected one of his most loyal backers of the war.[94]

After completing his review, Clifford concluded that Westmoreland could not guarantee victory with the additional soldiers, but only postpone a communist triumph. It reminded him of the discussions of July 1965. This time, though, he reverted to his earlier skepticism and advised the President not to endorse sending more soldiers to Vietnam. Instead, he pressed for negotiations initiated by a bombing halt. Clifford told Johnson that the request for 206,000 additional troops represented a decisive turning point in the war. Approval of the request meant continuing down the road of "more troops, more guns, more planes, more ships . . . without accomplishing our purpose." The United States had done "enormous damage" to the "country we are trying to save." Clifford voiced one of Johnson's greatest fears: if the President approved Westmoreland's latest request for troops, the General would come back in another month with a request for "another 200,000 or 300,000 with no end in sight."[95]

Johnson remained as torn as ever. At one of his regular Tuesday lunches with his senior foreign policy advisers, he alternated between telling the South Vietnamese "we will do no more until they do more" and calling up one hundred thousand reserves.[96] Seeking guidance and reassurance, the President convened another series of high level meetings in March to discuss options. Clifford presented the case for de-escalation while Rostow and Rusk counseled militancy. The National Security Adviser argued most vociferously for new and accelerated offensives by Westmoreland. An astonishingly strong showing by Senator McCarthy in the New Hampshire primary and Robert Kennedy's entry into the presidential race a few days later raised the stakes even higher. McCarthy favored a bombing halt and the opening of negotiations with Hanoi. Kennedy would go even farther, wresting control of Vietnam policy from Johnson with the creation of an independent commission to recommend future U.S. actions.[97] Rostow claimed to see a connection between Democratic Party challenges to Johnson and North Vietnamese troop movements. The reports of North Vietnamese pullbacks from the area surrounding Khe Sanh prompted him snidely to wonder if the communists leaders of the North had decided "to let McCarthy and Bobby Kennedy win the war for them."[98]

During the last week in March Johnson assembled the Wise Men for advice on the next move in Vietnam. He set them an impossible task: Create both movement toward negotiations with Hanoi and continuing U.S. offensive operations. He expected them to ratify whatever course he chose, just as they had done since 1965. He told them that there had been a "panic" in the country since the *New York Times* published news of Westmoreland's request for an additional 206,000 troops. He estimated the cost of such an additional deployment at $15 billion, which would affect the position of the dollar and the British pound. Already France demanded payment for its dollars in gold, costing the U.S. about $1 billion of its reserves. Johnson seemed nearly to weep as he told his advisers about Kennedy's plan to convene a commission of notables to decide future Vietnam policy. "I will have overwhelming disapproval in the polls and the election. I will go down the drain. I don't want the whole alliance and the military pulled down with it."[99]

Despite Johnson's expectations that the Wise Men would do what they always did (sympathize with his burdens and eventually ratify his choices), they reversed their earlier support for a militant course and urged the President to seek a negotiated settlement. They reasoned that the public had had its fill of war. Dean Acheson, usually one of the most militant of the Wise Men, reflected on his own agony during the Korean War and regretfully explained that the United States "could no longer do the job we set out to do in the time we have left and we must take steps to disengage."[100]

Johnson seemed bereft, surprised, and hurt by the desertion of trusted counselors who had been among the most forceful advocates of continuing the U.S. role in Vietnam. "Everybody is recommending surrender," he complained on March 28.[101] Similar gloom descended on Rostow as he surveyed the President's dismal political fortunes. "About the only thing we've got," he concluded, "is that the North Vietnamese *do* mount a big offensive." Then "the 101st [airborne division], the airmobile [cavalry] and the marines clobber them between now and May 15." With such a dramatic reversal of fortune Johnson could be "just like Lincoln in 1864."[102]

Johnson was no Lincoln, history did not repeat itself, and on March 31 the President capitulated. In a nationally broadcast speech that evening, he announced a partial bombing halt that would stop the U.S. attacks everywhere over North Vietnam with the exception of the immediate vicinity of the Demilitarized Zone. He sent Averell Harriman as a representative to explore prospects for opening negotiations with the North Vietnamese and NLF. Finally, he promised to devote himself to peace for the remainder of the year. Accordingly, "I shall not seek, nor will I accept the nomination of my party for another term as your president." Almost none of his senior advisers knew that he intended to leave at term's end, although he had said as much to Westmoreland when the commander visited Washington in the fall of 1967.[103]

OPENING PEACE TALKS

U.S. policy toward Vietnam in the remaining nine-and-one-half months of the Johnson administration recapitulated the tragic and farcical elements of the previous four-and-one-half years. Johnson continued to vacillate between hastening negotiations and increasing military pressure. His principal advisers disagreed more openly than ever before about whether to bomb the North more heavily or move more quickly toward negotiations. Their divisions caused policy to lurch back and forth more suddenly after Johnson announced he would not seek re-election. With the sharp diminution in his political power, public attention focused on the competition among Eugene McCarthy, Robert Kennedy, and Vice President Hubert Humphrey on the Democratic side and Richard Nixon and Nelson Rockefeller on the Republican side to elect his successor.

The President became a maudlin and forlorn figure shortly after his surprising announcement, and expressed second thoughts almost from the day he proclaimed the partial bombing halt and the appointment of Harriman. He complained that the first calls he received after his speech came from the wife of Senator McCarthy and Senators Edward Kennedy, Ernest Greuning, and George McGovern, all prominent dissenters from his policies in Vietnam. "I knew something was wrong," he told his senior advisers, "when all of them approved."[104] He met Robert Kennedy in the White House on the morning of April 3 to tell him that the "the situation confronted by the nation [was] the most serious he had seen in the course of his life." He "would do his very best to get peace," but "he was not optimistic." He assured Kennedy that he did not "hate him or dislike him" and that he would not play a major role in the upcoming presidential campaign.[105]

After a few weeks of discussion about where to hold preliminary conversations, Harriman and Cyrus Vance, his deputy, went to Paris in May to begin a frustrating six month exercise in opening substantive conversations with the North. Clifford and Harriman (the latter thinking that arranging peace in Vietnam would cap a distinguished career) wanted to go much farther than

Johnson's other aides in satisfying Hanoi's conditions. Harriman approached the negotiations with a view toward the forthcoming presidential election. His first priority was "not permitting [the continuation of the war] to elect Nixon as president."[106] Johnson, on the other hand, hardly cared who succeeded him. Humphrey's efforts to re-establish his old ties to the liberal wing of the Democratic party disappointed the President. Johnson came to believe that Nixon would be as good—or bad—as Humphrey, and he did not want to tip the balance to either. Feeling rejected yet indispensable, he ordered the peace delegation to "put aside all questions of domestic politics and keep out of them."[107]

Meanwhile, the American negotiators in Paris ran into suspicions from the North that the United States wanted to increase the bombing and fears from the South that Washington intended to exclude Saigon from the conversations. Harriman and Vance energetically tried to overcome communist objection to recognition of the legitimacy of the government of South Vietnam with plans for negotiations on the basis of "your side [the North and the NLF], our side [the South Vietnamese government and the United States]." The South tentatively accepted this formula in July, "so long as the Government of Vietnam played the major role in 'our' side."[108]

Saigon's reservations all but negated any progress Harriman and Vance made with the North Vietnamese, yet Harriman pressed Johnson to make concessions to Hanoi. In late July Harriman urged Johnson to stop all bombing of the North in response to the communists' apparent reduction in activity in the South. Vice President Humphrey, assured of the Democratic nomination after the murder of Robert Kennedy on June 6, concurred. According to Harriman, Johnson "went through the roof" when he learned that Humphrey endorsed a bombing halt.[109]

Disgusted with Humphrey, Harriman, and Democratic congressional critics of the war, the President thought that the Republicans had been "a lot more help to us than the Democrats in the last few months."[110] Johnson discussed Vietnam with Nixon in late July after the Republican Party nominated Nixon for President. The President did not trust the North Vietnamese, whom he thought were using the bombing halt to resupply their forces. He pointed out that the United States had previously had five or six bombing halts without a breakthrough in negotiations. The current pause lifted the bombing against 78 percent of the land and 90 percent of the people. What more did the North want, he wondered? Nixon seemed supportive, telling Johnson he had taken the right position against a complete halt and implying that he actually sided more with Johnson than with his own foreign policy advisers who "want to stop bombing." Nixon urged resisting such calls, because holding out the possibility of a complete bombing halt remained "the only piece of leverage you have left." Johnson loved to hear Nixon say, "You can only have one President'' at a time.[111] The President seemed so impressed with Nixon that Harriman and Clifford thought he wanted to see Humphrey defeated in the fall.[112] Their fears carried weight, but in fact Johnson was not eager to see Nixon succeed him—he doubted whether either Nixon or Humphrey was up to the job.

Johnson's militant advisers all opposed Harriman's call for a total halt to the bombing. Johnson himself thought that the ''Communists have a movement underway to get me to stop the bombing.'' Wheeler worried about another communist offensive if the bombing were completely stopped. He estimated that 30 percent more troops and supplies would get through once the bombing stopped. CIA Director Richard Helms warned against complacency because of a temporary lull in the fighting. He believed that the North needed time to resupply its badly decimated units in the South. He thought the war was at its ''tensest point'' and a new, even more ferocious ''attack could come at any time.''[113] Bunker, Rostow, and Rusk all opposed declaring a total bombing halt for fear of provoking a collapse in Saigon. Rostow predicted that ''any reduction of our bombing effort enables [the enemy] to increase the weight of his effort against us in the field.''[114] Johnson instructed Rusk to hold a press conference at which the Secretary of State condemned the communists for intransigence.

The spilt among his advisers, Johnson's continuing ambivalence and shocking events in Czechoslovakia and Chicago overshadowed the Paris negotiations in August. Soviet tanks rolled into Prague on August 21 to overthrow the liberal reform government of Alexander Dubcek. Harriman perceived a connection between Johnson's dithering over a total bombing halt and the invasion of Czechoslovakia. Keen to arrange a deal with the North, the Paris negotiator believed that the President's refusal to halt the bombing at the end of July represented ''a historic tragedy.'' It made ''Johnson look rigid regarding Vietnam,'' and may have convinced some fence-sitting Kremlin leaders that they had nothing to lose by going after Dubcek.[115]

THE ELECTION OF 1968

A week later the Democratic party nominated Hubert Humphrey for the presidency in a tumultuous convention in Chicago. Johnson refused Humphrey's entreaties to compromise with anti-war Democrats over a platform plank on Vietnam. He considered a compromise a personal rejection, and his militant advisers forecast another ''third wave'' of attacks from the North. CIA Director Helms thought the new wave ''will probably come out like measles'' in the last two weeks of August.''[116] The convention narrowly endorsed the administration's handling of the war. On the same night Humphrey was nominated the Chicago police force lost control, beating and tear-gassing a crowd of some ten thousand demonstrators who had come to the city to protest administration policy on Vietnam.[117]

Humphrey left Chicago badly trailing Nixon in public opinion surveys. The Republican nominee fed the widespread suspicion that Johnson had mishandled the war. Nixon had advocated escalation in the early days and now condemned the Johnson administration for stalemate. He refused to offer specific recommendations to break the impasse, because he claimed that to do so would interfere with the ongoing negotiations, yet he did reply affirmatively to a reporter's question asking if he had a plan to end the war.[118]

Humphrey remained loyal to Johnson's policy throughout September, while requesting permission to take a more independent position. None was forthcoming. Even as Humphrey sought Johnson's approval for advocating a complete bombing halt, the President heard voices urging an end to restrictions on bombing he had imposed on March 31. The Senate Committee on Armed Services was in a surly mood. Chairman John Stennis of Mississippi wanted to bomb and mine the port of Haiphong. Democratic Senator Richard Russell, once one of Johnson's closest friends in the Senate but now an adversary, seemed accurately to reflect the President's own ambivalence. "How do we get out of the predicament in Vietnam?" he asked. Russell could not decide between more bombing and the quest for a military victory or a complete halt and placing greater emphasis on the negotiations at Paris. Although his friendship with Russell was broken, Johnson respected his views. Like Russell, Johnson did not know what to do next, and he could give Humphrey no useful guidance.[119]

Finally unable to wait any longer for Johnson's permission if he were to have chance in the election, Humphrey separated himself from current policy at a speech in Salt Lake City on September 30. He endorsed a total bombing halt "as an acceptable risk for peace, because I believe that it could lead to a success in negotiations and a shorter war." In preparing his speech Humphrey relied on the advice of George Ball, who left his position as U.S. representative to the United Nations to serve as foreign affairs adviser to the Vice President's campaign. Ball told Clifford and Rusk that he could not "live with himself if he didn't work to defeat Nixon." But Johnson and Rusk considered Ball's resignation a slap in the face. Johnson snorted that Ball's support of Humphrey represented a movement on the Vice President's part toward the "dove side." Even Clifford, who favored a complete bombing halt, thought that Humphrey's speech was a "desperation move."[120]

Despite Johnson's irritation, Humphrey's presidential campaign gained momentum after his Salt Lake City speech. The tempo of negotiations in Paris picked up as well. In mid-October, Harriman and Vance reached what they considered to be a breakthrough with Xuan Thuy of North Vietnam. The United States promised to halt all bombing over the North, while the communists satisfied the Americans that they would not take advantage of a bombing halt to reinforce their forces in the South. The "our side, your side" formula seemed a basis for seating the delegates. In this way the North would give tacit recognition to the government of the South while the United States would extend the same sort of acknowledgment to the NLF. The North Vietnamese mocked the Americans for deferring to the South's concerns. "Usually the man leads the horse," complained the North's Le Duc Tho. "This time the horse is leading the man."[121]

Once more, however, the White House did not want to go as far as Harriman proposed. Johnson would "rather not stop the bombing" until the communist representatives actually arrived in Paris. "It could badly hurt us," he said, if they had a week in which to resupply their forces in the South.[122] The White House ordered Harriman and Vance to insist on negotiations opening no more than twenty-four hours after the bombing halt.

Harriman and Vance dutifully reported Washington's conditions, and negotiations continued. In Washington, Johnson found it as hard to choose as ever between negotiations and renewed military actions. He told his top advisers, "I won't continue fighting if there is any reasonable prospect of getting terms. But I am not as optimistic as my colleagues" who believed peace was guaranteed if he ordered a bombing halt. Johnson gained assurances from the Joint Chiefs that they could handle a bombing pause. Chairman Wheeler explained that the United States could easily restart bombing if the North began another offensive. He said that the other Chiefs would not oppose a bombing pause. Unlike the thirty-seven-day pause of December 1965–January 1966, undertaken on the basis of "pious hope," the current bombing halt was based on real assurances from the North.[123]

Rumors that Johnson was on the verge of announcing a bombing halt sent the Nixon campaign into a panic. Anna Chennault, representing the Nixon campaign, informed the South Vietnamese ambassador to the United States of the White House's plans to start negotiations before Election Day. Chennault suggested that South Vietnam's President Thieu should refuse to participate in the talks before the election, since a Nixon administration would show more sympathy for South Vietnam than would a government led by Humphrey.[124]

In the final days of October, three complex and interrelated sets of conversations went on simultaneously on three continents. In Paris Harriman negotiated with the North Vietnamese. In Saigon Thieu pondered ways to prevent the United States from stopping the bombing, refusing to attend a peace conference without explicit recognition of the South. In Washington Johnson met at 2:30 A.M. on October 29 with his foreign policy advisers to discuss the announcement of a bombing halt. Harriman reported that the North would agree to meet on November 2 if the bombing stopped on October 30. Johnson and his advisers received word that Nixon was trying to prevent a bombing halt before the election. Undersecretary of State Eugene Rostow wrote his brother Walt that Nixon wanted matters to get worse in Vietnam. An informant in the Republican campaign told Eugene Rostow that "these difficulties would make it easier for Nixon to settle after January. Like Ike in 1953, he would be able to settle on terms which the President could not accept, blaming the deterioration of the situation between now and January or February on his predecessor."[125]

Here was Johnson's chance to swing the election to Humphrey, and for a moment the President contemplated publicizing the connection between Thieu and Nixon. It "would rock the world if it were said he [Thieu] were conniving with the Republicans." But Johnson's heart was not in the Humphrey campaign. Unwilling to give his Vice President an edge, Johnson ultimately decided not to make an issue of Nixon's dealings with the South. Clark Clifford later claimed that Johnson actually wanted Nixon to win, even if he would not acknowledge the wish. More likely, the angry, isolated, and defeated Johnson simply did not care to choose between Nixon, a longtime untrustworthy political rival, and Humphrey, a Vice President he believed had betrayed him.[126] Johnson might have gone forward anyway with an early announcement of a bombing halt, a move bound to help Humphrey, but Ambassador Bunker's support of Thieu's refusal to go to Paris on November 2 forced Johnson to agree to delay his statement. He also dropped his insistence that the peace talks begin immediately after the bombing halt.

Johnson's mind simply was not on the upcoming presidential election. He did not think it was "of world shaking importance" whether the talks occurred before or after November 5, Election Day. Not that he had great faith in a Nixon presidency. "Nixon will doublecross them after November 5," he predicted to his senior advisers.[127] In Paris, Harriman relayed word from the White House to the North Vietnamese that the United States wanted negotiations to begin within four days after the proclamation of a bombing halt. On October 31 Johnson announced the bombing halt and the commencement of negotiations on Wednesday after Election Day. Humphrey's campaign took off in the public opinion polls, but the momentum slowed on Sunday when Thieu once more said that South Vietnam would not participate. On Election Day he lost the election to Nixon by a scant 510,000 votes, and Saigon agreed to come to Paris. Senator Charles Percy (R., Ill.) told Harriman that Nixon was certain Humphrey would have won the election had the bombing halt and the negotiations been announced three days earlier than they had been.

By the end of 1968 most Americans wanted relief from the endless war in Vietnam, although they disagreed on the methods for doing so. The war had exacted a terrible cost on the terrain, the people, and the society of Vietnam. Hundreds of thousands were dead and as many as two million were homeless. Successive governments of South Vietnam had proved corrupt and incapable of defending their citizens against the communists without massive American

intervention. Officials' persistently unfounded public optimism and the failure of a variety of plans for winning the war left many people radically
disillusioned with the government and other public institutions. What began
as an intervention to bolster the American position in the Cold War became by
1968 a major contributor to American dissatisfaction with the aims of post–
World War II foreign policy. Involvement in Vietnam also undermined the
global political and economic standing of the United States. Public disappointment with the war helped Richard Nixon win the presidency. When
Nixon and Henry Kissinger, his new National Security Adviser, took over in
January 1969 they pleaded for patience, but they agreed "it was essential to
reduce American casualties and get some of our troops coming home in order
to retain the support of the American people."[128]

11

* * * * * * * * * * *

Richard Nixon's War:

1969–1973

*B*Y *1969 THE WAR* had devastated the land and demoralized the people of Vietnam both north and south of the seventeenth parallel. It had also exhausted the patience of most Americans. The government of South Vietnam remained unpopular, but it was more stable than it had been before the election of President Nguyen Van Thieu and Vice President Nguyen Cao Ky in September 1967. Ordinary South Vietnamese continued to resent the avoidance of conscription by privileged young men. Village life in Vietnam had been turned upside down, as the fighting in the countryside drove over four million peasants from their traditional homes into the bloated cities. Many of these newcomers depended for their livelihoods on the jobs or handouts provided by hundreds of thousands of Americans in Vietnam, whose presence confronted ordinary Vietnamese with a heart-wrenching dilemma. As long as massive numbers of Americans remained in Vietnam, the war would continue. But their departure would leave hundreds of thousands of Vietnamese destitute.

Above the seventeenth parallel, the government retained the tight control over North Vietnamese society it had exercised since 1954. But Ho Chi Minh, the charismatic leader whose nationalist achievements had helped bind Northerners together, was not the man he had been after the Vietminh's victory over France. As his health had failed, the direction of life in North Vietnam had fallen to Ho's friends who had formed the Communist Party with him in

1940. These fervid old revolutionaries had an unshakable belief that they would eventually triumph, but they, too, were tired and wondered if their compatriots would exhibit the same spirit of self-sacrifice once Ho died. They wanted the fighting to end quickly, either with a cease-fire offering temporary respite from the burdens of war, or with a complete victory.

War-weariness also washed over the United States in 1968 and 1969. Richard M. Nixon owed his victory in the presidential election in November 1968 partly to the growing public frustration with Vietnam. Nixon envisioned his presidency as an enormous opportunity to realign American politics in favor of the Republican Party, yet he, too, faced the danger of becoming engulfed in Vietnam. His 43.5 percent of the popular vote barely topped Hubert Humphrey's total by five hundred thousand. When, however, Nixon's votes were added to those of George Wallace, the segregationist governor of Alabama who favored more assertive U.S. actions in Vietnam, well over a majority of the public rejected Humphrey's call for de-escalation. If public attention could be diverted from events in Vietnam, anything was possible. But if the war continued as the principal topic of public conversation, swallowing up resources and emotions, Nixon feared he might suffer the fate of his predecessor. No wonder Nixon told H. R. Haldeman, his Chief of Staff, early in 1969, "I'm not going to be like Lyndon Johnson, holed up in the White House, afraid to show my face. I'm going to end the war in Vietnam. Fast."[1]

NIXON, KISSINGER, AND VIETNAM

To reduce the obsession with Vietnam, Nixon quickly forged what *Time* magazine characterized as an "improbably partnership" with Henry Kissinger, whom he named his National Security Adviser.[2] On the surface the two men seemed to have little in common. Nixon, a Republican from Southern California, had built his reputation in international affairs as a rigid anticommunist. The eastern establishment—the network of government officials, academics, commentators, prominent journalists, and corporate business leaders who implemented and explained foreign policy from the Second World War until the 1960s—reviled Nixon as a crude, dishonest politician. Kissinger, on the other hand, had flourished as a public advocate of the sophisticated realist theories of international relations favored by the establishment. Kissinger embodied the bipartisan spirit in foreign policy perfected by the Wise Men, who had been advisers to both Democratic and Republican presidents since 1940. While a professor at Harvard, he had undertaken several diplomatic missions for the Johnson administration, most notably Pennsylvania, the unsuccessful effort to arrange a cease-fire with North Vietnam, in the summer and fall of 1967. He had accomplished the unlikely feat

of advising Republican Nelson Rockefeller (his first political patron), Democrat Hubert Humphrey, and eventually Republican Richard Nixon during the
election campaign of 1968. Nixon hoped the appointment of Kissinger would
provide him with some badly needed respect from the establishment, whose
members and mores Nixon envied as much as despised.[3]

Despite their differences in background and earlier associations, Nixon
and Kissinger had much in common politically and personally. Along with
most other prominent political figures and foreign policy experts in 1968, they
believed that Vietnam had diverted U.S. attention away from more pressing
problems and weakened the Western alliance. Excessive focus on the war had
limited efforts at improving relations with the Soviet Union and had contributed to the outbreak of the Middle East War in June 1967. At the same time,
fighting the war in Vietnam had not achieved one of the principal U.S. aims—
reducing the threat posed by the People's Republic of China, a nuclear power
since 1964. Nixon and Kissinger also shared a widespread belief that Vietnam
had damaged the institution of the presidency.

But Nixon and Kissinger went beyond conventional formulas regarding
the need for a strong president in the Cold War. Both men distrusted colleagues as much as enemies, and thought that unless they established tight,
personal control over policy-making their administration would fail. Kissinger's harrowing boyhood experiences in Nazi Germany convinced him that
the world was a dangerous place where inflamed passions often produced evil
results. Nixon remembered every slight, every negative editorial, every cruel
cartoon directed at him. He viewed political opponents as personal enemies
who hoped to see him fail, even if that meant destroying his beneficial foreign
policy achievements. These suspicions, sometimes bordering on paranoia,
led Nixon and Kissinger to conduct foreign policy in secret. The two men
quickly became soul mates, meeting daily and speaking on the phone dozens
of times a day at all hours.[4]

But Nixon and Kissinger did not see eye to eye on Vietnam policy. The
President, by far the more political of the two men, believed it was necessary
to turn the public's attention away from the war. Kissinger cared less for
managing public opinion but hoped to arrange an American exit from Vietnam in a manner that would fortify U.S. standing with other, more important,
countries. Yet despite their real differences, Nixon and Kissinger together
devised plans to reduce public attention paid to Vietnam while at the same
time continuing the fighting. Why did they not simply end the American role
at the beginning of their term? Like officials of every previous administration
Nixon and Kissinger believed U.S. credibility was at stake in Vietnam. While
they thought that the United States had become too heavily invested there,
they also believed that a forced departure from Vietnam would embolden
American rivals elsewhere in the world.

Neither man held out much hope for the formal negotiations at Paris to end the war. Kissinger's experience with Pennsylvania persuaded him that the gap between North Vietnam and the United States was too wide, and neither side felt compelled because of the military situation to yield. Instead he predicted the war was likely to "peter out" when one side, probably the North, decided that continuing the war was not worth it.[5] Nixon also believed that negotiations only would ratify a situation on the ground rather than it would create new facts.[6] In short, some sort of military solution remained a part of the administration's game plan.

VIETNAMIZATION AND WITHDRAWAL

Instead of negotiations, Nixon adopted another of the late proposals of the Johnson administration to reduce U.S. exposure to the war. In late 1967 Secretary of Defense Robert McNamara had proposed turning more of the fighting over to the South Vietnamese. The United States would gradually remove its troops from South Vietnam while at the same time providing more munitions and training for the ARVN. When Nixon became president the scheme received a name, Vietnamization. Melvin Laird, the new Secretary of Defense, thought that Vietnamization would be the best way to stop the deterioration in the performance of U.S. forces. Morale had sunk among American troops after the Tet Offensive.[7] The cost of maintaining 535,000 troops in South Vietnam had also drained resources from the ambitious program of upgrading the nuclear missiles aimed at the Soviet Union.[8]

As Vietnamization went forward the ARVN's strength rose from 850,000 to over 1,000,000 men, with another 100,000 South Vietnamese enrolling in military schools. Meanwhile, the United States encouraged South Vietnam to modernize the promotion and pay system of its armed forces, but the response was limited. The Americans turned over huge quantities of weaponry to the ARVN: one million rifles, twelve thousand machine guns, forty thousand grenade launchers, and two thousand heavy mortars. Washington also transferred hundreds of planes, ships, helicopters, and trucks to the South Vietnamese. Americans hoped Vietnamization would reduce the appalling level of desertion that had reached 139,670 in 1968. Although desertion rates declined slightly from 1969 until 1972, over 120,000 South Vietnamese soldiers deserted per year.[9]

While the U.S. turned over more of the fighting to the South Vietnamese, Washington explored ways of aggressively choking off North Vietnamese infiltration in the South. In March 1969 Kissinger recommended that U.S. troops enter the "Parrot's Beak" area of Cambodia (named for its distinctive shape) to thwart infiltration. Nixon, however, resisted such a highly visible escalation of the war at the very beginning of his administration. Instead, the President authorized B-52 air raids against infiltration routes through Cambodia. Simultaneously, the Joint Chiefs of Staff advocated bombing the sanctuaries of the North Vietnamese inside Cambodia. After a North Vietnamese offensive in February, Nixon decided that secret attacks on the North's forces inside Cambodia would slow the momentum of the North Vietnamese advance. The bombing, code-named Menu because the first raids, Breakfast, were followed by Lunch, Snack, and Dinner, were kept secret from the public at home and some of the crews who flew the planes, but the Cambodian government of Prince Norodom Sihanouk knew about them. Sihanouk did not object. When William Beecher of the *New York Times* revealed the fact of the bombing in May, his articles provoked no public interest.[10]

Ever the politician, Nixon tried to reduce public concern over the war. He acted as some Democratic members of Congress, who previously had refrained from opposing Lyndon Johnson's Vietnam policy out of party loyalty, prepared to restrict the new President's power to wage war without prior congressional approval. Senator J. William Fulbright, Chairman of the Foreign Relations Committee, and a few other Senate doves such as fellow Democrats Frank Church of Idaho, Ernest Greuning of Alaska, George McGovern of South Dakota, and Wayne Morse of Oregon, and Republicans George Aiken of Vermont and John Sherman Cooper of Kentucky, had long advocated restraints on the President's authority. Many Democrats had previously resisted tying the hands of a president of their own party; now that a Republican occupied the White House, more Democrats favored restricting the President's independence in foreign affairs. North Carolina's Sam Ervin, a fervent hawk during Johnson's presidency, supported a measure "preventing the president from involving the United States in undeclared wars in the future or any other foreign commitments without adhering to the constitutional process of affirmation by the Senate."[11]

Nixon believed that the secret bombing of Cambodia would provoke little opposition so long as casualties were low and no ground troops were involved. In May he delivered a televised address calling for a cease-fire throughout Indochina to be followed within a year by a withdrawal of both U.S. and North Vietnamese troops from Vietnam. His cabinet gave him a standing ovation, but Kissinger complained that foreign governments did not take a speech seriously—they preferred private communications. As for the public, Kissinger thought that the "whole thing was too complex with too many nuances that are totally unintelligible to the ordinary guy."[12]

In June, Nixon met President Thieu on Midway Island and publicly announced plans for Vietnamization. He said that the United States planned to withdraw twenty-five thousand troops over the next few months, and promised further withdrawals at "regular intervals." The pace of withdrawal depended on three factors: the progress made by the ARVN in training and re-equipment (that is, Vietnamization); progress in the Paris peace talks; and the level of communist military activity. Only the first two were under any control of the U.S.[13] A few days later Nixon responded to former Secretary of Defense Clark Clifford's proposal that the United States withdraw all of its troops from Vietnam before the end of 1970. The President assailed Clifford for not having pulled out of Vietnam when he had the chance. Nixon then upped the ante: he hoped the United States could beat that deadline, and he was not "wedded" to the Thieu regime. Kissinger believed that Nixon had gone too far. He thought that any public withdrawal of affection for President Thieu "will probably mean the collapse of the South Vietnamese government in the near future and will result in South Vietnamese troops fighting us."[14]

In its very first months, the Nixon administration set the pattern for the next four years. The President declared a military victory impossible but also said that the United States would not quit Vietnam until a negotiated settlement ended the fighting. The administration's actions raised hopes at home and anxieties in South Vietnam that the war would end soon. The pace of withdrawal was too slow to satisfy critics of the war but too fast for military commanders in the field. As withdrawals proceeded, more and more U.S. troops in the field came to see the war as futile. No one wanted to be the last man killed or wounded. Mutinies, or "combat refusals," as the army called them, rose dramatically as men refused to go on search-and-destroy missions. More and more combat soldiers took heroin. A frightening jump occurred in episodes of soldiers attacking officers with guns or hurling fragmentation bombs into their tents—"fragging," it was called. Racial tensions shot up at bases around the world. Nurses found the self-inflicted injuries and drug overdoses of the last years of the war sadder and more bewildering than the wounds suffered from enemy fire at the height of the fighting. A nurse said, "I just didn't expect to see a soldier shot from playing a game of Russian roulette or injured in a racial fight in a bar." An army study identified a "sociopathological riptide" among soldiers in the last years of the American presence in Vietnam.[15]

The South Vietnamese government also could see the handwriting on the wall, and became ever more demanding of demonstrations of support from the United States. The Nixon administration responded the way Johnson had done when it faced similar demands for shows of affection: it increased the bombing. At the same time, Hanoi's political leaders believed that time was on their side and they could only gain by waiting. The North made few concessions in the peace talks, something that Nixon and Kissinger had come to expect.

Nevertheless, the ground war seemed to slow in the summer of 1969. The United States wrote the North Vietnamese government offering to continue the dialogue begun in secret at the Paris peace talks. The North Vietnamese rebuffed the approach before Ho Chi Minh died on September 4. Upon the announcement of his death doves urged Nixon to declare a cease-fire. The United States did stop military activities for the day of Ho's funeral, but the

new leadership of North Vietnam did not come forward with any new proposals at the Paris peace talks.

Meanwhile, the anti-war movement, which had been badly damaged in
the public eye by the police riot at the Chicago convention (most Americans
blamed the anti-war protesters for the violence), gathered strength. Congressional critics assailed Nixon; some accused him of prolonging the war even
after officially ruling out a military victory. Senator Albert Gore (D., Tenn.)
complained that casualties continued to mount—''more than 42,000 killed
and wounded''—in the first five months of the Nixon administration. He
called on the administration to use its overwhelming power in Vietnam to
force the South Vietnamese government to heel rather than to ''use our forces
to support and maintain in power a regime which appears thoroughly cal-
loused to our losses and sacrifices [and is] unwilling to undertake its own
defense.''[16] Fulbright explored holding Foreign Relations Committee hearings on Vietnam with Clark Clifford as the star witness.[17] The former Defense Secretary declined to testify in public, but Fulbright continued to press
the administration to withdraw all U.S. forces as quickly as possible from
Vietnam. ''Conditions in the United States are deteriorating very rapidly,''
Fulbright privately told high administration officials.[18] Even Republicans
seemed restless. Margaret Chase Smith, a longtime supporter of the war,
complained that she had ''no idea what Nixon's Vietnam plan is and that
Nixon has asked the Republican leadership to take him on faith.''[19] In the fall
Fulbright announced that his hearings would occur soon. He complained that
Nixon was ''not making progress on his campaign promises to give birth to
his plans to end the war.''[20]

ANTI-WAR PROTESTS

Outside of Congress the revived antiwar movement became more visible in
late 1969. The presidents of seventy-nine colleges issued a public appeal
for Nixon to step up the timetable for the withdrawal of U.S. forces from
Vietnam. Otherwise they feared that their campuses would be engulfed in
a wave of anti-war protests. A one-day moratorium of customary activities was planned throughout the country for October 15, to be followed by
another moratorium each succeeding month with one day added to the moratorium activities each month. Organizers of the moratorium asked students
from elementary schools to universities to attend anti–Vietnam War rallies
rather than regularly scheduled classes. Working people, too, were encouraged to stop their ordinary activities in favor of participation in a variety of
anti-war activities, from listening to speeches, to letter writing campaigns, to
picketing draft boards and federal offices, to silent vigils in front of court
houses. Millions of people, mostly middle-class, many middle-aged, turned

out across the country. Tens of thousands marched around the White House.[21]

As if to prove his indifference to the demonstrations, Nixon let it be known that he spent the afternoon watching a football game. He also announced that draft calls were canceled for November and December because the withdrawals from Vietnam reduced the need for troops. He replaced the vastly unpopular General Lewis Hershey, director of the Selective Service system, with Curtis Tarr, a civilian. Tarr's task was to defuse protests against Selective Service. He quickly ended most student deferments, replacing them with an annual lottery whereby men were inducted on the basis of their birthdays. They were liable for induction for a single year, after which they would be safe. While many young men whose lottery numbers exposed them to the draft still objected to military service in a war which the President had publicly declared unwinnable, the lottery system removed some of the obvious inequities of the deferment system. Moreover, before the lottery, all young men felt some exposure to the draft. After the lottery took hold, over two thirds of men born in any year breathed more easily since only those with lower lottery numbers were likely to be drafted. This development alone substantially reduced the number of young men likely to engage in anti-war activities.[22]

For many anti-war activists, public demonstrations against the war seemed old, stale, and tired. Veteran War protesters had been marching against U.S. involvement for at least five years, yet the war went on endlessly. Some favored more militant actions to make the war impossible. Instead of picketing in front of draft boards, they favored disrupting the boards' operations. They suggested encouraging soldiers to leave their bases before they embarked for Vietnam. Some advocated sitting down on railroad lines to prevent the shipment of ammunition; others advised blocking the sailing of naval vessels bound for Vietnam. The Weatherman faction of the Students for a Democratic Society organized a violent protest in Chicago for October. They called it the "Days of Rage," designed to build a " 'white fighting force' to attack the beast from within as the peoples of the world attack it from without." Organizers of this pitifully small demonstration (barely three hundred people) expected it to lead to a revolution. Even many radicals considered the Days of Rage infantile, and liberals were appalled. But radical and liberal anti-war activists did forge another uneasy compromise, melding the moratorium scheduled for November with a more militant march on Washington.[23]

None of this had much impact on the war except to allow opponents of the anti-war movement to paint its activities as the work of extremists. Nixon proved able to manipulate public opinion to continue support for his course, however unclear it might be. The President sought to undermine the appeal of the mid-November anti-war march with a major speech on Vietnam on

November 3. The televised address recited the history of U.S. involvement in Vietnam since 1954. Nixon used some of the most overheated rhetoric of the war. He blamed the Johnson administration for neither winning nor ending the war. He professed respect for the idealism and desire for peace of young people, but then went on to claim that they preferred the "easy way" (withdrawal) to "the right way" (Vietnamization). He struck the note of credibility: "For the United States, the first defeat in our nation's history would result in a collapse of confidence in American leadership, not only in Asia, but throughout the world." He claimed that the "survival of peace and freedom" throughout the world depended on whether the "American people have the moral stamina and the courage" to continue their support for the government of President Nguyen Van Thieu. Finally, he asked "the great silent majority" of the American people for their support.[24] He temporarily achieved that backing. Three hundred representatives and fifty-eight senators signed a letter of support. The Gallup poll recorded a 68 percent approval rating for Nixon. The White House received eighty thousand telegrams and letters in favor of the speech. "The euphoria continues," Haldeman exulted. The mix of mail to the Senate Foreign Relations Committee also changed from its customary opposition to the President's policy to three-to-one in favor of Nixon's position.[25]

After the silent majority speech, the White House pressed to discredit the anti-war movement with middle Americans. Vice President Spiro Agnew delivered an angry blast at news commentators whom he accused of a liberal bias. He derided them as an "unelected elite" and "an effete corps of impudent snobs." According to Haldeman, Nixon "couldn't contain his mirth as he thought about" Agnew's speech.[26] The Vice President urged people to deluge the news organizations with letters of protests. Some of the letter-writing was organized by White House operatives. Ross Perot, an extremely wealthy Texas businessman, also helped by paying for ads and running a television show supporting Nixon's position. Haldeman considered Perot an "amazing resource," because his devotion to Nixon more than compensated for his "*total* lack of sophistication."[27]

Nixon's "silent majority" speech and Agnew's derision had the desired effects. The press carried less news of the massive demonstrations in Washington than they had of earlier protests. The White House staff, however, knew that the demonstration was huge. Some of the scenes made for compelling television pictures. On Friday, November 14, thousands of marchers, each carrying a candle, walked solemnly passed the White House. As they passed the presidential mansion every demonstrator uttered the name of a dead American soldier. Nixon watched the whole process for about two hours. At one point he suggested that helicopters fly low over the crowd to drown out their voices and blow out the candles.[28] The next day came the rally of 325,000 people on the Mall by the Lincoln Memorial. The President felt besieged. A solid barricade of buses, lined end to end, prevented people from getting to within two blocks of the White House. Hundreds of protesters mobbed the Justice Department, where police responded with mass arrests and tear gas. Once more Nixon responded by watching football and telling his staff to organize "our own monster rally, with 500,000, to outdo them once and for all."[29]

On Sunday, November 16, in the midst of the march on Washington, the *New York Times* broke the story of the My Lai massacre. Army investigators had known of the massacre for eighteen months, but had kept it secret. News of the massacre and the apparent coverup provoked more calls to remove American troops from Vietnam. Longtime critics of the war explained that the massacre demonstrated that the war had brutalized some American soldiers who fought there. Nixon responded by highlighting the Vietcong's "calculated and continual" use of "terror, murder and massacre."[30]

Once the *Times* reported on the delayed investigation, Lieutenant-General William Peers conducted a more thorough study. The Peers report laid most of the blame on twenty-four-year-old Lieutenant William Calley, who had led the American platoon that murdered over five hundred innocent Vietnamese civilians. Calley was eventually court-martialed, as were three of his superior officers. Only Calley was sentenced to prison, and sympathy for him as a scapegoat spread widely, especially in the generally hawkish South, where he had grown up. Calley's defenders pointed to the lax supervision of higher authorities, the poor training received by young lieutenants, and, most of all, the frustrating nature of the war. In the aftermath of Tet, jumpy American soldiers had come to consider nearly all Vietnamese as potential enemy fighters. Nixon capitalized on this sympathy by reducing Calley's life sentence to three years. While there was far less public outcry against the My Lai massacre than expected by Seymour Hersh, the reporter of the *New York Times* who broke the story, news of the massacre shook the confidence of many Americans who had supported of continuing American participation in the war. Even as Calley's defenders claimed that he had been made a scapegoat for every bad decision made by superiors, they realized that continuing the war could only produce more such episodes that had to be defended, excused, or ignored. Now that Nixon had acknowledged that the war could not be won militarily, what was the point of exposing young men to the possibility of engaging in similar atrocities?[31]

The media's generally muted handling of continued anti-war sentiment pleased Nixon. "We've got those liberal bastards on the run," he crowed, "and we're going to keep them on the run." Attorney General John Mitchell authorized the FBI to tap the telephones of the organizers of the moratoriums. Six months later Nixon approved a plan to infiltrate, burglarize, wiretap, trick, and provoke into violence a variety of anti-war and liberal groups "who pose a threat to our national security."[32]

As much as Americans disliked the anti-war movement, they loathed the idea of themselves, their sons, brothers, husbands, or boyfriends fighting in Vietnam. At the beginning of 1970 the U.S. government remained as committed as ever to supporting the continuation in office of President Nguyen Van Thieu, his ministers, and the chief military officers of the Republic of Vietnam. More and more ordinary Americans, however, despised the South Vietnamese government. Hundreds of thousands of veterans returned home from Vietnam with contempt for the fighting spirit of the allies and a grudging admiration for the toughness of the North Vietnamese and the resourcefulness of the Vietcong. Nothing resonated more with the American public than veterans' complaints of the hundreds of able-bodied Vietnamese men of draft age who never saw a day in uniform, yet when senators questioned military commanders in Vietnam about the disgust American grunts felt toward their ARVN counterparts, they "seemed to be out of touch not only with what Vietnamese thought but also with the way American soldiers feel."[33]

Of course, Americans had grumbled about the inequities of their own Selective Service system, which allowed many men of higher socio-economic status to avoid service, but the refusal of so many South Vietnamese men to join the armed forces rankled far more. It seemed as if the South Vietnamese and their government did not want to fight alone and might not even want the war to end.[34]

LAOS AND CAMBODIA

In early 1970, Nixon pursued a combination of secret diplomacy, a faster withdrawal of American forces from the war, and dramatic military gestures as ways of bringing the war to a conclusion. In February and March, Kissinger slipped away to Paris for two days of secret talks with North Vietnamese representatives. While Kissinger held out little hope for progress in the public talks with the North, he thought that secret diplomacy might work. In mid-March Kissinger told Nixon that if the North had anything positive to offer in the next round of secret talks "we'll be on the way to a settlement this year." For the first time the North agreed to discuss mutual troop withdrawals, effectively acknowledging the existence of North Vietnamese units in the South. This news was especially gratifying to Nixon, who had seen his approval rating slip eleven points over his handling of Vietnam since the Silent Majority speech of the previous November.[35]

Congressional pressure also mounted for a speedy end to American involvement. News of American B-52 attacks on northern Laos and reports that twenty-seven Americans had been killed in Laos in the past year set off a firestorm of congressional criticism. Senator Stuart Symington (D., Mo.) complained to Secretary of State William P. Rogers that "you cannot expect the public to continue to stand by unquestioning as the silent war in Laos escalates, while the public war in Vietnam is being de-escalated with great fanfare.''[36] Fulbright's position was that "Asia is for the Asians, and that an unequivocal American commitment to withdrawal from Mainland Asia is a *sine qua non* for negotiations leading to some kind of neutrality for the area of Indochina.''[37]

Nixon wanted to accelerate the pace of withdrawal to shore up his ebbing support and quiet congressional criticism. Kissinger, on the other hand, believed that the first signs of flexibility on the part of the North Vietnamese reflected desperation. He wanted to drag out negotiations, waiting four weeks rather than two before having another meeting, to make them sweat. Yet Kissinger stood virtually alone in believing that the North Vietnamese thought time was running out. Most observers agreed with a Soviet account of the North Vietnamese motives: they pursued a cautious strategy "geared to the U.S. political scene and looking toward the 1972 elections." They believed their position strengthened with every reduction of U.S. troops. Accordingly, "they want to get U.S. troops out and are not likely to do anything to stop the movement.''[38]

Both American withdrawals and engagement in battle intensified in March and April. In March Nixon announced plans to remove an additional 150,000 troops by the end of the year. At the same time Cambodia's chief of staff, General Lon Nol, overthrew the government of Prince Norodom Sihanouk. Lon Nol, unlike the neutral Sihanouk, sided clearly with the Americans and South Vietnamese and wanted them to rid neutral Cambodia of the North Vietnamese, who used Cambodia's border region to support insurgents in South Vietnam. Fighting spread when the ARVN conducted raids into Cambodia to disrupt the transportation of supplies down the Ho Chi Minh Trail. In response the North Vietnamese and their Cambodian allies, the Khmer Rouge, marched toward the Cambodian capital of Phnom Penh. By mid-April, the Khmer Rouge controlled about one fourth of Cambodia. Lon Nol panicked and asked the United States for military assistance to prevent the seizure of the capital.[39]

General Creighton Abrams, commander of the MACV since mid-1968, worried about the effect of the withdrawal of 150,000 American troops on the war, had also pressed Nixon for over a year for intervention in Cambodia to show the South Vietnamese that the United States was still willing to help them fight. The President had deferred Abrams's request for an invasion of the Parrot's Beak in March 1969. Now Nixon believed that an eye-catching military move could seize the initiative from the Democratic Senate, which over the past four months had rejected two of Nixon's nominees, Clement Haynsworth and G. Harrold Carswell, for positions on the Supreme Court.

In late April Nixon decided to invade Cambodia, despite reservations expressed by his own advisers. Kissinger, who had long recommended such a course, now thought that the President was "acting too rashly without really thinking through the consequences." The National Security Adviser feared that an invasion of Cambodia might expose weaknesses in the South Vietnamese armed forces. Over several days, however, Kissinger came aboard, convinced that Nixon wanted to invade. He did not care to undermine his credibility with the President by raising more objections. Other opposition to an invasion of the Parrot's Beak came from Secretary of State William P. Rogers, who feared that casualties would be high and little long-term political gain could be expected from the invasion. With Rogers expressing skepticism, Kissinger became one of the most ardent backers of the plan to attack the North Vietnamese in Cambodia. He considered the invasion a test of Nixon's authority. Haldeman believed that Kissinger "would go ahead even if [the] plan is wrong, just to prove that the President can't be challenged."[40]

On the evening of April 30, Nixon went before the American public to announce that thirty-one thousand U.S. troops had entered Cambodia to destroy the headquarters of the revolutionary forces. He pleaded for support. "If when the chips are down," he said, "the world's most powerful nation acts like a pitiful, helpless giant, the forces of totalitarianism and anarchy will threaten free nations and free institutions throughout the world."[41]

The invasion produced only modest military yields. The American and ARVN forces killed two thousand enemy troops and destroyed eight thousand bunkers. The attack into Cambodia may have bought some time for additional Vietnamization. In the operation's first ten days, U.S. and ARVN soldiers destroyed more ammunition than the North Vietnamese forces used in the first four months of 1970.[42] Supportive Republicans such as Barry Goldwater of Arizona told constituents that the operation "has had a decisive effect upon the enemy." Goldwater explained that invading Cambodia was "the only decision" Nixon could make "other than quitting and this we can't do."[43] The invasion failed completely, however, in its larger goal of reversing the military trend toward a victory for the North. The ARVN forces fought poorly, and their incompetence and unwillingness to fight were abundantly evident on evening news programs. The United States and ARVN forces also failed to find the headquarters of the North Vietnamese operations, a supposed "nerve center" located in Cambodia.

Worst of all, from Nixon's point of view, the Cambodian operation provoked some of the most furious anti-war demonstrations of the Vietnam era. On April 29, the day before the announcement, Missouri Democrat Thomas Eagleton warned that "a decision to intervene could be explosively decisive here at home."[44] The business community became galvanized against the war. Thomas Watson, chairman of the board of IBM, testified before the Senate Foreign Relations of Committee about the terrible toll the war had taken on the economy and morale of business people. Paul Harvey, a conservative radio commentator, told his huge following in small towns of the

Midwest and South, "America's 6 percent section of the planet's mothers cannot bear enough boy babies to police Asia—and our nation can't bleed to death trying."[45] The concern of such prominent, middle-of-the-road individuals heartened congressional opponents of U.S. involvement in the fighting. Fulbright considered their support "essential if we are ever to change our policy in Southeast Asia."[46]

KENT STATE

Protests against the war, the draft, military-sponsored research, and the Reserve Officers' Training Corps (ROTC) erupted on hundreds of college campuses across the country. The most horrifying events took place on the campus of Kent State University in northeastern Ohio. An angry crowd of about five hundred Kent State students gathered at the center of the campus on Friday, May 1, to denounce Nixon. That evening thousands of students celebrated the first warm evening of spring in downtown Kent. Later a few fist fights broke out among patrons at a downtown bar. Soon a mob of about four hundred rampaged through the downtown area, smashing store windows. The crowd grew to about fifteen hundred, and city police used tear gas to force them back to the campus. The mayor of the town declared a state of emergency and called out the National Guard. The next day, Saturday, there was a peaceful rally, but that night someone set the ROTC building ablaze. Afterwards, the National Guard occupied the campus and used tear gas to disperse the crowd of about fifteen hundred who had gathered to watch the ROTC building burn.

On Sunday Ohio Governor James Rhodes announced that the Guardsmen had gone to Kent State to "eradicate the communist element" from the campus. At 11:30 A.M. on Monday, May 4, two thousand students rallied against the presence of the Guardsmen on the campus while another ten thousand watched the confrontation. The Guardsmen fired tear gas into the crowd, forcing them to flee. The soldiers, many of whom had spent the last week putting down a rough strike by teamsters, were tired, nervous, and frightened. They consulted among themselves when the students gathered on a parking lot. Guardsmen marched away from the crowd, and then, without warning, abruptly turned around and fired sixty-one shots into the horrified crowd. Four students were killed instantly; another nine were wounded. The crowd was silent for a moment and then came the sounds of loud wailing. The students sat down on the lawn until guardsmen roughly ordered them to move.[47]

News of the slaughter at Kent State provoked the largest campus upheavals of the war. Across the country students rallied, attended vigils, and signed petitions. Demonstrations took place at 1,350 campuses, and more than four million people took part. About two thousand undergraduates at Harvard signed a petition calling for the immediate withdrawal of U.S. forces from Cambodia.[48] Over one hundred thousand young people spontaneously converged on Washington to petition Congress to end the war. Nixon appeared to be "very disturbed . . . afraid that his decision had set it off, and that [it] is the ostensible cause of the demonstrations."[49] When thousands of protesters gathered at the Lincoln Memorial, they were astonished to receive a pre-dawn visit from Richard Nixon, distraught over the outrage his actions had produced. The President did little to cool anger by an ineffectual gesture of reconciliation with protesters. Uncomfortable with strangers and in situations he could not control, Nixon made small talk about college football and surfing with young people who wanted the war to end. He asked the students to "try to understand what we are doing."[50] Haldeman found him "completely beat and just rambling on, but obviously too tired to go to sleep."[51] The President further strained relations with his opponents by publicly describing some protesters as "bums" who were more concerned with burning and looting their campuses than with studying.[52]

CONGRESSIONAL FRUSTRATION

Members of Congress were also infuriated by the Cambodian invasion. Fulbright thought that Nixon's policies were "undermining the security of our country." He thought "it might be a long time before the sun shines again for our country."[53] Congress responded to the public concern over the Cambodian invasion by initiating a repeal, which was official in January 1971, of the 1964 Gulf of Tonkin Resolution, used by Presidents Johnson and Nixon to justify continued American participation in the fighting.[54] Two Senate doves, Democrat Frank Church of Idaho and Republican John Sherman Cooper of Kentucky, introduced legislation blocking further funding of American operations in Cambodia after June 30. The amendment passed the Senate but failed in the House. In any event, Nixon had already said the troops would leave by that date. He also stated that the Cambodian mission "insured the continuance and success of our withdrawal program."[55] The President responded defiantly to lawmakers' efforts to restrict his actions in Vietnam: "If Congress undertakes to restrict me, Congress will have to assume the consequences."[56]

At the same time, Kissinger resumed his public relations campaign to undermine support for the anti-war movement. When three members of his staff resigned in protest over the Cambodian invasion, he told journalists that their departure marked "the epitome of the cowardice of the Eastern Establishment."[57] He also tried to calm his former colleagues in academia, asking for patience and warning that further protest against the war would provoke a backlash among conservative Americans who favored greater military force in Vietnam.[58]

Neither the counterattacks against the anti-war movement nor the invasion of Cambodia brought the end of the war any closer. The public peace talks in Paris stalled. The North Vietnamese delegation dismissed as a farce American proposals to withdraw troops if the North Vietnamese left the South. Willing to wait for a better proposal, the North Vietnamese threatened to remain in Paris "until the chairs rot."[59] In August 1969, hoping that North Vietnamese diplomat Xuan Thuy would be more forthcoming in private than in public, Kissinger opened secret conversations, but he returned home dispirited. The North insisted that the United States leave Vietnam and cease support for the Thieu regime. Because North Vietnam had not acknowledged the division of Vietnam into separate countries, it would not withdraw its forces from what it considered part of its own territory.

By the middle of 1970, therefore, Nixon's honeymoon with the public over Vietnam had ended. The expansion of the war into Cambodia had revived the domestic turmoil of 1968. Like Johnson before him, Nixon could not appear safely on college campuses across the country. Unlike his Democratic predecessor, however, Nixon appealed to the more hawkish section of the electorate. As long as that portion of the public was satisfied, the administration could progress toward other foreign policy goals. Because anti-war outbursts after the Cambodian invasion had polarized national opinion, hawkish Americans became even more committed to Nixon than before. A few days after National Guardsmen killed the Kent State protesters, New York construction workers rampaged through New York's financial district. They beat up anti-war demonstrators, forced officials at City Hall to raise the American flag (lowered in mourning after the Kent State killings), and smashed windows at nearby Pace College. Two weeks later the head of the New York Labor Council led an estimated sixty- to one hundred thousand flag-waving union members in a march supporting the invasion of Cambodia and opposing the anti-war demonstrations. Nixon received them warmly at the White House.[60]

The emotional exhaustion following the anti-war moratoriums and the shock of the Kent State killings, combined with the American withdrawal from Cambodia in June 1970, took their toll on the anti-war movement. As another 150,000 American troops left Vietnam and casualty figures dropped below one hundred per week, public concern about Vietnam fell slowly until early 1971. Then in February and March anger revived as the ARVN, encouraged by the American command, invaded another neighboring country, Laos, once more looking for the enemy's nonexistent headquarters. On February 8, 1971, approximately seventeen thousand ARVN troops crossed into Laos along National Highway 9. The raid, code-named Long Son 719, had the support of ten thousand U.S. troops located just inside South Vietnam, who bombarded communist positions with artillery and air strikes. U.S. army helicopters also ferried the ARVN troops into battle. Nevertheless, without the large contingent of Americans who had led them into Cambodia the year before, the ARVN forces stumbled badly as they confronted thirty-six thousand battle-hardened North Vietnamese troops. After six weeks of the bloodiest fighting of the war, in which the South Vietnamese suffered casualties of 50 percent of their forces, the ARVN retreated in disarray from Laos. Kissinger feared that the ARVN decided to "pull out as quickly as they can because they're afraid that the North Vietnamese are massing for a big attack and that their guys are going to get slaughtered."[61] Nixon hoped that the withdrawal of the ARVN from Laos would coincide with another American troop reduction. Yet administration statements that the ARVN had exercised an "orderly retreat" made no sense to television viewers who saw film clips of terrified South Vietnamese soldiers clinging to the skids of helicopters, desperately trying to get back to South Vietnam.[62] In the aftermath of the Laotian incursion, the House Democratic caucus adopted a resolution "to end the U.S. military involvement in Indochina and bring about the release of all prisoners" by the end of 1972.[63]

THE *PENTAGON PAPERS*

An even greater public relations disaster was in the making. On Sunday, June 13, 1971, the *New York Times* began a series of stories on the origins of United States involvement in the war in Vietnam. "My God, there it is!" said former Defense Department official Leslie Gelb when he opened his newspaper that morning.[64] "It" was the forty-seven-volume *History of U.S. Decision-making Process on Vietnam, 1945–1967,* popularly known as the *Pentagon Papers,* which Gelb had compiled at Secretary of Defense Robert McNamara's request in 1968.

Daniel Ellsberg, formerly a Defense Department official who had grown disillusioned with the war, had leaked copies of the *Pentagon Papers* to *Times* reporter Neil Sheehan earlier that spring. Casting a dark shadow over the foreign policy of every administration from Truman through Johnson, the documents revealed that American officials had ignored international agreements, manipulated the Saigon government, and deliberately misinformed Congress and the public. According to Haldeman, the *Times*'s excerpt "really blasts McNamara and Kennedy and Johnson" for their deceptions regarding U.S. intentions in the war.[65] The *Economist* of London observed that when Johnson decided to Americanize the war in the spring and summer of 1965, he "continued to soft soap the public, talking of negotiation when none was in mind, expressing optimism when none was justified, causing changes in policy to be denied when important decisions had, in fact, been taken."[66]

Publication of the *Pentagon Papers* convinced some people who had previously remained undecided about the war that the government had long known that the original commitment to Vietnam was a mistake. Once the *Pentagon Papers* became part of the public debate, it shortened the time remaining for Nixon to bring the war to an end. The documents confirmed what many people had suspected and Nixon had suggested since he had taken office: the originally stated reason for U.S. involvement in Vietnam was no longer valid. The only way officials could justify continued U.S. involvement in the war was to ask people to trust Nixon's skills as a master of foreign affairs, yet he could demonstrate that mastery only by ending U.S. participation.

The appearance of the *Papers* set off a debate within the higher circles of the Nixon administration about how to respond. Some of Nixon's political advisers, led by Charles Colson and John Ehrlichman, believed that the publication only helped the Nixon administration, because the information damaged Democrats from Truman to Johnson. Colson advised administration spokesmen to "point out that the bad guys and spies are all left wing Democrats. . . . Those who got us into trouble can't be counted on to get us out of trouble."[67] Ehrlichman believed that "it's going to come out anyway," and the public would blame the Democrats, not Nixon.[68]

Kissinger acknowledged some of these arguments (for example, he agreed the documents showed "Hubert Humphrey's yellow streak"), but he recommended a strong attack on Daniel Ellsberg and Neil Sheehan.[69] "The fact that some idiot can publish all of the diplomatic secrets of the country . . . is damaging to your image," he told Nixon. "It shows you're a weakling, Mr. President."[70] As Kissinger's deputy, Alexander Haig, told the President, publication of the documents caused "terrible problems with the South Vietnamese government. . . . [I]t's criminally traitorous that the documents got to the *New York Times,* and even more so that the *Times* is printing them."[71]

Nixon sided with Kissinger and ordered the Justice Department to seek an injunction against the *New York Times* and other newspapers, barring them from publishing additional excerpts. The newspapers appealed the injunction all the way to the Supreme Court, which decided the case with blinding speed. On June 30 the Court ruled that the administration had "not met the heavy burden of showing justification" for imposing prior restraint on publication of the documents. The newspapers helped sway a majority of the Court to its side by arguing that it had consciously withheld from publication sensitive material related to ongoing efforts to end the war by negotiations.[72] The Court's decision persuaded Nixon that "the establishment has a new intellectual arrogance which leads them to think that they know best and that the determination regarding what the public should know should be made by them." In the aftermath of the *Pentagon Papers* publication, White

House counselor John Ehrlichman ordered a break-in at the office of Daniel Ellsberg's psychiatrist to find discrediting information about Ellsberg. This burglary set in motion a series of abuses of presidential power culminating in the Watergate break-in of June 1972.[73]

PLANNING FOR 1972

A series of dramatic diplomatic and political developments in the second half of 1971 again shifted public attention away from Vietnam. In July Nixon announced that Kissinger had returned from a visit to Beijing to arrange a trip to the Chinese capital by Nixon. A month later Nixon announced a new economic policy, freezing wages and prices and ending the link of the dollar to gold that had prevailed since 1945. In October Kissinger returned to China to make final arrangements for Nixon's trip. The same month the General Assembly of the United Nations unseated the Republic of China (Taiwan) and granted exclusive membership to the People's Republic of China. All of these events combined to create a sense that Vietnam no longer dominated news and policy-making in Washington. This altered environment provided precisely the sort of presidential freedom of action in international and domestic affairs Nixon had hoped to restore when he took office. Yet all was not well politically. Despite the drama of late 1971, fewer than half the public approved of his job performance at the beginning of 1972.[74]

In January 1972, Nixon told Kissinger that he felt "under terrible pressure on Vietnam" from members of Congress who wanted to set a specific date for the withdrawal of all American troops. The President had promised an end to the war every year since 1969. While casualties, draft calls, and reports of the fighting all were down, the war went on. Nixon sought to reduce the influence of the doves with a speech on Vietnam, setting out the offers the United States had made in the secret negotiations. Kissinger thought this a bad idea because it would make it appear as if the President was so eager to remove a discussion of Vietnam from the political agenda of the 1972 election that he was "looking for a way to bug out." The National Security Adviser believed that "the North Vietnamese are ready to give, so we'd be totally wrong to show any nervousness. If we do the peace plan early in January, it'll spur the opponents to tear it to pieces."[75] Kissinger believed it was better to wait until later in the election year.

Nixon accepted the form but not the substance of Kissinger's advice. The President agreed briefly to postpone a speech on Vietnam but could not keep quiet about the subject. He told CBS interviewer Dan Rather on January 2 that he had no other choice but to bomb North Vietnam after the North had stepped up the rate of infiltration on the South and shelled Saigon on December 19. Nixon explained that he could not promise to remove all U.S. soldiers from South Vietnam by Election Day. Hanoi held the key to the continued presence of U.S. ground troops as well as to whether the United States would continue to bomb the North. Now, however, Nixon did not repeat his and Lyndon Johnson's assertion that Hanoi could continue to attack their neighbor to the South or it could see the withdrawal of U.S. forces, but it could not do both. Nixon said that he could not "withdraw all of our forces as long as the enemy hold one American prisoner of war."[76]

The North held about six hundred U.S. servicemen captives in squalid POW camps scattered across the DRV. Like their counterparts in the South, the North Vietnamese authorities paid little attention to the Geneva agreements on proper treatment of POWs. Food was scarce and unwholesome, medical care nearly non-existent, and many prisoners spent years wearing the tattered uniforms they had on when they were captured. Most U.S. POWs were flyers shot down in air raids, but there were also more than fifty soldiers captured in ground fighting. The authorities permitted few visits by the International Red Cross or family members, but anti-war activists met regularly with the POWs to encourage them to denounce U.S. conduct in the war. The North Vietnamese sometimes extracted from the captives ritualistic confessions of war crimes. Broadcasts of these condemnations by the servicemen of their own government shocked the American public, but they also allowed the Nixon administration to whip up emotions against the North Vietnamese. Hanoi's treatment of U.S. prisoners of war became Nixon's trump card in the domestic political debate over Vietnam. Thereafter, whenever a congressional resolution demanded a withdrawal of U.S. forces by a certain date, it qualified the withdrawal of U.S. troops in exchange for a return of prisoners of war.[77]

In January, Nixon made several additional announcements on Vietnam designed to confound his domestic opposition. He promised to pull seventy thousand more U.S. troops out by May, leaving sixty-nine thousand in the country. Secretary of Defense Laird, who initially resisted such a large pull-out because it would annoy some of the Joint Chiefs of Staff, told the press that the U.S. no longer had a ground combat role in Vietnam.[78] Nixon then delivered a major televised speech on January 25. He revealed Kissinger's secret talks in Paris with North Vietnam's Le Duc Tho and Xuan Thuy. He explained that the U.S. had offered to withdraw its forces six months after an agreement on a cease-fire and return of prisoners of war. He said that President Thieu had offered to step down one month before presidential elections. The North's negotiators rejected the proposal's call for a cease-fire throughout Indochina—they did not control the communist forces in Laos or Cambodia—and the demand that they remove their troops. Kissinger was certain that "the press is going to kick us on Vietnam, not because they think we're wrong, but because they know we're right and are furious because we're the ones who are doing it, the same way they did on Cambodia and to an extent on China."[79]

The reaction of the press and Democratic politicians was mixed but mostly positive. Newspapers praised Nixon for making a serious offer for peace. *New York Times* columnist James Reston noted that the North was unlikely to accept a cease-fire now that they were gaining on the battlefield. Only Senator George McGovern complained that Nixon had double crossed him. McGovern, along with Republican Senator Mark Hatfield of Oregon, had proposed to end the war in return for an exchange of prisoners. Nixon had opposed it. Nixon had also criticized McGovern for meeting North Vietnamese representatives in Paris in September 1971 and offering to set a date for withdrawal in return for the prisoners of war. Nixon made the same offer public in his January 25 speech, although the position the U.S. took in negotiations had far more qualifications. When Kissinger spoke with Le Duc Tho, he made it clear that the United States would never drop its support for the government of President Thieu. Nevertheless, Nixon's speech had the desired impact on public opinion. Trial heats between him and Senator Edmund Muskie of Maine, who seemed at the time to be the most likely Democratic presidential candidate, showed the president with a four-point lead. The public approved of his overall handling of the war by a margin of 52 percent.[80]

Nixon's standing with the public rose farther in February as he traveled to Beijing. Stunning television pictures of Nixon's toasting Chinese leaders and visiting the Great Wall consolidated Nixon's position as a statesman.[81] In Haldeman's view, he was "big league [and] has done it for years."[82] The Shanghai communiqué promised improvement in relations between the United States and China despite their abiding differences over Vietnam. The White House staff exulted at the obvious discomfort of Nixon's domestic political critics. Kissinger predicted that "the liberals will try to piss on" Nixon's success at removing Vietnam as an irritant in U.S.-Chinese relations. They would call Nixon's trip "an election year gimmick." The White House derided such objections as sour grapes. "You're not against *what* we're doing," Kissinger said, "you're just against the fact that *we're* doing it."[83]

The White House expected to build on the success at unfreezing relations with China with a summit meeting between Nixon and Soviet Communist Party General Secretary Leonid Brezhnev scheduled for late May. Nixon wanted to obtain the maximum dramatic impact from his visit to Moscow. In mid-March he warned Kissinger to dampen expectations about what might be accomplished when the President met Brezhnev. "What I am concerned about is not that we will fail to achieve the various goals" of arms control and a general warming of relations. Rather, Nixon feared, "when we do make the formal agreements there will be no real news value in them."[84]

THE NORTH'S SPRING OFFENSIVE

Yet the prospect of sealing detente with the Soviet Union suddenly dimmed at the end of March when the North Vietnamese army launched an offensive across the Demilitarized Zone (DMZ) using hundreds of tanks and artillery pieces. In terms of the amount of heavy weapons employed, the offensive dwarfed the attacks of Tet. Troops of the PLAVN rolled quickly toward the northern provincial capital of Quang Tri, an area once defended by U.S. marines but now controlled by the ARVN. Within days the North Vietnamese overran the two northernmost provinces of South Vietnam. The Defense Department's analysts believed that the ARVN had been taken by surprise and expected the situation to get worse.[85]

A few days later the situation did deteriorate when North Vietnam launched the second stage of the offensive with attacks from Cambodia in the center of South Vietnam. North Vietnamese tanks and artillery headed for Tay Ninh and An Loc. Although the ARVN was surprised tactically, the Americans had expected some sort of attack during the dry season. The upcoming U.S. presidential election set a deadline for a climax to the war. Moreover Hanoi could have been expected to respond somehow to the American-sponsored invasions of Cambodia in 1970 and Laos in 1971.

Nixon responded to the panic by ordering air and naval bombing of North Vietnam. B-52s and fighter bombers went into action against the North up to the eighteenth parallel and naval bombing attacked twenty-five miles north of the DMZ. "The bastards have never been bombed like they're going to be bombed this time," Nixon said. The United States increased its aircraft stationed in or near Vietnam to close to one thousand. The number of B-52s rose from 80 to 140. Six aircraft carriers were stationed off Vietnam. The number of air and naval personnel in and near Vietnam rose from 47,000 to 77,000 at the time when the number of ground troops had fallen from 95,000 to 68,100.[86]

Still the North Vietnamese tide rolled on. On May 2 the South Vietnamese fled the northern city of Quang Tri, giving the North Vietnamese control of the province of the same name.[87] In Saigon American military officials believed that the ARVN were not up to the fight. Three years of Vietnamization had failed to turn the ARVN into a modern fighting force capable of withstanding a conventional attack. South Vietnamese commanders were not encouraging their soldiers to do enough to repel the North Vietnamese. The city of Hué was filled with soldiers running about aimlessly without commanders. The *Economist* reported that most government officials deserted their posts, "mindful of the massacre of civilians by the communists in Hué during the Tet offensive of 1968."[88] The *New York Times* quoted a despondent student: "Right now, it's everyone for himself." An American adviser in Hué told a reporter, "We are desperately trying to dampen the panic, trying to get the local government to form an emergency committee to keep essential services going—police, health, feeding the refugees. I've got my fingers in the dike, but I've got more holes than dike." The road from Hué south to Da Nang, the second largest city in the South, was jammed with 150,000 refugees, many of whom were ARVN forces who had shed their uniforms to blend in with the civilian population.[89]

In Washington Nixon and Kissinger faced the terrible prospect of a North Vietnamese victory in Vietnam and a simultaneous collapse of detente. Nixon decided that a Northern victory was the worst possible outcome. Kissinger reluctantly agreed. "There's no choice on the summit," Kissinger said. "We have to drop it or else the Russians will." Kissinger wondered, "How can we have a summit meeting and be drinking toasts to Brezhnev while Soviet tanks are crumbling Hué?"[90]

After consulting with Kissinger, Haig, and Haldeman, Nixon ordered the mining of the port of Haiphong, even if it meant risking the collapse of the summit scheduled for the end of May. On the evening of May 8, he told members of Congress worried that an escalation would derail the summit that he had ordered the mining. He then went on national radio and television to announce that "all entrances to North Vietnamese ports will be mined. . . . Air and naval strikes against military targets in North Vietnam will continue." In his speech, Nixon seemed subtly to offer concessions for an end to the war. He told North Vietnam that the United States would stop bombing and remove the mines once there was a cease-fire in Indochina and the return of all prisoners. The United States would remove its forces from Vietnam within four months of a cease-fire, but Nixon did not demand a reciprocal withdrawal of North Vietnamese forces. Ever partial to the muscular metaphors of football, Nixon approved Linebacker as the code name for the bombing operation.[91]

Opponents of the war predictably were infuriated by the decision to mine Haiphong. Senator McGovern considered it a "flirtation with World War III." Senator Edward M. Kennedy called it "folly."[92] But it was the Soviet reaction that mattered most. Despite accusations that the United States had needlessly escalated the war and a protest over a Soviet ship accidentally sunk in Haiphong harbor, the Soviets said nothing about the upcoming summit. Fearful of U.S.-Chinese rapprochement, tired of the war, and eager to conclude an arms control agreement with Washington, Moscow wanted Nixon to visit. By May 11, Kissinger believed that Nixon had weathered the crisis over the summit. Haig thought that the mining of Haiphong "was not a knee-jerk action on the part of the president to save United States honor. It was the action of a world leader who has developed a worldwide concept in a way that it's tied to his ability to function."[93]

The meeting went forward as scheduled at the end of May. Nixon and

Brezhnev signed a treaty limiting deployment of anti-ballistic missile systems, and reached an interim agreement limiting the deployment of strategic nuclear missiles. Nixon and Kissinger returned from Moscow with their public image enhanced as men who had carried off the first meeting between a U.S. president and the Soviet leaders in five years. Vietnam no longer dominated the political and international news in the United States. Foreign observers believed noticed that "Vietnam just does not seem to matter that much any longer in American domestic politics."[94] At the end of June, Nixon announced that no more draftees would go to Vietnam unless they volunteered. He also said that the total U.S. ground troop strength would fall to thirty-nine thousand by September 1.[95]

THE ELECTION OF 1972 AND THE PARIS NEGOTIATIONS

The war went on in the midst of a presidential election, just as had been the case in 1968. The massive bombing of North Vietnam and the mining of the harbors had not forced the NVA to withdraw from the South, nor had the ARVN retaken the northern province of Quang Tri. Renewed bombing of the North had also led to more American POWS, the one issue the majority of the public seemed to care about. In July, the Senate passed a resolution calling for a total withdrawal of U.S. forces from Vietnam if negotiations failed to produce a settlement within four months. At the last minute administration supporters succeeded in including language linking a withdrawal to the return of prisoners of war. Nevertheless, it was clear that one house of Congress insisted on a deadline. Missouri Senator Thomas Eagleton, chosen as the vice presidential nominee by George McGovern, the Democratic presidential candidate, charged that Nixon was "keeping the troops in Vietnam until the last minute" and would then pull them out "just before the election."[96] Nixon's furious response was that the Senate doves had told the leadership of North Vietnam "Don't negotiate with the present administration; wait for us, we will give you what you want—South Vietnam."[97]

Such talk about an impending North Vietnamese victory made more of an impression at home, where public opinion polls showed Nixon widening his lead over McGovern, than they did with Hanoi. By August North Vietnam was in a mood to bargain seriously with Kissinger over an end to the war. The bombing had taken a heavy toll on the North, stalling the offensive into South Vietnam.

The late summer and early fall of 1972 bore an eery resemblance to the same months of 1968. In both years the upcoming presidential election forced the pace of negotiations between the United States and North Vietnam. While Lyndon Johnson was not a candidate in 1968 and Richard Nixon was in 1972, both Presidents were skeptical about the negotiating process they themselves had set in motion. In Nixon's case he reversed his earlier eagerness for a negotiated settlement before the war. Kissinger, on the other hand, who had urged patience on Nixon at the beginning of 1972, changed his mind in the summer and pushed for a settlement before the November election.

In August Kissinger negotiated with Le Duc Tho in Paris and Nguyen Van Thieu in Saigon. Both Kissinger and Tho changed their long-standing positions in the Paris talks. The United States no longer insisted that the North remove all of its troops from the South, while the North Vietnamese no longer demanded that the United States immediately drop its support for President Thieu. Differences opened between Kissinger and Nixon. The National Security Adviser believed that a deal should be struck before the election, because the North would be most prone to make concessions before November. Nixon, on the other hand, accepted the advice of Charles Colson, who reported that pollsters had determined that "any agreement we reached before the election would appear to be a political ploy."[98] Kissinger reported on August 14 that the North no longer insisted on removing Thieu before a cease-fire went into effect. He told Nixon that "we have gotten closer to a negotiated settlement than ever before." Nixon was not impressed. He told Haig that "Henry must be discouraged . . . until after the election."[99]

Kissinger traveled from Paris to Saigon to convince the South Vietnamese government to accept a deal based on a cease-fire in place (which would keep the Northern forces in the South) and the continuation in office of President Thieu. The South Vietnamese leader would have none of it. Despite the initial rout of the ARVN forces in the spring offensive, Thieu believed that the later stall in the Northern advance demonstrated the strength of the ARVN. The South Vietnamese President rejected the continued presence of the Northern forces in the South and Kissinger's proposal for a Committee of National Reconciliation to administer new elections. North Vietnamese troops in the South threatened the viability of Thieu's government, and free elections in which the NLF could participate undermined Thieu's legitimacy. The South Vietnamese President believed that Nixon would stand by him regardless of anything Kissinger said about progress in the Paris talks. A letter from Nixon to Thieu at the end of August promised that "the United States has not persevered all this way, at the sacrifice of so many American lives, to reverse course in the last few months of 1972."[100]

Kissinger returned to Paris for more secret negotiating sessions with Le Duc Tho in September and early October. By now Kissinger acted almost completely on his own. He waived aside Saigon's objections to a potential coalition government and Nixon's concerns "that the American people are no longer interested in a solution based on compromise. [They] favor continued bombing and want to see the United States prevail after all these years."[101] After marathon negotiating sessions from October 8 to 11, Kissinger and Le

Duc Tho reached an agreement between themselves. It contained a cease-fire for Vietnam (but not all of Indochina) and the return of prisoners of war. The United States agreed to leave Vietnam, and the North could keep its troops in the South but would guarantee not to raise their numbers. Thieu's government would remain in place, but it would acknowledge the legitimacy of the NLF and explore the prospect of a coalition government.[102]

Thieu persistently demanded to be part of the negotiations or at least be shown a draft of what Kissinger and Le Duc Tho had worked out, but Kissinger held him off. The National Security Adviser finally showed an English language version of the accord to Thieu on October 19. Shocked at what he read, Thieu said, "This is not what we expected," and he declined to join the agreement, thinking he had Nixon's support. Nixon cabled Kissinger in Saigon that Thieu's agreement to any accord "must be wholehearted so the charge cannot be made that we forced him into a settlement."[103]

Yet forcing the South Vietnamese into a settlement was precisely what Kissinger had in mind. He told Thieu that he had "never been subjected to such treatment as he had experienced" at the hands of the South Vietnamese while in Saigon. When he returned to Washington, he panicked after Hanoi radio announced the terms of the agreement. On October 26 he called Haldeman at 3 o'clock in the morning "in a state of very great concern." Later that day he called a press conference and invited the television cameras.[104] "We believe," Kissinger said, "that peace is at hand." His principal audience was in the two Vietnamese capitals. He wanted to convince Hanoi that despite Saigon's objections the United States remained committed to the document he had drafted with Le Duc Tho. He wanted Saigon to know that Thieu's objections could not scuttle the agreement. The United States was determined to leave Vietnam, with or without the blessing of the government of South Vietnam and on terms closer to those originally proposed by Hanoi than to the U.S. requirements.[105]

For Nixon, winning the election took precedence over the departure of U.S. forces from Vietnam. "Only great events can change things in the campaign now," he told Haldeman. "and Vietnam is the only great event happening." Nixon was unhappy that Kissinger had stolen the limelight with his announcement. Once Kissinger went before the cameras, there was no room for the President to explain his own achievement in ending the war. Nixon wanted to highlight the contrast between "our peace with honor" with McGovern's "peace by surrender."[106]

As he had done since he became president, Nixon did not explain fully what he meant by that phrase. He wanted to support the government of President Thieu yet considered the South Vietnamese an obstacle to ending the war. He thought that Vietnam no longer was important to the United States, and he believed that the public did not care about Vietnam so long as there were no ground troops there. He also believed, however, that more bombing of the North would show that the United States had not been forced out of the war. As Election Day approached, therefore, Nixon expressed much of the same ambivalence toward the war characteristic of U.S. presidents for the previous decade. He wanted to end the war, but only after having humiliated the North Vietnamese. The goal was impossible, given the patience of the North and Nixon's own acknowledgment that Vietnam no longer mattered that much either to the U.S. public or to U.S. foreign policy.

Despite Nixon's frustrations, Haldeman saw a silver lining in raising the profile of Vietnam late in the campaign. Vietnam now overshadowed the growing Watergate scandal. Kissinger's statement that peace was at hand had taken "the corruption stuff [that is, Watergate] off the front pages."[107] The North Vietnamese, too, saw the election as a turning point in their relations with the United States. "They have looked increasingly nervous as election day approaches in the United States," *The Economist* observed the week before voting. They feared that a Nixon re-elected with a large popular mandate would have no further popular restraint in his actions against the North.[108] On November 7, 1972, Nixon won reelection by a huge margin, gaining 60.5 percent of the popular vote and carrying every state with the exception of Massachusetts and the District of Columbia.

THE CHRISTMAS BOMBING

After the election, the United States resumed discussions with both South and North Vietnam. Nixon still had not made up his mind whether to force South Vietnam to accept the agreement worked out by Kissinger or bomb North Vietnam to demonstrate U.S. power and his own independence from congressional limitations. He used both approaches. He first sent Haig to Saigon to reassure and threaten Thieu. "Thieu has to go along with us now," Nixon said. "If he doesn't, we won't have Congressional support to back him later."[109] The South Vietnamese President presented Haig with sixty-nine modifications of the agreement designed to limit the role of the NLF in any future South Vietnamese government and force the evacuation of North Vietnamese troops from the South.[110] Haig also made it clear that the United States wanted an agreement with North Vietnam. He promised increased military aid to the South and additional bombing of the North if that would make Thieu feel any better. But one way or another, the United States would be out of Vietnam within six months.[111]

The scene then shifted to Paris where Kissinger presented the South Vietnamese demands to the North. He did so more for the record than with any expectation that they would be accepted. For their part, the North Vietnamese insisted that the United States keep the agreement negotiated in

October. Kissinger's mood shifted wildly between hope and gloom. If only the North would make a few cosmetic concessions, the whole deal could be made final. If they would not, they would feel as if they could dominate Washington and Saigon. He alternated between asking Nixon for more time to wrap up a firm agreement and telling the President to go on national television and announce the resumption of bombing the North.[112]

Back in Washington, Nixon, Haldeman, Ehrlichman, and John Connally thought Kissinger had become unglued. Nixon considered Kissinger's current wild oscillations between elation and despair "not very rational." Connally believed that "any agreement's better than no agreement." He thought that the main obstacle to signing an accord came from South Vietnam rather than Hanoi. No matter who was responsible, an impasse existed in Paris, and the high hopes of October seemed to have been dashed. Connally thought it was a terrible idea to have Nixon make a televised speech announcing the break-down in talks and renewed bombing. Nixon "should not personify that fail-ure," Connally advised. "He should jettison Kissinger instead, and let Kissinger do the briefing."[113]

The Paris talks continued inconclusively for a few more days, but eventu-ally they broke off on December 13. Kissinger flew back to Washington where he denounced the North Vietnamese to Nixon as "tawdry, filthy shits. They make the Russians look good." His reaction was far out of proportion to the provocation, since what the North Vietnamese wanted was a return to the October agreements. Kissinger had convinced himself, however, that had the Northern delegation really wanted to sign an agreement they would have shown some understanding of the delicacy of the U.S. position regarding South Vietnam. He thought Le Duc Tho wanted to make him sweat. Instead, Kissinger would make North Vietnam pay.[114]

On Friday, December 15, Nixon, Kissinger, and Haldeman met for sev-eral hours to decide how to announce the renewed bombing of North Viet-nam, code-named Linebacker II. They dickered over when to begin the attacks—Sunday or Monday. Nixon did not like the idea of "having a Sunday church service while he was bombing." Eventually they decided on announc-ing the campaign on Saturday, commencing light bombing on Sunday, and hitting Hanoi hard on Monday. For the first time, giant B-52 bombers would be used against the major cities of North Vietnam. They also decided that Kissinger, not Nixon, would announce the bombing. His press briefing would serve as a sort of atonement for his premature declaration that peace had arrived in October. Now that Nixon decided on bombing, Kissinger felt "better than he had in weeks, because now we're in control of things again instead of being in the position of the rabbit with two snakes, having one on each side."[115]

The Christmas bombing of North Vietnam began on December 18. There was a one day halt on Christmas, and the bombing stopped on December 29. Wave after wave of the B-52s attacked the bridges, power plants, railroad lines, and industrial installations of North Vietnam. Over one thousand Vietnamese civilians lost their lives. North Vietnamese surface-to-air missiles shot down fifteen of the B-52s. Ninety-three airmen were declared missing and presumed dead; thirty-one were captured as POWs. On one day of the bombing six of the ninety bombers were shot down.[116]

The bombing provoked outrage similar to the protests following the Cambodian intervention of April 1970. James Reston called it "war by tantrum," and an editorial in the *Washington Post* wondered if the President had lost his mind.[117] No one had prepared the public for the bombing, and most Americans believed that the war was nearly over, with only a few details needing to be worked out. Instead, the heaviest raids of the war occurred. Reports from the scene showed the devastation. The city government of Hanoi took visiting U.S. reporters on tours of schools and hospitals destroyed by the attacks. They showed them a crater where they said ten thousand people had once lived. These claims were grossly exaggerated, but approximately eleven hundred civilians were killed in the Christmas bombing.[118] The President affected an air of calm nonchalance. He went on his regularly scheduled vacation to Florida on December 22, encouraged by Kissinger's advice that his "best course is brutal unpredictability."[119]

Much of this toughness was for show. Nixon desperately wanted the war to end, but he remained just as anxious to demonstrate his own icy resolution. He believed that the air force could not sustain losses of the huge bombers for long. He complained that "it's going to be very tough to take" daily losses of three or more bombers. The bombing had been meant to persuade South Vietnam that the United States would come to its aid. Alexander Haig carried a letter to Thieu demanding that the South accept the deal worked out in October. If not, the U.S. would negotiate with the North alone, leaving the South to make the best deal it could. Thieu ignored Nixon's condition, and continued to insist that no deal occur without a complete withdrawal of North Vietnamese troops. In the midst of the bombing Nixon and Kissinger decided that they make a bilateral deal with the North if the South continued to balk. By the end of 1972, Kissinger had as little use for Thieu—"a complete SOB"—as he had for Le Duc Tho.[120]

The heaviest raids of the Christmas bombing took place on December 26. That evening, Hanoi sent a message to Washington that it was willing to resume the negotiations in Paris on January 8. After a few days of squabbling over the precise date—Nixon wanted January 2, the day before Congress reconvened—the two sides agreed that technical negotiations would begin on January 2, followed by a formal meeting on January 8. On December 30, Nixon announced the end to the bombing and the resumption of the talks.[121]

THE PARIS AGREEMENTS

On January 9 Kissinger and Le Duc Tho reached an agreement almost identical to the one scuttled by Thieu in November. The North Vietnamese negotiator accepted some changes in the language strengthening the dividing line at the Demilitarized Zone, but for all practical purposes the arrangement remained the same—as did the continuing obstacle to the agreement: the objections of President Thieu to the continued presence of North Vietnamese armed forces in the South. Nixon sent Haig again to Saigon to bully the South's President. Nixon and Kissinger told Haig to "take a very hard line with Thieu." He should make it clear that Nixon was going to go forward with the agreement with the North whether Thieu approved or not. Nixon and Kissinger wanted Haig to "trick Thieu" and stop him from "shooting his mouth off" against Kissinger or the agreement before Nixon's presidential inaugural on January 20.[122]

Haig personally delivered to Thieu a brutal letter demanding that he embrace the agreements. Nixon informed him that he had "irrevocably decided" to initial the agreements on January 23 and sign it on January 27. "I will do so, if necessary alone." Should Thieu agree, Nixon promised billions in military and economic aid and the possibility of renewed bombing to withstand any war from the North. While making this assurance, Nixon knew he could not keep it without congressional approval. By the beginning of 1973, both houses of Congress were on record opposing further U.S. participation in the war. Thieu resisted for several days, objecting to the continued presence of the Northern troops in the South and the official recognition of the NLF as the major flaws in the agreement. Neither Haig nor Nixon nor Kissinger would budge. On January 22 he sent word that he approved of the agreement between Kissinger and Le Duc Tho.[123]

On January 23 Kissinger and Le Duc Tho initialed the Paris agreements, and on January 27 Secretary of State William P. Rogers and Le Duc Tho signed them. The accords declared a cease-fire throughout Vietnam (not all of Indochina) beginning at midnight on January 27. POWs would be exchanged within sixty days of the cease-fire. The United States agreed to remove the last of its troops from South Vietnam sixty days after the return of POWs. The North Vietnamese would not be required to remove their troops from the South, but they promised not to "take advantage" of the cease-fire and raise their numbers. This provision proved to be the most contentious. The United States insisted that it meant the North agreed to send no more troops south of the seventeenth parallel, while Hanoi believed it entitled them to replace soldiers in the South as they returned home. The agreement left the government of President Thieu in place, but it created a Committee of National Reconciliation including representatives of the National Liberation Front. The Committee would sponsor elections for a new government in which all parties could participate. The Paris accords also created a four-nation International Commission for Supervision and Control of the Cease-fire. Representatives from Canada and Indonesia, two U.S. allies, joined delegates from Poland and Hungary, two Communist states, to oversee the cease-fire.[124]

At the conclusion of the cease-fire Nixon continued the war—against his critics at home. He told Kissinger that American doves "are disturbed, distressed, and really discouraged because we succeeded."[125] The White House press office exulted that Nixon and Kissinger received credit from the smaller newspapers, especially those farther away from Washington, for achieving an end to the war in Vietnam that would have eluded American doves. The *Birmingham News* praised an agreement representing "a much better bargain than Sen. George McGovern or other 'dove' critics were willing to settle for." The *Denver Post* extolled the Paris agreement as "a tribute to the skill and statesmanship of Henry Kissinger and to the determination, spirit and persistence of President Nixon."[126]

So ended direct U.S. participation in the fighting in Vietnam, although the fighting continued until 1973, in part because Nixon had diminished its importance to the American public. Nixon had also engendered more support from the public by raising the profile of the issue of prisoners of war. By so doing, however, he actually increased the number of Americans held captive. Four years of the Nixon administration had made only one change from the conditions available to the United States in 1968. The United States had not been forced to drop its support for the government of President Thieu, but that government now had agreed to share power. The final agreement allowed the government of President Thieu a fighting chance to remain in power—no more, no less. U.S. casualties had risen by twenty thousand dead in the four years of the Nixon administration, and an additional three hundred thousand Vietnamese had lost their lives. And still the war went on.

Chapter

* * * * * * * * * * *

The Bitter End: 1973–1975

*T*HE FOREIGN ministers of the Democratic Republic of Vietnam, the Republic of Vietnam, the Provisional Revolutionary Government of Vietnam, and the Secretary of State of the United States signed the Paris agreements on January 27, 1973. Expectations ran high in Europe and the United States that the cease-fire meant peace, but inside Vietnam the Paris accords signaled only a truce in which the combatants would regain their strength for a final, climactic battle. For the revolutionaries of the North the Paris agreements represented another in a series of respites going back to the war with France in their effort to unify Vietnam under communist rule. For the members of the government of Nguyen Van Thieu the Paris agreements held out the grim prospect of facing the revolutionaries alone. For years the official U.S. position in the war justified the presence of the American military in Vietnam as helping the government of the South stand alone. Now the Americans were ready to leave and few South Vietnamese officials believed they could face the North or the revolutionaries in the South.

According to the Paris agreements a cease-fire was scheduled to go into effect at eight o'clock Sunday morning Saigon time on January 28. Fighting was intense in the forty-eight hours before the guns were due to fall silent. The North Vietnamese and the NLF fighters attacked hundreds of villages, trying to gain territory before the shooting stopped. U.S. air force and navy planes flew nine hundred bombing sorties, and giant B-52s flew more than fifty-three plane missions, the heaviest U.S. assaults on the South since the Linebacker bombing of the previous May.

305

Then, for the briefest moment, there was silence. An American officer announced to hundreds of grateful reporters in a dingy office building in downtown Saigon, "All offensive military operations by U.S. forces in the republic of Vietnam stopped at 0800 today."[1] A few scenes of reconciliation took place. Here and there, ARVN soldiers and NLF fighters climbed out of holes, tunnels, and bunkers, stood up, and shyly waved to one another. Sometimes the ARVN allowed the National Liberation Front fighters to bury fallen comrades in a dignified way. Previously, government forces had often let enemy corpses rot in the streets for days as warnings to others who might contemplate taking up arms against Saigon. Some observers likened these moments to the profound relief felt on November 11, 1918, by Allied and German forces on the Western front at the end of World War I at the signing of the Armistice. But such joyful moments were rare. In most of South Vietnam, the cease-fire applied only to the United States. The war went on for the other three parties—the governments of South and North Vietnam and the NLF. One U.S. pacification official reported a few months later that the "ceasefire appeared to have initiated a new war, more intense and more brutal than the last."[2]

Indeed, the 25,473 South Vietnamese battle deaths in 1973 exceeded those of any previous year in the war with the exception of 1968, the year of the Tet Offensive, and 1972, the year of the spring invasion of the South by Northern armored forces.[3] The few American officials who remained in South Vietnam, led by Graham Martin, the ambassador who assumed his position in the summer of 1973, tried as hard as had their predecessors to have Washington increase its military support for the Republic of Vietnam. But Americans mostly ignored the fighting in the South in 1973 and much of 1974. Once more the United States followed the pattern set at the beginning of its involvement. What happened inside Vietnam or Indochina mattered only insofar as it affected the United States. Americans cared little for the complicated realities of Indochina, as had been the case for more than thirty years.

A series of events elsewhere in Southeast Asia, the Middle East, and inside the United States soon overshadowed Vietnam. First came the release of U.S. prisoners of war in February and March 1973.[4] Then the remaining U.S. military personnel left Vietnam. In the summer, public attention was fixed on the growing Watergate scandal as daily revelations of White House malfeasance overshadowed foreign affairs. This fascination with Watergate was interrupted only briefly by the visit of Soviet Communist Party General Secretary Leonid Brezhnev to the United States in June. Both President Richard Nixon and Brezhnev believed their summit consolidated progress in detente, so neither wanted a revival of differences over Vietnam. Foreign policy became an issue once more in the fall of 1973 when war broke out between Israel and Syria and Egypt. The oil embargo proclaimed by the

Organization of Arab Petroleum Exporting Countries (OAPEC) created a nasty economic slump in the United States and the rest of the industrial world in the winter of 1973–1974. Facing the worst economic conditions since the Great Depression, Americans largely ignored the awarding of the Nobel Peace Prize to Henry Kissinger and Le Duc Tho for arranging the 1973 ceasefire in Vietnam.

Then Watergate dominated the American consciousness, reaching its inexorable climax with the resignation of Richard Nixon on August 9, 1974. His successor, Gerald Ford, considered the fighting in Vietnam a distinctly secondary issue early in his presidency. By the time he focused on the growing war in the South at the beginning of 1975 it was too late. By the fall of 1974 the North Vietnamese leadership decided to abandon the few remaining efforts at reconciliation with the South Vietnamese government. "We can achieve peace only by defeating the enemy," North Vietnamese radio proclaimed. At the end of 1974 the North exhorted fighters in the South that "the entire enemy army and government must be totally expunged and the government put into the hands of the people."[5] As leaders of the North prepared for the final battle, the government of President Thieu feared abandonment, and most Americans wanted to hear as little as possible about Vietnam.

THE PHONY PEACE

March 26, 1973 was a more significant date for the United States than January 27 because it marked sixty days after the signing of the Paris agreements. By that date all prisoners of war were due to be repatriated. In the interim, prisoners of war were to be exchanged and each side was to provide an accounting of those who had died in captivity. By far, the largest number of POWs were Vietnamese held by the South and the Provisional Revolutionary Government. In the first sixty days after the cease-fire Saigon returned 26,880 POWs to the communists. This release did not satisfy the communists, who claimed that an additional 15,000 remained behind. The communists returned 5,336 South Vietnamese servicemen out of a total of 31,981 listed as missing. Negotiations continued between the PRG and the Saigon government over civilian detainees, and eventually the South freed another 5,081 and the communists 606. Anti-war activists in the United States complained that the South continued to hold in jail anywhere from one hundred- to two hundred thousand civilians suspected of supporting the Vietcong or simply opposed to the policies of the Thieu government.[6]

Americans cared far more about the return of their own captives. In accordance with the Paris agreements, the North Vietnamese authorities immediately turned over a list of 591 who would be returned by March 26.[7] These men all came back to the United States within the sixty-day time limit.

The first group flew from Hanoi to Clark Air Base in the Philippines on February 12. Some walked effortlessly, others hobbled down the ramp of the plane. All saluted the flag. The first to reach the microphone, navy captain Jeremiah Denton, a captive for seven years, said, "We are honored to have had the opportunity to serve our country." Much to the relief of President Nixon, who feared the POWs might blame him for prolonging their bondage, Denton added that "we are profoundly grateful to our Commander in Chief."[8] Over the next six weeks the remaining prisoners returned to warm homecomings, parades, and visits to the White House.

The situation differed markedly, however, for those Americans exiting South Vietnam. By the end of March, only 159 marines remained to guard the U.S. embassy in Saigon. The clandestine Liberation Radio, the voice of the Vietcong, characterized the American departure from the air base at Da Nang as an undignified retreat, in which unkempt officers and enlisted men boarded civilian air planes carrying the cheap consumer goods they had bought in their last days.[9] As groups of POWs were gradually repatriated in February and March, the last several thousand U.S. soldiers quietly departed from Tansonnhut, the major U.S. air base serving Saigon. On March 29 a modest ceremony took place for about fifty of the remaining GIS. Before an audience of Vietnamese clerical workers and scores of American news reporters, General Frederick Weyand, the last commander of U.S. forces in South Vietnam, announced the deactivation of the Military Assistance Command, Vietnam. He then flew home to the U.S. A few hours later hundreds of Vietnamese civilian employees of the base looted the storerooms, carrying off clothes, furniture, ceiling fans, lamps, electric appliances, books and papers, and anything else that could be sold on the black market of Saigon. Other Vietnamese went on a rampage, smashing what was left of the dining hall.[10] Arnold Isaacs, the reporter who described the looting of the dining hall at Tansonnhut, characterized the mess as "a tiny but telling metaphor . . . for the country we had sought to save with American technology and wealth but had never fully understood."[11]

But the destruction was one of the more comprehensible aspects of the ceasefire. Across South Vietnam the departure of the Americans represented less than and something far worse than the restoration of peace or a return to normal life. Over the previous decade hundreds of thousands, maybe as many as a million, South Vietnamese had come to depend on the presence of the United States for their livelihood. The first consequence of the departure of the United States from South Vietnam was a sharp economic decline, worse than a recession but not quite a calamity. The bars serving soldiers, the markets for cameras, watches, calculators, and motor scooters now had lost their best customers and were forced to depend on South Vietnamese soldiers. Nevertheless, an air of cautious hope that the economy would not collapse prevailed. Despite food shortages caused by the migration to the cities of hundreds of thousands of war refugees, the agricultural system remained intact. As many as ten thousand U.S. civilians remained, organizing aid programs.[12] One banker gave South Vietnam "a 50-50 chance of limping along—and that is all most developing countries are doing anyway."[13]

It was hard for anyone to know what to expect from the ARVN now that the Americans were gone. The South Vietnamese army still numbered over one million men, but it faced an uncertain future. The United States had promised to maintain its strength through the resupply of the most advanced American equipment. President Thieu had fought hard for Nixon's assurances that the United States would not let the South Vietnamese armed forces fall behind. Still, Thieu did not trust the Americans. He believed, with good reason, that neither Nixon nor most Americans considered Vietnam very important now that U.S. POWs had returned home. Moreover, the ARVN had learned to fight from the Americans who never had to worry about equipment, arms, or ammunition. Always assured of support, the ARVN fought a high-technology war, ready to sacrifice equipment but more careful of the lives of their soldiers. No one knew what the South Vietnamese fighters would do if they feared for their sources of supply. Would they be willing to endure the hardships, casualties, and backbreaking physical labor endured by the North Vietnamese on the Ho Chi Minh Trail? That was unlikely. Could they achieve the more realistic goal of fighting the war without the Americans' help in such a way that conserved their resources?

Southern anxiety about their ability to survive increased further in the wake of a visit to Hanoi by Henry Kissinger in February. Kissinger hoped to establish a rough "equilibrium" in Vietnam between the contending parties. This balance might resemble the achievement of detente with the Soviet Union, in which both Washington and Moscow believed they had a stake in maintaining a partnership. This stability required the reconciliation and creation of a new coalition government in the South, but the lingering animosities among the parties were so great that he doubted a coalition would work. Instead, he wanted both sides to live side by side yet separate.

When he visited Hanoi in early February, Kissinger expressed satisfaction with the North's release of U.S. prisoners of war. He also presented more details about reconstruction aid. The West German government promised a modest $30 million in reconstruction aid to all the countries of Indochina after "real peace" had been achieved.[14] Nixon offered $4.25 billion over the next decade to help North Vietnam. Northern leaders considered the promise to validate their claim for reparations, a term which later infuriated U.S. officials. Nixon mentioned the role Congress played in appropriations, but other officials doubted that Congress would block aid. Senator J. William Fulbright observed that "Vietnam is behind us," and Congress would be likely to fund an investment in reconstruction. Secretary of State William Rogers said "I don't think we are going to have any problems" in proceeding with "the business of peace and reconstruction" with the North.[15]

In fact, the promise of aid to North Vietnam produced a remarkable reversal in Congress. Members who had been most supportive of the U.S. actions in the war, such as Republican Senators Barry Goldwater or James Buckley, viscerally opposed aid to the North. On the other side, doves such as Democratic Senator Fulbright and 1972 Democratic presidential nominee George McGovern supported it.[16] Kissinger told the North's leaders that the United States recognized that a complete cease-fire would not occur immediately and so the U.S. would overlook minor breaches in the cease-fire. "After all," he said, "how are the two sides going to establish areas of control, except by testing one another."[17]

But the breaches were anything but minor. In the first three weeks after the cease-fire, over three thousand violations of the ceasefire left 7,653 soldiers dead on each side. Over two hundred thousand South Vietnamese were driven from their homes. Some returned quickly, but over sixty thousand were left permanently homeless by the fighting.[18] In the first weekend after the ceasefire the North captured 213 hamlets. Within days, the South had retaken all but thirty-six of them.[19] Both sides complained to the International Control Commission established by the Paris agreements to monitor compliance. The North and the prg accused the South of harassing members of their delegations to a joint military commission. A PRG representative claimed that ARVN soldiers "encircled and isolated the delegation . . . and sent its troops to dig combat fortifications close to the delegation's office."[20] At one point a rock-throwing mob attacked North Vietnamese delegates to the Four Party Joint Military commission at the airport at Ban Me Thuot in the central highlands.

The communist side also broke the cease-fire. The NVA had approximately 250,000 troops in South Vietnam, Laos, and Cambodia. North Vietnamese gunners shelled the provincial capital of Quang Tri in the north of the Republic of Vietnam. Another time communist fighters hurled hand grenades into a pre-dawn Buddhist ceremony in a temple in the Mekong Delta, killing seventeen people. By early March, the North Vietnamese, fed up with the constant harassment their representatives on the Four Power Joint Military Commission received, withdrew all of their personnel from the Commission's field offices, leaving only a token contingent at the headquarters at Tonsonnhut Air Base near the capital.[21] Meanwhile, the end of U.S. bombing of the Ho Chi Minh Trail enabled the North to send between twenty-five and thirty thousand soldiers through Cambodia toward the South in March.[22] After Kissinger returned from his visit to Hanoi in February, he acknowledged that the North Vietnamese had not changed their basic goal to reunify Vietnam under their leadership.[23]

THE SOUTH'S OFFENSIVE

President Thieu's suspicions of the support he could expect from the United States increased after he conferred with Nixon in early April. Earlier visits by South Vietnamese leaders had produced massive publicity and occasional angry demonstrations. By contrast, few Americans paid much attention to Thieu's visit to San Clemente. The POWs were home and, according to Admiral Thomas Moorer, Chairman of the Joint Chiefs of Staff, "Watergate was bubbling like mad."[24] Kissinger also found Nixon so distracted by Watergate that he could not focus on the violations of the cease-fire or the more ominous reports that the North's field units were preparing for a general offensive. "Nixon clearly did not want to add turmoil over Indochina to his mounting domestic perplexities."[25] Thieu found Nixon "preoccupied and absent minded" at their meeting. Nixon told Thieu that the United States would fund his ambitious program of modernization of the South Vietnamese armed forces. Nixon spoke of military aid at the "one billion dollar level" and "economic aid in the eight hundred million dollar range." Kissinger considered these numbers fanciful, since congressional support for aid to South Vietnam "was eroding fast." Nixon assured Thieu, "You can be sure that we stand with you." At the same time, however, Nixon encouraged Thieu to go forward with plans to establish an electoral commission to supervise the creation of the government of national reconciliation promised by the Paris agreements. Thieu left San Clemente for Washington, where his visit went virtually unnoticed. As Stephen Ambrose, Nixon's biographer, noted, Thieu and his supporters in Saigon "no longer mattered to the Americans."[26]

Back home, Thieu ignored Nixon's admonition to try to make the cease-fire and reconciliation with the revolutionaries work. Thieu's fear that the Americans eventually would abandon South Vietnam only fortified his efforts to gain every possible advantage over his local adversaries.[27] He went forward with his program of four no's: no negotiations with the enemy, no communist activity south of the Demilitarized Zone, no coalition government, and no surrender of territory to the North or the PRG. The first three principles were clearly incompatible with the spirit of reconciliation envisioned by the Paris agreements and recommended by Washington. The last *no* also undermined the Paris agreements by indicating that the Saigon government recognized no PRG rights to any territory they controlled at the end of the war. More significantly, the concentration on territory also represented a dramatic reversal of the strategy followed by the U.S. command while the war waged. American generals had ignored the importance of territory, concentrating instead on reducing the flow of men and supplies into the South and killing enemy soldiers. But the experience of the spring offensive of 1972 shocked Thieu's government. Officials feared the repetition of the panicked evacuation of the northern cities of South Vietnam. By refusing to yield an inch to the PRG, Thieu sought to demonstrate to the population of the South the power of his government. But the reverse also was true: should the government of the South be forced to yield ground such a withdrawal would prove its weakness.[28]

The ARVN went on the offensive for the remainder of 1973. Thieu wanted to weaken the revolutionaries and also convince the United States of the power of his forces. He believed that the North Vietnamese and Vietcong fighters were exhausted and wanted a cease-fire. Captured documents indicated some weakening in the North Vietnamese fighting spirit; one directive to Northerners fighting in the South explained that ''a number of our people have balked at making sacrifices when we are approaching the complete victory.''[29] War weariness was at least as evident among the Southern forces, but Thieu pressed forward. Desperate to renew Washington's interest in the plight of the South Vietnamese, Thieu acted as the Americans became more preoccupied with domestic affairs. On August 15, two weeks after a Senate Select Committee had concluded two months of riveting testimony on Watergate, Congress ordered a stop to any further U.S. bombing of Cambodia.[30]

The ARVN conducted offensives in the coastal lowlands, the Mekong Delta region, the western mountainous area close to the Cambodian border, and the provinces near the capital of Saigon. The heaviest fighting occurred near Saigon, where the government forces made little progress in clearing areas held by the PRG since the spring offensive of 1972. The Vietnamese air force (VNAF) went into action, bombing suspected enemy storage sites near Saigon. Most of the bombs landed harmlessly, miles from their targets. VNAF pilots flew high above the ground to avoid the withering anti-aircraft fire from the PRG fighters.

NORTHERN COUNTER-ATTACKS

The North Vietnamese and PRG responded with their own attacks designed to keep open their supply lines. In mid-October communist forces captured a South Vietnamese militia outpost in the northern part of the country between Da Nang and Hué.[31] Fighting reached its peak at the end of October, with both sides struggling to gain control of the ''rice road'' from the Mekong Delta to the capital. Thieu ordered his forces to ''consider every grain of rice as a bullet.''[32] Both sides lost thousands of soldiers.[33]

The North's leaders appealed to the Soviet Union and China for help. Le Duan, the First Secretary of the Vietnam Workers Party, traveled to Beijing and Moscow in June asking for additional military aid. His visit followed hard on the heels of Leonid Brezhnev's Washington summit with Nixon. While Watergate had preoccupied the American public, detente with the Soviet Union represented the most highly valued aspect of Nixon's foreign policy.

The Soviets, too, had gained enormous respect internationally through detente with the United States.[34]

Much to the dismay of leaders of the North, both China and the Soviet Union once more adopted the stance they had taken during the Genva conference of 1954: they valued improved relations with the United States more than the prospect of a communist victory in the Vietnam War. With the conclusion of the Paris agreements, the Chinese and the Soviets, like the Americans, seemed to believe that Vietnam mattered less than it had before. In October the Central Committee of the Vietnam Workers Party convened a plenary session to discuss the next step in the confrontation with the Thieu government. General Vo Nguyen Giap proposed an early offensive against Thieu, but the political leaders drew back from such a momentous decision as they had done in 1957 and 1958. They feared that the United States might still be drawn back into the fighting. As they had done in 1959 and 1960, the North's leaders decided to conduct a low-intensity military struggle against the South.

The Northern leaders followed what they characterized as "the path of revolutionary violence," authorizing sabotage against government targets designed to unnerve the South Vietnamese and scare off potential foreign investors. They directed communist units in the South to "strike back against the Saigon administration as long as it has not discontinued its war acts." To punctuate their confrontation with the South, the communist forces shelled the Bien Hoa air base near Saigon on November 4, destroying three fighter planes.[35] A North Vietnamese broadcast justified the attack as a "well deserved" rebuke to the "war-mongers [and] stubborn and bellicose group of traitors" who made up the Saigon administration.[36] Nevertheless, the communists did not authorize a final offensive against the South in late 1973.

THE NOBEL PRIZE

The deterioration in the ceasefire coincided with the awarding of the Nobel Peace Prize jointly to Henry Kissinger and Le Duc Tho. Kissinger gratefully accepted his share of the prize. The cease-fire may have been hanging by a thread, but the Paris accords had achieved the end of direct U.S. involvement and the return of U.S. POWs, the elements Americans cared most deeply about. The *Los Angeles Times* considered the prize well earned by "a professional and brilliant feat of diplomacy by two remarkable men."[37] For most people in the United States, the end of direct American involvement validated Kissinger's claim that Vietnam was, at most, a secondary area of the nation's foreign policy. For his part, Le Duc Tho rejected the honor, noting that "peace has not yet really been established in South Vietnam."[38] Some American observers also questioned the judgment of the Norwegian Nobel committee in highlighting a settlement just as it seemed to slip away. Edwin O. Reischauer, former U.S. ambassador to Japan, said that to put Kissinger "together with Le Duc Tho shows either that the people of Norway have a very poor understanding of what happened out there or a good sense of humor. There is no peace in Vietnam and the getting out was much too slow." Another Asia expert noted "I'm no fanatical enemy of Kissinger, but this is a bit much. I think he's done some good things, but the peace prize? There's no peace and we stayed much too long."[39]

THE FALL OF RICHARD NIXON

But public attention quickly shifted away from the Nobel Prize and Vietnam. So many dangerous foreign policy issues confronted Kissinger in the last months of 1973 that he did not go personally to Norway to accept his share of the prize in December. The war between Israel and Egypt and Syria, started on October 6, threatened to involve the superpowers. On the twenty-first of that month, while Kissinger was in Moscow trying to dampen tensions, Nixon ignited a firestorm of public anger when he dismissed Archibald Cox, the special prosecutor investigating Watergate. Congress received hundreds of thousands of telephone calls and telegrams denouncing Nixon, and the House of Representatives commenced impeachment proceedings against him. Nixon's authority in foreign affairs, which had prevailed with most of the public and a majority of lawmakers up to this point, suffered severely in the wake of the firing of Cox.[40] Graham Martin, the U.S. ambassador to South Vietnam, worried that preoccupation with the Middle East war would force Kissinger to neglect Indochina. He wanted an additional $1 billion in aid to the government of the South. "Time is crucial here," he cabled Kissinger. The Secretary of State tried to reassure Martin that Washington remained focused on Vietnam, but that was mostly a charade.[41]

On November 7 Congress overrode Nixon's veto to adopt the War Powers Act, a product of years of effort by congressional opponents of U.S. involvement in Vietnam to fortify the legislature's power to declare war. Under provisions of the new law, the President was required to notify Congress if possible before introducing U.S. forces into an area where hostilities might take place. Once the President engaged U.S. forces, they could stay no more than sixty days unless Congress granted specific authority to extend their stay.[42] While passage of the War Powers Act did not prohibit subsequent U.S. engagement in Vietnam should the position of the South Vietnamese decline further, the bar to future involvement had been raised higher than ever before.

As the Watergate drama unfolded in the United States in the first seven months of 1974, intense fighting continued in Vietnam. North Vietnam complained that the South had delayed the return of prisoners. Le Duc Tho blamed the United States because Washington still paid for Saigon's prison system and trained its police.[43] Meanwhile, the South faced an even worse economic situation. The world-wide recession brought about by the rise in oil prices hit the South especially hard. With Americans gone, spending by U.S. personnel on bars, taxis, prostitutes, servants, and souvenirs shrank from $400 million in 1971 to $100 million in 1973. Unemployment hit 27 percent and inflation roared along at 65 percent. ARVN soldiers felt the pinch; their month's pay was enough to support them for at most a week.[44] Preoccupied with saving himself from impeachment, Nixon never seriously considered the reintroduction of American fighting forces in Vietnam, but he did ask Congress for $850 million in military and economic assistance to support the South's war effort.[45] Congress resisted. Kissinger sensed Nixon's desire to avoid confrontation with the North. One of the Secretary of State's aides told Ambassador Martin that "Henry's attitude is that he wants to maintain a polite tone even when Ducky [Kissinger's nickname for Le Duc Tho] is vituperative."[46]

To reverse congressional opposition, Martin returned home to argue the case for more aid. Martin, the last U.S. envoy to South Vietnam, was one of the worst. Like scores of previous U.S. officials in South Vietnam, he insisted the government forces were making progress in their war. His relentlessly upbeat assessments of the South's progress were supposed to bolster the fighting spirit of the government and encourage a war-weary American Congress to spend $750 million ($100 million less than requested in the spring) over the next year to support the South's armed forces and economy. Martin spent the summer of 1974 in Washington arranging additional aid for the South. He painted a rosy picture of an army holding its own against communist attacks and an economy that had suffered but not collapsed with the departure of the U.S. forces: "Politically the South Vietnamese government is stronger than ever."[47] Martin seemed to some critics more a representative of the South Vietnamese government to the U.S. than the American ambassador. One editorial called him "our man from Saigon."[48]

Members of Congress remained unconvinced by Martin's pleadings. When a Defense Department official repeated Martin's rosy scenario, Representative Patricia Schroeder (D., Colo.) replied, "I have a feeling you believe in the Tooth Fairy."[49] At the end of August Congress approved $700 million in military and economic assistance, a reduction from the $1 billion originally requested but larger than the $400 million sought by some opponents of the war. *The Washington Post*'s editorial favoring the $700 million figure captured the lawmakers' mood: "The principle of American steadfastness deserves to be honored as best we can, even though the particular government benefitting from its application in this instance is far from a model regime."[50]

Throughout his tenure in Saigon, Martin rejected any criticism of the South as communist propaganda. A true believer in the cause, he questioned the judgment, motives, and patriotism of anyone who doubted the capacity of the South Vietnamese government. He tried to prohibit embassy personnel from speaking to reporters from the *New York Times* or the *Washington Post* because they wrote critical stories about President Thieu. He assailed the staff of Senator Kennedy for carrying out the wishes of "those whose objectives it is to aid Hanoi."[51] When Amnesty International complained about the South holding more than one thousand civilian political prisoners, Martin blasted the human rights organization for "unquestioningly pushing whatever propaganda line" the communist forces adopted. Representative Donald Fraser (D., Minn.), highly critical of the Saigon authorities, characterized Martin's hot-tempered defense of Saigon as "a disgrace." But Martin was unbowed. As time went on, he perceived a "conspiracy out there" of reporters, intellectuals, peace activists, and congressional opponents of further aid to South Vietnam.[52]

If Martin's relentless optimism failed to sway Congress, it did affect the perceptions of South Vietnamese authorities. They were less willing than ever to heed admonitions to negotiate with Hanoi and the PRG. They paid little attention when one member of Congress explained that the reduction from the original request for $1 billion signified to Saigon "that we're cutting you down to $700 million which is enough for you to defend yourself and sit down and work out a political settlement."[53] One of Thieu's associates explained that he "thought perhaps in his mind that if the U.S. Ambassador in Saigon showed no visible signs of concern, the situation could not be hopeless," even after Congress decreased aid.[54] The reduction in U. S. support had the greatest impact on the attitude of Southern commanders toward their stockpiles of ammunition. The government still had ten shells for every one the communists possessed.[55] The South had complete mastery of the air. But what would life be like if American aid diminished? The South relied on Martin to project the future. If he said Washington would support them, America would eventually come through. If he panicked, they would too. The hopes for an independent, viable South Vietnam, the original justification for the war, seemed also as remote as ever in August 1974.

Watergate reached its climax, and the war got hotter in late summer. Richard Nixon resigned the presidency on August 9, 1974, in the midst of the largest communist offensive since the cease-fire. On August 8 communist forces overran the outpost at Thuogduc, 330 miles north of Saigon and 30 miles south of Da Nang. The coastal plain South of Da Nang now was vulnerable. As many as an entire division of North Vietnamese troops took part in the battle.[56]

Nixon's resignation reverberated throughout Vietnam. The communists saw his demise as delicious retribution for a hated adversary. Liberation Radio, the voice of the PRG, claimed that U.S. involvement in Vietnam had intensified a profound economic and social crisis in the United States. Nixon paid the price for his "perfidious and cruel" activities in Vietnam. Nixon had been "unmasked . . . as a war criminal in Vietnam and as a deceitful, double dealing, cheating and crafty swindler."[57] In Saigon Nixon's resignation produced a more varied reaction, combining admiration for the peaceful transfer of power in the American democracy with apprehension over what to expect from Gerald Ford, his successor.[58]

AVOIDING PRESIDENT FORD'S WAR

President Ford's first statements on Vietnam seemed to reassure the South that he remained committed to Nixon's policies, but officials in Saigon could not be certain that the United States would mount a major campaign on their behalf. The new President called for "strict observance of the cease-fire in Vietnam." He encouraged Congress to fund the full amount of military aid requested by the Nixon administration, but he accepted the $700 million in aid eventually passed at the end of August.[59] The press reported that Kissinger urged him to respond forcefully to a North Vietnamese offensive expected in the fall,[60] but U.S. public opinion had shifted sharply away from support for involvement in Vietnam—if anything, the mood now reflexively indicated staying away. The *Philadelphia Inquirer* advised Ford to avoid the quagmire: "We are out and should stay out."[61] Similarly, the *Baltimore Sun* counseled the new President to acknowledge that neither U.S. military strength nor diplomacy could impose a settlement on Vietnam. The paper supported Congress's effort to reduce military assistance and "accept the peculiarly Vietnamese political solution that someday, somehow must come."[62]

In his first weeks in office, Ford concentrated more on healing festering wounds at home than on the burgeoning war in Indochina. Ambassador Martin grumbled that "the bureaucracy has the feeling that we shouldn't dirty our hands in Vietnam."[63] And despite his sympathy for the perilous situation in the South, Ford shared this sentiment. On September 8 he pardoned Richard Nixon for any crimes he might have committed during Watergate. One week later, the President tried to balance the pardon of Nixon, which angered the former President's many adversaries, by offering what he called "earned amnesty" to Vietnam war-draft or military-justice offenders. Both measures cost Ford dearly in popular opinion, and his standing in the polls dropped twenty points in September.[64]

CLEMENCY FOR DRAFT OFFENDERS

To offer draft evaders and military deserters a chance to wipe the slate clean, Ford created a Presidential Clemency Board chaired by former Senator Charles Goodell (R., N.Y.). The activities of the board did not go far enough to satisfy demands for a full amnesty or pardon raised by opponents of the war, yet it irritated many nationalists and conservatives within the Republican Party. One Louisiana Republican representative rejected any sort of amnesty "as a direct insult to those servicemen who . . . did not shirk their duty." Senator Ernest Hollings (D., S.C.) said that wives of servicemen listed as missing in action "went through the roof" when the heard Ford propose amnesty for draft offenders.[65]

But the board pushed forward despite such objections, accepting applications from about 21,500 men until April 1975. It reviewed cases until the end of 1975 and found 13,000 of the applications eligible for action. The President granted immediate pardons for 42 percent of these men; the bulk of the remainder received pardons after three to six months of alternative service. The profiles of the men who entered the clemency program defied the stereotype of draft evaders. Most were uneducated, and either had not answered draft calls or had gone absent without leave from their military units. While the program worked well for the men who participated in it, only 20 percent of those who might have sought clemency did so. Goodell constantly found himself defending the program from critics within the administration who believed that it undermined Ford's chances for re-election and from civil libertarians and anti-war groups who complained that the clemency program unjustly punished people who courageously opposed an unjust war.[66]

THE BEGINNING OF THE SOUTHERN COLLAPSE

As the Ford administration struggled to consolidate its power in the last months of 1974, President Thieu's authority continued to diminish in South Vietnam. Prime Minister Tran Thien Khiem advised visiting Deputy Secretary of Defense William P. Clements Jr. that the congressional reduction of aid to South Vietnam had wrecked morale. "The people," he complained, "recognize that the government of Vietnam could no longer count on U.S. air support."[67] Even worse, huge anti-government demonstrations, similar to the ones that had brought down Ngo Diem Dinh in 1963, broke out in Saigon in October and spread to other cities across South Vietnam. The cause this time was corruption. Marchers chanted "we want a president who serves the people, not a president who steals from the people!" A group called the People's Anti-Corruption Movement denounced the government as a "rotten, dictatorial family regime, worse than Diem's." Like Diem, Thieu responded with repression and concessions. He closed down critical newspapers, but he also dismissed hundreds of ARVN officers, including the commanders of three of the four military corps. In early November he banned further demonstrations, and a superficial calm returned to the capital.[68]

Thieu's difficulties emboldened the revolutionaries. The PRG announced its own version of one of Thieu's four no's: the PRG refused to negotiate with the government "as long as Nguyen Van Thieu and his gang remain in power in Saigon." Commanders in the North ordered their forces in the South to "liberate the people and hold the land"; before, they had had the more modest goal of harassing the ARVN. Since the South's armed forces were committed by one of Thieu's four "no's" never to abandon territory, the fighting was intense. Losses in the coastal plain south of Da Nang and the Mekong Delta in the final months of 1974 proved especially demoralizing.[69]

Then the dam burst, and the South Vietnamese armed forces collapsed in the first three months of 1975. On January 6 communist forces captured Phuc Binh, capital of Phuc Long province, eighty miles northwest of Saigon near the Cambodian border. Nearly all of the fifty-four hundred government soldiers were killed or captured, many of them elite airborne forces dispatched to the front to prevent the loss of territory to the communists. But few soldiers fought well, and many ground troops threw down their arms. South Vietnamese air force planes killed many government troops when they dropped their bombs from a high altitude to avoid communist anti-aircraft fire.[70] While Thieu and his top commanders recognized in late December that the communists held the advantage in Phuc Binh, the President's commitment not to yield an inch forced him to defend it. The loss of Phuc Binh was the first provincial capital to fall to the communists since the fall of Quang Tri during the Easter Offensive of 1973.[71]

Three days after Phuc Binh fell the communist forces launched a major attack on the coastal plain three hundred miles north of Saigon. This time, though, South Vietnamese officials could not expect American air strikes to relieve them. Yet they expressed the wistful hope that "the fall of Phuc Binh could prove a blessing in disguise if it could strengthen President Ford's hand in dealing with a hostile Congress." In late January the President submitted a request for an additional $300 million in military assistance. He told his cabinet that the United States would develop a guilt complex affecting other areas of U.S. foreign policy should the United States not provide additional aid to South Vietnam. He recognized the strong antipathy in Congress toward additional involvement in the Indochina war, so he justified his request as maintaining credibility of commitments elsewhere. Ron Nessen, the White House press secretary, said "the odds are in favor of a disaster" in South Vietnam "if we don't do anything" to support the Saigon military.[72]

As Congress considered Ford's request for additional money for South Vietnam, administration officials stressed the credibility of the U.S. word given to foreign governments. One of Ford's aides told cabinet secretaries to stress that the credibility of the word of the United States was at stake. "If our adversaries see our constancy and determination lacking here, they may be tempted to test our will in other areas of the world."[73] Ambassador Martin weighed in from Saigon. "Thank God," he cabled Kissinger, "you have got the guts to move and the understanding that there has never been a time when bold and aggressive action would produce more dividends."[74]

But it was hard to convince members of Congress that Vietnam mattered. The war now was the South's to win or lose. Longtime opponents of the U.S. effort in the war rejected administration arguments that the South Vietnamese armed forces were reluctant to commit their vastly superior reserves of ammunition and armor because they feared the U.S. would not make good their losses. Representative Robert Leggett (D., Calif.) observed that "by continuing to shower money on the war making machines we have created in Indochina, we encourage a profligate style of warfare that is expensive but not very effective." Mostly, Congress simply wanted no more of Vietnam. Congressman Richard Ottinger (D., N.Y.) concluded that "the commitment that the United States made in entering the Paris agreement was that we were going to get out." Congressman Les Aspin (D., Wis.) mentioned the greatest fear that the request for more aid was a prelude to the return of U.S. forces to Vietnam "followed by fighting, casualties, and maybe, worst of all, American POWs. We would be back in the quagmire."[75]

An eight-member congressional delegation, including supporters and opponents of further aid, visited both Cambodia and South Vietnam in early March. The situation in Cambodia seemed especially critical, with the possibility that the government of General Lon Nol might fall to the communist Khmer Rouge within weeks. The members of Congress heard chilling reports of hundreds of thousands of refugees fleeing the areas controlled by the Khmer Rouge in terror of a bloodbath. Representative Pete McCloskey (R., Calif.), an opponent of greater aid, expressed shock at what was happening in Cambodia. "If it collapses," he told Ford upon his return, "there will be a massacre."[76] President Lon Nol told the visitors he was willing to step down if that would stop the fighting, but most of the members doubted that a new government would stop the communists' advance.[77] While some of the antiwar members came away from Vietnam with heightened respect for the fighting spirit of the South Vietnamese, a consensus emerged that the war was approaching an unhappy climax. McCloskey said, "I fear that what we are negotiating is how to transfer power peacefully to the Communists."[78]

The North Vietnamese offensive rolled on. On March 14 they captured the provincial capital of Ban Me Thuot in the central highlands.[79] For the first time the government of South Vietnam announced a withdrawal of its forces to save a line near Saigon. Thieu adopted a strategy of "light at the top, heavy on the bottom," designed to save his best troops for a defense of Saigon.

Thieu acted without warning or planning, forcing his ill-prepared troops to execute one of the most difficult military maneuvers, withdrawal under enemy fire.[80] Thomas Polgar, the CIA station chief in Saigon, thought that "the South Vietnamese had no strategical concept . . . beyond putting a regiment here and putting a regiment there."[81] By March 20 the government had lost or abandoned without a fight ten of forty-four provinces. On that day the ARVN quit the northern city of Hué without a fight. The retreat from the north stunned and demoralized many commanders.[82] One officer told an American reporter, "We were very angry, very ashamed. " Another screamed at a South Vietnamese colonel who ordered a retreat, "Why are we withdrawing? We can fight!"[83]

Yet for every word of defiance, thousands of soldiers ran away. Half a million refugees—officials, deserting soldiers, farmers, businesspeople—crowded the roads from the north to the south and from the highlands to the coast. Hundreds of thousands of frightened soldiers and their families, officials, and civilians packed Da Nang. On March 26 officials of the U.S. Agency for International Development announced a civilian airlift of twelve thousand people a day out of Da Nang to Saigon. The pictures from the airlift were even more dispiriting, as ARVN soldiers clamored over old people, women, and children to secure some of the remaining seats on vastly overloaded transport planes.[84] CIA Director William Colby informed Ford of the "terrible mob scenes" at the airport and the port of Da Nang. "Some of the military have even shot their way onto ships." A small number of civilians had boarded the evacuation craft "but law and order has broken down completely and it's almost impossible" to save defenseless refugees.[85] Only the incurably optimistic Ambassador Martin saw hope in the situation. "Despite journalistic accounts," he cabled, "what happened here was a planned military withdrawal . . . to more defensible lines." He thought that the military equation in the remainder of the country, "roughly old Cochinchina, is now reasonably stable."[86]

By the beginning of April, hopes were lost for a compromise between Thieu and the advancing communist forces. U.S. efforts turned to humanitarian aid but that, too, ended in catastrophe. The Ford administration organized Operation Babylift to evacuate fifteen hundred children from Vietnam for adoption in the U.S. and Australia. The idea for the evacuation came from Edward J. Daly, a former CIA operative described as a "pistol-packing millionaire," who chaired World Airlines. Daly had flown the last planes out of Da Nang and wanted to do something to erase bad memories of the frenzied evacuation from that city.[87]

But the babylift provoked controversy as soon as it was announced. Although the youngsters were described as orphans, many were not. Some were sent by terrified parents to avoid what they feared would be a bloodbath after the war. One mother said, "Maybe some day the VC will be here. My children die. I like stay. But I worry too much with vc here.''[88] White House photographer David Kennerly, in Saigon at the end of March, said, ''I had old friends begging me to take their children out.''[89] Not surprisingly, the PRG condemned this attempt to ''force people to evacuate.'' Independent relief agencies also objected. An official of the Vatican's relief organization characterized the airlift as ''a deplorable and unjustified mistake . . . originated by an unmotivated hysteria.''[90] The first Operation Babylift plane, a giant air force c-5A transport, the world's largest aircraft, took off from Tansonnhut air base with 243 children on April 4. Ten children were strapped into seats that normally accommodated three adults. An air force officer said the scene at the airport before the plane took off was ''the most pathetic and touching sight I have ever seen.'' The sight was worse thirty-five minutes later when a pressure door at the rear of the plane failed, causing the aircraft to crash in flames. One-hundred-seventy-eight children died. An American nurse who unzipped body bags at a nearby hospital frantically trying to identify the dead called it ''the most shocking experience of my entire life.''[91] Americans saw it all on television. For many of them the plane crash symbolized much of the horror and futility of the American involvement in Vietnam. Whatever their good intentions, the American had never comprehended Vietnamese culture or politics. Modern technology seemed mocked and defeated by Vietnamese tenacity.

THE FINAL DAYS

In the aftermath of Operation Babylift, even top officials of the Ford administration wanted no more of Vietnam. Ron Nessen, Ford's press secretary, advised the President to break sharply and publicly with past policies on Vietnam by preparing the way for final withdrawal of the U.S. from Vietnam. In February Nessen had loyally advocated asking Congress for additional aid for Vietnam and Cambodia, but now he recommended against it, certain that Congress would refuse. Nessen warned that ''until now it is not 'Ford's war.' But it will be if he requests more aid to keep the war going.''[92]

On April 4 Army Chief of Staff Frederick Weyand provided one of the gloomiest assessments of the military situation in Vietnam. Ford had earlier dispatched his fact-finding mission with the admonition, ''You are not going over to lose.''[93] But Weyand returned from a one-week visit to South Vietnam to report that ''the Government of Vietnam is on the brink of a total military defeat.'' They were certain to go down if aid was not increased. Even if it were, he thought that the chance for their survival ''marginal at best.''[94] He also scotched an idea floated by General William C. Westmoreland, the former commander in Vietnam, for renewed U.S. air strikes over the North.[95] Weyand realized that Congress would forbid any air action over the North. He did propose, however, that Ford consider the use of troops to help the evacuation of the remaining six thousand U.S. personnel and some ten thousand South Vietnamese tied to the Americans. The madcap evacuation of Da Nang convinced Weyand that the United States needed to provide protection when Saigon fell.[96]

A few days later, on April 9, CIA Director Colby reinforced Weyand's grave assessment. The day before, a dissident officer of the South Vietnamese air force had used his F-5 fighter jet to bomb the presidential palace. He then flew the plane into communist-controlled territory and defected to the PRG with denunciations of Thieu and the Americans.[97] Thieu then tried to reorganize his government to bring in opposition leaders, but most of them were reluctant to join such an obviously lost cause. Any new government would probably only negotiate terms with the communists. Colby believed that, for its part, Hanoi "is not interested in a compromise but rather in a figleaf for a North Vietnamese takeover under military pressure."[98]

Faced with an impossible military situation, Ford agreed with Nessen and his other political advisers that a continuation of the war was the last thing the American public wanted. It was hardly a close call. Throughout the sixty days preceding the fall of Saigon, the White House had found widespread disapproval whenever it measured congressional and public attitudes toward a continuation of military aid to Saigon. Phnom Penh fell to the Khmer Rouge at the beginning of April.[99] The collapse of the Cambodian armed forces infected the South Vietnamese soldiers. U.S. military intelligence in South Vietnam believed that "Saigon can hold out only a few weeks. . . . Barring massive U.S. intervention or a deliberate North Vietnamese pause it is going to go."[100] Public opinion in the United States opposed such intervention. Illinois Republican Robert Michel reported that his constituents believed that the reluctance of the South Vietnamese armed forces to fight meant that "we can only provide humanitarian assistance."[101]

For the rest of April, Congress would only consider providing such humanitarian assistance. Ford addressed Congress on April 10 to ask for the additional $300 million in military aid, but there was little likelihood lawmakers would approve. Four days later, he met with the Senate Committee on Foreign Relations at the White House. Both Republicans and Democrats told him that the war was over. As Senator Howard Baker (R., Tenn.) put it, "An evacuation of the American citizens [is] so urgent that everything else— legality, Thieu's incumbency, everything else—[is] secondary to that."[102] Other members of Congress told the White House that only humanitarian assistance was possible. Representative Bella Abzug (D., N.Y.), one of the most vociferous critics of U.S. involvement in the war, called for an end to military assistance to the government of President Nguyen Van Thieu, but she said that "the human suffering and chaos in South Vietnam require prompt humanitarian and constructive action by the U.S. government, whose wrong policies and illegal intervention for the past decade are largely responsible for the current tragic plight of the South Vietnamese.'' Senator Walter Mondale (D., Minn.), who had expressed growing opposition to U.S. involvement in Vietnam over the previous four years, agreed that Congress would not provide military assistance but would be moved by the plight of Vietnamese children, who were the ''innocent victims of the conflict.''[103]

Even as Ford acknowledged the end of the South's ability to defend itself, Graham Martin employed a bewildering array of tactics, some at war with one another, to persuade some foreign power to come to the aid of the South Vietnamese. He flattered Kissinger for his speeches favoring additional aid to South Vietnam. He told the Secretary of State that he was like George Marshall advocating aid to Western Europe at the beginning of the Cold War— indeed, he was a ''genius.''[104] Martin also thought it might help to obtain aid for South Vietnam by aligning himself with Kissinger against professional Foreign Service officers who opposed aid. These people took ''great care to insure their intellectual hemlines are not one silly milimeter [sic] above or below the current conventional intellectual mode.''[105]

When it became clear to Martin that Congress would not approve additional aid, the Ambassador looked to other countries. He persisted in a yearlong effort to have Saudi Arabia, underwrite Saigon's war effort. He cabled the U.S. embassy in Jidda, Saudi Arabia, that South Vietnam was now a ''victim of a concerted propaganda campaign of distortion in the U.S. . . . fanned by the same elements of media which are so vocal in support of Israel.''[106] Despite the visit of a South Vietnamese representative to Saudi Arabia, the Saudis declined to back an obviously losing cause.[107]

While Martin desperately sought military aid for South Vietnam, he resisted efforts at humanitarian assistance, fearing such aid would convince the government of South Vietnam that U.S. officials had concluded their cause was hopeless. For the same reason, Martin resisted for as long as possible the evacuation of U.S. personnel, their dependents, and South Vietnamese who worked for the United States.[108]

The differences of opinion among Ford, his political advisers, Kissinger, and Martin about the appropriate course for the United States to follow in South Vietnam demonstrated that Vietnam still mattered at the upper levels of the U.S. government in 1975, but the issue no longer engaged the public the way it once had done. Now the major public concern was to avoid discussion of Vietnam. Such widespread revulsion helps understand why Ford chose to suppress discussion of the promises made by Richard Nixon to President Thieu at the time of the Paris agreements to provide military assistance to South Vietnam should the North violate the agreements. Once the existence of the letters from Nixon to Thieu became known in 1975, Ford's critics contended that he should have fully disclosed the contents of the letters to

Congress at the time of the final debate over providing aid to South Vietnam.[109]

Given Kissinger's general opposition to sharing confidential information with Congress, there was little likelihood that Ford would have turned the documents over to lawmakers. Having overruled Kissinger on a substantial matter—making an all-out push for aid to South Vietnam—Ford had little incentive to further irritate his Secretary of State by turning over documents to a hostile Congress.[110] Furthermore, it is hard to believe that anything, including the disclosure of these promises, would have altered the general public aversion to re-entering the war.

Meanwhile, North Vietnamese forces approached Saigon. Thieu's domestic opponents from the right, led by former Vice President Nguyen Cao Ky, to the neutralists, led by General Duong Van Minh, all wanted Thieu to leave. Even Ambassador Martin, his most steadfast supporter, believed that a new government might be able to work out an arrangement with the advancing communist forces to avoid a surrender of the city. On April 21 President Thieu finally resigned the presidency. Vice President Tran Van Huong replaced him. Thieu spoke on television to the nation that evening, seeking the vindication of history. He explained that he had always opposed the Paris agreements because it legitimized the Vietcong. He said that U.S. aid had been critical in blunting the communist attacks during Tet in 1968 and in the spring of 1972. Now that the United States could no longer be counted on to provide military aid, Thieu said he had no choice. He blamed Kissinger for not making good on Nixon's commitment to supply new military aid if the North violated the Paris agreements and angrily refused Kissinger's offer of asylum in the United States.[111]

Finally, on April 23, Ford received wild applause from six thousand young people in the audience at Tulane University and praise from political and foreign affairs analysts around the country when he announced that "the war in Vietnam is over as far as America is concerned." After Ford spoke, he pointedly informed the press that he reached the decision on his own, without consulting Kissinger, whose high reputation for foreign policy achievement had recently seemed to overshadow Ford's. The President was elated by the warm reception of his speech. Most Americans seemed relieved that the war had ended.[112]

But it had not. An unnatural calm hung over Saigon for the next few days. North Vietnamese and Vietcong tanks were on the outskirts of the city, but refrained from entering. In both Saigon and Washington, American officials delayed orders to evacuate Saigon for as long as possible. Ever the blind optimist, Martin thought that Saigon could hold out for another few weeks if the United States did not force a panic by withdrawal.[113] As Ford told the National Security Council on April 24, "I think it is very important to stay there as long as we can contribute, to evacuate in a way that will not promote panic." Until the end, Kissinger tried to enlist the Soviet Union to help the Americans out of a jam in Vietnam. This time he wanted them to arrange a lull in the fighting to permit U.S. personnel to leave peacefully.[114]

By now, events in Vietnam were more out of Soviet hands than ever. On April 27 President Huong resigned and was replaced by General Duong Van Minh. The war had come full circle. Minh, of course, had led the coup against Ngo Dinh Diem on November 1963. A presumed neutralist, he had been ousted himself by the Americans in January 1964. In 1967 Thieu had banned his participation in the presidential elections. Now Minh was president, trying to arrange a peaceful accommodation with the triumphant communists. He offered them a cease-fire but they refused.

On April 28 the final battle for Saigon began with North Vietnamese and Vietcong artillery attacks on Tansonnhut Airport. The shelling killed two U.S. marines helping to evacuate civilians and rendered all but one runway useless. On the morning of April 28, Kissinger met with the Washington Special Actions Group to decide what to do if Tansonnhut were to be closed. If that happened "we should pull out all the Americans" by helicopter from Saigon.[115]

That evening Ford and his principal foreign policy and military advisers made the fateful decision to evacuate the U.S. embassy. Secretary of Defense James Schlesinger opposed using American air power to cover the departure. There were four thousand North Vietnamese sappers in the capital, he said. "They will attack the embassy if we attack by fire." The NSC meeting also agreed with Kissinger to save the Americans before helping the South Vietnamese who depended on them. "If we have to go out, priority will go to the Americans," he said.[116]

On the morning of April 29 more than ten thousand Vietnamese who depended on the Americans surrounded the grounds of the U.S. embassy. They pushed papers that they thought authorized them passage out of the city onto the marine guards, who had orders not to let Vietnamese pass. About four thousand climbed over the walls and forced their way through the gates. "Can someone tell me what the hell is going on!" Kissinger exploded when he heard reports that Vietnamese had boarded helicopters leaving the roof of the embassy. "The orders are that only Americans are to be evacuated." But the Vietnamese would not let the nearly six hundred Americans remaining in Vietnam leave unless some of the Vietnamese went, too.[117]

The evacuation was also slowed by Martin's foot-dragging. The ambassador wanted Americans to stay until the very last minute to give heart to the Vietnamese. His delays infuriated General George Brown, Chairman of the Joint Chiefs of Staff. "The ambassador has got to get those people out of there. Can't you tell him to get them out of there?" he asked Kissinger. "Those are his bloody orders, goddammit!" Kissinger shouted. Exhausted, angry, fed up with Martin and the war, Kissinger explained, "Yes, I'll instruct the Ambassador to get those people out, but he's been ordered to get those people out a hundred times." Finally, Martin led the last of the Americans up the ladder of a helicopter on the roof of the U.S. embassy for evacuation to aircraft carriers waiting off the coast. In the end, about 5,000 people, including 4,100 Vietnamese and 900 Americans, were evacuated from the roof of the embassy on April 29.[118] Americans also ordered the South Vietnamese air force to land their helicopters on American ships to keep them from falling into the hands of the North Vietnamese. A few South Vietnamese pilots flew their crafts to the American vessels under the impression that they would refuel, regroup and rejoin the fighting. But when they landed marines told them, "Stand back, boys. The war is over." The Americans then pushed the craft into the sea.[119]

On April 30 a somber and angry Henry Kissinger predicted a catastrophic political aftermath for the country in general and for Ford in particular. Hours after television pictures flashed around the world showing the mad evacuation of the last U.S. civilians from the roof of the American embassy in Saigon, Kissinger took stock of the debacle in a speech in the East Room of the White House. He warned the assembled high officials that the United States would "pay a price for what happened in Southeast Asia." The United States would be tested by its adversaries over the next few months. He wondered whether the American public might not grow despondent at the burdens of leadership in international affairs. Yet he predicted a resurrection of firmness in U.S. foreign policy. Adversaries who celebrated America's discomfiture were "doing so prematurely." Angry and frustrated that his handiwork at the Paris negotiations had gone so publicly sour, Kissinger pointed the finger of blame at the top. Politicians basking in the glow of public approval for having ended U.S. participation in the war should reflect on the fate of British Prime Minister Neville Chamberlain. He was "the most popular man in England in 1938 [at the time of the Munich agreement]—eighteen months later he was finished."[120]

How fitting that the first post-mortem on the war by an American Secretary of State revived the memory of Munich. From the very beginning, U.S. policy in Vietnam had been linked to the analogy of the moral failing of the Western powers in appeasing Hitler's limitless ambitions. The comparison never fit reality but even at the very end Americans were not thinking about the country they were supposed to be helping. As always, they were preoccupied with something—be it domestic politics, containment, the Cold War, or credibility—other than what was actually happening in Vietnam.

Conclusion:

The United States and

Vietnam at War

*A*MERICANS and Vietnamese fought a twenty-year war to define themselves. For the Vietnamese their war was never about the United States. Their issues were clear: What kind of an independent Vietnam would emerge from the end of European colonialism? How would Vietnamese keep outsiders at bay? Who would rule?

Differences between the DRV and the Republic of Vietnam helped the revolutionaries win. Ho Chi Minh and his colleagues in the Vietnam Workers Party led a unified DRV. Vietnamese revolutionaries always predicted that the outsiders—French or American—would soon weary of engaging an adversary many thousands of miles from home. From 1947 until 1975 Vietnamese General Vo Nguyen Giap outlined his philosophy of protracted war. Their victory over French colonialism in 1954 validated their nationalism in the eyes of their fellow Vietnamese. They consolidated power in the DRV with authoritarian control and continuous appeals to resist a foreign presence. The Vietnamese revolutionaries in both the North and the South took a much longer view than did their more impatient foes. Their belief that they needed only to avoid losing in order to win their struggle eventually proved correct.

The unity, tight control, and popularity of the DRV contrasted sharply with the prevalent disorder in the Republic of Vietnam. Some of the problems of the South derived from poor leadership. Ngo Dinh Diem had several

328

strengths—notably, authentic nationalism, industriousness, and incorrupti-bility—but his deficiencies eventually undermined him. He could never de-velop broad popular appeal. His successors had even more trouble forging a nation in the midst of a war. More than Diem, they were seen as completely dependent on their American sponsors. Leadership deficiencies were a symp-tom rather than a cause of the Republic of Vietnam's disarray. The project of building a separate, viable nation in one half of Vietnam, a land with a long history, proved impossible.

Yet such nation-building was the task a series of U.S. officials set for themselves for nearly two decades. For the United States, the issues involved in participation in Vietnamese affairs were complicated, ambiguous, and conflicted. The war in Vietnam was never strictly about Vietnam for the Americans who directed it, fought in it, or opposed it. The United States became involved in Vietnamese politics and eventually fought in Vietnam because of the Cold War. For more than forty years after 1947, Americans advanced containment of the Soviet Union as the central principle of U.S. foreign relations. Had American leaders not thought that all international events were connected to the Cold War there would have been no American war in Vietnam. American leaders persistently believed that their credibility was at stake there.

But the Cold War alone does not explain completely the course of U.S. involvement in Vietnam. All wars have a domestic element, but the American war in Vietnam had more than most. Domestic politics, the timetable of presidential electoral cycles, and what Americans thought of their public institutions eventually came to dominate the way the United States fought the war. These factors both took the country into the war and brought it out.

The maintenance of U.S. credibility always seemed to be of paramount importance to policy-makers as they contemplated their next move in Viet-nam. From the beginning, the United States fought in Vietnam to influence others' opinions of what the United States would do elsewhere. To maintain French faith in the United States as an ally, the United States backed France's campaign in Indochina. To prevent vulnerable nations from falling like domi-noes to communist insurgencies and to show that such revolts would fail, the United States embarked on nation-building in South Vietnam. To demon-strate to the South Vietnamese government that the United States would stand behind it through thick and thin, thereby fortifying the South's desire to fight, the United States bombed the North. To demonstrate to the world that the United States had learned the lessons of Munich, the Johnson administration sent ground troops and Americanized the war. To show North Vietnam that it could not prevail in negotiations where it had not succeeded on the battlefield, the United States maintained its backing for various governments of South Vietnam.

For the United States the war seemed endless. Former Secretary of State

Dean Rusk often remarked that his greatest mistake was overestimating the patience of the American people and underestimating that of the Vietnamese. Rusk probably should not have been surprised at either. At every step up and down the ladder of escalation Americans heard a clock ticking ever more loudly.

Alarms began sounding at the very beginning. When the United States backed France's restoration of authority in Indochina in the early days of the Cold War, many American officials expressed impatience with the French refusal to yield real power to authentic Vietnamese nationalists. After the Vietminh defeated France at Dienbienphu in 1954, Americans briefly felt that their moment had arrived in Vietnam. The United States backed Ngo Dinh Diem as he created a new Republic of Vietnam south of the seventeenth parallel. Many U.S. officials believed that Diem represented the elusive Third Force—non-communist and truly nationalist—the United States had tried to find in Indochina since 1946. Diem tried hard, but his flaws became apparent as early as 1955. For the next eight years many Americans believed that Diem would not be able to consolidate his power, although they rarely could find an alternative. Time seemed to be running out for the American commitment to Vietnam in the administration of President John F. Kennedy—one of Diem's earliest and strongest supporters. In 1963 Kennedy and most of his principal Vietnam advisers believed that the only way to save the Republic of Vietnam from the NLF insurgents was to make the war an American operation. Eventually they took the fateful step of conspiring to overthrow Diem. Thereafter, successive South Vietnamese leaders increasingly became creatures of the United States.

From 1963 until the middle of 1967 everything the United States did in the war was designed to bolster the morale of the South Vietnamese government. The aim was to fortify the Republic of Vietnam so as to deny a Vietcong–North Vietnamese victory. U.S. leaders thought that such a victory would encourage the Soviet Union and its allies in other communist states and movements at the expense of the United States and its friends. The belief that the Vietnamese insurgency represented a major battleground of the Cold War turned out to be false. The United States and its allies would not have been utterly demoralized had the communists gained power in Vietnam twelve years earlier than they did. The Soviet Union and other communists would not have been able to use the victory of their sometime allies in Vietnam as a foundation for world revolution. But officials in the Johnson administration firmly believed that these dire consequences would follow if the revolutionaries unified Vietnam under Ho Chi Minh's leadership.

At each step along the way the top American advisers complained that time was running out. Secretary of Defense Robert S. McNamara, Secretary of State Dean Rusk, National Security Advisers McGeorge Bundy and Walt Rostow, Assistant Secretary of State William P. Bundy, and General Maxwell Taylor, came back from their many trips to Vietnam with tales of how conditions had deteriorated. Each month was worse than the one before; the United States had to do something to stop the rot. Their recommendations included plans for intervention to change the government, bombing the North, bombing the South, and eventually sending over five hundred thousand troops to Americanize the war.

Even as they climbed the ladder of escalation, Americans knew that they would not easily prevail. President Johnson was often more aware of the dangers than many of his more hawkish advisers. He knew the governments of South Vietnam were weak, and he recognized the fragility of domestic support for the war effort. But he could not bring himself to turn back; the Cold War and American credibility seemed to matter too much. Little the Johnson administration did worked. By 1967 the United States was in turmoil at home, and the Johnson administration at last seemed ready for negotiations with Hanoi. These talks could do little, however, to break the impasse, as long as American policy-makers continued to believe that they could deny the NLF and the North Vietnamese a large measure of political power in the South.

The ever-patient Vietnamese believed that eventually Americans would tire of the war, depart Vietnam, and leave the field to them. The North bet a lot on the Tet Offensive of early 1968. It did not ignite the general rising throughout South Vietnam many North Vietnamese leaders had wanted, but it ruined American expectations of seeing an end to the war any time soon. As Americans contemplated the horrible devastation left by Tet, they faced the sort of fighting they could not tolerate—a drawn-out war without clear progress but with high casualties.

American electoral politics—both the divisions among candidates and the ever-ticking clock of approaching elections—also affected the negotiations in both 1968 and 1972. During the three months before each election the United States varied the pace of negotiations with an eye to the electoral calendar. In 1968 Johnson, lonely, isolated, repudiated by much of his own party, did not much care who was elected—after me, nothing, he thought. In the last days of the campaign, Johnson had an opportunity to discredit Richard Nixon, the Republican nominee, and help elect Hubert Humphrey, but Johnson passed up the chance to help his Vice President assume his mantle because he was angry that Humphrey had disavowed so much of Johnson's Vietnam policy.

By 1968 the American public was heartily sick of the war. Richard Nixon won the presidency by focusing on the frustrations Americans felt toward the entire liberal agenda of the 1960s—domestic reform, civil rights, and involvement in Vietnam to contain the Soviet Union. Why, then, did the Nixon administration not simply end the war in 1969, instead of going through the elaborate negotiations and deceptions of the next four years? Why did the Nixon administration believe it preferable to divert public attention from Vietnam—by Vietnamization and dazzling foreign policy achievements elsewhere—than simply end the war? Why not, in the words of Senator George Aiken, "declare victory and leave"?

The answer is simple, but deeply sad. Nixon, Kissinger, Defense Secretary Melvin Laird—nearly everyone in power from 1969 to 1973—still thought the Cold War mattered as it had for the previous twenty years. While they accepted one of the realist dissenters' opinions of the Vietnam War—that it had diverted resources from more important aspects of the confrontation with the Soviet Union and communism—they agreed that the confrontation was important. So was the notion of credibility. Without the appearance of toughness, they feared the word of the United States would be devalued elsewhere in the world. Like their predecessors, Nixon and Kissinger believed that Vietnam mattered only insofar as it affected interests of the United States elsewhere.

For Nixon, winning re-election became a consuming passion in 1971 and 1972. If the war ended, his re-election would be assured, but if it raged on with no end in sight, he could become as discredited as Johnson had been in 1968. On one level Nixon wanted to support the government of President Thieu, but he considered the South Vietnamese an obstacle to ending the war. He thought that Vietnam per se no longer was important to the United States, and he believed that the public did not care about the war there so long as there were no ground troops there. He also believed, however, that more bombing of the North would show that the United States had not been forced out of the war. As Election Day approached, therefore, Nixon expressed much of the same ambivalence toward the war characteristic of U.S. presidents for the previous decade. He wanted to end the war, but only after defeating the North Vietnamese. The goal was impossible, given the patience of the North and Nixon's own acknowledgment that Vietnam no longer mattered that much either to the U.S. public or U.S. foreign policy.

The Paris accords signed in January 1973 proved to be only a temporary cease-fire. The war resumed in earnest in the winter of 1974–1975, and the NLF and the North Vietnamese completed their victory in April. By that time the American public wanted as little as possible to do with Vietnam. President Ford acknowledged that the United States could do nothing more to help the government of President Thieu. As the last American helicopters left the roof of the United States embassy in Saigon, Kissinger showed how Americans always thought about something else when it came to Vietnam. He resurrected the Munich analogy—the argument invoked so often during the Eisenhower, Kennedy, Johnson, and Nixon administrations to justify U.S. participation in the war. His fears that the United States would tear itself apart looking for scapegoats to blame for the failure in Vietnam proved to be unfounded. Domestically the United States proved to be a far more resilient society than feared by the many people who predicted that it would descend into an orgy of recrimination after 1975.

Turn away from the leaders at the top and examine the experience of the men and women, Vietnamese and Americans, who actually fought the war. International politics, containment, and credibility mattered little for them. But time was of the utmost importance. Just as time moved at a varied pace for different high policy-makers in Washington, Hanoi, and Saigon, time flowed unevenly for soldiers. For the North Vietnamese fighters, they were in it for the duration. No one recruited to go South knew how long he would be away. More than one third never returned to the North. Many stayed in the South for years; they never left the field. Many lived underground in tunnels for months or years at a time.

The troops of the ARVN rarely showed such tough endurance. Some fought well, but not enough and never for as long a time as did their foes in either the North Vietnamese army or the Vietcong. The ARVN came to depend too much upon the technological marvels provided by their American allies. The people of South Vietnam suffered from the disintegration of their society. Its traditional rural way of life was destroyed by war. Its cities swelled with three million refugees, and its fields were bombed. This vast destruction made it all the more difficult for ordinary South Vietnamese to continue to make the sacrifices necessary to prevail in a nearly endless war.

The Americans were even more impatient. They hoped their twelve-month tour of duty and their helicopters, fighter bombers, and heavy fire power would make the fighting bearable for an army of conscripts. American military leaders feared increased casualties and a weakening of the American will to fight. The search-and-destroy tactics they adopted purposely kept the American troops away from the very South Vietnamese they supposedly were helping. Isolated from the Vietnamese, often lonely and frightened, most American soldiers could not wait to leave Vietnam.

Back home, their loved ones and friends could not wait to have them return. Others dreaded the prospect of taking their place in an ugly, often brutal war that seemed to go on forever with few tangible results. Their fears, frustrations, and disillusionment with their leaders fueled a growing anti-war movement. Their protests against the fighting produced varied results. The anti-war movement contributed to general war-weariness, and from 1968 until 1975 all three American presidents knew that most of the public wanted to end U.S. involvement in the war. That did not mean, however, that there ever existed general agreement on the ways in which the anti-war movement suggested leaving Vietnam. While protests made continuing the war increasingly difficult, a backlash also arose against the anti-war movement. Leaders often used public opposition to some of the movement's tactics to fortify support for their own ways of dealing with the problem of Vietnam.

I have been teaching and writing about the war in Vietnam for more than fifteen years. It is remarkable to notice how many questions have changed and how many have endured in that time. Before the end of the Cold War, especially during the nationalistic Reagan years, students asked what the United States could have done to have won the war in Vietnam. The answer—nothing—was deeply dissatisfying. Embedded in the students' questions of the mid-1980s was a profound and often disturbing sense that a lone hero, untainted by a large, corrupt bureaucracy, could have prevailed. This disillusioned view held that evil men ran large organizations, and that their malfeasance led to the American catastrophe in Vietnam. Far fewer of today's students ask if the United States could have won the war. They understand that the perseverance of the NLF put them in an extraordinarily powerful position to prevail. Besides, with the end of the Cold War, it hardly seems to have mattered that the United States fought in Vietnam at all.

But earlier questions keep recurring. Robert S. McNamara's confession, in his memoir *In Retrospect: The Tragedy and Lessons of Vietnam,* of having been "terribly wrong" about escalating the war revives an old question often on the minds of young people today: Would the U.S. have lost the war in Vietnam had Kennedy lived? The easiest answer is: We cannot know; history happens only one way. The more complex answer is: Probably not. We should not forget the importance of the Cold War and containment. Just as Kissinger's predictions that the United States would tear itself apart over Vietnam did not come to pass, the reasoning behind American involvement in the war turned out to have been deeply flawed. The position of the United States in the world was not so precarious and that of the Soviet Union and other revolutionary movements not so dominant that an earlier communist victory in Vietnam would have changed the outcome of the Cold War. We know this now, and many people came to doubt the importance of U.S. involvement in Vietnam as the war went on. Yet given the depth of leaders' commitment to the principles of containment, it is hard to believe that the United States would not have participated the way it did in Vietnam, at least until 1968.

Clearly the fervor with which people long for a hero to have lived and saved them from the tragedy of Vietnam reveals how poignant a wound the war left. When McNamara spoke at Harvard University in the spring of 1995, observers noticed how Vietnam seemed to have taken place only yesterday for the people in the audience over forty. Their feelings were raw. For younger adults, including the hundreds of students in the audience, McNamara was a figure out of the past. Ernest May, one of the country's foremost diplomatic historians, gave the most dispassionate explanation of why he thought McNamara was wrong to have claimed that Kennedy would not have become as deeply involved as Johnson. McNamara seemed to have forgotten the powerful spell of the Cold War. It was as if, May observed, a Crusader wrote his memoirs without mentioning Christianity.[1]

So, was the war in Vietnam worth it—for the Americans or the Vietnamese? The immediate response is: Of course not. Vietnam was unified; the nationalists / revolutionaries won. But the cost included three million dead, as many as fifteen million made refugees at different times throughout the war, horrible physical devastation, over one million people, including some of the most industrious and educated, forced to flee, and the creation of one of the world's poorest economies. Despite the fears expressed by American officials, Vietnam did not endure a bloodbath after the communist triumph, but the victors did impose an authoritarian, repressive regime. Much of the death and damage was the responsibility of the United States. The victorious revolutionaries bore responsibility for the forced departure of the refugees, the terrible economic mismanagement, and the political repression of postwar Vietnam.

Was the war worth it for the United States? Again, of course, the predominant answer is no. There were fifty-eight thousand dead and far more severely wounded than in earlier wars (primarily because of the improvements in medical evacuation.) The U.S. economy suffered years of inflation because of government policies pursued during the Vietnam years. In the aftermath of the Cold War, it is also hard to see that the investment in Vietnam had anything much to do with the demise of the Soviet Union. The most enduring legacy of all, perhaps, was a persistent distrust of public institutions and the officials who ran them.

But the United States emerged stronger than many people expected from the crucible of Vietnam. The recriminations over the war never reached the level of the debate in Weimar Germany over responsibility for Germany's defeat in World War I, despite fears expressed in 1975 that they would. While both Dan Quayle, the successful vice presidential candidate in 1988, who had been a hawk, and Bill Clinton, the victorious presidential candidate in 1992, who had been a dove, generated furious opposition for avoiding the draft, both won their elections.

Ironies abound. The public institution that learned the lessons of the Vietnam war best was the military. Its reputation by the mid-1970s had reached its nadir; within the following two decades it became one of the most highly esteemed organizations in the United States. Moreover, the five hundred thousand Vietnamese and other Southeast Asians who came to the United States after 1975 became one of the country's greatest human resources.

Finally, the prevalent hostility and skepticism—some people characterize it as cynicism—Americans express toward their leaders and their public institutions is partly a consequence of the war in Vietnam. An old anti-war slogan—"I love my country but fear my government"—reverberates. The coarsening of political discourse during the past generation has some of its roots in the agony of U.S. involvement in Vietnam. But the positive side of this distrust of public institutions and officials is a deeply felt desire for accountability and responsiveness, and a willingness to use the influence of the media, the courts, and the government to meet popular needs. The United States is a louder place now. It is a more diverse society, with fewer enforced norms. It is also, surprisingly, a more democratic place, in large measure because the country went through the agonizing experience of Vietnam.

Notes

ABBREVIATIONS

DDEL   Dwight D. Eisenhower Library. Abilene, Kansas.
FRUS   *Foreign Relations of the United States.*
GRFL   Gerald R. Ford Library. Ann Arbor, Michigan.
HSTL   Harry S. Truman Library. Independence, Missouri.
JFKL   John F. Kennedy Library. Boston, Massachusetts.
LBJL   Lyndon B. Johnson Library. Austin, Texas.
MEMCON   Memorandum of Conversation.
NA   National Archives. Washington, D.C.
NCCEWVN   National Coordinating Committee to End the War in Vietnam Papers.
OH   Oral History.
POF   President's Office Files.
PRO   Public Record Office. London.
PUL   Princeton University Library. Princeton, New Jersey.
SMCEWV   Student Mobilization Committee to End the War in Vietnam Papers.
WHCF/CF   White House Central Files/Country File.
WHSMOF   White House Staff Members' Office Files.

PREFACE

1. John Kenneth Galbraith to President Johnson, 22 July 1965, *FRUS, 1964–1968*:3, p. 221.

CHAPTER 1

1. Herring, *America's Longest War: The United States and Vietnam, 1950–1975;* Harrison, *The Endless War: Vietnam's Struggle for Independence.*
2. Steinberg, et al., p. 69.
3. Ibid., p. 38; Taylor, pp. 37–44.
4. Olson and Roberts, p. 2; Taylor, pp. 267–95.
5. Turley, p. 2.
6. Steinberg, et al., pp. 69–75, 128–29.
7. Ibid., pp. 130–34; Ennis, pp. 38–41.
8. Ennis, pp. 52–61.
9. Ibid., p. 53.
10. Steinberg, et al., p. 313; Duiker, *Sacred War,* pp. 16–18.

11. Marr, *Vietnamese Anticolonialism*, pp. 133, 137, 170.
12. Lacouture, *Ho Chi Minh*, p. 12.
13. Duiker, *Sacred War*, pp. 21–22.
14. Lacouture, *Ho Chi Minh*, pp. 3–52.
15. Ibid., pp. 21–24.
16. Fall, ed., *Ho Chi Minh*, p. 6; Ulam, p. 310; Page, *Geopolitics*, pp. 164–81; Page, *Lenin*, pp. 141–53.
17. Duiker, *Sacred War*, pp. 33–35.
18. Harrison, pp. 54–57.
19. Macdonald, pp. 25–36.
20. LaCouture, *Ho Chi Minh*, pp. 71–84.
21. Hess, p. 48.
22. Ibid., p. 72; Louis, pp. 40–43.
23. Hess, pp. 69–83, 142–43; Thorne, pp. 202–28; Louis, pp. 28–29, 157, 273–75.
24. Kimball, pp. 142–43; Roosevelt-Stalin meeting, 28 November 1943, *FRUS, Tehran*, pp. 485–86; Dallek, *Franklin D. Roosevelt*, p. 429.
25. Hess, p. 81.
26. Ibid., p. 92.
27. Campbell and Herring, eds., pp. 37–40; Kimball, p. 146.
28. Kimball, p. 146.
29. Dallek, *Franklin D. Roosevelt*, pp. 363, 376; Louis, pp. 28, 41, 552.
30. Tonnesson, p. 160.
31. Kimball, pp. 148–49.
32. Ibid.; Hess, p. 130.
33. Hess, p. 141.
34. Ibid., p. 142.
35. Quoted in Tonnesson, p. 238.
36. Hess, p. 170; Fenn, pp. 72–80; Patti, pp. 45–58.
37. Hess, pp. 145–49; Tonnesson, pp. 220–21, 238–56.
38. Hess, p. 145.
39. Ibid., pp. 148–49.
40. Tonnesson, p. 284; Smith, "Japanese Period," p. 299.
41. Quoted in Tonnesson, p. 288.
42. Marr, "Vietnam, 1945," pp. 155–93; Tonneson, p. 293.
43. Hess, p. 171; Fenn, pp. 80–83; U.S. Senate, Committee on Foreign Relations, *Hearings on the Causes*, pp. 243–51.
44. Tonnesson, p. 378.
45. Hess, p. 174; Tonnesson, p. 393; Duiker, *U.S. Containment Policy*, pp. 37–38.
46. Donovan to Truman, 28 September 1945, box 15, Rose Conway Files.
47. Hess, pp. 178–79; U.S. Senate, Committee on Foreign Relations, *Hearings on the Causes*, pp. 296–98.
48. Hess, p. 182; U.S. Senate, Committee on Foreign Relations, *Hearings on the Causes*, pp. 144–48.
49. Hess, p. 181; Caffrey to Secretary of State, 16 August 1945, *FRUS*, 1945:4, pp. 703–5.
50. *FRUS*, 1946:8, pp. 15–20.

CHAPTER 2

1. Leffler, pp. 100–81.
2. Hunt and Levine, pp. 12–33.
3. Hickey, *Sons of the Mountains*, p. 387.

4. Buttinger, *Vietnam: A Dragon Embattled*, pp. 308–18; Buttinger, *Vietnam: A Political History*, pp. 226–27; Harrison, pp. 107–9.

5. Duiker, *U.S. Containment Policy*, pp. 39–40; Hess, p. 195.

6. Buttinger, *Vietnam: A Dragon Embattled*, pp. 368–72; Gardner, *Approaching Vietnam*, pp. 74–75.

7. Hess, p. 197.

8. Hickey, *Sons of the Mountains*, p. 393.

9. Karnow, p. 154.

10. Hess, pp. 199–200.

11. Karnow, p. 155.

12. Ibid., p. 159.

13. Hess, p. 201; Duiker, *U.S. Containment Policy*, pp. 40–47.

14. Karnow, p. 159; Lacouture, *Ho Chi Minh*, p. 170.

15. Hess, p. 203; Duiker, *U.S. Containment Policy*, pp. 45–46, 49.

16. Karnow, p. 159; Hammer, *Struggle for Indochina*, p. 204.

17. Hess, p. 206.

18. Marshall to U.S. embassy, Paris, 17 June 1946, State Department Records, RG59, 851G.00/6-1747, NA.

19. Abbott Low Moffat to Department of State, 23 July 1947, State Department Records, RG59, FW851G.00/6-1447, NA.

20. "Southeast Asia Conference," 21 June 1948, box 9, Melby Papers.

21. O'Sullivan to State Department, 21 June 1947, RG59, 851G/6-2047, NA.

22. O'Sullivan to State Department, 20 June 1947, RG59, 851G.00/6-2047, NA; Rotter, pp. 90–93.

23. Reed to State Department, 27 June 1947, RG59, 851G.00/6-2747, NA; O'Sullivan to State Department, 16 July 1947, 851G.00/6-2147, NA.

24. Hess, p. 317; Rotter, p. 91.

25. Hammer, *Struggle for Indochina*, pp. 208–10.

26. O'Sullivan to State Department, 1 July 1947, 851G.00/7-147, NA.

27. Hammer, *Struggle for Indochina*, p. 213.

28. Ibid.; George D. Hopper to Secretary of State, 30 December 1947, RG59, 851G.00/12-3047, NA.

29. Hess, p. 320.

30. Hammer, *Struggle for Indochina*, pp. 222, 225.

31. Caffery to Secretary of State, 11 August 1947, RG59, 851G.00/8-1147, NA.

32. Hammer, *Struggle for Indochina*, p. 225.

33. E. C. Rendall, MEMCON, 27 December 1947, RG59, 851G.00/12-2447, NA.

34. Hammer, *Struggle for Indochina*, p. 228.

35. Buttinger, *Vietnam: A Dragon Embattled*, p. 722.

36. Ibid., pp. 724–25.

37. Leffler, pp. 142–46; Gaddis, *United States*, pp. 346–52.

38. Hixson, pp. 41–44, 73–74; Steel, pp. 444–46; Miscamble, pp. 64–70; Mayers, pp. 113–14, 129–30; Gaddis, *Strategies of Containment*, pp. 36–39.

39. Schaller, *American Occupation*, p. 122; Miscamble, pp. 250–54; Gardner, *Approaching Vietnam*, pp. 82–83.

40. Charles Deane to President, 19 October 1949, box 177, President's Security File.

41. Hess, p. 319; Rotter, pp. 92, 94–95.

42. "Proposed Solution of Indochina Problem," n.d. [Summer 1948], box 9, Melby Papers.

43. Hess, p. 322; Duiker, *U.S. Containment Policy*, pp. 81–83.

44. Hess, pp. 324, 329, 330; Rotter, pp. 117–19.

45. Bruce to Secretary of State, 1 January 1950, *FRUS, 1950:*6, p. 704.

46. Secretary of State to President, 2 February 1950, ibid., p. 717.

47. Dean Rusk to James H. Burns, 7 March 1950, box 212, President's Security File.

48. Omar Bradley to Secretary of Defense, 10 April 1950, box 212, ibid.

CHAPTER 3

1. Merchant, "Estimate of a Princeton Graduate Interested in the Far East, July 1951," Merchant Papers.
2. Dulles, "Far Eastern Problems," 5 May 1952, box 14, Dulles Papers; Joseph Jones to Harlan Cleveland, "The Conditions of Success of U.S. Policy in Asia," 18 September 1950, RG286, box 55, Economic Cooperation Agency Papers; Richard Bissell to Harlan Cleveland, 10 October 1950, ibid.
3. Stueck, pp. 348–70.
4. Gardner, *Approaching Vietnam,* p. 92; Stueck, p. 367; Kaufman, pp. 349–57; Schaller, *American Occupation,* pp. 278–86.
5. Military Aid for Indochina, 1 February 1950, *FRUS, 1950:*6, pp. 711–14.
6. NSC-64, Report to the NSC by the Department of State, February 27, 1950 adopted by the NSC April 18 and approved by President Truman, 24 April 1950, ibid., pp. 744–47.
7. Gullion to Secretary of State, 18 March 1950, ibid., pp. 764–65.
8. Charlton Ogburn Jr. to Assistant Secretary of State for Far Eastern Affairs, 21 March 1950, ibid., pp. 766–67.
9. Gullion to Secretary of State, 8 April 1950, ibid., pp. 774–75.
10. Gullion to Secretary of State, 9 April 1950, 18 June 1950, ibid., pp. 777, 823.
11. Gullion to Secretary of State, 23 June 1950, RG59, 751G.00/6-2350, NA; Acting Secretary of State to Saigon, 10 May 1950, *FRUS, 1950:*6, p. 813.
12. MEMCON, 18 June 1950, ibid., p. 830.
13. Truman to Acheson, 1 May 1950, ibid., p. 791.
14. Gullion to Secretary of State, 29 June 1950, reports that "no Vietminh or Chinese Commie action of unusual character yet observed following Korea development," ibid., p. 831.
15. Editorial note, ibid., p. 836.
16. Heath to Secretary of State, 25 July 1950, ibid., p. 839; Heath to Secretary of State, 7 August 1950, ibid., pp. 847–48.
17. Secretary of State to the U.S. embassy in France, 15 August 1950, ibid., p. 855.
18. Memorandum prepared in the Policy Planning Staff, "U.S. Policy toward Indochina in the Light of Recent Developments," 16 August 1950, ibid., pp. 856–57.
19. Bruce to Secretary of State, 17 August 1950, ibid., p. 859.
20. McMahon, pp. 33–34; Foot, pp. 113–15; Leffler, pp. 403–6; Schaller, *Douglas MacArthur,* pp. 206–23.
21. Buttinger, *Vietnam: A Dragon Embattled,* pp. 751–52.
22. Ibid., p. 750.
23. Fall, *Street without Joy,* p. 30; Canadian ambassador to France to External Affairs, 12 December 1950, Canadian Mission to Tokyo to External Affairs, 28 December 1950, RG25, box 4621, file 50052.40, part 10, Canadian National Archives.
24. Omar Bradley to Secretary of Defense, 28 November 1950, box 212, President's Security File.
25. Unsigned memorandum for Undersecretary for External Affairs, 29 November 1950, RG25, box 4621, file 50052.40, part 9, Canadian National Archives.
26. Webb to James Lay, progress report on NSC-64, 15 March 1951, box 212, President's Security File.
27. Blancke to Secretary of State, 23 January 1951, *FRUS, 1951:*6, p. 358.
28. Minutes of 13th meeting of the Southeast Asia Aid Policy Committee, 7 February 1951, ibid., p. 376.
29. Heath to Secretary of State, 23 May 1951, ibid., p. 420.
30. Heath to Secretary of State, 29 June 1951, ibid., pp. 419–20, 432–33.
31. Blancke to Secretary of State, 31 May 1951, ibid., p. 424.
32. MEMCON by Livingston Merchant, 8 August 1951, ibid., p. 480. See n.1 above.
33. Merchant to Secretary of State, 12 September 1951, ibid., pp. 494, 499–521.
34. Minutes of the 2d meeting with General de Lattre de Tassigny, 17 September 1951, ibid., p. 513.
35. Buttinger, *Vietnam: A Political History,* pp. 328–32.

36. Defense of Southeast Asia, 1 January 1952, box 116, President's Security File; Oliver Franks to Foreign Office, 27 March 1952, FO371/10157, PRO.
37. William Hayter to Foreign Office, 2 April 1952, FO371/101057, PRO.
38. Hayter to Foreign Office, 30 May 1952, FO371/101058, ibid.
39. Leffler, pp. 453–63.
40. Foreign Office to Saigon, 30 May 1952, F0371/101058 PRO; also Minute, C. G. Harris, 4 May 1952, ibid.
41. Selwyn Lloyd to Foreign Office, 15 May 1952, ibid.
42. National Intelligence Estimate, "Probable Developments in Indochina through Mid-1953," 29 August 1952, *FRUS, 1952–1954*:13, pp. 243–49, 253–90.
43. *FRUS, 1952–1954*:13, p. 298, quoting Harry Truman memoirs, vol. 2, *Years of Trial and Hope, 1946–1952*, p. 519.
44. Fall, *Hell in a Very Small Place*, pp. 47–50; Simpson, *Tiger in the Barbed Wire*, pp. 94–99.
45. John W. O'Daniel to Admiral Arthur Radford, 30 June 1953, *FRUS, 1952–1954*:13, pp. 624–26; Canadian embassy in Paris to Department of External Affairs, 23 July 1953, RG25, box 4621, National Archives of Canada; Memo to Foreign Office, 28 July 1953, file 50052.40, part 17, National Archives of Canada.
46. Fall, *Hell in a Very Small Place*, pp. 30, 42–45.
47. Department of State to the National Security Council, 5 August 1953, *FRUS, 1952–1954*:13, pp. 714–17.
48. Discussion of the 161st meeting of the NSC, 9 September 1953, box 46, Whitman File; *FRUS, 1952–1954*:13, pp. 780–89.
49. Richard Nixon, handwritten notes, Trip to Far East, December 1953, series 378, box 1, Richard Nixon Papers.
50. Richard Nixon, television and radio speech, 23 December 1953, series 369, Richard Nixon Papers.
51. Discussion of the 177th meeting of the NSC, 23 December 1953, *FRUS, 1952–1954*:13, pp. 929–31.
52. Meeting of the NSC, 8 January 1954, *FRUS, 1952–1954*:13, p. 949.
53. Trapnell to Army Chief of Staff, 29 December 1953, Department of State Records, RG59, 751G.5/12-2453, NA; Drumright to Secretary of State, 26 December 1953, *FRUS, 1952–1954*:13, pp. 931–33.
54. Fall, *Hell in a Very Small Place*, pp. 43–45, 47–50.
55. Ibid., pp. xi, 76, 102.
56. Ibid., pp. 24–25, 51, 125, 128–29.
57. Billings-Yun, p. 11.
58. Meeting of the NSC, 8 January 1954, *FRUS, 1952–1954*:13, p. 963.
59. Billings-Yun, p. 11; D. Anderson, *Trapped by Success*, p. 24.
60. Herring, "Franco-American Conflict," p. 41; Fall, *Hell in a Very Small Place*, pp. 125–32; Billings-Yun, pp. 29–31.
61. Billings-Yun, p. 31; Herring, "Franco-American Conflict," pp. 43–44.
62. Billings-Yun, p. 34; Radford Oral History; Cesari and de Folin, pp. 107–9.
63. Radford, pp. 403–4; Radford Oral History; Billings-Yun, p. 35.
64. Dulles telephone conversation with Admiral Radford, 10:00 A.M., 24 March 1954, Telephone Conversations Memoranda Series, Dulles Files.
65. D. Anderson, *Trapped by Success*, pp. 17–40; Billings-Yun, pp. 53–122; Herring and Immerman, pp. 81–103.
66. Billings-Yun, pp. 61–62.
67. George and Smoke, pp. 256–57.
68. *New York Times*, 31 March 1954, p. 26.
69. Foreign Office to Washington, 1 April 1954, FO371/112049, PRO; Canadian embassy in Washington to Department of External Affairs, 13 April 1954, RG25, box 4622, file 50052.40, part 21, Canadian National Archives.

70. Secretary of State for Commonwealth Relations, London to High Commissioner for United Kingdon in Canada, 13 April 1954, Embassy in Washington to External Affairs, 13 April 1954, RG25, box 4622, file 50052.40, part 21, Canadian National Archives.
71. Billings-Yun, pp. 66–68. Immerman and Herring, p. 88.
72. Billings-Yun, p. 76.
73. Hagerty diary, 26 March 1954, Hagerty Papers.
74. Italics added. Presidential News Conference, 31 March 1954, *Public Papers of the President: Dwight David Eisenhower, 1954,* pp. 364–70.
75. Discussion at the 191st meeting of the NSC, 1 April 1954; Whitman File.
76. Ridgeway to Joint Chiefs of Staff, 2 April 1954, *FRUS, 1952–1954:*13, p. 1220.
77. Hagerty diary, 1 April 1954. Hagerty Papers.
78. Memorandum of conversation, Drumright, 2 April 1954, *FRUS, 1952–1954:*13, pp. 1214–17.
79. Gardner, *Approaching Vietnam,* pp. 186–90; Gilbert, p. 968.
80. Billings-Yun, pp. 90–92; O'Connor, "Conference with Congressional Leaders Concerning the Crisis in Southeast Asia, April 3, 1954," White House Memo Series, Dulles Files; Richard Russell, Notes from 3 April 1954 meeting at the State Department, Russell Papers; Herring and Immerman, pp. 91–93.
81. Billings-Yun, p. 100.
82. Press conference, 7 April 1954, *Public Papers of the President: Dwight D. Eisenhower, 1954,* p. 383.
83. Dillon to Department of State, 5 April 1954, *FRUS, 1952–1954:*13, pp. 1236–37.
84. Herring and Immerman, pp. 91–96; Billings-Yun, pp. 123–47; Dulles to Department of State, 22 April 1954, *FRUS, 1952–1954:*13, p. 1361.
85. *FRUS, 1952–1954:*13, pp. 1411–15.
86. Herring and Immerman, p. 95.

CHAPTER 4

1. G. Greene, pp. 18, 23.
2. D. Anderson, *Trapped by Success,* pp. 75–80; Currey, pp. 196–98; Sherry, vol. 2, pp. 416–17, 423.
3. G. Greene, p. 63.
4. Liebling, p. 141.
5. D. Anderson, *Trapped by Success,* pp. 199–209.
6. Fall, *Hell in a Very Small Place,* p. 384.
7. Radio and Television address to the nation by Secretary of State Dulles, 7 May 1954, *FRUS, 1952–1954:*16, pp. 720–21.
8. Herring, "'A Good Stout Effort'"; Immerman, ed., *John Foster Dulles,* p. 220 (quoting Evelyn Schuckburgh, diaries).
9. Conference with the President, 5 May 1954. Special Assistant to the President, box 11.
10. Immerman, "United States," p. 55; Gardner, *Approaching Vietnam,* 256–58; Dulles-Molotov meeting, 27 April 1954, *FRUS, 1952–1954:*16, pp. 579–80.
11. Dulles to Walter Bedell Smith, 12 May 1954, *Pentagon Papers,* House of Representatives version, book 9, pp. 457–59.
12. Dulles to U.S. Delegation, 8 May 1954, *FRUS, 1952–1954:*16, pp. 728–29.
13. Meeting of the NSC, 13 May 1954, ibid., pp. 1548–49.
14. Dulles conversation with President, 19 May 1954, ibid., p. 1583.
15. Meeting of the NSC, 20 May 1954, ibid., vol. 12, pp. 498–99.
16. J. Cable, pp. 66–69; Randle, pp. 192–93.
17. Outline of General Smith's remarks to the President and Bipartisan Congressional Group, 23 June 1954, Special Assistant for National Security Affairs, box 11, NSC Briefing Notes.
18. Randle, pp. 228–46; J. Cable, pp. 66–79.

19. Buttinger, *A Dragon Embattled,* p. 833.
20. Dillon to Secretary of State, 20 June 1954, *FRUS, 1952–1954:*16, p. 1188.
21. Churchill to Eisenhower, 21 June 1954, ibid., pp. 1728–29.
22. Hagerty diary, 8 July 1954, Hagerty Papers.
23. Immerman, "United States," pp. 62–63.
24. Smith-Molotov meeting, 18 June 1954, *FRUS, 1952–1954:*16, pp. 11898–90; Immerman, "United States," p. 61; Randle, pp. 280–91; Devillers and Lacouture, pp. 232–42.
25. Immerman, "United States," p. 64; U.S.-French communique on the Paris Talks, 13–14 July 1954, *FRUS, 1952–1954:*13, pp. 1829–30.
26. NSC meeting, 15 July 1954, *FRUS, 1952–1954:*13, pp. 1835–40.
27. J. Cable, pp. 116–17.
28. Eden to Foreign Office, 20 July 1954, FO371/112080, PRO.
29. Quoted in J. Cable, p. 122.
30. Meeting of the NSC, 22 July 1954, *FRUS, 1952–1954:*13, p. 1869.
31. Randle, pp. 332–49; J. Cable, pp. 115–28; Eden to Prime Minister, 19 July 1954, FO371/112080, PRO.
32. Shaplen, p. 104.
33. Ngo Dinh Diem, Briefing Book on Ngo Dinh Diem Visit, 8 May, 1957, box 73, Subject Series, Confidential Files, White House Central Files.
34. D. Anderson, *Trapped by Success,* pp. 53–55.
35. Meeting of the NSC, 22 July 1954, *FRUS, 1952–1954:*13, p. 1868.
36. J. E. Cable minute on *New York Times* clipping, 24 Octover 1954, FO371/112118, PRO.
37. O'Daniel to Department of the Army, 27 July 1954, *FRUS, 1952–1954:*13, pp. 1883–85.
38. Duiker, *U.S. Containment Policy,* pp. 194–212.
39. D. Anderson, *Trapped by Success,* pp. 48–49; Fall, "Political-Religious Sects," pp. 235–49.
40. Kahin, p. 76; Cooper, p. 130.
41. *Pentagon Papers,* vol. 1, p. 579.
42. Kahin, p. 77; Minutes of Meetings of the International Commission for Supervision and Control of the Cease-fire in Indochina, 8, 9, 11 March 1955, RG25, box 4649, file 50052.A12.40, Canadian National Archives.
43. D. Anderson, *Trapped by Success,* pp. 82–83; U.S. Senate, Committee on Foreign Relations, *Vietnam, Cambodia, and Laos,* p. 11.
44. Eisenhower to Collins, 3 November 1954, *FRUS, 1952–1954:*13, p. 2206.
45. Memo for the record by General J. Lawton Collins, 3 November 1954, ibid., p. 2208.
46. Lansdale to Collins, 3 January 1955, box 28, Collins Papers.
47. D. Anderson, *Trapped by Success,* pp. 92–97; Kahin, pp. 81–83.
48. Kidder to Department of State, 15 November 1954, *FRUS, 1952–1954:*13, p. 2250.
49. Collins to Secretary of State, 20 January 1955, *FRUS, 1955–1957:*1, p. 55.
50. Discussion of the NSC, 27 January 1955, ibid., pp. 62–66.
51. Quoted in D. Anderson, *Trapped by Success,* p. 99.
52. Ibid., p. 102.
53. Collins to Secretary of State, 30 March 1955, *FRUS, 1955–1957:*1, p. 162; Memorandum of conversation with General Ely, 31 March 1955, box 29, Collins Papers.
54. Italics added. Collins to Secretary of State, 7 April 1955, *FRUS, 1955–1957:*1, p. 219.
55. Dulles to Collins, 20 April 1955, box 24, Collins Papers.
56. D. Anderson, *Trapped by Success,* p. 110; Shaplen, pp. 122–23; Dulles to Dillon, 27 April 1955, *FRUS, 1955–1957:*1, pp. 294–96, 297–98, 337–38.
57. *Pentagon Papers,* vol. 1, p. 574; D. Anderson, *Trapped by Success,* p. 113; Shaplen, pp. 122–24.
58. Dulles to Dillon, 30 April 1955, *FRUS, 1955–1957:*1, p. 340.
59. Collins to Secretary of State, 5 May 1955, ibid., p. 368.
60. Robert Zimmerman to State Department, 13 May 1955, RG59, 751G.00/5-1355, NA.
61. Minute on *Washington Star* column, 30 June 1955, FO371/117143, PRO.

62. Alexander Haig to President, 26 March 1971, President's Office Files, Nixon Presidential Materials Project.
63. Severeid to Alsop, 14 November 1955; Alsop to Severeid, 17 November 1955, part 1, box 12, Joseph and Stewart Alsop Papers.
64. Canadian delegation in Tan Chau to Canadian delegation in Hanoi, 17 October 1955, RG25, box 4627, file 50052.40, part 40, Canadian National Archives.
65. D. Anderson, *Trapped by Success,* pp. 128–29; Canadian delegation to the International Commission on Control and Supervision of the Cease-fire in Indochina to Department of External Affairs, 20 December 1955, Canadian Embassy in Washington to Department of External Affairs, 9 December 1955, RG25, box 4627, file 50052.40, part 40, Canadian National Archives.
66. U.S. Views on All-Vietnam Elections, 5 May 1955, RG59, 751G.00/5-655, NA.
67. Herbert Graves to Foreign Office, 4 June 1956, FO371/123429, PRO; John F. Kennedy, "America's Stake in Vietnam," American Friends of Vietnam, *Symposium on America's Stake in Vietnam,* pp. 8–14.
68. Duiker, *Communist Road,* p. 172.
69. MEMCON, Harold Macmillan and Vu Van Mau, Foreign Minister of Republic of Vietnam, 25 November 1955, RG25, box 4627, file 50052.40, part 40, Canadian National Archives.
70. Minute on Roger Makins to Foreign Office, 27 June 1956, FO371/123429, PRO.
71. D. Anderson, *Trapped by Success,* pp. 143–48; Minutes of Meetings of International Commission for Control and Supervision of the Cease-fire in Indochina, 11, 21 July 1956, RG25, box 4650, file 50052.A12.40; A. A. Duff to John McCormick, 25 June 1957, Collins to Holmes, 13 March 1959, RG25, box 4627, file 50052.40, parts 42, 43; Minutes of Meetings of International Commission for Control and Supervision of the Cease-fire in Indochina, 8 February 1957, 23 March 1957, RG25, box 4652, file 50052.A12.40, Canadian National Archives.
72. Saigon Embassy to State Department, 20 August 1957, RG59, 751G.00/8-2057, NA.
73. D. Anderson, *Trapped by Success,* p. 152–52.
74. Kahin, p. 86; Herring, *America's Longest War,* pp. 60–61.
75. Herter to Eisenhower, 6 March 1957, International Series, box 50, Whitman Files.
76. Memorandum of conversation at the White House, 9 May 1957, *FRUS, 1955–1957:*1, pp. 794–99.
77. Duiker, *Communist Road,* p. 174.
78. Memorandum of conversation with Ngo Dinh Nhu, 17 October 1959, RG59, 751G.00/11-1959, NA.
79. Duiker, *Communist Road,* p. 179.
80. Saigon embassy to State Department, 18 September 1956, RG59, 751G.00/9-1956, NA; Memorandum of conversation, Pierre Landy, Paul Kattenburg, 4 October 1956, RG59, 751G.00/10-456, NA; Embassy to Department of State, 11 December 1956, RG59, 751G.00/12-1156, NA.
81. Duiker, *Communist Road,* pp. 177–79.
82. Ibid., pp. 178–82; Kahin, pp. 109–110; Thomas Corcoran to Kenneth Young, 2 November 1956, RG59, 751G.00/11-256, NA.
83. Norman Thomas to John Foster Dulles, 26 July 1957, RG59, 751G.00/7-2657, NA; Saigon to the Department of State, 21 May 1957, RG59, 751G.00/5-2157, NA.
84. Spector, *Advice and Support,* pp. 337–43; Kahin, pp. 91–92, 101–3, 105, 107–9; Buttinger, *Vietnam: A Dragon Embattled,* p. 1172; Duiker, *Communist Road,* p. 183.
85. Elbridge Durbrow, Evaluation Report on Vietnam, 5 December 1957, RG59, 751G.00/12-557, NA.
86. Duiker, *Communist Road,* p. 187.
87. American embassy in Paris to State Department, RG59, 751G.00/7-2259, NA.
88. Duiker, *Communist Road,* pp. 188–89.
89. Durbrow to State Department, 7 March 1960, *FRUS, 1958–1960:*1, p. 330.
90. Memorandum of Lansdale to Lional Marr, 11 August 1960, *FRUS, 1958–1960:*1, p. 500.
91. Duiker, *Communist Road,* p. 190.
92. McGarr to Felt, 12 November 1960, *FRUS, 1958–1960:*1, pp. 645–46.

93. D. Anderson, *Trapped by Success,* p. 192; Durbrow to State Department, 12 November 1960, *FRUS, 1958–1960:*1, pp. 644–45; Canadian delegation to International Commission of Control and Supervision of the Cease-fire in Indochina to Department of External Affairs, 19 November 1960, RG25, box 4640, file 50052.A.2, part 5, Canadian National Archives.

94. Lansdale to Gates, 12 November 1960, *FRUS, 1958–1960:*1, p. 653; Durbrow to Department of State, *FRUS, 1958–1960:*1, pp. 708–9; U.K. Ambassador in Saigon to Foreign Office, 19 November 1960, RG25, box 4640, file 50052.A.2.40, part 5, Canadian National Archives; Spector, *Advice and Support,* pp. 369–73.

95. Duiker, *Communist Road,* pp. 196–97; Pike, pp. 82–84.

96. Duiker, *Sacred War,* pp. 128–37.

CHAPTER 5

1. Smith, *International History,* vol. 1, pp. 224–25.

2. Hellmann, pp. 15–29; Lederer and Burdick.

3. *FRUS, 1961–1963:*1, p. 12.

4. Rostow Oral History, p. 44; *FRUS, 1961–1963:*1, p. 16.

5. Kennedy to McGeorge Bundy, 6 February 1961, box 1, Vietnam, National Security File, JFKL.

6. Meeting between the Secretary of State and the Assistant Secretary of State for Far Eastern Affairs, J. Graham Parsons, 28 January 1961, *FRUS, 1961–1963:*1, p. 19.

7. Castle, pp. 17–23; Greenstein and Immerman, pp. 568–87.

8. Walt Rostow to President, 10 March 1961, box 1, Laos Files, National Security File, LBJL; Castle, pp. 25–31.

9. Castle, p. 31; Duiker, *U.S. Containment Policy,* pp. 252–57; Kenneth Landon to Walt W. Rostow, 7 March 1961, Rostow to President, 9, 10, 21 March 1961, Landon to Rostow, 13 March 1961, box 18, National Security File, JFKL.

10. John Denson, British Embassy in Washington to F. A. Warner of the Foreign Office, FO371/160130, 20 December 1961, PRO.

11. National Intelligence Estimate, 28 March 1961, *FRUS, 1961–1963:*1, pp. 58–59.

12. Persons meeting with Rusk, 28 January 1961, ibid., p. 20.

13. Lansdale to Diem, 30 January 1961, ibid., p. 22.

14. Rostow to President, 12 April 1961, ibid., p. 68.

15. *Pentagon Papers,* vol. 2, p. 36.

16. Sorensen to President, 28 April 1961, Komer to Rostow, 28 April 1961, *FRUS, 1961–1963:*1, pp. 84–85.

17. A Program of Action to Prevent Communist Domination of South Vietnam, 1 May 1961, ibid., pp. 93–115.

18. Ibid., p. 100.

19. NSAM-52, 11 May 1961, ibid., pp. 132–33.

20. Gardner, *Pay Any Price,* pp. 52–53.

21. U.S. embassy in Vietnam to Department of State, 13 May 1961, *FRUS, 1961–1963:*1, pp. 136–37.

22. Joint communique following the visit of Lyndon B. Johnson to Vietnam, 13 May 1961, FO371/160128, PRO; Duiker, *U.S. Containment Policy,* pp. 260–61.

23. *New Times* (Hanoi), 18 May 1961, Saigon to External Affairs, 5 May 1961, Washington embassy to External Affairs, 15, 27 May 1961, RG25, box 4641, file 50052.A.40, part 6, Canadian National Archives.

24. Report by the Vice President, n.d., *FRUS, 1961–1963:*1, pp. 152–53; Browne, pp. 93–97.

25. Report by the Vice President, n.d., *FRUS, 1961–1963:*1, pp. 151–55.

26. Canadian Embassy in Saigon, "Report on the Situation in Vietnam," 31 July 1961, RG25, box 4641, file 50052.A.40, part 7, Canadian National Archives.

27. Report by the Vice President, n.d., *FRUS, 1961–1963:*1, pp. 151–55.

28. Ibid.
29. Canadian delegation to the International Commission of Supervision and Control to External Affairs, 26 August 1961, RG25, box 4641, file 50052.A.40, part 7 FP, Canadian National Archives.
30. Walt Rostow to President, 26 May 1961, *FRUS, 1961–1963:*1, p. 157.
31. Bassett and Pelz, p. 231.
32. Gibbons, pt. 2, p. 104.
33. Blaufarb, p. 104.
34. FO371/160130, 20 December 1961; Letter of J. I. McGee to A. S. Fare of the Commonwealth Relations Office in Canterbury, Australia, 4 January 1962, PRO; *Pentagon Papers,* vol. 2, p. 140; Washington embassy to External Affairs, 6 April 1962, RG25, box 4641, file 50052.A.40, part 7, Canadian National Archives.
35. Nolting to State Department, 30 November 1961, *FRUS, 1961–1963:*2, pp. 698–700.
36. Canadian Prime Minister's conversation with Deputy Prime Minister of Australia, 31 March 1962, RG25, box 4641, file 50052.A.40, part 7 FP, Canadian National Archives.
37. Walt Rostow to President, 11 November 1961, *FRUS, 1961–1963:*2, pp. 573–75.
38. Duiker, *U.S. Containment Policy,* pp. 280–82.
39. Shapley, pp. 88, 118.
40. Draft instructions from the President to his military representative (Taylor), 11 October 1961, *FRUS, 1961–1963:*1, p. 345. Taylor himself prepared this draft.
41. For an earlier recommendation about more aggressive use of the helicopter see Walt Rostow to President, 3 April 1961, ibid., p. 61. For Vietcong fear of the helicopter, see Duiker, *Communist Road,* pp. 215–16.
42. Editorial note, *FRUS, 1961–1963:*1, p. 380; *Pentagon Papers,* vol. 2, pp. 83–84.
43. Nolting to Department of State, 18 October 1961, *FRUS, 1961–1963:*1, p. 392.
44. Memorandum for the record, Taylor, 19 October 1961, ibid., pp. 395–96.
45. Memo prepared in the Department of State, 20 October 1961, ibid., pp. 408–9.
46. Barrett and Pelz, p. 223.
47. Galbraith to President, 3 November 1961, *FRUS, 1961–1963:*1, pp. 474–75.
48. Mansfield to President, 2 November 1961, ibid., pp. 467–70.
49. *Pentagon Papers,* vol. 2, p. 93.
50. Paper prepared by Taylor, 3 November 1961, *FRUS, 1961–1963:*1, pp. 480–81.
51. Cottrell to Taylor, 27 October 1961, ibid., pp. 505–7. A handwritten note on the document, probably by Taylor, reads: "This writer later has inconsistent observation, it must be said."
52. Ibid., p. 505.
53. Lansdale to Taylor, n.d. [October 1961], ibid., pp. 522–32.
54. Draft memorandum from McNamara to President, 5 November 1961, ibid., pp. 538–40.
55. Notes by Secretary of Defense McNamara, 6 November 1961, ibid., p. 543.
56. McNamara to President. 8 November 1961, Draft memo to President, 8 November 1961, ibid., pp. 559–66; McNamara, pp. 40–41.
57. Lyman Lemnitzer, notes of a meeting, Department of State, 9 November 1961, ibid., pp. 572–73.
58. MEMCON of meeting at the White House, 7 November 1961, ibid., pp. 544–45.
59. Notes of a meeting at the White House, 11 November 1961, ibid., p. 577; *Pentagon Papers,* vol. 2, pp. 108–9; Kahin, pp. 138–39.
60. Notes on the NSC meeting, 15 November 1961, Vice President's Security File, NSC II; Meeting of the NSC, *FRUS, 1961–1963:*1, p. 607.
61. Abraham Chayes (State Department legal adviser) to Secretary of State, 16 November 1961, ibid., p. 629.
62. NSAM-111, 22 November 1961, ibid., pp. 656–57.
63. Lyman Lemnitzer to Harry Felt, 7 February 1962, *FRUS, 1961–1963:*2, p. 109; Sheehan, p. 117; McNamara, p. 47.
64. Sheehan, p. 122.

65. CIA station to Department of State, 27 February 1962, *FRUS, 1961–1963:*2, p. 181.
66. Nolting, memo for the record, 1 March 1962, ibid., pp. 187–93.
67. Rusk to embassy in Vietnam, 1 March 1962, ibid., p. 194–95.
68. Nolting, memo for the record, 1 March 1962, ibid., p. 193.
69. Memorandum from Heavner to Chalmers Wood, 3 August 1962, ibid., pp. 575, 571.
70. Draft Action Plan for Vietnam, 3 July 1962, ibid., pp. 499–504.
71. NSAM-178, 9 August 1962, ibid., pp. 586–87.
72. Rachel Carson's articles later were published as *Silent Spring.* Murrow to Bundy, 16 August 1962, *FRUS, 1961–1963:*2, pp. 590–91; Buckingham, pp. 9–22.
73. McNamara to President, 16 November 1962, *FRUS, 1961–1963:*2, pp. 732–33.
74. Forrestal to Bundy, 8 August 1962, *FRUS, 1961–1963:*2, p. 583.
75. Canadian delegation to the International Commission of Control and Supervision to External Affairs, 21 June 1962, RG25, box 4641, file 50052.A.1.40, Canadian National Archives.
76. Sheehan, pp. 75–76, 117.
77. Memo for the record, 14 September 1962, *FRUS, 1961–1963:*2, pp. 636–37.
78. Nolting to Cottrell, 15 October 1962, ibid., pp. 698–99.
79. Task Force Saigon weekly progress report, 18 September 1962, ibid., p. 703.
80. Forrestal to Bundy, 8 August 1962, ibid., p. 583.
81. Harriman to Nolting, 12 October 1962, ibid., pp. 693–96.
82. Robert H. Johnson to Eugene Rostow, 16 October 1962, ibid., pp. 703–4.
83. Worth H. Bagley to Maxwell Taylor, 12 November 1962, Taylor Papers.
84. Nolting to State Department, 29 October 1962, John Mecklin to USIA, 5 November 1962, Nolting to Wood, 6 November 1962, *FRUS, 1961–1963:*2, pp. 721–25; Canadian delegation in Saigon to External Affairs, 14 August 1962, RG25, box 4641, file 50052.A.1.40, Canadian National Archives.
85. Sheehan, pp. 121–25.
86. Sheehan, pp. 203–265; Halberstam, pp. 77–81.
87. *Washington Post,* 3 January 1963; *New York Times,* 4 January 1963.
88. Halberstam, pp. 82–84.
89. Embassy in Vietnam to State Department, 5 February 1963, *FRUS, 1961–1963:*3, p. 100.
90. Sheehan, pp. 269–386.
91. Wheeler to JCS, January 1963, ibid., pp. 73–94.
92. Forrestal to President, 1, 4 February 1963, *FRUS, 1961–1963:*3, pp. 95, 97.
93. Roger Hilsman and Michael Forrestal to President, ibid., pp. 49–61.
94. Reeves, pp. 526–27; Giglio, p. 248.
95. Department of State to embassy in Vietnam, 26 June 1963, *FRUS, 1961–1963:*3, p. 415.
96. Duiker, *U.S. Containment Policy,* pp. 294–96; Hilsman, p. 468; Hammer, *Death in November,* pp. 103–19; Mecklin, p. 153; Consulate at Hué to Department of State, 9 May 1963, *FRUS, 1961–1963:*2, p. 277.
97. Manifesto of Buddhist Clergy and Faithful, 10 May 1963, *FRUS, 1961–1963:*3, p. 287.
98. Embassy in Vietnam to the Department of State, 1 June 1963, *FRUS, 1961–1963:*3, p. 339; Hammer, *Death in November,* p. 140.
99. Embassy to Department of State, 11 June 1963, *FRUS, 1961–1963:*3, p. 375; Hammer, *Death in November,* pp. 144–48.
100. Hammer, *Death in November,* p. 145; Ashby and Gramer, p. 168.
101. Lodge Oral History.
102. Embassy in Vietnam to Department of State, 11 June 1963, *FRUS, 1961–1963:*3, p. 376.
103. Truehart to Department of State, 14, 15 June 1963, ibid., pp. 393, 395.
104. Memorandum of conversation at the White House, 14 July 1963, ibid., pp. 451–53.
105. Forrestal to President, 9 August 1963, ibid., p. 559.
106. Department of State to Embassy in Vietnam, 24 August 1963, ibid., p. 629.
107. Bassett and Pelz, pp. 247–48.
108. Karnow, "Edge of Chaos."

109. George Mc.T. Kahin to Frank Church, 30 September 1963, series 2.2, box 26, Frank Church Papers.
110. Roger Hilsman to Secretary of State, 16 September 1963, box 200, Vietnam Country File, National Security File, JFKL.
111. Giglio, p. 251.
112. Central Intelligence Agency, Events and Developments in Vietnam, 5–18 October 1963, box 200, Vietnam Country File, National Security File, JFKL.
113. *Pentagon Papers*, vol. 2, p. 257; "Checklist," box 200, Vietnam Country File, National Security File, JFKL.
114. Blair, p. 69.
115. Hammer, pp. 300–301.
116. Newman, p. 322.
117. Berman, "Battle over Historical Interpretation"; Reeves, pp. 652–54; Olson, *Mansfield*, pp. 117–21.

CHAPTER 6

1. Suggested draft of presidential letter, n.d. [October 1963], box 200, Vietnam Country File, National Security File, JFKL.
2. Memorandum of discussion at the special meeting on Vietnam, Honolulu, 20 November 1963, *FRUS, 1961–1963:*4, pp. 608–24.
3. Discussion at the daily White House staff meeting, 22 November 1963, *FRUS, 1961–1963:*4, p. 625.
4. *New York Times,* 25 November 1963, p. 1; Gardner, *Pay Any Price,* pp. 90–93.
5. Shapley, pp. 276–79; McGeorge Bundy Oral History; Rostow Oral History.
6. McGeorge Bundy Oral History.
7. Memo of meeting, 24 November 1963, *FRUS, 1961–1963:*4, pp. 635–36.
8. Newman, pp. 345–47, makes these changes in the wording of NSAM-273 the core of his argument that Johnson significantly Americanized the war.
9. NSAM-273, 26 November 1963; Hilsman to Secretary of State, 5 December 1963, *FRUS, 1961–1963:*4, pp. 637–39, 667.
10. President to Taylor, 2 December 1963, President to John McCone, 2 December 1963, telephone conversation between Harriman and McGeorge Bundy, 4 December 1963, Taylor to President, 6 December 1963, ibid., pp. 651, 665, 579.
11. Rusk to Lodge, 6 December 1963, ibid., p. 685.
12. McNamara and Rusk, telephone conversation, 7 December 1963, ibid., p. 690; Press conference, 7 December 1963, *Public Papers of the President: Lyndon B. Johnson, 1963–1964,* pp. 34–38.
13. Chester Cooper (Chairman of the CIA's working group on Vietnam) to McCone, 6 December 1963, *FRUS, 1961–1963:*4, pp. 680–82.
14. Lyndon Johnson and Senator J. William Fulbright, telephone conversation, 2 December 1963, tape K6312.02, Johnson and Don Cook, telephone conversation, 30 November 1963, tape K6311.06, LBJL.
15. Forrestal to President, 11 December 1963, *FRUS, 1961–1963:*4, pp. 698–99.
16. Hilsman to Rusk, 20 December 1963, ibid., p. 719.
17. Embassy in Vietnam to Department of State, 7 December 1963, *FRUS, 1961–1963:*4, p. 687; Race, pp. 128–29.
18. Report on the situation in Long An Province (delivered to McNamara in Saigon), 20 December 1963, *FRUS, 1961–1963:*4, pp. 714–15.
19. Minutes of a meeting of the Special group for Counterinsurgency, 12 December 1963, ibid., pp. 704–5.
20. Carroll to McNamara, 13 December 1963, ibid., p. 707; McNamara, pp. 103–5.

21. CIA information report, 16 December 1963, *FRUS, 1961–1963*:4, p. 711.

22. Forrestal to President, 11 December 1963, ibid., p. 700.

23. Mansfield to Kennedy, 19 August 1963, *FRUS, 1961–1963*:3, p. 585.

24. Olson, *Mansfield*, pp. 115–16; Mansfield to President, 7 December 1963, *FRUS, 1961–1963*:4, p. 691.

25. Memo by William Sullivan, 21 December 1963, ibid., pp. 728–31.

26. MEMCON, 20 December 1963, ibid., pp. 716–18.

27. McNamara to President, 21 December 1963, ibid., pp. 732–33; McNamara, pp. 105–6; Blair, pp. 86–93.

28. McCone to President, 23 December 1963, *FRUS, 1961–1963*:4, p. 735.

29. McCone, highlights of a discussion in Saigon, 18–20 December, ibid., pp. 736–38.

30. Jorden to Harriman, 31 December 1963, ibid., pp. 753–54.

31. President to Lodge, 30 December 1963, State Department to Lodge, 31 December 1963, ibid., pp. 444–45.

32. Bundy to President, 9 January 1964, *FRUS, 1964–1968*:1, p. 9.

33. Olson, *Mansfield*, pp. 125–29; Mansfield to President, 6 January 1964, 7 December 1963, box 1, Vietnam, National Security File, LBJL.

34. Bundy to President, 6, 9 January 1964, ibid.

35. Rusk to President, 9 January 1964, ibid.

36. McNamara to Johnson, 7 January 1964, *FRUS, 1964*:1, pp. 12–13.

37. Gibbons, pt. II, p. 218; Sorensen to President, 14 January 1964, Country Files, box 1, Vietnam, Vietnam Memos, misc. vol. II, National Security File, LBJL.

38. Ibid., p. 1.

39. Rostow to President, 10 January 1964, *FRUS, 1964–1968*:1, p. 15.

40. Taylor to McNamara, 22 January 1964; *Pentagon Papers*, vol. 3, pp. 496–99.

41. CINCPAC to Joint Chiefs of Staff, 25 January 1964, box 1, Vietnam, National Security File, LBJL.

42. McGeorge Bundy to President, 9 January 1964, *FRUS, 1964–1968*:1, pp. 8–9. Italics in original.

43. CIA station in Saigon to CIA, 28 January 1964, ibid., pp. 36–37.

44. Lodge to Department of State, 29 January 1964, box 1, Vietnam, National Security File, LBJL.

45. Saigon to Department of State, 30 January 1964, box 2, ibid.

46. Denney to Acting Secretary of State, 29 January 1964, Forrestal to President, 30 January 1964, Green to Secretary of State, 30 January 1964, *FRUS, 1964–1968*:1, pp. 40–44.

47. Heble to Secretary of State, 30 January 1964, box 2, Vietnam, National Security File, LBJL.

48. *New York Times*, 30 January 1964, p. 1.

49. Saigon to State Department, 30 January 1964, box 2, Vietnam, National Security File, LBJL.

50. Press conference, 1 February 1964, *Public Papers of the President: Lyndon B. Johnson, 1963–1964*, vol. 1, pp. 257–60.

51. Green to Secretary of State, 30 January 1964, *FRUS, 1964–1968*:1, pp. 43–44.

52. Saigon to State Department, 5 February 1964, box 2, Vietnam, National Security File, LBJL.

53. Lodge to State Department, 1 February 1964, *FRUS, 1964–1968*:1, pp. 54–55; Lodge to Secretary of State, 5 February 1964, box 2, Vietnam, National Security File, LBJL.

54. Rusk to Lodge, 1 February 1964, *FRUS, 1964–1968*:1, p. 53.

55. Colby to Rusk, McNamara, Bundy, 14 February 1964, box 2, Vietnam, National Security File, LBJL.

56. Richard Helms (Deputy Director for Plans, CIA) to Rusk, 18 February 1964, *FRUS, 1964–1968*:1, p. 84.

57. Forrestal to McNamara, 14 February 1964, ibid., p. 77.

58. Taylor to McNamara, 18 February 1964, FRUS, pp. 86–87; Joint Chiefs of Staff Historical Division, *The History of the Joint Chiefs of Staff, The War in Vietnam, 1960–1968*, pt. 1, pp. 23–24.

59. Lodge to President, 20 February 1964, box 2, Vietnam, National Security File, LBJL.

60. Memorandum for the record of a conversation at the White House, 20 February 1964, President to Lodge, 21 February 1964, *FRUS, 1964–1968*:1, pp. 93–94, 96.

61. McNamara to Taylor, 21 February 1964, ibid., p. 97.
62. Taylor to McNamara, 2 March 1964, ibid., pp. 112–13.
63. Taylor to McNamara, 21 March 1964, ibid., pp. 110–11.
64. Walt Rostow, "Habana and Hanoi," 22 February 1964, ibid., p. 105.
65. Memorandum of a conversation between the Joint Chiefs of Staff and the President, 4 March 1964, Taylor Papers.
66. John McCone, memorandum on Vietnam, 3 March 1964, *FRUS, 1964–1968*:1, 120–27.
67. McNamara to the members of the McNamara-Taylor mission to Vietnam, 5 March 1964, ibid., p. 133.
68. Lodge to Department of State, 13 March 1964, ibid., pp. 142–44.
69. McNamara to President, 5, 13 March 1964, box 2, Vietnam, National Security File, LBJL.
70. McNamara to President, 16 March 1964, *FRUS, 1964–1968*:1, p. 157.
71. McNamara to President, 16 March 1965, ibid., p. 167.
72. Record of the 524th meeting of the NSC, 17 March 1964, box 1, NSC Meetings, LBJL; NSAM-288, 17 March 1964, *FRUS, 1964–1968*:1, pp. 172–73.
73. Forrestal to Bundy, Political Scenario in Support of Pressures on the North, 31 March 1954, box 2, Vietnam, National Security File, LBJL.
74. Forrestal to Bundy, 16 April 1964, *FRUS, 1964–1968*:1, pp. 242–43.
75. Conversation between Secretary Rusk and Prime Minister Khanh, 18 April 1964, ibid., pp. 244–45.
76. Lodge to Department of State, 4 May 1964, ibid., pp. 284–85.
77. William Bundy to Secretary of State, 4 May 1964, box 2, Vietnam, National Security File, LBJL.
78. Lodge to President, 7 May 1964, *FRUS, 1964–1968*:1, pp. 296–97.
79. Memorandum of a meeting, Saigon, 11 May 1964, ibid., pp. 304–5.
80. Memorandum of a meeting, Saigon, 11 May 1964, ibid., p. 309.
81. Memorandum of a meeting, Saigon, 11 May 1964, ibid., pp. 312–13.
82. Lodge to Department of State, 14 May 1964, ibid., pp. 315–17.
83. Notes prepared by the Secretary of Defense, 14 May 1964, ibid., pp. 324–27.
84. LBJ to Lodge, 14 May 1964, box 2, Vietnam, National Security File, LBJL. Lodge replied on May 15, 1964, *FRUS, 1964–1968*:1, p. 333.
85. Meeting of the NSC, 15 May 1964, National Security File, LBJL.
86. Memorandum prepared by the Directorate of Intelligence, CIA, 15 May 1964, *FRUS, 1964–1968*:1, p. 336.
87. Rusk to Lodge, 21 May 1964, ibid., pp. 344–45.
88. Lodge to Rusk, 22 May 1964, ibid., p. 346.
89. Draft congressional resolution prepared in the Department of State, 24 May 1964, *FRUS, 1964–1968*:1, pp. 356–57.
90. Bundy to President, 22 May 1964, box 2, Memos to the President, National Security File, LBJL.
91. *New York Times*, 25 May 1964, p. 1.
92. Steel, p. 549.
93. Ball to Rusk, 31 May 1964, *FRUS, 1964–1968*:1, pp. 400–403.
94. Forrestal to President, 29 May 1964, box 5, Vietnam, National Security File, LBJL.
95. Meeting, Honolulu, 1 June 1964, *FRUS, 1964–1968*:1, p. 418.
96. Record of a meeting, Honolulu, 2:15–6:15 P.M., 1 June 1964, ibid., pp. 421–24.
97. Rostow to Secretary of State, 6 May 1964, box 4, Vietnam, National Security File, LBJL.
98. Bundy to Rusk, 3 June 1964, *FRUS, 1964–1968*:1, pp. 442–43.
99. Lodge to President, 5 June 1964, ibid., pp. 459–61.
100. Bundy to President, 6 June 1964, Bundy Memos to President, vol. 5, National Security File, LBJL.
101. Lodge cabled Rusk on June 18 that he wanted to return to the United States to help Governor

William Scranton of Pennsylvania secure the Republican presidential nomination. He thought
he could help Scranton defeat Goldwater, whose nomination would turn the Republicans over to
a man whose conduct of foreign affairs would be "imprudent and impulsive." Goldwater, he
said, could not be trusted with the atomic bomb. Lodge to Rusk, 18 June 1964, *FRUS, 1964–
1968:*1, pp. 521–22; President Johnson's press conference of 23 June 1964, *Public Papers of
the Presidents: Lyndon B. Johnson, 1963–1964,* vol. 1, pp. 802–8.

102. Summary record of a meeting at the White House, 10 June 1964, *FRUS, 1964–1968:*1, pp. 487–
92; Sullivan, pp. 202–4.
103. Bundy to President, 10 June 1964, *FRUS, 1964–1968:*1, pp. 493–95.
104. William P. Bundy, memorandum on the Southeast Asian situation, 12 June 1964, *FRUS, 1964–
1968:*1, 507–12.
105. Paper prepared by William Bundy, 13 June 1964, ibid., pp. 515–16.
106. NSAM-308, 22 June 1964, ibid., p. 523.
107. Editorial note, ibid., pp. 523–24.
108. McGeorge Bundy to President, 25 June 1964, President to Taylor, 2 July 1964, ibid., pp. 530–
31, 538.
109. Taylor to State Department, 25 July 1964, ibid., pp. 563–65.
110. Ibid.; Saigon to Secretary of State, 25 July 1964, box 6, Vietnam, National Security
File, LBJL.
111. Gibbons, pt. 2, pp. 280–96; Goulden, pp. 100–20; Windchy, pp. 54–70; Gardner, *Pay Any
Price,* pp. 134–40; Prados, *Hidden History,* pp. 48–59.
112. Editorial note, *FRUS, 1964–1968:*1, p. 589.
113. Wheeler to Sharp, 2 August 1964; Forrestal to Secretary of State, 3 August 1964, ibid., pp. 591,
599.
114. Goulden, p. 160.
115. Tonkin Gulf Chronology, 28 August 1964, History of Tonkin Gulf, National Security File,
LBJL.
116. Kahin, p. 220; *Hearings, The Gulf of Tonkin;* Shapley, pp. 304–8; McNamara, pp. 135–43;
Duiker, *U.S. Containment Policy,* pp. 321–22.
117. Notes of the 538th meeting of the NSC, 4 August 1964, *FRUS, 1964–1968:*1, pp. 611–12.
118. Notes of a leadership meeting at the White House, 4 August 1964, White House staff meeting, 5
August 1964, ibid., pp. 615, 631–32.
119. 538th meeting of the NSC, 4 August 1964, Editorial note, ibid., pp. 611, 664; Van De Mark,
p. 18.
120. Goulden, p. 52; Wayne Morse to Virginia Green, 6 August 1968, Morse Papers.
121. *Congressional Record,* 7 August 1964, p. 18413.
122. His remarks covered ten pages in the *Congressional Record.* One irate constituent complained
that the day after the debate Morse inserted thirty pages of letters he had received in support of
his position. "This is wasteful and you have cost the taxpayers $2940 for that date alone. And
you have done it many times before." David Brosser to Wayne Morse, 11 August 1964, box B
122, Morse Papers.
123. 7 August 1964, *Congressional Record,* 88th Cong., 2d sess., pp. 18423, 18425.
124. Ibid., p. 18427.
125. Morse to Helen Mears, 15 September 1964. Morse's mail ran approximately 200 to 1 in favor of
his opposition to the Gulf of Tonkin Resolution. Morse to Elbert Bird, 29 August 1964, box B
122, Morse Papers.
126. Morse to Rudy Frank, 18 December 1964, box B 122, Morse Papers.
127. Frank Church Rebo letter to names on petition, 1 October 1964, series 2.2, box 27.3, Frank
Church Papers.
128. William Bundy, memo, 13 August 1964, *FRUS, 1964–1968:*1, p. 674.
129. Moyers to President, 3 October 1964, box 8. President's Office File, LBJL.
130. Kahin, pp. 226–27.

CHAPTER 7

1. Rusk Oral History.
2. Speech at Akron, Ohio, 21 October 1964, *Public Papers of the President: Lyndon B. Johnson, 1963–1964,* vol. 2, pp. 1390–91.
3. Gibbons, pt. 2, p. 359.
4. Fulbright, pp. 51–52; Woods, pp. 354–56.
5. Dellinger Oral History; De Benedetti, pp. 92–93, 98–99.
6. Maxwell Taylor to Department of State, 31 August 1964, *FRUS, 1964–1968:*1, p. 719.
7. McGeorge Bundy to President, 31 August 1964, Bundy Files, National Security File, LBJL.
8. Taylor to Rusk, 6 September 1964, Taylor Papers.
9. Westmoreland to Taylor, 6 September 1964, *FRUS, 1964–1968:*1, p. 737.
10. Taylor to W. W. Rostow, 5 October 1964, box 13, Rostow Papers.
11. Rostow to Taylor, 23 September 1964, ibid.
12. Taylor to Rusk, 6 September 1964, Taylor Papers.
13. Special National Intelligence Estimate, 8 September 1964, Country Files, Vietnam, box 6, National Security File, LBJL.
14. Bundy to President, 8 September 1964, *FRUS, 1964–1968:*1, pp. 746–48.
15. Memorandum of a meeting at the White House, 9 September 1964, ibid., pp. 749–55.
16. NSAM-314, 10 September 1994, ibid., pp. 58–59.
17. Sullivan, pp. 199–202; Johnson, pp. 414–15.
18. Taylor to State Department, 16 September 1964, *FRUS, 1964–1968:*1, pp. 774–75.
19. State Department to Taylor, 13 September 1964, ibid., pp. 766–67.
20. Taylor to State Department, 24 September 1964, ibid., pp. 789–91.
21. Taylor to State Department, 24 September 1964, ibid., pp. 787–89.
22. McGeorge Bundy, memo for the record, 20 September 1964, Bundy Files, National Security File, LBJL.
23. Ball, pp. 381–85.
24. Paper prepared at the Department of Defense, 25 September 1964, *FRUS, 1964–1968:*1, pp. 793–94.
25. Rusk to Taylor, 26 September 1964, ibid., pp. 797–98.
26. Taylor to Rusk, 28 September 1964, ibid., pp. 798–800.
27. Bundy to Johnson, 30 September 1964, Country Files, box 6, Vietnam, National Security File, LBJL.
28. Special National Intelligence Estimate, 1 October 1964, *FRUS, 1964–1968:*1, pp. 806–8.
29. Westmoreland to Wheeler, 17 October 1964, ibid., pp. 838–39.
30. Ball, pp. 381–83.
31. Editorial note, *FRUS, 1964–1968:*1, p. 813.
32. Wheeler to McNamara, 27 October 1964, ibid., 847–49.
33. Taylor to State Department, 15 October 1964, 16 October 1964, ibid., pp. 832–37.
34. Taylor to State Department, 16 October 1964, ibid., pp. 834–37.
35. Taylor to State Department, 25 October 1964, ibid., pp. 845–46.
36. Taylor to President, 28 October 1964, ibid., pp. 858–59.
37. Taylor to State Department, 31 October 1964, ibid., pp. 860–61.
38. Westmoreland to Taylor, 31 October 1964, ibid., pp. 861–62.
39. Ibid.
40. Taylor to State Department, 1 November 1964, ibid., pp. 873–75.
41. Wheeler to Sharp, 2 November 1964, box 7, Vietnam, National Security File, LBJL.
42. Memo of a meeting at the White House, 19 November 1964, *FRUS, 1964–1968:*1, pp. 914–16.
43. *Pentagon Papers,* vol. 3, pp. 656–66.
44. Taylor to President, 24 November 1964, ibid., p. 666.
45. Paper prepared by the NSC Working Group, 21 November 1964, *Pentagon Papers,* vol. 3, pp. 656–66.

46. Ibid.

47. U. Alexis Johnson to Rusk, 24 November 1964, *FRUS, 1964–1968:*1, p. 937.

48. Paper prepared by Maxwell Taylor, n.d., ibid., pp. 948–55.

49. Notes of a meeting at the White House, 1 December 1964, ibid., pp. 965–69.

50. Position paper on Southeast Asia prepared by the Executive Committee of the NSC, 2 December 1964, ibid., pp. 969–74.

51. Instructions from President to Ambassador Taylor, 3 December 1964, ibid., pp. 974–78.

52. Taylor to State Department, 7 December 1964, ibid., pp. 982–84.

53. Bundy to Johnson, 5 December 1964, box 2, Bundy memos to President, National Security File, LBJL.

54. Memorandum of conversation, 8 December 1964, *FRUS, 1964–1968:*1, pp. 985–87.

55. Mansfield to President, 9 December 1964, box 6, Name File, National Security File, LBJL.

56. Van De Mark, pp. 40–41; President to Mansfield, 17 December 1964, *FRUS, 1964–1968:*1, pp. 1009–12.

57. Taylor to State Department, 23 December 1964, ibid., p. 1031.

58. Taylor to State Department, 20 December 1964, ibid., pp. 1014–17.

59. Ibid.; *Pentagon Papers,* vol. 2, pp. 343–45.

60. *Department of State Bulletin,* 11 January 1965, pp. 34–39.

61. Embassy to State Department, 28 December 1964, Wheeler to Westmoreland, 28 December 1964, *FRUS, 1964–1968:*1, pp. 1049–50; McGeorge Bundy, "Pros and Cons of a Reprisal Raid," 28 December 1964, box 4, Bundy Files, National Security File, LBJL; Gibbons, pt. 3, pp. 382–83.

62. Douglas Cater to President, 26 January 1965, box 12, Vietnam, National Security File, LBJL.

63. PBS, *Vietnam: A History,* episode 5: "America Takes Charge—1965–1967"; President to McNamara, 7 January 1965, *FRUS, 1964–1968:*2, p. 42.

64. Bundy to President, 27 January 1965, box 39, NSC History, National Security File, LBJL.

65. McGeorge Bundy, notes of meeting, 27 January 1965, box 2, Bundy Papers, LBJL; Intelligence memo, 26 January 1965, *FRUS, 1964–1968:*2, pp. 89–90.

66. Kahin, pp. 260–63.

67. Taylor to State Department, 6 February 1965, box 13, Vietnam, National Security File, LBJL.

68. Gibbons, pt. 3, p. 61.

69. Bundy to President, 7 February 1965, Memos to President, box 2, Bundy Files, National Security File, LBJL.

70. Ball to President, 13 February 1965, box 37, NSC History, National Security File, LBJL.

71. Gordon Chase to McGeorge Bundy, 16 February 1965, box 13, Vietnam, National Security File, LBJL.

72. Special National Intelligence Estimate, 4 February 1965, *FRUS, 1964–1968:*2, pp. 143–48; Bundy to President, 17 February 1965, Memos to President, 2, Bundy Files, National Security File, LBJL; Olson, *Mansfield,* pp. 145–46.

73. Full mailing, 16 March 1965; Editorial, WFBM radio station, 31 March 1965, box 367, Bayh Papers; Gibbons, pt. 3, p. 129; Ashby and Gramer, p. 199.

74. McGeorge Bundy to President, 5 May 1965, Memos to President, box 2, Bundy Files, National Security File, LBJL.

75. Pearson to Johnson, 28 February 1965; Pearson Papers.

76. McGeorge Bundy to President, 6 March 1965, box 1, Bundy Papers, LBJL.

77. Bundy to President, 6 March 1965, Memos to President, box 2, Bundy Files, National Security File, LBJL.

78. Thomson to Bundy, 19 February 1965, box 39, NSC History, National Security File, LBJL.

79. Bundy to President, 6 March 1965, box 1, Bundy Papers, LBJL.

80. PBS, *Vietnam,* episode 5: "America Takes Charge—1965–1967."

81. Speech of 7 April 1965, *Public Papers of the President: Lyndon B. Johnson, 1965,* vol. 1, pp. 394–99; Goodwin, pp. 365–66; Steel, pp. 562–67; Turner, p. 118.

82. Gibbons, pt. 3, p. 218; President to Mansfield, 12 April 1965, *FRUS, 1964–1968:*2, pp. 547–48.

83. Goodwin to President, 27 April 1965, box 5, President's Office File, LBJL.
84. McNamara to President, 21 April 1965, Memos to President, box 4, Bundy Files, National Security File, LBJL.
85. Kahin, pp. 320–21; Berman, *Planning a Tragedy,* p. 62; Van De Mark, pp. 178–83.
86. Wheeler to McNamara, 11 June 1965, box 43, NSC History, National Security File, LBJL.
87. McNamara to President, 20 July 1965, box 8, Meetings on Vietnam, National Security File, LBJL.
88. Meeting in the Cabinet Room, noon, 22 July 1965, box 2, Notes of meetings, National Security File, LBJL.
89. McGeorge Bundy to President, 23 July 1965, box 43, NSC History, National Security File, LBJL.
90. McGeorge Bundy to President, 19 July 1965, ibid.
91. Jack Valenti to President, 22 July 1965, box 12, President's Office File, LBJL; Gardner, *Pay Any Price,* pp. 242–51.
92. Meeting in the Cabinet Room, 21 July 1965, Meeting Notes File, box 2, National Security File, LBJL.
93. Kahin, p. 373; Berman, *Planning a Tragedy,* pp. 111–21.
94. Louis Harris to White House, 17 June 1965, WHCF/CF, box 71, LBJL.
95. Meeting in the Cabinet Room, noon, 22 July 1965, box 2, Notes of meetings, National Security File, LBJL.
96. Ball to President, 18 June 1965, box 42, NSC History, National Security File, LBJL.
97. Ball to Secretary of State, 28 June 1965, box 43, ibid.
98. Kahin, pp. 374–75; Berman, *Planning a Tragedy,* pp. 119–21.
99. Chester Cooper, memo for the record, Meetings on Vietnam, 21 July 1965 [dated July 22, 1965], box 1, National Security File, LBJL.
100. Ball's informal notes on bombing [June 1965], boxes 92–94, Country Files, Vietnam, National Security File, LBJL.
101. Cooper to Bundy, 30 June 1965, box 43, NSC History, National Security File, LBJL.
102. Views of Clark Clifford on Vietnam, taken down by Jack Valenti, Camp David, 25 July 1965, box 1, Reference File, Vietnam, National Security File, LBJL.
103. Galbraith to President, 22 July 1965, WHCF/CF, box 71, LBJL.
104. Vietnam panel, 10 July 1965, box 43, NSC History, National Security File, LBJL.
105. Lodge to President, 20 July 1965, ibid.
106. Meeting in the Cabinet room, 21 July 1965, box 2, National Security File, LBJL.
107. Notes of meeting, 22 July 1965, *FRUS, 1964–1968:*3, pp. 209–17; Chester Cooper, memo of meeting on Vietnam, 21 July 1965, boxes 74–75, Vietnam, National Security File, LBJL.
108. Busby to President, 10:00 P.M., 21 July 1965, box 3, Horace Busby Files, LBJL.
109. Kahin, pp. 395–96; notes of meeting, 22 July 1965, *FRUS, 1964–1968:*3, pp. 219–20.
110. Mike Mansfield to President, 27 July 1965, box 6, Name File, National Security File, LBJL.
111. Olson, *Mansfield,* pp. 157–61; Notes of telephone conversation, Secretary Fowler and Bill Moyers, 18 November 1965, box 1, Fowler Files.
112. *The Papers and the Papers;* Gelb, pp. 272–97; Berman, *Planning a Tragedy,* pp. 79–128; Kahin, pp. 399–401; Janis; May and Neustadt, pp. 88–90; Van De Mark, pp. 219–21; Young, pp. 158–60.

CHAPTER 8

1. Clarke, pp. 109, 145.
2. Krepenivich, pp. 164–92.
3. "Cincinnatus," p. 76.
4. Terry, p. 45.
5. L. Cable, p. 22.
6. Chanoff and Daon, p. 48.

7. Press Conference Statement, 28 July 1965, *Public Papers of the President: Lyndon Johnson, 1965,* vol. 2, pp. 794–803.
8. Moore and Galloway, pp. 27–29.
9. Clarke, p. 109.
10. Lanning and Cragg, p. 69.
11. Ibid., p. 103.
12. Moore and Galloway, p. 51.
13. Ibid., p. 53.
14. Mason, p. 175.
15. Moore and Galloway, pp. 232–33.
16. Ibid., 399.
17. *Pentagon Papers,* vol. 4, pp. 304–6; McGarvey, pp. 73–74, 94.
18. *Pentagon Papers,* vol. 4, p. 304; Post, pp. 351–52; Buzzanco, pp. 242–44.
19. Ibid., p. 307.
20. McNamara to President, 30 November 1965, 7 December 1965, ibid., pp. 622–24.
21. Clarke, pp. 21–23, 127–28.
22. Lodge to Secretary of State, 9 March 1966, box 41, Vietnam, National Security File, LBJL.
23. Lodge to Secretary of State, 8 April 1966, ibid.
24. Clarke, p. 133.
25. Wheeler to Westmoreland, 20 May 1966, History File 6-D1, Westmoreland Papers.
26. Westmoreland to Wheeler, 22 May 1966, History File 6-D7, Westmoreland Papers.
27. Prados, *Hidden History,* p. 64; S. Sheehan, pp. 140–44.
28. Clarke, pp. 45–46.
29. Ibid., pp. 40–41, 93; Collins, p. 76; Karnow, *Vietnam,* p. 457.
30. Bergerud, pp. 72–76; Collins, pp. 75–79.
31. Koch, p. 142.
32. Krepenivich, p. 170.
33. Ibid., pp. 170–71.
34. Institute of Medicine, p. 27; Buckingham, pp. 86–135.
35. Wynn F. Foster, pp. 50–57; Bob Stoffey, pp. 51–113.
36. Bergerud, p. 72.
37. Hayslip, pp. 68–69.
38. Hensler, p. 95; Young, p. 170.
39. Karnow, *Vietnam,* pp. 454–55; Edward Marks, "Saigon: The Impact of the Refugees," series 2, box 1, War Refugees, 1967, Pike Collection.
40. Krepenivich, pp. 170–71.
41. Baskir and Strauss, p. 5.
42. Norman, p. 18.
43. Appy, pp. 121–23; Young, p. 195.
44. Caputo, pp. 38–43; Santoli, pp. 38–39; Zumwalt and Zumwalt, p. 52; Spiller, p. 55; Wilson, p. 9.
45. Puller, p. 75; Maurer, pp. 151, 153, 162, 173; Santoli, p. 94.
46. "Cincinnatus," p. 155.
47. Wolff, p. 7.
48. Appy, pp. 238–40; Grady, pp. 50–55.
49. Maurer, p. 165.
50. "Cincinnatus," pp. 85, 136–37.
51. Marshall, pp. 4, 7, 12.
52. Norman, p. 67.
53. Ibid., pp. 21, 27–28, 35, 73.
54. Lanning and Cragg, p. 49.
55. Henderson, pp. 40–47; Mangold and Penycate, p. 63.
56. R. W. Chandler, pp. 47, 49.

57. Leaflet 4115, ibid., p. 55.
58. Leaflet SP 927, ibid., p. 63.
59. Leaflets 4-132-68 and 4-133-68, ibid., pp. 21–22.
60. Valentine, pp. 13, 348; Young, pp. 240–41.
61. Valentine, p. 93.
62. Ibid., p. 95.
63. Gardner, *Pay any Price,* pp. 219, 222; Bundy to President, 24 July 1965, *FRUS, 1964–1968:*3, p. 235.
64. Krepenivich, p. 190.
65. Schell, p. 87.
66. Mangold and Penycote, pp. 166–67; Schell, pp. 57–186.
67. Mangold and Penycate, pp. 162–77, 70–71.
68. Komer to President, 1 July 1966, box 1, Warnke Papers.
69. *Pentagon Papers,* vol. 4, pp. 419–20.
70. Vo Nguyen Giap, "The Big Victory, the Great Task," in McGarvey, ed., p. 213.
71. Moyers to President, 9 June 1966, box 12, Office Files of Bill Moyers, LBJL.
72. Valentine, pp. 123, 130–37.
73. Komer to President, 1 July 1966, box 1, Warnke Papers; Herring, *LBJ and Vietnam,* pp. 71–74.
74. *Pentagon Papers,* vol. 4, p. 420.
75. Ibid., p. 421.
76. Rostow to President, 7 March 1967, boxes 92–94, Country Files, Vietnam, National Security File, LBJL.
77. *Pentagon Papers,* vol. 4, pp. 29–30; Mark Clodfleter, pp. 117–46.
78. *Pentagon Papers,* vol. 4, p. 28.
79. Ibid., p. 30.
80. Ibid., p. 31.
81. Ibid., p. 53.
82. Bundy to President, 14 December 1965, boxes 92–94, Country Files, Vietnam, National Security File, LBJL.
83. William Jorden to President, 7 March 1967, ibid.
84. *Pentagon Papers,* vol. 4, p. 34; Rusk to President, 19 December 1965, NSF memo to President, box 5, Bundy Papers, vol. 17.
85. Jorden to President, 7 March 1967, boxes 92–94, Country Files, Vietnam, National Security File, LBJL.
86. *Pentagon Papers,* vol. 4, pp. 39, 47.
87. *New York Times,* 27, 30 January 1966, Op-ed page; Woods, pp. 400–401.
88. McGeorge Bundy to President, 27 January 1966, boxes 92–94, Country Files, Vietnam, National Security File, LBJL.
89. McGeorge Bundy to President, 26 January 1966, ibid.
90. McGeorge Bundy to President, paper for discussion with congressional leadership, 24 January 1966, ibid.
91. Jorden to President, 7 March 1966, ibid.
92. McGeorge Bundy to President, memo of conversation with Walter Lippmann, 20 January 1966, ibid.
93. *Pentagon Papers,* vol. 4, pp. 52–53; Clodfleter, pp. 92–100.
94. *Pentagon Papers,* vol. 4, pp. 55–57; Ellsworth Bunker to Secretary of State, 17 June 1967, box 17, Rostow memos to President, vol. 31, National Security File, LBJL.
95. *Pentagon Papers,* vol. 4, p. 71.
96. Ibid., pp. 78, 96.
97. Lodge to Rostow, n.d. [April 1966], box 260, Vietnam, National Security File, LBJL.
98. Rostow to Harriman, 28 January 1966, box 13, Rostow Papers.
99. *Pentagon Papers,* vol. 4, p. 101.
100. Ross, pp. 280–89; *Wall Street Journal,* 27 June 1966, p. 2.
101. *Pentagon Papers,* vol. 4, pp. 105–7; *Wall Street Journal,* 24 June 1966.

102. *Pentagon Papers,* vol. 4, p. 110.
103. Leaflet 54, R. W. Chandler, p. 110.
104. Leaflet 51, ibid., p. 111.
105. JUSPAO, leaflet 7, ibid., p. 107.
106. Leaflet 134, ibid., p. 104.
107. R. W. Chandler, pp. 149, 151.
108. *Pentagon Papers,* vol. 4, p. 116; Jian, pp. 378–79; Whiting, pp. 194–95.
109. Ibid., pp. 111–12.
110. *Pentagon Papers,* vol. 4, p. 117.
111. Ibid.; Perry, pp. 177–79; Shapley, pp. 362–63.
112. *Pentagon Papers,* vol. 4, p. 127.
113. Ibid., p. 128.
114. Ibid., p. 131; Westmoreland, pp. 117–18.
115. *Pentagon Papers,* vol. 4, p. 136.
116. Lodge to Secretary of State, 10 August 1966, box 110, Country Files, Vietnam, National Security File, LBJL.

CHAPTER 9

1. Baskir and Strauss, p. 5.
2. Hallin, pp. 106–10; Halberstam, pp. 80–81.
3. Small, pp. 20–22.
4. See chap. 3. Notes of meeting at State Department, 7 April 1954, Russell Papers; Dallek, *Lone Star Rising,* pp. 443–44.
5. 12 September 1963, *Congressional Record,* 88th Cong., 2d sess., 16824. Liberal Democrats, such as Birch Bayh of Indiana, Joseph Clark of Pennsylvania, Ernest Gruening of Alaska, George McGovern of South Dakota, Wayne Morse of Oregon, Claiborne Pell of Rhode Island, Gaylord Nelson of Wisconsin, Ralph Yarborough of Texas, and Stephen Young of Ohio, later became, at one time or another, doves who opposed the deepening U.S. involvement in Vietnam. Moderate Democrats, such as Quentin Burdick of North Dakota, Frank Moss of Utah, Edmund Muskie of Maine, and Maureen Neuberger of Oregon, were genuinely outraged by Diem's behavior and thought that he was ruining the chances to achieve a victory over the communists. Several conservative Democrats and Republicans also supported the resolution because they opposed foreign aid. Democrat Allen Bible of Nevada, Republican Carl Carlson of Kansas, Democrat Russell Long of Louisiana, Democrat Olin Johnston of South Carolina, and Republican Milward Simpson of Wyoming generally opposed foreign aid. They also supported presidents who followed an assertive policy against communist states and movements. Later, as the United States's involvement in Vietnam deepened, they set aside their reservations about the quality of the Diem regime and supported escalation of the U.S. role under Lyndon Johnson.
6. Ashby and Gramer, pp. 169–71.
7. Ely, pp. 19–21; Senate Committee on Foreign Relations, *Hearing on Supplemental Foreign Assistance,* 28 January–18 February 1966, p. 591.
8. 6 August 1964, *Congressional Record,* 88th Cong., 2d sess., 18470. All ten of the absent senators announced that they supported passage of the resolution.
9. Ibid., p. 18415.
10. Church press release, 6 August 1964, Church letter to names on petition, 1 October 1964, series 2.2, box 27.3, Church Papers; Ashby and Gramer, pp. 183–84.
11. 6 August 1964, *Congressional Record,* p. 18408.
12. Gibbons, pt. 3, p. 304.
13. Carl Marcy to Fulbright, 22 June 1965, series 48, box 3:16:2, Fulbright Papers.
14. Woods, pp. 384–85.
15. Marcy to Fulbright, 17 August 1965, series 48, box 3:16:2, Fulbright Papers.

16. Woods, pp. 386–98.
17. Carl Marcy to J. William Fulbright, 21 January 1966, Record Group 46, Senate Committee on Foreign Relations Files, Carl Marcy Files, NA.
18. Fulbright to William C. Baggs, 12 January 1966, series 48, box 1:8:1, Fulbright Papers.
19. Marcy to Fulbright, 21 January 1966, ibid.
20. Senate Committee on Foreign Relations, *Supplemental Foreign Assistance*, 28 January–18 February 1966, p. 9.
21. Ibid., pp. 332–35. For McNamara's reaction to Kennan's testimony see McNamara, p. 215.
22. Gavin, "The Easy Chair."
23. Senate Committee on Foreign Relations, *Supplemental Foreign Assistance*, 28 January–18 February 1966, pp. 227–28, 239.
24. Ibid., p. 231.
25. *Executive Sessions of the U.S. Senate Foreign Relations Committee*, p. 233.
26. Estelle Wrock to Frank Church, 11 February 1966, series 2.2, box 30.3, Church Papers.
27. *Executive Sessions of the U.S. Senate Committee on Foreign Relations*, vol. 12, 1966, p. 233.
28. Robert Bernstein to Fulbright, 28 February 1966, series 48, box 1:8:1, Fulbright Papers.
29. Schlesinger to Fulbright, 10 March 1966, series 2.2, box 30.12, Church Papers.
30. Carl Marcy to J. William Fulbright, 2 November 1966, series 48, box 3:16:3, Fulbright Papers.
31. 16 February 1966, *Congressional Record*, 89th Cong., 2d sess., 2966; Transcript of a CBS News discussion moderated by Eric Severeid, including Senators Frank Church, Jacob Javits, Stuart Symington, and John Tower, "Vietnam Perspective," 15 February 1966, series 2.2, box 29.15, Church Papers.
32. Jacob Javits, press release, 2 February 1966, series 2.2, box 29.17, Church Papers.
33. Page Belcher to I. V. Horner, 9 December 1964, box 76.1, Belcher Papers.
34. Page Belcher to Alva A. Smith, 3 July 1965, Box 93.14, ibid.
35. Ervin to Hickman, 10 August 1965, Ervin to Lewis Sainsing, 21 October 1965, box 136, Ervin Papers.
36. "Must Face Realities in Vietnam Ervin Says," 3 February 1966, box 156, Ervin to Mrs. Francis Harper, 13 January 1965, Ervin to Zelma Farlow, 25 January 1965, Ervin to Geoffrey Walsh, 26 January 1965, Ervin Papers.
37. Shapley, p. 449. Thomas L. McNaugher, *The M-16 Controversies*.
38. Herring, *LBJ and Vietnam*, pp. 37, 17–20.
39. Rostow Oral History; Rusk Oral History.
40. Meeting with senior foreign policy advisers, 3 April 1968, box 1, Tom Johnson's notes of meetings, LBJL.
41. Harry McPherson to President, 3 March 1966, box 52, McPherson Files.
42. Small, pp. 80–81.
43. Woods, pp. 252–56, 360–75, 389–90, 402–9.
44. 16 February 1966, *Congressional Record*, p. 2966. Douglas MacArthur II to Church, 25 March 1966, series 2.2, box 9.5, Church Papers.
45. Averell Harriman to Robert Kennedy, Memorandum of telephone conversation, 6:00 P.M., 27 February 1967, box 520, Harriman Papers.
46. Statement of Senator Robert F. Kennedy, 21 March 1967, 1968 Campaign Files, box 5, Speech Writers' Files, Robert F. Kennedy Papers.
47. Rostow to President, 15 March 1967, box 14, National Security File, LBJL; Memos to the President, ibid.
48. Manashe and Radosh, eds., p. 14.
49. De Benedetti, pp. 115–16.
50. Ibid., p. 108.
51. Chester Cooper to Jack Valenti, 24 April 1965, box 1, Reference File, Vietnam, LBJL.
52. See chap. 5.

53. Among the most popular works published in 1965 were Bernard Fall and Marcus Raskin, *The Vietnam Reader*, Bernard Fall, *The Two Vietnams*, and Robert Scheer, *How We Got Involved in Vietnam*.
54. Richard Ichord to George Brown, 14 October 1965, box 86.70, Albert Papers.
55. Bundy to Robert Buckhout, 16 April 1965, box 7, Bundy Files; Menashe and Radosh, p. 141.
56. Small, pp. 50–51; McGeorge Bundy Oral History.
57. Wells, pp. 67, 242; De Benedetti, pp. 25–26, 59–61, 66–68; T. H. Anderson, pp. 136–39, 166.
58. Frank Church, speech, 11 September 1963, series 2:2, box 25.2, Church Papers.
59. Committee of Inquiry into Meaningful Election in Vietnam [1966], box 33, Lowenstein Papers.
60. Dellinger, pp. 216–27.
61. De Benedetti, pp. 117, 126; Dellinger, p. 215.
62. T. H. Anderson, pp. 127–28, 208.
63. Small, pp. 89–90, 150.
64. Gitlin, pp. 97–101.
65. Register, MSS 278, National Coordinating Committee, State Historical Society of Wisconsin.
66. NCCEWVN steering committee minutes, 18–20 September 1965, box 1.2, NCCEWVN Papers.
67. De Benedetti, p. 131; Katz, pp. 97–100.
68. NCCEWVN steering committee minutes, 18–20 September 1965, box 1.2, NCCEWVN Papers; Michael Klare to Frank Emspak, 12 October 1966, box 2.6, ibid.
69. Michael Klare to Joan Levenson, 19 September 1966, ibid.
70. Register, Fifth Avenue Peace Parade Committee Papers.
71. De Benedetti, p. 127.
72. Ibid., pp. 129–30.
73. Ibid., p. 137; Gitlin, pp. 180–85; T. H. Anderson, pp. 146–49.
74. Mansfield to President, 29 June 1966, Name File, box 6, National Security File, LBJL.
75. De Benedetti, pp. 161–62; Matusow, pp. 385, 389; Rieder, pp. 243–47; Chafe, pp. 262–75.
76. Memo to the President, 6 April 1967, box 16, Douglas Cater Files.
77. Hall, *Because of their Faith;* Wells, pp. 48–49, 67–68, 122–23.
78. Some Reasons for a Massive Mobilization to End the War in Vietnam [April 1967], box 5.12, SMCEWV Papers.
79. De Benedetti, pp. 172–73; Hall, p. 43.
80. De Benedetti, pp. 173–74; Small, pp. 99–100; Hall, p. 44.
81. Sidney Peck, "Some Reasons for a Massive Mobilization to End the War in Vietnam," n.d. [April 1967], box 5.12, SMCEWV Papers.
82. *New York Times*, 16 April 1967, p. 1; *San Francisco Examiner*, 16 April 1967, p. 1.
83. De Benedetti, p. 176; Wells, pp. 133–35; *New York Times*, 16 April 1967; Zaroulis and Sullivan, pp. 111–12.
84. Some Reasons for a Massive Mobilization to End the War in Vietnam, [April 1967], box 5.12, SMCEWV Papers.
85. Gallup, pp. 2062–63, 2083, 2089.
86. Working committee meeting, Student Mobilizing Committee, 6 June 1967, box 1.1, SMCEWV Papers.
87. *New York Times*, 16 April 1967, p. 2.
88. De Benedetti, pp. 180–86; Wells, pp. 138–39, 168–70.
89. De Benedetti, pp. 181–82; T. H. Anderson, pp. 166, 176.
90. Baskir and Strauss, p. 16.
91. Ibid., p. 17.
92. *U.S. v. Seeger*, 380 *U.S.* 163 (1965).
93. Hershey to Douglas Cater, 6 December 1967, Logan Wilson, "Statement by the President of the American Council on Education," Douglas Cater to the President, 17 December 1967, box 17, Cater Files; Bobbie G. Kiberg to President Gerald R. Ford, 13 January 1977, box 41, Connor Papers; Information on Clemency Procedures, box 9, Hartmann Papers.
94. Cater to the President, 10 July 1967, box 16, Cater Files. Among those attending was Strobe

Talbott, editor of the Yale *Daily News,* who later went on to a prominent career in journalism and became Deputy Secretary of State in 1994. Lowenstein consistently opposed leftist influences, first in his career as director of the National Student Association and later in the anti-war movement. Once *Ramparts* magazine revealed that the CIA had secretly funded the activities of the NSA in the 1950s, anti-war leftists voiced their own suspicions, the mirror image of President Johnson's, that Lowenstein worked secretly for the U.S. government. Chafe, pp. 97–99.

95. T. H. Anderson, pp. 214, 314; Gitlin, pp. 22–27, 245; De Benedetti, pp. 191–93.
96. De Benedetti, p. 192.
97. Ibid., p. 196; Zaroulis and Sullivan, pp. 139–40; Wells, pp. 170–74.
98. Small, p. 112.
99. David McGiffert to Warren Christopher, 9, 11 October 1967, Roger Wilkins to Ramsey Clark, 5 October 1967, Christopher to Joseph Califano et al., 4, 5 October 1967, box 8. Christopher Papers.
100. Mailer, pp. 11–12, 37–63.
101. De Benedetti, pp. 197–98; Wells, pp. 195–201.
102. De Benedetti, pp. 198–99.
103. Vietnamese students in France to organizers and participants in the march on Washington, 16 October 1967, box 44.4, SMCEWV Papers.
104. Chafe, pp. 262–63; Goodwin, pp. 480–89; Zaroulis and Sullivan, pp. 125–26.
105. *New York Herald Tribune,* 13 August 1965; *Science,* vol. 150 (December 1965); series II, U.S. Economy, box 1, Pike Collection.
106. Campagna, p. 32; *Newsweek,* 10 July 1967, p. 49, *Washington Post,* 30 January 1968, series II, U.S. Economy, box 1, Pike Collection.
107. Riddell. pp. 43, 51.
108. Bowen, p. 14.
109. Eliot Janeway, *Chicago Tribune,* 24 January 1966, *Wall Street Journal,* 18 January 1966, series II, U.S. Economy, box 1, Pike Collection.
110. Friends Committee on National Legislation Newsletter, December 1966, series II, box 1, Economics, Pike Collection.
111. Rusk Oral History; Russell Papers.

CHAPTER 10

1. Shapley, pp. 436–37; McNamara, p. 271.
2. Rusk interview, 5 October 1991. Rusk Oral History.
3. Harriman to President and Secretary of State, 14 January 1967, box 12, Rostow Memos to President, National Security File, LBJL.
4. Harrison Williams to President, 6 March 1967, box 14, ibid.
5. Rusk to President, 8 March 1967, ibid.
6. Herring, ed., *Secret Diplomacy,* p. 211.
7. Memo of conversation, McNaughton-Zinchuk, 3 January 1967, box 12, Rostow Memos to President, National Security File, LBJL.
8. Herring, *Secret Diplomacy,* p. 285.
9. Ibid., p. 231.
10. MEMCON, 22 December 1966, William P. Bundy and Alexander Zinchuk, Bundy Files, LBJL.
11. *Washington Post,* 19 January, 2 February 1967; *International Herald Tribune,* 20 January 1967.
12. *Public Papers of the President: Lyndon B. Johnson, 1967,* press conference, 2 February 1967, pp. 128–34.
13. Statements regarding conditions for negotiations, n.d. [March 1967], box 14, Rostow Memos to President, National Security File, LBJL.
14. Ashmore and Baggs, p. 25.

15. Ibid., pp. 44–47.
16. Ibid., pp. 79–80; Rostow to Lodge and Westmoreland, 8 March 1967, box 14, Rostow Memos to President, National Security File, LBJL.
17. Herring, ed., *Secret Diplomacy,* p. 722.
18. Ibid., p. 537.
19. Ibid., p. 723.
20. Rostow to President, 9 September 1967, box 22, Rostow Memos to President, National Security File, LBJL.
21. Herring, ed., *Secret Diplomacy,* p. 724.
22. Shapley, pp. 425–33; McNamara, pp. 291–95; Rostow to Johnson, 18 August 1967, box 3, Rostow to Johnson, 7 August 1967, box 4, Rostow Memos to President, National Security File, LBJL.
23. Herring, ed., *Secret Diplomacy,* p. 726.
24. Speech at San Antonio, 29 September 1967, *Public Papers of the President: Lyndon B. Johnson, 1967,* pp. 876–81.
25. Gibbons, vol. 4, p. 784; Marcovich to Kissinger, 2 October 1967, Read memo for record, 6 October 1967, box 4, Rostow Papers.
26. Herring, ed., *Secret Diplomacy,* p. 737.
27. Notes of President's Wednesday night meeting, 18 October 1967, box 1, Tom Johnson's notes of meetings, LBJL.
28. Tom Johnson's notes of meetings, 4 October 1967, LBJL.
29. Notes of President's Wednesday night meeting, 18 October 1967, box 1, Tom Johnson's notes of meetings, LBJL.
30. Herring, ed., *Secret Diplomacy,* p. 768.
31. Ibid., p. 770.
32. PBS, *Vietnam: A History,* episode 5: "America Takes Charge, 1965–1967."
33. Gibbons, vol. 4, p. 269.
34. Luce and Sommer, p. 314.
35. Lodge to Secretary of State, 7 February 1967, box 240, Vietnam, National Security File, LBJL.
36. Lodge to President, 1 March 1967, box 14, Rostow Memos to President, National Security File, LBJL.
37. Rusk to Lodge, 12 January 1967, Box 240, Vietnam, National Security File, LBJL.
38. Joiner, p. 155.
39. Rusk to Lodge, 12, 31 January 1967, Lodge to Rusk, 9 February 1967, box 240, Vietnam, National Security File, LBJL.
40. Lodge to President, 29 March 1967, box 14, Bunker to President, 22 May 1967, box 16, Rostow Memos to President, National Security File, LBJL; Wheeler to Westmoreland, 24 June 1967, Messages File, Westmoreland Papers.
41. Bunker to State Department, 26 May 1967, box 16, Rostow Memos to President, National Security File, LBJL.
42. Shaplen, *Road from War,* pp. 156–57; Rostow to President, 30 June 1967, box 18, Rostow Memos to President, National Security File, LBJL.
43. Bunker to President, 12 July 1967, box 17, Rostow Memos to President, National Security File, LBJL.
44. Gibbons, vol. 4, p. 772; Joiner, p. 117.
45. Joiner, p. 125.
46. Gibbons, vol. 4, p. 772.
47. "The Elections in South VN," Lowenstein Papers.
48. Turner, p. 189.
49. Joiner, pp. 150–55; Gibbons, vol. 4, p. 775.
50. Gibbons, vol. 4, pp. 894–95.
51. Ibid., pp. 895–96.
52. McNamara to President, 1 November 1967, Vietnam, National Security File, LBJL.

53. Gibbons, vol. 4, pp. 883–85.
54. Ibid. (Italics in original); Ball Oral History.
55. McGeorge Bundy to President, 17 October 1967, Vietnam–October 1967, Vietnam, National Security File, LBJL.
56. Notes by Jim Jones of meeting of 2 November 1967, Meeting Notes File, LBJL.
57. Gibbons, vol. 4, p. 877; Notes by Jim Jones of meeting of 2 November 1967, Meeting Notes File, LBJL.
58. Meeting with senior advisers, 5 December 1967, box 1, Tom Johnson's notes of meetings, LBJL.
59. *New York Times,* 16 November 1967; Gibbons, vol. 4, pp. 896–97.
60. Meeting with Saigon advisers, box 1, Tom Johnson's notes of meetings, LBJL.
61. Gibbons, vol. 4, p. 898.
62. Ibid., pp. 940–42.
63. Ibid., pp. 942–43.
64. Oberdorfer, p. 8.
65. Notes of the President's foreign affairs luncheon, 30 January 1968, Tom Johnson's notes of meetings, box 3, LBJL.
66. Macdonald, pp. 263–65; Oberdorfer, pp. 157–236; Wirtz, pp. 60–74.
67. Obderdofer, pp. 344–51.
68. MACV report, 28 February 1968, box 2, Clifford Papers.
69. Oberdorfer, pp. 45–46.
70. Macdonald, p. 263.
71. CIA report, 20 February 1968, box 2, Clifford Papers.
72. Macdonald, pp. 285–87; Prados and Stubbe, pp. 343–93; Wirtz, pp. 76–79.
73. Andrew Goodpaster, meeting with General Eisenhower, 8 February 1968, box 28, Rostow Memos to President, National Security File, LBJL.
74. Macdonald, pp. 289–91.
75. MACV report, 28 February 1968, box 2, Clifford Papers.
76. Rostow to President, 12 February 1968, box 6, Rostow Memos to President, National Security File, LBJL.
77. Notes of the President's meeting to discuss General Wheeler's trip to Vietnam, 28 February 1968, box 3, Tom Johnson's notes of meetings, LBJL.
78. Macdonald, pp. 266–69.
79. Braestrup, pp. 169–84; Spector, *After Tet,* p. 99; MACV Report, 28 February 1968, box 2, Clifford Papers; Hammond, p. 352.
80. Hersh, *My Lai 4,* pp. 38–39, 49–51, 53, 76.
81. *U.S. News and World Report,* 4 February 1968, pp. 23–28; *Newsweek,* 12 February 1968, pp. 23–31; *New York Times,* 2 February 1968, p. 35.
82. *New York Times,* 2 February 1968, p. 35.
83. Hammond, pp. 353–60; Notes of the President's meeting with senior foreign policy advisers, 6 February 1968, box 3, Tom Johnson's notes of meetings, LBJL; *The Economist,* 3 February 1968, p. 10.
84. Macdonald, p. 269.
85. Chafe, pp. 282–86; Goodwin, pp. 490–99.
86. *New York Times,* 10 March 1968, p. 1.
87. Lodge to Rusk, 5 March 1968, box 26, Clifford Papers.
88. Taylor to Clifford, 6 March 1968, ibid.
89. Harold Brown for the Deputy Secretary of Defense, 4 March 1968, ibid.
90. Warnke to Clifford, 8, 14 March 1968, Hoopes to Clifford, 14 March 1968, ibid.
91. Wheeler to President, 11 March 1968, ibid.; Notes of the President's meeting to discuss General Wheeler's trip to Vietnam, 28 February 1968, box 3, Tom Johnson's notes of meetings, LBJL.
92. Leslie Gelb Oral History; McNamara, pp. 306–8; Gelb, pp. 170, 176.
93. Clifford, pp. 419–22, 448–52.
94. Herring, *LBJ and Vietnam,* p. 154.

95. Clifford, p. 495; Berman, *Lyndon Johnson's War,* pp. 176–80; Gardner, *Pay Any Price,* pp. 432–36; Isaacson and Thomas, pp. 704–6; Notes of President's meeting with senior foreign policy advisers, 5:33 P.M., 4 March 1968, box 3, Tom Johnson's notes of meetings, LBJL.

96. Meeting of March 5, 1968 [notes dated March 6, 1968], Tom Johnson's notes of meetings, box 3, LBJL.

97. Chester, Hodgson, and Page, pp. 142–45; Schlesinger, p. 930; McNamara, p. 260.

98. Rostow to President, 21 March 1968, box 6, Rostow Memos to President, National Security File, LBJL.

99. Meeting with Generals Wheeler and Abrams, 26 March 1968, box 1, Tom Johnson's notes of meetings, LBJL.

100. Clifford, p. 517.

101. CIA-DoD Briefing by General Dupuy and Geroge Carver, 28 March 1968, box 1, Tom Johnson's notes of meetings, LBJL.

102. Walt Rostow's handwritten notes, advisory group meeting at State Department, 25 March 1968, box 6, Rostow Files, Vietnam, National Security File, LBJL.

103. *Public Papers of the President: Lyndon B. Johnson, 1968–1969,* vol. 1, p. 476.

104. Meeting with senior foreign policy advisers, 2 April 1968, box 1, Tom Johnson's notes of meetings, LBJL.

105. The President, Robert F. Kennedy, and others, memorandum of conversation, 10:00 A.M., 3 April 1968, box 5, Rostow Files, National Security File, LBJL.

106. Averell Harriman, "General Review of the Last Six Months," 14 December 1968, box 562, Harriman Papers.

107. Johnson to Harriman, 3 October 1968, box 6, Rostow Files, National Security File, LBJL.

108. Daniel Davidson and Richard Holbrooke to State Department, 9 July 1968, box 558, Harriman Papers.

109. Harriman, "General Review of the Last Six Months," box 562, Harriman Papers.

110. Notes of President's meeting with his foreign policy advisers, 24 July 1968, Tom Johnson's notes of meetings, box 4, LBJL.

111. President's meeting with Richard Nixon, 26 July 1968, box 3, ibid.

112. Clifford, pp. 563; Harriman, "General Review of the Last Six Months," box 562, Harriman Papers.

113. President's meeting with foreign policy advisers, 30 July, 10 August 1968, box 3, Tom Johnson's notes of meetings, LBJL.

114. Rostow to Clifford, 19 August 1968, box 6, Rostow Files, National Security File, LBJL.

115. Averell Harriman, memorandum for personal files, 22 August 1968, box 558, Harriman Papers.

116. Notes of the President's Tuesday luncheon group, 20 August 1968, box 5, Tom Johnson's notes of meetings, LBJL.

117. Farber, pp. 182–83.

118. Ambrose, *Nixon,* vol. 2, pp. 175, 180.

119. President's Tuesday lunch, 17 September 1968, box 6, Tom Johnson's notes of meetings, LBJL.

120. George Ball, Oral History; Chester, Hodgson, and Page, p. 726; Notes of the President's weekly luncheon meeting, 15 September 1968, box 5, Tom Johnson's notes of meetings, LBJL.

121. Averell Harriman and Robert Shaplen, memorandum of conversation, 1 November 1968 [memo dated November 30, 1968], box 562, Harriman Papers.

122. Notes of the President's meeting, 22 October 1968, box 1, Tom Johnson's notes of meetings, LBJL.

123. Notes on meeting with foreign policy advisory group, 14 October 1968, box 5, Tom Johnson's notes of meetings, LBJL.

124. Sieg, pp. 322–70; Ambrose, vol. 2, pp. 213–16; De Loach, pp. 398–400; Gardner, *Pay Any Price,* p. 502.

125. Notes of the President's meeting, 2:30 A.M., 29 October 1968, box 1, Tom Johnson's notes of meetings, LBJL.

126. Ibid.
127. Notes on Tuesday luncheon, 29 October 1968, box 1, Tom Johnson's notes of meetings, LBJL.
128. Averell Harriman and William Rogers, memorandum of conversation, 21 January 1969, box 562, "General Review of the Last Six Months," Harriman Papers.

CHAPTER 11

1. Haldeman, *Ends of Power,* p. 81.
2. *Time,* 13 December 1968, p. 18.
3. Schulzinger, pp. 25–28.
4. Schulzinger, pp. 25–27; Hoff, pp. 149–57; Isaacson, 129–52.
5. Kissinger, "Vietnam Negotiations," *Foreign Affairs* (January 1969): 215–20.
6. Nixon, *In the Arena,* pp. 339–40; Ambrose, vol. 2, pp. 148–49; Hoff, pp. 161–64.
7. Spector, *After Tet,* pp. 249–53; Cincinnatus, pp. 75–77.
8. Garthoff, p. 104.
9. Collins, pp. 85–109.
10. Isaacson, pp. 177, 256–67; Shawcross, p. 34.
11. Sam Ervin to Lloyd Tyler, 26 February 1969, box 220, Ervin Papers.
12. Haldeman, *Diaries,* p. 56.
13. Ambrose, vol. 2, p. 278.
14. Haldeman, *Diaries,* p. 65; Ambrose, vol. 2, p. 278.
15. Norman, p. 100; Cincinnatus, p. 156.
16. Albert Gore to Clark Clifford, 19 June 1969 (copy to J. William Fulbright), Fulbright Papers.
17. Fulbright to Clark Clifford, 21 June 1969, Fulbright to Jerome F. Thompson, 2 July 1969, ibid.
18. Carl Marcy, memorandum for the file, 29 July 1969, ibid.
19. Norville Jones to Fulbright, 21 October 1969, ibid.
20. Ambrose, vol. 2, p. 301.
21. De Benedetti, pp. 255–57.
22. Ambrose, vol. 2, pp. 300–81; Baskir and Strauss, pp. 27–29.
23. De Benedetti, pp. 232–33, 244–46; Wells, pp. 296–97, 335, 339, 367–68.
24. Speech of 3 November 1969, *Public Papers of the Presidents: Richard M. Nixon, 1969,* vol. 1, pp. 901–9.
25. Ambrose, vol. 2, p. 311; Bob Dockery to Fulbright, 26 November 1969, box 44:2, Fulbright Papers; Haldeman, *Diaries,* pp. 105, 107.
26. Haldeman, *Diaries,* p. 107; Safire, pp. 177–80.
27. Haldeman, *Diaries,* p. 106.
28. Ibid., p. 108.
29. Ibid., pp. 108–9.
30. Ambrose, vol. 2, p. 313.
31. Hersh, *My Lai 4,* pp. 151–55; Ambrose, vol. 2, p. 313; De Benedetti, pp. 265–66.
32. Kutler, p. 101.
33. Norville Jones, James Lowenstein, and Richard Moose to Fulbright, 31 March 1970, Fulbright Papers.
34. Baskir and Strauss, pp. 47–48.
35. Haldeman, *Diaries,* pp. 134–35; Ellsworth Bunker to State Department, 11 April 1970, box 1, NSC Convenience File.
36. Symington to Rogers, 31 February 1970, box 46:1, Fulbright Papers.
37. Haldeman, *Diaries,* pp. 128, 130, 138; Marcy to Fulbright, 30 March 1970, box 45:1, Fulbright Papers.
38. Haldeman, *Diaries,* p. 146; Norville Jones to Fulbright and Aiken, 8 April 1970, box 46:1, Fulbright Papers; MEMCONS, Bunker meeting with President Thieu, 11, 21 March 1970, Bunker to Kissinger, 11, 21 March 1970, box 1, NSC Convenience File.

39. D. P. Chandler, pp. 197–206; Bunker to Kissinger, 2, 11 April 1970, box 1, NSC Convenience File.
40. Haldeman, *Diaries,* pp. 154–55.
41. Speech of 30 April 1970, *Public Papers of the President: Richard M. Nixon, 1970,* pp. 470–71.
42. D. P. Chandler, pp. 204–5; *New York Times,* 10 May 1970, p. 1.
43. Form letter from Goldwater to constituent supporting President's actions in Cambodia, May 1970, Goldwater to Ruth MacGregor, 22 May 1970. This constituent, who opposed the action in Cambodia, shot back, "And why can't we quit? Better than spilling the blood of our men and that of other innocent victims of our tragic mistake in going into this unnecessary and stupid war!" Box 91:11, Goldwater Papers.
44. Thomas Eagleton to Nixon, 29 April 1970, box 46:2, Fulbright Papers.
45. *New York Times,* 1 June 1970.
46. Fulbright to Thomas Watson, 8 May 1970, box 17:4, Fulbright Papers.
47. Heinemann, pp. 246–49.
48. Marcy to Fulbright and Aiken, 5 May 1970, box 17:4, Fulbright Papers.
49. Haldeman, *Diaries,* p. 159.
50. *New York Times,* 10 May 1970, p. 1.
51. Haldeman, *Diaries,* 9 May 1970, p. 163.
52. Ambrose, vol. 2, p. 348.
53. Fulbright to Charles Eichebaum, 5 May 1970, box 17:1, Fulbright Papers.
54. Ely, pp. 28, 32.
55. Speech from oval office, 3 June 1970, *Public Papers of the President: Richard M. Nixon, 1970,* pp. 476–83.
56. Brandon, pp. 146–47.
57. Ibid., p. 106.
58. Isaacson, pp. 275–81; Schulzinger, p. 44.
59. Shaplen, *Road from War,* pp. 300–301, quoted in Herring, *America's Longest War,* p. 248.
60. De Benedetti, p. 283.
61. Haldeman, *Diaries,* p. 256.
62. Castle, pp. 108–9; Fulbrook, pp. 3–16.
63. Resolution of the Democratic Caucus, 31 March 1971, Joseph Clark to Democratic members of Congress, 26 March 1971, box 152, Albert Papers.
64. Ungar, p. 12; Rudenstine, pp. 48–65.
65. Haldeman, *Diaries,* p. 300.
66. *The Economist,* 10 July 1971, p. 51.
67. Haldeman notes, 8 July 1971, box 43, Haldeman Files.
68. Ehrlichman notes, 21 June 1971, box 21, Ehrlichman Files.
69. Haldeman notes, 23 June 1971, box 43, Haldeman Files.
70. Quoted in Ambrose, vol. 2, p. 447.
71. Haldeman, *Diaries,* p. 300.
72. Rudenstine, pp. 301–2.
73. Haldeman, *Diaries,* p. 313.
74. Ambrose, vol. 2, p. 495; Bunker to Kissinger, 3, 28 July 1971, box 1, NSC Convenience File.
75. Haldeman, *Diaries,* p. 391.
76. Ambrose, vol. 2, p. 494.
77. Szulc, p. 383; Keating, pp. 10–13.
78. Haldeman, *Diaries,* p. 394; Ambrose, vol. 2, p. 508.
79. Haldeman, *Diaries,* p. 401.
80. Ambrose, vol. 2, pp. 509–11.
81. Schulzinger, pp. 90–101.
82. Haldeman notes, 2 March 1972, Haldeman Files.
83. Haldeman notes of meetings, 15 July 1971, ibid.

84. President to Kissinger, 11 March 1972, box 45, Haldeman Files.
85. Presidential news summary, 3 April 1972, Nixon Presidential Materials Project.
86. Hersh, *Price of Power*, p. 506; *New York Times*, 5 May 1972, p. 1.
87. *New York Times*, 2 May 1972, p. 1.
88. *The Economist*, 6 May 1972, p. 39.
89. *New York Times*, 4 May 1972, pp. 1, 5.
90. Haldeman, *Diaries*, p. 452.
91. *Public Papers of the President: Richard M. Nixon, 1972*, p. 587.
92. Ambrose, vol. 2, pp. 540–41.
93. Haldeman, *Diaries*, pp. 458–59.
94. *The Economist*, 8 April 1972, p. 15.
95. *New York Times*, 29 June 1972.
96. Haldeman, *Diaries*, p. 485.
97. *Public Papers of the President: Richard M. Nixon, 1972*, pp. 744–54.
98. Isaacson, p. 441.
99. Ambrose, vol. 2, p. 593; Isaacson, p. 443.
100. Ambrose, vol. 2, p. 595.
101. Kissinger, *White House Years*, pp. 1313, 1330–32, 1341–53; Szulc, p. 626.
102. Isaacson, pp. 450–54.
103. Ibid., p. 454.
104. Bunker to Haig, 22 October 1972, box 1, NSC Convenience File; Haldeman, *Diaries*, p. 523.
105. Isaacson, p. 459.
106. Haldeman, *Diaries*, p. 524.
107. Ibid.
108. *The Economist*, 4 November 1972, p. 16.
109. Haldeman, *Diaries*, p. 535.
110. Isaacson, p. 462.
111. Hung and Schechter, pp. 120–24.
112. Isaacson, pp. 464–65.
113. Haldeman, *Diaries*, pp. 549–50.
114. Nixon, *RN*, p. 733; Isaacson, p. 467.
115. Haldeman, *Diaries*, p. 556.
116. Ambrose, vol. 3, p. 43; *New York Times*, 21 December 1972.
117. Ambrose, vol. 3, p. 41.
118. *New York Times*, 26 December 1972.
119. Haldeman, *Diaries*, pp. 557–59.
120. Ibid., p. 558; Ambrose, vol. 3, p. 41.
121. Isaacson, pp. 470–71.
122. Haldeman, *Diaries*, p. 569.
123. Hung and Schechter, p. 148.
124. *Department of State Bulletin*, vol. 67, no. 1755, 12 February 1973, pp. 169–88.
125. Ambrose, vol. 3, p. 53.
126. Herbert Klein to President, 3 February 1973, box 27, Vietnam, Zeigler Files.

CHAPTER 12

1. Isaacs, p. 12.
2. Ibid., p. 11; Bunker to Kissinger, 2 March 1973, box 3, NSC Convenience File.
3. Isaacs, p. 311.
4. C. S. Whitehouse to Kissinger and Bunker, 6 March 1973, box 3, NSC Convenience File.
5. Isaacs, p. 327.
6. Ibid., p. 92.

7. Senate Select Committee on POW/MIA Affairs, *Report*, p. 81.
8. Ambrose, vol. 3, p. 65.
9. Liberation Radio broadcast, 17 March 1973; *Express News*, 28 March 1973, box 33, Pike Collection.
10. *Japan Times*, 16 March 1973, series 2, box 33, Pike Collection; Isaacs, p. 124.
11. Isaacs, p. 124.
12. *Los Angeles Times*, 29 March 1973, box 33, Pike Collection.
13. *U.S. News and World Report*, 19 March 1973, ibid.
14. *Baltimore Sun*, 1 February 1973, series 2, box 32, ibid.
15. *Washington Star*, 16, 26 February 1973, ibid.
16. *Washington Star*, 12 March 1973, series 2, box 33, ibid.
17. Snepp, p. 51.
18. *Stars and Stripes*, 1 February 1973, *Washington Star*, 18 February 1973, *Chicago Daily News*, 20 February 1973, series 2, box 32, Pike Collection.
19. *Washington Post*, 1 February 1973, ibid.
20. Vietnam News Agency, 17 February 1973, ibid.
21. *Chicago Daily News*, 10, 15 February 1973, box 32, *Stars and Stripes*, 4 March 1973, *New York Times*, 16 March 1973, box 33, ibid.
22. *Washington Star*, 7 March 1973, box 33, ibid.
23. *Washington Star*, 12 March 1973, ibid.; Bunker to Whitehouse, 25 May 1973, box 5, NSC Convenience File.
24. Senate Select Committee on POWS, *Report*, p. 121.
25. Kissinger, *Years of Upheaval*, p. 318.
26. Ambrose, vol. 3, pp. 98–99; Isaacs, p. 138; Snepp, p. 58.
27. C. S. Whitehouse to Kissinger, 4, 7, 10 June 1973, Sullivan to Kissinger, 3 June 1973, box 5, NSC Convenience File.
28. Isaacs, p. 139; Whitehouse to Thieu transmitting Nixon to Thieu, 10 June 1973, Kissinger to Whitehouse, 4, 7, 8 June 1973, Whitehouse to Kissinger, 11 June 1973, Whitehouse to Tran Van Lam, 10, 12 June 1973, Whitehouse to Kissinger, 7, 8, 12 June 1973, boxes 5, 6, NSC Convenience file.
29. Captured VC/NVA document, February, 1973, series 2, box 32, Pike Collection.
30. Isaacs, p. 142.
31. *Stars and Stripes*, 15 October 1973, series 2, box 33, Pike Collection.
32. *Express News*, 24 October 1973, series 2, box 33, Pike Collection.
33. Isaacs, p. 139; Snepp, pp. 91–92.
34. Garthoff, pp. 330–34.
35. Isaacs, p. 143; Snepp, p. 93.
36. Liberation Press Agency (clandestine) broadcast in English to East Europe and the Far East, series 2, box 33, Pike Collection.
37. *Los Angeles Times*, 17 October 1973.
38. Isaacs, p. 142.
39. *Christian Science Monitor*, 18 October 1973.
40. Kutler, pp. 405–13.
41. Martin to Scowcroft, 12 October 1973, 6, 12 November 1973, 15, 17 December 1973, Kissinger to Martin, 16 October 1973, box 6, NSC Convenience File; Charles J. Tull, "Present at the Collapse," Paper delivered at GRFL, 31 March 1995.
42. Ely, pp. 48–53.
43. Scowcroft to Martin, 6 February 1974, box 5, NSC Convenience File.
44. Isaacs, pp. 300–302.
45. Snepp, p. 105.
46. W. R. Smyser to Graham Martin, 28 February 1974, box 6, NSC Convenience File.
47. House Subcommittee on Asian and Pacific Affairs, *The Situation in Southeast Asia*, 31 July 1974, pp. 2–3; Martin to Scowcroft, 7 July 1974, box 6, NSC Convenience File.

48. *New York Post,* 7 August 1974, series 2, box 35, Pike Collection.
49. Isaacs, p. 303.
50. *Washington Post,* 11 August 1974, box 35, Pike Collection.
51. Isaacs, pp. 304–7; Snepp, p. 101.
52. House Subcommittee on Asian and Pacific Affairs, *The Situation in Southeast Asia,* 31 July 1974, pp. 15, 22; Snepp, p. 145; Martin to Scowcroft, 16 January 1975, box 7, NSC Convenience File, GRFL.
53. *Washington Post,* 8 August 1974, box 35, Pike Collection.
54. Isaacs, p. 309.
55. *Christian Science Monitor,* 2 August 1974, p. 5A, box 35, Pike Collection.
56. *The Economist,* 3 August 1974, *Baltimore Sun,* 3 August 1974, *Vietnam Press,* 5 August 1974, *Washington Post,* 8 August 1974, ibid.
57. Liberation Radio, 9, 14 August 1974, ibid.
58. *New York Times,* 1 August 1974, ibid.
59. Speech of 13 August 1974, *Public Papers of the President: Gerald R. Ford, 1974.*
60. *New York Times,* 14 August 1974, box 35, Pike Collection.
61. *Philadelphia Inquirer,* 18 August 1974, ibid.
62. *Baltimore Sun,* 18 August 1974, ibid.
63. Memorandum of conversation at the White House, 13 September 1973, box A5, Kissinger/Scowcroft Parallel Files.
64. Cannon, pp. 367, 376–83; Kutler, "Clearing the Rubble: The Nixon Pardon", pp. 25–38; J. R. Greene, pp. 53–58.
65. Gene Ainsworth to Bill Timmons, 6 September 1974, box 1, Loen and Lippert Files, William Timmons to Brent Scowcroft, box A7, Kissinger/Scowcroft Parallel Files.
66. William Strauss to Lawrence Baskir, 4 August 1975, box 5, Goodell Papers; Statement of Charles Goodell, 15 January 1976, box 6, ibid.; Henry Schwarzschild to Theodore Marrs, 19 November 1974, Briefing memo for the President, 20 January 1975, Charles Goodell to Philip Buchen, 28 February, 16 May 1975, Buchen to Goodell, 22 May 1975, Message dictated by John Marsh, 26 August 1975, Russ Rourke to Philip Buchen, 12 September 1976, boxes 4, 6, Buchen Files; Richard Lawson to Jerry Jones, 24 January 1975, Theodore Marrs to Jerry Jones, 11 April 1975, box 35, Connor Files.
67. Prime Minister Tran Thien Khiem, Ambassador Martin, and William P. Clements, memorandum of conversation, 2 October 1974, box 5, NSC Convenience File.
68. Isaacs, pp. 322–25; Martin to Scowcroft, 1, 9 November 1974, box 6, NSC Convenience File.
69. Isaacs, p. 327; *Washington Post,* 14, 18 December 1974, box 35, Pike Collection.
70. *New York Times,* 1 February 1975, series 2, box 35, Pike Collection.
71. Isaacs, p. 332.
72. *Washington Post,* 4, 8 January 1975, *Far East Economic Review,* 17 January 1975, *Baltimore Sun,* 30 January 1975, series 2, box 35, Pike Collection; Notes of Cabinet meeting, 29 January 1975, box 4, Connor Files; Isaacs, p. 333.
73. James E. Connor to Vice President et al., 5 February 1975, box 4, Connor Files.
74. Martin to Scowcroft, 9 January 1975, box 7, NSC Convenience File.
75. House Committee on Appropriations, *Hearings on Aid,* p. 111.
76. Memorandum of conversation, President Ford and members of the congressional Vietnam delegation, 5 March 1975, box A5, Kissinger/Scowcroft Parallel File; Engelmann, pp. 26–32.
77. *Washington Post,* 4 March 1975, series 2, box 35, Pike Collection.
78. President Ford and members of the congressional Vietnam delegation, memorandum of conversation, 5 March 1975, box 5A, Kissinger/Scowcroft Parallel File.
79. *Washington Star,* 14 March 1975, series 2, box 35, Pike Collection.
80. Snepp, p. 185; Rowland Evans and Robert Novak, "Why the Vietnamese Collapsed," *Washington Post,* 5 April 1975, series 2, box 37, Pike Collection.
81. Engelmann, p. 62.

82. *The Economist,* 22 March 1975, *Washington Star,* 20 March 1975, box 35, Pike Collection.

83. *New York Times,* 27 March 1975, ibid.; Engelmann, p. 229.

84. *The Economist,* 5 April 1975, series 2, box 37, Pike Collection.

85. Minutes of the NSC Meeting, 28 March 1975, box 5, NSC Convenience File.

86. Martin to Akins, 9 April 1975, box 5, NSC Convenience File.

87. *Washington Post,* 5 April 1975, series 2, box 37, Pike Collection.

88. *Washington Post,* 4 April 1975, series 2, box 1, Refugees and civilian casualties, April 1975, Pike Collection.

89. *Newsweek,* 14 April 1975, p. 18.

90. *Washington Star,* 6 April 1975, series 2, box 1, Refugees and civilian casualties, Pike Collection.

91. *Washington Star,* 4 April 1975, ibid.; *Washington Post,* 4 April 1975, series 2, box 37, Pike Collection; Engelmann, p. 22.

92. Ron Nessen to Donald Rumsfeld, 8 April 1975, box 11, Nessen Papers.

93. Ford, Kissinger, Weyand et al., meeting at the White House, 25 March 1975, box A5, Kissinger/Scowcroft Parallel Files.

94. Weyand to President, 4 April 1975, box 4, Kissinger/Scowcroft Parallel File.

95. *Washington Post,* 14 March 1975, box 36, Pike Collection.

96. Weyand to President, 4 April 1975, box 4, Kissinger/Scowcroft Parallel File.

97. *Wall Street Journal,* 9 April 1975, New China News Agency Broadcast, 10 April 1975, series 2, box 37, Pike Collection.

98. Minutes of NSC Meeting, 9 April 1975, GRFL.

99. Henry Kissinger to President, 25 February 1975, box 7, President's Handwriting File, Charles Leppert to John Marsh, 2 April 1975, box 43, Marsh Files, Jim Shumway to Ron Nessen, box 12, Nessen Files.

100. Cincpac Hawaii to JCS Washington, 2 April 1975, box 33, President's Handwriting Files.

101. Charles Leppert to John Marsh, 21 April 1975, box 43, Marsh Files.

102. Ford, members of the Senate Foreign Relations Committee, et al., memorandum of conversation, 14 April 1975, box A5, Kissinger/Scowcroft Parallel Files.

103. Robert McCloskey to John Marsh, 26 April 1975, box 13, Friedersdorf Files.

104. Perhaps it was no surprise that the "genius" comment occurred in a cable in which Martin angled for an appointment as Deputy Secretary of State. Martin to Kissinger, 27 January 1975, box 5, Copies of Materials from the U.S. Embassy in Saigon, NSC Convenience File.

105. Martin to James Akins, 14 April 1975, ibid.

106. Ibid.

107. Akins to Martin, 12 April 1975, box 5, NSC Convenience File. In November 1974, Martin also tried to encourage Japan to raise its level of aid to South Vietnam from $64 million to $120 million for the year April 1, 1974–March 31, 1975. Martin to Kissinger, 16 November 1974, box 6, NSC Convenience File.

108. Martin to Kissinger, 11, 13, 26, 27, 28 April 1975, box 5, NSC Convenience File.

109. Schechter, p. 549.

110. Kissinger to President, 7 May 1975, box 13, Friedersdorf Files.

111. Snepp, pp. 392–97; *Washington Post,* 22 April 1975, *Japan Times,* 23 April 1975, series 2, box 38, Pike Collection.

112. Schulzinger, *Henry Kissinger,* pp. 200–201. Issacson, *Kissinger,* pp. 643–45. *Washington Post,* 25 April 1975, series 2, box 38, Pike Collection.

113. Washington Special Actions Group Meeting, 28 April 1975, box A4, Kissinger/Scowcroft Parallel Files.

114. NSC Meeting, 24 April 1975, ibid.

115. Washington Special Actions Group Meeting, 28 April 1975, ibid.

116. NSC Meeting, 28 April 1975, ibid.

117. In the midst of these frantic discussions, Kissinger tried wisecracks to break the tension. When informed that Catholic and Mormon relief organizations still had American civilians in the

vicinity of Saigon, Kissinger asked Ambassador Dean Brown, "Are the Mormons in danger?" The Ambassador replied that all sorts of groups "like that look to us to get them out." Kissinger replied, "Well, I feel sure that as long as Brent Scowcroft [a Mormon] is Deputy Assistant to the President, the Mormons will get out of there. How about the Jews? Does anybody care about the Jews?" Washington Special Action Group meeting, 28 April 1975, box A4, ibid.

118. Washington Special Actions Group Meeting, 29 April 1975, box A5, ibid.
119. Engelmann, p. 247.
120. Henry Kissinger, remarks in the East Room, 30 April 1975, box 4, Raoul-Duval Files. Kissinger had used the same technique—pointing the finger of blame while advocating reconciliation—for weeks before the fall of Saigon. He advised Ford to take the high road in explaining the deteriorating situation in South Vietnam, and thought it appropriate to avoid "trying to assess blame." He then advocated not letting Congress "escape responsibility" for the collapse of the South Vietnam government. "He feels that it is necessary to recount a number of legislative actions in recent years that led to the straw the broke the camel's back. For example, the bombing halt, the steady cuts in aid, other Congressional limitations." Jack Marsh to Donald Rumsfeld, 3 April 1975, box 33, Marsh Files.

CONCLUSION

1. *New York Times,* 27 May 1995, p. A16.

Select Bibliography

The literature on the war in Vietnam is large and growing. The following select bibliography lists the manuscript sources and the principal secondary works cited. Two recent guides to the literature of the Vietnam War are available for those wishing to explore further. They are: Gary R. Hess, "The Unending Debate: Historians and the Vietnam War," Michael J. Hogan, ed., *America in the World: The Historiography of American Foreign Relations since 1941* (New York: Cambridge University Press, 1995), pp. 358–94; and Stanley I. Kutler, ed. *Encyclopedia of the Vietnam War* (New York: Scribner, 1996).

MANUSCRIPT COLLECTIONS

Albert, Carl. Papers. Carl Albert Congressional Research Center, University of Oklahoma.
Alsop, Joseph and Stewart. Papers. Library of Congress, Washington, D.C.
Ball, George. Oral History. LBJL.
———. Papers. LBJL.
Bayh, Birch. Papers. Lilly Library, Indiana University, Bloomington.
Belcher, Page. Papers. Carl Alpert Congressional Research Center. University of Oklahoma.
Buchen, Philip. Files. GRFL.
Bundy, McGeorge. Oral History. LBJL.
———. Files. LBJL.
———. Papers. LBJL.
Bundy, William. Oral History. LBJL.
Canadian Ministry of Foreign Affairs. RG25, Canadian National Archives, Ottawa.
Cater, Douglas. Files. LBJL.
Christopher, Warren. Papers. LBJL.
Church, Frank. Papers. Boise State University, Boise, Idaho.
Clifford, Clark. Papers. LBJL.
Collins, J. Lawton. Papers. DDEL.
Connor, James E. Files. GRFL.
———. Papers. GRFL.
Conway, Rose. Files. HSTL.
Dellinger, David. Oral History. LBJL.
Dulles, John Foster. Files. DDEL.
———. Papers. PUL.
Economic Cooperation Agency Papers. RG286, NA.
Ehrlichman, John. Files. WHSMOF. Nixon Presidential Materials Project. NA.
Ervin, Sam. Papers. University of North Carolina, Chapel Hill.
Fifth Avenue Peace Parade Committee Papers. Swarthmore Peace Collection. Swarthmore College, Swarthmore, Penn.

Foreign Office Records. PRO. London.

Fowler, Henry. Files. LBJL.

Friedersdorf, Max. Files. GRFL.

Fulbright, J. William. Papers. University of Arkansas, Fayetteville.

Gelb, Leslie. Oral History. LBJL.

Goldwater, Barry. Papers. Arizona State University, Tempe.

Goodell, Charles. Papers. GRFL.

Hagerty, James. Papers. DDEL.

Haldeman, H. R. Files. WHSMOF. Nixon Presidential Materials Project. NA.

Harriman, Averell. Papers. Library of Congress, Washington, D.C.

Hartmann, Robert. Papers. GRFL.

Johnson, Tom. Notes of meetings. LBJL.

Kennedy, Robert F. Papers. JFKL.

Kissinger/Scowcroft Parallel File. GRFL.

Lodge, Henry Cabot. Oral History. JFKL.

Loen, Vernon, and Charles Lippert. Files. GRFL.

Lowenstein, Allard. Papers. University of North Carolina, Chapel Hill.

Mansfield, Mike. Papers. University of Montana, Missoula.

Marcy, Carl. Files. RG46. NA.

Marsh, John. Files. GRFL.

McGovern, George. Papers. PUL.

McPherson, Harry. Files. LBJL.

Meeting Notes Files. LBJL.

Melby, John F. Papers. HSTL.

Merchant, Livingston. Papers. PUL.

Morse, Wayne. Papers. University of Oregon, Eugene.

Moyers, Bill. Files. LBJL.

National Coordinating Committee to End the War in Vietnam Papers. State Historical Society of Wisconsin, Madison.

National Security File. JFKL.

National Security File. LBJL.

Nessen, Ron. Papers. GRFL.

Nixon, Richard. Papers. Southwest Region, Laguna Niguel, Calif. NA.

NSC Briefing Notes. DDEL.

NSC Convenience File. GRFL.

Pearson, Drew. Papers. LBJL.

Pike, Douglas. Collection, Vietnam Archive. Texas Tech University, Lubbock.

President's Handwriting Files. GRFL.

President's Office File. LBJL.

President's Office Files. Nixon Presidential Materials Project. NA.

President's Security File. HSTL.

Radford, Arthur. Oral History. Dulles Oral History Collection. PUL.

Raoul-Duval, Michael. Files. GRFL.

Rostow, Walt Whitman. Oral History. JFKL.

———. Oral History. LBJL.

———. Files. LBJL.

———. Papers. LBJL.

Rusk, Dean. Oral History. LBJL.

Russell, Richard. Papers. University of Georgia, Athens.

Special Assistant for National Security Affairs. National Security Council, Briefing Notes. DDEL.

Special Assistant to the President. National Security Council, Briefing Notes. DDEL.

State Department Records. RG59. NA.

Student Mobilization Committee to End the War in Vietnam. Papers. State Historical Society of
    Wisconsin, Madison.
Taylor, Maxwell. Papers. National Defense University, Washington, D.C.
Vice President's Security File. LBJL.
Warnke, Paul. Papers. LBJL.
Westmoreland, William C. Papers. Center for Military History, Washington, D.C.
White House Central Files. DDEL.
Whitman, Ann. Files. DDEL.
Zeigler, Ron. Files. WHSMOF. Nixon Presidential Materials Project, NA.

GOVERNMENT PUBLICATIONS

Congressional Record
Department of State Bulletin
Public Papers of the President
    Dwight David Eisenhower
    Gerald R. Ford
    Lyndon B. Johnson
    John F. Kennedy
    Richard M. Nixon
U.S. Congress. Senate. Committee on Foreign Relations. *Executive Sessions of the U.S. Senate
    Foreign Relations Committee*, vol. 12, 1966.
———. Commitee on Foreign Relations. Files. RG46. NA.
———. Committee on Foreign Relations. *Hearings on the Causes, Origins and Lessons of the
    Vietnam War.* 92d Cong., 2d sess., 9–12 May 1972.
———. Committee on Foreign Relations. *Hearings, The Gulf of Tonkin, the 1964 Incident.* 90th
    Cong., 2d sess., 20 February 1968.
———. Committee on Foreign Relations. *Hearings on Supplemental Foreign Assistance, Vietnam,
    1966.* 89th cong., 2d sess., 28 January–18 February 1966.
———. Committee on Foreign Relations. *Vietnam, Cambodia, and Laos: Report by Senator Mike
    Mansfield.* 6 October 1955.
———. Select Committee on POW/MIA Affairs. *Report of the Select Committee on POW/MIA Affairs.*
    103d Cong., 1st sess., 13 January 1993.
U.S. Department of State. *Foreign Relations of the United States.*
U.S. Congress. House. Committee on Appropriations. *Hearings on Aid to Vietnam and Cambodia.*
    94th Cong., 1st sess., 3 February 1975.
———. Subcommittee on Asian and Pacific Affairs. *The Situation in Southeast Asia.* 93d cong., 2d
    sess., 31 July 1974.

NEWSPAPERS AND NEWS MAGAZINES

Christian Science Monitor
The Economist
Los Angeles Times
New York Times
Newsweek
San Francisco Examiner
Time
U.S. News and World Report
Wall Street Journal
Washington Post

BOOKS, ARTICLES, AND MEDIA BROADCASTS

Ambrose, Stephen. *Nixon.* Vols. 2, 3. New York: Simon & Schuster, 1989, 1991,

Anderson, David L., ed. *Shadow on the White House: Presidents and the Vietnam War, 1945–1975.* Lawrence: University Press of Kansas, 1993.

———. *Trapped by Success: The Eisenhower Administration and Vietnam, 1953–1961.* New York: Columbia University Press, 1991.

Anderson, Terry H. *The Movement and the Sixties.* New York: Oxford University Press, 1995.

Appy, Christian. *Working Class War: American Combat Soldiers and Vietnam.* Chapel Hill: University of North Carolina Press, 1993.

Ashby, LeRoy, and Rod Gramer. *Fighting the Odds: The Life of Senator Frank Church.* Pullman: Washington State University Press, 1994.

Ashmore, Harry, and William C. Baggs. *Mission to Hanoi: A Tale of Deception and Double-dealing In High Places.* New York: Putnam, 1968.

Ball, George. *The Past Has Another Pattern.* New York; Norton, 1982.

Baskir, Lawrence, and William Strauss. *Chance and Circumstance: The Draft, the War and the Vietnam Generation.* New York: Knopf, 1978.

Bassett, Lawrence J., and Stephen E. Pelz. "The Failed Search for Victory: Vietnam and the Politics of War." In *Kennedy's Quest for Victory,* edited by Thomas Paterson. New York: Oxford University Press, 1989.

Bergerud, Eric M. *The Dynamics of Defeat: The Vietnam War in Hau Nghia Province.* Boulder, Colo.: Westview Press, 1991.

Berman, Larry. "The Battle over Historical Interpretation: NSAM 263 and NSAM 273." Paper delivered at conference, "Vietnam: The Early Decisions, 1961–1964," 17 October 1993. LBJL.

———. *Lyndon Johnson's War: The Road to Stalemate in Vietnam.* New York: Norton, 1989.

———. *Planning a Tragedy: The Americanization of the War in Vietnam.* New York: Norton, 1982.

Billings-Yun, Melanie. *Decision Against War: Eisenhower and Dien Bien Phu, 1954.* New York: Columbia University Press, 1988.

Blair, Anne E. *Lodge in Vietnam: A Patriot Abroad.* New Haven, Conn.: Yale University Press, 1995.

Blaufarb, Douglas. *The Counterinsurgency Era, U.S. Doctrine and Performance.* New York: Free Press, 1977.

Blum, Robert M. *Drawing the Line: The Origin of the American Containment Policy in East Asia.* New York: Norton, 1982.

Bowen, William. "The Vietnam War. A Cost Accounting." *Fortune,* April 1966.

Braestrup, Peter. *Big Story: How the American Press and Television Reported and Interpreted the Crisis of Tet 1968 in Vietnam and Washington.* Boulder, Colo.: Westview Press, 1977.

Brandon, Henry. *The Retreat of American Power.* New York: Norton, 1973.

Browne, Malcolm W. *Muddy Boots and Red Socks: A Reporter's Life.* New York: Times Books, 1993.

Buckingham, William, Jr. *Operation Ranch Hand: The Air Force and Herbicides in Southeast Asia, 1961–1971.* Washington, D.C.: Office of Air Force History, 1982.

Buttinger, Joseph. *Vietnam: A Dragon Embattled.* New York: Praeger, 1967.

———. *Vietnam: A Political History.* New York: Praeger, 1968.

Buzzanco, Robert. *Masters of War: Military Dissent and Politics in the Vietnam Era.* New York: Cambridge University Press, 1996.

Cable, James. *The Geneva Conference of 1954 on Indochina.* New York: St. Martin's Press, 1986.

Cable, Larry. *Unholy Grail: The US and the War in Vietnam, 1965–68.* New York: Routledge, 1991.

Campagna, Andrew S. *The Economic Consequences of the Vietnam War.* Westport, Conn.: Praeger, 1991.

Campbell, Thomas, and George C. Herring, eds. *The Diaries of Edward Stettinius.* New York: New Viewpoints, 1975.

Cannon, James. *Time and Chance: Gerald Ford's Appointment with History.* New York: Harper Collins, 1994.

Caputo, Philip. *A Rumor of War.* New York: Ballantine, 1978.

Castle, Timothy N. *At War in the Shadow of Vietnam: U.S. Military Aid to the Royal Lao Government, 1955–1975.* New York: Columbia University Press, 1993.

Cesari, Laurent, and Jacques de Folin. "Military Necessity, Political Impossibility: The French Viewpoint on Operation *Vautour.*" In Kaplan, Artaud, and Rubin.

Chafe, William H. *Never Stop Running: Allard Lowenstein and the Struggle to Save American Liberalism.* New York: Basic Books, 1993.

Chandler, David P. *The Tragedy of Cambodian History: Politics, War and Revolution since 1945.* New Haven: Yale University Press, 1991.

Chandler, Robert W. *War of Ideas: The U.S. Propaganda Campaign in Vietnam.* Boulder, Colo.: Westview Press, 1982.

Chanoff, David, and Daon Van Toi. *Portrait of the Enemy.* New York: Random House, 1986.

Chester, Lewis, Godfrey Hodgson, and Bruce Page. *An American Melodrama: The Presidential Campaign of 1968.* New York: Viking, 1969.

"Cincinnatus." *Self-Destruction: The Disintegration and Decay of the U.S. Army During the Vietnam Era.* New York: Norton, 1981.

Clarke, Jeffrey J. *Advice and Support: The Final Years, 1965–1973.* Washington, D.C.: Center for Military History, 1988.

Clifford, Clark. *Counsel to the President.* New York: Random House, 1991.

Clodfleter, Mark. *The Limits of Air Power.* New York: Free Press, 1989.

Cohen, Warren, and Akira Iriye. *The Great Powers in East Asia, 1963–1960.* New York: Columbia University Press, 1990.

Collins, James Lawton, Jr. *The Development and Training of the South Vietnamese Army, 1950–1972.* Washington, D.C.: Department of the Army, 1975.

Cooper, Chester. *The Lost Crusade: America in Vietnam.* New York: Dodd Mead, 1970.

Currey, Cecil B. *Edward Lansdale: The Unquiet American.* Boston: Houghton Mifflin, 1988.

Dallek, Robert. *Franklin D. Roosevelt and American Foreign Policy, 1932–1945.* New York: Oxford University Press, 1979.

———. *Lone Star Rising: Lyndon Johnson and His Times, 1908–1960.* New York: Oxford University Press, 1991.

De Benedetti, Charles, with Charles Chatfield. *An American Ordeal: The Antiwar Movement of the Vietnam Era.* Syracuse, N.Y.: Syracuse University Press, 1990.

Dellinger, David. *From Yale to Jail: The Life Story of a Moral Dissenter.* New York: Pantheon, 1993.

DeLoach, Cartha. *Hoover's FBI: The Inside Story.* Washington, D.C.: Regnery, 1995.

Devillers, Philippe, and Jean Lacouture. *End of a War: Indochina, 1954.* New York: Praeger, 1969.

Duiker, William J. *Sacred War: Nationalism and Revolution in a Divided Vietnam.* New York: McGraw Hill, 1995.

———. *The Communist Road to Power in Vietnam.* Boulder, Colo.: Westview Press, 1981.

———. *U.S. Containment Policy and the Conflict in Indochina.* Stanford, Calif.: Stanford University Press, 1994.

Ely, John Hart. *War and Responsibility: Constitutional Lessons of Vietnam and Its Aftermath.* Princeton, N.J.: Princeton University Press, 1993.

Engelmann, Larry. *Tears Before the Rain: An Oral History of the Fall of Saigon.* New York: Oxford University Press, 1990.

Ennis, Thomas E. *French Policy and Developments in Indochina.* Chicago: University of Chicago Press, 1936.

Fall, Bernard B. *Hell in a Very Small Place: The Siege of Dien Bien Phu.* Philadelphia: J. B. Lippincott, 1967.

———, ed. *Ho Chi Minh on Revolution: Selected Writings, 1920–1966.* New York: Praeger, 1967.

———. "The Political-Religious Sects of Vietnam." *Pacific Affairs* 28 (September 1955).

————. *Street without Joy*. Harrisburg, Pa.: Stackpole Press, 1964.

Farber, David. *Chicago, '68*. Chicago: University of Chicago Press, 1988.

Fenn, Charles. *Ho Chi Minh: A Biographical Introduction*. New York: Charles Scribner's Sons, 1973.

Firestone, Bernard J., and Alexej Ugrinski. *Gerald R. Ford and the Politics of Post-Watergate America*. Westport, Conn.: Greenwood Press, 1993.

Foot, Rosemary. *The Wrong War: American Policy Dimensions and the Korean War*. Ithaca, N.Y.: Cornell University Press, 1985.

Foster, Wynn F. *Captain Hook: A Pilot's Tragedy and Triumph in the Vietnam War*. Annapolis, Md.: Naval Institute Press, 1992.

Fulbrook, Jim E. "Lam Son 719, Part III: Reflections and Values." *United States Army Aviation Digest* (August 1986).

Gaddis, John Lewis. *The United States and the Origins of the Cold War*. New York: Columbia University Press, 1972.

————. *Strategies of Containment: A Critical Appraisal of Postwar American Security Policy*. New York: Oxford Univesity Press, 1982.

Gallup, George H. *The Gallup Poll: Public Opinion, 1935–1971*. Vol. 3. New York: Random House, 1972.

Gardner, Lloyd C. *Approaching Vietnam: From World War II through Dienbienphu*. New York: Norton, 1988.

————. *Pay Any Price: Lyndon Johnson and the Wars for Vietnam*. Chicago: Ivan Dee, 1995.

Garthoff, Raymond. *Detente and Confrontation: American-Soviet Relations from Nixon to Reagan*. Washington, D.C.: The Brookings Institution, 1985.

Gavin, James M. "The Easy Chair: A Communication on Vietnam from General James M. Gavin." *Harper's*, February 1966.

Gelb, Leslie H., with Richard K. Betts. *The Irony of Vietnam: The System Worked*. Washington, D.C.: The Brookings Institution, 1979.

Gibbons, William C. *The U.S. Government and the Vietnam War*. 4 vols. Princeton, N.J.: Princeton University Press, 1985–1995.

Giglio, James N. *The Presidency of John F. Kennedy*. Lawrence: University Press of Kansas, 1991.

Gitlin, Todd. *The Sixties: Years of Hope, Days of Rage*. New York: Bantam, 1987.

Goodwin, Richard. *Remembering America: A Voice from the Sixties*. Boston: Little Brown, 1988.

Goulden, Joseph C. *Truth Is the First Casualty: The Gulf of Tonkin Affair—Illusion and Reality*. Chicago: Rand McNally, 1969.

Grady, Bernard E. *On the Tiger's Back*. Brunswick, Maine: Biddle Publishing Company, 1994.

Greene, Graham. *The Quiet American*. New York: Penguin, 1955.

Greene, John Robert. *The Presidency of Gerald R. Ford*. Lawrence: University Press of Kansas, 1995.

Greenstein, Fred I., and Richard H. Immerman. "What Did Eisenhower Tell Kennedy about Indochina? The Politics of Misperception." *Journal of American History* 79:2 (September 1992).

Halberstam, David. *The Making of a Quagmire: America and Vietnam During the Kennedy Era*, rev. ed. New York: Knopf, 1988.

Haldeman, H. R. *The Haldeman Diaries*. New York: Putnam, 1994.

————, with Joseph di Mona. *The Ends of Power*. New York: Times Books, 1978.

Hall, Mitchell K. *Because of their Faith: CALCAV and Religious Opposition to the War in Vietnam*. New York: Columbia University Press, 1990.

Hallin, Douglas. *The "Uncensored War:" The Media and Vietnam*. New York: Oxford University Press, 1986.

Hammer, Ellen J. *A Death in November: America in Vietnam, 1963*. New York: Oxford University Press, 1987.

————. *The Struggle for Indochina, 1940–1954*. Stanford, Calif.: Stanford University Press, 1954.

Hammond, William M. *Public Affairs: The Military and the Media.* Washington, D.C.: Center of Military History, 1988.

Harrison, James P. *The Endless War: Vietnam's Struggle for Independence.* New York: Columbia University Press, 1989.

Hayslip, Le Ly, with Jay Wurts. *When Heaven and Earth Changed Places.* New York: Plume, 1989.

Heinemann, Kenneth J. *Campus War: The Peace Movement at American State Universities in the Vietnam Era.* New York: New York University Press, 1993.

Hellmann, John. *American Myth and the Legacy of Vietnam.* New York: Columbia University Press, 1986.

Henderson, William D. *Why the Vietcong Fought: A Study of Motivation and Control in a Modern Army in Combat.* Westport, Conn.: Greenwood Press, 1979.

Hensler, Paul G., with Jeanne Wakatsuki Houston. *Don't Cry, It's Only Thunder.* Garden City, N.Y.: Doubleday, 1984.

Herring, George C. *America's Longest War: The United States and Vietnam, 1950 1975,* 3d ed. New York: McGraw Hill, 1996.

———. "Franco-American Conflict in Indochina, 1950–1954." In Kaplan, Artaud, Rubin.

———. " 'A Good Stout Effort': John Foster Dulles and the Indochina Crisis, 1954–55." In Immerman.

———. *LBJ and Vietnam: A Different Kind of War.* Austin: University of Texas Press, 1994.

———, ed. *The Secret Diplomacy of the Vietnam War.* Austin: University of Texas Press, 1982.

———, and Richard Immerman. "Eisenhower, Dulles and Dienbienphu: 'The Day We Didn't Go to War' Revisited." In Kaplan, Artaud, And Rubin.

Hersh, Seymour M. *My Lai 4: A Report on the Massacre and Its Aftermath.* New York: Random House, 1970.

———. *The Price of Power: Kissinger in the Nixon White House.* New York: Summit Books, 1983.

Hess, Gary R. *The United States' Emergence as a Southeast Asia Power.* New York: Columbia University Press, 1987.

Hickey, Gerald C. *Sons of the Mountains: Ethnohistory of the Vietnamese Central Highlands to 1954.* New Haven, Conn.: Yale University Press, 1982.

Hilsman, Roger. *To Move a Nation: The Politics of Foreign Policy in the Administration of John F. Kennedy.* Garden City, N.Y.: Doubleday, 1967.

Hixson, Walter. *George F. Kennan: Cold War Iconoclast.* New York: Columbia University Press, 1989.

Hoff, Joan. *Nixon Reconsidered.* New York: Basic Books, 1994.

Hung, Nguyen Tien, and Jerrold Schechter. *The Palace File.* New York: Harper & Row, 1986.

Hunt, Michael H., and Steven I. Levine. "The Revolutionary Challenge to Early U.S. Cold War Policy in Asia." In Cohen and Iriye.

Immerman, Richard, ed. *John Foster Dulles and the Diplomacy of the Cold War.* Princeton, N.J.: Princeton University Press, 1990.

———. "The United States and the Geneva Conference of 1954: A New Look." *Diplomatic History* 14:1 (Winter 1990).

Institute of Medicine, Committee to Review the Health Effects in Vietnam Veterans of Exposure to Herbicides. *Veterans and Agent Orange: Health Effects of Herbicides Used in Vietnam.* Washington, D.C.: National Academy Press, 1994.

Isaacs, Arnold R. *Without Honor: Defeat in Vietnam and Cambodia.* New York: Vintage, 1984.

Isaacson, Walter. *Kissinger: A Biography.* New York: Simon & Schuster, 1992.

———, and Evan Thomas. *The Wise Men: Six Friends and the World They Made.* New York: Simon & Schuster, 1986.

Jian, Chen. "China's Involvement in the Vietnam War." *China Quarterly* (June 1995).

Johnson, U. Alexis. *The Right Hand of Power.* Englewood Cliffs, N.J.: Prentice Hall, 1981.

Joiner, Charles. *The Politics of Massacre.* Philadelphia: Temple University Press, 1974.

Kahin, George McT. *Intervention: How America Became Involved in Vietnam.* New York: Knopf, 1986.

Kaplan, Lawrence, Denise Artaud, and Mark Rubin, eds. *Dien Bien Phu and the Crisis of Franco-American Relations, 1950–1954*. Wilmington, Del.: Scholarly Resources, 1990.

Karnow, Stanley. "The Edge of Chaos." *Saturday Evening Post*, 28 September 1963.

———. *Vietnam: A History*. New York: Penguin, 1991.

Katz, Milton. *Ban the Bomb: A History of SANE, the Committee for a Sane Nuclear Policy*. Westport, Conn.: Greenwood Press, 1986.

Kaufman, Burton I. *The Korean War: Challenges in Crisis, Credibility and Command*. Philadelphia: Temple University Press, 1986.

Keating, Susan Katz. *Prisoners of Hope: Exploiting the POW/MIA Myth in America*. New York: Random House, 1994.

Kimball, Warren F. *The Juggler: Franklin Roosevelt as Wartime Statesman*. Princeton, N.J.: Princeton University Press, 1991.

Kissinger, Henry. *White House Years*. Boston: Little, Brown, 1979.

———. "The Vietnam Negotiations." *Foreign Affairs* (January 1969).

———. *Years of Upheaval*. Boston: Little, Brown, 1982.

Koch, Christopher J. *Highways to a War*. New York: Viking, 1995.

Krepenivich, Andrew F., Jr. *The Army and Vietnam*. Baltimore: Johns Hopkins University Press, 1986.

Kutler, Stanley I. "Clearing the Rubble: The Nixon Pardon." In Firestone and Ugrinsky.

———. *The Wars of Watergate: The Last Crisis of Richard Nixon*. New York: Knopf, 1990.

Lacouture, Jean. *End of a War: Indochina, 1954*. New York: Praeger, 1969.

———. *Ho Chi Minh: A Political Biography*. New York: Random House, 1968.

Lanning, Michael Lee, and Dan Cragg. *Inside the NVA: The Real Story of North Vietnam's Armed Forces*. New York: Fawcett Columbine, 1992.

Lederer, William, and Eugene Burdick. *The Ugly American*. New York: Norton, 1958.

Leffler, Melvyn P. *A Preponderance of Power: National Security, The Truman Administration and the Cold War*. Stanford, Calif.: Stanford University Press, 1991.

Liebling, A. J. "A Talkative Something-or-Other." *New Yorker*, 7 April 1956.

Louis, Wm. Roger. *Imperialism at Bay: The United States and the Decolonization of the British Empire, 1941–1945*. New York: Oxford University Press, 1978.

Luce, Don, and John Sommer. *Vietnam: The Unheard Voices*. Ithaca, N.Y.: Cornell University Press, 1969.

Mailer, Norman. *The Armies of the Night: History as a Novel, the Novel as History*. New York: New American Library, 1968.

Manashe, Louis, and Ronald Radosh, eds. *Teach-ins USA: Reports, Opinions and Documents*. New York: Praeger, 1967.

Mangold, Tom, and John Penycate. *The Tunnels of Cu Chi*. New York: Random House, 1985.

Marr, David G. *Vietnamese Anticolonialism, 1885–1925*. Berkeley: University of California Press, 1971.

———. "Vietnam, 1945, Some Questions." *The Vietnam Forum* 6 (Summer/Fall 1985).

Marshall, Kathryn. *In the Combat Zone: An Oral History of American Women in Vietnam, 1966–1975*. Boston: Little, Brown, 1987.

Mason, Robert, *Chickenhawk*. New York: Penguin, 1983.

Matusow, Allen J. *The Unraveling of America*. New York: Harper & Row, 1984.

Maurer, Harry. *Strange Ground: Americans in Vietnam, 1945–1975, An Oral History*. New York: Henry Holt, 1989.

May, Ernest, and Richard Neustadt. *Thinking in Time: The Uses of History for Decision-Makers*. New York: Free Press, 1986.

Mayers, David. *George F. Kennan and the Dilemmas of U.S. Foreign Policy*. New York: Oxford University Press, 1988.

Macdonald, Peter. *Giap: The Victor in Vietnam*. New York: Norton, 1993.

McGarvey, Patrick J., ed. *Visions of Victory: Selected Vietnamese Communist Military Writings, 1964–1968*. Stanford, Calif.: Hoover Institution, 1969.

McMahon, Robert J. "Truman and the Roots of U.S. Involvement in Indochina, 1945–1953." In Anderson, *Shadow.*

McNamara, Robert S., with Brian Van De Mark. *In Retrospect: The Tragedy and Lessons of Vietnam.* New York: Times Books, Random House, 1995.

McNaugher, Thomas L. *The M-16 Controversies: Military Organization and Weapons Acquisition.* New York: Praeger, 1984.

Mecklin, John. *Mission in Torment: An Intimate Account of the U.S. Role in Vietnam.* Garden City, N.Y.: Doubleday, 1965.

Miscamble, Wilson D. *George F. Kennan and the Making of American Foreign Policy, 1947–1950.* Princeton, N.J.: Princeton University Press, 1992.

Moore, Harold G., and Joseph L. Galloway. *We Were Soldiers Once . . . and Young.* New York: HarperPerennial, 1992.

Newman, John M. *JFK and Vietnam: Deception, Intrigue and the Struggle for Power.* New York: Warner Books, 1992.

Nixon, Richard. *In the Arena: A Memoir of Victory, Defeat and Renewal.* New York: Simon & Schuster, 1990.

———. *RN: The Memoirs of Richard Nixon.* New York: Grossett & Dunlap, 1978.

Norman, Elizabeth M. *Women at War: The Story of Fifty Military Nurses Who Served in Vietnam.* Philadelphia: University of Pennsylvania Press, 1990.

Oberdorfer, Don. *Tet!* Garden City, N.Y.: Doubleday, 1971.

Olson, Gregory A. *Mansfield and Vietnam: A Study in Rhetorical Adaptation.* East Lansing: Michigan State University Press, 1995.

Olson, James, and Randy Roberts. *Where the Domino Fell: America and Vietnam, 1945–1990.* New York: St. Martin's Press, 1996.

Page, Stanley. *The Geopolitics of Leninism.* Boulder, Colo.: East European Monographs, 1982.

———. *Lenin and World Revolution.* Gloucester, Mass.: Peter Smith, 1968.

Patti, Archimedes. *Why Vietnam? Prelude to America's Albatross.* Berkeley: University of California Press, 1980.

Pentagon Papers: The Defense Department History of United States Decisionmaking on Vietnam. Senator Gravel ed. 5 vols. Boston: Beacon Press, 1971–72.

Perry, Mark. *Four Stars: The Inside Story of the Forty-Year Battle Between the Joint Chiefs of Staff and America's Civilian Leaders.* Boston: Houghton Mifflin, 1989.

Pike, Douglas. *Viet Cong: The Organization and Techniques of the National Liberation Front of South Vietnam.* Cambridge, Mass.: MIT Press, 1966.

Post, Ken. *Revolution, Socialism, and Nationalism in Vietnam.* Vol. 3, *Socialism in Half a Country.* Belmont, Calif.: Wadsworth Publishing, 1989.

Prados, John. *The Hidden History of the Vietnam War.* Chicago: Ivan Dee, 1995.

———, and Ray Stubbe. *Valley of Decision: The Siege of Khe Sanh.* Boston: Houghton Mifflin, 1991.

Public Broadcasting System (PBS). *Vietnam: A History.* Television documentary, 1983.

Puller, Lewis, Jr. *Fortunate Son.* New York: Grove Weidenfield, 1991.

Race, Jeffrey. *War Comes to Long An: Revolutionary Conflict in a Vietnamese Province.* Berkeley: University of California Press, 1972.

Radford, Arthur W. *From Pearl Harbor to Vietnam: The Memoirs of Admiral Arthur W. Radford.* Stanford, Calif.: Hoover Institution Press, 1980.

Randle, Robert. *Geneva 1954: The Settlement of the Indochina War.* Princeton, N.J.: Princeton University Press, 1969.

Reeves, Richard C. *President Kennedy: Profile of Power.* New York: Simon & Schuster, 1993.

Riddell, Tom. "Inflationary Impact of the Vietnam War." *Vietnam Generation* (Winter 1989).

Rieder, Jonathan. "The Rise of the Silent Majority." In Steve Fraser and Gary Gestle, *The Rise and Fall of the New Deal Order, 1930–1980.* Princeton, N.J.: Princeton University Press, 1989.

Ross, Douglas A. *In the Interests of Peace: Canada and Vietnam, 1954–1973.* Toronto: University of Toronto Press, 1984.

Rotter, Andrew J. *The Path to Vietnam: Origins of the American Commitment to Southeast Asia*. Ithaca, N.Y.: Cornell University Press, 1987.

Rudenstine, David. *The Day the Presses Stopped: A History of the Pentagon Papers Case*. Berkeley: University of California Press, 1996.

Safire, William. *Before the Fall*. Garden City, N.Y.: Doubleday, 1978.

Santoli, Al. *Everything We Had: An Oral History of the Vietnam War*. New York: Ballantine Books, 1981.

Schaller, Michael. *The American Occupation of Japan*. New York: Oxford University Press, 1984.

———. *Douglas MacArthur: The Far Eastern General*. New York: Oxford University Press, 1989.

Schechter, Jerrold L. "The Final Days: The Political Struggle to End the War in Vietnam." In Firestone and Ugrinsky.

Schell, Jonathan. *The Real War*. New York: Pantheon, 1987.

Schlesinger, Arthur M., Jr. *Robert Kennedy and His Times*. Boston: Houghton Mifflin, 1978.

Schulzinger, Robert D. *Henry Kissinger: Doctor of Diplomacy*. New York: Columbia University Press, 1989.

Shaplen, Robert. *The Lost Revolution*. New York: Harper & Row, 1965.

Shapley, Deborah. *Promise and Power: The Life and Times of Robert McNamara*. Boston: Little, Brown, 1993.

Shawcross, William. *Sideshow: Nixon, Kissinger and the Destruction of Cambodia*. New York: Simon & Schuster, 1979.

Sheehan, Neil. *A Bright Shining Lie: John Paul Vann and America in Vietnam*. New York: Random House, 1988.

Sheehan, Susan. *Ten Vietnamese*. New York: Knopf, 1967.

Sieg, Kent. "A Straw in the Wind: The Johnson Administration and the Paris Peace Talks on Vietnam, 1968–1969." Ph.D. diss., University of Colorado, Boulder.

Simpson, Howard R. *Tiger in the Barbed Wire: An American in Vietnam, 1952–1991*. New York: Kodanshan International, 1992.

Small, Melvin. *Johnson, Nixon and the Doves*. New Brunswick, N.J.: Rutgers University Press, 1988.

Smith, Ralph B. *An International History of the Vietnam War*. New York: St. Martin's Press, 1983. Vol. 1.

———. "The Japanese Period in Indochina and the Coup on March 9, 1945." *Southeast Asian Studies* 9:2 (1978).

Snepp, Frank. *Decent Interval: An Insider's Account of Saigon's Indecent End*. New York: Random House, 1977.

Spector, Ronald. *Advice and Support: The Early Years of the U.S. Army in Vietnam, 1941–1960*. New York: Free Press, 1985.

———. *After Tet: The Bloodiest Year of the Vietnam War*. New York: Free Press, 1993.

Spiller, Harry. *Death Angel: A Vietnam Memoir of a Bearer of Death Messages to Families*. Jefferson, N.C.: McFarland, 1992.

Steel, Ronald. *Walter Lippmann and the American Century*. Boston: Little, Brown–Atlantic Monthly Press, 1980.

Steinberg, David, et al. *In Search of Southeast Asia*. Honolulu: University of Hawaii Press, 1987.

Stoffey, Bob. *Cleared Hot! A Marine Combat Pilot's Vietnam Diary*. New York: St. Martin's Press, 1992.

Stueck, William W. *The Korean War: An International History*. Princeton, N.J.: Princeton University Press, 1995.

Sullivan, William H. *Obligato, 1939–1979: Notes on a Foreign Service Career*. New York: Norton, 1984.

Szulc, Tad. *The Illusion of Peace: Foreign Policy in the Nixon-Kissinger Years*. New York: Viking, 1978.

Taylor, Keith Waller. *The Birth of Vietnam*. Berkeley: University of California Press, 1983.

Terry, Wallace. *Bloods: An Oral History of Vietnam*. New York: Random House, 1984.

Thorne, Christopher. *Allies of a Kind: The United States, Britain and the War Against Japan, 1941–1945*. New York: Oxford University Press, 1978.

Tonnesson, Stein. *The Vietnamese Revolution of 1945: Roosevelt, Ho Chi Minh and de Gaulle in a World at War*. Newbury Park, Calif.: Sage Publications, 1991.

Turley, William S. *The Second Indochina War: A Short Political and Military History*. Boulder, Colo.: Westview Press, 1986.

Turner, Kathleen J. *Lyndon Johnson's Dual War: Vietnam and the Press*. Chicago: University of Chicago Press, 1985.

Ulam, Adam B. *The Bolsheviks: The Intellectual and Political History of the Triumph of Communism in Russia*. New York: Macmillan, 1965.

Ungar, Sanford, *The Papers and the Papers*. New York: Columbia University Press, 1989.

Valentine, Douglas. *The Phoenix Program*. New York: William Morrow, 1990.

Van De Mark, Brian. *Into the Quagmire: Lyndon Johnson and the Escalation of the Vietnam War*. New York: Oxford University Press, 1991.

Wells, Tom. *The War Within: America's Battle over Vietnam*. Berkeley: University of California Press, 1994.

Westmoreland, William C. *A Soldier Reports*. Garden City, N.Y.: Doubleday, 1976.

Whiting, Allen S. *The Chinese Calculus of Deterrence: India and Indochina*. Ann Arbor: University of Michigan Press, 1975.

Wilson, George C. *Mud Soldiers: Life Inside the New American Army*. New York: Scribner, 1989.

Windchy, Eugene G. *Tonkin Gulf*. Garden City, N.Y.: Doubleday, 1971.

Wirtz, James J. *The Tet Offensive: Intelligence Failure in War*. Ithaca, N.Y.: Cornell University Press, 1991.

Wolff, Tobias. *In Pharaoh's Army: Memories of the Lost War*. New York: Knopf, 1994.

Woods, Randall Bennett. *Fulbright: A Biography*. New York: Cambridge University Press, 1995.

Young, Marilyn B. *The Vietnam Wars*. New York: HarperCollins, 1991.

Zaroulis, Nancy, and Gerald Sullivan. *Who Spoke Up? American Protest against the War in Vietnam, 1963–1975*. Garden City, N.Y.: Doubleday, 1984.

Zhai, Qiang. ''Beijing and the Vietnam Conflict, 1964–1965.'' *Cold War Information Project Bulletin* (Winter 1995/1996).

Zumwalt, Elmo, Jr., and Elmo Zumwalt III. *My Father, My Son*. New York: Collier Macmillan, 1986.

Index

Abbott, George M., 41
Abrams, Creighton, 285
Abzug, Bella, 323–24
Acheson, Dean:
  and Bao Dai, 42
  and France, 21, 55, 56
  and Ho, 29, 30
  as Wise Man, 257
Agent Orange, 193
Agnew, Spiro, 282
Agrovilles, 94
Air war, U.S.:
  bombing as negotiation inducement,
    202–14, 258–52
  bombing North, decision on, 157–
    60, 162, 166–67, 169
  bombing North, first strikes, 171–
    73
  Christmas bombing, 300–302
  escalation of, 205–14
  halts in, 268–69, 272
  and infiltration routes, 203–4, 209–
    11, 277–78, 292–93
  and industrial targets, 207–10
  in South, 182
  and spring offensive 1972, 295–97
  Tonkin Incident, 151, 153
Allied plans for Southeast Asia, 12–19
Alsop, Joseph, 88
American Communist Party, 232
American Friends of Vietnam, 78, 89,
  93, 97
Americanization of war, 127, 134,
  154, 179, 329

*American Ordeal: the Antiwar Move-
  ment of the Vietnam Era* (De
  Bendetti), 244
Amnesty for draft offenders, 317–
  18
Amnesty International, 316
André, Max, 26, 27
Another Mother for Peace, 236
Anti-war movement, 226–42, 269–70,
  280–84, 287–89
Ap Bac, battle of, 117–19
Argenlieu, Thierry d', 24, 26–30,
  33
Army of the Republic of Vietnam
  (ARVN):
  in battle of Ap Bac, 117–19
  conditions in, 191–92
  desertion in, 140
  formation of, 86–87
  government weakness and, 131,
    137–38
  vs. NLF, 128–29, 131, 139–40
  Phuc Binh, battle of, 319
  religion in, 191
  Saigon, battle for, 320–21, 325–
    27
  after U.S. pullout, 309–12
  U.S. view of, 128, 191
Ashmore, Harry, 249–50
Aspin, Les, 320
Associated States of Indochina, 49,
  52, 57
Attrition strategy, 176, 182–83
Aubrac, Raymond, 250